LONDONI
SYLHETI
DICTIONARY

PART ONE
SYLHETI - ENGLISH

First edition June 2014
Second edition January 2016
Third edition October 2016

© Roger Gwynn

Acre Press
<rogwynn27@gmail.com>

INTRODUCTION

The scope and purpose of this dictionary need some explanation. What exactly is meant by Londoni Sylheti, and what justification is there for placing this small collection of words in the public domain?

In order to give a satisfactory answer to the first question I will have to start with some geographical and historical facts. Sylhet was an administrative District in British India, with an area similar to that of Northern Ireland, lying between the alluvial plains of Bengal and the hills of Assam in the north-eastern part of India. It was named after its chief town, which was called Srihatta [*shree-hot-taw*] in formal Bengali and Silot [*see-lot*] in local dialect. The spelling "Sylhet" was somewhat capricious, invented by British settlers with the same dash of fantasy as "Delhi" for Dilli and "Bombay" for Mumbai. Before British rule the area in question had at different times been part of various kingdoms large and small. It had never been a political unit on its own. While the Mughal emperors were paramount over most of India the kingdom of Jaintia, containing part of modern Sylhet, remained independent, as a vassal state of the kingdom of Ahom (Assam), though the rest of the region was controlled by Mughal governors. The East India Company took over the Mughal dominions in this area in 1765, and annexed the zone under Jaintia control in 1835. From then until 1874 the British colonial district called Sylhet was included in the province of Bengal; while from 1874 to 1947, except for a short interlude between 1905 and 1911, it was administered as part of Assam. In 1947 almost the whole of the British district of Sylhet was transferred to the new independent state of Pakistan, along with most of East Bengal. In 1971 East Pakistan achieved its own independence as Bangladesh. Not long after that the old colonial district of Sylhet was divided into four new districts: Sylhet, Sunamganj, Habiganj and Moulvibazar. For the purposes of this book "Sylhet" describes the former district, nowadays often referred to as "Greater Sylhet".

"Sylhet", then, is essentially a modern administrative term, and the culture and language of its inhabitants must be viewed within a wider context. The dominant languages of the north eastern corner of India – Bengali, Assamese and Oriya – belong to the Eastern Magadhi branch of the Indo European language family and are closely related to each other. Grass root dialects throughout that region blend into one another without respecting political or administrative boundaries (just as the local dialects of south eastern France blend into those of north western Italy). The official language in use in Sylhet, as in the rest of Bangladesh, is Bengali, but the spoken dialect of most of its people is considerably different from standard Bengali, tending more towards Assamese. It also varies slightly from one locality to the next, so that the vernacular of a village in western Sunamganj is markedly different from that of a village in Beanibazar, a hundred miles to the east.

Some enthusiasts maintain that "Sylheti" deserves the status of a language in its own right, but as the dialect on the ground is far from uniform throughout the area of Greater Sylhet, and no standard or literary form of it has ever been established, it seems more reasonable to argue that what exists is a fairly distinct cluster of dialects which can be conveniently, if not very precisely, labelled with that term. An important point to note is that a majority of people who use a Sylheti dialect have a strong sense of their own identity as "Sylhetis" and of their speech as "Sylheti", and it is perhaps this more than anything else which gives these terms their validity.

Remarkably, a form of Devnagari script unique to the Sylhet area does exist, and this fact is often quoted in support of the argument that Sylheti is not just a dialect cluster but a language in its own right. Nagri, as it is generally called, is one of the simplified "second class" forms of the Devnagari script which, centuries ago, were used by ordinary people – such as tradesmen and ballad singers – for their own modest purposes, whilst the more elaborate "first class" forms, like the Bengali and Assamese scripts, were monopolized by priests and ministers for important religious and official work. In Sylhet we know that the Nagri script was used quite widely to preserve the texts of spiritual ballads, though no other uses of it are recorded. There is no evidence that it was ever used for general communication, or even that it was particularly linked to the local dialect, for the ballads written in it tend to be framed in a more general eastern Bengali idiom. So although its existence is noteworthy it has little relevance to the subject of spoken Sylheti.

And what about *Londoni* Sylheti? In Sylhet, individuals and families who have migrated to Britain and settled here are generally described as "Londonis", inhabitants of London - "London" being commonly used, especially by non-migrants, as a synonym for Britain. There is, in the United Kingdom today, a large and well established community of people who trace their origins to Sylhet, have at least some command of a Sylheti dialect and consider themselves, at least in certain contexts, as Sylhetis. By and large their Sylheti speech lacks much of the "quaint" and rural vocabulary which can still be heard in Sylhet itself, but comprises a basic stock of common Sylheti words plus a large number of terms derived from English, reflecting features of life in Britain. An English speaker who wishes to converse with "Londonis" in their own idiom can get by with this relatively limited vocabulary. It has to be said that even in Sylhet itself, as a result of modern communications and formal education, local dialects are rapidly losing their richness and idiosyncrasy, and more and more words from English and standard Bengali are finding their way into everyday speech.

This dictionary cannot and does not reflect the full variety of traditional Sylheti vernacular speech. Its aim is modest: to provide just enough vocabulary to sustain a simple conversation on everyday matters with a British Sylheti-speaker. The material for it was collected in Birmingham over a period of about twenty years, during which I was living in a Sylheti household and working within the local Sylheti community. Most of my contacts were with people originating from those specific parts of Greater Sylhet which happen to have contributed most migrants to Birmingham: Jagannathpur, Balaganj, Biswanath, Golapganj, Beanibazar, Moulvibazar. The wordlist includes many words borrowed from standard Bengali, particularly abstract nouns, which are in common use nowadays but have no Sylheti equivalent.

It has been necessary to choose a method of representing in written form an idiom which is normally only spoken. Details of the system I have employed are given in the phonetics section below.

I would like to take this opportunity to record my deepest gratitude to all the people in the Birmingham Sylheti community who so generously accepted me as an honorary kinsman and shared with me everything I could ever hope for – from tea and *handesh* to folk tales and cherished personal memories. They unwittingly provided the material for this book. I must also thank Liz Anderton of the St James Language Project for facilitating the first Sylheti classes which started the ball rolling in 1980, and James and Sue Lloyd-Williams for their constant support and encouragement.

NOTES ON THE CONTENTS

The words in the dictionary are arranged in normal alphabetical order, with the addition of three special characters: **d̦**, coming immediately after **d** ; **ṭ**, coming after **t** ; and **ŋ** which follows **n**. The sounds represented by these letters and others are explained in the section on phonetics, below. Each entry in the wordlist may contain up to ten elements, as follows.

1. **Headword** In most cases this is a whole word. Where it is a verb stem, it ends with a hyphen, *e.g.* **kor-** . If it is a prefix it ends with a plus sign, *e.g.* **be+** . If it is a suffix it is preceded by a hyphen, *e.g.* **–ala** .
2. **Pronunciation hint** This is contained in square brackets. If the word consists of more than one syllable the stressed syllable is preceded by a small vertical line ' . In the great majority of cases, the stress falls on the first syllable. Instead of symbols from the international phonetic alphabet a small number of easily recognizable characters have been used to provide a rough guide to pronunciation. These are explained in the phonetics section. However, written symbols are of limited use for illustrating sounds, and the help of a Sylheti speaker should be sought when in doubt.
3. **Part of speech** The following categories and abbreviations have been used:

(adj)	adjective	**gorom** ca – *hot* **tea**
(adj/adv)	adjective or adverb	**asfas** gor – *nearby* **house** / **house** *nearby*
(adv)	adverb	**joldi** auka – *come* **quickly**
(conj)	conjunction	afne **ar** ami – *you* **and** *I*
(int)	interjection	**kobordar!** – *watch out!*
(n)	noun	gorom **ca** – *hot* **tea**
(n adj)	adjective derived from a noun	**rukor** tebul – *a* **wooden** *table*
(n adv)	adverb derived from a noun	**ufre** touka – *put it* **on top**
(n/adv)	noun or adverb	**aij** tanda – *today* **is cold** / *it's cold* **today**
(n°)	numeral	**tin** gonta – *three* **hours**
(post)	postposition	tin ta **fojonto** – *until* **three o'clock**
(pre)	preposition	**ana** cini – *without* **sugar**
(pron)	pronoun	afne **amar** bai – *you are* **my** *brother*
(pron adj)	pronominal adjective	afne **amar** bai – *you are* **my** *brother*
(v)	verb	tain besi **kain** – *he* **eats** *too much*
(vi)	intransitive verb	**joldi auka** – *come quickly*
(vt)	transitive verb	kut **anouka** – *bring* **a coat**
(v adj)	adjective derived from a verb	**baŋga** tebul – *a* **broken** *table*
(v adv)	adverb derived from a verb	lati **doria** atoin – *he walks* **holding** *a stick*
(v n)	noun derived from a verb	boi **fora** bala – *reading* **books** *is good*

4. **Meaning** English words which convey the basic sense of the headword, and if appropriate any different shades of meaning associated with it, are given in italics. If further details are offered, including subheadings and examples, these follow a vertical line | .
5. **Subheadings** Standard phrases incorporating the headword, including verbal compounds, appear within the entry paragraph in bold type. The use of verbal compounds is extremely common in Sylheti (as in Bengali and all its close cognates). In one typical pattern the principal verb becomes a past participle and an auxiliary verb takes over as the part which is inflected for person and tense. This is similar to the way English forms its future tenses with the auxiliary verb "will", and its perfect tenses with "have". Another kind of compound is found when a noun is coupled with a verb (often **kor-**) to form the noun's verbal equivalent: *e.g.* **imel kora**, literally "to make or do email", thus *to email*.
6. **Other parts of speech** If the same form as the headword can also function as a different part of speech, this will appear either in another paragraph or as a separate entry within the same paragraph, in which case it is preceded by a ¶ sign.

7. **Examples of use** Wherever deemed necessary or helpful, each suggestion of meaning has been followed by one or more examples of the word or phrase in practical use. These examples add flesh to the bare bones of the wordlist, and should repay any time spent examining them.
8. **Etymology** At the end of many entries, within square brackets, is an indication of the origin of the word in question, where this can reasonably be inferred. References to Bengali, however, serve to point out an equivalent rather than an origin, as Sylheti dialect and standard Bengali are cognate descendants of the same ancient language, and Sylheti is not in any way derived from standard Bengali. The sign < has been used where necessary to point to a more remote origin, e.g. [B. acar < S. ācāra] – the Bengali word **acar** is derived from Sanskrit **ācāra**. The following abbreviations have been used for languages:

    A. Arabic   P. Persian
    B. Bengali   Pg. Portuguese
    C. Chinese   S. Sanskrit
    E. English   T. Turkish
    H. Hindi   U. Urdu
    O. Old Indo-Aryan

Where a source word in the language of origin has been specified, a Romanized transcription has been given. The Romanized transcriptions incorporate a few special characters to represent sounds not found in English; keys to the systems used are given in Annexe 2.

9. **Cross reference** In many cases an entry ends with a cross-reference to a related item which appears in the dictionary. The following examples illustrate the formats used.

    < **kor-**   *formed from the verbal stem* **kor-**
    = **aḍa**   *equivalent to the word* **aḍa**
    = **ḍuḍ + -ala**   *composed of the word* **ḍuḍ** *plus the suffix* **-ala**
    cf **baje**   *compare with the word* **baje**

10. **Notes** In some cases an explanatory note has been attached to an entry to give additional information, for example about a particular social context with which a word is connected.

THE PHONETICS OF SYLHETI

Language is based on distinctive speech sounds used to communicate meaning. *Sounds,* not written words or symbols, are the material from which language is made. Speaking and hearing come before writing and reading. Anybody who wants to master another language needs to be able to recognise and reproduce accurately the speech sounds of that language, and this is particularly true when it is not a standardized written language but a normally unwritten dialect that one is studying. Hence this section on the sound system, or phonetics, of Sylheti. The notes below may be too technical for some people's liking, and can be ignored by anyone already familiar with the sounds of Sylheti. They can also be skipped by learners who are able to get help from an experienced Sylheti speaker – oral practice with a teacher is far more valuable than any amount of written explanation.

As Sylheti is normally only spoken, and not written down, it has been necessary to devise a suitable alphabet for representing its sounds on paper. The Bengali alphabet could have been used, but Sylheti uses some very characteristic sounds which are not found in standard Bengali and cannot be reproduced by any tool in the Bengali writing system. Apart from which, not many of the people interested in studying Sylheti are familiar with Bengali. Again, the Nagri script could have been used, and might seem rather appropriate as it belongs specifically to Sylhet, but it too is not particularly good at representing speech sounds, and virtually nobody is familiar with it. So I have preferred to use the Roman alphabet, with some straightforward rules and just three modified letters.

I have adopted the phonetic principle of *one symbol for one sound* : for example, the sound "sh" is represented by a single letter **s**. This may seem perverse, but it avoids the ambiguity which can arise when several letters are used to portray a single sound. Another rule which I have followed is that of *economy of symbols* : for example, if the sound [s] is heard in combination with [t] but never with [ṭ], and the sound [š] occurs with [ṭ] but never with [ṭ], then it may make sense to consider [s] and [š] as alternative forms of the same phoneme, each belonging to a specific, definable phonetic context, rather than as "two different letters".

Any scheme which codifies the speech sounds of a language into a small set of phonemes (whose written form is an alphabet) must necessarily be a simplification. Far from reflecting every nuance of pronunciation in the actual speech of real people, a phoneme list is an abstraction, a generalization, which has the practical purpose of reducing overabundance and complexity to a manageable form. This is particularly true in the present work: the scheme I have adopted is a brutal simplification of a varied and complicated reality. Pedants and purists may be shocked, but the average learner will perhaps forgive me for making his or her life a little easier.

There is one particularly difficult feature of everyday speech, not only in Sylhet but in Bangladesh generally, which I have more or less avoided. Like all the languages derived from Old Indo-Aryan, Bengali makes use of "aspiration" in its phonetic system. In standard Bengali the difference between the unaspirated and aspirated forms of the plosive consonants has to be observed; at least in theory, many pairs of words are differentiated solely by the presence or absence of aspiration. For example, [gā] with the [g] unaspirated means "*body*", while [g¨ā] with aspirated [g] means "*wound*". So important has this distinction always been considered that from Sanskrit onwards all the main Indo-Aryan languages have represented the unaspirated and aspirated forms of the same consonant with entirely different symbols in their alphabets. But whatever "aspiration" may originally have involved in Old Indo-Aryan or Sanskrit, it has become an elusive phenomenon in modern spoken Bengali, particularly in local dialects like Sylheti. In some cases the extra breath which characterizes orthodox aspiration can be heard, but in many cases it cannot. Interestingly, modern experts are divided in their opinion about whether and how near-homophones like [gā] and [g¨ā] are contrasted in the speech of ordinary Sylheti people. Implosion, laryngealization, tone change have all been posited, along with the use of aspiration in certain situations. My own feeling is that in some cases no phonetic distinction is maintained, it being perfectly possible to distinguish homophones purely by context – as we distinguish "bear" from "bare" in English. In other cases there may be added stress or elongation of the vowel, and in yet other cases true aspiration. I believe that the issue has very little practical importance, so for the most part I have ignored it.

In general vowel length has no significance in Sylheti, as in modern Bengali where no pair of words is ever distinguished solely by the length of the vowel. The contrasts between short [i] and [u] and long [i:] and [u:] which were observed in Old Indo-Aryan are still shown in Bengali writing, but not maintained in speech. The old contrast between short [a] and long [a:] has been replaced by a contrast in quality, [ò] versus [ā]. Although in standard Bengali a medial, rounded [ô] contrasts with the deeper [ò], in Sylheti this contrast is never exploited. Thus I have distinguished only five vowel phonemes in Sylheti, **a, e, i, o, u,** against six in Bengali.

Nasalization is another feature which was significant in Old Indo-Aryan, and is still represented in written standard Bengali though it has virtually disappeared from normal speech throughout Bangladesh. It plays no role in Sylheti.

v

More details of the sounds represented by each of the twenty-two letters used in this dictionary are given in Appendix 1 below.

Those who are familiar with Sanskrit, Old Indo-Aryan or Bengali will recognize in this dictionary numerous words derived from those languages appearing in a somewhat modified form. There are certain general rules of morphophonemic change which it may be helpful to know.

(1) Sylheti speakers (in common with speakers of many other northern Indian dialects) tend to dislike pronouncing any word which begins with a combination of consonants, and to avoid this they either add an introductory vowel or insert a vowel to separate the consonants. Thus, O. **strī** becomes Sylheti **istiri** and O. **prīti** becomes Sylheti **firiti**. The same rule is followed with modern borrowings from English, for example E. **school** becomes Sylheti **iskul** and E. **front** becomes Sylheti **feront**.

(2) Often a pure vowel in standard Bengali is represented in Sylheti by a diphthong with /i/ as its second component. For example, final -år in Bengali (derived from –ara in Old Indo-Aryan) sometimes becomes –oir in Sylheti. Thus O. **uttara** > B. **uttår** > Sylheti **uttoir**. Final –ôx in Bengali, where x stands for a consonant, often becomes –oix in Sylheti, for example B. **rôd** > Sylheti **roid**, B. **bôn** > Sylheti **boin**. Similarly a final –ax in Bengali sometimes becomes –aix in Sylheti, for example B. **dal** > Sylheti **dail**, B. **majh** > Sylheti **maij**.

(3) A different kind of rule concerns internal change within certain Sylheti words. When a case ending is added to a monosyllabic noun containing a diphthong with /i/ as the second component, the diphthong usually changes to its first component and the /i/ joins the case ending. Thus when **boin** is put in the possessive case, instead of becoming **boinor** it becomes **bonir**. The locative case of **lair** is **larit** rather than **lairo**. The rule is often applied to English loan words too. E. **queen** is Sylheti **kuin**, possessive **kunir** rather than **kuinor**. However, this rule is not invariably followed; some speakers avoid the transposition of vowels out of choice, or where there is a possibility of confusion: for example, most people will say **jeilo** rather than **jelit** for "in jail", as **jelit** could also mean "in jelly".

(4) Another rule comes into play when a consonant is preceded by /ai/ or /ei/ or /oi/, or followed by /ia/ or /ie/ or /io/. A kind of mirror pattern often emerges, consisting of a first diphthong followed by a doubled consonant followed by a second diphthong which is the reverse of the first one. Take for example the past participle of **bat-**, which is basically **batia**. Although it can be pronounced without modification, ['bātıā], it is more often pronounced ['bāıt-tıā]. Similarly **kaliana** is generally pronounced ['χāıl-lıāna]. Likewise the Sylheti word **soitto** is pronounced ['sòıt-tıò], and **aicca** is pronounced ['āıtš-šıā]. Words borrowed from English are subject to the same rule. E. **baby** is Sylheti **bebi**. and when this noun appears in its "instrumental" form with an /e/ added at the end, i.e. **bebie**, this is pronounced ['béıb-bıé]. And the same mirror phenomenon can be observed when a consonant is preceded by /au/ or followed by /ua/ – for example, **auka** is often pronounced ['āuk-kuā]. As the mirror effect is a matter of phonetic interpretation rather than morphology, it has *not* been overtly indicated in the phonemic notation ("spelling") employed in this dictionary.

APPENDIX 1: SYLHETI PHONEME LIST

a	[ā] back, as in Southern English "bath"	in most cases:	**mat, kan**
	[a] light, as in English "rota"	in final unstressed position:	**beta, kila**
b	[b] as in English "boy"		**baba, boi**
	[f] as "f" in English "	in some final positions:	**cib**
c	[tš] as "ch" in English "chip"	when combined with another consonant: **baicca, inci**	
	[s] as in English "cell"	in all other cases:	**ca, koci, gece**
d	[d] as in English "dog"		**dail, dor**
ḍ	[ḍ] produced with tongue on teeth		**din, dol, dui, baḍa**
e	[é] forward, as in French "zéro"	at the end of a word:	**he, amare**
	" "	if followed by another vowel:	**cear, ein, neul**
	[ɛ] back, as in English "bed"	if followed by a consonant:	**ek, jel, beta**
f	[f] as in English "fit"		**fet, falao, afa**
	[p] as "p" in English "cup"	when doubled:	**coffor, goffo**
g	[g] as in English "go"		**gan, gor, age**
	[k] as "ck" in English "sick"	in some final positions:	**dig**
h	[h] more breathy than in English		**hala, he, aha**
i	[ī:] long, like "ee" in English "see"	in monosyllabic words:	**fit, bil**
	[ī] shorter, as in French "dix"	elsewhere:	**beti, kila, cini**
j	[j] as in English "jug"	at the beginning of a word:	**jal, jele**
	" "	in combination:	**raijjo, hanje, korjo**
	[z] as "z" in English "zoo"	elsewhere:	**saja, baje, biji**
k	[k] as in English "king"	before /i/ or /u/:	**kila, kula, baki**
	" "	after /u/:	**ruk, couk, auka**
	" "	usually after /i/:	**bik, tika, nikot**
	[χ] scraped, as "ch" in Scottish "loch"	elsewhere:	**kal, ke, kola, ikta**
l	[l] as in English		**log, bala, fal, calla**
m	[m] as in English		**mac, lama, hal, amma**
n	[ṇ] retroflex	before /t/ or /d/:	**gonta, anda**
	[n] as in English	elsewhere:	**nam, one, jan, onno**
ŋ	[ŋ] as "ng" in English "bang"		**baŋla, doŋ, joŋgol**
o	[ô] rounded, as in English "go"	when stressed at the end of a word:	**mai-go**
	" "	if followed by /u/:	**bou**
	[w] as "w" in English "wool"	beginning a word and followed by /a/:	**oal**
	[ò] far back, rather like "aw" in "caw"	elsewhere:	**gor, hori, mora. one**
r	[r] tapped, as in Spanish "rey"		**rait, jur, tara**
	[ɽ] retroflex		**bari, bura**
s	[s] as in English "sit"	before /t/:	**besto, obosta**
	[š] as in English "tension"	elsewhere:	**sat, asi, bes, gussa**
t	[t] as in English		**tin, taun, mati**
ṭ	[ṭ] dental, as in Spanish		**tin, tara, mat**
u	[ū] long, like "oo" in English "cool"	in monosyllabic words:	**ful, kun**
	[u] shorter, as in Spanish "cruz"	elsewhere:	**uri, huru**

APPENDIX 2: TRANSCRIPTION SYSTEMS

SANSKRIT

Vowels

a   ā   i   ī   u   ū   e   o   ŕ

Consonants

guttural:	k	kh	g	gh	ŋ
palatal:	c	ch	j	jh	ň
retroflex:	ṭ	ṭh	ḍ	ḍh	ṇ
dental:	t	th	d	dh	n
labial:	p	ph	b	bh	m
liquid:		y	r	l	v
spirant:		š	ś	s	h

BENGALI

Vowels

å   a   i   u   e   o

Consonants

guttural:	k	kh	g	gh	ŋ		
palatal:	c	ch	j	jh			
retroflex:	ṭ	ṭh	ḍ	ḍh	ṇ	ṛ	ṛh
dental:	t	th	d	dh	n		
labial:	p	ph	b	bh	m		
liquid:		y	r	l			
spirant:		s	h				

nasalization: ṅ

ARABIC

ا alif	a		ر ra	r		ف fa	f
ب ba	b		ز za	z		ق qaf	q
ت ta	t		س sin	s		ك kaf	k
ث tha	θ		ش shin	š		ل lam	l
ج jim	j		ص sad	ṣ		م mim	m
ح ha	ḥ		ض dad	Ḏ		ن nun	n
خ kha	ḳ		ط ta	ṭ		ه ha	h
د dal	d		ظ za	ż		و waw	u, w
ذ dhal	ð		ع ain	ʿ		ى ya	i, y
			غ ghain	ğ			

a

a- [ā] (vi) *come* | coffori ao! – *come quickly* : ke aicoin – *someone has come (to the door)* : auka tain – *let him come; let's wait till he comes* : aitam ni? – *may I come in?* : amar muke di aice – *it came out of my mouth; it just slipped out* : ami ai – *I'll come; I'll be back in a moment* : amra guri aibo – *we'll go and come back again* : ami ou deki aici – *I've just been and seen it* : afne taiar oia auka – *go and get ready, and then come back here* : lain aito nae – *the cord won't reach this far* : fotu sundor aice – *the photo has come out well* : isab ae na – *the sum doesn't work out* : hou nam arbi tone aice – *that name comes from Arabic* : **aite** – *in coming; while coming* : afnar aite kosto oice – *you surely had trouble coming here* : tan aite diron oibo – *there'll be some delay in his coming* : **aite aite** – *while coming; on the way* : amra aite aite kai lici – *we had something to eat on the way* : **aibar** – *of coming; for coming* : tai aibar lagi beus – *she's desperately keen to come* : aibar somoe fan anoin jen – *please bring some paan when you come* : **kam ae** – *a useful purpose is served* : ou kafor dia kam aibo – *this cloth will come in useful* : **a- ja-** – *come and go* : tara hamesa ae jae – *they frequently come and go* : aite jaite ek gonta lage – *it takes an hour to get there and back* : **ae jae** – *comes or goes; makes a difference* : kunta ae jae na – *it doesn't make any difference* : kita aito jaito? – *what difference would it make?* : **a- gi** – *go and come back again* : afne auka gi – *go now, and come back later* : **ai ar-** – *come; arrive* : tain kun somoe ai arcoin – *he arrived some time ago* : **aia for-** – *come; arrive* : one boirati aia forbo – *the bridegroom's retinue will soon arrive* : **aia ja-** – *come and go away again* : tain tinbar aia gecoin – *he called round three times*. [B. as-]

a+ (adv prefix) *un-* | adua – *unwashed* : asokti – *lack of strength*

aa [ā:] (int) *ah! oh!* | aa, ki sundor! – *oh, how lovely!* : **aa kor-** – *say "aah"* : aa koro! – *open your mouth wide!* : betae aa kori roicoin – *the old fellow was left gaping.*

aajari ['ā: zārī] (n) *sighing and wailing; lamentation* | kodae tan aajari hune na ni – *God surely hears her crying* : **aajari kor-** – *sigh and wail; lament* [P. āh-o-zārī]

aar ['ā-ār̥] (n) *the month of Ashar (June-July)* [B. asar̥h < S. āśār̥ha]

aat [ā:t] (n) *bowels; entrails* [H. ānt < O. antra]

abad ['ābād] (n) *cultivation* [P. ābād – *habitable*]

abadi ['ābādī] (adj) *cultivable; arable* | abadi jomi – *arable land* ¶ **abadi** (n) *settler; migrant farmer* : ino abadi aice – *migrants have settled here.* < **abad**

abaoa ['ābāwa] (n) *climate; weather* | i desor abaoa bala – *the climate in this country is good.* [P. āb-o-havā – *water and air; climate*]

abba ['āb-bā] (n) *father; Dad*

abiskar ['ābiṣ̌ār] (n) *discovery; invention* | **abiskar kor-** – *discover; invent* : tain noea jatir gac abiskar korcoin – *she's discovered a new species of plant* : kompiutar ke abiskar korcoin? – *who invented the computer?* [B. abiskar < S. aviśkāra]

abita ['ābita] (adj) *unmarried* [B. ābibahitā < S. avivāhita]

abo ['ābò] (adv) *still now* = **abu**

aboltabol ['ābòl tābòl] (n) *nonsense*

abra ['ābra] (adj) *dumb* | abra fua – *a dumb boy* : tai jonom taki abra – *she's been dumb from birth* | **abra** (n) *dumb person* [B. haba]

abritti [ā-'brīt-tī] (n) *recital* | **abritti kor-** – *recite* [B. abritti < S. āvŕtti – *turning around, reversion*]

abu ['ābū] (adv) *still now; even now* | abu meg der – *it's still raining* : tain abu aicoin na : she hasn't arrived yet [H. abhī]

ac ['ās] (n) *vague notion; intuition* | ac kor- – *sense; guess* [B. aⁿc]

ac- ['ās] (vi) *be; exist; be present* | afne bala acoin? – *are you well?* : ji oe, ami bala aci – *yes, I am well* : ami bemar aclam – *I was ill* : tain kuk acla – *he used to be a cook* : tumi kuae aclae? – *where were you?* : alla ace – *God exists; God is out there* : tumar abba acoin? – *is your Dad in?* : amar dada abu acoin – *my grandfather is still alive* : .. **ace** – *there is* .. :

ino tel ace – *there's some oil here* : tebulo borton ace – *there are plates on the table* :   (**kar**) **.. ace** – *(someone) has ..* : amar gori ace – *I have a watch* : afnar hurutta ace? – *do you have any children?* : tair budḍi ace – *she's got brains* : tarar gari acil – *they used to own a car* : (**ke**) (**korto**) **acil** – *(someone) should have (done)* : tain testa korta acla – *he should have tried* : ami jaitam aclam – *I should have gone* : tara bujto acil – *they should have understood* : tumi balatike huntae aclae – *you ought to have listened properly*   [B. ach-]
 Note: Defective verb having only present (indefinite) and past (historic) tenses. Replaced by **o-, tak-, ro-** in other tenses. Replaced by **nae** for negative of present tense.
acar[1] ['āsār] (n) *manners*   [B. acar < S. ācāra]
acar[2] (n) *pickles*   [B. acar]
acar[3] (n) *stumbling* | **acar ka-** – *trip, stumble* : ami acar kaiclam – *I stumbled*   [B. acaṛ]
acar-beboar (n) *behaviour*   = **acar**[1] + **beboar**
aclam alekum [as 'lām-ālāıkūm] (int) *peace be upon you; greetings* (standard Muslim form of salutation)   [A. as-salāmu ¿alaikum – *peace upon ye*]
acman ['ās-mān] (n) *sky*   [P. āsmān]
acor ['āsòr] (n) *evening prayer time* | acoror nomaj – *evening prayers*   [A. ¿aṣr]
acra- ['āsra-] (vt) *scratch; comb* | murgi-hokol mati acrar – *the hens are scratching the soil* : tumar cul acraico ni? – *have you combed your hair?* : **acrai le-** – *comb* : rinar cul balatike acrai lao – *give Rina's hair a good combing*   [B. acṛa-]
adda ['ād-da] (n) *gathering place; idle assembly* | curor adda – *a haunt of thieves* : fuainte adda boaice – *the lads are loafing about together* : **adda mar-** – *loiter in a group* : tara haridin adda mare – *they hang about in a gang all day*   [B.]
ad [ād] (n°) *half* | ad kear jaega – *half a kedar of land* : ad gonta : *half an hour*   = **ada**[2]
ada[1] ['ādā] (n) *ginger*   [B. aḍa]
ada[2] (n°) *half* | aḍa fon moeḍa – *half a pound of flour* : aḍa camuc – *half a spoonful* : aḍa gonta – *half an hour* : **aḍa·kan** – *a half* : aḍa·kan kao, aḍa·kan rako – *eat half and put the other half aside* ¶ **aḍa** (adv) *half; partly* | beta aḍa fagol – *the man's half mad* : tai aḍa gumo – *she's half asleep* : aḍa ḍuḍ aḍa fani – *half milk and half water*   [B. aḍha]
adab ['ādāb] (n) *courtesy* | **adab kor-** – *give a greeting other than "salaam"* : tain amare aḍab korcoin – *he greeted me politely* ¶ **adab** (int) *good day! greetings!*   [A. ādāb – *politeness*]
adacada ['ādā-sādā] (adv) *partially; incompletely* | he aḍacaḍa kam korce – *he did the job incompletely* : tain aḍacaḍa bujcoin – *he hasn't fully understood*   = **ada**[2]
adae ['āḍāy] (n°) *settlement of dues; release from an awkward situation* | **adae oe** – *relief is obtained* : afne aicoin, amar aḍae oice – *thank goodness you've come, now I'm off the hook* : kam·ta oi gele ek aḍae oibo – *it will be a relief when the job's done* : **adae kor-** – *pay (a due); obtain payment (of a due)* : tan fauna aḍae kortam oimu – *I must pay him what I owe* : afnar fauna aḍae korcoin ni? – *have you got back the money you were owed?*   [A. adā' – *discharge*]
adalot ['āḍālòt] (n) *law court*   [A. ¿adāla – *justice*]
adi ['āḍī] (adj) *traditional; original*   [A. ¿ādī – *usual*]
admi ['āḍ-mī] (n) *human being*   [U. āḍmī < A. ādamī – *one of Adam*]
adob ['āḍòb] (n) *good manners; courtesy*   [A. adab]
adob-kaeda ['āḍòb-χāéḍa] (n) *good manners and behaviour*   = **adob** + **kaeda**
adom ['āḍòm] (n) *Adam; Man* | aḍomor jat – *mankind*   [A. ādam]
adomsumari ['āḍòm-šumārī] (n) *population census*   [P. mardumšumārī]
ador ['āḍòr] (n) *affection* | **adoror** – *cherished, beloved* : amar aḍoror natin – *my dear granddaughter* : **ador kor-** – *show affection to* : tain amare bout aḍor koroin – *she is very kind to me* : **ador de-** – *pet; caress*   [B. aḍår < S. āḍara – *esteem*]
ador-jotno ['āḍòr-jotnò] (n) *love and care*   = **ador** + **jotno**
adumcudum ['āḍūm-sūḍūm] (adj) *silly* | aḍumcuḍum mat – *silly talk* : **adumcudum kor-** – *behave foolishly*

ae [āy] (n) *income* | amrar ae komi gece – *our income has decreased* : «ae buji bee koro» – *cut your coat according to your cloth* : **ae kor-** – *earn* : tain aftat dui ajar fon ae koroin – *he earns two thousand pounds a week* [B. ay < S. āya]

aefol ['āy-fòl] (n) *apple* [E.]

ae-unnoti ['āy-ūn-nòtī] (n) *prosperity* | **ae-unnoti kor-** – *make a living; prosper; do well* = **ae** + **unnoti**

afa ['āfā] (n) *elder sister* [U. āpā]

afa- ['ā: fā] (vi) *pant* | **afai ja-/afai ut-** – *become short of breath* : sirit utle ami afai jai – *I get breathless going up stairs* : tain afai utcoin – *she's got all out of breath* = **hafa-**

afani ['ā: fānī] (v n) *panting; asthma* = **hafani**

afatoto ['āfā-tòtò] (adv) *for the time being* | afatoto tauk – *let it be for now* : amra afatoto ino roimu – *we'll stay here for the time being* [B. apatåtå < S. āpātatah – *on occasion*]

afcuc ['āfsūs] (n) *regret; matter of regret* | koto boro afcuc! – *what a pity!* : **afcuc lage** – *regret is felt* : tumar afcuc lage na? – *don't you feel any regret?* : **afcuc oe** – *regret is felt* : tan lagi amar afcuc oe – *I feel bad about him* : amar afcuc nae – *I have no regrets* : **afcuc kor-** – *regret; express regret; feel sorry* : bade afne afcuc korba – *you'll regret it later* : tain afnar lagi afcuc korcoin – *he said he was sorry about you* [P. afsos]

afil ['āfīl] (n) *appeal* | amar afil oice na – *my appeal hasn't succeeded* : tan keic afilo gece – *his case has gone to* appeal : **afil kor-** – *lodge an appeal* : afil kora jaibo – *it will be possible to appeal* : **afil fa-** – *win an appeal* : amar afil faici – *I've won my appeal* [E.]

afnar ['āf-nār] (pron adj) *your* see **afne**

afne[1] ['āf-né] (pron) *you* (honorific) | afne age jauka – *you go first* : **afnar** – *your; of you* : afnar furi kuae? – *where is your daughter?* : afnar bodole tain jaiba – *he will go instead of you* : **afnare** – *you; to you* : tain afnare cinoin : *he knows you* : ami cinci na afnare – *I'm afraid I can't recall who you are* : afnare na! – *sorry, my remark wasn't addressed to you* : **afnera/afnara/afnain** – *you* (plural) : afnera bouka – *please sit down, all of you* : afnarar nam kouka – *please tell me your names* : **afnerare/afnarare/afnaintore** – *(to) you all* : afnaintore kita ditam? – *what can I offer you all?* [B. apni]

afne[2] (adv) *on its own* | **afne afne** – *all on its own; of its own accord* : afnar aŋgul afne afne tik oibo – *your finger will recover automatically* < **afon**

afon ['āfòn] (adj) *one's own* | tain amar afon cacar goror bai – *he is my own first cousin* : ein amrar afon – *she is one of our own; she's one of the family* [B. apån]

afos ['āfòš] (adv) *back again* | tain amar boi·kan afos dicoin – *he's given my book back* : amar hori afos aicoin – *my mother-in-law has come back* [P. vāpas]

afot ['āfòt] (n) *mishap* [B. apåd < S. āpada]

afot-bifot ['āfòt-bīfot] (n) *danger or mishap*

afotti ['āfòt-tī] (n) *objection* | amar afotti nae – *I have no objection (to that)* : **afotti kor-** – *make an objection; protest* : tara butor befare afotti korce – *they made objections about the voting* [B. apåtti < S. āpatti – *mishap*]

afta ['āf-ta] (n) *week* | ekod afta lagbo – *it will take a week or so* : gelo afta / goto afta – *last week* : samnor afta – *next week* : dui aftar bitre – *within two weeks* : tin afta bade – *three weeks later* = **hafta**

ag [āg] (n) *forepart; beginning* | **ag taki/ag tone** – *from before* : bout ag taki coler – *it's being going on since long before* : ami ag tone koiclam – *I said so beforehand* : **agor** – *of before; previous* : agor din – *the previous day* : **age** – *at the fore; before*

ag- [ā:g] (vi) *defecate* | bebi agce – *the baby's done a poo* : **agi le-** – *defecate* [B. hag-]

aga[1] ['āga] (n) *tip; point* [B. aga]

aga[2] ['ā:ga] (v n) *defecation; excreta* | **aga dore** – *an urge to void the bowels is felt* : tumar furir aga dorce – *your daughter needs to go to the toilet* < **ag-**

agaca ['āgasa] (n) *weeds* [B. agacha]

agaj ['āgāz] (n) *beginning* [P. āġāz]

agami ['āgamī] (adj) *coming; next* | agami bocor – *next year* : agami sombar – *next Monday* : agami masor fac tarik – *the 5th of the coming month* [B. agami < S. āgāmī – *coming*]

agat ['āgat] (n) *wound; harm* | **agat fa-** – *be hurt* : he tar ato agat faice – *he's been hurt in the arm* : tain monor maje agat faiba – *she will be hurt (emotionally)* : **agat đe-** – *hurt* : tare agat đio na – *don't hurt him* [B. aghat < S. āghāta – *blow*]

age ['āgé] (n adv) *before; in front; earlier* | afne age jauka – *you go first* : he amar age boicil – *he sat down in front of me* : tumi age koilae na kilagi? – *why didn't you say so before?* : taintain age london takta – *they previously used to live in London* : tain ektil age gecoin gi – *he left a short while ago* : tain afnar age aicoin – *he came before you did* : noe·tar age ain jen – *please come before nine* : **age đi** – *in front; ahead; in future* : tain age đi kam koroin – *he works in the front (of the restaurant)* : tolet kunano? age đi – *where's the WC?* *straight ahead* : age đi aro balo oibo – *it will be even better in the future* : **age col-** – *go ahead; go too fast* : ou gori age coler – *this clock is fast* : **age mat-** – *speak too forwardly* : age matio na! – *don't speak out of turn!* < **ag**

age-bade ['āgé bādé] (adv) *before and after* = **age** + **bade**
age-fice ['āgé fīsé] (adv) *in front and behind* = **age** + **fice**
agkan ['āg-χān] (n) *fore; front* = **ag** + **kan** ³
agkano ['āg-χānò] (n adv) *before* | tura agkano – *a short while before* < **agkan**
ag-kor ['āg-χòr] (n) *time latitude* | **ag-kor oe** – *unpunctuality occurs* : amar aite tura ag-kor oito fare – *I may arrive a bit early or a bit late* = **ag** + **kor**
agla ['āgla] (adj) *separate* = **alga**
agla- (v) *separate; set apart; hive off* | tumar boi aglaitam ni? – *shall I put your books separately?* : cacara aglaice – *uncle's family have split off from the joint family* : **aglai le-** – *separate* : boro·guin furu·guin taki aglai limu – *we'll separate the big ones from the smaller ones* < **agla**
agloc ['āglos] (adv) *apart* | he agloc boice – *he's sitting on his own* = **algoc**
agon ['āgon] (n) *Agrahayan (November-December)* [B. ågråhayån < S. agrahāyaṇa]
agor ['āgòr] (n adj) *of before; previous; olden* | agor đin – *the day before* : agor fira tarik foesa đicil – *last time Tariq paid* : afnar agor tikana kita acil? – *what was your previous address?* : agor jumana bala acil – *the old days were best* : ou gori bout agor – *this watch is antique* : larair agor fotu – *a photo from before the war* : goto aftar agor afta – *the week before last* : agor ag! – *first come, first served!* < **ag**
agorbatti ['āgòr-bat-tī] (n) *incense stick* [H. agarbattī]
agtari ['āk-tārī] (adv) *from before; in advance* | agtari janai đile bala acil – *it would have been better if you'd let us know beforehand* = **ag** + **taki**
agua- ['āg-wā] (v) *advance; bring forward* | kam·ta aguaice – *the job has made progress* : tara tarik aguaice – *they've brought the appointment forward* : **aguai đe-** – *hold out; lead forward* : tan at aguai đicla – *he held out his hand* : afnare aguai đitam ni? – *shall I see you on your way?* < **ag**
aguan ['āg-wān] (adv) *in advance* | tara amar tolof aguan đi laice – *they've paid my wages in advance* : baccainte aguan gumaice – *the children have gone to bed early* < **agua-**
aguin ['āgūın] (n) *fire* | aguin joler – *the fire is burning* : auka, agunor kanđat bouka – *come and sit near the fire* : aguin·ta maro – *turn the fire off* : tura aguin đeuka – *please give me a light* : **aguin đore** – *fire catches on* : lakrit aguin đorce – *the firewood has ignited* : **aguin lage** – *fire bursts out* : kukaro aguin lagce – *the stove has caught fire* : **aguin laga-/aguin lagai đe-** – *set fire (to)* : he kotono aguin lagaice – *he set the curtains on fire* : **aguin o-/aguin oi ja-** – *to become enraged* : betae aguin oi gecoin – *the old man's furious* = **agun**
agun ['āgūn] (n) *fire* | agun kuna – *the fire quadrant; south east* [B. agun < S. agni]
aha [ā-'hā] (int) *tut! bother!* | aha, amar kut falai aici! – *drat, I left my coat behind!*
ahaha ['ā-hāhā] (int) *oh dear oh dear!*
ahare [ā-hā-'ré] (int) *dear me!* | ahare, koto đukko! – *dear dear, so sad!* : ahare! – *oh, for goodness' sake!*
aia ['āıā] (v adv) *having come* | tara aia kita korto? – *having come, what will they do? what's the point in their coming?* : tain aia bidio đekoin – *he comes and watches videos* : tain roibbar aia sombar gecoin gi – *she came on Sunday and left on Monday* < **a-**

aialle ['āɪal-lɛ́] (v adv) *once having come* | tara aialle amra kaimu – *once they've arrived we shall have our meal* = **aia** + **arle**
aiari ['āɪārī] (v adv) *having come* | Rina goro aiari fon korcil – *having come home Rina made a phone call* : tain biane aiari bat kaicoin – *he had a meal when he came this morning* = **aia** + **ari**
aiat ['āɪāt] (n) *ayat; verse of the Quran* [A. ayāh – *sign*]
aicc- ['āɪtš] (vi) *(have) come* | aicci – *I've arrived; I'm on my way; I'm just coming* : meman aiccoin! – *the guests have arrived!* : id aicce – *Eid has come round again*
   Note: A frequently used irregular form of the past root of **a-** .
aicca ['āɪtšɪa] (int) *all right; okay; oh; very well; by the way* | kail deka oibo! aicca – *see you tomorrow! yes, okay!* : aicca, testa kormu – *oh very well, I'll try* : aicca, ek·ta kota jikai – *by the way, let me ask you something* : aicca, jai gi – *well, I'll be off now* : aicca re ba, deo! – *oh come on Dad, please, let me have it!* : tara gari loice .. aicca? – *they've bought a car .. oh, really?* [B. accha]
aicla ['āɪs-la] (n) *fish scales* [B. aⁿs < O. aŋšu]
aij [āɪz] (n/adv) *today; now* | aij sonibar – *today is Saturday* : ami aij jaimu – *I shall go today* : aij kiba kail – *today or tomorrow* : age doni acla, aij tain fokir – *he used to be rich, now he's a beggar* : **aijku** – *today* : aijku meg dibo – *it will rain today* : **aijkur** – *today's; of today* : aijkur kagoj kunano? – *where's today's paper?* : aijkur din bala nae – *the weather today is no good* : aijkur lagi ses – *that's all for today* [B. aj]
aijkail ['āɪz-χāɪl] (adv) *nowadays* | aijkail kesed beshi cole na – *cassettes aren't much in demand these days* : ranare deki na aijkail – *I don't see Rana around nowadays* : **aijkailku** – *nowadays* : **aijkailkur** – *contemporary; of these days* : aijkailkur hututta bout calak – *kids these days are very clever* = **aij** + **kail**
ailsa ['āɪl-šɪa] (adj) *lazy* [B. alse]
ailsemi ['āɪl-šemī] (n) *laziness* [B. alsemi]
ain [āɪn] (n) *law; rule* | noea ain fas oice – *a new law has been passed* : ino gari colar ain nae – *cars aren't allowed here* : **anir** – *of the law* : anir befar – *a matter of law* : anir manus – *a law-abiding person* : anir bifokke – *against the law* : **anit** – *in the law* : anit nae ita – *it's not in the rules* : he anit dora force – *he's fallen foul of the law* [P. āīn]
aina ['āɪna] (n) *looking-glass; glass pane* | aina bae cao! – *look in the mirror!* : janlar aina fati gece – *the window pane is cracked* [P. āīna]
aini ['āɪnī] (adj) *legal* = **ain** + **-i** ²
ain-kanun ['āīn-χānūn] (n) *laws and regulations* = **ain** + **kanun**
air [āɪ-r] (n) *a species of fish (Mystus aor)* [B. air]
aittio ['āɪt-tɪò] (n) *relative* | tain afnar kunu aittio ni? – *is she a relative of yours?* [B. attia < S. ātmiya – *one's own*]
ajab ['āzāb] (n) *torment; great pain* [A. ¿aðāb]
ajad ['āzād] (adj) *free* [P. āzād]
ajadi ['āzādī] (n) *freedom* [P. āzādī]
ajaira ['āzāɪra] (adj) *useless* ¶ **ajaira** (n) *useless person*
ajan ['āzān] (n) *the call to prayer; adhan* | **ajan de-** – *give the adhan; recite the prayer call* [A. āðān]
ajar ¹ ['āzār] (n) *illness* [P. āzār – *harm*]
ajar ² ['ā:zār, 'āzār] (nº) *thousand* | ek ajar tin so callis – *one thousand three hundred and forty* : fac ajar fon – *five thousand pounds* : ajaror maje ek·jon – *one person in a thousand* : ajare ek·ta – *one per thousand; one for every thousand* = **hajar**
ajebaje ['āzé-bāzé] (adj) *worthless* cf **baje**
ajma- ['āzmā] (vt) *try out; test* | tumar kismot ajmao na kitar lagi – *why don't you try your luck* [U. āzmānā < P. āzmūdan]
ajob ['āzòb] (n) *wonder* | ajob lage – *amazement is felt* : hunia amar ajob lagce – *I was amazed to hear it* ¶ **ajob** (adj) *wondrous, amazing* | ajob kando! – *what an amazing affair!* : ajob tokdir – *a wonderful stroke of fate* [A. ¿ajab]

ajor ['āzòr] (n) *divine reward for good deeds* [A. ajr]

ak [āχ] (n) *pen mark; line* | akor ufre cain ɖi lauka – *please sign on the line* : **ak ɖe-** – *make a mark* : i kolome ak ɖee na – *this pen won't write* [B. aⁿk < O. aŋka – *mark*]

aka- ['āχā] (v) *draw* | ek·ta fotu akao! – *draw me a picture!* : tain sunɖor ful akaita faroin – *she can draw flowers nicely* : **akai ɖe-** – *draw (for someone)* : tain goror noksa akai ɖiba – *he'll draw you a plan of the house* [B. aⁿk-]

akam ['āχām] (n) *bad deed* [O. akarma]

akama ['āχama] (adj) *useless* [O. akarmā]

akam-kukam ['āχām-kūχām] (n) *bad deeds* = **akam + kukam**

akar ['āχār] (n) *shape; form; symbol for 'a' in Bengali writing* | je kunu akare – *in any shape or form* [B. akar < S. ākāra]

akas ['āχāš] (n) *sky* [B. akas < S. ākāša]

aker ['āχɛr] (adj) *final; last* [A. āḵir]

akerat ['āχɛrāt] (n) *doomsday* [A. āḵira]

akli ['āχlī] (n) *piece of wisdom; advice* | tura akli ɖeuka amare – *please give me some advice* < **akol**

akni ['āχnī] (n) *dish of fried rice; biryani* [P. yaḵnī]

akol ['āχòl] (n) *sense* | betar akol nae – *the fellow has no common sense* : (tumar) akol ace! – (to child) *that's a good boy!* : tumar akol ɖekao! – (to baby) *smile and show us your teeth!* : **akol ɖe-/akol ɖi la-** – *give advice* : tain bala akol ɖicoin amare – *he gave me some useful advice* : ek·ta akol ɖi lauka – *please give me some advice* [A. ¿aql – *wisdom*]

akol-buɖɖi ['āχòl-būɪɖ-ɖī] (n) *common sense* = **akol + buɖɖi**

akolɖat ['āχòl-ɖāt] (n) *wisdom tooth* = **akol + ɖat**

akt [āχt] (n) *marriage rite* | **akt oe** – *the marriage sacraments are performed* : tair akt oice – *her formal marriage has taken place* : akt oice, bia baɖe oibo – *the sacraments have taken place but the social celebration will be later* [A. ¿aqd – *tying together*]

akta ['āχta] (adv) *suddenly* | akta amar buk lagcil – *I suddenly felt hungry* : akta ɖeki janla kula – *all of a sudden I noticed the window was open* [B. acâmka]

al¹ [ā:l] (n) *plough; ploughing; a measure of land* | beta al jane na – *that man doesn't know how to plough a field* : «al-o cine na, jal-o cine na» – *he's no good at any type of work* : ek al jomin – *one haal of land* : **alor** – *of the plough; for ploughing* : alor goru – *oxen used for ploughing* : «na alor na bicor» – *fit neither for ploughing nor for breeding; useless* : **al ba-** – *wield a plough; plough land* : jelera al bae na – *fisherfolk don't cultivate any land* [B. hal]

al² (n) *tiller (of boat)* | **al car-/al cari ɖe-/al cari ja-** – *let go of the tiller; relinquish control; give up* : al cari ɖicoin ni? – *have you thrown in the sponge?* [B. hal]

al- [āl] (vi) *move away* | alo, tumra! – *move back, you lot!* : **ali ja-** – *move away* : tain amrar gec tone ali gecoin – *he has distanced himself from us* cf **alog**

-ala [-āla] (noun suffix) *-man* | ɖuɖala – *milkman* : lamfa culala – *fellow with long hair* : venala – *man with a van* [H. vālā]

ala ['ā:la] (n) *wife's younger brother; undistinguished person* | ɖur ala! – *get away with you, you creep!* = **hala** [vulgar when used as a term of abuse]

alaɖa ['ālaɖa] (adv) *separately* | tara alaɖa takto – *they used to live separately* ¶ **alaɖa** (adj) *separate; dissimilar* | tan alaɖa bet ace – *she has a separate bed* : tan karbar alaɖa – *his dealings are idiosyncratic; he's a quirky individual* : **alaɖa kor-/alaɖa kori le-** – *make separate; sequestrate; separate* : tumar boi alaɖa korci – *I've separated your books from the rest* [A. ¿alā ħīda – *on its own*]

alaf ['ālaf] (n) *conversation; talk; matter to discuss* | biar alaf coler – *marriage negotiations are going on* : afnar loge amar alaf ace – *there's something I want to discuss with you* : **alaf kor-** – *have conversation; discuss* : cacar loge ami forae alaf kori – *I often have a chat with uncle* : tan loge morgejor kota alaf korcoin ni? – *have you discussed the subject of the mortgage with him?* [B. alap < S. ālāpa]

alaf-alucona ['ālaf-ālūsona] (n) *discussions* = **alaf + alucona**

alafsalaf ['ālaf-šālaf] (n) *talk, chatting* = **alaf**
alcar ['āl-sār] (n) *gastric ulcer* | cacar alcar oi gece – *uncle's got a stomach ulcer* [E.]
alfin ['āl-fīn] (n) *pin* [Pg. alfinete]
alga ['ālga] (adj) *separate; loose; unfixed* | tan alga gor ace – *she has a separate house* : tumar cul alga kene? – *why is your hair untied?* : butolor difa alga roice – *the stopper of the bottle is off* : **alga kor-** – *make separate; separate; loosen* [B. alga]
algoc ['ālgos] (adv) *apart* | ami algoc taki – *I keep myself to myself* [H. alag se]
alhamdulilla [al-'hāmdu-lil-lā] (int) *praise to God!* [A. alhamdu li l-lāh]
ali[1] ['ālī] (n) *laziness* cf **ailsemi**
ali[2] (n) *lazy person* | alir goro kali – *a lazy person has an empty larder*
ali[3] ['ā:lī] (n) *set of four* | ek ali am – *four mangoes* : tin ali enda – *a dozen eggs* [B. hali]
alia ['ālīa] (adj) *lazy* cf **ailsa**
alif [ā-'līf] (n) *Arabic "A"; alpha* [A. alif]
alif-be [ā-'līf-bé] (n) *Arabic ABC* [P. alif, be < A. alif, ba]
alim ['ālīm] (n) *Islamic scholar* [A. ¿ālim – *knower; learned person*]
alkatra [āl-'χāt-ra] (n) *pitch; tar* [A. al-qaṭrān]
alla ['āl-lā] (n) *God* | alla malik : *God is sovereign* : alla hafij – *God is the protector; God protect you* : alla oaste – *for the sake of God* : allar rohmote – *by the mercy of God* : allar icca – *(let it be) as God wishes* : allar ukum – *(let it be) as God ordains* : allar bari – *Mecca* : ek allae jane – *only God knows* : allae dein jodin – *if God permits* : allae dile kail jaimu – *if God permits I shall go there tomorrow* : ore alla! – *oh my God!* : **alla alla kor-** – *recite God's name in supplication* [A. al-lāh – *The Sole Deity*]
alla talla ['āl-la-tāl-la] (n) *God* [A. al-lāh ta'ālā – *God, Who is Exalted*]
alle ['āl-lé] (v adv) *on completion of an action; when it is done* | for oi alle deka jaibo – *when the day has dawned it will be possible to see* : tumi kam·ta kori alle foesa faibae – *you'll get your money when you've done the work* : tara ai alle amra kaimu – *when they have arrived we shall eat* = **arle**
almari ['āl-marī] (n) *cupboard* [Pg. armario]
-aloe ['ālòɛ] (n) *abode* [B. alåy < S. ālaya]
alog ['ā-lòg] (adv) *separately* | tara alog take – *they live apart* [H. alag]
alu ['ālū] (n) *potato* | gul alu – *potato* : mita alu – *sweet potato* : sak alu – *leguminous potato* : mou alu – *yam* : simul alu – *cassava* [B. alu < P. ālū – *plum*]
alu bukara ['ālū-būχāra] (n) *prune* [P. ālū boχārā – *Bokhara plum*]
alucona ['ālūsona] (n) *discussion* | alucona coler – *discussions are going on* : **alucona kor-** – *discuss; criticize* : murobbiain alucona korra – *the elders are having a discussion* : tain besi alucona koroin – *he criticizes too much* [B. alocåna < S. ālocanā – *assessment*]
am [ām] (n) *mango* [B. am < O. āmra]
amantu billah [ām'āntūbīl-lā] (int) *I believe in God* (first words of the declaration of faith or "imaan") [A. amantu bi l-lāhi]
amar ['āmār] (pron adj) *my* < **ami**
amare ['āmāré] (pron) *me; to me* < **ami**
amasa ['āmāša] (n) *dysentery* [B. amasa < S. āmāšaya – *stomach*]
am cifara ['ām-sīfāra] (n) *final section of the Quran* (the last and best known of the thirty sections into which the Quran has been divided for the purposes of recitation) [P. sī pāra – *thirty parts* × P. pāra-e-amm – *the part beginning with "amm"*]
amda ['ām-da] (adj) *plentiful* | amda fol ace – *there's plenty of fruit* [P. āmāda – *ready*]
amdani ['ām-danī] (n) *coming; arrival; import; income* | ino bout mainsor amdani oe – *a lot of people come here* : tarar foesar amdani ace – *they make plenty of money* : **amdani o-** – *be acquired; be imported* : kajur arob taki amdani oe – *dates are imported from Arabia* : **amdani kor-** – *acquire; import* : ota kunan tone amdani korcoin? – *wherever did you get that from?* [P. āmadanī – *coming*]
amdani-roftani ['ām-danī-rof-tanī] (n) *import and export* = **amdani + roftani**

ami ['āmī] (pron) *I* | ami ino taki – *I live here* : ke jaito? ami! – *who wants to go? I do!* : **amar** – *of me; my* : amar nam Ali – *my name is Ali* : amar samne ubao – *stand in front of me* : **amare** – *to me; me* : afne amare cinoin na – *you don't know me* : kagoj·kan amare deuka – *please give the paper to me* [B. ami]

-ami [-āmī] (noun suffix) *-ness* | buka, bukami – *foolish, foolishness* : dustu, dustami – *naughty, naughtiness* : fagol, faiglami – *crazy, craziness*

amkori ['ām-χòrī] (n) *crawling* | **amkori de-** – *crawl* : gedae one amkori dee – *the baby can crawl now* [B. hamaguri]

amma ['ām-mā] (n) *Mum*

amol ['āmòl] (n) *deeds; conduct; behaviour; administration* | afnar amol dekia bicar korbo allae – *God will judge you according to your deeds* : fua·tar amol bala nae – *the boy's conduct is not very good* : bitisor amol – *the British Raj; the period of British rule* : agor amolor foesa – *coins of a previous era* [A. ¿amal – *work; deeds; moral conduct*]

amoli ['āmolī] (adj) *observant of religious duties; of good character* | tain boro amoli manus – *he is a very upright person* [A. ¿amalī]

amra ['ām-ra] (pron) *we* | amra inor manus – *we are local people* : **amra amra** – *we ourselves; we as a group* : amra amra tik kormu – *we'll fix it on our own* : **amrar** – *of us; our* : ein amrar ticar – *she is our teacher* : amrar bodole era jaibo – *they will go instead of us* : **amrare** – *to us; us* : tain amrare iŋlis hikain – *she teaches us English* [B. amra]

an- [ān] (vt) *bring; fetch; get; buy* | kut anci na – *I haven't brought a coat* : kolom ano cai – *please fetch a pen* : goro cetelait antam – *we want to get satellite TV installed in our home* : aij tain katol anba – *he's going to buy a jackfruit today* : **ani le-** – *bring; fetch; get* : tain fandan ani lira – *she's bringing the paan salver* : **gia an-/an- gi** – *go and get* : amar cosma ano gi cai – *please fetch my spectacles* [B. an-]

ana¹ ['āna] (pre) *without* | tain ana karone rag koroin – *he gets angry without any reason* : i boi·ta ana foesae faici – *I got this book free of charge* : he ana kame aicil – *he came with no purpose in mind* : tara ana koia gece gi – *they left without saying goodbye* : ana dekia kila koitam? – *how can I say without having seen it?* : «ana foria fondit» – *a pundit without having gone to the trouble of studying*

ana² (n) *anna; sixteenth part* | tin teka at ana – *three rupees and eight annas; three and a half rupees* : ek ana – *one sixteenth* : cair ana – *four sixteenths; one quarter* : ou amor baro ana bad – *three quarters of these mangoes are rotten* : dus at ana amar, at ana tumar – *the fault is half mine, half yours* : **sullo ana** – *sixteen sixteenths; the whole* : tan foesa sullo ana kuaicoin – *he's lost all of his money* : afne sullo anar malik – *you are the sole owner* : kota·ta sullo ana mica – *that statement is entirely false* [B. ana]

ana³ (v n) *coming; to come* | tara ruj ana dorce – *they've started coming every day* : tan goro ana jorur – *it's vital for him to come home* < **a-**

ana⁴ (v n) *bringing* < **an-**

ana- (vt) *cause to be brought; send for* | ca anairam – *I'm having tea brought here* : tain ranare dia fail anaicoin – *he got Rana to fetch the file* : mestoir anaitam ni? – *shall I send for a workman?* : **anai le-** – *cause to be brought; send for* : tain sof taki mal anai licoin – *he had stuff brought from the shop* [B. ana-]

anaj ['ānāz] (n) *vegetables* [H. anāj – *grain*]

ana-jana (n) *coming and going* = **ana**³ + **jana**²

ana-loa (n) *fetching and carrying* = **ana**⁴ + **loa**¹

anamot ['ānāmot] (adv) *wholly; entirely* | karfit anamot nata kori lice – *they've totally ruined the carpet* : kam·ta anamot ses kortam – *I want to finish off the job*

ananac ['ānānas] (n) *pineapple* [Pg. ananas]

anbita ['ān-bita] (adj) *unmarried* [B. ábibahitá < S. avivāhita]

andar ['ān-dār] (n) *underpants* [E.]

andare ['ān-dāré] (adv) *under one's control; in a position of reliance* | afnar andare koe·jon huruta roice? – *how many children are under your authority? / how many dependent children have you?* [E. under]

anda ['āndā] (adj) *blind; unseeing; ignorant* | tain anda, couke dekoin na – *she's blind, she can't see* : ami anda manus – *I'm an ignorant fellow* ¶ **anda** (n) *blind person* | ek andare codga dicla – *he gave alms to a blind man* [H. andhā < O. andha]
andair ['āndāɪr] (n) *darkness* | tain andairor maje goro gecoin – *he went home in the dark* **andair** (adj) *dark* | andair lage – *it seems dark* : tan couk andair oi gecil – *her vision had blacked out* [H. aⁿdherā < O. andhikāra]
andu ['ān-dū] (adj) *uninformed* | andu kota – *wild talk; baseless statement* : he andu mat mate – *he talks without knowing the facts* [H. andhā]
andulon ['ān-dūlòn] (n) *movement; campaign* | andulonor somoe – *the time of the Bangladesh independence movement* : **andulon kor-** – *wage a campaign* : tara beton baraibar lagi andulon korer – *they're campaigning for an increase in wages* [B. andolån < S. āndolana – *swinging; oscillating movement*]
ani[1] ['ānī] (v n) *coming* | one tan ani dorkar – *his coming is needed now; he needs to come now* : tara anit – *they are on the way* : tain anir kalo kandicla – *she wept when coming away* < **a-**
ani[2] (n) *law* see **ain**
anondo ['ānondò] (n) *joy; pleasure* | **anondo oe** – *pleasure is felt* : amar bakka anondo oice – *I really did enjoy it* : **anondo kor-** – *enjoy oneself* : huruta anondo korer – *the children are having a good time* [B. anåndå < S. ānanda]
antaj ['āntāz] (n) *estimation; guesswork* | tan antaj bala – *he has a good eye (in estimating)* : antaj ni na jana kota? – *was that a guess, or something you know for a fact?* : **antaj kor-** – *estimate; guess* : antaj kori kouka, koto – *say roughly how much* : ami antaj korclam, afne aiba bule – *I guessed you'd come* [B. andaj < P. andāza – *size; measurement*]
antaje ['āntazé] (adv) *by guesswork; without exact knowledge* | antaje kita koitam – *what can I say, without actually knowing* : tain antaje matoin – *he makes ill-informed statements* : antaje! – *fiddlesticks!* < **antaj**
aŋgaj ['āŋgāz] (n) *fortitude; resilience* = **aŋgej**
aŋgej ['āŋgéz] (n) *fortitude; resilience* | tair aŋgej ace – *she has a lot of resilience; she can put up with a lot* : **aŋgej kor-** – *endure; bear* : tanda aŋgej kortam fari na – *I can't stand the cold* [P. angez < angektan – *to provoke*]
aŋgul ['āŋgūl] (n) *finger; toe* | buri aŋgul – *thumb* : kuti aŋgul – *little finger* : faur aŋgul – *toe* : **buri aŋgul deka-** – *flash one's thumb; make a rude gesture* [B. aŋgul < O. aŋgula]
aŋguli ['āŋgūlī] (n) *finger* [B. åŋguli < S. aŋguli]
aŋgur ['āŋgūr] (n) *grape; grapes* [P. aŋgūr]
aŋkur ['āŋkūr] (n) *crawling* | **aŋkur de-** – *crawl* : one bebie aŋkur dito fare – *now baby is able to crawl* = **amkori**
aoa ['āwā] (v n) *coming; arrival* | jani na, tan aoa kundin oibo – *I don't know when his arrival will take place* : tair lagi na aoa bala – *it's better for her not to come* : tara aoar somoe ful ancil – *they brought some flowers when they came* : afne aoar age fon koroin jen – *please phone before you come* : Mina aoat lab nae – *there's no point in Mina's coming* : afne aoat amra bacci – *we've been saved by your arrival* < **a-**
aoaj ['āwāz] (n) *sound; noise* | kunu aoaj nae – *not a sound to be heard* : **aoaj oe** – *sound is made* : besi aoaj or – *there's too much noise* : **aoaj fa-** – *hear a sound* : ami tura aoaj faici – *I heard a small sound* : **aoaj kor-** – *make a noise* : aoaj korio na – *don't make any noise* [P. āvāz – *voice*]
aoa-jaoa ['āwā-jāwā] (n) *coming and going* | **aoa-jaoa kor-** – *come and go* : boce haridin aoa-jaoa koroin – *the boss keeps coming and going all day*
aoara ['āwāra] (n) *vagrant* [P. āvāra – *wandering; homeless*]
aoban ['āwbān] (n) *call; appeal* [B. ahban < S. āhvāna]
aola ['āola] (n) *custody; care* = **haola**
aolad ['āolād] (n) *progeny; children* [A. aulād]
aolat ['āolāt] (n) *loan* [A. hawāla – *assignment; draft*]
aona ['āonā] (n) *things to come; fate in store; predestiny* < **a-**

aorot ['āoròt] (n) *woman* [P. aurat < A. ¿aura – *pudendum*]
ar [ā-r] (conj) *and* | mina ar runa – *Mina and Runa* : suɖu kani ar gum – *nothing but eating and sleeping* : ami geci ar aici – *I've been there and back* : ɖuɖ ɖorkar ar cini ɖorkar – *we need milk and also sugar* ¶ **ar** (adv) *more; in addition; still* | ar ace ni? – *is there any more? are there any left?* : ar nae – *there's no more, there are none left* : ar kaita ni? – *would you like any more (to eat)?* : ar fartam nai – *I can't manage any more* : ar ke jaita? – *who else wants to go?* : tain ar aita nae – *he won't come after all* : ar tin·ta am roice – *there are still three mangoes left* : ar somoe nae – *there's no time left* : te ar kita? – *so what else? that's all, isn't it?* ¶ **ar** (adj) *additional; remaining* | ar mainse baɖe kaiba – *the remaining people will eat later* : ar·guin kuae? – *where are the rest?* : **ar keu** – *someone else; anyone else* : tai korce, na ar keu korce? – *did she do it, or someone else?* : ar keu aicoin na – *nobody else has come* : **ar kunta** – *something else; anything else* : ar kunta cain ni? – *do you want anything else?* : na, ar kunta nae – *no, nothing else* : **ar kunu** – *some more; some other; any more; any other* : ar kunu torkari nae ni? – *aren't there any other vegetables?* : ar kunu somoe aiba – *come some other time* : ami ar kunu ɖin koitam nai – *I'll never say it again* : **ar ar** – *many more* : am jam licu ar ar koto – *mangoes, jaams, lychees and so many more things* [B. ar]
ar² [ā:r] (n) *necklace* [B. har < O. hāra]
ar³ [ā:r] (n) *defeat* | **ar man-/ar mani le-** – *admit defeat* : afne ar mani licoin ni? – *have you met your match?* [B. har < O. hāri]
ar-¹ [ā-r] (v) *complete an action; finish; already have done* | ami kam·ta kori arci – *I've completed the job* : arco ni? – *have you finished? are you done?* : tain ai arcoin – *he has already come* : tar boes sullo oi arle .. – *when he has turned sixteen* [B. sar-]
ar-² (vi) *get lost; be a loser* | ikan are na jen – *make sure this doesn't get lost* : tara foela kelat arcil – *they lost in the first match* : **ari ja-** – *get lost* : furi·ta ari gecil – *the girl had got lost* : tumar kad ari jaito fare – *your card may get lost* [B. har-]
-ara (noun suffix) *those people; that lot* | silfi-ara kuae? – *where are Shilpi and her lot?* : abul-ara london gece – *Abul and his family have gone to London*
ara- ['āra] (vt) *lose* | tumar rumal araio na – *don't lose your hankie* : **arai le-** – *lose* : tain hamesa catti arai lein – *he keeps losing his umbrella* : amra aijkur kela arai lici – *we lost today's match* [B. hara-]
arai ['ārāī] (n°) *two and a half* | arai mas – *two and a half months* : arai so – *two hundred and fifty* : arai ajar – *two thousand five hundred* : arai·ta baje – *it's two thirty* : tair arai bocor boes – *she's two and a half years old* [B. aɽai]
aram ['ārām] (n) *comfort* | tarar goro aram nae – *there's a lack of comfort in their house* : **aram lage** – *comfort is felt* : ino afnar aram lager ni? – *are you feeling comfortable here?* : **aramor** – *of comfort; comfortable* : ou cear aramor – *this chair is comfortable* : tain bout aramor kam koroin – *he has a cushy job* : **aram kor-** – *make oneself comfortable; take it easy* : one tura aram korouka – *please relax for a bit now* : **aram fa-** – *feel at ease* : afnar goro aram fai – *I feel at ease in your house* [P. ārām]
aramce ['ārām-sé] (adv) *comfortably; easily* | aramce bouka – *please seat yourself comfortably* : aramce jaita farba – *you'll get there with ease* [U. ārām se]
arbar ['ār-bār] (adv) *again* | arbar kouka – *say that again* : amar cafi arbar kuaici – *I've lost my key again* = **ar**¹ + **bar**¹
arbi ['ārbī] (n) *Arabic* [A. ¿arabī]
are ['ā-ré] (int) *well I never!* | are! haca-u forto fare! – *my goodness, he really can read it!* : are! Malik sab ni? – *well, if it isn't Mr Malik!* : are! are! – *well, this is quite amazing!*
arek ['ārɛχ] (adj) *another* | arek beta – *another man* : arek·jon – *another one; a different person* : arek bar – *another time; once again* = **ar**¹ + **ek**
ari¹ ['ārī] (n) *handsaw* [H. ārī]
ari² (v adv) *having done; after doing* | tain ɖeki ari jaiba gi – *after having a look he'll go* : tara kai ari gumaice – *after having a meal they went to sleep* : afne gi ari citi ɖein jen – *please write after you've got there* < **ar-**¹

ari[3] (n) *neighbour* cf **fori**
ari[4] (n/adj) *ascendant* | ari kuna – *north west compass point* [? O. ārohī]
arifori ['ārī-fòrī] (n) *neighbour* | tain amar gaur arifori – *he's a village neighbour of mine*
¶ **arifori** (adj) *of one's neighbourhood* | amar arifori caca – *my neighbourhood "uncle"* cf **fori**
arji ['ārjī] (n) *petition; request* [U. arzī < A. ¿arƉ – *submission*]
armoni ['ār-mònī] (n) *harmonium* [E.]
aro ['ā-rò] (adv) *even more* | aro ɖao! aro! – *give me some more! more, more!* : ota aro sunɖor – *this one is even prettier* : london taki daka aro boro – *Dhaka is even bigger than London* : **aro besi** – *even more* : tai Runar caite aro besi jane – *she knows even more than Runa* = **ar**[1] + **-o**
arob ['āròb] (n) *Arabia; the Arab lands* | arob ɖesor manus – *an Arab* [A. ¿arab]
aroj ['āròz] (n) *petition; request* [A. ¿arƉ – *submission*]
arok ['āròχ] (adj) *another* | arok beta ar – *another man is coming* : tar arok nam acil – *he used to have a different name* : arok bar ɖektam ni? – *shall we try one more time?* :
  arok·ta/arok·kan – *another one* : arok·ta ɖeuka – *please give me another one* : **arok·jon** – *another person* : hok sab nae, arok·jon – *it's not Mr Haq, it's someone else* : ota arok·jonor – *that belongs to someone else* = **ar**[1] + **ek**
arombo ['āròm-bò] (n) *beginning* | **arombo o-/arombo oi ja-** – *begin; start* (intransitive) : maramari arombo oi gece – *fighting has begun* : **arombo kor-** – *begin; start* (transitive) : tain kam arombo korta – *he wants to start working* : hurutae fora arombo korce – *the children have started to study* [B. aråmbhå < S. ārambha]
arua ['ārŵa] (adj) *foolish*
as[1] [āš] (n) *fibre* [B. aⁿs]
as[2] [ā:š] (n) *duck; goose; swan* [B. haⁿs < S. haŋsa – *goose*]
as- [ā:š] (vi) *laugh; smile* | aso kitar lagi ? – *why are you laughing?* : ɖekrae ni, bebi ase! – *see, the baby is smiling!* : **asi le-** – *laugh* : fuae akta asi licil – *the boy suddenly burst out laughing* [B. has-]
asa ['āšā] (n) *hope; expectation; prospect* | tan monor maje boro asa – *she is nurturing great hopes* : tain aiba, kunu asa ace ni? – *is there any likelihood of his coming?* : amra jitbar asa kom – *there's not much hope of our winning* : ek minitor asa nae – *we can't take even the next minute for granted* : **asa kor-** – *hope; expect* : asa kori hokoloe bala acoin – *I hope everyone is well* : tain london jaiba asa korra – *she's hoping to go to London* : asa kori baro·tar age aiba – *I expect she'll come before twelve* [B. asa < S. āšā]
asa- ['ā:šā] (vt) *make (someone) laugh* | ci, asaio na amare – *come off it, don't make me laugh* [B. hasa-]
asaasi ['ā:šā-āšī] (n) *laughter* < **as-**
asam ['āšam] (n) *Assam* [B. asam]
asami ['āšamī] (n) *accused person* | fouɖari keicor asami – *the accused in a criminal case* [A. al-`asāmī – *the names*]
ascuijjo ['āš-tšuɪjjɪò] (n) *extraordinary thing; astonishment* | ki ascuijjo! – *what an extraordinary thing!* : ascuijjor kota – *a matter of amazement; an extraordinary matter* : **ascuijjo lage** – *it seems extraordinary; it's astonishing* : **ascuijjo o-/ascuijjo oi ja-** – *be astonished* : ami hunia ascuijjo oici – *I was amazed to hear it* [B. ascårjå < S. āšcarya]
asefase ['āšé-fāšé] (adv) *nearby* | rina tara asefase take – *Rina and her family live close by* [B. asepase]
asfas ['āš-fāš] (adj/adv) *nearby* | asfas goror manus – *neighbours* : asfas kunu sof ace ni? – *is there any shop nearby?* [H. āspās]
asfatal ['āš-fatāl] (n) *hospital* | kail afnar asfatalor tarik – *tomorrow is your hospital appointment* : tain asfatalo borti oicoin – *she has been admitted to hospital* [E.]
asi ['āšī] (nº) *eighty* [B. asi]

11

asi ['āːšī] (n) *smile; laughter* | sunɖor asi – *a nice smile* : muta asi – *loud laughter* : **asir** – *laughable; funny* : asir kicca – *a funny story* : asir koṭa – *a laughable thing* : **asi ɖe-** – *smile; laugh* : geɖae asi ɖice – *the baby smiled* [B. hasi < O. hasi]
asi-kusi ['āːšī-kūšī] (n) *merriment* = **asi + kusi** [1]
asi-tatta ['āːšī-tat-tā] (n) *jesting* = **asi + tatta**
askari ['ās-χārī] (n) *soldier* [A. ¿askarī]
asman ['āš-mān] (n) *sky* [P. āsmān]
asokti ['āšòχtī] (n) *weakness* | **asokti lage** – *weakness is felt* : amar faur maje asokti lage – *I feel a weakness in my legs* : **asokti kore/asokti kori lee** – *weakness is felt* : amar asokti kori lice – *I'm feeling quite weak* [B. asåkti < S. ašakti]
asol ['āšòl] (n) *original thing; original amount* | asol·ṭa oilo .. – *the main thing is* .. : ṭin ajar fon asol – *£3000 principal* : **suɖe asole** – *including both interest and capital* : suɖe asole cair ajar fon – *principal plus interest, £4000* : **asole** – *basically; really; in fact* : asole ṭain bul kam korcoin – *he's done the wrong thing, basically* : asole manus bala – *he's a sound person, in reality* ¶ **asol** (adj) *basic; main* : asol koṭa oilo .. – *the main point is* .. : asol jinis buli geclam! – *I forgot the most important thing!* [A. aṣl – *root, origin, basis*]
assin ['āš-šīn] (n) *Aswin (September-October)* [B. assin < S. āšvina]
asto ['āštò] (nº) *eight* = **at**
asta ['āsta] (adj) *whole; entire* | amra asta gor caf korci – *we've cleaned the whole house* : asta gaur maje ɖukan nae – *there's no shop in the entire village* : enda·ṭa asta roice – *the egg has stayed intact* [B. asta]
aste ['ās-té] (adv) *slowly; softly; gently* | gari aste coler – *the bus is moving slowly* : aste maṭo! – *speak softly!* : aste! – *carefully now! gently does it!* : **aste aste** – *very slowly; very softly* : ṭain aste aste aṭoin – *she walks very slowly* : tara aste aste matcil – *they were talking very quietly* [B. aste < P. āhista]
aste-ɖire ['āsté-ɖīré] (adv) *slowly* | aste-ɖire kam korouka – *work slowly; take your time* = **aste + ɖire**
astin ['āstīn] (n) *sleeve* [P. āstīn]
asto ['āštò] (adj) *whole; entire* = **asta**
astor ['āstòr] (n) *covering* | lefor astor – *quilt cover* : **astor ɖe-** – *apply a coating* : oalo astor ɖeoa – *the wall has been plastered* [P. āstar]
at [1] [āt] (nº) *eight* [B. at]
at [2] [āːt] (n) *village market* [B. hat]
at- [1] [āt] (vi) *fit; fit in* | baskoṭ ɖui·ṭa gelas aṭbo – *two glasses will fit in the box* : oṭo boro ṭebul ino aṭto nae – *such a large table won't fit in here* : **ati ja-** – *fit; fit in* : ek·kan cear ino ati jaibo – *one chair will fit in here* [B. at-]
at- [2] [āːt] (vi) *walk* | aṭo! – *start walking! off you go!* : ṭain aste aste aṭoin – *she walks very slowly* : ou fekor maje ata jae na – *it's impossible to walk in all this mud* : aij amra aṭmu – *today we'll go on foot* : **atia/aittia** – *by walking; on foot* : afne kila aicoin? aittia – *how did you come? on foot* : **ati ati** – *by walking; on foot* : tara ati ati goro gece gi – *they walked all the way home* [B. haⁿt-]
ata [1] ['āta] (n) *wholemeal wheat flour* [B. ata]
ata [2] (n) *stickiness; glue* | ata lage – *it feels sticky* : ata ɖi lagaici – *I've stuck it with glue* [B. atha]
ata- [1] (vt) *tidy away; fit in; close up; finish off; tighten up* | kagjain ataitam ni? – *shall I tidy away the papers?* : ṭumar bejal aṭao – *clear up your mess* : cear·kan ono atani lagbo – *the chair will have to be fitted in here* : ɖoroja atkauka – *please close the door* : gira·ṭa ataiṭa farcoin na – *he hasn't managed to fasten the knot properly* : **atai le-** – *tidy away; fit in; close up; finish off; tighten up* : afnar kam atai louka – *please finish your work; time to pack it all up* [B. ata-]
ata- [2] (vt) *cause to walk; force to walk* | aij ar koṭo ataiṭa amare? – *how much further are you going to make me walk today?* [B. haⁿta-]

ataati[1] ['āta-ātī] (n) *shortage* | calir ataati oito fare – *there may be a shortage of rice* : **ataati kor-** – *make economies; be niggardly* : tain jobor ataati koroin – *he is awfully tight* < **at-**[1]

ataati[2] ['ā:ta-ātī] (n) *walking about* | **ataati kor-** – *walk about* : tain bianku ataati koroin – *he goes for a walk in the morning* : tumar lagi bout ataati korci – *I've done a lot of running about for you* < **at-**[2]

atais ['āt-āɪš] (n°) *twenty-eight* [B. atais]

atanno ['ātan-nò] (n°) *fifty-eight* [B. atannå]

atanobboi ['āta-nòb-bòī] (n°) *ninety-eight* [B. atanåbbåi]

ataro ['ātarò] (n°) *eighteen* [B. atharå]

atasi ['ātašī] (n°) *eighty-eight* [B. åstasi]

atattoir ['ātat-tòɪr] (n°) *seventy-eight* [B. atattår]

atcallis ['āt-sal-līš] (n°) *forty-eight* [B. atcållis]

atk- (vi) *get stuck* | cakka atkice – *the wheel has got stuck* : **atki ja-** – *get stuck; get held up* : gari jemor maje atki gecil – *the car was stuck in a jam* : afnar kam atki jaibo – *your work will get held up* : he majemaje forat atki jae – *he sometimes gets stuck in his reading*

atka ['ātχa] (v adj) *stuck; held up* | **atka for-** – *get held up* : amra atka forclam – *we got held up* < **atk-**

atka- ['ātχa] (vt) *stick; fasten; detain; hold back* | istem ono atkauka – *stick the stamp here* : doroja atkaicoin ni? – *have you fastened the door?* : hurutae amare atkaicil – *the children held me up* : gari atkao! – *make the bus wait!* : **atkai rak-** – *fasten; detain* : tar jama ceftin dia atkai rake – *he fastens his shirt with a safety pin* : fulise gari atkai rakce – *the police have detained the car* : **atkai đe-** – *stick; fasten* : hurutae oalo fotu atkai đer – *the kids are sticking pictures on the wall* [B. atka-]

atok ['ātòχ] (adj) *detained; confined* | tai hariđin goror maje atok take – *she is shut up inside the house all day* : **atok kor-** – *detain; hold captive* : curare atok korce – *they've held the thief* : **atok kori rak-** – *keep in detention; keep captive* : he tar boure atok kori rake – *he keeps his wife imprisoned* [B. atåk]

atsotti ['āt-šòt-tī] (n°) *sixty-eight* [B. atsåtti]

atu ['ātū] (n) *knee* [B. ha^{n}tu]

attis ['āt-tīš] (n°) *thirty-eight* [B. attris]

at [āt] (n) *hand; arm; cubit* | tumar at caf koro – *clean your hands* : tar at lamfa – *he has long arms* : cuic afnar ator daine – *the switch is on your right hand* : rumor maf coe at – *the room measures six cubits (nine feet)* : hokoltir maje tar at ace – *he has a hand in everything* : selait tair at bala – *she's a dab hand at sewing* : **ator** – *of the hand* : ita tan ator kam – *this is her handiwork* : hokolti ek ator – *it's all the work of one single person* : ou keik afnar ator ni? – *did you make this cake yourself?* : ita kar ator leka? – *whose handwriting is this?* : boro ator leka – *writing done in block letters* : afnar ator kagoj·kan đi lauka – *please give me the paper you've got in your hand* : afnar ator·kan – *the one you're holding* : tain amar ator manus – *he is a man in my hand; he is someone I can control* : **ato** – *in the hand* : tumar ato kita? – *what's that you're holding?* : tan ato foesa ace – *he has money in hand* : **ato đe-/ato đi la-** – *hand over* : amar ato đi lao – *give it to me* : **ato lo-** – *take; pick up* : ato loia đekouka – *pick it up and have a good look* : tain bout kam ato loicoin – *he's taken on a lot of work* : **ate** – *by hand; with one's hand* : ami nijor ate lekmu – *I shall write it with my own hand* : **at đe-/at đi la-** – *touch; interfere; lend a hand* : at đio na – *don't touch it* : tan kamor maje at đein na jen – *please don't interfere in his dealings* : tura at đi lauka amare – *please give me a hand* : **at đi** – *by hand* : tain at đi malaicoin – *she made it by hand* : **at đek-** – *read a palm* : tain mainsor at đekoin – *she can read people's palms* : **at đeka-** – *have one's palm read* : ek sađure at đekaiclam – *I got a sadhu to read my palm* : **at kor-** – *bring under control* : tare ami at kortam farci na – *I haven't been able to get him in hand* : **at mila-** – *shake hands* : amar loge at milauka. – *shake hands with me!* [B. hat]

ata ['āta] (n) *sleeve* [B. hata]

ata- (vt) *touch with the hand; stroke* | amar boi atao kene? – *why are you touching my books?* : tai bilaire atar – *she's stroking the cat* : he mac ataia ɖore – *he catches fish by tickling them* : **ataia ɖek-** – *feel with the fingers* : ataia ɖekouka norom koto – *feel it and see how soft it is*   [B. hatṛa-]
ataati ['āta-ātī] (n) *touching; fisticuffs* | **ataati kor-** – *scuffle* : galagali baɖe ataati korce – *they exchanged insults and then had a scrap*   < **ata-**
atane ['ātanɛ́] (n adv) *by agency* | tar cacar atane kam·ta koraici – *I got the job done through his uncle*
ate ['ātɛ́] (n adv) *by hand* | tan ate taiar korcoin – *she made it by hand* : **ate ate** – *from hand to hand* : tain ate ate ɖi laicoin – *he has handed it over*   < **at**
atgori ['āt-gòrī] (n) *wrist watch*   = **at + gori**
ati ['ātī] (n) *hiccups* | **ati ute** – *hiccuping starts* : amar ati utce – *I've got the hiccups* : **ati far-** – *hiccup* : he kanir somoe ati farcil – *he hiccuped while eating*
atiar ['ātīār] (n) *weapon; tool*   [B. hatiar]
atkoroc ['āt χòròs] (n) *trivial expenses* | atkorocor foesa – *pocket money*   = **at + koroc**
atmuja ['ātmūza] (n) *gloves*   = **at + muja**
atol ['ātòl] (n) *handle*   [B. hatål]
ator ['ātòr] (n) *bowels; entrails* | atoror maje bis – *pain in the bowel*   [H. ā^{n}t < O. antra]
atra ['ātra] (adj) *separate* | tarar atra bari ace – *they have a separate homestead* : **atra o- /atra oi ja-** – *become separate* : fua·ta atra oi gece – *the son has set up on his own*   [O. antara]
atra- (v) *separate* | tara ɖui bai atraice – *the two brothers have split up* : **atrai le-** – *make separate; put apart* : bala·guin atrai louka – *separate the good ones from the rest*
atta ['āt-tā] (n) *spirit; soul*   [B. atta < S. ātmā]
attali ['āt-tālī] (n) *clapping* | **attali mar-** – *clap*   [B. hattali]
atti ['āt-tī] (n) *elephant*   [B. hati < O. hastī]
attor ['āt-tòr] (n) *fragrant oil; perfume*   [A. ¿iṭr]
atur ['ātūr] (adj) *disabled*   [B. atur < O. atura – *afflicted*]
atura ['ātura] (n) *hammer*   [B. haturi]
au ['āū] (adj) *this too* | au cear noea – *this chair is new too* : au furin baŋla jane – *these girls too, they know Bengali*   = **ou + -u**
aujubilla ['āūzūbil-lā] (int) *God help me*   [A. a¿ūðu bi l-lāh – *I seek refuge in God*]
auka ['āūkŵa] (imperative) *come! come in!* | auka, bouka! – *come in and sit yourself down!* : obae auka – *please come this way*   < **a-**
aula ['āūlŵa] (adj) *dishevelled; devastated; daft* | aula cul – *dishevelled hair* : fua morce taki tain aula oi gecoin – *she's gone to pieces since her son died* : hou beta aula – *that old fellow is a simpleton*   [B. elo < O. ākula]
aula- (vt) *mess up*   < **aula**
aulia ['āūlīā] (n) *spiritual leaders; saints*   [A. auliyā' – *guardians*]
aur- ['āūr] (vi) *disappear* | **auri ja-** – *disappear; get lost* : amar muja auri gece – *my socks have gone missing*
aura ['āūra] (adj) *hidden; lost* | aura foesa – *lost coins*   ¶ **aura** (n) *cover; shelter* | ino aura nae – *there's nowhere to shelter here* : mege bijoin na jen, aurat takouka – *don't get wet in the rain, stay under cover*   [O. āvŕta – *covered*]
auta ['āūta] (pron) *this one too* | auta baɖ – *this one is spoilt too*   = **au + -ta** [2]
auua [1] ['āūŵa] (a) *simple-minded*   [B. haba]
auua [2] (n) *goose*

b

ba [bā] (int) *dad; sir; son* | aicca, d̯eo ba! – *go on Dad, give it to me, please!* : o ba, hunouka! – *excuse me, sir, there's something I want to say to you* : ao ba! – *come here, sonny!* = **baba** Note: Interjection used to address males only. Informal and familiar.

ba [2] (conj) *or* | d̯ui·ta ba tin·ta – *two or three of them* [B. ba]

ba- (vt) *ply; wield* | caca al baita janoin – *uncle knows how to use a plough* : burae nau bain – *the old man operates a boat* : jelera jal bae – *fishermen use nets* [B. ba-]

baad̯uri ['bāad̯ūrī] (n) *braggadocio* | **baad̯uri kor-** – *swagger* [P. bahādurī – *valour*]

baanno ['bāan-nò] (n°) *fifty-two* [B. bahannå]

baar ['bāar] (n) *bloom; splendour* [P. bahār – *spring*]

baattoir ['bāat-tòır] (n°) *seventy-two* [B. bahattår]

bab [bāb] (n) *manner; mien* | he murobbi bab d̯ekaito cae – *he's trying to adopt an air of seniority* : befsar bab bala nae – *business isn't looking good* : tan monor bab bala – *she's in a happy frame of mind* : **bab kore** – *it presents an appearance; it seems* : megor bab korer – *it looks like rain* : **(kar loge) bab ace** – *an affinity exists (with someone)* : tan loge amar bab ace – *I get on well with him* : **babe** – *in manner; in a manner* : babe tain rukko – *he is rough in manner* : tan babe buja jae – *you can tell from his manner* : sokto babe d̯orouka – *hold it firmly (in a strong manner)* : kam sund̯or babe coler – *the work is going fine* : he bala babe bujce na – *he hasn't understood properly* : **bab kor-** – *acquire an affinity; get friendly* : he cearmenor loge bab korce – *he's made friends with the chairman*
[B. bhab < S. bhāva – *existence; state*]

bab- (v) *ponder; think; worry* | tumi kita babirae? – *what are you thinking about?* : babia d̯ekouka – *think it over* : tain besi baboin – *she worries too much* : babio na! – *don't worry!* [B. bhab-]

baba ['bābā] (n) *father; ancestor; son* | baba-ji! – *o father! o goodness!* : baba go! – *help!* : baba ad̯om – *Adam* : na baba, ita korio na – *no, son, don't do that* [P. bābā]

babaji ['bābāzī, 'bābājī] (n) (vocative) *Father* ¶ **babaji** (int) *oh goodness!* = **baba + ji**

babe ['bābé] (n adv) *in a manner* | bala babe kam koro – *do your work in a satisfactory manner* : tik babe colo – *behave in a proper manner* : ila babe na – *not like that* : jeca babe – *any old how* : sund̯or babe – *nicely* < **bab**

babi ['bābī] (n) *elder brother's wife* [H. bhābī]

babna ['bābnā] (n) *thinking; worrying* | foesar babna – *financial worries* : babnar kunta nae – *there's nothing to worry about* : kior babna? – *why worry? what is there to worry about?* [B. bhabna < S. bhāvanā – *perception*]

babot ['bābòt] (n) *subject heading* | **babot/babote** – *under the heading (of); concerning* : kanir babot kita oito? – *what is to be done about food?* – garir babote bout koroc oice – *a great deal has been spent on the car* [A. bāba – *category*]

bac [1] [bās] (adv) *enough* | amar bac oe na – *I don't get enough* : bac, bac! tamo! – *that's enough, stop, stop!* [P. bas]

bac [2] (n) *bus* | londonor bac noe·tat care – *the bus for London leaves at nine o'clock* : tara noe·tar bac d̯orto – *they want to catch the nine o'clock bus* : **baco** – *in a bus; by bus* : amra baco jaimu – *we'll go by bus* [E.]

bac- [1] (vi) *survive; stay alive; be left over* | bicara bacta nae – *the poor fellow isn't going to survive* : afne bout d̯in bacba! – *you will live long!* [said when someone just mentioned by name suddenly appears in person] : tura calon bacce – *a small amount of curry is left* : **jane bac-** – *escape with one's life* : tain kunumote jane baccoin – *somehow he came through it alive* : **baci ja-** – *survive; be saved; be left over* : d̯os·jon baci gecoin – *ten people survived* : baci gelam! – *phew! I'm off the hook!* : kicu kani baci jaito fare – *some food may be left over* [B. baⁿc-]

bac- [2] (vt) *pick out; select; sort out* | tara ukuin bacer – *they're picking nits* : caul·gula baca lagbo – *the rice grains will need picking over* : he macor goca bacto fare na – *he isn't able* *to pick out the fishbones* : sunḋor ek·kan kaḋ bacouka – *select a nice card* : oto·gula kafor bactam kila? – *how am I to sort out all this clothing?* : **baci le-** – *pick out; select* : tai kok·kan kafor baci lice – *she has chosen a few saris*   [B. bach-]

baca ['bāsā] (v adj) *selected* | baca am – *selected mangoes* : iguin baca baca – *these ones are individually selected*   < **bac-** ²

baca- (vt) *save; rescue; let live; preserve* | bacauka amare! – *help, save me!* : tanre bacaibar testa korer – *they're trying to save his life* : afne bacaicoin amare – *thanks, you've got me out of a fix* : alla bacaile ḋeka oibo – *if God lets us live, we shall meet again* : tain kali foesa bacaita – *he just wants to save money* : **bacai ḋe-** – *save* : tarare bacai ḋeuka – *please save them* : alla amrare bacai ḋice – *God has preserved us*   [B. baⁿca-]

bacabici ['bāsabīsi] (n) *picking and choosing* | **bacabici kor-** – *pick and choose; be particular*   < **bac-** ²

bacbara ['bās-bāra] (n) *bus fare* | londonor bacbara koto? – *how much is the bus fare to London?*   = **bac + bara** ²

bacca ['bātša] (n) *child*   = **baicca**

bacon ['bāsòn] (n) *living; survival*   < **bac-** ¹

bacur ['bāsūr] (n) *calf*   [B. bachur < O. vatsa]

baḋ ¹ [bāḋ] (n) *aftermath* | baḋ·ta bala nae – *the sequel is unpleasant* : **baḋ taki** – *since afterwards; ever since* : biar baḋ taki – *ever since the wedding* : tumi aoar baḋ taki – *ever since you came* : **baḋor** – *of afterwards; subsequent* : baḋor din – *the following day* : ou citi baḋor – *this letter is a later one* : **baḋe** – *afterwards* : baḋe koimu tumare – *I'll tell you afterwards*   [A. ba¿d]

baḋ ² (adv) *left out* | tumi baḋ – *you're not included* : **baḋ ḋe-/baḋ ḋi la-** – *leave out; give up* : cacare baḋ ḋeoa jae na – *uncle mustn't be left out* : tain cigret kani baḋ ḋi laicoin – *he's given up smoking cigarettes* : baḋ ḋi lao! – *oh, forget it!* : **baḋ for-/baḋ fori ja-** – *get left out* : ek·jonor nam baḋ fori gecil – *one person's name had been left out*   [? A. ba¿d]

baḋ ³ (adj) *bad* | gor·ta ekebare baḋ – *this house is altogether lousy* : **baḋ o-/baḋ oi ja-** – *become bad; get spoilt* : fua·ta baḋ oi jar – *the boy is going astray* : tibi baḋ oi gece – *the television is out of order* : **baḋ kor-/baḋ kori le-** – *spoil* : deko, jama baḋ kori libae – *mind out or you'll spoil your shirt*   [P. bad]

-baḋ (noun suffix) *-ism; tendency* | cufibaḋ – *Sufism* : moulbaḋ – *radicalism* : sontrasbaḋ – *terrorism*   [B. -baḋ < S. vāda – *speech; doctrine*]

baḋa ¹ ['bāḋa] (n) *rubbish; rubbish container* | ho·guin baḋa – *that lot's just trash* : baḋar maje falai ḋao – *throw it in the bin* : **baḋa kor-** – *make a mess* : ino baḋa korio na – *don't make a mess here*

baḋa ² (n) *extreme case* | fua·ta ailsemir baḋa – *the boy is idleness personified*

baḋa ³ (n) *obstacle; objection* | amar kunu baḋa nae – *I have no objection* : ilagi baḋa nae – *that's no problem* : **baḋa ḋe-** – *create obstacles; make objections* : amra jaitam, tain baḋa ḋein – *he objects to our going*   [B. baḋha < S. bādhā – *obstacle*]

baḋam ['bāḋām] (n) *nut*   [P. bādām – *almond*]

baḋami ['bāḋāmī] (adj) *nut-brown*   [P. bādāmī]

baḋ-baki (adj) *remaining* | baḋ-baki·tuku kail ḋekmu – *we'll see to the rest tomorrow* : baḋ-baki jara, baco jaiba – *everyone else will go by bus*   = **baki**

baḋe ¹ ['bāḋé] (n adv) *afterwards; after* | baḋe tara buji lice – *afterwards they realised* : tain kaicoin, baḋe gumaicoin – *he ate, and after that he slept* : tin afta baḋe – *three weeks later* : caca gecoin baḋe tai kanḋice – *she wept after uncle had left* : afne amar baḋe aicoin – *you arrived after me* : kanir baḋe ata bala – *it's good to walk a bit after eating* : **baḋe baḋe** – *just after; in succession* : baḋe baḋe tin·jon morcoin – *three people died one after the other* : ek din baḋe baḋe – *on alternate days*   < **baḋ** ¹

baḋe ² (n adv) *in exclusion; apart* | caca baḋe hokoloe bala – *uncle apart, everyone is well* : foesa baḋe aro koto·ta ace – *there are many things besides money*   < **baḋ** ²

baḋi ['bāḋī] (n) *plaintiff*   [B. baḋi < S. vādī – *speaker*]

16

-badi (adj suffix) *-speaking; -istic; exemplifying a type* | micabadi – *untruth-speaking; mendacious* : sartobadi – *egoistic; selfish* : moulbadi – *radical* ¶ **-badi** (noun suffix) *-ist; exemplar of type* | santibadi – *pacifist* : moulbadi – *radical(ist)* : sontrasbadi – *terrorist* [B. -badi < S. vādī – *speaker; proponent of doctrine*]
badia ['bādīa] (n) *serving dish* [P. bādiya – *bowl*]
bado ['bādò] (n) *Bhadra (August-September)* [B. bhadrå < S. bhādra]
badol ['bādòl] (n) *rain* [P. bādal – *cloud*]
bador ['bādòr] (n adj) *of after; following; next* | bador din – *the following day* : bador·ta – *the next one* : ou garir bador gari – *the train after this one* : idor bador din – *the day after Eid* : ein amrar bador – *he is after us (in line)* < **bad** [1]
badsa ['bādša] (n) *king; emperor* | «hokoloe badsa oile hukum manto ke?» – *if everyone is king, who will be there to obey?* [P. pādšāh]
badsagiri ['bādšagīrī] (n) *kingship; regal airs* [P. pādšāhīgīrī]
badua ['bādūā] (n) *bad one* cf **bad** [3]
bae ['bāɛ] (n adv) *in a way; in a direction; towards* | hou bae jauka – *go in that direction* : afne kun bae jaita? – *which way do you want to go?* : amar bae cauka – *look towards me* : tain goror bae atira – *he is walking towards his house* : (**kuntar**) **bae ca-** – *pay attention (to something)* : tara gorir bae caia kam kore – *they work with their eyes on the clock* : hurutar bae caia goro auka – *come home for the children's sake* : foesar bae cain na jen – *don't think about the cost* = **babe** < **bab**
baf [bāf] (n) *father* | baf ar beta – *father and son* : **boro baf** – *great grandfather* : **baf to baf! / baf re baf!** – *good gracious!* [B. bap]
bafa ['bāfā] (n) *dandruff* [H. bafā]
bafdada ['bāf-dādā] (n) *forebears; ancestors* = **baf** + **dada**
bag [1] [bāg] (n) *share; part; fraction* | munafar ek bag faiba afne – *you'll receive one share of the profit* : fosolor boro bag nata oi gece – *a large part of the crop has been spoilt* : tin bagor ek bag – *one third* : sat bagor dui bag – *two sevenths* : **bag kor-/bag kori le-** – *share; divide* : tara tin boine bag korce – *the three sisters shared it* : otare tin bag kormu – *we'll divide it into three* : barore cair dia bag koro – *divide twelve by four* : ita cair·jonor maje bag kori lita – *you're to share it among four people* [B. bhag < S. bhāga]
bag [2] (n) *leopard; tiger* [B. bagh < O. vyāghra]
bag- (vi) *run away* | fua·ta bagce – *the boy has run away* : he amar foesa loia bagbo – *he's going to run off with my money* : tain jan loia bagcoin – *he ran for dear life* : bago! – *buzz off!* : bagi ja- – *run away* : is, bagi gece! – *oh dear, he's scarpered!* [B. bhag-]
baga [1] ['bāga] (v n) *fleeing; running away* | **baga mar-** – *run away; desert one's post* : fuainte baga marce – *the boys have run away* : kamlain baga marto fare – *the workers may do a bunker* < **bag-**
baga [2] (n) *sharing* ¶ **baga** (adj) *shared* | baga gor – *a shared house* < **bag** [1]
baga- (vt) *cause to run; chase away* | tain fuaintore bagaicoin – *he has chased the boys away* [B. bhaga-]
bagabagi ['bāgā-bāgī] (n) *division* | **bagabagi kor-** – *divide* : tarar jaega bagabagi korce – *they've divided up their land* = **baga** [2]
bagan ['bāgān] (n) *garden; orchard* | ca bagan – *tea garden* : amor bagan – *mango orchard* : **bagan kor-** – *cultivate a garden* : goror kore di bagan korce – *they've made a garden behind the house* [B. bagan < P. bāġ]
bagar ['bāgār] (n) *spice fried in oil* | dalir maje bagar dein – *people add fried spices to their dhal* [H. baghār]
bagi ['bāgī] (n) *sharecropping* | **bagit de-/bagit di la-** – *let out on a sharecropping basis* : tan jaega bagit di laicoin – *he has let out his land to a sharecropper* : **bagit rak-** – *rent land as a sharecropper* < **bag** [1]
bagol ['bāgòl] (n) *running away* | **bagol mar-** – *run away* : fua·ta bagol marce – *the boy has run away* cf **baga** [1]
bahi ['bāhī] (adj) *stale* [B. basi]

bai [bāɪ] (n) *brother; male cousin; age-mate* | saikkat bai – *full brother* : cacar goror bai – *paternal cousin: son of father's brother* : fufur goror bai – *paternal cousin: son of father's sister* : mamar goror bai – *maternal cousin: son of mother's brother* : moir goror bai – *maternal cousin: son of mother's sister* : arifori bai – *neighbourhood "brother"* : **baiain** – *brothers* : tumar baiain koe·jon? – *how many brothers have you got?* : **baiaintor** – *of brothers* : tair baiaintor nam jani na – *I don't know the names of her brothers* [B. bhai]
baibai ['bāɪbāɪ] (n) *leave-taking* | **baibai de-/baibai di la-** – *say goodbye* : tumar cacare baibai di lao! – *say bye-bye to your uncle!* [E.]
bai-berador ['bāɪ-bɛ́rādòr] (n) *brothers; brethren* = **bai + berador**
baibun ['bāɪbūn] (n) *brothers and sisters* = **bai + bun**
baic [bāɪs] (n) *race; competition* | baic lagce – *the race is on* [B. baic]
baicca ['bāɪtšɪa] (n) *child; young animal* | dudor baicca – *a suckling child* : bilair baicca – *kitten* : kuttar baicca – *puppy* : murgir baicca – *chick* : **baiccain** – *children* : baiccainte kali cillae – *the children keep yelling* : baiccaintor kafor – *the children's clothes* : baiccaintore dekouka – *keep an eye on the children* : **baicca oe** – *a child is born* : tan boro furir baicca oice – *her elder daughter's had a child* : **baicca de-** – *produce offspring* : bilaie baicca dice – *the cat has had kittens* [B. bacca < P. bacca]
baiccakaicca ['bāɪtšɪa-χāɪtšɪa] (n) *children* = **baicca**
baiddo ['bāīd-dò] (adj) *bound* | tain aita baiddo – *he is bound to come* : **baiddo o-/baiddo oi ja-** – *be obliged; be forced* : afne baiddo oiba, jaita – *you will be obliged to go* : tara kor lamto baiddo oi gece – *they've had to back down* : **baiddo oia** – *perforce; of necessity* : ami baiddo oia curi korci – *I stole it because I had no alternative* : **baiddo kor-/baiddo kori le-** – *oblige; force* : tura foesa loito baiddo korci tare – *we forced him to take some money* [B. baddhå < S. bādhya – *trammeled; obstructed*]
baifut ['bāɪfūt] (n) *(woman's) brother's son* = **bai + fut**
baiggo ['bāɪg-gɪò] (n) *luck; fortune; fate* | koto boro baiggo! – *what a stroke of luck!* : tumar baiggo bala – *you're in luck* : ita baiggo – *it's simply fate* : tan baiggor dus – *he's just unlucky* : amrar baiggot nae, noea gor faitam jene – *it's not in our stars that we should get a new house* [B. bhaggå < S. bhāgya – *portion*]
baigna ['bāɪgnā] (n) *sister's son* [B. bhagina < O. bhāgineya]
baigni ['bāɪgnī] (n) *sister's daughter* [B. bhagini]
baijan ['bāɪzān] (n) *(respected) brother* = **bai + jan**
baiji ['bāɪzī] (n) *(woman's) brother's daughter* = **bai + ji**
bain [1] [bāɪn] (n) *divorce* | **tin talak bain kor-** – *divorce a wife by saying "talak" three times* [A. bain – *separation*]
bain [2] (n) *wrongdoing* | amra kunu bain korci ni? – *I ask you, have we done anything wrong?* = **beain**
baini ['bāɪnī] (n) *militia* | mukti baini – *freedom fighters* : rejakar baini – *pro-government paramilitary force* [B. bahini < S. vāhinī – *army*]
baiŋgon ['bāɪŋ-gòn] (n) *aubergine* [H. baingan < Pa. vātiŋgaṇa]
baiof ['bāɪòf] (n) *brotherhood; palliness* cf **bai**
bair [bāɪr] (n) *outside* | tara bair tone aice – *they have come from outside* : **bair o-/bair oi ja-** – *come out; go out* : afne kun somoe bair oiba? – *at what time will you be going out?* : kobor·ta bair oi gece – *the news has leaked out* : **bair kor-/bair kori le-** – *take out; bring out* : jeb taki kad bair korce – *he got a card out of his pocket* : haca·kan bair kori litam – *I want to extract the truth* : **bair kor-/bair kori de-** – *put out; throw out* : tare gor taki bair kori dice – *they have thrown him out of the house* [B. bahir]
baira ['bāɪrā] (n) *wife's sister's husband*
baira-bai ['bāɪrā-bāī] (n) *wife's sister's husband*
baire ['bāɪrɛ́] (n adv) *outside* | tain baire ubaicoin – *he's standing outside* : iskulor baire – *outside the school* : londonor baire – *outside London* : niomor baire – *outside the rules* < **bair** cf **bara**
bais [bāɪš] (n°) *twenty-two* [B. bais]

baisab ['bāɪšāb] (n) *elder brother* = **bai + sab**
bait ['bāɪt] (n) *vomiting* | **bait bait kore** – *nausea is felt* : amar bait bait korer – *I feel I'm going to be sick* . **bait kor-** – *vomit* : bebie bait korce – *the baby's thrown up* [O. vanti]
baj [bāz] (n) *falcon* [P. bāz – *falcon*]
-baj (noun suffix) *practicant; one who indulges* | tokabaj – *one who goes in for cheating; a swindler* : furtibaj – *one who likes having fun* : doŋbaj – *joker* : rendibaj – *one who consorts with prostitutes* [P. bāz – *player*]
baj- [1] (vi) *resonate* | **baje** – *resonates; rings; sounds; clashes* : gonta bajer – *the bell is ringing* : armoni bajer – *a harmonium is being played* : redio bajer – *a radio is playing* : coe·ta bajer – *six is striking / it's six o'clock* : naur tole bajer – *the boat is scraping the bottom* : malikor loge bajbo – *there will be a clash with the owner* : hono bajce! – *there's the rub!* : tar baro·ta bajce – *midnight has struck for him / he's done for* : **baji jae** – *resonates; rings; sounds; clashes* : elam baji jar – *the alarm is going off* : dos·ta baji gece – *ten has struck / it's gone ten o'clock* : dui dole baji jaibo – *there'll be a clash between the two groups* [B. baj-]
baj- [2] (vt) *fry* [B. bhaj-]
baja ['bāza] (v adj) *fried* < **baj-** [2]
baja- (vt) *cause to resonate; ring (a bell); play (music)* | gonta bajao – *ring the bell* : he tobla bajaito fare – *he can play the tabla* : tara kecet bajaice – *they played music on a cassette player* : tain elam bajaicoin – *he made the alarm go off* : **bajai de** – *cause to resonate; cause to ring; cause to play* : tara amar baro·ta bajai dice – *they have caused my ruination* [B. baja-]
bajan ['bāzān] (n) *father* = **baba + jan**
bajar ['bāzār] (n) *shopping centre; bazaar* | kandat bajar nae – *there are no shops nearby* : tain bajaro gecoin – *he's gone to the shops* : **bajar kor-** – *do shopping* : amrar ruj bajar kora lage – *we have to shop every day* : ou bajar kori aice – *he's just come back from shopping* [P. bāzār]
bajar-at (n) *shops* = **bajar + at** [2]
baje ['bāzé] (adj) *worthless; low* | baje mat – *idle talk* : baje kota – *nonsense, rubbish* : baje manus – *a worthless person* [A. waÐī ¿ - *vile, mean*]
bajeaft ['bāzéaft] (n) *confiscation* | **bajeaft o-/bajeaft oi ja-** – *be confiscated* : tarar mal bajeaft oi gece – *their goods have been confiscated* : **bajeaft kor-** – *confiscate* : fulise bajeaft korce – *the police confiscated it* [P. bāz yāft – *recovery*]
baji [1] ['bāzī] (n) *gaming* | **baji dor-** – *lay a wager; bet* : tar loge bajī dorclam – *I made a bet with him* [P. bāzī – *playing*]
baji [2] (n) *fried vegetables* [B. bhaji]
-baji (noun suffix) *practice; indulgence (in)* | tokabaji – *practice of deceit* : calakbaji – *habit of craftiness* : doŋbaji – *indulgence in joking* [P. bāzī - *playing*]
bajna ['bāznā] (n) *playing (of instruments); music* | gan bajna – *singing and music* : «kajnar caite bajna besi» – *more words than deeds* [B. bajna]
baju ['bāzū] (n) *arm; side* | tain foria bajut duk faicoin – *he fell and hurt his arm* : ek bajut gaŋ ar ek bajut kal – *there's a river on one side and a canal on the other* : kun baju jaitam? – *which way should I go?* : hou baju jauka – *go in that direction* : mocjid hou bajut – *the mosque is that way* [P. bāzū – *arm*]
bak- (vi) *bend; get bent* | **baki ja-** – *get bent* : ou camuc baki gece – *this spoon has become bent* [B. baⁿk-]
baka ['bāχa] (v adj) *bent; crooked* < **bak-**
baka- (vt) *cause to bend; make bent* | at bakaito fare na – *he can't bend his arm* : **bakai le-** – *make bent; bend* : catti ke bakai lice – *someone has bent the umbrella* [B. baⁿka-]
baka-tera ['bāχa-téra] (adj) *crooked; awry* = **baka + tera**
baki ['bākī] (adj) *outstanding; remaining; left* | baki foesa – *money outstanding* : baki jinis – *remaining things* : baki cear kunano? – *where are the rest of the chairs?* : tin·ta camuc baki – *three of the spoons are missing* : fac fon baki roice – *there's five pounds still owing* : ebo

ɖui minit baki – *there are still two minutes to go* : (**kunta oibar**) **baki roice** – *there's still some way to go (before something happens)* : kam ses oibar baki roice – *there's some way to go before the job will be completed* : tin·ta bajbar baki roice – *it's not yet three o'clock* : amar bujbar baki roice – *I haven't yet fully understood* ¶ **baki** (n) *money outstanding; credit* | amrar gece baki nae – *we don't give credit* : ino baki cole na – *purchase on credit is not allowed here* : «bakir arok nam faki» – *credit is just another name for evasion* : **baki ɖia** – *on credit* : tara baki ɖia cail ance – *they bought rice on credit* : **bakit** – *on credit; on tick* : camana bakit anmu – *we'll purchase the furniture on tick* [A. bāqī – *remaining*]

bakka ['bāk-ka] (adv) *positively; greatly* | hou kafor bakka sunɖor – *that cloth is really pretty* : aij bakka gorom force – *it's turned out really hot today*

bakol ['bāχòl] (n) *rind; bark* [B. bakål < O. valkala]

bakor ['bāχòr] (n) *coriander plant*

bal[1] [bāl] (n) *child* [B. bal < O. bāla]

bal[2] (n) *pubic hair* [H. bāl < O. vāla]

bala[1] ['bāla] (n/adv) *time of day; time; occasion* | biankur bala – *(in) the morning* : hanje bala – *(in) the evening* : je bala faroin – *at whatever time you can manage* : tara kun bala aibo? – *at what time will they come?* : i bala ɖekouka – *now have a look* : ruj tin bala kaiba – *you must eat three times a day* : tin balar kani – *three daily meals* : afnar bala suja oibo – *in your case it will be quite straightforward* [B. bela]

bala[2] (adj) *good; fine; correct; considerable* | bala manus – *a good person* : bala kota – *a good point / a good thing* : ɖin·ta bala – *it's a fine day* : afne bala ni? – *are you well?* : tar bala nam jani na – *I don't know his real name* : tumar bala at ɖia kao – *eat with your right hand* : restono bala biji oe – *business is brisk at the restaurant* : bala gorom force – *it's got really hot* : hou gori bala nae – *that clock isn't working properly* : amar soril bala nae – *I'm not well* ¶ **bala** (adv) *well* | tarar bala coler – *they are doing well* : he oŋkot bala korer – *he is doing well in maths* : **bala lage** – *it feels good* : ino tumar bala lage ni? – *do you like it here?* : amar kunta-u bala lage na – *I'm fed up* : **bala o-/bala oi ja-** – *get well; turn out well* : tain bala oi gecoin – *she's got well again* : bala oice! – *that's just fine!* : **bala kori ɖe-** – *put right* : amar gori bala kori ɖeuka – *please put my watch right* : **bala fa-** – *like* : ami gua bala fai na – *I don't care for betelnut* : tumi tare bala fao ni? – *do you like him?* : **bala jan-** – *judge to be good* : tane ami bala jani – *I think he's a decent person* : **bala ko-** – *speak favourably* : mainse bala koibo – *people will approve* : he afnar bala koice – *he spoke well of you* ¶ **bala** (n) *welfare* | alla tumar bala koruk – *may God grant you well-being* : tumar balar lagi koilam – *I said it for your own good* : tain mainsor balar lagi kam koroin – *he works for the benefit of others* [H. bhalā]

balabura ['bālabūra] (n) *weal or woe; state of being* | tara amar balabura buje na – *they don't care what state I'm in* : tumar cacir balabura jikaitae – *you should ask your aunt how she is* = **bala**[2] + **bura**[1]

balafta ['bālafta] (adv) *well; in good health* | afne balafta acoin ni? – *how are you?*

balaile ['bālāılɛ́] (adv) *well; properly* | tain balaile gecoin ni? – *has he arrived there all right?* : balaile ɖekouka – *have a really good look*

balatike ['bālatikɛ́] (adv) *well; properly* | balatike bouka – *please sit nice and comfortably* : balatike leko na kene? – *why don't you write it properly?* : ami balatike bujci na – *I haven't really understood*

bal-baicca ['bāl-bāıtšıa] (n) *children* = **bal**[1] + **baicca**

balega ['bālegā] (adj) *nubile (girl)* [A. bāliġ – *come of age*]

bali ['bālī] (n) *sand* [B. balu < O. vālukā]

balis ['bālīš] (n) *cushion; pillow* [P. bāliš]

balluk ['bāl-lūk] (n) *bear* [B. bhalluk]

balti ['bāltī] (n) *bucket* [H. bāltī < Pg. balde]

bam [bām] (adj) *left; lefthand* | bam fase – *on the left side* : almarir bam saite – *to the left of the wardrobe* : bam at ɖi likclam – *I wrote it with my left hand* ¶ **bam** (n) *left side* | bam taki gari aicil – *a car came from the left* : **bame** – *on the left; to the left* : bame jauka – *go*

left : bame ɖukan faiba – *you'll find a shop on the left* : **bamor** – *of the left; lefthand* : bamor rasta ɖorouka – *take the lefthand road* [B. bam < O. vāma]
ban [bān] (n) *flood* [B. ban < O. vāna]
bana- (vt) *cause to be made; make; make up; spell* | afnar fasfut banaicoin ni? – *have you had a passport made?* : tain beakuf banaicoin amare – *he has made a fool of me* : tara gor banar – *they are constructing houses* : ca banao! – *make some tea!* : tain kobor·ta banaia koicoin – *he made up that bit of news* : betfut kila banain? – *how do you spell "Bedford"?* : **banai le-** – make : ca banai lici – *I've made the tea* : **banaia de-/banai de-** – *make (for someone)* : caci amare toki banai ɖicoin : *auntie has made me a hat* [B. bana-]
banail ['bānāıl] (v adj) *made up; artificial* | banail ɖat – *false teeth* : hou ful banail ni? – *are those flowers artificial?* : i ɖoi goro banail – *this yogurt is homemade* < **bana-**
banan ['bānān] (v n) *construction; spelling* < **bana-**
band- (vt) *bind; tie; fasten; close; switch off* | tumar cul banɖo – *tie up you hair* : ɖori ɖi banɖci – *I've tied it with string* : ɖuar banɖo! – *shut the door!* : cuic banɖtam ni? – *shall I switch off?* : **banɖi le-** – *bind; fasten; close* : tara gait banɖi lice – *they've tied up their bags (ready to depart)* : tibi banɖi lao – *turn the TV off* [B. baⁿɖh-]
banda ¹ ['bānɖā] (v adj) *bound; tied up* | amar at-fau banɖa – *my hands are tied (I have no freedom of action)* < **band-**
banda ² (n) *slave* | allar banɖa – *servants of God; Muslims* [P. banda]
bandi ['bānɖī] (n) *female slave* cf **banda**
bandobi ['bānɖobī] (n) *girlfriend* [B. banɖhabi < S. bānɖhavī – *kinswoman*]
bandor ['bānɖòr] (n) *monkey* [H. banɖar]
baŋ- [bāŋ-] (v) (transitive) *break; break open; break up; break off; fold* | fuainte aina baŋce – *the boys have broken a windowpane* : arok foget baŋtam oimu – *we'll have to open another packet* : afne fac fon baŋta farba ni? – *can you give change for a five pound note?* : ou ceg baŋtam – *I want to cash this cheque* : tain ruja baŋta cain na – *she doesn't want to break her fast* : kad baŋa lagto nae – *there's no need to fold the card* : kota·ta baŋoin na jen – *you won't tell anyone, will you* | (intransitive) *get broken; break up; dissipate; be resolved* | ɖui·ta gelas baŋce – *two glasses have got broken* : tar at baŋbo – *he's going to break an arm* : mitiŋ baŋce – *the meeting has broken up* : cacar gum baŋce – *uncle's sleep has dissipated; uncle has woken up* : aste aste tumar ɖor baŋbo – *your fear will gradually wear off* : amar bul baŋce – *my illusions have been shattered* : tair mon baŋcil – *her spirits were dashed* : tar gola baŋce – *his voice has broken; he's gone hoarse* : asa kori bera·ta baŋbo – *I hope the mix-up will be resolved* : **baŋgi ja-** – *get broken* : gelas baŋgi gece – *a glass has got broken* : tan gum baŋgi jaibo – *his sleep will be disturbed* : **baŋgi le-** – *break* : ɖeko, cear baŋgi libae – *watch out, you'll break the chair* : **baŋgia an-** – *ache* : amar fau baŋgia aner – *my leg is aching* : **baŋgia ko-** – *tell in detail; make explicit* : baŋgia kouka amare – *tell me the whole story* [B. bhaŋ-]
baŋga ['bāŋ-ga] (v adj) *broken; damaged; creased* | baŋga tebul – *a broken table* : baŋga gori – *a clock which is not working* : tair mon baŋga – *her mind is upset; she is downhearted* : tair ceara baŋga – *her face is emaciated* : kagoj·kan baŋga – *the paper is creased* < **baŋ-**
baŋgali ['bāŋ-galī] (n) *Bengali person* [B. baŋgali]
baŋgi ¹ ['bāŋ-gī] (v adv) *having been broken* < **baŋ-**
baŋgi ² (n) *melon*
baŋla ¹ ['bāŋ-la] (n) *Bengali (language)* | afne baŋla janoin ni? – *do you know Bengali?*
¶ **baŋla** (adj) *Bengali* | baŋla kobita – *Bengali poetry* [B. baŋla]
baŋla ² (n) *loose change* < **baŋ-**
baŋlaɖes ['bāŋlaɖéš] (n) *Bangladesh* = **baŋla** ¹ + **ɖes**
baŋli ['bāŋ-lī] (n) *bangle* = **baŋri**
baŋri ['bāŋ-rī] (n) *bangle* [H. baŋrī]
baŋti ['bāŋ-tī] (n) *loose change* | amar gece baŋti foesa nae – *I haven't got change*
bao ¹ ['bāò] *wind; weather* [B. bayu < O. vāyu]

bao² (n) *price; rate*   [H. bhāv < O. bhāva – *state*]
bar¹ [bār] (n) *occasion; time (of repetition); day of the week* | tain tin bar aicoin – *she's come three times* : koto bar koici tumare – *how many times have I told you* : foela bar – *the first time* : tin baror bar – *the third time* : ek so bar – *a hundred times* : haca-u jaiba? ek so bar! – *are you really going to go? Yes, most certainly!* : aij ki bar? – *what day is it today?* : aij jumma bar – *today is Friday* : **bare** – *at a time; on a day* : ek bare korci – *I did it in one go* : tain ki bare aiba? – *on what day will he come?* : **bare bare** – *on repeated occasions; again and again* : tara bare bare jikaice – *they enquired repeatedly*   [B. bar < O. vāra]
bar² (n) *outside* | tain bar taki aicoin – *he's come from outside* : **bar o-/bar oi ja-** – *go out; come out* : tain gor taki bar oicoin – *he's gone out (of the house)* : bar oo ikan taki! – *get out!* : fera bar oice – *measles have broken out* : ek·ta kagoj bar oice – *a leaflet has come out* : tura lab bar oice – *a little profit has issued (from the business)* : amar jan bar oi gece – *my vitality has gone out / I'm knackered* : **bar kor-** – *take out; bring out; come out with* : jeb taki cakku bar korce – *he pulled a knife from his pocket* : asol bisoe bar kortam kila? – *how can I find out the real truth?* : tara isab bar korce – *they have worked out the calculation* : tain fasfut bar korba – *he's going to take out a passport* : tara fotrika bar korce – *they've published a newssheet* : kotota bar korer! – *so many things they're inventing!* : **bar kori de-** – *put out; eject* : tare bar kori đeuka! – *chuck him out!* : **bar kori le-** – *bring out; extract* : bici bar kori lici – *I've got the seeds out* : tumar jan bar kori limu! – *I'll spifflicate you!* : **bar ca-** – *keep watching out; wait* : tar lagi bar caitam nai – *we're not going to wait for him* : tain afnar bar caira – *he's expecting you* : tura somoe bar caia đeki – *let's wait a while and see*   = **bair**
bar³ [bā:r] (n) *weight* | koto bar! – *what a weight!* : ou bostar bar nae besi – *this sack isn't very heavy*   [B. bhar]
bar- (vi) *get bigger; grow; increase; go forward* | Mina tin inci barce – *Mina has grown three inches* : tar ujon barer – *his weight is increasing* : tumar cul barce – *your hair has grown* : đin barer – *the days are getting longer* : age baro! – *move forward!* : **bari ja-** – *get bigger; grow; increase; go forward* : tai đin đin bari jar – *she's getting taller every day* : calir đor bari gece – *the price of rice has gone up*   [B. baṛ-]
bara¹ ['bārā] (n) *outside* | goror bara·ta sunđor – *the outside of the house is attractive* : **barar** – *of the outside; external* : barar tolet – *an outside toilet* : barar manus – *outsiders* ¶ **bara** (adv) *outside* | bara jaita ni? – *are you going to go out?* : bara meg đer – *it's raining outside* : caca kuae? tain bara – *where's uncle? he's out*   cf **bair**
bara² (n) *rent; fare* | ou goror bara haftat asi fon – *the rent for this house is eighty pounds per week* : bac bara koto? – *how much is the bus fare?* : **bara de-** – *pay rent; pay a fare* : mase mase bara đena lage – *the rent must be paid monthly* : tara bara đia take – *they pay rent to stay / they are tenants* : amra ebo bara đici na – *we haven't yet paid our fare* : **bara đi la-** – *rent out; let* : tarar gor bara đi laito – *they want to let their house* : **bara kor-** – *rent; hire* : tain boro gor bara korba – *he's going to rent a large house* : tara gari bara kori luton gece – *they hired a car and went to Luton*   [B. bhaṛa]
bara- (vt) *make bigger; enlarge; increase* | amra gor·ta baraimu – *we're going to enlarge the house* : tara fasfutor miaiđ baraice – *they extended the passport's validity* : sofo calir đor barar – *they're putting up the price of rice in the shops* : betae kota barae – *the fellow talks too much*   [B. baṛa-]
barabae ['bārabāy] (adv) *outside* | barabae cauka – *look outside* : **barabae đi** – *outside* : barabae đi manus coler – *people are walking about outside*   = **bara**¹ + **bae**
barabari ['bārabārī] (n) *inflation; exaggeration; excessive behaviour* | **barabari kor-** – *exaggerate; go too far; behave immoderately* : tain besi barabari koroin – *he goes a bit too far; he's too big for his boots; he's offensive*   < **bar-**
baratia ['bārātīa] (n) *tenant; lodger*   [B. bhaṛatia]
barbar ['bār-bār] (adv) *again and again* | ekoi beta barbar ae – *the same man comes again and again* : tumare barbar koa lage kene? – *why do I have to keep telling you?*   < **bar**¹
barebare ['bārɛ-bārɛ] (adv) *again and again*   < **bar**¹

bari [¹ ['bārī] (n) *homestead; family home; village home* | tara bondor maje bari korce – *they have set up a homestead in the open fields* : amrar bari nobigonj – *our home is in Nabiganj* : barir hokoloe bala ni?– *is everyone at home well?* : tain barit gecoin – *he's gone home (to his village)* [B. bari < O. vātikā]
bari ² (n) *knock; blow* | **bari mar-** – *knock; strike a blow* : tarar dorjat bari marclam – *we knocked on their door* : betar matat bari marce – *he struck the man on the head* : **bari ka-** – *take a knock* : tain bukut bari kaicoin – *he received a blow on the chest* [H. vār]
bari ³ ['bā:rī] (adj) *heavy* [B. bhari]
barik ['bārīk] (adj) *slender; slim; fine* | barik bas – *thin bamboo* : barik tonai – *a slim body* : barik leka – *delicate handwriting; small print* [P. bārīk]
barinda ['bārīnda] (n) *verandah* [B. baranda < Pg. varanda]
bariola ['bāriòla] (n) *landlord* [B. barioala]
baris ['bārīš] (n) *rain* [P. bāriš]
barisa ['bārīša] (n) *rainy season* [P. bāriš × B. bårsa]
baro ['bārò] (n°) *twelve* | tin cair·guna baro – *four threes are twelve* : baro mas – *twelve months* : baro·ta am – *twelve mangoes* : baro·jon manus – *twelve people* : rait baro·ta – *twelve o'clock midnight* [B. barå]
baromaia ['bāròmaıa] (adj) *twelve-month-long; all-year* | baromaia kola – *banana which fruits all year round*
barot ['bāròt] (n) *India* [B. bharåt < S. bhārata]
barti ['bārtī] (n) *increase* | **barti o-** – *increase* : mainsor barti or – *the population is increasing* ¶ **barti** (adj) *extra; excessive* | huruta aile barti koroc oibo – *if the children come there'll be extra expense* : barti kagjain falai deuka – *throw away the excess bits of paper* [B. barti]
bas ¹ [bāš] (n) *aroma; smell* | **bas kore** – *it smells* : sundor bas kore – *it smells lovely* : kerejor bas kore – *it smells of kerosene* [B. bas < S. vāsa – *fragrance*]
bas ² (n) *bamboo* | muta bas – *stout bamboo* : basor kuti – *bamboo post* : **(kamor maje) bas hara-** – *undermine (an operation)* : tain amar kamor maje bas haraicoin – *he's put a spanner in my works* [B. baⁿs < O. vaŋša]
bas ³ (n) *habitation* | **bas kor-** – *dwell* [B. bas < O. vāsa]
bas- ¹ (vi) *be felt* | **base** – *it feels; it seems; it looks* : bad base – *it looks bad* : lal sundor basbo tumar tonut – *red will look good on you* [B. bas-]
bas- ² (vi) *float* | nau basce – *the boat is afloat* : **basi ja-** – *start floating; overflow; get flooded* : cacir couk basi jar – *auntie's eyes are brimming with tears* : asta gor basi gece – *the whole house is awash* [B. bhas-]
basa ¹ ['bāšā] (n) *dwelling* [B. basa < O. vāsa]
basa ² (n) *language; style of speech; stylish Bengali* | dakaia basa – *Dhaka speech; standard Bengali* : tain basa matoin – *he speaks in posh Bengali* [B. bhasa < S. bhāśā]
basa- (vt) *get to float; flood* | tara lonc basaito farce na – *they couldn't get the launch afloat* : hurutae batrum basaice – *the children have flooded the bathroom* : **basai de-** – *overwhelm; flood* : nani ador dia basai dira – *granny is overwhelming us with kindness* [B. bhasa-]
basinda ['bāšīnda] (n) *inhabitant* [P. bāšinda]
basko ['bāšχò] (n) *box* [E.]
bason ¹ ['bāšòn] (n) *vessels; pots* [B. basån < O. vāsana]
bason ² (n) *speech* | **bason de-** – *make a speech* : cearmen sab sundor bason dira – *the Chairman is making a fine speech* : **bason huna-** – *deliver a lecture* : tain amrare bason hunaicoin – *he gave us a lecture* [B. bhasån < S. bhāśaṇa]
basosti ['bāšòstī] (n°) *sixty-two* = **basotti**
basotti ['bāšòt-tī] (n°) *sixty-two* [B. basåtti]
bassa ['bāš-šā] (n) *king; emperor* | «hokoloe bassa oile ukum manto ke?» – *if everyone is king, who will be there to obey?* = **badsa**
bat [bāt] (n) *apportionment; lot* | ei lao tumar bat – *here, take your portion* : **bate** – *by apportionment* : bate dos fon faiba – *you'll get ten pounds in the share-out* : **(kar) bate**

fore – *it falls to (someone's) lot* : amar bate koto forbo? – *how much will I get as my share?* : tar bate ran force – *he got a leg portion (of a chicken)* : **bat kor-/bat kori le-** – *share out* : hokolor maje bat kori louka – *share it out among everyone* : tara jaga·ta bat kori lice – *they have shared the land among themselves*   [B. baⁿt < O. vanta]

bat- ¹ (vt) *pound (spices)*   [B. bat-]

bat- ² (vt) *apportion; dole out* | kani bato! – *dole out the rice!* : tain ek·ta goru batcoin – *he shared out (the meat from) a cow*   [B. baⁿt-]

batail ['bātāıl] (n) *chisel*   [B. batali]

bat-batuara ['bāt-batwārā] (n) *sharing out*   = **bat** + **batuara**

bate ['bāté] (n adv) *in allowance* | koroc bate foesa dice – *they've given some money to allow for expenses* : aij rait kanir bate ain jen – *come prepared for a meal tonight*   < **bat**

bati ¹ ['bātī] (n) *bowl*   [B. bati]

bati ² (n) *lowland*   [B. bhati]

batiala ['bātīāla] (n) *lowlander*   = **bati** ² + **-ala**

batiol ['bātīòl] (adv) *downwards; downstream* | nao batiol coler – *the boat is going downstream* : **batiol o-** – *go down; back down* : obosta deki tara batiol oice – *seeing the situation, they backed down*   cf **bati** ²

batra ['bātra] (n) *portion*   cf **bat**

batti ['bāt-tī] (adj) *short* | batti manus – *person of short stature* : tumar fen batti oi gece – *your trousers are too short* : tandar somoe din batti take – *the days are short in winter* : **batti kor-/batti kori le-** – *shorten; trim; keep short* : amar cul batti kortam – *I want to have my hair cut* : kota·ta batti kori louka – *keep it short / get to the point* : **batti kori** – *in brief* : amare batti kori koicoin – *he told me in a few words*   [B. beⁿte]

battiol ['bāt-tīòl] (adv) *downwards*   = **batiol**

batua ['bātua] (n) *wanderer*

batuara ['bātwārā] *sharing out*   [H. batvārā]

bat ¹ (n) *boiled rice; meal; food* | bat randci – *I've cooked some rice* : bat torkari – *rice and curry* : dail bat – *lentils and rice; a basic meal* : bat kaicoin ni? – *have you had a meal?* (often asked in the course of a friendly exchange of greetings) : bat dao! – *give me some grub!* : cair·ta bat kauka – *do have something to eat*   [B. bhat < O. bhakta]

bat ² (n) *rheumatism* | **bate dore** – *rheumatism afflicts* : bate dorce amare – *I've got rheumatism*   [B. bat < O. vāta – *wind*]

bat ³ (n) *bathtub* | tain bato hamaicoin – *he's in the bath* : **bat kor-/bat kori le-** – *have a tub bath* : aij bat korco ni? – *have you had your bath today?*   [E.]

bata ['bātā] (n) *living allowance* | haftat foncas fon bata fae – *he gets an allowance of fifty pounds a week*   [B. bhata]

bata- (vt) *make explicit; explain* | kita oice, batao amare – *tell me what's happened* : **batai de-/batai di la-** – *explain* : tanre fura befar·ta batai dici – *I've explained the whole matter to him*   [H. batā-]

batas ['bātāš] (n) *air; wind; airborne humours* | i rumo batas hamae na – *this room doesn't get any air* : amar muko batas lagce – *I can feel a breeze on my face* : tanda batas boice – *a cold wind is blowing* : tair feto batas jomce – *she's got wind in her belly* : tare ulta batase faice – *an evil affliction has taken hold of him* : **batas ka-** – *take the air* : bara gia tura batas kai – *let's go out and get some fresh air* : **batas de-/batas di la-** – *supply air; ventilate* : tain furir muko batas dira – *she is fanning her daughter's face*   [B. batas < O. vāta]

batera ['bātɛrā] (n) *quail (bird)*

batija ['bātīzā] (n) *brother's son*   [B. bhatija]

batiji ['bātīzī] (n) *brother's daughter*   [B. bhatiji]

batil ['bātīl] (adj) *invalid; futile* | i tikit batil oi gece – *this ticket has become invalid* : afnar hokol kam batil – *all your work is in vain*   [A. bāṭil]

batti ['bāt-tī] (n) *lamp; light* | tan rumo batti joler – *a lamp is burning in his room* : andair lage, batti jalaitam ni? – *it's dark, shall I turn on the light?* : onku batti marta faroin – *now you can switch the lights off*   [H. batti < O. vartikā]

bau ['bāū] (n) *left side* | **baue** – *on the left; to the left* : baue bidior sof – *on the left is the video shop* : dainɛ baue caia far oiba – *look to the right and left, then cross over* ¶ **bau** (adj) *lefthand* | bau at – *the left hand* : bau fas – *the left side* : bau at ɖi! – *(excuse me for passing this) with my left hand!* [B. ba^n < O. vāma]

baucar ['bāūsār] (n) *voucher; 1960s work permit* | tain baucar dia london aicla – *he came to England on a work permit* [E.]

bauedi ['bāuɛɖī] (adv) *to the left* | bauedi cauka – *look to the left* = **bau + dia**

baug ['bāug] (n) *repair* | **baug kor-** – *repair* : tain amar gori baug korcoin – *he has repaired my clock* : **baug o-/baug oi ja-** – *get repaired* : tumar leftof baug oice ni? – *has your laptop been repaired?*

baunia ['bāunɪa] (n) *dwarf; midget* [B. bamån < O. vāmana]

baur ['bāūr] (n) *husband's elder brother* [B. bhasur]

baurcuta ['bāūrsūta] (n) *son of husband's elder brother*

bauta ['bāūta] (adj) *stale; malodorous* | bauta dud – *gone-off milk*

be [bé] (int) *dear (child)* | kita be? – *what is it, dear?* : ka be! – *eat up, darling!* : ac na be! – *get a move on, child!* **Note**: Interjection used for addressing children. The tone is affectionate and familiar.

be+ (adv prefix) *lacking; without* | beadob / beaddob – *lacking manners* : bedin – *without religion* : beakol – *without any sense* : besundor – *devoid of beauty* [P. be]

beaddob [bé-'ād-dòb] *rude; impolite* = **beadob**

beadob ['bé-adòb] *rude; impolite* [P. be – *without* + A. adab – *manners*]

beadobi ['bé-adòbī] *rudeness; impoliteness* | beadobi maf korouka – *excuse me (for butting in, etc)* : koto boro beadobi! – *what uncouth behaviour!* [P. beadabī]

beafar ['bé-afār] (n) *affair* = **biafar**

beain ['bé-āɪn] (n) *wrongdoing* | **beain kor-** – *do wrong; break the law* : ami kunu beain korci ni? – *have I done anything wrong?* [P. beāin]

beaini ['bé-āɪnī] (adj) *illegal* | beaini karbar – *illicit goings-on* = **beain + -i** ^{2}

beakol ['bé-āχòl] (adj) *witless; distraught; foolish* | kobor hunia tain beakol oicoin – *after hearing the news he was at his wits' end* : beakol fua! – *oh you silly boy!*
[P. be – *without* + A. ¿aql – *wisdom*]

beakuf ['bé-ākūf] (adj) *foolish* [P. be – *without* + A. wuqūf – *sense*]

beam ['bé-ām] (n) *physical exercise* | **beam kor-** – *do exercises* [S. vyāyāma]

bearam ['bé-ārām] (n) *illness* | tar bearam kita? – *what's wrong with him?* : **bearam oe/bearam oi jae** – *one falls ill* : afnar cinta taki bearam oibo – *you're going to get ill with worry* : cacar fetor bearam oi gecil – *uncle had a stomach illness* : **bearam kore** – *one falls ill* : amar bearam korce – *I'm ill* [P. beārām – *without comfort*]

bebi ['bébī] (n) *baby* | **bebin** – *babies* : bebintor kafor – *babies' clothes* [E.]

beboar ['bɛbòār] (n) *use; behaviour* | tar beboar bala – *his behaviour is good* : **beboar kor-** – *use; behave* : tara saban beboar kore na – *they don't use soap* : he maje maje karaf beboar kore – *he sometimes behaves badly* [B. bɛbåhar < S. vyavahāra – *action*]

bebodan ['bɛbòɖān] (n) *interval; space; difference* | ɖui goror maje suɖu coe futor bebodan – *there's only a six foot space between the two houses* : erar maje kunu bebodan deki na – *i can't see any difference between them* [B. bɛbådhan < S. vyavadhāna – *spacing out*]

bebosa ['bɛbòšā] (n) *commerce; business* | tain ek bebosar malik – *he is the owner of a business* : bebosa kila coler? – *how's trade?* : **bebosa kor-** – *do business* : tain age kafror bebosa korta – *he used to be in the clothing trade* : tara londonor ufre bebosa korce – *they've started a business based in London* [B. bɛbåsa < S. vyavasāya – *activity*]

bec- [bɛs] (vt) *sell* | ino ɖuɖ bece na – *they don't sell milk here* : amar gari bectam – *I want to sell my car* : **beci le-** – *sell* : tan gor beci licoin – *she's sold her house* [B. bec-]

becakena ['bɛsakɛna] (n) *buying and selling* < **bec- + kin-**

bedin ['béɖīn] (adj) *irreligious* [P. be – *without* + A. dīn – *religion*]

bedisa ['bédīša] (adj) *senseless; crazed* | fua·ta bedisa oi gece – *the boy has gone crazy (with excitement)* ¶ **bedisa** (n) *senseless person; fool* | bedisar lakan matio na – *don't talk like a fool* [P. be – *without* + B. disa – *direction*]
bedna ['bɛdnā] (n) *pain* | **bedna kore** – *it hurts* : amar bukut bedna kore – *I have a pain in my chest* = **bedona**
bedokol ['bédòχòl] (adj) *out of control* | **bedokol o-/bedokol oi ja-** – *get out of control; slip from one's control* : fua·ta bedokol oice – *the boy has got out of control* : gor·ta amar bedokol oi gece – *I've lost possession of the house* [P. be – *without* + A. daḳl – *access*]
bedona ['bɛdònā] (n) *pain* [B. bedåna < S. vedanā]
bedorkari ['bédòrχārī] (adj) *unnecessary* [P. bedarkārī]
bee [béy] (n) *expenditure* | **bee oe/bee oi jae** – *expenditure is incurred* : olidor somoe besi bee oi jae – *more money gets spent during the holidays* : **bee kor-/bee kori le-** – *spend* : forat bakka somoe bee kore – *she spends a lot of time studying* : tara hokol foesa bee kori lice – *they have spent all the money* [B. bey < S. vyaya]
beest [bɛ'ɛst] (n) *heaven* | alla tane beest nocib koruk – *may God grant him/her a place in heaven* (said on the death of a good person) : sat beest – *the seven heavens* [P. bahišt]
befaeda ['bɛfāyda] (adj) *futile; fruitless* | cinta kora befaeda – *worrying is fruitless* : jana befaeda oibo – *it'll be no use going* [P. be – *without* + A. fā'ida – *profit*]
befana ['bɛfāna] (adj) *helpless; without provision; at a loss* | rari beti ekere befana – *the widow is totally without resources* : befana oia kandira – *she is sobbing helplessly and unconsolably* [P. bepanāh – *shelterless*]
befar ['bɛfār] *affair; matter* | ita tumar kunu befar nae – *it's no business of yours* : koto boro befar – *a big deal* : kusir befar – *a matter for rejoicing* : **befare** – *in the matter (of)* : tain tumar befare cinta korra – *he's worrying about you* : gor loar befare kita kortam? – *what are we to do about buying a house?* = **biafar**
befari ['bɛfārī] *merchant* | «ada befari jajor kobor rakoin» – *a small trader talking like a shipping magnate* [B. bɛpari < S. vyāpārī]
beforoa ['bɛfòrowā] (adj) *careless* [P. beparvāh]
befsa ['bɛfsa] (n) *business* | tarar befsa bala coler – *their business is doing well* : **befsa kor-** – *do business* : tain emrikat befsa korra – *he's running a business in America* = **bebosa**
beg[1] [bɛg] (n) *speed* | **bege** – *at a speed* : gari bege aicil – *a car came speeding along* : foncas mail bege colram – *we're moving at 50 mph* [B. beg < S. vega – *velocity*]
beg[2] [bɛg] (n) *bag* | foesar beg – *moneybag* : camrar beg – *a leather bag* : ek beg cini – *one bag of sugar* : bego touka – *put it in the bag* [E.]
beg[3] [bɛk] (n) *return trip; return* | **beg kor-** – *return; come back* : tara hou din-u beg korce – *they returned the very same day* [E. back]
begar ['bɛgār] (adv) *without remuneration* | **begar kat-** – *work for nothing* : amra ni begar kattam? – *are we expected to work for nothing?* [P. begār]
begedec ['bɛgɛdɛs] (n) *return address* | kore di begedec leka ace – *the sender's address is written on the back* [E. back address]
begna ['bɛgna] (adj) *not one's own* | tara begna manus – *they're strangers; they are not relatives of ours* [P. begāna]
begom ['bɛgòm] (n) *lady; Begum* [P. begam < T. begam]
begor ['bɛgòr] (pre) *without* [P. ba-ġair]
begrum ['bɛgrūm] (n) *back parlour* [E. back room]
behaia ['bɛhāiā] (adj) *shameless* [P. be – *without* + A. hayā' – *modesty*]
behuda ['bɛhuda] (adj) *senseless* [P. behūda]
beijjot ['béɪj-jòt] (adj) *disgraced; shamed* | **beijjot o-/beijjot oi ja-** – *be shamed* : tain beijjot oicoin – *he has been put to shame* : **beijjot kor-** – *shame; humiliate* : amrare beijjot korco – *you have humiliated us* [P. be – *without* + A. ¿izza – *honour*]
beijjoti ['béɪj-jòtī] (n) *disgrace* = **beijjot + -i**[1]
beila ['béɪla] (n) *young mother* | beilar dus – *obstetric illness* [O. bālikā – *girl*]

beiman ['béɪmān] (adj) *perfidious; untrustworthy; dishonest* | he beiman oi gece – *he has shown himself to be untrustworthy* ¶ **beiman** (n) *dishonest person* | koto boro beiman! – *what a scoundrel!* [P. be – *without* + A.'īmān – *faith*]
beimani ['béɪmanī] (n) *perfidy* | **beimani kor-** – *behave treacherously* : amrar loge beimani korce – *he let us down; he betrayed our trust* = **beiman + -i** [1]
beisaf ['béɪšāf] (adj) *countless* [P. be – *without* + A. hisāb – *accounting*]
bej- [bɛz] (vt) *send* | **beji le-** – *send* : tare goro beji lici – *I sent him home* [H. bhej-]
bejal ['bɛzāl] (n) *hassle; mess; adulteration* | ami bakka bejalor maje – *I'm in quite a fix* : boro bejal lagce – *things are in a right mess* : i telor maje bejal – *there are impurities in this oil* : **bejal kor-** – *cause complications* : tain kali bejal koroin – *he keeps making things more difficult* : **bejal de-/bejal di la-** – *adulterate* : ou gir maje bejal di laice – *they've adulterated this ghee* [B. bhejal]
bejali ['bɛzalī] (adj) *unstraightforward* | bejali manus – *a trouble maker* = **bejal + -i** [2]
bejan ['bɛzān] (adv) *greatly; awfully* | fuainte bejan marce tare – *the boys gave him a terrible beating* : baiccae bejan kander – *the poor child is crying her head off* [P. ba-jān – *with life and soul; wholeheartedly*]
bejar ['bɛzār] (adj) *vexed; dismayed* | **bejar o-/bejar oi ja-** – *get annoyed; be dismayed* : bejar oin na jen – *please don't be annoyed; please don't take me wrong* : tain bejar oi gecoin – *he's got fed up* [P. bezār – *weary; disgusted*]
bejjoti ['bɛj-jòtī] (n) *disgrace* = **beijjoti**
bejuit ['bɛzuīt] (n) *unfittingness; impropriety* | bejuit lagbo – *it will look odd; it won't be appropriate* [P. be – *without* + B. jut – *suitable arrangement; propriety*]
bejuita ['bɛzuɪta] (adj) *inappropriate; awkward; odd (number)* | afne bejuita somoe aicoin– *you've come at an awkward time* ¶ **bejuita** (n) *odd thing; odd number* | cair jura oile, fac bejuita oibo – *if four is an even number, five must be an odd number* < **bejuit**
bekaeda ['bɛɣāyda] (n) *irregularity; awkward situation* | ofiso bekaeda coler – *things are not going as they should in the office* : amra boro bekaedar maje – *we are in a very embarrassing situation* [P. be – *without* + A. qā'ida – *basis; rule*]
bekar ['bɛɣār] (adj) *unemployed; out of service* | ami bekar – *I'm without a job* : bekar manus – *unemployed people* : **bekar o-/bekar oi ja-** – *become unemployed; become inoperative* : ou gori bekar oi gece – *this clock isn't working any more* [P. bekār]
bekeal ['bɛɣéāl] (n) *inadvertence* | **bekeale** – *inadvertently* : tain bekeale bici kai licoin – *she swallowed some seeds by mistake* [P. be – *without* + A. ḵayāl – *notion*]
bekuf ['bɛkūf] (adj) *foolish* = **beakuf**
bel [1] [bél] (n) *wood-apple (Aegle marmelos)* [B. bel < O. bailva]
bel [2] (n) *spade; shovel* [P. bel]
bel- (v) *perform a rolling action* | tain cafatti belra – *she's rolling out chapatis* [B. bel-]
belain ['bɛlāɪn] (n) *rolling pin* cf **bel-**
belat ['bɛlāt] (n) *blood* [E.]
belek ['bɛlɛk] (n) *the black market* | **beleko** – *on the black market; by illicit means* : tumi beleko loiclae ni? – *did you buy it on the black market?* : tain beleko aicoin – *he entered the country illegally* : **belekor** – *obtained on the black market; illicit* : belekor mal – *black market goods* : belekor karbar – *black marketeering; illegal dealings* [E.]
belet ['bɛlɛt] (n) *razor blade* [E. blade]
belfoi ['bɛlfòɪ] (n) *olive-like fruit (Elaeocarpus serratus)* [B. jålpai]
belkoi ['bɛlχòɪ] (n) *olive-like fruit* = **belfoi**
beltif ['bɛltīf] (n) *bell-push* cf **tif**
belun ['bɛlūn] (n) *balloon* [E.]
bemar ['bɛmār] (adj) *ill* | goro hokoloe bemar – *everyone in the house is ill* : bemar soril loia colra – *she's carrying on despite ill health* ¶ **bemar** (n) *illness* | tan bemar kita? – *what's wrong with him?* : **bemar oe/bemar oi jae** – *illness occurs* : gorome besi bemar oe – *there is more illness in hot weather* : **bemar care/bemar cari jae** – *illness desists* : tan

bemar care na – *her illnesses never cease; she's constantly ill* : **bemar for-/bemar fori ja-** – *fall ill* : caca bemar fori gecoin – *uncle has fallen ill*   [P. bīmār – *ill*]
bemar-ajar ['bɛmār-āzār] (n) *illnesses*
bemari ['bɛmārī] (n) *sick person; invalid* | hator bemari – *a heart patient*   = **bemar + -i** ³
bemarsemar ['bɛmār šɛmār] (n) *illnesses*   = **bemar**
ben [bɛn] (n) *van*   [E.]
benami ['bɛnāmī] (adj) *recorded in another's name*   [P. benām – *anonymous*]
benela ['bɛnɛla] (n) *van driver; man with a van*   = **ben + -ala**
beŋ ¹ [bɛŋ] (n) *frog; toad*   [B. beŋ < O. viyaŋga]
beŋ ² (n) *bank* | sunali beŋ – *Sonali Bank* : **beŋko** – *in a bank; at a bank* : foesa beŋko toita – *you should put the money in a bank* : tai beŋko kam kore – *she works in a bank* : **beŋkor** – *of a bank* : beŋkor isab – *bank statement*   [E.]
beŋceŋ ['bɛŋ-sɛŋ] (n) *confusion; mix-up*   = **beŋga**
beŋekaunt ['bɛŋɛkāunt] (n) *bank account*   [E.]
beŋga ['bɛŋga] (n) *confusion; mix-up* | **beŋga lage/beŋga lagi jae** – *confusion or complication occurs* : tain gele gi beŋga lagbo – *if he leaves everything will get into a mess* : **beŋga laga-/beŋga lagai de-** – *cause confusion or complication* : ila kori beŋga lagaicoin – *by doing that he's messed everything up*
beŋgacera ['bɛŋga-sɛra] (n) *confusion; mix-up*   = **beŋga**
beokt ['béòχt] (n) *the wrong time* | **beokte** – *at the wrong time* : tain beokte nomajo gecoin – *he did his prayers at the wrong time*   [P. be – *without* + A. waqt – *time*]
ber [bɛr] (n) *encirclement* | **ber de-/ber di la-** – *encircle*   [B. beɽ]
ber- (vt) *surround; hem in* | **beri le-** – *surround; hem in* : baiccainte beri lice tare – *the children have crowded round him*   [B. beɽ-]
bera ['bɛra] (n) *fence; tangle; imbroglio* | rukor bera – *wooden* fence : **bera de-/bera di la-** – *put up a fence* : ou caite bera ditam – *we want to put up a fence on this side* : **bera lage/bera lagi jae** – *confusions arise* : tain aile bera lagi jaibo – *if he comes, everything will be messed up* : tin bera lagce – *things have got into a real mess* : **bera laga-/bera lagai de-** – *cause confusion* : caca bera lagaiba – *uncle is going to muddle things up*   [B. beɽa]
bera (n) *ram; sheep*   [B. bheɽa]
bera- (vi) *make loops; move around* | taintain tauno beraira – *they are gadding about town* : **beranit** – *on a trip; on a visit* : kala beranit aira – *aunt is coming for a visit* : london beranit gecoin – *he's gone on a trip to London* : **guri bera-** – *wander around; gad about* : he kali guri berae – *he does nothing but roam around*   [B. beɽa-]
beracera ['bɛra-sɛra] (n) *complication; confusion* | **beracera lage/beracera lagi jae** – *confusions arise* : age buddi korle hese beracera lagto nae – *if you make plans first, things won't end in chaos* : **beracera laga-/beracera lagai de-** – *cause confusion* : tan fatnar aia beracera lagaice – *his business partner came and messed things up*   = **bera**
berador ['bɛradòr] (n) *brethren*   [P. birādar]
berail ['bɛrāɪl] (v adj) *looped; convoluted*   < **bera-**
berani ['bɛranī] (v n) *moving about; going on trips*   < **bera-**
berber ['bɛr-bɛr] (n) *mumbling* | **berber kor-** – *mumble* : berber koro kita? – *what's that you're mumbling about?*
beret ['bɛrɛt] (n) *baker's bread*   [E.]
beri ['bɛrī] (n) *ewe; sheep*   [B. bheɽi]
bes [béš] (adj) *much* | bes foesa ace tan – *he has lots of money* ¶ **bes** (adv) *very; quite; well* | fani·ta bes foriskar – *the water's very clear* : amar soril bes bala nae – *my health is not particularly good* : gari·ta bes boro – *the car is quite large* : tan befsa bes coler – *his business is doing well* : **bes kori** – *in good measure; in plenty* : bes kori kain jen – *please do eat plenty* ¶ **bes** (n) *a lot; more* | tain bes hikcoin – *he's learned a lot* : afne amar taki bes janoin – *you know more than I do* : ek so; na, aro bes oibo – *one hundred; no, it'll be more than that* ¶ **bes** (int) *fine!* | afne kail aiba? bes! – *you'll come tomorrow? excellent!*   [P. beš – *more*]

besa- ['bɛšā] (vt) *increase; make large* | isab besaia ɗekaice – *they presented an inflated account* < **bes**
besat ['bɛšāt] (n) *small trade* [A. bisāt – *spread out carpet*]
beseba ['bɛšeba] (n) *inconvenience* | beseba lage – *inconvenience is felt* : amar boro beseba lagcil – *I felt very awkward* = **be + seib**
besi [1] ['bɛšī] (n) *excess* [P. bešī]
besi [2] (adj) *much; many; more; most; too much* | besi fani force – *a lot of water has leaked out* : tara besi din takto nae – *they won't stay for many days* : niom taki besi lobon ɗicoin – *she's put in more salt than normal* : hokol taki besi foesa faice he – *he got the most money of all* : tumar besi buɗɗi – *you have too much intelligence; you're too damned smart* ¶ **besi** (adv) *much; too much; very* | tai besi kanɗice na – *she didn't cry much* : i kam besi kotin – *this job is too hard* : rum·ta besi boro nae – *the room isn't very big* : **besi kori** – *much; excessively* : he besi kori gumae – *he sleeps too much* ¶ **besi** (n) *a lot; an excessive amount* | ami besi cai na – *I don't want a great deal* : tumi besi loico – *you've taken too much* [B. besi < P. beš]
beskom ['bɛšχòm] (n) *variance; difference* | tarar maje rait-ɗin beskom – *there's a huge difference between them* : **beskom oe/beskom oi jae** – *discrepancy occurs* : lekar maje beskom oi gece – *there are discrepancies in the texts* : **beskom ɗore/beskom ɗori lee** – *discrepancy occurs* : isabe beskom ɗori lice – *there is some inconsistency in the accounts* = **bes + kom**
besto ['bɛstò] (adj) *busy; occupied; eager* | tara besto manus – *they are busy people* : one tain besto – *he's busy at the moment* : **besto o-/besto oi ja-** – *be busy; be eager* : tara london jaibar lagi besto oice – *they're eager to go to London* : **besto tak-** – *be kept busy* : tain huruta loia besto takoin – *she's always busy with the children* [B. bɛstå < S. vyasta – *thrown apart*]
besumar ['bɛšumār] (adj) *countless* [P. bešumār – *without reckoning*]
besundor ['bɛšunɗòr] (adj) *ugly* = **be + sundor**
bet [1] [bɛt] (n) *bed* | **beto ja-** – *go to bed* : beto jao gi! – *go to bed!* : tain beto gecoin – *he's gone to bed* [E.]
bet [2] (n) *waterlily* [B. bhe^{n}t]
beta ['bɛtā] (n) *son; uncle; man; he; He* | ek bafor tin beta – *three sons of one father* : a beta! – *come here, son!* : o beta, huno! – *listen to me, old fellow!* : hanif beta jaiba – *Uncle Hanif will be going* : ek beta aicoin – *a man has come* : oto boro beta! – (sarcastically) *such an important fellow!* : kun beta koice tumare? – *whoever told you that?* : beta jobor menot kore – *he works very hard* : beta jane – *He (God) knows* : **tar beta** – *himself; he* : tar beta bout testa korce – *he himself has tried very hard* : **betar ma** – *(one's own) mother* : **betae** – *son; man; he* (instrumental) : betae ɗekce amrare – *that man has spotted us* : betae kita koe? – *what does he say?* : **betain** – *sons; men* : hokol betain gecoin gi – *the men have all gone* : **betainte** – *sons; men* (instrumental) : amar betainte hokolti tik korbo – *my sons will fix everything* : **betaintor** – *sons'; men's* : betaintor juta – *men's shoes* : **betaintore** – *(to) sons; (to) men* (objective) : afnar betaintore bujauka – *explain it to your sons* [B. beta]
betaim ['bɛtāɪm] (n) *the wrong time* | **betaime** – *at the wrong time* : afne boro betaime aicoin – *you've come at a very odd time* = **be + taim**
beti ['bɛtī] (n) *daughter; aunt; girl; woman; she* | amar ɗui beti – *I have two daughters* : kita beti, bala aco ni? – *hi Auntie, how are you?* : kamla beti – *servant girl* : sofo je beti kam kore – *the woman who works in the shop* : beti manus – *womenfolk* : beti kunano take? – *where does she live?* : **tar beti** – *herself; she* : tar beti hokol kota jane – *she knows all about it* : **bettie** ['bɛt-tɪɛ́] – *daughter; woman; she* (instrumental) : bettie koice – *it was the woman who said so* : **betin** – *daughters; women* : hokol betin ino – *all the women are here* : **betinte** – *daughters; women* (instrumental) : afnar betinte kita korer? – *what are your daughters doing?* : **betintor** – *daughters'; women's* : betintor gori – *a ladies' watch* : **betintore** – *(to) daughters; (to) women* (objective) : tan betintore ɗekcoin ni? – *have you seen his daughters?* [B. beti]

betrik ['bɛtrik] (n) *battery* [E.]
betrum ['bɛtrūm] (n) *bedroom* | tin betrumor gor – *a three bedroom house* [E.]
bet [bɛt] (n) *rattan; cane* | bet ɖi cear malae – *they make chairs out of cane* : **bet mar-** – *beat with a cane* : fuaintore bet marto – *they used to cane boys* [B. bet]
betaia ['bɛtāia] (adv) *excessively* | tara curre betaia marce – *they gave the thief a terrible beating* [P. be – *without* + A. tahā́sā́ – *abstinence*]
betala ['bɛtāla] (adj) *irregular; odd* | betala gorom force – *it's got extraordinarily hot* : tain boro betala manus – *he's a very odd person* [P. be – *without* + B. tal – *rhythm*]
beton ['bɛtòn] (n) *wages; pay* | tar beton tin so fon – *his salary is three hundred pounds* : tumi beton koto faibae? – *how much will you earn?* : kamlaintor beton dici – *we've paid the workmen's wages* [B. betån < S. vetana]
betor ['bɛtòr] (n) *witr (prayers)* | betor nomaj – *the witr prayers* [A. witr – *uneven*]
bettomij ['bɛt-tòmīz] (adj) *ill-mannered* [P. be – *without* + A. tamyīz – *distinction; discernment*]
bettomiji ['bɛt-tòmīzī] (n) *rude behaviour* = **bettomij + -i** [1]
beu [béū] (n) *shoulder-bar; yoke*
beuɖa ['béwɖa] (adj) *senseless* = **behuɖa**
beufae ['béūfāy] (adj) *helpless* [P. be – *without* + B. upay – *recourse*]
beus ['béūš] (adj) *senseless; frantic* | tara jaibar lagi beus – *they are raring to go* : tain beus, afnare ɖekta – *he's dying to see you* : **beus o-/beus oi ja-** – *become senseless* : tain akta beus oi gecoin – *she suddenly became unconscious* : **beus kor-/beus kori le-** – *render senseless* : ɖaktor tare beus kori lice – *the doctor anaesthetized him* [P. behoš]
beusi ['béūšī] (n) *senseless behaviour* [P. behošī]
bia ['bīā] (n) *marriage; wedding* | bia oe/bia oi jae – *a wedding takes place; marriage is solemnized* : kail ninar bia oibo – *Nina's wedding will be tomorrow* : ranar loge runar bia oi gece – *Runa has got married to Rana* : **bia lage** – *marriage is in the making* : henar bia lagce – *plans for Hena's wedding are afoot* : **bia kor-/bia kori le-** – *get married* : afne bia korta nae ni? – *don't you want to get married?* : **bia bo-** – *undergo a marriage ceremony* : tara tin ɖin baɖe bia boibo – *they'll be getting married in three days' time* : **bia ka-** – *attend a wedding* : afnar bia kaitam – *we'd like to be there when you get married* : **bia laga-** – *arrange a marriage* : tan fuar bia lagaita – *she wants to find a marriage partner for her son* [B. biya < S. vivāha]
biafar ['bīāfār] (n) *affair; matter; thing* | biafar kita? – *what's the matter / what's going on?* : biafar oilo .. – *the thing is this* .. : arok biafar oilo .. – *and there's another thing* .. : afcucor biafar – *a regrettable thing* : kusir biafar – *a matter for rejoicing* : ita kunu biafar nae – *that's no matter / that doesn't matter* : **biafare** – *in the matter of; regarding; about* : amar biafare kita koicla? – *what did he say regarding me?* : goror biafare kunta korci na – *we haven't done anything about the house* [B. bɛpar < S. vyāpāra]
biai ['bīāi] (n) *son's wife's father; daughter's husband's father* [B. behai < O. vaivāhika]
biain ['bīāin] (n) *son's wife's mother; daughter's husband's mother* [B. behan < O. vaivāhinī]
biakol ['bīāχòl] (adj) *witless* = **beakol**
bial ['bīāl] (n) *afternoon* | bial fojonto – *until the afternoon* : **biale** – *in the afternoon* : tara biale goro take – *they stay at home in the afternoon* : **bialku** – *in the afternoon* : kun somoe aiba? bialku – *what time will you come? in the afternoon* : **bialkur** – *of the afternoon* : bialkur ca kani – *afternoon tea* : bialkur bala – *the afternoon* [B. bikal < O. vaikāla]
biallis ['bīāl-līš] (nº) *forty-two* [B. biallis]
bian ['bīān] (n) *forenoon; morning* | bian taki – *since morning time* : **biane** – *in the morning* : biane utia kamo lagcoin – *she got up early and set to work* : **bianku** – *in the morning* : tara bianku aia gece – *they dropped by in the morning* : **biankur** – *of the morning* : biankur fora – *morning lessons* : biankur bala – *morning time* : **biante** – *in the morning* : biante kita korcla? – *what did you do in the morning?* [H. bihān < O. vibhāna – *dawn*]

bia-saḍi ['bīā-šāḍī] (n) *marriage* | **bia-saḍi kor-** – *get married* : afne bia-saḍi korcoin ni? – *are you married?* = **bia + saḍi**

bibad ['bībād] *dispute* | **bibad lage/bibad lagi jae** – *contention arises* : tara ḍui baie bibad lagi gece – *the two brothers have fallen out* : **bibad kor-** – *have a dispute; quarrel* : tara hamesa amrar loge bibad kore – *they often quarrel with us* [B. bibad < S. vivāḍa]

bibaḍi ['bībāḍī] (n) *disputant; plaintiff* [B. bibaḍi < S. vivāḍī]

bibaito [bī 'bāɪtò] (adj) married [B. bibahitå < S. vivāhita]

bibecona [bī 'bɛsòna] *consideration* | **bibecona kor-** – *consider; ponder* : tain bisoe·ta bibecona korra – *he's thinking the matter over* : **bibecona kori ḍek-** – *have a good think (about something)* : afne jaita ni na, bibecona kori ḍekouka – *will you go or not? please think it over carefully* [B. bibecåna < S. vivecanā – *discrimination*]

bibi ['bībī] (n) *grandmother* [P. bībī – *lady; grandame*]

bibinno ['bībin-nò] (adj) *various different* | bibinno jaega – *various different places* : bibinno somoe – *(at) various different times* : bibinno rokom – *various kinds* : bibinno rokomor gac – *various kinds of plants* : bibinno jator mac – *various different species of fish* [B. bibhinnå < S. vibhinna]

bic [¹ ['bīs] (n) *seed* | **bicor** – *seed-bearing* : bicor alu – *seed potato* : bicor goru – *stud bull* : «na alor, na bicor» – *not fit for ploughing, not fit for breeding; good for nothing* = **bij**

bic ² (n) *midst* | **bice** – *in the midst (of)* [H. bīc]

bica ['bīsā] (n) *caterpillar*

bica- (vt) *spread out* | tain jaenomaj bicaira – *he's spreading out his prayer mat* : **bicai ḍe-** – *spread out* : tantan boibar lagi kombli bicai ḍici – *I've spread out some blankets for them to sit on* [B. bica-]

bical ['bīsāl] (n) *bull* cf **bic¹**

bicar ['bīsār] (n) *judgment; justice* | ami bicar cai – *I want a fair deal; I want a fair hearing* : **bicar oe/bicar oi jae** – *judgment is passed; justice is done* : jauk, bicar oice – *anyway, justice has been done* : ek ḍin tar bicar oibo – *some day he will be called to account* : i kun bicar oilo? – *so what kind of justice is that? that's just not fair* : **bicar kor-** – *pass judgment; judge* : afne nije bicar korouka – *judge for yourself* : **bicar bo-** – *sit in judgment* : gaur murobbiain kail bicar boiba – *the village elders will hold court tomorrow* : **bicar ḍe-** – *appeal to a third party for adjudication* : tain cacar gece bicar ḍicoin – *he's asked uncle to declare who's in the right* : **bicar an-** – *file an appeal for arbitration* : tara bicar anto cae – *they want to have the matter adjudicated* [B. bicar < S. vicāra – *thought; opinion*]

bicara ['bīsāra] (n) *poor fellow; bloke* | bicara mara kaicoin – *the poor bloke has died* : bicarar nam jani na – *I don't know the fellow's name* [P. becāra – *helpless; deprived*]

bicari ['bīsārī] (n) *poor woman; poor girl* cf **bicara**

bice ['bīsé] (n adv) *in the midst; between* | sooror bice – *in the middle of the town* : ḍui ḍolor bice – *between two factions* < **bic²**

bici ['bīsī] (n) *seed; bean; pip; fruit stone* | urir bici – *beans* : lembur bici – *lemon pip* : katolor bici – *jackfruit stone* [B. bici]

bicmilla ['bis-mil-la] (int) *in the name of God* (the formula customarily pronounced by a Muslim before eating and before commencing any task) | **bicmilla kor-** – *say "bismillah" and begin; make an auspicious start* [A. bi smi l-lāhi – *by the name of the Deity*]

bicna ['bīs-na] (n) *bedding; bed* | tumar bicna tik koro – *tidy your bed* : **bicna fala-** – *spread out bedding; prepare a bed* : tan lagi feronto bicna falaici – *I've made up a bed for him in the front room* [B. bicana]

bicon ['bīsòn] (n) *seedling* cf **bic¹**

bicra ['bīs-ra] (n) *seed bed* [H. bīcṛā]

bidio ['bīḍiò] (n) *videotape; video film* | sof taki biḍio anci – *I've got a video from the shop* : afne biar biḍio ḍekta ni? – *would you like to see the video of the wedding?* : **bidio tul-** – *make a video recording* : kelar biḍio tulmu – *I'm going to videotape the match* [E.]

biḍae ['bīḍāy] (n) *farewell; leavetaking* | biḍaer somoe aicce – *the time for farewells has come* : **biḍae o-/biḍae oi ja-** – *take one's leave; be dismissed* : tara biḍae oi gece – *they've* *departed* : **biḍae le-** – *take one's leave* : biḍae liram – *I'm saying goodbye; I'm off now* : **biḍae de-/biḍae ḍi la-** – *say goodbye (to); allow to go; dismiss* : tane biḍae ḍi lauka – *say goodbye to him; let him go; don't detain him any longer* : amare biḍae ḍi laito – *they want to dismiss me* : **biḍae kor-/biḍae kori de-** – *see off; dismiss* : tarare biḍae kori ḍeuka – *see that they leave; get rid of them*   [B. biḍay < A. wadā¿]

biḍḍa ['bīḍ-ḍa] (n) *learning; knowledge*   [B. biḍḍa < S. viḍya]

biḍḍan ['bīḍ-ḍān] (n) *learned; well educated*   [B. biḍḍan < S. viḍvāna]

biḍes ['bīḍɛš] (n) *foreign land* | ḍes biḍes – *home and abroad* : tain biḍes bala fain na – *she doesn't like foreign parts* ¶ **biḍes** (adv) *abroad* | tara biḍes take – *they live abroad* : tain biḍes gecoin – *he has gone abroad*   [B. biḍes < S. viḍeša]

biḍesi ['bīḍɛšī] (adj) *foreign* ¶ **biḍesi** (n) *foreigner*   [B. biḍesi]

biḍisa ['bīḍīša] (adj) *senseless* = **beḍisa**

bifokko ['bīfok-kò] (n) *opposite side* | **bifokke** – *in opposition* : tain amrar bifokke maticoin – *he spoke against us*   [B. bipåkkå < S. vipakśa]

bifot ['bīfòt] (n) *danger; predicament* | amra boro bifotor maje – *we're in great danger; we're in an awful fix* : tara bifoto force – *they're in trouble* : amrare bifoto falaice – *they have put us in danger; they have put us in a predicament*   [B. bipåḍ < S. vipaḍa]

biforit ['bīfòrit] (adj) *contrary* | biforit manus – *a contrary person; an awkward fellow* : biforit orto – *opposite meaning*   [B. bipårit < S. viparīta – *inverse*]

big [bīg, bīk] (n) *subtraction* | **big kor-** – *subtract*   [B. biog < S. viyoga]

biggafon ['bīg-gāfòn] (n) *advertisement*   [B. biggapån < S. vijñāpana – *information*]

biggen ['bīg-gɛn] (n) *science*   [B. biggɛn < S. bijñāna – *discernment; natural science*]

bigr- (vi) *go out of line* | **bigri ja-** – *go out of line; go off* : tar mata bigri gece – *he's gone off his head* : amrar kactomar bigri jar – *our customers are turning away*   [H. bigɽ-]

bij [bīz] (n) *seed; kernel*   [B. bij < O. bīja]

bij- (vi) *get wet* | afne mege bijcoin – *you've got all wet from the rain* : **biji ja-** – *get wet* : caḍḍor biji gece – *the sheet's got wet*   [B. bhij-]

bija ['bīza] *wet; damp* | bija kafor – *wet clothes* : goro bija lage – *it feels damp in the house* : tumar at bija – *your hands are wet* : **bija bija** – *damp*   [B. bheja]

bija- (vt) *wetten; dampen; soak* | tumar juta bijaico – *you've got your shoes wet* : age tena·ta bijaita – *you should dampen the cloth first* : dail fanir maje bijaimu – *I'm going to let the lentils soak in water*   [B. bhija-]

biji ['bīzī] (n) *busyness; trading* | aij biji nae – *there's not much trade today* : biji cole ni? – *do you get plenty of custom?* : bala biji or – *business is good*   [E. busy]

bijli ['bīz-lī] (n) *lightning; electricity*   [B. bijli]

bik¹ [bīk] (n) *subtraction* = **big**

bik² (n) *embrocation* | **bik laga-** – *apply embrocation* : tar bukut bik lagaici – *I've rubbed embrocation on his chest*   [E. Vick's]

bik- (vi) *be on sale; be sold* | ino kafor bike – *clothes are sold here* : lembu bike ni? – *do the lemons sell well?* : gor bikce – *the house has been sold*   [H. bik-]

bikal ['bīkāl] (n) *afternoon*   [B. bikal < O. vaikāla]

bikka ['bīk-ka] (n) *begging* | **bikka kor-** – *beg* : he bikka kori kae – *he lives by begging* : «keur jonom baḍsar gore, keur bafe bikka kore» – *some people are born in a royal palace, some people's parents beg for a living*   [B. bhikka < S. bhikśā]

bikol ['bīkòl] (adj) *out of order*   [B. bikål]

bil [bīl] (n) *bill* | ilektikor bil aice – *the electricity bill has arrived* : ola gec jalaile boro bil utbo – *if you use gas like that you'll run up a big bill* : **bil tul-** – *run up bills* : sofo gia bil tule – *he goes to the shops and runs up big bills*   [E.]

bila- ['bīlā] (vt) *distribute; hand out*   [B. bila-]

bilai ['bīlāi] (n) *cat*   [H. bilāī]

bilat [bī'lāt] (n) *Britain*   [B. bilat < A. wilāya – *ruling power*]

bilati ['bīlātī] (adj) *British*   < **bilat**

bil-baḍol ['bīl-bāḍòl] (n) *bills*

bili ['bĭlī] (n) *delivery* | **bili kor-** – *deliver* [B. bili]
bilic ['bĭlīs] (n) *bleach* [E.]
bilkul ['bĭl-kūl] (adv) *altogether; completely* | bilkul tik – *absolutely correct* : bilkul fagol – *totally crazy* [A. bi l-kull – *by the total, in totality*]
biman ['bĭmān] (n) *Bangladesh Airlines* | kila jaira? bimano – *how are you going? By Bangladesh Biman* [B. biman < S. vimāna – *aerial chariot*]
bimar ['bĭmār] (adj) *sick* = **bemar**
bin¹ [bĭn] (n) *dustbin* | bino falaici – *I threw it in the bin* [E.]
bin² (n) *choking* | **bin ka-** – *choke* : kanir somoe bin kaicla – *she choked while eating*
bina ['bĭnā] (pre) *without* | bina kame – *without a job; pointlessly* : bina dorkare – *unnecessarily* : bina foesae – *without money; free of charge* : «bina batase gacor fata lore na» – *the leaves on the trees don't flutter without wind; there's no smoke without fire* [B. bina < S. binā]
binas [bĭ'nāš] (n) *ruination* | **binas o-/binas oi ja-** – *get ruined; be spoilt* : karfit binas oi gece – *the carpet has been ruined* : **binas kor-/binas kori le-** – *ruin; mess up; waste* : hokolta binas kori lirae – *you're making a great mess* [B. binas < S. vināša – *total destruction*]
binno ['bĭn-nò] (adj) *separate; different* | binno gor – *a separate house* : binno jat – *a different kind* : binno jator manus – *a different kind of people; people of a different race* : tan ekaunt amar taki binno – *his account is separate from mine* [B. bhinnå < S. bhinna – *separated*]
bir¹ [bĭr] (n) *hero* [B. bir < S. vīra]
bir² [bĭ:r] (n) *crowd; crowding; thronging* | mainsor bir – *crowds of people* : garir bir – *heavy traffic* : biror somoe – *the time of crowding; the rush hour* : **bir oe/bir take** – *there is a crowd; it is crowded* : bajaro hokol somoe bir take – *the market is always crowded* : **bir kor-** – *crowd together; throng* : cinemar samne mainse bir korra – *people are thronging in front of the cinema* [B. bhir̥]
biram ['bĭrām] (n) *pause; break* | **biram kor-** – *have a break* [B. biram]
biran ['bĭrān] (n) *fried dish* | mac biran – *fried fish* : **biran kor-/biran kori le-** – *fry; grill* : alu biran kori liba – *he is going to sauté the potatoes* [P. biryān – *roasted*]
biranobboi [bĭrā-'nòb-bòı] (n°) *ninety-two* [B. biranåbbåi]
birasi ['bĭrāšī] (n°) *eighty-two* [B. birasi]
birat ['bĭrāt] (adj) *huge; vast* | birat haor – *a vast floodplain* : **birat boro** – *very big; enormous* : birat boro dolan – *a great big building* [B. birat < S. virāt]
biri ['bĭrī] (n) *cigarette; bidi* | desi biri – *bidi (miniature cigar)* : **biri ka-** – *smoke cigarettes* : afne biri kain ni? – *do you smoke?* : ino biri kani cole na – *smoking is not allowed here* [B. bir̥i]
biroin ['bĭròın] (n) *a type of rice* = **birun**
birokto ['bĭròχtò] (adj) *disturbed* | **birokto o-** – *be annoyed* : caca birokto oicoin – *uncle is vexed* : birokto oin na jen – *please don't be annoyed* : **birokto kor-** – *disturb; annoy; bother* : tumar ammare birokto korio na – *don't pester your Mum* : afnare birokto korci – *sorry if I disturbed you* [B. biråktå < S. virakta – *detached*]
birombona [bĭ'ròmbònà] (n) *botheration* [B. bir̥åmbånà < S. vidambanā – *irony*]
birosfoti ['bĭròš-fòtī] (n) *Jupiter; Thursday* [B. brihåspati < S. br̥haspati]
birosfotibar ['bĭròš-fòtī-bār] (n) *Thursday* [B. brihåspåtibar]
biruddo ['bĭrūd-dò] (adj) *opposed* | **birudde** – *in opposition; against* : tain amrar birudde kam korra – *he is working against our interests* : hou desor birudde lorai oicil – *there was a war against that country* [B. biruddhå < S. viruddha]
birudi ['bĭrūdī] (adj) *opposed* | birudi dol – *opposition party* [B. birodhi < S. virodhi]
birudita ['bĭrūdita] (n) *opposition; enmity* | **birudita kor-** – *oppose; be hostile (to)* : tara tan birudita kore – *they are against him* [B. birodhita < S. virodhitā]
birun ['bĭrūn] (n) *binni (a type of rice)* | birun cail – *husked binni rice* : birun bat – *glutinous boiled binni rice* [B. binni]

bis¹ [bīš] (nº) *twenty* [B. bis]
bis² (n) *pain; ache; poison* | fetor bis – *stomach ache* : matar bis – *headache* : cun asole bis – lime is really a poison : **bis kore** – *it hurts; it aches* : kunano bis kore? – *where does it hurt?* : amar matat bis korer – *my head is aching* : **bis ka-** – *consume poison* : bis kaia morto acil – *he took poison and nearly killed himself* [B. bis < S. viśa – *poison*]
bisa ['bīšā] (n) *visa* | afne bisa loicoin ni? – *have you obtained a visa?* : tara bisa dito na korce – *they have refused to issue a visa* [E.]
bises ['bīšeš] (adj) *particular; special* | bises dorkar – *a particular need* : bises kunta nae – *nothing in particular* : **bises bises** – *very particular; quite special* : bises bises kani – *very special food* ¶ **bises** (adv) *particularly* | bises sundor – *particularly beautiful* : bises boro nae – *not particularly big* [B. bises < S. viśeṣa – *distinction, peculiarity*]
bis-bedna (n) *aches and pains* = **bis + bedna**
bisi ['bīšī] (adv) *much* = **besi**
bisoe ['bīšòy] (n) *matter; subject* | tain hokol bisoe janoin – *he knows all about everything* : kanir bisoe loia maticlam – *we discussed the subject of food* : bisoe kita? – *what's up? what's all this about?* : **(kuntar) bisoe** – *in the matter of (something); about (something)* : tara befsar bisoe jikaicil – *they asked about the business* : amra cacir bisoe hokol somoe cinta kori – *we always worry about auntie* [B. bisåy < S. viśaya]
bisram ['bīš-rām] (n) *rest; repose* | **bisram kor-** – *take a rest* [B. bisram < S. biśrāma]
bisriŋkola ['bīš-rīŋ-χòlā] (n) *disorder; indiscipline* [B. bisriŋkhåla < S. viśṛŋkhala - *unfettered*]
bissas ['bīš-šāš] (n) *belief; confidence* | tain aiba, amar bissas – *it's my belief he will come* : ou befare amar fura bissas – *I have full confidence regarding this matter* : **bissas ace** – *one has confidence* : tar ufre amar bissas acil – *I used to have confidence in him* : tare dia bissas nae – *there's no trusting him* : **(kar) bissas oe** – *it is believable (to someone)* : amar bissas oe na – *I can't believe it* : **bissas kor-** – *believe* : bissas korouka ... – *believe me ...* : amra allare bissas kori – *we believe in God* : tar kota bissas kori na – *I don't believe what he says* [B. bissas < S. viśvāsa]
bisu ['bīšū] (n) *joint cooking arrangement; common mess* | amra ek bisut kaitam – *we used to cook and eat jointly* [E. ?]
bisudbar ['bišūd-bār] (n) *Thursday*
bit [bīt] (n) *bird's droppings* [H. bīt]
bit- (vi) *(bird) defecate*
biti ['bītī] (n) *daughter; lass* = **beti**
bitis ['bitiš] (n) *the British* | **bitisor** – *British* : bitisor jaaj – *a British ship* : bitisor amole – *under British rule; during the British era (in India)* [E.]
bitla ['bīt-la] (adj) *naughty*
bit ['bīt] (n) *homestead site* [B. bhita – *base*]
bitantor ['bītantòr] (n) *detailed account* [B. brittantå < S. vṛttānta – *end of act*]
bitor ['bītòr] (n) *interior; inside* | tara bitor taki bar oice – *they emerged from inside* : folor bara·ta kala, bitor·ta dola – *the outside of the fruit is black, the inside is white* : tar bitor·ta bala – *he has a good heart* : **bitror** – *of the interior; inner* : bitror rum tala mara – *the inner room is locked* : **bitre** – *in the interior; inside* [B. bhitår]
bitre ['bīt-rɛ́] (n adv) *inside; in; within* | bitre jauka – *go inside* : tolet bitre na bara? – *is the toilet inside or outside?* : kunta nae bitre – *there's nothing inside* : goror bitre – *inside the house* : almarir bitre – *in the cupboard* : ek gontar bitre – *within an hour* : tar kemotar bitre – *within his capacity* : sombobor bitre – *within the bounds of possibility* : **bitre bitre** – *inwardly* : bitre bitre iŋsa kore – *deep down inside he's jealous* < **bitor**
bitta ['bīt-ta] (n) *wealth; property* [B. bittå < S. vitta]
bitu ['bītū] (adj) *timid* [B. bhitu]
bo-¹ [bò] (vi) *sit down; be set down; settle* | bouka! – *please be seated!* : cacare boibar dao – *let uncle sit; offer uncle a seat* : ami boitam nai – *I'm not going to sit; I won't stop, thankyou* : amra boite boite heran – *we're tired of sitting* : sil ino boito – *the rubber stamp*

34

should go here : kolomor ak boe na – *the pen's mark doesn't settle / the pen isn't making a mark* : dakni·ta boice na – *the lid isn't on properly* : keic boice – *a lawsuit has been instituted* : tain arbar bia boicoin – *he's got married again* : **boi tak-/boi ro-** – *remain seated* : boi tako! – *stay sitting where you are!* : tain boi roicoin – *he's just sitting there* : **boia ja-/boi ja-** – *sit before leaving; sit for a while* : boi jauka! – *do sit a while (before you go)* : betae dos minit boia gecoin – *the man stayed for ten minutes, then left* [B. bås-]

bo- ² (vi) *(water) flow; (air) blow* | gaŋ kun dike boice? – *which way does the river flow?* : raitku haoa boe – *a breeze blows at night* [B. båh-]

bo- ³ (vt) *carry* | oto boro buja ke boito? – *who's going to carry such a heavy load as this?* : amra mal boite boite ses – *we're worn out from lugging stuff around* [B. båh-]

boa ['bòa] (v n) *(act or state of) sitting* | afnar boa·ta oice na – *the way you are sitting is not right* : **boat** – *in a seated position; sitting* : tara goro boat – *they are sitting waiting at home* : tain boat roicoin – *he's sitting tight* < **bo-**

boa- (vt) *make to sit; offer a seat to; set in place* | memanre boao – *offer seats to our guests* : tantanre feronto boaici – *I made them sit in the front room* : dostokot kunano boaitam? – *where should I put my signature?* : ketli boaici – *I've put the kettle on* : tara tifkol boaice – *they've installed a tubewell* : tain keic boaiba – *he's going to start a lawsuit* : **boai de-** – *get to sit; put in place* : cacare boai dao – *offer uncle a seat* : tara keic boai dice – *they've started legal proceedings* : **boai rak-** – *keep (someone) sitting* : amrare dui gonta boai rakce – *they kept us sitting and waiting for two hours* [B. båsa-]

bobisot ['bòbišòt] (n) *future* | tair bobisot bala – *her future looks promising* : bobisot cinta – *concerns about the future* : tara bobisot cinta kore na – *they don't pause to think about the future* : **bobisote** – *in future* : bobisote kita oibo ke jane? – *who knows what may happen in the future?* [B. bhåbisåt < S. bhaviśyat]

boc ¹ [bos] (adv) *enough* | boc, oice! – *that's enough!* : tar boc oe na – *it's not enough for him; he doesn't get enough* : tara boc korto fare na – *they can't do enough; they can't manage adequately* = **bac**

boc ² (n) *boss; employer* | boce koicoin – *the boss said so* : afnar bocre jiggauka – *ask your employer* [E.]

bocor ['bòsòr] (n) *year* | tin bocor lagbo – *it will take three years* : ek bocor bade – *one year later* : tair boes coe bocor – *her age is six years; she's six years old* : bocor sese – *at the end of a year* : bocor sese isab kora lagbo – *accounts must be drawn up at the end of the year* : **bocor din** – *about one year* : tain bocor din bade aiba – *he'll return after a year or so* : **bocoro** – *per year* : bocoro fac ajar fon – *£5000 per year* : bocoro tin bar – *three times a year* : **bocore bocore** – *year by year; every year* : bocore bocore bare – *it gets bigger every year* [B. båcår < S. vatsara]

bod [bòd] (adj) *bad* [P. bad]

bodar ['bòdār] (n) *heed* | bodar kor- – *take heed; bother* : he bodar kore na – *he doesn't bother; he can't be bothered* [E.]

bodboe ['bòd-bòy] (n) *bad smell* [P. badbo]

bodcurot ['bòd-sūròt] (adj) *bad-looking; ugly* **bod + curot**

bodjat ['bòd-zāt / 'bòj-jāt] (adj) *low; mean-minded* [P. bad – *evil* + A. ðāt – *nature*]

bodl- ['bòd-l] (vi) *change; be altered* | din-kail bodler – *times are changing* : tarar lombor bodlice – *their number has changed* : **bodli ja-** – *change; be altered* : tar ceara bodli gece – *his appearance has changed* [H. badal-]

bodla ['bòd-la] (n) *replacement; equivalent; exact replica* | bacmotir bodla nae – *there's no substitute for basmati* : ita rou macor bodla – *this looks exactly like ruhi fish* : tain afnar bodla – *he's your double* : **bodla lo-/bodla loi le-** – *take an eye for an eye; take revenge* : tara bodla loi lito – *they want to get their own back* ¶ **bodla** (adj) *interchangeable; very similar* | bodla cakka – *a replacement wheel* : bodla tajmol – *the spitting image of the Taj Mahal* ¶ **bodla** (adv) *instead (of)* : ein amar bodla matba – *he will do the talking on my behalf* < **bodol**

boḍla- (vt) *exchange; swap; change* | teka boḍlaitam – *I want to exchange some money* : cidi boḍlauka – *please change the CD* : tumar kafor boḍlani lagbo – *you'll have to change your clothes* : **boḍlaia de-/boḍlai de-** – *exchange; provide a replacement (for)* : rajai boḍlai ḍeuka – *please change the bedcover* : **boḍlai le-** – *change; obtain a replacement (for)* : tar nam boḍlai lice – *he's changed his name* [B. bå̃ḍla-]
boḍla-boḍli ['bòḍ-lā-bòḍ-lī̃] (n) *chopping and changing; exchange* = **boḍla + boḍli**
boḍlail ['bòḍ-lāıl] (v adj) *changed; exchanged* < **boḍla-**
boḍli ['bòḍ-li] (n) *exchange* | **boḍli o-/boḍli oi ja** – *be exchanged; be transferred* : tan lombor boḍli gece – *his number has been changed* : tain boḍli oi gecoin – *she has been transferred (to another post)* [H. baḍli]
boḍloe ['bòḍ-lòy] (n) *bad habit* | tumar ita boḍloe – *that's a bad habit of yours* : he tar boḍloe care na – *he won't give up his bad habits* **boḍ + loe**
boḍmais [bòḍ-'māıš] (adj) *evil; lascivious* | hou beta boro boḍmais – *that fellow is quite vicious* : boḍmais luk·ta – *that depraved man* ¶ **boḍmais** (n) *evil person* | koto boro boḍmais! – *what a scoundrel!* [P. bad – *evil* + A. ma¿āš – *way of life*]
boḍmejaj ['bòḍ-mezāz] (n) *bad temper* [P. bad – *evil* + A. mizāj – *disposition*]
boḍmejaji ['bòḍ-mezāzī] (adj) *bad-tempered* = **boḍmejaj + -i** ²
boḍnam ['bòḍ-nām] (n) *ill repute* | tan boḍnam hunci na kunuḍin – *I've never heard any ill of him* : **boḍnam kor-** – *vilify; speak ill (of someone)* : he afnar boḍnam korer – *he is blackening your name* : mainsor boḍnam koro kene? – *why do you speak ill of others?* [P. badnām – *of bad repute*]
boḍnocib ['bòḍ-nòsīb] (adj) *ill fated* [P. bad – *bad* + A. naṣīb – *fate*]
boḍoibbas [bòḍ 'òıb-bāš] (n) *bad habits* = **boḍ + oibbas**
boḍojmi ['bòḍòzmī] (n) *indigestion* [P. bad – *bad* + A. haḎm – *digestion*]
boḍol ['bòḍòl] (n) *exchange; change* | tar halotor maje boḍol nae – *there's been no change in his condition* : **boḍole** – *instead (of)* : cinir boḍole gur diclam – *instead of sugar I added molasses* : tumar boḍole ke jaibo? – *who will go in your stead?* : **boḍol kor-/boḍol kori le-** – *exchange; change* : sokal sokal betrik boḍol kora lagbo – *the battery will very soon have to be changed* [A. badl]
boḍro ['bòḍ-rò) (adj) *decent; polite* [B. bhå̃ḍrå̃ < S. bhaḍra – *good; worthy*]
boe [bòy] (n) *odour; smell* | **boe kore** – *it smells; it stinks* : hutkir boe kore – *there's a smell of dried fish* : **boe fa-** – *discern a smell* : telor boe faici – *I smell petrol* [P. bo]
boeam ['bòyām] (n) *jar* [Pg. boião]
boean ['bòyān] (n) *account; narrative* [A. bayān – *explanation*]
boes ['bòyš] (n) *age* | tumar boes koto? – *how old are you?* : amar boes ḍos bocor – *my age is ten years; I'm ten years old* : sare at bocor boes – *eight and a half years of age* : **boes oe/boes oi jae** – *one becomes (sufficiently) old* : tair iskulo jaibar boes oice na ebu – *she's not yet old enough to go to school* : ḍaḍir raijjir boes oi gece – *grandmother is very old indeed* [B. bå̃yås < S. vayas]
boesal ['bòyšāl] (adj) *of considerable age* < **boes**
boesko ['bòyšχò] (adj) *of considerable age* [B. bå̃yåska < S. vayaska]
boga ['bògā] (n) *egret* [O. baka]
bogi ¹ ['bògī] (n) *female egret;* (vulgar male slang) *woman*
bogi ² (n) *penis*
bogol ['bògòl] (n) *armpit* | **bogole** – *in arms; close beside* : beti geḍare bogole loicoin – *the woman took the child in her arms* : tarar barir bogole gaŋ – *there's a river right beside their homestead* [P. baġal – *side; arm*]
bogorbogor ['bògòr-bògòr] (n) *muttering* | **bogorbogor kor-** – *mutter; grumble* : burae kali bogorbogor kore – *the old man keeps mumbling away*
boi ¹ [bòı] (n) *book* [B. bå̃i < O. vahikā]
boi ² (v adv) *in a seated state* | boi tako! – *stay sitting!* < **bo-**
boical ['bòısāl] (n) *earthquake* = **buical**
boi-fustok ['bòı-fūs-tòχ] (n) *books* = **boi + fustok**

boin [bòɪn] (n) *sister; female cousin of the same generation* | saikkat boin – *full sister* : cacar goror boin – *paternal cousin: father's brother's daughter* : fufur goror boin – *paternal cousin: father's sister's daughter* : mamar goror boin – *maternal cousin: mother's brother's daughter* : moir goror boin – *maternal cousin: mother's sister's daughter* : **bonir** – *sister's* : tumar bonir nam kita? – *what's your sister's name?* : **bonain/bonin** – *sisters* : tara boinain cair·jon – *they are four sisters* : **bonaintor/bonintor** – *of sisters* : bonintor maje Minara boro – *Minara is the eldest of the sisters* [B. bon]
boinari ['bòɪnarī] (n) *(woman's) female friend*
boinfut ['bòɪnfūt] (n) *(woman's) sister's son* = **boin + fut**
boinjamai ['bòɪn-jāmāɪ] (n) *younger sister's husband* = **boin + jamai**
boinji ['bòɪn-jī] (n) *(woman's) sister's daughter* = **boin + ji** ²
boirati ['bòɪrātī] (n) *bridegroom's delegation; son-in-law's visit* | boirati aice – *the bridegroom's party have arrived (for the wedding)* : amar baisab boirati gecoin – *my big brother has gone on a visit to his in-laws* [B. bårjatri < S. varayatrī]
bois [bòɪš] (n) *water buffalo* [H. bhaiⁿs]
boisak ['bòɪšāχ] (n) *Vaisakh (April-May)* [B. boisakh < S. vaišākha]
boisnob ['bòɪšnòb] (n) V*aisnava* [B. boisnåb < S. vaiṣṇava]
boisot ['bòɪšòt] (n) *future* = **bobisot**
boitol ['bòɪtòl] (n) *vagabond* [B. betal < S. vaitāla – *goblin*]
bojjat ['bòj-jāt] (adj) *low; mean-minded* = **bodjat**
bok- (v) *scold; grumble* | caci fuaintore bokcoin – *aunt has given the boys a ticking off* : tain hariɖin bokoin – *he keeps grumbling all day long* : ar bokio na! – *do stop carrying on about it* [B. båk-]
boka ['bòχa] (n) *scolding* | **boka ɖe-/boka ɖi la-** – *scold* : tain hurutare boka ɖira – *she's scolding the children* < **bok-**
bokaboki ['bòχābòkī] (n) *scolding; chatter* < **bok-**
bokar [bòχ'ār] (n) *fever* [A. buḳār – *vapour*]
bokbok ['bòχ-bòχ] (n) *idle talk; nattering* | **bokbok kor-** – *natter; chatter*
bokea ['bòχéa] (n) *arrears* [A. baqīya – *residue*]
bokoaj [bòχ'wāz] (n) *big talker; windbag* [H. bakvāsī – *chatterer*]
bokor ['bòχòr] (n) *fever* = **bokar**
bokri ['bòχ-rī] (n) *female goat* [H. bakrī]
bokriɖ ['bòχ-rīɖ] (n) *Eid-ul-Adha* [U. baqarīɖ < A. ¿īd al-baqar – *festival of cattle*]
boksis ['bòχ-šīš] (n) *gratuity; tip* [P. baḳšīš]
bokti ['bòχ-tī] *devotion; reverence* [B. bhåkti < S. bhakti]
bokto ['bòχ-tò] (n) *devoted* | tain sa furanor bokto – *she is devoted to Shah Puran; she is a devotee of Shah Puran* : ein afnar bokto – *he's a fan of yours* [B. bhåktå < S. bhakta]
bokula ['bòkūla] (n) *egret* [O. baka]
bol [bòl] (n) *bodily strength; vigour* | tar sorilo bol nae – *he has no physical strength; he is puny* [B. bål < O. vala]
bol- (vi) *grow larger; increase* | gac·ta ɖin ɖin boler – *the plant is getting taller day by day* : amrar beton bolto nae – *our wages aren't going to go up* : **boli ja-** – *grow larger; increase* : nati boli gece – *grandson has got bigger* cf **bar-**
bola ['bòlā] (n) *wasp* [B. bolta]
bola- (vt) *make greater; increase* | boce amar beton bolaicoin – *the boss has put up my wages* : **bolaia ɖe-** – *make greater; increase* : tara calir ɖam bolaia ɖice – *they have put up the price of rice* : **bolaia ko-** – *overstate* : tar boes bolaia koicil – *he exaggerated his age* cf **bara-**
bolon [bòlòn] (n) *increment; increase* | ɖui tin incir bolon – *an increase of two or three inches* : bolon komon – *increase and decrease; going up and down; fluctuation* : **bolon o-** – *increase; grow larger* : befsar tura bolon oice – *business has increased a little* : ar bolon oito nae tumar – *you're not going to get any bigger* < **bol-**
boltu ['bòltū] (n) *(engineering) bolt* [E.]

37

bomi ['bòmī] (n) *vomiting* | **bomi lage** – *nausea is felt* : amar bomi lagce – *I've got a queasy feeling* : **bomi bomi kore** – *nausea is felt* : amar bomi bomi korer – *I feel bilious* : **bomi kor-** – *vomit; get sick* : tumi bomi korco ni? – *did you get sick?* [B. båmi < S. vami]

bon [bòn] (n) *wild vegetation* [B. bån < O. vana – *wilderness*]

bon- (vi) *be made; be cast in a role* | tarar gor bonce – *their house has been built* : tan fasfut boner – *his passport is being processed* : tain raja bonba – *he will play the role of the king* : caca bekuf boncoin – *uncle has been made to look a fool* : **(kar loge) bone** – *things work out (with someone else)* : jonor loge lilur bone – *Lilu gets on well with John* : tarar loge amar bonto nae – *I won't be able to get on with them* : **boni ja-** – *get made; get done* : fonor lain boni gece – *the phone line has been installed* : kam boni gece – *the job has been completed* [H. ban-]

bonaji ['bònāzī] (adj) *herbal* | bonaji ousuđ – *herbal medicine* [B. bånåj]

bonđ[1] [bòn] (adj) *closed; closed down; at a standstill* | aij ofis bonđ – *the office is closed today* : laibri soni-roibbare bonđ – *the library is closed on Saturdays and Sundays* : hokol kam bonđ – *everything has come to a halt* : **bonđ o-/bonđ oi ja-** – *close down; cease* : fektri bonđ oi gece – *the factory has closed down* : **bonđ kor-** – *close; stop* : keced bonđ kortam ni? – *shall I stop the cassette player?* : muk bonđ kor! – *shut your mouth!* (offensive) [B. båndhå]

bonđ[2] (n) *open arable lowland*

bonđa ['bòn-đa] (n) *slave; devotee* | allar bonđa - *servants of God; Muslims* = **banđa**

bonđegi ['bòn-đɛgī] (n) *servitude; devotion* [P. bandagī]

bonđi ['bòn-đī] (n) *prisoner* | **bonđi kori rak-** – *hold prisoner* : tare tin đin bonđi kori rakce – *they kept him prisoner for three days* [P. banđī]

bonđobost ['bòn-đòbòst] (n) *arrangement* | **bonđobost kor** – *make arrangements* : tara kanir bonđobost korce – *they provided a meal* [P. band-o-bast – *conclusion*]

bonđok ['bòn-đòχ] (n) *pawned item; mortgaged item* | **bonđok đe-/bonđok đi la-** – *pawn; mortgage* : amar gori bonđok đitam – *I want to pawn my watch* : tarar fura jaga bonđok đi laice – *they have mortgaged all their land* [B. båndhåk < S. banđhaka]

bonđor ['bòn-đòr] (n) *bazaar* [P. banđar – *port*]

bonđu ['bòn-đū] (n) *friend* [B. båndhu < O. banđhu – *relative*]

bonđu-banđob (n) *friends* [B. båndhu- bandhåb]

bonđuk (n) *rifle; gun* [P. bunđūq]

bonibonaf ['bònī bònāf] (n) *compatibility; getting on together* | tar loge amar bonibonaf nae – *I don't get along well with him* cf **bon-**

bonin ['bònīn] (n) *sisters* = **boinain**

bonir ['bònīr] (n adj) *sister's* < **boin**

bon-joŋgol ['bòn-jòŋ-gòl] (n) *rough vegetation; wilderness*

bonna ['bòn-na] (n) *flooding* | **bonna oe/bonna oi jae** – *flooding occurs* : sunamgonjo bonna oi gece – *there have been floods in Sunamganj* [B. bånna < O. vanyā]

boon ['bò-on] (v n) *state of sitting* | tare boono faici – *I found him sitting there* : tara boonor maje – *they're having a sit down* < **bo-**

bor [bòr] (n) *application of weight; burdening* | **(kuntar ufre) bor đe-** – *rest weight (on something)* : tain latir ufre bor đia atoin – *he walks leaning on a stick* [B. bhår]

bor- (v) *fill; fill up; fill in; put in* | tar fet borce – *his stomach has filled; he's eaten enough* : kamlae gat borer – *the workman is filling in a hole* : tar beton borta kila? – *how will you make up his full wage?* : citi kamo borouka – *put the letter in an envelope* : **bori ja-** – *get filled; get covered in dirt* : balti bori gece – *the bucket has filled up* : tumar jama bori gece – *your clothes have got filthy* : **bori le-** – *stuff in* : tumar jebo bori lao – *stick it in your pocket* : **bori đe-** – *fill in; make up in full* : fuae amar ren bori đee – *my son makes up any shortfall in my rent payments* [B. bhår-]

bora[1] ['bòra] (v adj) *filled; full* | bora gelas – *a full glass* : bosta caile bora – *the sack is full of rice* : bosta bora cail – *a sackful of rice* : ek bocor bora – *a whole year* : amar fet bora – *I'm full; I've eaten enough* < **bor-**

38

bora [2] (n) *fried dal cake*   [B. båɽa]
bora- (vt) *fill; fill up; fill in; cover with dirt* | ɖui buṭol boraici – *I've filled two bottles* : fani ɖia boraici – *I filled them with water* : garir ɖam ke boraita? – *who would cover the full cost of the car?* : karfiṭ boraico tumra – *you lot have messed up the carpet* : **borai de-/borai le-** – *fill in; cover with dirt* : tara gaṭ borai ɖice – *they have filled in the holes* : tumar kafor borai lico – *you've dirtied your clothes*   [B. bhåra-]
borabor ['bòrabòr] (adv) *regularly; exactly; straight* | tain borabor ain – *he comes regularly* : borabor tik – *quite correct* : borabor tin·tat – *at three o'clock sharp* : borabor jauka – *go straight ahead*   [P. barābar – *equally*]
boraf ['bòrāf] (n) *frost; ice; snow* | boraf lage – *it feels freezing* : boraf jomce – *ice has formed* : boraf forer – *snow is falling*   [B. båråf < P. barf – *snow*]
borail ['bòrāıl] (v adj) *filled; covered in dirt* | basko kagoje borail – *the box is full of paper* : tumar kafor borail – *your clothes are dirty*   < **bora-**
boraŋ ['bòraŋ] (n) *silted channel; creek*
borbaḍ [bòr-'ḍāḍ] (adj) *gone to waste* | **borbaḍ o-/borbaḍ oi ja-** – *be wasted; get spoilt* : afnar hokol kam borbaḍ oibo – *all your work will be wasted* : **borbaḍ kor-/borbaḍ kori le-** – *waste; spoil* : foesa borbaḍ kore – *he wastes money* : amar kafor borbaḍ kori lico – *you've ruined my sari*   [P. bar bād – *on the wind*]
borḍas [bòr-'ḍāš] (n) *endurance; long-suffering* | betir jobor borḍas – *the girl has great endurance; she is very long-suffering* : **borḍas kor-** – *endure; suffer; put up (with)* : borḍas korta kilagi? – *why should you put up with it?*   [P. bardāšt – *taking up; acceptance*]
bori ['bòrī] (n) *pill; tablet*   [B. båɽi < O. vaṭika]
borisa ['bòrīšā] (n) *rain; the rainy season*   = **borsa**
borkot ['bòr-χòt] (n) *blessing from God*   [A. baraka]
boro ['bòrò] (a) *large; larger; senior; older; rich; generous; important* | boro gac – *a large tree* : kun mac boro? – *which fish is the biggest?* : ein amar boro fufu – *she is my senior paternal aunt* : tain amar boro – *he is older than me* : tara boro luk – *they are rich people* : tan ɖil boro – *she has a generous heart* : boro ofisar – *a high-ranking official* : foesa boro na iman boro? – *which is more important, money or integrity?* ¶ **boro** (adv) *very; exceedingly* | boro bala manus – *a very good person* : boro sunɖor jaega – *a very beautiful place* : boro muskil! – *what a great nuisance!* : **boro o-/boro oi ja-** – *become bigger; be too big* : natin boro oi jar – *granddaughter is getting older* : i fen amar lagi boro oi gece – *these trousers are too big for me* : **boro kor-/boro kori le-** – *enlarge; extend* : amrar gor boro kori litam – *we want to enlarge our house*   [B. båɽā]
boroc ['bòròs] (n) *year* | ɖui-tin boroc age – *two or three years earlier* : tain aicoin fac boroc coler – *it's now the fifth year since she came*   [H. baras < O. varśa]
boron ['bòròn] (n) *boil; abscess*   [B. brån < S. vraṇa]
borosa ['bòròšā] (n) *trust; reliance* | alla borosa – *God for reliance* : **(kar ufre/kare ɖia) (kar) borosa ace** – *(someone) has trust (in someone)* : allar ufre borosa – *we place our trust in God* : cacar ufre amar borosa ace – *I have confidence in my uncle* : tare ɖia borosa nae – *there is no trusting him at all* : **(kar ufre) borosa kor-** – *rely (on someone); trust (someone)* : beṭar ufre fura borosa korclam – *I had put my entire trust in that fellow; I was fully relying on him*   [H. bharosā < O. bharavašya]
borsa ['bòr-šā] (n) *rain; the rainy season*   [B. bårsa < S. varśā]
borsi ['bòr-šī] (n) *fish hook*   [B. båɽsi]
borti ['bòr-tī] (adj) *filled; full* | ek bosta borti cail – *a sack full of rice* : ɖukan mainse borti – *the shop is full of people* : tar maṭaṭ ukuin borti – *his head is teeming with lice* ¶ **borti** (n) *filling-up; admission* | tara bortir lagi aice – *they have come for admission* : **borti o-/borti oi ja-** – *get admitted* : tain asfatalo borti oicoin – *she's been admitted to hospital* : **borti kor-/borti kori le-** – *put in; have (someone) admitted* : bego borti kori loo – *pop it in your bag* : tare aij borti kormu – *we'll admit him today* : **borti kora-** – *get (someone) admitted* : taire iskulo borti koraitam – *I want to get her enrolled in school*   [B. bhårti]

bortoman ['bòr-tòmān] (adj) *present* | bortoman somoe – *the present time* : tain bortoman acla – *he was present* ¶ **bortoman** (n) *the present (time)* | otit, bortoman ar bobisot – *the past, the present and the future* : **bortomane** – *at present* : afne bortomane kunano takoin? – *where do you live at present?* [B. bårtåman < S. vartamāna]

borton ['bòr-tòn] (n) *plate; dish* [H. bartan]

borui ['bòrūɪ] (n) *jujube (Zizyphus jujuba), a small tree with greenish fruit resembling miniature apples or plums* [B. båråi]

bosobas ['bòsòbāš] *habitation* | **bosobas kor-** – *dwell* = **bas** [3]

bosonto ['bòsòn-tò] (n) *spring (season); pox* | bosonto coler – *spring is in progress* : bosonto bar oice – *the pox has broken out* [B. båsåntå < S. vasanta – *spring*]

bosot-bari ['bòsòt-bārī] (n) *home; settled abode* | tarar bosot-bari nobigonjo – *their home is in Nabiganj* [B. båsåt-bati]

bosoti ['bòsòtī] (n) *habitation* | faaro mainsor bosoti kom – *not many people live in the hills* [B. båsåti]

bossa ['bòš-šā] (n) *rain; the rainy season* = **borsa**

bosta ['bòs-tā] (n) *sack* | ek bosta cail – *a sack of rice* : calir bosta koto? – *how much (in price) is a sack of rice?* [P. basta – *bundle*]

bostu ['bòs-tū] (n) *thing* [B. båstu < S. vastu]

bot [bòt] (n) *banyan* [B. båt < S. vata]

botgac ['bòt-gās] (n) *banyan tree* = **bot** + **gac**

boti ['bòtī] (n) *lump of meat* [H. botī]

botla ['bòt-lā] (adj) *rotund; plump*

botoi ['bòtòɪ] (n) *penis*

botris ['bòt-rīš] (n°) *thirty-two* [B. båtris]

bottis ['bòt-tīš] (n°) *thirty-two* = **botris**

bou [bôu] (n) *bride; (young) wife; daughter-in-law* | tan fuar lagi bou tukaira – *he's looking for a bride for his son* : jamai-bou ekloge aicoin – *husband and wife arrived together* : boro bou bala randa jane – *my elder daughter-in-law cooks well* [B. båu < O. vadhu]

bou-baicca ['bôw-bāɪtšɪa] (n) *wife and children* = **bou** + **baicca**

boud [bôud] (n) *signboard* | **boud laga-** – *put up a signboard; advertise for sale* : tara restono boud lagaice – *they've put the restaurant up for sale* : **boud mar-** – *put up a signboard; advertise for sale* : goro boud marci – *we've put our house on the market* [E.]

bout [bôut] (adj) *much; many* | bout foesa – *a lot of money* : bout manus – *many people* ¶ **bout** {adv} *much; very* | bout sundor – *very beautiful* : bout age – *much earlier; long before* : bout besi – *much too much* [H. bahut]

boutta ['bôut-tā] (pron) *much; a lot* | boutta roice – *there's a lot left over* : tain amrar lagi boutta korcoin – *she has done a lot for us* : boutta matci – *(forgive me if) I've said more than I should* = **bout** + **-ta** [2]

briddo ['brid-dò] (adj) *old; elderly* ¶ **briddo** (n) *old person* | juan briddo hokoloe – *everyone, young and old alike* [B. briddho < S. vṛddha – *grown*]

brikko ['brik-kò] (n) *tree* [B. brikkå < S. vṛkśa]

bu [bū] (int) *dear (child)* | kita re bu? – *what is it, darling?* Note: Interjection used for addressing a girl or woman. Informal and familiar.

buai ['būāɪ] (n) *elder sister* = **bubai**

buba ['būba] (adj) *dumb* [B. boba]

bubai ['būbāɪ] (n) *elder sister* [B. bubu]

budda ['būd-dā] (n) *old man* [H. būddhā < O. buddha]

bud [1] [būd] (n) *awareness* | **bud oe** – *it seems; I think* : bud oe meg dibo – *it seems it's going to rain* : farba ni? bud oe – *will you be able? I think so* : tain aicoin, bud oe – *he's arrived, I think* : **bud kor-** – *feel* : itar kunu jorurot bud korra ni? – *do you feel there's any real necessity for it?* : **bud fa-** – *realise* : he aice kori bud faiclam na – *I didn't realise he had come* : bud faico ni? – *see what I mean?* [B. bodhi < S. bodha]

bud [2] (n) *Mercury; Wednesday* [B. budh < S. budha]

budbar ['būd-bār] (n) *Wednesday* [B. budhbar]
buddi ['būd-dī] (n) *intelligence; idea; advice* | tair buddi ace – *she has brains; she's smart* : tumar buddi! – *how frightfully clever of you!* : buddi deko – *oh, that's clever, that is* : amar kunu buddi nae – *I have no bright ideas* : bala buddi! – *what a brilliant idea!* : cacar buddi moto kam koro – *act in accordance with uncle's advice* : buddir kota – *words of intelligence; a good idea; a good point* : **buddi de-** – *give ideas; give advice* : amare ek·ta buddi deuka – *please give me some advice* : **buddi lo-** – *take advice* : afnar buddi loitam – *I'd like to get some ideas from you* : hokol somoe forar buddi loia cole – *he always follows other people's lead* [B. buddhi < S. buddhi]
buddi-foramosso ['būd-dī-fòrāmòš-šò] (n) *advice*
buddiman ['būd-dīmān] (adj) *intelligent* [B. buddhiman < S. buddhimāna]
bug [būg] (n) *suffering* | **bug kor-** – *undergo (suffering); suffer* : caci nanan ruge bug korra – *my aunt is suffering from various ailments* : tain bout din bug korcoin – *she was suffering for a long time* [B. bhog < S. bhoga – *enjoyment*]
bug- (vi) *undergo suffering; suffer* | tain bate bugcoin – *he suffers from rheumatism* : tain ek mas dori bugra – *he has been suffering (from it) for a month* [B. bhog-]
bugi ['būgī] (n) *one who suffers; sufferer* [B. bhogi]
bugol ['būgòl] (n) *geography* [B. bhugol < S. bhū – *earth* + B. gol – *sphere*]
bui [būɪ] (n) *land; the earth* [B. bhumi < O. bhūmi]
buical ['būɪsāl] (n) *earthquake* = **bui + cal**
buiddi ['būɪd-dī] (n) *intelligence* = **buddi**
buj [būz] (n) *estimation; adequacy* | tumar buj moto kam koro – *act as you see fit* : afnar buj oice ni? – *are you satisfied?* : kanir buj ace – *there's enough food to go around* : **buj lo-** – *take over; accept (something proffered)* : he buj loe na – *he refuses to take it from me* : **buj man-/buj mani le-** – *accept (an offer, an argument, a situation); agree* : hese tara buj mani lice – *in the end they conceded* : **buj mana-/buj manai de-** – *get (someone) to agree* : tare buj manani lagbo – *we'll have to talk him round* [B. bujh]
buj- (v) *accept; acknowledge; weigh up; understand* | tumar banla foesa bujo – *here, take your change* : ami buji na ikan – *no, I won't have any of that* : ami buji-suji na – *I don't know at all; I don't accept that* : he bujto cae na – *he refuses to see the point* : tara bujto raji nae – *they just don't want to know* : cutti buji na – *I don't care if it's your day off or not* : bujtam oimu – *I'll have to think it over* : afnar loge bujtam – *I want to talk it over with you* : bujbar baki roice – *we haven't got to the bottom of it yet* : tain ana bujia kam koroin – *he does things without thinking* : afne kita bujoin? – *what do you reckon?* : jekta bala bujoin – *whatever you think best* : he dibo kori buji na – *I hardly imagine he's going to pay up* : tain bujcoin amra goro – *he thought we were at home* : ami bujci kali! – *oh, I thought it was empty!* : kila bujlae? – *what made you think that?* : tain kunta bujoin na – *he doesn't understand anything* : bujram – *yes, I get what you're saying* : bujci na – *I haven't understood, sorry, I'm not with you* : bujcoin ni? – *know what I mean?* : bujco? – *have you got that?* : buja muskil – *it's hard to say* : tain kusi, buja jae – *you can tell he's pleased* : tara aito nae buji – *I take it they're not going to come* : tain gecoin gi buji? – *so he's gone, has he?* : **buji lo-** – *accept (something handed over)* : cafi buji loo – *here, take the key* : **buji le-** – *take on board (an idea)* : buji lao tumi bemar forlae, te kita korlae ne? – *just suppose you fell ill, what would you do then?* : aicca, buji lici – *oh, I see* [B. bujh-]
buja[1] ['būzā] (n) *burden* [B. bojha]
buja[2] (v n) *understanding* | buja muskil – *to understand is difficult; it's hard to say* : **buja jae** – *it can be understood; it is evident* : tumi rag korco, buja jae – *it's clear that you have become angry; I gather you're annoyed* : buja jae na – *you just can't tell* : tain age kuk acla buja jae na – *you'd never guess he used to be a cook* < **buj-**
buja- (vt) *hand over; get (someone) to understand; explain* | cacare cafi bujaici – *I've handed the keys over to uncle* : afnare bujai .. – *let me explain ..* : fagolre bujaita kila? – *how can you get a madman to see sense?* : taire bujaite ek gonta lagce – *it took an hour to persuade her* : **bujaia de-** – *hand over; explain* : tane kota·ta bujaia dici – *I've made him*

understand my point : **bujaia rak-** – *reassure; make satisfied* : betare bujaia rakci – *I gave the fellow reassurances; I soothed him; I calmed him down* : hurutare bujaia raktam kila? – *how am I to keep the children satisfied?* [B. bojha-]

bujabuji ['būzā būzī] (n) *mutual explication; exchange of views* | bujabuji coler – *negotiations are going on* : bul bujabuji – *misunderstanding; acrimony* : erar maje bul bujabuji oi gece – *a misunderstanding has arisen between them* : **bujabuji kor-** – *debate; argue* : tara bout somoe ɖori bujabuji korce – *they thrashed things out together at great length* < **buj-**

bujafora ['būzā fòrā] (n) *discussion of terms; negotiation* | bujafora lagbo – *discussion will be necessary; we'll have to talk things over* : bujafora coler – *negotiations are going on* : **bujafora kor-** – *negotiate* : tara ɖui gonta ɖori bujafora korer – *they've been talking things over for two hours* [B. bojhapâṛa]

bujra ['būz-rā] (n) *one who understands* | ita bujra koe·jon acoin? – *how many people are capable of understanding that?* ¶ **bujra** (adj) *capable of understanding* : ek·jon bujra manus ani louka – *fetch someone who can understand* < **buj-**

buk[1] [būk] (n) *breast; chest* | tar buk fulae kila! – *how he does puff out his chest!* : **bukur** – *of the chest* : bukur maje ɖuk faici – *I was hurt in the chest* : **bukut** – *in the chest* : amar bukut bis korer – *there's a pain in my chest* [B. buk < O. vakśa]

buk[2] (n) *book; orderbook* | tain buk ɖia foesa tuloin – *he draws his benefit by orderbook* : bukor maje fata nae – *there are no pages left in the book* [E.]

buk[3] (n) *hunger* | **buk lage** – *hunger is felt* : amar feto buk lagce – *I feel hungry* : tumar buk lagle koibae – *tell me if you get hungry* [B. bhukh < O. bubhukśā]

buka[1] ['būkā] (adj) *foolish* [B. boka < O. bakka – *goat*]

buka[2] (adj) *hungry* [B. bhukha]

bukami ['būkāmī] (n) *foolishness* = **buka**[1] + **-ami**

bul[1] [būl] (n) *mistake; wrong thing* | lekar maje bul – *there are mistakes in the script* : tumar bul tik koro – *correct your mistakes* : ami bul koiclam – *I said the wrong thing; what I said was incorrect* : tain amar bul ɖorcoin – *he pointed out my mistake* : ola bul maf korta kila? – *how could you pardon such a mistake?* : **bul oe/bul oi jae** – *a mistake is made; something goes wrong* : amar bul oito fare – *I may have made a mistake; I may be wrong* : tan koat bul oice – *he erred in speaking; he got his words wrong* : amar bujte bul oi gece – *I understood wrong; I got the wrong end of the stick* : **bul oia** – *as a result of a mistake* : citi bul oia ino aice – *the letter arrived here by mistake* : **bul fore/bul fori jae** – *a lapse of memory occurs* : amar bul fori gece – *I've forgotten* : amar bul forto nae – *I shan't forget* : **bule** – *by mistake* : bule goro falaici – *I left it at home by mistake* : **bul kor-/bul kori le-** – *make a mistake* : tumi birat bul kori lirae – *you're making a huge mistake* : ami aia bul korci – *I made a mistake in coming; I was wrong to come* : tain matia bul korcoin – *he should never have said anything* : **bul kori** – *by mistake* : tai bul kori cini ɖi laice – *she put sugar in by mistake* : **bul buj-** – *get the wrong idea* : cacae bul bujcoin – *uncle has taken it the wrong way* ¶ **bul** (adj) *mistaken; wrong* | he bul kagoj·ta ance – *he's brought the wrong document* : afne bul kam korcoin - *you've done the wrong thing* [B. bhul]

bul[2] [būl] (n) *time* = **bala**[2]

bul- (v) *be unmindful; forget* | ami bultam nai – *I won't forget* : kanir kota bulio na – *don't forget about eating; don't forget to eat* : bultam kila? – *how could I forget?* : ita bulbar nae – *it's not something one could forget about* : **buli le-** – *forget* : tumi karakara buli libae – *you'll soon forget* : tan nam buli lici – *I've forgotten his name* : **buli ja-** – *forget* : tain buli jain – *she forgets things* : tan kota ami buli geclam – *I had forgotten all about him* : buli jauka – *forget it* [B. bhul-]

bule[1] ['būlɛ] (v) *(someone) says; they say; according to what people say* | afne bule london gecla? – *I hear you went to London?* : afne bule jaita tarar goro – *they said you're to go to their house* : (in reported speech) jikaici, farba ni? bule oe – *I asked "will you be able?" "yes," says he* [B. bâle – *one says, they say*]

bule ² (n adv) *by mistake* | bule tain agor baco utcoin – *he boarded the earlier bus by mistake* < **bul ¹**
buma ['būmā] (n) *bomb* [B. boma < Pg. bomba]
bumi ['būmī] (n) *ground; earth; land* [B. bhumi < S. bhūmi]
bun [būn] (n) *sister* = **boin**
bun- (v) *plait; knit* [B. bun-]
buna ¹ ['būnā] (v adj) *plaited; knitted* < **bun-**
buna ² (adj) *fried* [H. bhūnā – *roasted*]
buni ['būnī] (n) *breast (mamella)*
bur [bū:r] (n) *early morning* | **bure** – *in the early morning* : tain bure uti nomaj foroin – *she gets up very early and says her prayers* ¶ **bur** (adj) *of the early morning* | bur bala – *the time of early morning* : bur fac·ta – *five a.m.* : amra bur tin·tat utclam – *we got up at three o'clock in the morning* [B. bhor < O. bhorā]
bura ¹ ['būra] (adj) *bad* | bura lage – *it feels bad; it looks bad* : kobor bala ni bura? – *is the news good or bad?* [H. burā]
bura ² (n) *old man* | burae hono take – *the old man lives over there* ¶ **bura** (adj) *old* | bura manus ototuku kain – *an old person eats so little* [B. buṛa < O. buddha]
bura-buri (n) *old man and old woman; old couple* = **bura + buri ¹**
buraki ['būrākī] (n) *old age* | burakir kalo santi cai – *we want peace in our old age*
burbala ['būr-bāla] (n) *early morning* = **bur + bala ¹**
buri ¹ ['būrī] (n) *old woman* [B. buṛi]
buri ² (n) *pot belly* [B. bhuⁿṛi]
burka ['būrkā] (n) *women's head-covering, veil and cloak; burqa* [A. burqūː]
buro ['būrò] (adj) *elderly* [B. buṛo]
buru ¹ ['būrū] (n) *marsh rice* [B. boro]
buru ² (n) *eyebrow* [B. bhru < S. bhrū]
but ['būt] (n) *voting; elections* | kail but oibo – *the elections will take place tomorrow* : but coler – *voting is going on* : **but de-/but ɖi la-** – *cast a vote* : ami but ɖi laici – *I've voted* : afne but kare ɖiba? – *whom will you vote for?* [E.]
butabuti ['būtābūtī] (n) *voting; elections* | butabuti coler – *voting is going on* < **but**
butbuta- ['būt-būtā] (vi) *moan* | butbutaia haoa dake – *the wind is moaning*
butbuti ['būt-būtī] (v adv) *moaning* | butbuti dake – *it's moaning*
but ¹ [būt] (n) *idol; dumb figure* | monɖiro but ace – *there are idols in the temple* : beta but oia roice – *the fellow remained as an idol; he stood dumbfounded* [P. but]
but ² (n) *spirit* | bute ɖorce tare – *a spirit has possessed him* : but jara lagbo – *the spirit needs to be exorcised* [B. bhut < S. bhūta – *past; figment*]
butaŋ ['būtaŋ] (n) *button* [B. botam < Pg. botão]
but-ferot ['būt-fɛròt] (n) *ghosts; hobgoblins* = **but ² + ferot**
butol ['būtòl] (n) *bottle* | ek butol ɖuɖ – *one bottle of milk* : ɖuɖor butol – *a milk bottle* [E.]
butu ['būtū] (n) *dumb fool* | butur lakan cao kene? – *why are you staring like a fool?* = **but ¹**

c

ca¹ [sā] (n) *tea* | tain ca kain na – *she doesn't drink tea* : ca kaia jauka – *do have some tea before you go; do stay for tea* : memanre ca dico ni? – *have you offered tea to the visitors?* : lal ca – *brown tea; tea without milk* [B. ca < P. cā'e < C. ch'a]

ca² (n) *baby animal* | kuttar ca – *puppy* [B. cha]

ca- (v) *look; look for; ask for; want; wish; be willing* | hobae cauka! – *look over there!* : caio na! – *don't look!* : couk dia caito fare na – *he can't open his eyes* : hou beta kali car – *that man keeps staring* : he amar muka caice – *he looked at me* : amar bae cauka – *look at me* : afne kare caira? – *whom are you looking for? whom do you want?* : tara fani caice – *they have asked for water* : tara somoe car – *they are requesting extra time* : amra santi cai – *we want peace* : afne boita cain ni? – *do you wish to sit down?* : ami boitam cai – *I want to sit down* : he boito cae – *he wants to sit down* : tara cae aito – *they would like to come* : tumi haca-u cao ni jaitae? – *would you really like to go?* : tai dito cae na – *she refuses to give it back* : tain jaita caira – *he is asking for permission to leave* : amra bujtam cairam – *we are trying to understand* : tain bidio anta caicla – *he offered to bring a video cassette* : **(kunta) cai** – *one expects (something)* : ca gorom oa cai – *one expects tea to be hot* : gor caf taka cai – *a house should be kept clean* : **cai/cain** – *if you please* : deko cai! – *just look at that, will you!* : auka cain – *come with me, please* : **caia** – *looking out; by choice; selectively* : caia far oin jen – *look out as you cross (the road)* : sundor caia ek·ta am deuka – *please pick out a nice mango for me* : boro caia dui·ta mac anci – *I got two fish which I selected for their size* : amar bae caia koroin na jen – *don't do it with me in mind; don't do it for my sake* : **caite** – *in comparison* : tar caite tai bala – *compared to him, she is better; she is better than him* : lecur caite am boro – *mangoes are larger than lychees* : **caia tak-/caia ro-** – *stare; stay staring* : huruta caia roice – *the children watched intently* : gorir bae caia take – *he keeps his eyes on the clock* [B. ca-]

caba ['sābā] (n) *rind; peel*

caba- (v) *masticate; chew* | guc balatike cabao – *chew your meat thoroughly* : **cabae** – *it aches* : amar faur maje cabae – *it aches in my leg; my leg aches* [H. cabā-]

cabagan ['sābāgān] (n) *tea garden* = **ca + bagan**

cabal ['sābāl] (n) *infant; baby* [B. chaoal]

cabbis ['sāb-bīš] (nº) *twenty-six* [B. chabbis]

cac- [sās] (vt) *scrape; scour* | handi caca lagbo – *the pot will need scouring* : **caci ja-** – *get scraped; be grazed* : tar at caci gece – *his hand has been grazed* [B. caⁿch-]

caca ['sāsā] (n) *father's brother; father's* bai | **cacar goror** – *descended from father's brother* : cacar goror bai – *paternal cousin; father's brother's son* [H. cācā]

caca- (v) *cause abrasion; grate; smart* | **cacae** – *it smarts; it causes sharp pain* : amar faur maje cacae – *there's a sharp pain in my leg*

caci ['sāsī] (n) *wife of father's brother; wife of* caca [H. cācī]

caddor ['sād-dòr] (n) *shawl; sheet* [P. cādar – *tent; cloak*]

cadi ['sādī] (n) *wedding; marriage* = **sadi**

cae [sāy] (n) *ash* [B. chay]

caea¹ ['sāya] (n) *shade; shadow; reflection; protection* | ino caea ace – *there is some shade here* : caeat bouka – *sit in the shade* : fanit afnar caea dekci – *I saw your reflection in the water* : allar caea dorkar – *we need God's protection* [B. chaya < S. chāyā]

caea² (n) *petticoat* [Pg. saia]

caf¹ [sāf] (adj) *clean; clear; light* | caf kagoj – *clean paper; blank paper* : caf gola – *a clear voice* : caf ceara – *a light complexion* : caf kota – *clear, unambiguous words; plain speaking* : **caf o-/caf oi ja-** – *become clean; become clear; (photos) be developed* : ou kafor caf oito nae – *these clothes will never get clean* : asman caf oi jar – *the sky is clearing* : afnar fotu caf oice ni? – *have your photos been developed?* : **caf kor-/caf kori le-** – *clean* :

tain gor caf korra – *she's cleaning the house* : amra moela caf kori lici – *we've cleaned up the mess*   [A. ṣāf]
caf² (n) *pressure* | **caf de-** – *apply pressure* : tara foesa aḍaer lagi caf der – *they're pressing for payment*   [B. cap]
caf-¹ (v) *press; squeeze together* | elam cafo – *press the alarm button* : tura cafouka – *please squeeze up a bit (to make room)*   [B. cap-]
caf-² (vt) *print* | nijor foesae boi cafoin – *he prints books at his own expense*   [B. chap-]
cafa ['sāfā] (v adj) *printed* | cafa kafor – *printed sari* : biar daot kato cafa – *the wedding invitation is printed on card*   < **caf-**²
cafa-¹ (vt) *load onto; burden with*   [B. capa-]
cafa-² (vt) *press; suppress; hush up*   [B. chapa-]
ca-fani ['sā-fānī] (n) *refreshments* | ca-fani kauka – *do have something to eat or drink* : tare ca-fani kaibar lagi tura ḍici – *I gave him a little something to buy himself a drink*
cafatti ['sā-fāt-tī] (n) *chapati*   [H. capātī]
cafcofa ['sāf-sòfa] (adj) *clean; spotless; clear* | tebul·kan cafcofa – *the table is quite clean* : cafcofa na kori ḍeuka – *give a clear refusal*   = **caf + cofa**
cafi ['sāfī] (n) *key* | **cafi de-/cafi ḍi la-** – *wind up* : gorit cafi ḍi laicoin ni? – *have you wound up the clock?*   [B. cabi < Pg. clave]
cagi ['sāgī] (n) *nanny goat* | «cagi cenaite ḍoiro» – *catch your goat while she's urinating; make hay while the sun shines*   [B. chagi]
cagol ['sāgòl] (n) *billy goat*   [B. chagål < O. chāgala]
cai [sāɪ] (int) *will you; if you please* | huno cai! – *listen, will you!* : ou neo cai! – *well, I say! how about that!* : amar cosma ano cai – *please will you bring me my spectacles*   < **ca-**
caiḍa ['sāɪḍa] (n) *demand; requirement* | guar caiḍa kom – *there's not much demand for betelnut* : moeḍar caiḍa barer – *the demand for flour is increasing* : hurumainsor nanan caiḍa take – *children expect all kinds of different things*   [B. cahiḍa < H. cāhetā – *desired person or thing*]
caikel ['sāɪkɛl] (n) *bicycle* | caikel kori – *by bicycle* : tara caikel kori aice – *they came by bike* : **caikel cala-** – *ride a bicycle* : afne caikel cailaita faroin ni? – *can you ride a bike?* : **caikel mar-** – *ride a bicycle; go for a bike ride*   [E.]
cail [sāɪl] (n) *rice (husked rice grains)* | ek bosta cail – *a sack of rice* : **calir** – *of rice* : calir ḍor koto? – *what's the price of husked rice?* : **calit** – *in rice* : calit fattoir roice – *there are bits of grit in the rice*   [B. caul < O. cāvala]
cain¹ [sāɪn] (int) *will you; if you please* | ḍorouka cain – *hold this for me, will you* : i kun bicar oilo, kouka cain? – *what kind of justice is that, I ask you?* : cini·ta ḍeuka cain – *please pass me the sugar*   < **ca-**
cain² (n) *signature* | ita kar cain? – *whose signature is this?* : **canit** – *in relation to signature* : canit beskom – *a discrepancy in the signatures* : tain canit gecoin – *he's gone to sign on* : **cain ḍe-/cain ḍi la-** – *sign* : ino ḍeuka – *sign here* : ami cain ḍi laici – *I have signed* : **cain kor-/cain kori le-** – *sign; sign on* : cain korcoin ni? – *have you signed on?* : ḍolil·ta cain kora nae – *the deed isn't signed*   [E.]
cain³ (n) *sieve*   [B. cakni]
caina- ['sāɪnā] (vt) *sieve; riddle; go through minutely*   < **cain**³
caincora ['sāɪnsòrā] (n) *(small species of) bat*
cair [sāɪr] (n°) *four* | cair gonta – *four hours* : cair·jon manus – *four people* : cair·ta baje – *it's four o'clock* : cair·ta bat kauka – *please partake of a little rice*   [B. car]
cairo ['sāɪrò] (n°) *all four* | cairo fua bettomij – *all four of the boys are naughty* : cairo·ta noea – *all four of them are new*   = **cair + -o**
cairobae ['sāɪròbāy] (adv) *on all sides* | cairobae gari ar gari – *there are cars everywhere* : amra cairobae tukaici – *we've searched for it everywhere* : **cairobae di** – *on all sides* : tarar goror cairobae di faka – *there is open space all round their house*   = **cair + -o + bae**
cairtala ['sāɪr-tālā] (adj) *four-storeyed*   = **cair + -tala**

caite ['sāɪtɛ́] (v adv) *in comparison; than; rather than* | hota caite ita noea – *compared with that one, this one is newer* : i gor caite hou gor boro – *that house is bigger than this* : tumi amar caite bala jano – *you know better than I do* : lab caite luskan oice – *there has been loss rather than gain* : ita caite hota neuka – *take that one rather than this* < **ca-**

cak- (vt) *sieve; strain* | ou cail caka lagbo – *this rice will need to be sieved* : ros cakia rakci – *I've strained the juice off* : tara mesin dia rokto cake – *they dialyse blood by machine* : **caki le-** – *sieve; strain* : moeda age caki louka – *sieve the flour first* [B. chaⁿk-]

caka¹ ['sāχā] (n) *wheel; tyre* | garir koror caka kulce – *they've taken the rear wheels off the car* : dui·ta caka bast oice – *two tyres have burst* : tain caka bodlaira – *he is changing the tyre / wheel* [B. caka < O. cakra]

caka² (v n) *coagulation* | **caka bande** – *coagulation occurs* : dudor maje caka bandce – *the milk has clotted* < **cak-**

cakka ['sāk-kā] (n) *wheel* = **caka**¹

cakki ['sāk-kī] (n) *wheel; hoop* cf **caka**¹

cakku ['sāk-kū] (n) *knife* | **cakku mar-** – *wield a knife (in fighting)* [H. cākū < T. çaki]

cakni ['sāχnī] (n) *sieve* [B. chaⁿkni]

cakor ['sāχòr] (n) *servant* [P. cākar]

cakri ['sāχrī] (n) *service; employment; office job* | sorkari cakri – *government service* : tain cakri tukaira – *he is looking for a job* : beŋko cakri faice – *she has got a job in a bank* : cakri dorci – *I've taken a job* : cakri carci – *I've left my job* : **cakri kor-** – *be in employment* : tain kauncilo cakri koroin – *he works for the council* [P. cākrī – *servitude*]

cakri-noukri ['sāχrī-nôukrī] (n) *employment* = **cakri + noukri**

cal¹ [sāl] (n) *sloping roof* [B. cal]

cal² (n) *ploy; move (in a game); manner* | buddir cal – *an intelligent stratagem* : tumar cal! – *it's your move!* : tar murobbi cal deko – *just look at his air of importance* : **cal cala-** – *make one's move; carry out a stratagem* : emon cal calaicoin! – *what a clever move he made!* [H. cāl]

cal³ (n) *skin; peel* | lembur cal – *lemon rind* : fiaijor cal – *onion skin* : amar cal uti jar – *my skin is peeling* : tain jamiror cal tulra – *she's peeling the oranges* [B. chal]

cala ['sālā] (n) *ploy; stratagem* = **cal**²

cala- (vt) *cause to run; drive; operate* | fektrit mesin calaitam – *I used to operate machinery in the factory* : tai gari calae – *she drives a car* : cacae amrar soŋsar calain – *uncle manages our family affairs* : ali sab befsa calaira – *Mr Ali is running a business* : tar boue tare calae – *his wife makes him do as she wants* : calao! calao! – *get on with it, quick!* : calai ao! – *do hurry up!* : **calaia de-/calai de-** – *get (something) going; keep (something) going* : mesin calaia ditam ni? – *shall I get the machine going?* : tain befsa calai dira – *he is keeping the business going* : **calaia ne-/calai ne-** – *keep (something) going* : soŋsar kunumote calaia niram – *I'm keeping the household going somehow or other* [B. cala-]

cala-cokkor ['sālā-sòk-kòr] (n) *devious behaviour* | tar cala-cokkor bala nae – *his crafty carryings-on are not good* = **cala + cokkor**

calafi ['sālāfī] (n) *Salafi (pertaining to a Muslim reformist movement)* [A. salafī]

calak ['sālāχ] (adj) *cunning* [B. calak < P. cālāk – *nimble*]

calaki ['sālākī] (n) *guile* | **calaki kor-** – *act cunningly* : he amrar loge calaki korce – *he's pulled a fast one on us* [P. cālākī – *quickness*]

calam ['sālām] (n) *valediction; salaam* | amar calam louka – *please accept my salutations* : **calam kor-** – *salute; greet with a salaam* : tumar cacare calam korco ni? – *have you saluted your uncle (as you should)?* : **calam de-** – *give a salaam* : kanir somoe calam dein na – *one doesn't give salaams when people are eating* [A. salām – *peace; safety*]

calamalekum [sā'lāmalékūm] (int) *greetings!* [A. salām ¿alaikum – *peace upon you*]

calamot ['sālāmòt] (n) *well-being; safety* [A. salāma]

calan ['sālān] (n) *despatch; despatch note* | calano dostokot deuka – *please sign the despatch note* : **calan o-/calan oi ja-** – *be despatched* : afnar mal kail calan oibo – *your goods will be despatched tomorrow* : **calan de-/calan di la-** – *send off; despatch; incite* :

mal calan đici – *we've despatched the goods* : tare goro calan đi lao! – *send him home!* : tar bai hokol tare calan đer – *his brothers are egging him on*   [B. calan]
calani ['sālānī] (v n) *operating; running; driving* | mesin calani hikci – *I've learned how to operate the machine* : tain gari calanit – *he's out driving the car*   < **cala-**
cal-colon ['sāl-sòlòn] (n) *lifestyle; behaviour* = **cal** [2] + **colon**
calla ['sāl-la] (n) *pushing on; incitement* | forar callae ita korce – *he did this at someone else's instigation* : **calla đe-/calla đi la-** – *incite; egg on* : tar mamae tare calla đira – *his uncle is egging him on*   cf **cal** [2]
callis ['sāl-līš] (n°) *forty* (*an auspicious number in Muslim tradition*) | callis kođom – *forty steps* : callis đin – *forty days and forty nights*   [B. cållis]
callisa ['sāl-līša] (n) *ceremony of the fortieth day* (*traditional Muslim feast held forty days after a death*)
calok ['sālòχ] (n) *driver* | gari calok – *car driver*   [B. calåk]
calon ['sālòn] (n) *stew; meat curry*   [H. sālan]
caltiket ['sāl-tīkɛt] (n) *certificate*   [E.]
calu ['sālū] (adj) *running; working; operating; smart; clever* | calu mesin – *machine in operation* : centel hitiŋ calu nae – *the central heating isn't on* : afnar befsa calu ni? – *is your business up and running?* : fua·ta bes calu – *the lad is quite smart* : **calu kor-/calu kori đe-** – *set in motion; start up* : mesin calu kori đao – *start the machine* : tara ek·ta somiti calu korce – *they have started up an association*   [B. calu]
camana ['sāmānā] (n) *belongings; chattels*   [P. sāmān]
camra ['sām-ra] (n) *skin; hide; leather* | kala camra – *dark skin* : gorur camra – *cowhide* : camrar juta – *leather shoes*   [B. camɽa < O. carma]
camic ['sāmīs] (n) *spoon; spoonful* = **camuc**
camuc ['sāmūs] (n) *spoon; spoonful* | car camuc – *teaspoon* : boro camuc – *tablespoon; dessertspoon* : ek camuc cini – *one spoonful of sugar* : đui camuc đine tinbar – *two spoonfuls three times a day*   [B. camåc < P. camca – *ladle*]
can- [sān] (vt) *touch* | kagjain canio na! – *don't touch those papers!*   [B. choⁿ-]
canđ [sānđ] (n) *moon* | canđ utce – *the moon has risen* : canđ đeka jae na – *the moon is not visible* : battir canđ – *the night of lamps* (*festival of Shab-e-Barat, held at full moon the month before Ramadan, when fates are believed to be sealed*)   [B. caⁿđ < O. canđra]
canđa ['sān-đā] (n) *subscription; contribution* | **canđa tul-** – *raise subscriptions* : tain mocjiđor lagi canđa tulra – *he is collecting donations for the mosque* : **canđa ute** – *subscriptions are raised* : fac so fon canđa utce – *five hundred pounds has been raised*   [B. caⁿđa]
cani ['sānī] (n) *duplicate; match* | tan cani nae – *there is nobody who can match him* : er cani kunta ace? – *could anything equal that?*   [A. θānī – *second*]
canni [1] ['sān-nī] (n) *sneezing; hay-fever*
canni [2] (n) *moonlight*   [H. cāⁿđnī]
caŋga ['sāŋ-ga] (adj) *robust; hale*   [H. caŋgā < O. caŋga – *intact; pure*]
car [sār] (v adv) *having released* | **car đe-** – *release; give up; send off* : citi car đicoin ni? – *did you post the letter?* : car đeuka! – *oh, let it be! forget it!* = **caria**
car- (v) *leave; leave go; leave out; give up; release; discharge* | amra ou gor carmu – *we are going to leave this house* : amar at caro – *let go of my hand* : ami cartam nai tare – *I won't let him get away with it* : i kota carouka! – *let it pass!* : keur nam caroin na jen – *don't leave anyone's name out* : tumi ek lain carco – *you skipped a line* : ami ruja ek·ta-o carci na – *I haven't missed a single day of fasting* : mama cigret kani carcoin – *uncle has given up smoking* : tain kam carta kene? – *why does he want to quit his job?* : afnar kut carouka – *do take your coat off* : murgi cara lagbo – *the chickens must be let out* : fani caro – (a) *let the water out;* (b) *turn on the tap, let the water run* : ke fotka carcil – *somebody had let off a firework* : citi carcoin ni? – *have you posted the letter?* : tar boure bule carce – *they say he's divorced his wife* : **care** (intransitive) – *it leaves; it departs* : bemar care na – *illness never leaves us* : gari đos·tat carbo – *the train will depart at ten o'clock* : **cari đe-** – *release;*

discharge; divorce; omit : taire asfatal taki cari dice – *they've discharged her from the hospital* : tar boure cari dito koe – *he says he's going to divorce his wife* : tain citi cari diba – *he will post the letter* : tar ufre cari dici – *I've left it to him* : cari deuka! – *leave it! forget about it!* : cari dicoin – *she's hung up (on the telephone)* : dui nam cari diclam – *I had omitted two names* : tura jaega cari deuka – *leave a little space* : **cari ja-** – *leave behind; abandon; go beyond* : he tar bou-baiccare cari gece – *he has abandoned his wife and children* : mur cari gecoin – *he's overshot the turning* : **cari jae** – *it leaves; it departs* : tar jor cari gece – *his fever has passed* : gari noe·tat cari jaibo – *the bus will depart at nine o'clock* [B. chaṛ-]

cara¹ ['sārā] (v adj) *released; divorced* | cara beti – *a divorced woman* < **car-**

cara² (v adv) *left without; excepted; besides* | tai tin din kani cara – *she has been without food for three days* : foesa cara colta kila? – *how will you get by without money?* : afne cara hokoloe jaira – *everyone is going except you* : ek alla cara keu jane na – *none but God knows* : sukkur soni cara jeca din – *any day apart from Friday and Saturday* : tumi cara aro bout manus acoin – *there are many others besides you* : tain cara ami mattam nai – *unless he's there I won't say anything* : lab cara keti oibo – *far from any gain, there will be some loss* < **car-**

cara³ (v n) *release* | afnar cara nae! – *I'm not going to let you go!* : **cara fa-** – *obtain one's release; get away free* : he cara faito nae – *he's not going to get away with it* < **car-**

cara⁴ (n) *recourse* | ar kunu cara nae – *there's no other way* [P. cāra]

cara-¹ ['sārā] (vt) *cause to quit; force to relinquish* | tara gor caraito amrare – *they want to make us leave our home* : hese tar cakku caraice – *in the end they made him let go of his knife* [B. chaṛa-]

cara-² (vi) *be finished* | meg caraice – *the rain has stopped* [B. sar-]

caracari ['sārāsārī] (n) *release; separation; divorce* | aij caracari nae! – *I won't let you get away today!* : jamai-boue caracari oice – *the couple have got divorced* < **car-**

cari ['sārī] (v adv) *having left* < **car-**

caria ['sārīā] (v adv) *having left* | **caria ja-** – *leave behind; go beyond* : gari luton caria jaibo – *the train will go beyond Luton* : tain sima caria gecoin – *he's gone over the limit; he's gone too far* < **car-**

caroŋ ['sāròŋ] (n) *head seaman; foreman of lascars* [P. sarhang – *head of troop*]

cas [sāś] (n) *ploughing* | **cas kor-** – *plough; cultivate* : tara goru di jomi cas kore – *they plough the land using oxen* [B. cas < O. carśa]

cas-abad ['sāśābād] (n) *cultivation; agriculture* = **cas** + **abad**

cat [sāt] (n) *trap* | unduror cat – *mousetrap*

cat- (v) *lick; lap up* [B. cat-]

cata- ['sātā] (v) *trim; cut back* [B. chaⁿta-]

catni ['sāt-nī] (n) *fresh savoury appetizer* | fiaijor catni – *onion salad* : bakoror catni – *relish based on fresh coriander leaf* : macor catni – *fish paste with herbs* [B. catni]

cat [sāt] (n) *roofing; ceiling* [B. chat]

cata- ['sātā] (v) *pester* | huruta catar ni? – *are the children bothering you?* : hou beta jobor catae amare – *that chap is a pain in my neck* [H. sata-]

catri ['sāt-rī] (n) *schoolgirl; female student* [B. chatri]

catro ['sāt-rò] (n) *schoolboy; male student* [B. chatrå < S. chātra]

catti ['sāt-tī] (n) *umbrella* [H. chatrī < O. chatra]

caund ['sāund] (n) *sound; volume* | caund baraitam ni? – *shall I increase the sound output?* : caund komao! – *turn down the volume!* : **caund de-** – *provide sound; increase the sound* : tura caund deuka – *please turn up the volume a bit* [E.]

cauni ['sāunī] (n) *roofing* [B. chauni]

cear ['séār] (n) *chair* | tin·kan cear ano cai – *please bring three chairs* : cearo bouka – *please sit on the chair* [E.]

ceara ['sɛ̄ārā] (n) *appearance; looks; face* | sunɗor ceara – *a fair complexion; a pretty face* : tar ceara anɗair – *his face is dark; he looks grim* : tan firor lakan ceara – *he has a saint-like look* : dinor ceara bala nae – *the weather doesn't look promising* [P. cehra]

cearmen ['sɛ̄ār-men] (n) *chairman; (in Bangladesh) local council boss* [E.]

ceɗ [sɛɗ] (n) *cleaving* | **ceɗ kor-** – *cleave; sever* [B. cheɗ < S. cheɗa]

ceɗa- ['sɛɗā] (vt) *cleave; slice; cut to bits* [H. cheɗ-]

ceeri ['sɛ̄ɛrī] (n) *pre-dawn meal (in Ramadan)* [P. saharī < A. sahar – *dawn*]

cef [sɛf] (n) *spittle* | **cef fala-** – *spit* [B. chep]

cefta ['sɛf-tā] (adj) *flattened* | **cefta kor-/cefta kori le-** – *flatten* [B. cepta]

ceftin ['sɛf-tīn] (n) *safety-pin* [E.]

ceg[1] [sɛg] (n) *cheque* | tan furire ɗia ceg lekaicoin – *he got his daughter to write a cheque* : kail ceg joma ɗi laimu – *I'll deposit the cheque tomorrow* : ceg kes oice ni? – *has the cheque been cashed?* [E.]

ceg[2] (n) *dismissal; the sack* | **ceg ɗe-/ceg ɗi la-** – *sack; dismiss* : tare ceg ɗi laice – *they've sacked him* : **ceg ka-** – *get sacked* : tara hokoloe ceg kaice – *they've all been sacked* [E.]

cega ['sɛgā] (adj) *bent; crooked* | tar fit cega oice – *his back has become crooked*

cega-[1] (v) *become crooked; adopt a crooked posture* | cegaia boico kene? – *why are you sitting crooked?*

cega-[2] (vi) *jump; leap*

ceil [sɛil] (n) *sale* | **ceil laga-** – *hold a sale (with prices reduced)* : **ceilo ɗe-/ceilo ɗi la-** – *put on offer at a sale price* : aij cidi ceilo ɗi laice – *they're selling CDs cheap today* [E.]

cein [sɛin] (n) *necklace* [E. chain]

cek [sɛχ] (n) *application of heat; fomentation* | matir cek – *clay fomentation; poultice* : fanir cek – *warm water application* : fanir cekor butol – *hot water bottle* : **cek ɗe-/cek ɗi la-** – *apply a fomentation* : tair faur maje matir cek ɗice – *they've put a hot poultice on her leg* [B. se^{n}k]

ceka ['sɛχā] (adj) *bent; crooked* | ceka camuc – *a bent spoon*

cela ['sɛlā] (n) *disciple; follower; side-kick* [B. cela]

cele ['sɛ́lɛ́] (n) *son; boy* [B. chele]

cen [sɛn] (n) *penis*

cena ['sɛnā] (n) *urine (of ungulates)* [B. cona]

cena- (vi) *(ungulates) urinate* | «cagi cenaite ɗoiro» - *catch your goat while she's urinating; make hay while the sun shines*

cenan ['sɛnān] (n) *bathing* | **cenan kor-** – *have a bath; bathe* [B. snan < S. snāna]

ceŋguj ['sɛŋgūz] (n) *sandwich* [E.]

cera[1] ['sɛrā] (n) *boy; lad* [H. cerā]

cera[2] (n) *seedling* [B. cara]

cera[3] (n) *appearance* = **ceara**

cera-cobi ['sɛrāsòbī] (n) *appearance*

cerbi ['sɛr-bī] (n) *fat; suet* [P. carbī]

cesta ['sɛs-tā] (n) *endeavour; attempt* | cesta cara fol nae – *there are no fruits without effort* : **cestat** – *in the process of endeavouring* : amra gor loar cestat – *we're trying to buy a house* : **cesta kor-** – *make efforts; try* : ke hamaibar cesta korer – *someone's trying to get in* : amrar lagi bout cesta korcoin – *he has made great efforts on our behalf* [B. cesta < S. cestā – *activity*]

cet [sɛt] (n) *penis*

ceta ['sɛtā] (adj) *idle*

cetelait ['sɛtɛlāit] (n) *satellite TV* [E.]

cet [sɛt] (n) *spiritedness; vigour; irascibility* | amar sorilo cet nae – *I feel drained of energy* : oto cet kene? – *why are you so peevish?* : **cet lage** – *irritability is felt* : cacar cet lagce – *uncle has got hot under the collar* [H. cet < O. cetas – *consciousness*]

cet- (vi) *be aroused* [B. cet-]

ceta- ['sɛtā] (vt) *arouse* [B. ceta-]

cetni ['sɛt-nī] (n) *mould* | goror oalor maje cetni ɖorce – *mould has started growing on the walls of the house* [B. chaṭla]
cetona ['sɛtònā] (n) *consciousness* [B. cetåna < S. cetanā]
ci [sī'] (int) *yuck!* | ci! coic na! – (to baby) *yucky! don't touch!* [B. chi]
cianno ['sī ān-nò] (n°) *fifty-six* [B. chappannå]
cianobboi ['sīānòb-bòɪ] (n°) *ninety-six* [B. chiannåbbåi]
ciasi ['sī āšī] (n°) *eighty-six* [B. chiasi]
ciattoir ['sī āt-tòɪr] (n°) *seventy-six* [B. chiaṭṭår]
cib [sīb] (n) *spoon* = **cif**
ciɖri ['sīɖ-rī] (n) *hole* | handir maje ciɖri oi gece – *the saucepan has a hole in it* : rukor maje ciɖri korci – *I've made a hole in the wood* [B. chiɖrå < O. chiɖra]
cif [sīf] (n) *spoon* [H. sīf]
cif- [sīf] (v) *squeeze; wring* | lembu cifci – *I've squeezed the lemon* : kafor cifa lagto nae – *there's no need to wring the clothes*
cifa [1] ['sīfā] (v adj) *squeezed; confined* | cifa am – *a squashed mango* : cifa jaga – *a confined place* < **cif-**
cifa [2] (n) *narrow space; crevice* | foesa cifat fori gece – *the money has fallen into the gap*
cifacifi ['sīfāsīfī] (n) *confinement; cramping* | ou rumo cifacifi lage – *one feels cramped in this room* < **cif-**
cifai ['sīfāɪ] (n) *soldier* [P. sipāhī]
cifara ['sīfārā] (n) *section (literally "thirty sections") of the Holy Quran* | hurutae cifara forer – *the children are studying the Quran in sections* : tai cifarat utce – *she has progressed* (from studying the Arabic alphabet) *to memorizing the Quran itself* : am cifara – *the "amm para"* (final section of the Quran) [P. sī pāra – *thirty parts*]
cifaris ['sīfārīš] (n) *commendation* | **cifaris kor-** – *commend; recommend* : amar lagi cifaris korba – *please put in a word for me* [P. sifāriš]
cii [sī:] (int) *yuck!* | cii cii cii! – *oh, how disgusting!* : **cii cii kor-** – *express disgust* : cii cii kori lab nae – *making disgusted noises doesn't get you anywhere* [B. chi]
cik [sīk] (n) *shriek* | **cik mar-** – *shriek; yelp* [H. cīk̠h]
cika ['sīkā] (adj) *small; slight*
cikon ['sīkòn] (adj) *thin; lean* [B. cikån]
cikor ['sīkòr] (n) *baked clay* (tablets of which are consumed for medical purposes)
cikra- ['sīk-rā] (vi) *shriek; cry out*
cilan ['sīlān] (n) *whore* [H. chināl]
cilla- ['sīl-lā] (vi) *shout; talk loudly* | huruta kali cillae – *the children keep shouting* cillaio na! – *keep your voice down!* [H. cillā-]
cillacilli ['sīl-lā sīl-lī] (n) *shouting* | **cillacilli kor-** – *shout; talk loudly* < **cilla-**
cilok ['sīlòχ] (n) *adage; proverb; riddle* [B. slok < O. šloka – *verse*]
cilot ['sīlòt] (n) *Sylhet* [O. šrī haṭṭa]
ciloti ['sīlòtī] (adj) *Sylheti* ¶ **ciloti** (n) *Sylheti language; Sylheti person*
cimta ['sīm-tā] (n) *tongs; forceps* [B. cimta]
cimta- (vt) *gather together; tidy up* | tumar kam cimtao – *gather up your work and tidy it away* [H. simtā-]
cimti ['sīm-tī] (n) *pinch* | **cimti mar-** – *pinch* [B. cimti]
cin [sīn] (n) *recognizable mark* | amar namor kanɖat ek·ta cin ɖi lauka – *put a mark next to my name* [B. cinnå < S. cihna]
cin- (vt) *be acquainted with; recognize; know* | hou betare cini – *I know that man* : cincoin ni amare? – *have you managed to recognize me?* : afnare cinci na – *I don't recognize you* : rasta cini – *I know the way* : afnar gor cintam kila? – *how am I to know which is your house?* : he kunta-u cine na – *he doesn't know anything at all* : **cini le-** – *recognize; get to know* : cini lici tumare! – *now I realise who you are / what you're like!* : hurutare aste aste cini liba – *you'll gradually get to know the children* [B. cin-]
cina [1] ['sīnā] (v adj) *known* | cina manus – *a known person* < **cin-**

50

cina[2] (n) *chest; breast* [P. sīna]
cina- (vt) *cause to recognize; point out* | lebumia kun·gu, amare cinauka – *please show me which one is Lebu Miah* : tumare cinaimu, ami kijat manus! – *I'll show you what sort of person I am!* : **cinai đe-** – *cause to recognize; point out* : tan goror rasta cinai đicoin – *he has shown me the road to his house* [B. cena-]
cina-jana ['sīnā zānā] (v adj) *known; familiar* = **cina**[1] + **jana**[1]
cinajuk ['sīnāzūk] (n) *leech; importunate person* [B. china joⁿk]
cinakt ['sīnāx̱t] (n) *recognition; identification* [P. sanāk̄t]
cincina- ['sīnsīnā] (vi) *sift down; drizzle* | cincinaia meg đer – *it's drizzling*
cin-foricoe ['sīn-fòrisòy] (n) *acquaintance* | tar loge amar cin-foricoe nae – *I'm not acquainted with him* = **cin** + **foricoe**
cini ['sīnī] (n) *white sugar* [B. cini < P. cīnī – *Chinese*]
cini-fan ['sīnīfān] (n) *engagement ceremony (at which culinary items such as fish, sugar and betel leaf are given to the bride's family as a symbol of domesticity)* = **cini** + **fan**
cinta ['sīntā] (n) *thinking; worry; care* | cintar somoe nae – *there's no time for reflection* : cintar bisoe – *a worrying thought* : tan cinta nae – *he has no worries; he doesn't care* : kior cinta? – *worry about what? who's bothered?* : tain cinta taki bemar – *she's sick from worry* : tain boro cintar maje – *he's in a state of great anxiety* : tumar cintae ami baci na – *I'm dead from worry about you* : **cinta kor-** – *think; worry* : balaile cinta korouka – *think about it carefully* : tain besi cinta koroin – *she worries too much* : cinta koroin na jen – *please don't worry yourself* : **cinta kori đek-** – *think things over; reach a considered opinion* : cinta kori đekouka! – *just imagine!* : ami cinta kori đekci, jaoa jaito nae – *I've thought it over and decided it won't be possible for us to go* [B. cinta < S. cintā]
cinta-babna ['sīntābābnā] (n) *thinking; worry* | **cinta-babna kor-** – *think hard; worry* : tain bout cinta-babna koroin – *he worries a lot* = **cinta** + **babna**
ciŋgol ['sīŋgòl] (n) *withy; switch; cane*
ciŋla ['sīŋlā] (n) *withy; switch; cane*
cir- [sīr] (v) *tear; be torn; slit; pluck* | amar kafor circe – *my clothes have got torn* : he tar fen cire barebare – *he's always ripping his trousers* : iŋblaf ke circe? – *who slit the envelope open?* : tara jarjir cul cirer – *they're tearing each other's hair out* : ful cirio na – *don't pluck the flowers* : bon cirer – *they're pulling up weeds* : **ciri ja-** – *get torn* : amar firon ciri gece – *my shirt has got ripped* : **ciri le-** – *tear; tear up* : fotu ciri lice – *he's torn up the photo* [B. chir̥-]
cira ['sīrā] (v adj) *torn* < **cir-**
cirat ['sīrāt] (n) *path of righteousness* [A. ṣirāṭ]
ciri ['sīrī] (n) *piece of cultivated land* [H. chīr]
ciroin ['sīròın] (n) *comb* [B. ciruni]
cirođin ['sīròđīn] (adv) *always; for ever* [B. cirådin]
cirokal ['sīròχāl] (adv) *always; for ever* [B. ciråkal < S. cirakāla – *a long time*]
ciron ['sīròn] (n) *comb* = **ciroin**
cit[1] [sīt] (n) *piece (of cloth)* [B. chit]
cit[2] (n) *seat; place* | iskulo cit kali nae – *there are no vacant places at the school* : amra hutelo cit rakmu – *we will book rooms at the hotel* [E. seat]
citi ['sītī] (n) *letter* | tain kauncilor gece citi lekra – *he's writing a letter to the council* : citi carcoin ni? – *have you posted the letter?* : amar citir juaf faici na – *I haven't received a reply to my letter* [B. cithi]
citi-cear ['sītīséār] (n) *settee* [E.]
citin ['sītīn] (n) *sitting room* | citino bouka – *please take a seat in the lounge* : caca citino – *uncle is in the sitting-room* [E.]
citkari ['sīt-χārī] (n) *door bolt* | **citkari laga-** – *bolt the door* [B. chitkini]
cit [sīt] (adj) *lying face up* | **cit o-/cit oi ja-** – *lie on one's back* : cit oita faroin na – *he can't lie on his back* : **cit oia** – *face up* : tain cit oia gumain – *he sleeps face up* [B. cit]

cita ['sītā] (n) *macula; spot* | kaforor maje cita force – *there are spots on the cloth* ¶ **cita** (adj) *spotted* | cita oriŋ – *spotted deer* : cita bag – *leopard* [B. cita]
citka- ['sītχā] (vi) *scream; yell*
citkar ['sītχār] (n) *screaming* | **citkar kor-** – *scream* [B. citkar < S. citkāra]
citol ['sītòl] (n) *a species of fish (Notopterus chitala)* [B. citål]
citr- ['sīt-r] (vi) *get scattered* | **citri ja-** – *get scattered; spread* : kagoj citri gece – *the paper has got scattered* : kobor citri jaibo – *the news will spread* [H. chitar-]
citra- ['sīt-rā] (vt) *scatter* | kagoj citraio na – (to child) *don't scatter paper all over the place* : **citrai ɖe-/citrai le** – *scatter; spread* : matit lobon citrai ɖice kegu? – *who's been sprinkling salt on the floor?* [H. chitrā-]
citrail ['sīt-rāil] (v adj) *scattered* | fuar somosto kafor citrail – *that boy's clothes are scattered everywhere* < **citra-**
clamalekum ['slāmalékūm] (int) *greetings!* = **calamalekum**
co- [sò] (v) *touch* | coio na! – (to child) *don't touch!* : **coia ɖek-** – *gauge by touching; feel* : coia ɖekouka, norom koto – *feel it for yourself and see how soft it is* [B. chuⁿ-]
cobi ['sòbī] (n) *picture* [B. châbi < A. šabīh – *similar; likeness*]
codga ['sòdgā] (n) *almsgiving* [A. ṣadaqa]
codma ['sòdmā] (n) *shock* [A. ṣadma]
codri ['sòd-rī] (n) *village headman; Choudhury* [H. cauɖhrī]
coe ['sòy] (nº) *six* [B. chây]
coecallis ['sòy-sal-līš] (nº) *forty-six* [B. checållis]
coesosti ['sòy-šòstī] (nº) *sixty-six* = **coesotti**
coesotti ['sòy-šòt-tī] (nº) *sixty-six* [B. chesåtti]
coetis ['sòy-tīš] (nº) *thirty-six* [B. chåytris]
cofa ['sòfā] (adj) *clean* | **cofa kor-** – *clean* [A. ṣafā' – *clarity; purity*]
coffor ['sòp-pòr] (n) *slap* | **coffor laga-** – *slap* [B. cåpet]
coffori ['sòp-pòrī] (adv) *quickly; briskly* [H. caparī]
coi [sòɩ] (adj) *correct; all right* [A. ṣahīh]
coi-calamot ['sòɩ-salamòt] (n) *safety* | **coi-calamote** – *in safety; safe and sound* : tain coi-calamote ai arcoin – *he has arrived safely*
coin [sòɩn] (n) *neck-chain* [H. cain < E. chain]
coioɖ ['sòyòɖ] (n) *Sayyid; Syed (title used by families claiming descent from the Prophet Muhammad)* [A. sayyid – *lord; master*]
coit [sòɩt] (n) *Chaitra (March-April)* [B. cåitrå < S. caitra]
cok [sòχ] (n) *fields* [H. cak – *land estate*]
cokcok ['sòχ sòχ] (n) *shine; glitter* | **cokcok kore** – *it shines; it glitters*
cokcoke ['sòχ sòχɛ] (adj) *brilliant* | cokcoke lal – *bright red*
coki ['sòkī] (n) *platform bed* [H. coukī]
cokkor ['sòk-kòr] (n) *circuit* | **cokkor ɖe-** – *spin; go round* : amar matae cokkor ɖer – *my head is spinning* : tara farko tin cokkor ɖice – *they went round the park three times* : **cokkor laga-** – *go round in circles; do the rounds* : tain ruj ɖuibar cokkor lagain – *he comes round twice a day* : **cokkor mar-** – *go round in circles; do the rounds* : he caikel ɖi cokkor marto – *he used to go round and round on his bike* : amar matae cokkor marer – *my head is spinning* [B. cåkkår < O. cakra – *circle; circuit*]
cokku ['sòk-kū] (n) *eye* | tumar cokkut kita? – *what's that you've got in your eye?* : tar cokkur ɖus – *he has something wrong with his eyes* : cokkur fani – *tears* : nani-ji cokkur fani falaira – *grandmother is shedding tears* : amar cokkut ao – *come near so I can see you* [B. cåkku < S. cakśu]
cokrat ['sòχ-rāt] (n) *death throes* | cokrat mout – *throes of death* [A. sakra]
col [sòl] (n) *custom* | amrar nacbar col nae – *it's not our custom to dance* [B. cålån]
col- (vi) *get moving; go; run; function; carry on* | colouka! – *come on, let's get going!* : rastat gari coler – *cars are going along the road* : i gori cole na – *this clock isn't working* : i foesa ɖi kila coltam? – *how am I to get by on this amount of money?* : tarar befsa bala coler

– their business is running smoothly : amra kunumote colram *– we are getting along somehow* : lorai je somoe colcil *– when the war was going on* : **cole** *– it goes; it's all right; it's permissible* : tarar bala coler *– all is well with them; they're getting on well* : ino juta fora cole na *– it's not permissible to wear shoes here* : ca colbo? *– will tea be in order?* : caca na aile colbo *– it will be okay if uncle doesn't come* : caca na aile cole *– it's okay as long as uncle doesn't come* : meg na ɖile cole *– so long as it doesn't rain; let's hope it won't rain* : **kam cole** *– things are managed satisfactorily* : kali ek kamla oile kam colbo *– we can manage with only one worker* : ota ɖi amar kam coler *– I'm managing with this* : **colte colte** *– while going; on the way* : colte colte gari baɖ oi gece *– while going along the car broke down* : **colte firte** *– while moving about* : colte firte tan loge amar ɖeka oito fare *– I may bump into him while on my rounds* : **coli ja-** *– go away; be adequate* : tara coli gece *– they have gone away* : ek butol oile amar coli jaibo *– if I get one bottle that'll be enough for me* : **coli a-** *– come away* : amra jolɖi coli aici *– we came away quickly*   [B. cǎl-]

cola ['sòlā] (v n) *going; proceeding; carrying on* | aste aste cola bala *– driving slowly is best* : ou foesae cola jae na *– it's not possible to manage on this money* : colar somoe sabɖan! *– careful how you go!* : **colar fote** *– on the way* : colar fote kai limu *– we shall eat on the way*   < **col-**

colacol ['sòlāsòl] (n) *movement; flow* | roktor colacol *– blood circulation* : garir colacol *– vehicle movement; traffic*   < **col-**

colafira ['sòlāfīrā] (n) *coming and going; walking about; movement* | raitku mainsor colafira kom ino *– there aren't many people walking around at night here* : **colafira kor-** *– go here and there; move about* : hariɖin colafira kore *– she's on the move all day long* : taror maje jilki colafira kore *– electricity runs along inside the wire* : nana colafira korta faroin na *– grandad can't get about; grandad can't walk*   < **col-** , **fir-**

colam ['sòlām] (n) *valediction*   = **calam**

colon ['sòlòn] (v n) *movement; carrying on; behaviour*   < **col-**

colonsokti ['sòlòn-sòχtī] (n) *ability to move about; mobility* | tan colonsokti nae *– he has no power to move around; he has no mobility*   = **colon + sokti**

colti ['sòl-tī] (adj) *current* | colti masor ɖos tarik *– the tenth of this (current) month* : colti ain-kanun *– current laws* : colti mat *– common usage*   [B. cǎlti]

comk- ['sòmk] (vi) *be startled* | **comki ja-** *– be startled* : hunia comki geclam *– I was startled when I heard it*   [H. camak-]

condo ['sòn-ɖò] (n) *rhythm*   [B. chǎnɖǎ < O. chanɖas *– metre*]

condon ['sòn-ɖòn] (n) *sandalwood*   [B. cǎnɖǎn < S. canɖana]

condoni ['sòn-ɖònī] (n) *moonlight*   [B. caⁿɖni]

coora ['sòôrā] (adj) wide   [B. cǎoɽa]

cor-¹ [sòr] (vi) *move around* | haoror maje goru corer *– cattle are roaming on the floodland* : fanir maje mac core *– fish swim around in the water*   [B. cǎr-]

cor-² (v) *get up on; ride* | he gurae corce *– he has mounted a horse; he rode a horse* : tain caikel corta faroin na *– he can't ride a bike*   [B. cǎɽ-]

cor-³ (vi) *spread; get spread out* | rug cori gece *– the disease has spread*   [B. chǎr-]

cora ['sòrā] (n) *sparrow*   [B. cǎɽui]

cora-¹ (vt) *mount; set on high* | tare gurae coraice *– they put him on a horse*   [B. chǎra-]

cora-² (vt) *scatter; spread around* | tara gujob coraicil *– they spread rumours*   [B. chǎɽa-]

corhoɖɖo ['sòr-hòɖ-ɖò] (n) *boundary*   [P. sarhadd < A. hadd]

cori ['sòrī] (n) *begging of pardon* | cori koo! *– say sorry!* : cori-uri nae *– it's no use your saying sorry* : **cori ca-** *– ask forgiveness; beg pardon* : tain cori caicoin *– he has begged to be forgiven*   [E. sorry]

corta ['sòr-tā] (n) *betelnut clipper*   [H. sarotā]

cosma ['sòš-mā] (n) *spectacles; glasses* | afnar cosma lage ni? *– do you need to wear glasses?* : **cosma de-** *– put on spectacles; use glasses* : tain hokol somoe cosma ɖein *– she uses glasses all the time* : **cosma laga-** *– put on spectacles* : one tain cosma lagaicoin *– now he's put on his spectacles*   [P. cašma]

cot ['sòt] (n) *snap* | **cot kori** – *with a snap; quickly* : he cot kori ani lice – *he went and got it in a trice* [B. càt]

cotfot ['sòt-fòt] (n) *fidgeting; palpitation* | **cotfot kore** – *palpitation occurs* : amar gurdae cotfot korer – *my heart is palpitating* : amar jane cotfot korer – *I'm feeling nervous; I'm feeling restless* [B. càtpàt]

cotkona ['sòt-χònā] (n) *slap*

cotur ['sòtūr] (adj) *crafty* [B. càtur < O. catura – *quick*]

coucallis ['sôu-sal-līš] (n°) *forty-four* [B. cuallis]

coudi ['sôudī] (n) *Saudi Arabia* | tain coudit kam koroin – *he works in Saudi Arabia* ¶ **coudi** (adj) *Saudi Arabian* [E.]

couk ['sôuk] (n) *eye; evil eye; eyesight* | kala couk – *dark eyes* : amar couk karaf – *my eyesight is poor* : coukor fani – *tears* : **couke** – *with the eyes* : tain couke dekoin na – *he can't see; he is blind* : ami nijor couke dekci – *I saw it with my own eyes* : **cukut** – *in the eye* : tar cukut dula hamaice – *some dust has got into his eye* : **couk fore** – *the evil eye is cast* : tar fuar ufre couk forcil – *the evil eye had fallen on his son* [B. cokh < O. cakśu]

cousosti ['sôu-šòst-tī] (n°) *sixty-four* = **cousotti**

cousotti ['sôu-sòt-tī] (n°) *sixty-four* [B. cousàtti]

coutis ['sôu-tīš] (n°) *thirty-four* [B. coutris]

cuab [sū 'āb] (n) *merit from good deeds* | **cuab oe** – *merit is gained* : ila korle afnar cuab oibo – *if you do so you will gain merit* : **cuab hacil kor-** – *gain merit* : tain bout cuab hacil korcoin – *she has earned a lot of merit* [A. θawāb]

cuacui ['suā-suī] (n) *touching; contagion* < **co-**

cuanno ['sūan-nò] (n°) *fifty-four* [B. cuannà]

cuari ['suārī] (n) *palanquin* [H. soārī]

cuattoir ['suāt-tòır] (n°) *seventy-four* [B. cuattår]

cuba ['sūbā] (n) *early morning* | cuba kal – *early morning time* [A. şubħa]

cubanalla [su 'bān-al-lā] (int) *glory to God* [A. subhāna l-lāhu – *God is glorified*]

cubbis ['sūb-bīš] (n°) *twenty-four* | dukan din rait cubbis gonta kula – *the shop is open twenty-four hours a day* [B. càbbis]

cud- [sūd] (v) *copulate* [B. cud-] (indecent)

cudacudi ['sūdāsūdī] (n) *sexual intercourse* < **cud-** (indecent)

cuddo ['sūd-dò] (n°) *fourteen* [B. couddà]

cuddofurus ['sūd-dò-fūrūš] (n) *ancestors* | amrar cuddofurus codri acla – *our forebears were all Choudhurys* : tar cuddofurus galice – *they cursed him and all his tribe* : **cuddofurus taki** – *since generations ago* : tara cuddofurus taki amrar gaut – *they've been in our village for generations* [B. couddà purus – *fourteen generations*]

cuddogusti ['sūd-dò-gūstī] (n) *lineage; clan* | tan cuddogusti loia gecoin – *off he went, taking all his family and clansmen with him* : tarar cuddogusti-u kanjis – *they're misers, the whole clan of them* [B. couddà gosti – *fourteen families*]

cudi ['sūdī] (n) *whore* | cudir fua – *son of a bitch* (indecent)

cudri ['sūdrī] (n) *village headman; Choudhury* = **codri**

cuf [sūf] (n) *quietness; silence* | cairobae cuf – *there is silence all round* : cu-uf! – *si-lence, please!* : **cuf tak-** – *keep quiet* : betae hamesa cuf take – *the fellow always keeps very quiet* : **cuf kor-** – *be silent* : one tara cuf korce – *now they've gone silent* : cuf koro! – *quiet! shut up!* [B. cup]

cufa ['sūfā] (n) *bushes* [B. jhop]

cufcaf ['sūf-sāf] (adj) *quiet* | kita be, boro cufcaf deki? – *what is it, son, you seem to be keeping very quiet?* [B. cup-cap]

cui [sūı] (n) *needle* [H. suī]

cuic [suīs] (n) *switch* | cuic on korci – *I've turned the switch on* : cuic maro – *switch it off* [E.]

cuk [sūk] (n) *anger* | **cuk kor-** – *get angry* : cuk koro kene? – *why are you getting so worked up?* : tain kanoka cuk korcoin – *he lost his temper for no reason*

cuka ['sūkā] (adj) *sharp; sour* | i curi cuka nae – *this knife isn't sharp* : am·ta cuka lage – *the mango tastes sour*
cukani ['sūkānī] (n) *helmsman* [A. sukkān – *rudder*]
cukcuki ['sūk-sūkī] (n) *annoyance* | oto cukcuki kita? – *why are you so worked up?* : **cukcuki kor-** – *get annoyed* < **cuk**
cukra ['sūk-rā] (n) *lad* [H. chokrā]
cukri ['sūk-rī] (n) *lass* [H. chokrī]
cukti ['sūk-tī] (n) *contract; agreement* | **cukti kor-/cukti kori le-** – *make a contract; seal an agreement* : tarar loge mal ani dibar cukti korci – *I've made a contract with them to supply materials* [B. cukti]
cukut ['sūkūt] (n adv) *in the eye* < **couk**
cul [sūl] (n) *hair* | car maje cul force – *a hair has fallen in the tea* : tumar cul acrao – *comb your hair* : kukra cul – *curly hair* : lal cul – *brown hair* : **ek cul** – *a tiny amount* : ek cul kor lamtam nai – *I won't give in an inch* : **cul cir-** – *tear out hair* : tara cul cirat lagce – *they've started fighting tooth and nail* [B. cul]
cula ['sūlā] (n) *fireplace designed for cooking; cooking hearth* [B. cula]
cula- (vt) *peel; shave* | alu culaici – *we've peeled the potatoes* : **culail** – *peeled; shaven* : tar kolla culail – *his head is shaved bald*
culka- ['sūl-χā] (v) *tickle; itch* | amar at culkaice – *she tickled my hand* : **culkae** – *it itches* : amar kanor maje culkar – *I've got an itch in my ear* [B. culka-]
culkani ['sūl-χānī] (n) *itching* < **culka-**
cumu ['sūmū] (n) *kiss* | **cumu ka-** – *kiss* : tain amar ato cumu kaicoin – *he kissed my hand* : **cumu de-/cumu di la-** – *give a kiss* : tumar nanire ek·ta cumu di lao – *give your granny a kiss* [B. cumu < O. cumbā]
cun [sūn] (n) *quicklime* | tain fanor loge cun kain – *she eats lime with her paan* : **cun de-** – *apply lime; whitewash* : fanor maje cun dein na jen – *please don't put any lime on the paan* : goro cun deoa – *the house has been whitewashed* [B. cun < O. cūrṇa – *milled powder*]
cun- [sūn] (vt) *select* [H. cun-]
cunia ['sūnīā] (v adv) *selectively* < **cun-**
cunu ['sūnū] (n) *nose-rub* cf **cumu**
cur [sūr] (n) *thief; swindler; profiteer* | goro cur hamaicil – *a thief had broken into the house* : afnar gari kuae? cure nice gi – *where's your car? someone has stolen it* : murgi cur – *chicken thief* : «cur firre-o cur jane» – *to a thief, everyone else is a thief too* [B. cor]
cur- (vt) *release; throw* | ou kota curo – *leave that subject alone; just forget it* : ke fattoir curce – *someone threw a stone* [H. chor-]
cura [¹] ['sūrā] (n) *thief* cf **cur**
cura [²] (n) *chapter of the Holy Quran; sura* | cura fatia – *sura al-Fatiha* : iacin cura – *sura Ya Sin* : cura eklac – *sura al-Ikhlas* [A. sūra]
cura- (vt) *cause to release* [H. churā-]
curak ['sūrāχ] (n) *hole* [P. sūrāḵ]
curani ['sūrānī] (n) *key* cf **cura-**
curanobboi ['sūrānòb-bòi] (nº) *ninety-four* [B. curanåbbåi]
curasi ['sūrāšī] (nº) *eighty-four* [B. curasi]
cur-dakait ['sūr-dāχāit] (n) *thieves and robbers* = **cur + dakait**
curemi ['sūremī] (n) *cheating; dishonest behaviour* cf **cur**
curi [¹] ['sūrī] (n) *theft; swindling; dishonest behaviour* | gor curi – *burglary* : curit dora force – *he was caught in the act of stealing* : curir karbar – *crooked dealings* : **curi oe/curi oi jae** – *theft is committed* : ino forae curi oe – *things often get pinched here* : amar gor curi oi gece – *my house has been burgled* : amar gari curi oi gece – *my car has been stolen* : **curi kor-** – *steal* : fua·ta foesa curi korcil – *the boy stole some money* : **curi kori** – *surreptitiously; secretly* : he curi kori biri kae – *he smokes on the sly* : **curi kori ne-** – *take secretly and without permission* : ke amar mubail curi kori nice gi – *someone's gone off with my mobile phone* [B. curi]

curi ² (n) *knife* | curi dia kato – *cut it with a knife* : **curi mar-** – *attack with a knife; stab* : ek·gu arek·gure curi marce – *one of them stabbed the other* [B. churi]

curi ³ (n) *bracelet* [B. cuṛi]

curi-camari ['sūrī-sāmārī] (n) *dishonest dealings*

curot ['sūròt] (n) *way; means; appearance* | faibar curot nae – *there's no way of getting it* : tar curot bala nae – *his appearance is no good; he looks evil* : **kunu curot** – *somehow or other* – amra kunu curot goro aici – *somehow or other we reached home* : **kub curot** – *beautiful* : **bod curot** – *ugly* [A. ṣūra – *form; manner*]

cus- [sūš] (vt) *suck; absorb* | aŋgul cuse – *she sucks her thumb* : mati fani cuse – *the soil absorbs water* : **cusi le-** – *suck; absorb; drain* : tara goribor rokto cusi ler – *they are sucking the blood of the poor* [B. cus-]

cut [sūt] (n) *sharp knock; hurt* | **cut lage** – *hurt is done* : tar cut lagce – *he got hurt* : **cut fa-** – *get hurt* : ami cut faiclam – *I got hurt* [B. cot]

cut- (vi) *come unstuck; flow out; run off* | fotu cutce – *the photo has come unstuck* : handi taki moela cute na – *the dirt won't come off the saucepan* : amar gam cuter – *my perspiration is flowing; I'm in a sweat* : oi deko, cutce! – *see, he's running away!* : **cuti ja-** – *come unstuck; flow out; run off* : moela cuti gece – *the dirt has come off* : amar rokto cuti jar – *my blood is flowing out; I'm bleeding* : murgi hokol cuti gece – *all the hens have escaped* [B. chut-]

cuta- ['sūtā] (vt) *unstick; cause to flow; get rid off* | moela cutaitam kila? – *how am I to get the dirt off?* : roŋ·ta cutail jae na – *the paint won't come off* : hou bokoajre cutaicoin ni? – *have you got rid of that chatterbox?* [B. chuta-]

cutar ['sūtār] (n) *sweater* [E.]

cuto ['sūtò] (adj) *small; younger* | cuto gor – *a small house* : gor·ta besi cuto – *the house is too small* : cuto bai – *younger brother* : cuto caca – *junior uncle* : hurutar maje cuto ke? – *which is the youngest of the children?* : **cuto cuto** – *very small* : cuto cuto baicca – *a wee child* : **cuto boro** – *big and small* : mac ace, cuto boro – *there are fish of all sizes* : **cuto kor-/cuto kori le-** – *make smaller; reduce* : tar cul cuto kortam – *I want to cut his hair short* [B. chotå]

cuto-muto ['sūtò-mūtò] (adj) *small; unimportant*

cutti ['sūt-tī] (n) *leave; time off; holiday* | onku tumar cutti – *you can knock off now* : cuttir din – *a holiday* : tain cuttit – *he's on holiday* : **cutti lo-** – *take time off; take a holiday* : ami ek aftar cutti loici – *I've taken a week off* : tain cutti loia deso gecoin gi – *he's gone to Bangladesh on holiday* : **cutti de-/cutti di la-** – *allow to go; discharge* : baiccaintore cutti di laicoin – *they've let the children go home* [H. chuttī]

cutu ['sūtū] (adj) *small* = **cuto**

cuta ['sūtā] (n) *cotton yarn; thread* | cui cuta – *needle and thread* : cuta di ful malaicoin – *she made floral designs in thread* : cutar kafor – *cotton cloth* [B. suta]

cuti ['sūtī] (adj) *made of cotton* | cuti kafor – *cotton cloth* [H. sūtī]

cutli ['sūtlī] (n) *twine* [B. sutli]

cutmarauli ['sūt-mārāulī] (n) *whoring wretch* (indecent)

cutra ['sūtrā] (n) *a stinging plant*

d

dac [dās] (n) *dustbin* | daco falao – *throw it in the bin* [E.]
dacala ['dāsālā] (n) *dustman* = **dac** + **-ala**
daf [dāf] (n) *prestige* | **daf mar-** – *show off one's status* [B. ḍap]
dail [dāil] (n) *pulses; dhal* | mosur dail – *red lentils* : cana dail – *lentils* : butor dail – *chick-peas* : mug dail – *moong dhal* : dail bat – *rice and lentils; a humble meal* : dalir maje macor kolla – *fish heads in dhal* : **dail o-/dail oi ja-** – *turn into a mess; be ruined* : amrar id dail oi gece – *our Eid has been wrecked* [B. dal]
dain [dāin] (adj) *right-hand* | dain at – *the right hand* : dain fau – *right leg* ¶ **dain** (n) *the right* | **daine** – *on the right* : afnar ator daine – *on your right* : daine jauka – *go to the right; turn right* : baue daine cao – *look left and right* [B. dahin < O. dakśiṇa]
dak¹ [dāχ] (n) *postal service; items of post* | dak aice na ebu – *the post hasn't arrived yet* : amrar dak laga goro di laice – *they delivered our post next door* : dos·tat dak tule – *they collect the post at ten o'clock* : **dake** – *by post; in the post* : dake di laici – *I sent it by post* : baro·tar dake aice – *it came in the midday post* : **dake car-/dake cari de-** – *put in the post; send by post* : kafor dake carmu – *I shall send the clothes by post* : afnar citi dake cari dici – *I've posted your letter for you* [B. dak]
dak² (n) *call; sound; bidding; auction* | keur dak hunco ni? – *did you hear anyone calling?* : telifonor dak hunci – *I heard the phone ringing* : fakir dak huna jae – *birdsong is audible* : dak suru oice – *bidding has commenced* : dak uter – *the bids are mounting up* : ou gari dako loici – *I bought this car at an auction* : **dak de-/dak di la-** – *make a sound; call* : uetarre dak dao cai – *call the waiter, will you* : **dak dee/dak di lae** – *inflammation occurs* : fute dak dice – *the pimple has got inflamed* : amar kane dak di laice – *an abscess has formed in my ear* : **dak tul-** – *make a competitive bid* : ami dak tulci, to faici na – *I bid for it, but I didn't get it* [B. dak]
dak- (v) *call; beckon; address; invite; summon; bid* | tumar ammare dako cai – *please call your Mum* : afnare coe·tat dakmu – *I'll call you at six* : hou beta afnare daker – *that man is beckoning you* : afnare kila daktam? – *how should I address you?* : amare caca dakio – *call me Uncle* : tar cacare baf dakcil – *he passed his uncle off as his father* : tain amrare kanit dakcoin – *he has invited us for a meal* : teski dakouka – *call a taxi* : tara fulis daker – *they are calling the police* : afnare kouto dakce – *they have summoned you to the court* : tain tin ajar dakcoin – *he bid three thousand* : **dake** – *something makes a noise* : injilo dake – *the engine is making a noise* : tumar jutae daker – *your shoes are squeaking* : kutta daker – *a dog is barking* : bag dakcil – *a tiger roared* : age fakinte dakto – *the birds used to sing* : **daki le-** – *call; summon* : tare daki litam ni? – *shall I call him?* : tain bocre daki licoin – *he has called for the manager* [B. dak-]
daka ['dāχā] (n) *Dhaka, capital of Bangladesh* | daka gecoin ni? – *have you ever been to Dhaka?* : tara daka take – *they live in Dhaka* [B. dhaka]
daka- (vt) *cause to make a noise* | kagoj ola dakao kene? – *why are you making such a noise with the paper?* : kuttare ke dakaice – *someone has made the dog bark* [B. daka-]
dakaia ['dāχāyā] (n) *person from Dhaka*
dakait ['dāχāit] (n) *robber; bandit* | raitku dakait gure – *robbers roam about in the night* : dakait era! – *they're daylight robbers (they charge far too much)!* [H. dakait]
dakat ['dāχāt] (n) *robber; bandit* = **dakait**
dakati ['dāχātī] (n) *robbery; banditry* | ino dakatir dor nae – *there's no danger of banditry here* : dakati nae te kita! – *that's nothing but daylight robbery!* : **dakati oe/dakati oi jae** – *robbery takes place* : sooror maje-o dakati oe – *you get robberies even in the city* : **dakati kor-** – *commit a robbery* : fulis-u dakati korcil – *the policemen themselves carried out the robbery* [H. dakaitī]
daknam ['dāχ-nām] (n) *nickname* | tar bala nam arif, daknam rifu – *his proper name is Arif, his nickname is Rifu* [B. daknam]

dakna ['dāχ-nā] (n) *lid* = **dakni**
dakni ['dāχ-nī] (n) *lid* [B. dhakni]
dal [dāl] (n) *branch; bough* | «ou dal cari hou dal ɗore at ficlia foria more» – *one who keeps swinging from this branch to that, his hand will slip and he'll come to grief; a rolling stone gathers no moss* [B. dal]
dal- (v) *pour; pour out; dispense* | ca dalci – *I've poured out the tea* : sira daltam ni? – *shall I dish out some gravy?* : tain garit tel dalcoin – *he has put petrol in the car* : foesa dalo! – *put another coin in the slot!* [B. dhal-]
dalcini ['dāl-sīnī] (n) *cinnamon* [B. ɖarucini]
danda ['dān-dā] (n) *stick; staff* | **danda mar-** – *strike with a stick* [B. danda]
danda- (vt) *beat with sticks; drub*
daŋga ['dāŋ-gā] (n) *fighting; affray* = **ɖaŋga**
dari ['dārī] (n) *beard* [B. daⁿri]
dat [dāt] (adj) *firm; hard; strong* | tain dat kota maticoin – *he spoke strong words; he made a good point* : dat kelaura – *a strong player* : tain kamo dat acoin – *he's good at his job* : boro dat manus – *an able person; a smart fellow* [B. daⁿto]
dat- (v) *scold*
data ['dātā] (adj) *firm; hard; tough* | ou bet besi data – *this bed is too hard* : hanɗes data oi gece – *the rice-cakes have turned out rather tough* = **dat**
datta ['dāt-tā] (adj) *hard; tough* = **data**
deg [dɛg] (n) *cauldron* [P. deg]
dega ['dɛgā] (adj) *young (animal)* | dega goru – *calf; heifer*
deki ['dɛkī] (adj) *young (animal)* = **dega**
dekoir ['dɛχòir] (n) *belch* | **dekoir ute** – *a burp comes up* : mamar ɖuibar dekoir utcil – *uncle burped twice* : **dekoir tul-** – *bring up a burp; belch* [B. dhekur]
dem [dɛm] (n) *dampness* | **dem oe/dem oi jae** – *dampness develops* : goro dem oi gece – *the house has become affected by damp* [E.]
deu [dɛū] (n) *wave* | deu utce – *waves have risen; the water is choppy* : batase deu tuler – *the wind is whipping up waves* [B. dheu]
dibi ['dībī] (n) *small box; jar* [B. diba]
difa ['dīfā] (n) *stopper; cork* | butoler difa kuae? – *where's the stopper for the bottle?* : difa lage na – *the cork won't fit* : difa lagaici – *I've put a stopper in*
dil [dīl] *dealing* | **dil kor-** – *deal with* : tara koe, afnar keic one dil korto – *they say they're going to deal with your case now* : tan eflai dil korer – *they're processing his application* [E.]
dila ['dīlā] (adj) *loose; lax* | cutar dila oi gece – *the sweater is too loose* : boro dila manus – *a very lax person* [B. dhila]
dim [dīm] (n) *egg* [B. dim < O. dimba]
dimak ['dīmāχ] (n) *state of mind; mood; conceitedness* | amar dimak bala nae – *I'm not in a good mood* : tar dimak boro – *he has a swollen head* : **dimak kor-** – *be conceited* : he besi dimak kore – *he is too big-headed* [A. dimāġ]
distab ['dīs-tāb] (n) *disturbance* | **distab de-** – *cause disturbance; disturb* : afnare distab ɖiram – *sorry, I'm disturbing you* [E.]
dobol ['dòbòl] (n) *duplicate amount* | ɖui dobol – *twice as much* : tin dobol – *three times as much* : ɖam tin dobol barce – *the price has trebled* : amar taki ɖui dobol faico – *you got twice as much as I did* [E. double]
dol- [dòl] (vi) *get wrenched* | **doli ja-** – *get wrenched* : tair ator kobja doli gece – *her wrist has been sprained* [B. dhāl-]
doŋ [dòŋ] (n) *jesting; foolery* | besi doŋ bala nae – *too much joking is not a good thing* : **doŋ kor-** – *jest; be flippant* : fua kali doŋ kore – *the boy is always making fun* : cori, ami doŋ korclam – *sorry, I was only joking* [H. dhoŋ – *hoax*]
doŋbaj ['dòŋ-bāz] (n) *joker; prankster* = **doŋ + -baj**
doŋbaji ['dòŋ-bāzī] (n) *joking; foolery*

doŋdaŋ ['dòŋ-dāŋ] (n) *jesting; foolery* = **doŋ**
dor [dòr] (n) *fear* | **dor kore** – *one feels afraid* : raitku dor kore amar – *I feel scared at night* : **dor hamae/dor hamai jae** – *one gets frightened* : tar dor hamai gece – *he has got scared* : **dor baŋge** – *one's fears are overcome* : aste aste tar hafor dor baŋce – *gradually he lost his fear of snakes* : **dor deka-** – *frighten* : is, amare dor dekaiclae! – *oh, you scared me!* [B. dår]
dora- (vi) *be afraid; get scared* | doraici! – *I'm frightened!* : doraio na! – *don't be afraid!* : tain haf dorain – *she's scared of snakes* : **doraia** – *being afraid; out of fear* : tara doraia goro roicil – *being scared, they stayed at home* : tain doraia matoin na – *he's too scared to say anything* : **doraia ja-/dorai ja-** – *get frightened* : bilai dorai jaibo – *the cat will be frightened* : dorai geci! – *I got scared; you made me jump!* [B. dåra-]
draibar ['drāibār] (n) *driver; rickshaw-puller* [E.]
droar ['drò-ār] (n) *chest-of-drawers* [E.]
dub [dūb] (n) *immersion* | **dub de-/dub di la-** – *immerse oneself; take a dip* [B. dub]
dub- (vi) *be immersed; sink* | nau dubto nae – *the boat won't sink* : **dubi ja-** – *be immersed; sink* : koto jaaj dubi gecil – *many ships sank* : sujjo dubi jar – *the sun is going down* : utan dubi gece – *the yard has gone under water* [B. dub-]
duba ['dūbā] (n) *pond* [B. doba]
duba- (vt) *immerse; cause to sink* | fanir maje kafor dubaimu – *I'll immerse the cloth in water* : tufane nau dubaicil – *the storm made the boat sink* : dubaicoin amare! – *you've scuppered me!* : **dubail** – *immersed; submerged* : **dubai de-/dubai le-** – *immerse; cause to sink* : tin ta jaaj dubai dicil – *they sank three ships* : amrare dubai dice – *they have done us down* [B. duba-]
dufi ['dūfī] (n) *turtle-dove*
duk- [dūk] (vi) *go in* | cafi duke na – *the key won't go in* : **duki ja-** – *go in* : duki jauka! – *go on in!* : tara goro duki gece – *they've entered the house* [B. dhuk-]
duka- ['dūkā] (vt) *put in; insert* | basko kila dukaitam? – *how can I get the box in?* : **dukai de-** – *put in; insert* : cear hono dukai dao – *push the chair in there* [B. dhoka-]
dul [dūl] (n) *drum* [B. dhol]
dul- (n) *move away* | **duli ja-** – *move away; move house* : tara duli gece – *they have moved (to another house)*
dula- ['dūlā] (vt) *move; shift* | **dulai le-** – *move; shift* : bet ota dulai litam – *I want to move that bed elsewhere*
dulli ['dūl-lī] (n) *curtained palanquin* [B. duli]
dumur ['dūmūr] (n) *fig* [B. dumur]
dus [dūš] (n) *head-bump* | **dus ka-** – *bump one's head* [B. dhus]

ḑ

ḑa [ḑā] (n) *chopper; bill-hook* [B. ḑa]
ḑa- (v) *reap*
ḑaba ['ḑābā] (n) *chess* [B. ḑaba]
ḑaba- (v) *scold* [B. ḑaba- — *reprove*]
ḑabi ['ḑābī] (n) *claim; right* | i goror ufre tumar ḑabi nae — *you have no claim to this house* : amar ino takar ḑabi ace — *I have a right to remain here* : tara amar ḑabi mane na — *they won't acknowledge my rights* : **ḑabi kor-** — *claim; demand* : tain foesa ḑabi korcoin — *he has demanded money* [B. ḑabi < A. da¿āwā, da¿āwī — *demands*]
ḑabi-ḑaoa ['ḑābīḑāwā] (n) *rights* = **ḑabi**
ḑabidar ['ḑābīḑār] (n) *claimant* [P. da`vādār]
ḑac [ḑās] (n) *manner; technique; fashion* | tain i kamor ḑac faicoin na — *he hasn't got the hang of this job* : noea ḑacor kafor — *clothes in a new style* [B. ḑhaⁿc]
ḑad [ḑād] (n) *ringworm; tinea* [B. ḑaḑ]
ḑaḑa ['ḑāḑā] (n) *grandfather; great-uncle; brother* (Among Muslims this kinship term refers to one's paternal grandfather, or any brother or same-generation male cousin of either parent of one's father; also, in some cases, it may be used to refer to an elder brother. Among Hindus it refers to any grandfather or other male relative of one's grandparents' generation; but also to any elder brother.) [B. ḑaḑa]
ḑaḑi ['ḑāḑī] (n) *grandmother; great-aunt* (Among Muslims the term refers to one's father's mother, or any sister or same-generation female cousin of either parent of one's father, or the wife of any *ḑaḑa*. Among Hindus it refers to any grandmother or other female relative of one's grandparents' generation.) [B. ḑaḑi]
ḑae ['ḑāɛ́] (n adv) *on account (of); for* | megor ḑae geci na — *I didn't go, because of the rain* : tumar ḑae tain boutta korcoin — *she has done a lot for you* : tar tekar ḑae maea besi — *he is too fond of money* [B. ḑay < O. ḑāya — *given*]
ḑae-dorbar ['ḑāɛ́-dòr-bār] (n) *strife* | **ḑae-dorbar kor-** — *quarrel* = **dorbar**
ḑaf¹ [ḑāf] (n) *prestige* | **ḑaf mar-** — *show off one's status* [B. ḑap]
ḑaf² (n) *step; rung* [B. ḑhap]
ḑafon ['ḑāfòn] (n) *burial* | **ḑafon o-/ḑafon oi ja-** — *be buried (in a grave)* : **ḑafon kor-** — *bury (in a grave)* [A. ḑafn]
ḑafor ['ḑāfòr] (n) *screen; fence*
ḑag [ḑāg] (n) *mark; stain; (marked) lot; plot of land* | kolomor ḑag — *mark made by a pen* : kalir ḑag — *ink spot* : ḑostokotor jagae ḑag ḑici — *I've put a mark where the signature should go* : kafito ḑag lagce — *a stain has got on the carpet* : ḑag ute na — *the stain won't come off* : ḑos ḑag mal — *ten lots of goods* : ou ḑag amrar — *this plot belongs to us* : **ḑag fore/ḑag fori jae** — *a mark is made* : kaforor maje ḑag force — *a stain has got on the cloth* : tar name ḑag fori gece — *his name is blemished* : **ḑag tul-** — *remove a stain* : ḑag tultam farci na — *I couldn't get rid of the stain* [P. ḑāġ]
ḑaii ['ḑā-ī] (adj) *responsible; to blame* | amrar nirafottar lagi ke ḑaii oiba? — *who will take responsibility for our safety?* : illagi tumi ḑaii — *you are to blame for this; this is all your fault* [B. ḑayi < S. ḑāyī]
ḑaitto ['ḑā-īt-tò] (n) responsibility [B.ḑayittå < S. ḑāyitva]
ḑair [ḑāīr] (n) *perimeter of house; verandah* cf **ḑar**
ḑakil ['ḑākīl] (adj) *entering* | ḑakil kelas — *entry level class (in Islamic school)* : **ḑakil o-/ḑakil oi ja-** — *enter; be admitted* : kolijo ḑakil oice — *he has been admitted to college* : **ḑakil kor-/ḑakil kori le-** — *submit (a document)* : kecir hokol kagoj ḑakil korci — *I've submitted all the papers for the lawsuit* [A. dāḵil]
ḑakila ['ḑākīla] (n) *entrance* [A. dāḵila]
ḑakka ['ḑāk-kā] (n) *shove; push* | **ḑakka lage** — *a sudden push is felt* : kor taki ḑakka lagce — *I felt a shove from behind* : befsat ḑakka lagce — *there's been a surge in business* : **ḑakka de-/ḑakka di la-** — *shove; push* : ḑorojat ḑakka ḑeuka — *give the door a push* : **ḑakka laga-** — *shove; bump* : koror gari ḑakka lagaice — *the car behind bumped into us* [B. ḑhakka]

daktari ['dāχtārī] (adj) *medical* | daktari kad – *medical card* ¶ **daktari** (n) *medical treatment* | tan hafanir lagi daktari coler – *treatment for her asthma is going on* : **daktari kora-** – *get treatment* : daktari koraita nae ni? – *won't you seek treatment?* < **daktor**

daktor ['dāχtòr] (n) *doctor* | joini daktor – *registered family doctor; GP* : asfatalor boro daktor – *hospital consultant* : cokkur daktor – *eye specialist* : fosur daktor – *veterinary doctor* : **daktor deka-** – *consult a doctor* : afne daktor dekaicoin ni? – *have you seen a doctor about it?* [E.]

daktorni ['dāχtòr-nī] (n) *lady doctor* = **daktor** + -**ni**

dalal ['dālāl] (n) *hanger-on; tout* [A. dallāl – *broker*]

dam [dām] (n) *price; value* | itar dam koto? – *what's the price of this?* : hotar dam besi – *that one is too expensive* : muta dam – *high price* : kom dam – *low price* : lekaforar dam ace – *education has its value* : **damor** – *of a price; of value* : boro damor jinis – *a thing of much value* : kom damor juta – *low priced shoes; cheap shoes* : **dame** – *at a price* : kom dame loici – *I bought it at a low price* : tain bala dame beccoin – *he has sold it for a decent amount* : **dam ca-** – *demand a price* : tara dos fon dam caicil – *they were asking ten pounds (for it)* : **dam dor-** – *charge a price* : amra besi dam dortam nai – *we won't charge much* : **dam kor-** – *haggle over price* : tara ebu dam korer – *they're still arguing over the price* : **dam de-** – *pay (for); accord value (to)* : hotar dam dico ni? – *have you paid for that?* : tan kotar kunu dam dee na – *they take no heed of what he says* [B. dam]

dama ['dāmā] (n) *bullock* [B. damɾa]

dama- (vt) *suppress* [B. daba-]

dama-cafa ['dāmāsāfā] (n) *suppression; concealment* | kota·ta dama-cafa dia rakce – *they have hushed the matter up* < **dama-, cafa-** ²

damadami ['dāmādāmī] (n) *haggling* | damadami kor- – *haggle* < **dam**

damand ['dāmānd] (n) *son-in-law* [P. dāmād]

dami ['dāmī] (adj) *costly; expensive* | dami gori – *an expensive watch* : **kom dami** – *cheap* : ou kafor kom dami – *this cloth is cheap* < **dam**

dan ¹ [dān] (n) *gift; donation* | dan basko – *donation box* : **dan kor-/dan kori le-** – *donate* : tara ek bosta cail dan korto – *they want to donate one sack of rice* : **dan kori ja-** – *donate; bequeath* : ek mocjidor jaega dan kori gecoin – *he donated land for a mosque* [B. dan]

dan ² (n) *rice plant; paddy; unhusked rice grain* | tara dan ruito – *they're going to plant some rice* : kiran era dan tuler – *the farmers are harvesting the paddy* : dui bosta dan – *two sacks of unhusked rice* [B. dhan]

dana ¹ ['dānā] (n) *grain; corn; daily bread* | calir dana – *a grain of husked rice* : cinir dana – *a grain of sugar* : murgi dana kar – *the hens are eating corn* : rijekor dana – *one's daily bread (as allotted by God)* [P. dāna – *grain*]

dana ² (adj) *wise* | dana luke koe .. – *wise men say ..* [P. dānā]

dana-bina ['dānābīnā] (adj) *wise* [P. dānā o bīnā – *knowing and seeing*]

dana-fani ['dānāfānī] (n) *daily bread and water* = **dana** ¹ + **fani**

danda ['dāndā] (n) *clever trick* [B. dhandha]

dandamanda ['dāndāmāndā] (n) *trickery* = **danda**

dani ['dānī] (v n) *reaping* < **da-**

danga ['dāŋ-gā] (n) *fighting; affray* [B. danga]

dao ¹ ['dāò] (v) *give* (present imperative) < **de-**

dao ² (n) *opportunity* | tara dao tukar – *they're looking for their chance* : tain matbar dao faicoin – *he's found an excuse to start talking* [B. daⁿo]

daoa ['dāw̃ā] (n) *claim* [A. daʿwā]

daoai ['dāw̃āı] (n) *medicament* [A. dawā']

daot ['dāòt] (n) *invitation* | kanir daot – *invitation to eat* : takar daot – *invitation to stay* : **daot de-** – *invite* : tarare daot dici (kaibar lagi) – *I've invited them (for a meal)* : kojonor daot dicoin? – *how many people have you invited?* : **daot fa-** – *receive an invitation* : amra bidio dekar daot faici – *we've been invited to watch a video* : **daot ka-** – *have a meal by* *invitation* : tain ɖaot kaita gecoin – *he's gone for a meal to which he had been invited* [A. daʑwā]

ɖar¹ ['ɖār] (n) *edge; sharpness; current; indebtedness* | tebulor ɖar – *the edge of the table* : curir ɖar nae – *the knife isn't sharp* : gaŋgor ɖar ace – *the river has a strong current* : afnar ɖar fuctam fartam nai – *I could never repay you for all that I owe you* : **ɖaro** – *in proximity; nearby; beside* : amrar ɖaro – *in our neighbourhood; near us* : cinemar ɖaro – *near the cinema* : **ɖar de-/ɖar ɖi la-** – *lend* : tain ek so fon ɖar ɖicoin amare – *he has lent me a hundred pounds* : **ɖar kor-/ɖar kori an-** – *borrow* : tarar gec tone bidio ɖar kori anci – *I've borrowed a videotape from them* [B. ɖhar]

ɖar² (n) *door* = **ɖuar**

ɖara¹ ['ɖārā] (n) *flow* | fanir ɖara – *a flow of water* : megor ɖara – *pouring rain; buckets of rain* [B. ɖhara < S. ɖhārā]

ɖara² (n adv) *by agency (of); by* | jur ɖara – *by force* : calaki ɖara – *by guile* : tan ɖara – *by him* : ita kar ɖara sombob? – *by whom could this possibly be done?* : amar ɖara oito nae – *it can't be done by me; I personally cannot do it* [B. ɖara < S. ɖvārā]

ɖare ['ɖārɛ] (n adv) *nearby* = **ɖaro**

ɖare-kace ['ɖārɛχāsɛ] (n adv) *nearby* = **ɖare + kace**

ɖari ['ɖārī] (n) *beard* | **ɖari rak-** – *grow a beard* [B. ɖaɽi]

ɖariola ['ɖārɪòlā] (n) *bearded man* = **ɖari + -ala**

ɖaro ['ɖārò] (n adv) *nearby; beside* | tara ɖaro take – *they live nearby* : fektrir ɖaro sof ace – *there is a shop next to the factory* < **ɖar**¹

ɖaroan ['ɖārwān] (n) *gatekeeper* [P. darbān]

ɖaroga ['ɖāròɡā] (n) *police inspector* [P. dāroga – *commander*]

ɖarona ['ɖārònā] (n) *conception; idea* | i somonɖe afnar ɖarona kita? – *what do you think about it?* : amar kunu ɖarona nae – *I have no idea* [B. ɖharȧna < S. ɖhāranā]

ɖaru ['ɖārū] (n) *wood* [B. ɖaru < O. ɖāru]

ɖarun ['ɖārūn] (adj) *terrific* [B. ɖarun < S. ɖāruɳa – *fearsome*]

ɖat [ɖāt] (n) *tooth; teeth* | akol ɖat – *wisdom tooth* : geɖar ɖat uter – *baby's teeth are coming up* : amar ɖui·ta ɖat force – *two of my teeth have fallen out* : tain ufri ɖat lagaicoin – *he's had false teeth fitted* [B. daⁿt < O. ɖanta]

ɖatra ['ɖātra] (adj) *clever*

ɖatu ['ɖātū] (n) *matter; metal* [B. ɖhatu < S. ɖhātu – *element*]

ɖe- (v) *give; pay; add; send; emit; put; put on; put up; allow; supply; perform* | taire foesa ɖao – *give her some money* : tain kota ɖicoin – *he has given his word* : ami orɖek ɖam ɖici – *I have paid half the price* : koto ɖena lagbo? – *how much will have to be paid?* : tura lobon ɖeuka – *add a little salt* : tara citi ɖice – *they have sent a letter* : tare aij goro ɖimu – *I shall send him home today* : he cik ɖice – *he let out a scream* : kolom muko ɖio na – *don't put the pen in your mouth* : tain cosma ɖicoin – *she has put her spectacles on* : sunɖor ek·ta gan ɖeuka – *put on a nice song* : hono oal ɖimu – *we're going to put up a wall over there* : tara bajaro ɖukan ɖice – *they've set up a shop in the bazaar* : cacare boibar ɖao – *let uncle sit down* : tara kam korbar ɖee na – *they won't let me get on with my work* : alla ɖein joɖin .. – *if God permits ..* : allae ɖile amra kail jaimu – *God willing, we'll go there tomorrow* : amare buɖɖi ɖeuka – *give me some ideas* : tara juaf ɖice – *they have given a reply* : ke saɖ ɖibo? – *who will give a helping hand?* : cacire calam ɖao! – *give auntie a salaam; pay your respects to auntie!* : hou fua ɖakka ɖice amare – *that boy gave me a shove* : one geɖae asi ɖer – *now the baby is giving a smile* : fal ɖao! – *take a jump!* : he ɖuka ɖice – *he has practised deception* : tain cigret kani baɖ ɖicoin – *he has given up smoking cigarettes* : **ɖi ɖe-** – *hand over; give* : boi·kan tare ɖi ɖici – *I have given him the book* : **ɖia ja-** – *deliver* : tain sinni ɖia gecoin – *he delivered a portion of ritual feast food* : amare goro ɖia jauka – *please drop me off at my house* [B. ɖe-] Note: Used as an auxiliary in numerous verbal compounds. **ɖi la-** (q.v.) is a frequently used alternative, which can be substituted for **ɖe-** in most contexts.

ɖean ['ɖɛ́ān] (n) *meditation* | **ɖean kor-** – *meditate; think deeply* : afne kita ɖean korra? – *what are you thinking about so deeply?* [B. ɖhyan < S. ɖhyāna]

dean-darona ['dɛ́ān-dārònā] (n) *thought; idea* | amar kunu dean-darona nae – *I have no idea at all; I haven't the foggiest* = **dean + darona**
deb [dɛb] (n) *god; idol* [B. deb < S. deva]
debi ['dɛbī] (n) *goddess* [B. debi < S. devī]
debta ['dɛbtā] (n) *god; idol* [B. debâta < S. devatā]
deg [dɛg] (n) *cauldron* [P. deg]
dein [dɛ́ın] (n) *debt; obligation* [A. dain]
deir [dɛ́ır] (n) *delay* | besi deir oito nae – *there won't be much delay* [P. der]
dek- [dɛχ] (v) *see; look at; watch; look out; look out for; imagine; examine; try; stand the sight of* | deki? – *may I see?* : tain couke dekoin na – *he is unable to see; he is blind* : cacare dekcoin ni? – *have you seen uncle anywhere?* : ami kunu faeda deki na – *I don't see any advantage in it* : dekcoin ni karbar? – *have you seen the affair? do you see what is going on?* : dekcoin ni? – *see what I mean?* : tumi deki boro calak! – *you're quite a crafty one, I see!* : tain fotu dekra – *she's looking at some photos* : tumra bidio dektae ni? – *do you all want to watch a video?* : deko, forbae! – *watch out, you'll fall!* : amar lagi ek·ta kam dekouka – *please look out for a job for me* : ami kunta deki na – *I can't think of anything* : at dia dekouka – *feel it with your hand and see what it's like* : kaia dekouka – *eat it and see; taste it* : cesta kori dekouka – *try and see; have a try* : ami tare dektam fari na – *I can't stand the sight of him* : **deki deki** – *by seeing; by following an example* : cacare deki deki hikci – *I learnt by watching uncle do it* : **deki le-** – *catch sight of; look at* : deki lici tumare! – *I've spied you; I can see you!* : arbar deki louka – *have another look at it* : **deki a-** – *go and see* : tarar gor deki aici amra – *we've been to see their house* : **deki ja-** – *come and see* : amar nati deki jauka! – *come in and meet my new grandson!* [B. dekh-]
deka ['dɛχā] (v n) *seeing* | **deka jae** – *seeing is possible; (something) can be seen* : kacra deka jae – *some dirt can be seen* : osubida deka gece – *problems have come to light* : aij cand deka jaito nae – *the moon won't be visible tonight* : afne boro besto deka jae – *you're very busy, it seems* : deka jauk – *let's wait and see* : **deka oe** – *a face to face meeting occurs* : minar loge runar deka oice – *Runa met Mina* : tan loge tumar deka oito fare – *you may bump into him* : tan loge amar deka nae bout din dori – *I haven't seen him for a long time* : kocit deka oe – *we seldom meet* : kail deka oibo – *I'll see you tomorrow* : **(kar loge) deka kor-** – *go to see (someone); pay a visit (to someone)* : cacar loge deka korci – *I've been to see Uncle* : tan loge deka koroin jen – *make sure you go and call on him* < **dek-**
deka- (vt) *cause to see; allow to see; point out; show* | allae dekae, te dekmu – *if God permits me to see it, then I shall indeed see it* : ou kota tarare dekaitam kila? – *how can I get them to see this point?* : tan goena dekaicoin amare – *she let me look at her jewelry* : afnare ek·kan fotu dekaitam – *there's a photo I want to show you* : amare ek·ta rasta dekauka – *show me a way forward* : tain kali jukti dekain – *he keeps producing facile arguments* : ek·ta kota dekailam – *I was just making a point* : tara dekaibar lagi ota kore – *they do it in order to show off* : hokolere dekaia canda dicoin – *he made his donation in an ostentatious way* : daktor dekaicoin ni? – *have you been to see a doctor?* : **dekai de-** – *show; point out* : amare rasta dekai dice – *they showed me the way* : tarar gor dekai deuka – *please point out their house* [B. dekha-]
deka-saikkat ['dɛχā-šāık-kat] (n) *meeting* | **deka-saikkat oe** – *a face to face meeting occurs* : en loge amar kail deka-saikkat oibo – *I shall be seeing him tomorrow* : **(kar loge) deka-saikkat kor-** – *go to see (someone); pay a visit (to someone)* : nanar loge deka-saikkat korcoin ni? – *have you been to see Grandfather?* = **deka + saikkat**
deka-suna ['dɛχā-šūnā] (n) *attention; care* | **deka-suna kor-** – *look after; take care of* : tan deka-suna ke koroin? – *who looks after her?* : hokoltir deka-suna tain korba – *he will take care of everything* [B. dekha-sona – *seeing and hearing*]
dekbal ['dɛχbāl] (n) *attention; care* | **dekbal kor-** – *look after; take care of* [H. dekh-bhāl]
dekte ['dɛχ-tɛ́] (v adv) *in seeing; to look at* | tain dekte kirom? – *what does he look like?* : tai dekte sundor – *she is good-looking* : amar juta kila lage dekte? – *how do my shoes look?* : **dekte dekte** – *while you watch; in a trice* : dekte dekte kam·ta ses oibo – *the job will be*

63

finished in a moment : ḑekte ḑekte jaoar somoe ailo – *the time for departure has come already* < **dek-**
ḑem [ḑɛm] (n) *(plant) shoot*
ḑen [ḑɛn] (n) *obligation* = **dein**
ḑena[1] ['ḑɛnā] (v n) *giving; to give* < **de-**
ḑena[2] (adj) *to be given; due* | ḑena foesa – *money owed* : ḑos fon ḑena roice – *ten pounds are still owing* cf **dein**
ḑeneala ['ḑɛnɛālā] (n) *giver; sender* = **ḑena + -ala**
ḑeo[1] ['ḑέò] (n) *ghost; demon* = **ḑeu**
ḑeo[2] (v) *give* (future imperative) < **de-**
ḑeoa- ['ḑɛwā] (vt) *cause to give* | tare kani ḑeoaimu – *I'll get someone to feed him* : barit kobor ḑeoaicoin – *he's arranged to get the news home* [B. ḑeoa-]
ḑeoal ['ḑɛwāl] (n) *wall* [B. ḑeoal < P. dīvār]
ḑeoan ['ḑɛwān] (n) *court; revered gentleman* | ḑeoan ḑorbar – *litigation* : ḑeoan sab – *husband's father* [P. dīvān – *court*]
ḑeoana ['ḑɛwānā] (adj) *mad* [P. dīvāna]
ḑeoar ['ḑɛwār] (n) *wall* [P. dīvār]
ḑeor ['ḑέòr] (n) *husband's younger brother* [B. debår]
ḑer [ḑέr] (n°) *one and a half* | ḑer ḑin – *one and a half days* : ḑer fon cail – *a pound and a half of rice* : ḑer so mail – *one hundred and fifty miles* : ḑer ajar – *one thousand five hundred* : ḑer·ta baje – *it's half past one* [B. ḑeɽ]
ḑeri ['ḑɛrī] (n) *delay; lateness* | tin gonta ḑeri – *three hours' delay* : oto ḑeri? – *why are you so late?* : tar ḑerir karon kita? – *what's the reason for his being late?* : **ḑerit** – *with a delay; belatedly* : caca ḑerit aicoin – *uncle arrived late* : **ḑeri ace** – *a delay is due; further time will elapse* : ebu ḑos minit ḑeri ace – *there's still ten minutes to go* : tarar aite ḑeri ace – *it's not yet time for them to arrive* : **ḑeri oe/ḑeri oi jae** – *there is delay; it gets late* : tura ḑeri oito fare – *there may be a little delay* : bakka ḑeri oi jar – *it's getting very late* : cacar aite ḑeri oibo – *uncle will be late (in arriving)* : afnar fac minit ḑeri oi gece – *you are five minutes late* : **ḑeri kor-/ḑeri kori le-** – *make delay; be tardy; wait* : tumi ḑeri koro kene? – *why are you shilly-shallying?* : ami bes ḑeri kortam nai – *I won't be long* : aro ḑui minit ḑeri korouka – *please hang on for another couple of minutes* : tara bout ḑeri kori lice – *they have lost a lot of time* : **ḑeri kori** – *with delay; belatedly* : tain ḑeri kori aicoin – *he arrived late* : **ḑeri kora-** – *cause delay; make (someone) late* : fon koria tain aro ḑeri koraicoin amrare – *by phoning us he made us even later* [P. derī]
ḑeria ['ḑɛrīā] (adj) *excess; surplus; spare* | ḑeria kota – *superfluous words* : ḑeria kani – *left over food* : ḑeria rum – *a spare room*
ḑes [ḑɛš] (n) *country; homeland* | tarar kun ḑes? – *which country are they from?* : ou ḑesor manus – *a native of this country* : arok ḑesor beti – *a woman from a foreign country* : tain ḑeso gecoin – *he has gone home (to Bangladesh)* [B. ḑes < S. ḑeša – *region*]
ḑes-biḑes ['ḑɛš-biḑɛš] (n) *home and abroad* | tain ḑes-biḑes gurcoin – *he's travelled all over the place* = **ḑes + biḑes**
ḑesi ['ḑɛšī] (adj) *indigenous; local* | ḑesi fol – *indigenous fruits* : ḑesi kagoj – *paper produced within the country* : ḑesi cail – *locally grown rice* : ḑesi kafor – *homespun cloth* [B. ḑesi < S. ḑešī – *regional*]
ḑeslai ['ḑɛš-lāi] (n) *matches* [H. diyāsalāī]
ḑeu ['ḑέū] (n) *ghost; demon* [P. dev]
ḑeu-but ['ḑέūbūt] (n) *hobgoblins* = **ḑeu + but**[2]
ḑeura ['ḑέūrā] (n) *one who gives; sender; vendor* | ou citir ḑeura ke? – *who is the sender of this letter?* : tain ḑeura, ami loura – *he is the vendor, I'm the purchaser* < **de-**
ḑi- (v) *give* = **de-**
ḑia ['ḑīā] (v adv) *having given; by giving; by; with; along; in respect of* | tain kani ḑia coli gecoin – *having given the food, she went away* : tare foesa ḑia kusi koraici – *I made him happy by giving him money* : jur ḑia kam oito nae – *the job can't be accomplished by force*

: tara mesin dia malaice – *they made it by machine* : amra at dia kai – *we eat with our hands* : tain dail dia bat kaiba – *he will eat his rice with dhal* : tara lakri dia mailaice – *they have made it with wood* : jotno dia kam kore – *she works with care* : tara sorok dia ati aice – *they came walking along the road* : amra kamlare dia tik koraici – *we got it repaired by workmen* : boes dia kota nae – *it's not a question of age* : tare dia amar bissas nae – *I've no confidence in him* : afnar huruta dia maea nae ni? – *have you no affection for your children?* : korouka, afnar subida dia – *do it at your convenience*   < **de-**

didar ['dīdār] (n) *sight*   [P. dīdār]

dif [dīf] (n) *lamp*   [B. dip < S. dīpa]

dig [dīg] (n) *direction* | **dige** – *in a direction; in a way; towards* : afne kun dige jaita? – *in which direction do you want to go?* : ek dige bala oice – *in one way it's just as well* : tain bajaror dige jaira – *he's going towards the marketplace*   = **dik**

digdari ['dīgdārī] (n) *importunacy*   = **dikdari**

digol ['dīgòl] (adj) *long*

dik [dīk] (n) *direction; length* | cair dik – *the four points of the compass* : fub kun dik? – *which way is east from here?* : jomir dik foncas at – *the length of the plot is fifty cubits* : **dik lo-** – *head in a particular direction* : tumi ek·ta dik loitae – *you should choose a particular course of action*   [B. dik < S. dik]

dikdari ['dīkdārī] (n) *importunacy* | **dikdari kor-** – *bother; pester* : afnar dikdari korci – *sorry I've been such a bother to you*   [P. diqqdārī]

dil [dīl] (n) *heart; mind; soul; vital organ* | tar dil bala – *he is good-hearted* : tar dil kula – *he is frank and open-hearted* : caf dil – *a pure soul* : murgir dil – *chicken's heart or sweetbread* : **dile** – *in one's heart* : amar dile sondeo roice – *I feel doubts deep down inside* : **dile jane** – *with heart and soul* : dile jane bissas kori – *I believe with all my heart* : tain dile jane kusis korra – *he is trying wholeheartedly* : **dilor** – *of the heart* : dilor bondu – *bosom friend* : **dilor maje** – *in one's heart* : amar dilor maje dor – *I'm inwardly afraid* : **dil koe/dile koe** – *one feels; one thinks* : amar dil koe na kaibar – *I don't feel like eating* : amar dile koe, tara aito nae – *I reckon they won't come* : **dile dake** – *one feels; one thinks* : afnar dile kita dake? – *what do you think?*   [P. dil]

di la- ['dīlā] (v) *give; give away; hand over; add; send; emit; dismiss* | tan firon ek fokirre di laicoin – *he's given his shirt to a beggar* : tan ato di lauka – *hand it over to him* : tura lobon di lauka – *add a little salt* : tare goro di laitam ni? – *shall I send him home?* : he tar boure di laice – *he has divorced his wife* : ke cik di laice – *someone let out a shriek* : bai bai di lao! – *say bye-bye!* : di lai bicmilla – *let's say "bismillah"; let's make a start* : tara juaf di laice – *they have given a reply* : fuainte fot di laice – *the boys have set off on their way* : he cigret kani bad di laice – *he has given up smoking cigarettes*   Note: Derivative of **de-**, which is often used in place of **de-** in the affirmative. It is not normally used in the negative.

dimag ['dīmāk] (n) *brain; mental condition; conceit* | tan dimag karaf – *he's out of his right mind* : tan dimag besi – *he's too conceited*   [P. dimāġ – *brain*]

dimagi ['dīmāgī] (adj) *conceited*   < **dimag**

din [dīn] (n) *day; daylight; weather; time* | din takte jauka gi – *go while it's still daylight* : aij din·ta bala – *the weather's fine today* : tain dui-tin din takba – *she will stay for two or three days* : tin dinor din – *the third day* : bout din – *many days; a long time* : koto din oice? – *how long has it been?* : afne kun din jaiba? – *when will you go?* : je din fari – *whenever I can* : afne kunu din dekcoin tare? – *have you ever seen him?* : caci kok din dori bemar – *aunt has been ill for some time* : **dino** – *by day; per day* : tain dino gumain – *he sleeps by day* : tain dino foncas fon fain – *he receives fifty pounds per day* : **dinku** – *by day; on a day* : tain roibbar dinku aicla – *he came on Sunday* : **dinor** – *of day; of daytime* : dinor kamla – *a day worker* : dinor bala – *daytime* : fac dinor baicca – *a five day old baby* : ou dud koe dinor? – *how many days old is this milk?* : tin dinor lagi aicoin – *she's come for three days* : **dinkur** – *of day; of daytime* : dinkur kamla – *a day worker* : ek dinkur kani – *food for one day* : **din din** – *daily* : din din kali barer – *it's getting bigger every day* : **bocor**

din – *about a year* : **mas din** – *about a month* : **din ute** – *day breaks; daylight appears* : **din jae** – *time passes*   [B. din]
din [2] (adj) *poor*   [B. din < S. dīna – *needy*]
din [3] (n) *the Faith (Islam)*   [A. dīn]
din-dukki ['dīn-dūk-kī] (adj) *poor and wretched*   = **din** [2] + **dukki**
din-dunia ['dīn-dūnıā] (n) *the world*   = **dunia**
dinkedin ['dīn-kédīn] (adv) *day by day*   cf **din din**
din-rait ['dīn-rāıt] (adv) *day and night* | tain din-rait kam koroin – *he works night and day* : din-rait kula – *open day and night* : din-rait cobbis gonta – *24 hours a day*   = **din** + **rait**
dio [dıô] (v) *give* (future imperative)   < **de-**
di-o ['dī̀ò] (n°) *both* | amar di-o at bija – *both my hands are wet* : tain di-o·ta nicoin – *he has taken them both* : tara di-o·gu fagol – *they're mad, both of them*   = **dui-o**
dir [dīr] (adj) *slow and steady* | **dire** – *slowly and steadily* : ektu dire colouka – *please go a bit slower and steadier* :   [B. dhir < S. dhīra – *steadfast*]
dire ['dīrɛ́] (n adv) *slowly and steadily* | tara dire cole – *they proceed slowly* : dire matouka – *please speak more slowly* : **dire dire** – *very slowly* : tain dire dire kam koroin – *he works very slowly*   < **dir**
dire-suste ['dīrɛ́šūstɛ́] (adv) *slowly and surely*   = **dire** + **suste**
diroŋ ['dīròŋ] (n) *delay* | **diroŋ oe/diroŋ oi jae** – *delay occurs; it gets late* : kam suru oite bakka diroŋ oi gece – *there's been much delay in starting the job* : amrar diroŋ or – *we are getting late* : **diroŋ kor-/ diroŋ kori le-** – *make delay; dally* : besi diroŋ koroin na jen – *please don't make too much delay*   [P. dirang]
disa ['dīšā] (n) *orientation* | **disa fa-** – *find one's bearings; make sense of things* : ami kunu disa fairam na – *I can't make head or tail of it* : **disa le-** – *choose a direction* : afne ek disa loita oiba – *you must choose a course of action*   [B. disa < S. dišā]
do [dò] (int) *anyway* | tain auka do – *wait till he's arrived, at least*
do- (vt) *wash* | tain kafor doira – *she's washing clothes* : tumar at muk do – *wash your hands and face*   [B. dhu-]
doba ['dòbā] (n) *chess*   = **daba**
dobij ['dòbīz] (adj) *thick; tough*   [P. dabīz]
dobol ['dòbòl] (n) *duplicate amount* | tan boes amar taki dui dobol – *his age is twice mine* : dam tin dobol barce – *the price has risen by a factor of three*   [E.]
doea ['dòyā] (n) *compassion; kindness; pity* | afnar kunu doea nae ni? – *don't you have any heart?* – tain doea dekaicoin – *he has shown mercy* : tan dilo doea hamailo – *compassion entered her heart; she took pity* : ita tan doear ufre – *it depends on his kindness; it's up to him* : **doea kor-/doea kori le-** – *be kind; show mercy* : caci kila doea korcoin – *aunt has shown such kindness* : **doea kori** – *kindly; if you please* : afne doea kori ek kaf ca diba – *would you be so kind as to give me a cup of tea* : doea kori bad deuka – *please leave off*   [B. dåya < S. dayā]
doeal ['dòyāl] (adj) *kind-hearted*   [B. dåyal]
doealu ['dòyālū] (adj) *kind-hearted*   [B. dåyalu < S. dayālu]
doea-maea ['dòyāmāyā] (n) *compassion*   = **doea** + **maea**
dofa ['dòfā] (n) *instalment; occasion; point* | amra tin dofa ren dici – *we have paid three instalments of rent* : tain kok dofa aicla – *he came a few times* : fac dofa dabi – *a five-point demand* : **dofae dofae** – *in instalments*   [A. duf¿a – *push; spurt; instance*]
dofon ['dòfòn] (n) *burial*   = **dafon**
doi [dòı] (n) *yogurt*   [B. dåi]
doinik ['dòınīk] (adj) daily   [B. dåinik < S. dainika]
doijjo ['dòıj-jò] (n) *patience* | cacar doijjo kom – *uncle has little patience* : amar doijjor sima ace – *there are limits to my patience* : **doijjo dor-** – *be patient* : afne doijjo dorta oiba – *you'll just have to be patient*   [B. dhoirjå < S. dhairya]
doijjosil ['dòıj-jò-šīl] (adj) *patient*   [B. dhoirjåsil < S. dhairyašīla]
doinik ['dòınīk] (adj/adv) *daily*   [B. doinik < S. dainika]

doira¹ ['dòɪrā] (n) *sea* = **doria¹**
doira² (v adv) *having caught; holding* < **doria²**
dokkin ['dòk-kīn] (adj) *south; southern* | dokkin kuria – *South Korea* : dokkin muka cauka – *look in a southerly direction* ¶ **dokkin** (n) *the south* | dokkin kun dik? – *which way is south?* : **dokkine** – *in the south; to the south* : amrar barir dokkine gaŋ ace – *there is a river to the south of our homestead* [B. dåkkin < S. dakśiṇa]
dol [dòl] (n) *group; gang; political party* | ek dol kamla – *a gang of workmen* : hurutar dol aice – *a throng of children have arrived* : hacinar dol bute fas oice – *Hasina's party won the election* [B. dål]
dola¹ ['dòlā] (adj) *white* | dola manus – *a white person* : dola roŋgor kafor – *white cloth; a white sari* [B. dhåla < O. dhavala]
dola² (v adj) *gathered together; assembled* | **dola o-/dola oi ja-** – *be assembled* : hokoloe dola oicoin – *everyone gathered in a crowd* : bout foesa dola oi gece – *a lot of money has been amassed* : **dola kor-/dola kori rak-** – *gather together; assemble* : hurutare dola kori raktam oimu – *we must gather the children together* < **dol-**
dolan ['dòlān] (n) *edifice; big building* | tara dolan tuler – *they are erecting a large building* : fac tola dolan – *a five storeyed building* [P. dalān – *entrance hall*]
dolil ['dòlīl] (n) *legal deed; document* | jagar dolil – *land deeds* : dolilo cain lagbo – *a signature is needed on the document* [A. dalīl – *evidence*]
dom [dòm] (n) *breath* | **dom bond oe/dom bond oi jae** – *breathing becomes difficult* : gorome amar dom bond oi gecil – *I was suffocating in the heat* : **dom lo-** – *draw breath; take a breather* : caci dom loita farra na – *aunt cannot breathe properly* : dom louka! – *pause for breath; wait a minute!* [P. dam]
domka- ['dòm-χā] (v) *scold* [B. dhåmka-]
domok ['dòmòχ] (n) *scolding* | **domok de-** – *give a scolding; scold* : tain hurutare domok dira – *he's ticking off the children* [B. dhåmåk]
don [dòn] (n) *wealth; precious child* | tara bout donor malik – *they own considerable wealth* : tumi amar janor don – *you are the treasure of my heart* : **don kor-/don kori le-** – *amass wealth; get rich* [B. dhån < S. dhana]
don-doulot ['dòn-dôulòt] (n) *wealth* = **don** + **doulot**
doni ['dònī] (adj) *wealthy* [B. dhåni < S. dhanī]
dono ['dònò] (int) *anyway* | tain auka dono – *anyway, wait till he comes*
doŋso ['dòŋ-šò] (n) *destruction* | **doŋso kor-** – *destroy; ruin; waste* : tar nijor bobissot doŋso korer – *he is ruining his own future* [B. dhåŋså < S. dhvaŋśa]
dor [dòr] (n) *price* | aij calir dor koto? – *what's the price of rice today?* : atar dor boli gece – *the price of chapati flour has gone up* [B. dår]
dor- (v) *catch; seize; take hold of; hold; pick up; take; include; suppose; decipher; charge* | jelera mac dore – *the fishermen catch fish* : fulise cur dorce – *the police have caught a thief* : amra noe·tar bac cormu – *we shall catch the nine o'clock bus* : daktorre dortam fari na – *I can't get hold of the doctor* : rimut ulto dorcoin – *you're holding the remote control upside-down* : dorouka! – *here, hold this; take this!* : doroin na jen! – *don't touch it!* : taire culo dorcil – *he grabbed her by the hair* : fon dorouka – *pick up the phone; answer the phone* : keu dore na – *nobody is answering (the phone)* : tara hou kota dorce – *they have seized on that particular point* : isabor maje bieti dorclam na – *we hadn't included VAT in the calculation* : dorouka, fulis ailo – *and just suppose the police arrived* : tain dorcoin, amra ino nai – *he is assuming we aren't here* : cacar leka dortam fari na – *I can't make out uncle's handwriting* : tara kofir lagi besi dorce – *they've charged too much for the coffee* : betae kam dorce – *the fellow's taken a job* : tain ukil dorta – *he wants to engage a lawyer* : allar nam dorouka – *take God's name; say "bismillah"* : he dibar nam-u dore na – *he doesn't even mention the idea of paying up* : he cigret kani dorce – *he's started smoking cigarettes* : tain ruj ana dorcoin – *he's taken to coming here every day* : jani, tara dus dorbo – *I know they're going to find fault* : tain fot dorcoin – *he has got on his way* : **dore** (impersonal) – *fits; hurts; catches; takes hold* : ou garit coe·jon dore – *six people fit in this*

vehicle; this vehicle holds six : moulobi bajaror maje sirimoŋgol dore – *Srimangal is included in Moulvibazar* : bet ino dorto nae – *the bed won't fit here* : amar matat dore – *it hurts in my head; my head aches* : gaco fata dorce – *leaves have sprouted on the trees* : foesa gaco dore na – *money doesn't grow on trees* : goro aguin dorcil – *fire took hold in the house; the house caught fire* : bac ino dore na – *the bus doesn't stop here* : **dora for-** – *be caught; be found* : dakait dora force – *the robbers have been caught* : kicu bul dora force – *some mistakes have come to light* : **dora de-** – *allow oneself to be caught* : kuttae dora dee na – *the dog won't let itself be caught* : tain dora dein na – *he is evasive*   [B. dhår-] Note: A verb with many idiomatic uses. The compound form **dori le-** (q.v.) can be substituted in many contexts.

dora ['dòrā] (v n) *catching; taking; aching* | mac dora oto suja nae – *catching fish isn't that easy* : kam dora bala – *it's good to take employment* : amar faue dora suru oi gece – *my leg has started to ache* : mata dora – *headache* : komore dora – *low back pain* : bate dora – *rheumatic pain*   < **dor-**

dora- (v) *cause to catch; cause to take; cause to fit* | daroga ek din na ek din doraiba tare – *the police inspector will have him arrested some day or other* : fuainte citi-cearo aguin doraice – *the boys made the settee catch fire* : hou tebul ino dorail jaito nae – *that table can't be made to fit in here*   [B. dhåra-]

doraj ['dòrāz] (adj) *wide; deep (voice)*   [P. darāz]

dorbar ['dòr-bār] (n) *quarrel* | **dorbar lage** – *quarreling starts* : tarar maje dorbar lagce – *a quarrel has broken out among them* : **dorbar laga-** – *instigate a quarrel* : he cae dorbar lagaito – *he wants to spark off a quarrel* : **dorbar kor-** – *quarrel* : furinte kali dorbar kore – *the girls are forever squabbling*   [P. darbār – *royal court*]

dorbari ['dòr-bārī] (adj) *quarrelsome* = **dorbar** + **-i** ²

dorbes [dòr-'béš] (n) *religious mendicant*   [P. darvīš]

dorga ['dòr-gā] (n) *tomb-shrine* | sajalalor dorga – *the shrine of Hazrat Shah Jalal (in Sylhet)*   [P. dargāh – *threshold*]

dori ¹ ['dòrī] (n) *twine; string*   [B. dåṛi]

dori ² (v adv) *having caught; holding; including* | mac dori kai licoin – *having caught a fish, he ate it* : caca lati dori atoin – *uncle walks holding a stick* : afnare dori cair·jon – *four people including you* : dui afta dori – *for two whole weeks* : **nam dori** – *by name* : tane nam dori daki na – *I never address him by name* : **akta dori** – *suddenly* : amar akta dori keal oice – *I suddenly realised* : **dori le-** – *catch; seize; take hold of; hold; take; suppose* : fulise dori lice tare – *the police have caught him* : rossi dori louka – *hold onto the rope* : tai kam dori lice – *she has taken a job* : dori louka, aij meg dilo – *suppose it rains today*   < **dor-**

doria ¹ ['dòrīā] (n) *sea; wide river*   [P. daryā]

doria ² (v adv) *having caught; holding; including* | he mac doria carce – *after catching the fish he let it go* : tain lati doria atoin – *he walks holding a stick; he walks with a stick* : cacire doria cair·jon – *four people including auntie* : tin afta doria – *for three whole weeks*   < **dor-**

dorja ['dòr-jā, 'dòr-zā] (n) *door* = **doroja**

dorjon ['dòr-jòn, 'dòr-zòn] (n) *dozen*   [E.]

dorkar ['dòr-χār] (n) *need* | dorkar kita? – *what's the need? what's the use?* : dorkar nae – *there's no need* : dorkaror somoe – *in time of need; when necessary* : **bina dorkare** – *without need; unnecessarily* : **(kar)(kuntar) dorkar (ace)** – *one has need (of something)* : somoer dorkar – *one needs time* : amar tebulor dorkar – *I need a table* : afnar kunta dorkar ni? – *do you need anything?* : amar jaoar dorkar – *I need to go* : tumar jikaibar dorkar acil – *there was a need for you to ask; you should have asked* : kunta koibar dorkar nae – *there's no need to say anything* : maje maje cuttir dorkar oe – *sometimes one needs a break* : amar foesar dorkar oito fare – *I may need some money* : **dorkar oile** – *if needs be; if necessary* : dorkar oile fon korba – *you can phone me if necessary* : **(kar) loge dorkar take** – *one needs to see (someone)* : bocor loge amar dorkar – *I need to see the boss* : afnar loge amar bises dorkar acil – *I really did need to have a word with you* : **dorkar fore** – *a need arises* :

akta ita-otar dorkar fore – *one suddenly finds oneself in need of this or that* : tumar kafror dorkar forto fare – *you may need some clothes* [P. darkār]

dorkari ['dòr-χārī] (adj) *necessary; essential; important* | dorkari kagoj-fotro – *essential documents* : ou basko bout dorkari – *this box is indispensable* [P. darkārī]

dorkast ['dòr-χāst] (n) *application* | **dorkast kor-** – *make an application; apply* : amra goror lagi dorkast korci – *we've applied for a house* [P. darkౖvāst]

dorkasto ['dòr-χāstò] (n) *application* = **dorkast**

dormo ['dòr-mò] (n) *religion* [B. dhårmå < S. dharma – *right way of life*]

dorod ['dòròd] (n) *compassion* [P. dard – *pain*]

doroja ['dòròja, 'dòròza] (n) *door* | doroja kula – *the door is open* : doroja kulo – *open the door* : doroja gocao – *open the door (to let someone in)* : doroja lagao – *close the door* : doroja atkao – *latch the door* [P. darvāza – *gate*]

doron ['dòròn] (n) *type; sort* | **doronor** – *type of; sort of* : ita kun doronor gulaf? – *what type of rose is this?* : tain ki doronor manus? – *what sort of person is he?* : nanan doronor fol – *various kinds of fruit* [B. dhårån]

dos [dòš] (n°) *ten* | dos din – *ten days* : dos·ta am – *ten mangoes* : dos·ta bajce – *ten o'clock has struck* : dos·jon – *ten people; the general public* : dos·jonor balar lagi – *for the good of the community; for everyone's benefit* [B. dås]

dostokot ['dòstòχòt] (n) *signature* | **dostokot de-** – *give one's signature; sign* : ou lanit dostokot deuka – *please sign on this line* [P. dast kౖat – *handwriting*]

doulot ['dôulòt] (n) *wealth* [P. daulat < A. daula – *fortune*]

doulotkana ['dôulòt-χāna] (n) *princely abode; home* | afnar doulotkana kunano? – *where is your (most honourable) home?* [P. daulat kౖāna – *treasury*]

dour ['dôur] (n) *running; hurrying; race* | kali dour – *incessant rush* : tain douror maje takoin – *he's always in a hurry* : caikel dour – *bicycle race* : gurar dour – *horse race* : **dour de-/dour di la-** – *run* : hurutae farko dour der – *the children are running around in the park* : dour di lao! – *run! hurry!* : **dour dia** – *by running; at the double* : tara dour dia aice – *they came running; they came at the double* : **dour mar-** – *start running; make a dash* : fuae akta dour marce – *the boy suddenly dashed off* [B. dourౖ]

dour- (vi) *run* | hurutae dourer – *the children are running* : dource! – *he's run away!* : **douria/douri** – *by running; at the double* : kila geclae? douria – *how did you get there? by running* : tara douri aice – *they came running* [B. dourౖa-]

douradouri ['dôurā-dôurī] (n) *running about* | **douradouri kor-** – *run around; rush about; be busy* < **dour-**

dristi ['drīštī] (n) *sight* [B. dristi < dŕsti]

druto ['drūtò] (adj) *speedy; fast* ¶ **druto** (adv) *rapidly; fast* | gari druto cole – the car is moving fast [B. drutå < S. druta]

du- (v) *wash* | afnar kafor duici – *I've washed your clothes* : tumar at duitae ni? – *do you want to wash your hands?* [B. dhu-]

dua¹ ['dūā] (v adj) *washed* | dua kafor – *washed clothes* : ota dua nae – *this one isn't washed* < **du-**

dua² (n) *prayer; blessing* | afnar duar borkote tain tik acoin – *thanks to your prayers she is all right* : hokolor duae bala aci – *I am well, by the blessings of all and sundry* : **dua kor-** – *say a prayer; pray* : amrar lagi dua koroin jen – *please pray for us* : dua·kan korba amar lagi – *do say a prayer for me* : **dua rak-** – *pray (for someone)* : tan lagi dua rakci – *I have made a prayer for her* : afne kila? jela dua rakcoin – *how are you? I'm just as you prayed for me to be* : **dua de-/dua di la-** – *pass on a blessing* : hurutare amar dua dio – *give the children my blessings* : **dua ne-** – *accept someone's blessing* : cacir dua nitae – *you're to accept aunt's blessings; aunt says to give you her blessings* [A. du¿ā']

dua-durud ['dūā-dūrūd] (n) *prayers* = **dua²** + **durud**

duar ['dūār] (n) *door* | duar kulo – *open the door* : duar gocao – *open the door (to let someone in)* : duar lagao – *close the door* : duar kato – *close the door* : duar atkao – *latch the door* : duar hokol somoe kula – *the door is always open* [B. duar < S. dvāra]

ɖucra ['ɖūs-rā] (adj) *other; different* | ɖucra gor – *another house* : ɖucra manus – *a different person* : ɖucra ek·jon – *somebody else* : ita ɖucra – *that's different* [H. ɖusrā – *second*]

ɖud [ɖūɖ] (n) *milk* | gabir ɖuɖ – *cow's milk* : cagir ɖuɖ – *goat's milk* : ɖuɖor baicca – *suckling child; baby* [B. ɖudh < O. dugdha]

ɖuɖala ['ɖūɖālā] (n) *milkman* = **ɖuɖ + -ala**

ɖuɖel ['ɖūɖɛl] (adj) *milch (cow)* | ɖuɖel gabi – *milch cow* : «gabi·ta oilo ɖuɖel» - *I smell a rat; there's more in it than meets the eye* [B. ɖuɖhel]

ɖufur ['ɖūfūr] (n) *midday; noon* [B. dupur < O. dviprahara]

ɖu·gca ['ɖūk-sā] (pron) *two (things)* = **ɖui + gaca**

ɖu·gu ['ɖūgū] (pron) *two (things or persons)* = **ɖui + gu** [1]

ɖugun ['ɖūgūn] (adv) *twice (in degree or extent)* | tain amar ɖugun boro – *he's twice as tall as me* : tumar ɖugun besi – *you have twice as much* [B. ɖuigun]

ɖuguna ['ɖūgūna] (adj) *doubled* | tin ɖuguna coe – *twice three is six*

ɖui ['ɖūī] (n°) *two; both* | ɖui furi – *two daughters* : ɖui kaf ca – *two cups of tea* : ɖui·ta enda – *two eggs* : ɖui·jon ɖaktor – *two doctors* : ɖui ato ɖorouka – *hold it in both hands* : ɖui tarik – *the second (of the month)* : ɖui lombor – *number two; the second* : **ɖui ek** – *about two* : ɖui ek mail – *a couple of miles* : **ɖui arai** – *about two; two and a bit* : ɖui arai gonta – *two hours or so* : ɖui so arai so – *two hundred or thereabouts* : **ɖui tin** – *two or three* : ɖui tin bar – *two or three times* : ɖui tin·ta aefol – *two or three apples* : **ɖui cair** – *two to four; a few* : ɖui cair·jon beti acla – *there were a handful of women there* [B. ɖui]

ɖuibar ['ɖūībār] (adv) *two times; twice* | tumare ɖuibar ɖakci – *I called you two times* : tain ɖuibar toga kaicoin – *he was cheated twice* = **ɖui + bar**

ɖui·jon ['ɖūīzòn] (pron) *two (persons)* | era koe·jon? ɖui·jon – *how many of them are there? two* : ino ɖui·jonor jaega ace – *there's room for two here*

ɖuinna ['ɖūīn-nıā] (n) *the world* = **ɖunia**

ɖui-o ['ɖūīò] (n°) *both* | ɖui-o fau – *both feet* : ɖui-o bar – *both times* : **ɖui-o·ta, ɖui-o·gu, ɖui-o·kan** – *both (things)* : ɖui-o·ta ek – *both are the same* : ɖui-o·kan amar – *they're both mine* : **ɖui-o·jon, ɖui-o·gu** – *both (persons)* : tara ɖui-o·jon ekmot – *they're both in agreement* : ami ɖui-o·gure ɖekci – *I saw both of them* = **ɖui + -o**

ɖui·ta ['ɖūītā] (pron) *two (things); two o'clock* | ou ɖui·ta tumar – *these two are yours* : jarjir ɖui·ta – *two each* : ɖui·ta oito fare – *it could be either of two things* : ɖui·ta bajce – *two has struck; it's two o'clock*

ɖujok ['ɖūzòχ] (n) *hell* [P. dozak̦]

ɖuk [ɖūk] (n) *pain* | **ɖuk lage** – *it hurts* : **ɖuk mile** – *it hurts* : tumar ɖuk mile ni? – *does it hurt (you)?* : **ɖuk ɖe-** – *cause pain; hurt* : amare ɖuk ɖio na – *don't hurt me* [B. ɖukh]

ɖuka ['ɖūkā] (n) *deception* | **ɖuka ɖe-** – *deceive* : tara ɖuka ɖice tumare – *they've tricked you; they've had you on* [B. ɖhoka]

ɖukabaji ['ɖūkābāzī] (n) *deception; trickery* | **ɖukabaji kor-** – *practise deception* : he majemaje ɖukabaji kore – *he sometimes pulls a fast one* = **ɖuka + -baji**

ɖukan ['ɖūkān] (n) *shop* | muɖir ɖukan – *grocery shop* : kaforor ɖukan – *clothing shop* : tara ɖukan korto – *they want to set up a shop* : tain bajaro ɖukan kulcoin – *he has opened a shop in the marketplace* [A. dukkān]

ɖu·kan ['ɖū χān] (pron) *two (things)* = **ɖui + kan** [2]

ɖukka- ['ɖūk-kā] (vi) *be painful; hurt* | ɖukkae ni? – *does it hurt?* : amar bukut ɖukkae – *it hurts in my chest; I feel a chest pain* < **ɖuk**

ɖukki ['ɖūk-kī] (adj) *wretched* [B. ɖukkhi < S. ɖuhkhī]

ɖukkit ['ɖūk-kīt] (adj) *disappointed; displeased; sorry* | ami tumar ufre ɖukkit – *I am disappointed with you* : ami ɖukkit – *I'm sorry* : **ɖukkit o-** – *be displeased; be offended* : afne ɖukkit oiba na – *please don't take offence* = **ɖukkito**

ɖukkito ['ɖūk-kitò] (adj) *disappointed* [B. ɖukkhitā < S. ɖuhkhita]

ɖukko ['ɖūk-kò] (n) *disappointment; regret* | ilagi ɖukko nae – *there's no regret for that; that doesn't matter* : **ɖukko lage** – *one feels regret* : cacir lagi amar jobor ɖukko lage – *I feel very sorry for auntie* : **ɖukko kor-** – *express regret; be dismayed* : baɖe tain ɖukko

korcoin – *afterwards he said how sorry he was* : ami ek jara ɖukko kori na – *I'm not in the least disappointed; I'm simply not bothered* [B. ɖukkhå < S. ɖuhkha]
ɖukko-kosto ['ɖūk-kò-χòštò] (n) *sorrow and pain* | ɖukke-koste amrar ɖin jar – *our days are passing in misery* : **ɖukko-kosto kor-** – *undergo suffering* : tara koto ɖukko-kosto korer – *what hardships they are enduring* = **ɖukko + kosto**
ɖul [ɖūl] (n) *pendant* | kanor ɖul – *earring* [B. ɖul]
ɖula ['ɖūlā] (n) *dust* [B. ɖhula]
ɖulabai ['ɖūlābāı] (n) *elder sister's husband* [H. ɖūlhā bhāi]
ɖuma [¹] ['ɖūmā] (n) *tail* [P. dum]
ɖuma [²] (n) *smoke; steam* | habon taki ɖuma bar or – *smoke is coming out of the oven* : «jino ɖuma hino aguin» – *where there's smoke, there's fire* [B. ɖhum < S. ɖhūma]
ɖun [ɖūn] (n) *trance; stupor* | gumor ɖun – *the fog of sleep; drowsiness* : **ɖun lage** – *one is entranced or stupefied* : gan huni tar ɖun lagce – *he's got carried away by the music he's listening to* [H. ɖhun]
ɖunɖ [ɖūnɖ] (n) *mental conflict; worry; care* | tain ɖunɖor maje – *she is in a quandary; she is worried* : he ɖunɖo nae – *he's not bothered; he doesn't give a damn* : tain ek ɖunɖe ses – *he's overcome with worry* [B. ɖånɖå < S. dvanɖva – *dichotomy*]
ɖunɖa [¹] ['ɖūn-ɖā] (n) *quarreling* [H. ɖunɖ < O. ɖuvaɳɖva]
ɖunɖa [²] (n) *searching* [H. ɖhunɖ]
ɖunɖaɖundi [¹] ['ɖūn-ɖā-ɖūn-ɖī] (n) *quarreling* = **ɖunɖa** [¹]
ɖunɖaɖundi [²] (n) *searching* = **ɖunɖa** [²]
ɖunia ['ɖūnıa] (n) *(this) world* | aijkur ɖunia – *today's world* : ɖunia ostaii – *this world is transitory* : ɖuniar maje ɖekci na – *I've never seen such a thing anywhere* : **ɖuniar** – *of the whole world; vast; countless* : ɖuniar kam baki – *there's a lot of work still to do* : ɖuniar manus aicoin – *ever so many people came* [A. dunyā – *nether zone*]
ɖuniaɖar ['ɖūnıāɖār] (n) *person of this world; man of the world* [P. dunyādār]
ɖuniaɖari ['ɖūnıāɖārī] (n) *worldly affairs; everyday life* [P. dunyādārī]
ɖunniti ['ɖūn-nītī] (n) *corruption* = **ɖurniti**
ɖur [ɖūr] (n) *distance* | on taki london bakka ɖur – *from here to London is a great distance; London is a long way from here* : ɖur taki ɖekci afnare – *I saw you from a distance* : **ɖuroe** – *at a distance; far off* : caca ɖuroe takoin – *uncle lives a long way away* : **ɖuror** – *of the distance; distant* : ɖuror faar – *distant hills* : ami ɖuror lagi jai na – *I don't go, because of the distance* [B. ɖur < O. ɖūra]
ɖurbol ['ɖūrbòl] (adj) *without strength; weak* [B. ɖurbål < S. ɖurbala]
ɖurbolota ['ɖūrbòlòtā] (n) *weakness* [B. ɖurbålåta < S. ɖurbalatā]
ɖur-ɖuran ['ɖūr-ɖūrān] (adj) *far off* [P. ɖūr darāz – *distant*]
ɖurgotona ['ɖūr-gòtònā] (n) *mishap; accident* [B. ɖurghåtåna < S. ɖurghatanā]
ɖurgoti ['ɖūr-gòtī] (n) *plight; adverse situation* | ou ɖurgoti tarar – *that's the unfortunate state they're in* [B. ɖurgåti < S. ɖurgati]
ɖurniti ['ɖūr-nītī] (n) *corruption* [B. ɖurniti < S. ɖurnīti – *bad policy*]
ɖuro ['ɖūrò] (int) *get away with you!* [P. ɖūr bāš]
ɖuroe ['ɖūròy] (adv) *far away* | tara ɖuroe take – *they live far away* < **ɖur**
ɖurud ['ɖūrūd] (n) *prayer* [P. darūd – *greeting; praise*] Note: Specifically, a prayer for the Prophet Muhammad.
ɖus [ɖūš] (n) *fault; defect; transgression* | matar ɖus – *mental defect; insanity* : tar matar fura ɖus – *he's completely bonkers* : cokkur ɖus – *something wrong with the eyes* : kanor ɖus – *defective hearing* : cii! ɖus! – *tut-tut! you shouldn't do that!* : amar ɖus nae – *it's not my fault* : baɳle tumar ɖus – *it will be your fault if it breaks* : he tar ɖus mani lice – *he has admitted he was to blame* : **ɖus ɖor-** – *find fault* : cacae amar ɖus ɖoroin kali – *uncle keeps finding fault with me* : **ɖus ɖeka-** – *point out faults; criticize* [B. ɖos < S. ɖośa]
ɖus- [ɖūš] (v) *attribute fault (to); blame* | afnare kanoka ɖusbo – *they will blame you for no reason* = **ɖusa-**

dusa- ['ḍūšā] (v) *attribute blame (to); blame* | tain hokol somoe amare ḍusain – *he always puts the blame on me* [B. ḍosa-]
dusaruf ['ḍūšārūf] (n) *laying of blame* | **dusaruf kor-** – *censure; criticise* : tare ḍusaruf kori lab nae – *there's no point in criticising him* [B. ḍosarop < S. ḍośāropa]
dusi ['ḍūšī] (adj) *blameworthy* [B. ḍosi < S. ḍośī]
dusmon ['ḍūš-mòn] (n) *enemy* [P. dušman]
dusmoni ['ḍūš-mònī] (n) *enmity* [P. dušmanī]
dusta ['ḍūš-tā] (adj) *malevolent; evil* [B. ḍustå < S. ḍuśta]
dustu ['ḍūš-tū] (adj) *mischievous; naughty* [B. ḍustu]
dust [ḍūst] (n) *friend* [P. dost]
dusti ['ḍūstī] (n) *friendship* [P. dostī]
dutala ['ḍūtālā] (adj) *two-storeyed* = **dui** + **-tala**

e

e¹ [ɛ́:] (int) *hey!*

e² (pron) *this; he; she; it* | e ke? – *who's this?* : e jane na – *he doesn't know* : **er** – *of this; of him; of her; of it* : er mane kita? – *what's the meaning of this?* : er nam Runa – *her name is Runa* : **ere** – *(to) this; (to) him; (to) her* : ere koin na jen – *don't tell him* [B. e]

ebla ['ɛblā] (adv) *now* | roid utce ebla – *now the sun has come out* : ebla jaitae gi faro – *you may go now* : **eblaku** – *now* : eblaku meg dibo – *now it's going to rain* : **eblakur** – *of now; present* : eblakur cinta – *worries of the present moment*   = **ei + bala**

ebo ['ɛbò] (adv) *still now; yet* | dadi ebo acoin – *grandmother is still living* : caca ebo aicoin na – *uncle hasn't arrived yet*   = **ebu**

ebotiri ['ɛbòtīrī] (adv) *still now; yet* | caci ebotiri roicoin – *auntie is still here* : tara ebotiri gece na – *they haven't gone yet*   = **ebo + tiri²**

ebu ['ɛbū] (adv) *still now; yet*   [H. abhi]

ebul ['ɛbūl] (adv) *now* | ebul suru kora jauk – *let's make a start now*   = **ei + bul**

eci ['ɛsī] (n) *sneezing* | **eci de-** – *sneeze* : **eci mar-** – *sneeze*   [B. haⁿci]

ecii ['ɛsī:] (int) *ugh! yuck!*

edig ['ɛdīg] (n) *this direction; this side* | **edige** – *in this direction; this side; this way* : edige auka – *come this way* : edige jaega ace – *there's room on this side*   = **edik**

edik ['ɛdīk] (n) *this direction; this side*   = **ei + dik**

edik-hodik ['ɛdīk-hòdīk] (n) *this way and that*   = **edik + hodik**

eflai ['ɛflāī] (n) *application* | amar eflai goce na – *they won't accept my application* : **eflai kor-/eflai kori le-** – *make an application; apply* : caca entir lagi eflai korcoin – *uncle has applied for entry clearance* : joldi eflai kori louka – *hurry up and apply*   [E.]

egaro ['ɛgàrò] (n°) *eleven*   [B. egarā]

egeinste [ɛg'ɛɪn-stɛ] (adv) *in opposition to; against* | tain amar egeinste kara oicoin – *he's running against me (in the election)*   [E.]

egna ['ɛg-nā] (adj) *one's own* | amrar egna manus – *our own kith and kin* : «egna taki begna bala» – *strangers are more reliable than relatives*   [P. yagāna]

ehe ['ɛ́-hɛ́:] (int) *oh, drat it!* | ehe, bat joli gece! – *drat it, the rice has burned!*

ehudi ['ɛhūdī] (adj) *Jewish* ¶ **ehudi** (n) *Jewish person; Jew*   [A. yahūdī]

ei¹ ['ɛ́ī] (int) *oy!* | ei fua! – *(to boy) oy, you!* : ei beta! – *watch it, mate!*   (impolite)

ei² (adj) *this* | ei fira tik oibo – *this time it'll be all right* : **ei·kan** – *this (one)* : **ei·ta** – *this (one)* : ei·ta dekouka – *just look at this* ¶ **ei** (pron) *this* | ei dekouka – *just look at this* : ei na sei na boke – *he goes on about this, that and the other*   cf **e²**

eiia ['ɛɪyā] (n) *Yahya; John*   [A. yahyā]

eije ['ɛɪjɛ́, 'ɛɪzɛ́] (int) *look! see here!* | amar cosma kuae? eije! – *where are my spectacles? they're here, look!*   = **ei + je**

ei·kan ['ɛɪχān] (pron) *this one; this*   = **ei + kan²**

ein [ɛɪn] (pron) *this (person); he; she* (respectful) | ein amar bai – *this is my brother* : ein bala manus – *she's a good person* : **enar** – *of this person; his; her* : enar nam kita? – *what's his name?* : enar samne ubauka – *stand in front of him* : **enre** – *to him; to her; him; her* : enre diram – *I'm giving it to her* : age dekci na enre – *I haven't seen him before* : **enain** – *these people; they* : enain amar aittio – *these people are relatives of mine* : enaintore jikauka – *ask them*   [B. ini]   Note: **ein** is the respectful form of **e²**.

ei·ta ['ɛɪtā] (pron) *this one; this*

ejmali ['ɛzmālī] (adj) *jointly held (property)*   [A. ijmālī]

ek [ɛχ] (n) *the number one* | ek jug ek oilo dui – *one plus one makes two* : ekor bade dui – *after one comes two* : **eke** – *one* (instrumental) : tin eke tin – *three ones make three* : «eke fare am, onne hota kae» - *one picks the mango, another gets to eat it* : **eke onnere** – *(to) each other* : tara eke onnere dusar – *they are blaming each other* : amra eke onnere cini – *we know each other* ¶ **ek** (adj) *one; united; the same; alone* | ek butol dud – *one bottle of*

73

milk : amra hokoloe ek – *we are all as one* : ɖui-o·tae ek – *both are the same* : ek kota – *one and the same point; the same thing* : ek allae jane – *God only knows* : ek london cara milto nae – *it won't be available except in London (alone)* : **ek·ta, ek·kan, ek·gaca** – *one (thing)* : ek·kan amar, ek·kan afnar – *one for me, one for you* : **ek·gu** – *one (thing or person)* : **ek·jon** – *one person* : meman aicla, ek·jon roicoin – *visitors came, and one has stayed* : **ek ek** – *each* : ek ek kofo ɖuɖ ɖeuka – *put some milk in each cup* : **ek ek·ta** – *each one* : ek ek·tar ɖam fac fon – *they cost five pounds each* : taintain ek ek·jon biɖɖan – *each one of them in educated* : **ek·ta ek·ta kori** – *one by one* : tain ek·ta ek·ta kori kaicoin – *she ate them one by one* : ek·jon ek·jon kori hamaira – *they're coming in one by one* [B. ek]
eka ['ɛҳā] (adj) *lone; single* | eka manus – *a lone person; a single person* : eka ek ma – *a lone mother* : ɖaɖi boro eka – *great-aunt is very lonesome* ¶ **eka** (adv) *alone; on one's own* | ami eka farmu – *I can manage on my own* : eka takte dor kore – *it's frightening to be alone* : hokoloe gecla, na afne eka? – *did everyone go, or only you?* [B. eka]
ekan ['ɛҳān] (pron) *one (thing)* = **ek·kan**
ekanno ['ɛҳān-nò] (n°) *fifty-one* [B. ekannå]
ekanobboi ['ɛҳanòb-bòı] (n°) *ninety-one* [B. ekanobbåi]
ekanto ['ɛҳān-tò] (adj) *particular; private* ¶ **ekanto** (adv) *particularly* | tara ekanto gorib – *they really are very poor* [B. ekantå < S. ekānta – *a solitary place; a sole purpose*]
ekasi ['ɛҳāšī] (n°) *eighty-one* [B. ekasi]
ekattoir ['ɛҳāt-tòır] *seventy-one* [B. ekattår]
ekaunt ['ɛkāunt] (n) *(bank) account* | tan alaɖa ekaunt ace – *she has a separate account* : **ekaunt kor-** – *set up an account* : **ekaunt kul-** – *open an account* : tain noea ekaunt kulta – *he wants to open a new account* [E.]
ekbar ['ɛҳ-bār] (adv) *once* | ami ekbar geclam – *I went there once* : **ekbarku** – *once* : tain ekbarku barmiɲam aicla – *he came to Birmingham once* = **ek + bar**
ekbarta ['ɛҳ-bār-ta] (adv) *one time; for once* | afne ekbarta aia ɖeki jaiba – *you must come and visit us one day* = **ekbar + -ta** [2]
ekcallis ['ɛҳ-sāl-līš] (n°) *forty-one* [B. ekcållis]
ekcor ['ɛҳ-sòr] (adv) *a lot* [P. yaksar – *altogether*]
ekɖin ['ɛҳ-ɖīn] (n/adv) *one day; someday* | caci ekɖin bala, ekɖin bemar – *aunt is well one day, ill the next* : ami ekɖin jaimu beranit – *I shall go for a visit someday* = **ek + ɖin**
ekɖinku ['ɛҳ-ɖīn-kū] (n/adv) *one day; someday* | tane bajaro ɖekci ekɖinku – *I saw him in the marketplace one day* : **ekɖinkur** – *of one day; concerning one day* : caca ekɖinkur lagi roicla – *uncle stayed for one day* = **ekɖin + ku**
ekɖom ['ɛҳ-ɖòm] (adv) *altogether; completely; entirely* | ekɖom foca – *totally rotten* : ami ekɖom baɖ ɖi laice – *I've given it up altogether* [P. yak dam – *one moment*]
ekebare ['ɛҳɛbārɛ] (adv) *altogether; completely; entirely* | fua·ta ekebare baɖ – *the boy is altogether ruined* : **ekebare nae** – *not existing at all* : cail ekebare nae – *there's absolutely no rice at all* : tar buɖɖi ekebare nae na – *he's not altogether without intelligence* < **ekbar**
ekere ['ɛҳɛrɛ] (adv) *altogether; completely; entirely* | gor·ta ekere kali – *the house is totally empty* : ekere ses kora lagbo – *it must be finished of completely* = **ekebare**
ek·gca ['ɛk-ksā] (pron) *one (thing)* = **ek + gaca**
ek·gu ['ɛg-gū] (pron) *one (thing); one person* (not respectful) = **ek + gu** [1]
ekin ['ɛkīn] (n) *belief; faith; confidence* | tan ufre amar ekin ace – *I have faith in him* : amar ekin oice na abu – *I'm not yet confident* [A. yaqīn]
ekjara ['ɛҳ-zārā] (n/adv) *a small amount; a bit* | ekjara lobon faici – *I've found a tiny bit of salt* : ekjara bissas kori na – *I don't believe it at all* [B. ek + A. ðarra – *particle*]
ek·jon ['ɛҳ-jòn, 'ɛҳ-zòn] (pron) *one (person)* = **ek + jon**
ek·kan ['ɛҳ-ҳān] (pron) *one (thing)* = **ek + kan** [2]
ekkan ['ɛk-kān] (n) *one place* | **ekkan kor-** – *gather together* : tumar hokolti ekkan koro – *gather all your stuff together* = **ek + kan** [3]

ekkano ['ɛk-kānò] (adv) *in one place; somewhere* | kagjain ekkano torakouka – *keep the papers together in one place* : ami jani, ekkano toiclam – *I'm sure I put it somewhere* < **ekkan**

ekkere ['ɛk-kɛrɛ] (adv) *altogether; completely; entirely* = **ekere**

ekla ['ɛχ-la] (adv) *alone* | tain ekla takoin – *he lives on his own* : ami ekla korci – *I did it all by myself* [B. ekla]

eklaga ['ɛχ-lāgā] (adj) *adjacent; consecutive* | amrar ɖui gor eklaga – *our houses are next door to each other* : eklaga tin ɖin meg ɖice – *it rained for three days in succession* = **ek + laga**

eklaguli ['ɛχ-lāgūlī] (adv) *alone* | afne eklaguli kita koroin? – *what do you do, all on your own?* : tain eklaguli aicoin – *he came on his own* = **ekla**

eklakan ['ɛχ-lāχān] (adv) *in the same state* | tara ɖui bai eklakan – *both brothers are the same* : amra eklakan kafor loici – *we bought the same kind of cloth* : tara eklakan mate – *they speak in the same way* : afne kila acoin? eklakan – *how are you? so-so* = **ek + lakan**

ekloge ['ɛχ-lògɛ] (adv) *together* | tara ekloge take – *they live together* : ekloge tin·jon aicoin – *three of them came together* = **ek + loge**

ekmaɖrir ['ɛχ-mādɽīr] (adj) *having the same mother* | tara ekmaɖrir bai – *they are full brothers* [P. yakmādrī]

ekmot ['ɛχ-mòt] (adv) *in one mind; in agreement* | amra ɖui-o·jone ekmot – *we are both of the same opinion* : tara ekmot oice – *they have reached an agreement* [B. ekmåt]

ekmoto ['ɛχ-mòtò] (adv) *in the same state; so-so* = **ek + moto**

ekoɖ ['ɛχòɖ] (adj) *about one* | ekoɖ ajar – *about one thousand* : ekoɖ afta – *about a week* : ekoɖ fon – *a pound or so* [B. ek-aɖh – *one or half of one*]

ekoi ['ɛχòı] (adj) *one and the same* | ekoi kagoj – *the very same paper* : ekoi manus – *the same person* : ekoi kota – *the same thing* : ekoi ɖin – *the same day* : tara ɖui-o bai ekoi – *both of those brothers are the same* [B. ek-i]

ekois ['ɛχòıš] (n°) *twenty-one* [B. ekus]

ekotro ['ɛχòtrò] (adj/adv) *united; unified; commensal* | hokol bai ekotro – *all the brothers live together* : **ekotro kor-/ekotro kori le-** – *place together; gather into one place* : kagoj hokol ekotro kori lici – *I've gathered all the papers together* [B. ekåtrå < S. ekatra]

ekou ['ɛχòu] (adj) *one and the same* = **ek + -u**

ekruka ['ɛχ-rūχā] (adj) *selfish; obstinate* [P. yak ruḳa – *one faced*]

eksosti ['ɛχ-šòstī] (n°) *sixty-one* = **eksotti**

eksotti ['ɛχ-šòt-tī] (n°) *sixty-one* [B. eksåtti]

ek·ta ['ɛχ-tā] (pron) *one (thing)* | ek·tar baɖe ar ek·ta – *one thing after another* : ek·tar ufre ar ek·ta – *one thing on top of another* : ek·ta cai suɖu – *I only want one* : ek·ta ek·ta kori – *one by one* = **ek + ta**

ektu ['ɛχ-tū] (adj/adv) *a bit* | ektu santi ɖeuka – *please give me a bit of peace* : ektu bar cai – *let's wait a bit* [B. ektu]

ektuk ['ɛχ-tūk] (pron) *a bit* | ektuk roice – *a little bit is left* : ektuk ɖeuka – *give me a bit* ¶ **ektuk** (adv) *a bit* | ektuk barce – *it's grown a bit* : aoaj ektuk komao – *turn down the volume a bit* : tain kila? ektuk bala – *how is he? a bit better* = **ektuku**

ek·tuku ['ɛχ-tūkū] (pron) *one piece; a bit* = **ek + tuku**

ekta ['ɛχ-tā] (pron) *one (thing); something* | ino ekta ace – *there's one here* : afnare ekta koitam – *I want to tell you something* = **ek + -ta** ²

ektala ['ɛχ-tālā] (adj) *one storeyed* | ektala gor – *a house with one storey only* = **ek + -tala**

ektil ['ɛχ-tīl] (adv) *a little bit* = **ek + til**

ektis ['ɛχ-tīš] (n°) *thirty-one* [B. ektris]

ektisa ['ɛχ-tīša] (adj) *(month) having thirty-one days* = **ek + tisa**

ektorofa ['ɛχ-tòròfa] (adj) *one-sided; partisan; biassed* | joje ektorofa rae ɖicoin – *the judge delivered a biassed judgment* ¶ **ektorofa** (adv) *in a monopolistic manner* | tara ektorofa kai lito – *they want to consume it all themselves* : tain ektorofa ek gonta matcoin – *he talked for an hour without giving anyone else a chance* [P. yak tarafa]

elac ['ɛlās] (n) *cardamom* [B. elaci]
elau ['ɛlāu] (adj) *allowed; authorized* | ita elau nae – *that's not allowed* : **elau kor-** – *allow* : ino tara mubail elau kore na – *they don't allow mobile phones here* [E.]
emdi ['ɛm-d̄ī] (adv) *this way* = **emnedi**
emla ['ɛm-la] (adv) *in such a way* = **emola**
emne ['ɛm-nɛ] (adv) *this way; as it is; in any case; for no reason* | emne bala – *it's best the way it is* : tara emne-u aibo – *they'll come in any case* : kitar lagi jikaira? emne-u – *why do you ask?* oh, *for no particular reason* : ota emne-u oice – *it happened just like that, quite by chance* < **emon**
emne-hemne ['ɛm-nɛ-hɛm-nɛ] (adv) *this way and that* = **emne + hemne**
emnedi ['ɛm-nɛd̄ī] (adv) *this way* | eije, emnedi jauka – *look, go this way* = **emne + dia**
emola ['ɛmòlā] (adj) *such* | emola beakuf dekci na – *I've never seen such an idiot* ¶ **emola** (adv) *in such a way; thus; like this* | emola baŋgo – *fold it like this* : ami emola korci – *I went like this (demonstrating a gesture)* = **emon lakan**
emon ['ɛmòn] (adj) *such* | emon kota oito fare na – *such a thing cannot be* : emon mair oibo – *there will be such a big battle* [B. emån]
emontike ['ɛmòn-tīkɛ] (adv) *in such a way* | emontike coluk – *let it carry on just like that* : emontike mato kene? – *why are you talking like that?*
emrika ['ɛm-rīkā] (n) *America* | emrikar manus – *an American* : emrikar cail – *American rice* [E.]
enain ['ɛnāın] (pron) *these people; they* | enain amar mamain – *these are my maternal uncles* : **enaintor** – *of these people; their* : enaintor bari catok – *their home is in Chatak* : **enaintore** – *these people; them* (objective) : enaintore cini na – *I don't know them* < **ein**
enar ['ɛnār] (pron adj) *of this person; his; her* < **ein**
enda ['ɛndā] (n) *egg* [H. andā < O. anda]
enre ['ɛnrɛ] (pron) *to this person; (to) him; (to) her* < **ein**
enti ['ɛntī] (n) *entry clearance; visa* | tara enti dice na taire – *they haven't granted her a visa* : tain enti fai licoin – *he has obtained his entry clearance* : cacar enti oi gece – *uncle has got entry clearance* : tain daka gia enti tulta oiba – *she'll have to go to Dhaka to collect her visa* [E.]
entain ['ɛntāın] (pron) *these people; they* = **ein + tain**
eo ['ɛò] (pron) *this too* = **eu**
eota ['ɛòtā] (pron) *this too* = **euta**
er [ɛr] (pron adj) *of this; of him; of her* | er karon kita? – *what's the cause of this / the reason for this?* : er baf daktor – *this one's father is a doctor* < **e**
era ['ɛrā] (pron) *these people; they* | era mucolman – *these people are Muslims* : (as an indication of plurality) malik era kuae? – *where are the proprietors?* : fulis era tukar – *the police are searching* : **erar** – *of these people; their* : erar mat buji na – *I don't understand their language* : **erare** – *(to) these people; (to) them* : erare deuka – *give it to these people* : erare cinoin ni? – *do you know them?* < **e**²
ere¹ ['ɛrɛ́] (int) *hey!* | ere, huno! – *hey, listen!* : ere nu! – *look, here it is!*
ere² (pron) *(to) this; (to) him; (to) her* | ere ditam cai na – *I don't want to give it to this person* : ere cinoin ni? – *do you know him?* < **e**²
etec ['ɛtɛs] (n) *attestation* | diglaresono etec lage – *attestation is required on an affidavit* : **etec de-** – *attest; authenticate; countersign* : fotut ke etec dicoin? – *who has countersigned the photograph?* [E.]
etim ['ɛtīm] (n) *orphan* [A. yatīm]
etimkana ['ɛtīmχānā] (n) *orphanage* [P. yatimḵāna]
eto ['ɛtò] (adj/adv) *so much; so many* | eto deri? – *(why are you) so late?* : eto din kuae acla? – *where were you all this time?* : eto besi anoin na jen – *please don't bring so much* : eto manus aicoin! – *so many people have come!* [B. etā]

etotuk ['ɛtòtūk] (pron) *as much as this; so much* | etotuk kaoa jaito nae – *it won't be possible to eat this much* : tain etotuk bujta acla – *he should have realised as much* : etotuk cai na – *I don't want so much*   = **eto + tuk**

etotuku ['ɛtòtūkū] (adj) *as much as this; so much* | etotuku bat – *as much rice as this* : etotuku somoe – *so much time* ¶ **etotuku** (pron) *as much as this; so much* | etotuku boitam kila? – *how can we carry this much?*   = **eto + tuku**

etto ['ɛt-tò] (adj/adv) *so very much* | etto manus! – *so-o many people!* : etto boro beiman! – *such a great scoundrel!*   = **eto**

eu [1] ['ɛū] (pron) *this too* | eu tik – *it's true, indeed*   = **i + -u**

eu [2] (adv) *still now; yet* | eu coler befsa – *the business is still running* : eu faici na – *I haven't received it yet*   = **ebu**

euta ['ɛūtā] (pron) *this too* | tara euta nito gi – *they want to take this too* : euta afnar – *this one is also yours*   = **eu + -ta** [2]

f

fa- [fã] (v) *get; receive; find; obtain; win; be owed; recall; feel* | afne amar citi faicla ni? – *did you receive my letter?* : tain tin so fon tolof fain – *he gets £300 wages* : tair mar ceara faice – *she's inherited her mother's looks* : tara ek·kan dolil faice – *they've found a legal document* : faici! – *found it! ah, I get it!* : tane goro faiba – *you'll find him at home* : taire boono faiclam – *I found her sitting there* : afnare kila faitam? – *how can I get hold of you?* : cacare faitam oimu – *I must get hold of uncle* : betar nam fai na – *I can't recall the fellow's name* : tumar fora fao ni? – *do you remember all you've studied?* : tain keic faicoin – *he's won his lawsuit* : afne batas faira ni? – *are you feeling a draught?* : ami lora faici – *I heard a movement; I heard something moving* : tar gec tone ami foesa fai – *I'm owed some money from him* : cilot korimgonj fae na – *Sylhet does not include Karimganj* : **fae** (impersonal) – *afflicts* : taire bute faice – *a ghost has afflicted her; she's been possessed by a spirit*: afnare ferae faito fare – *measles may afflict you; you may catch the measles* : **fai le-** – *get; find; recall* : afne ceg fai liba – *you'll receive a cheque* : fai lici! – *I've found it! I've got it!* : **tukaia fa-** – *find (after searching)* : ami kagoj·kan tukaia faici na – *I couldn't find the document anywhere* : **lagal fa-** – *be able to reach* : he cuicor lagal fae na – *he can't reach the switch* : tan lagal faici na – *I couldn't get hold of him* : **buḍ fa-** – *become aware; realise* : ji oe, ami buḍ faici – *yes, I realise that* : afne buḍ faicoin ni? – *do you see? do you get it?* : **bala fa-** – *like* : caci mac bala fain na – *auntie doesn't like fish* : ami taire bala fai – *I like her* [B. pa-]

faar ['fã-ār] (n) *hill; mountain* | tara faaro utcil – *they went up a mountain* : faaror des – *a mountainous country* [B. pahaṛ]

fac [fãs] (n°) *five* | fac okt nomaj – *the five daily prayers* : bur fac·ta – *five o'clock in the morning* : «amrar fac aŋgul homan nae» – *our five fingers aren't all the same; it takes all types to make a world* [B. pãⁿc]

faccallis ['fãt-tšāl-līš] (n°) *forty-five* [B. påⁿtallis]

facasi ['fãsāšī] (n°) *eighty-five* [B. påⁿcasi]

facfoncas ['fãs-fòn-sāš] (n°) *fifty-five* [B. påⁿcannå]

facfoni ['fãs-fònī] (n) *five pound note*

facorbad ['fãsòr-bād] (adj) *ostracised* | **facorbad o-/facorbad oi ja-** – *be ostracised* : tain facorbad oi gecoin – *he has been sent to Coventry*

factala ['fãs-tālā] (adj) *five-storeyed* | factala gor – *a five-storeyed building; a massive building* = **fac + -tala**

fad [fãd] (n) *fart* | **fad mar** – *fart* [H. pād]

faeḍa ['fãy-ḍā] (n) *profit; gain; advantage* | i kamo faeḍa oibo – *there will be profit in this job* : ola befsat faeḍa kom – *there's little profit in that kind of business* : gussa kori faeḍa nae – *there's nothing to be gained by getting angry* : bar canit faeḍa kita? – *what's the point in waiting?* : faeḍa oe – *some advantage is gained* : jaoat afnar faeḍa oito fare – *there may be profit for you in going; you may gain something by going* : ita kori amar faeḍa oice – *I have benefited from doing that* : **faeḍa kor-** – *make a profit* : reston dia tara bout faeḍa korce – *they've done very well out of setting up a restaurant* [A. fã'ida]

faejama ['fãy-jāmā, 'fãy-zāmā] (n) *pyjamas* [P. pāe jāma]

faekana ['fãy-χānā] (n) *latrine; faeces* | faekana kuae? – *where is the toilet?* : fesab-faekana – *urine and stools* : **faekana ḍore** – *one feels the need to defecate* : amar faekana ḍorce – *I need to go to the toilet* : **faekana kor-** – *defecate* [P. pāe χāna]

faf [fãf] (n) *sin* | **faf kor-** – *commit sins* [B. pap < S. pāpa]

fafra ['fãf-rā] (n) *starch crackers* [B. papåṛ]

fagla ['fãg-lā] (n) *madman* < **fagol**

faglami ['fãg-lāmī] (n) *madness; folly* = **fagol + -ami**

fagli ['fãg-lī] (n) *madwoman* < **fagol**

fagol ['fāgòl] (adj) *mad; crazy; eccentric* | fagol beta – *madman* : fagol beta aicoin! *– watch out, the bogey man is coming!* : he fura fagol *– he's quite barmy* : fagol na kita? *– are you quite out of your mind?* : he cinemar lagi fagol *– he's crazy on the cinema* : **fagol o-/fagol oi ja-** *– go mad* : ami fagol oi jairam *– I'm going crazy* : **fagol kori le-** *– drive mad* : tain amare fagol kori lira *– he is driving me mad* [B. pagål]
fai-focondo ['fāi-fòsòn-dò] (n) *choice* = **focond**
faiglami ['fāig-lāmī] (n) *madness; folly* | ita faiglami! *- this is madness!* : **faiglami kor-** *– behave foolishly* : faiglami korio na *– don't do anything crazy* = **faglami**
faijlami ['fāiz-lāmī] (n) *silliness* | **faijlami kor-** *– be silly; be flippant* = **fajil + -ami**
faikka ['fāik-kıā] (n) *bird* [B. pakhi]
fail [fāil] (n) *(office) file* | afnar fail ari gece *– your file has been lost* : amar kabin tarar falit *– my marriage deed is in their file* [E.]
fainjabi ['fāin-jābī] (n) *Punjabi; type of loose cotton shirt* [H. panjābī]
faji ['fājī, 'fāzī] (adj) (of a person) *tiresome; vile* [H. pājī]
fajil ¹ ['fāzīl] (adj) *learned (in Islamic matters)* [A. fāÐil]
fajil ² (adj) *over-smart; impertinent* [A. fāÐil *– superabundant; excessive*]
fak ¹ [fāχ] (n) *ripeness; maturity* | **fak dore** *– ripeness develops* : dane fak dorce *– the paddy has started to ripen* : **fak kor-** *– (of food) make toothsome; cook* : birani fak korcoin *– she has cooked some biryani* [B. pak < O. pāka]
fak ² (n) *twist; turn; circuit* | kicmotor fak *– a twist of fate* : tara tin fak gurce *– they went round three times* : **fak di** *– there and back; recurrently; again* : tain fak di aicoin *– he came back again* : tara fak di mica mate *– they keep telling lies* : **fak ka-** *– be turned; roll over* : gari kotobar fak kaice *– the car rolled over several times* [B. pak]
fak ³ (n) *gap; fissure; crack* [B. phaⁿk]
fak ⁴ [fāk, pāk] (adj) *pure* | fak mucolman *– a pure Muslim* [P. pāk]
fak- ¹ (vi) *ripen; mature* | dan fakce *– the paddy has ripened* : dadar cul fakce *– great-uncle's hair has turned grey* : **faki ja-** *– ripen; mature* : kola faki jar *– the bananas are ripening* : boron faki gece *– the boil has come to a head* [B. pak-]
fak- ² (vi) *become twisted* | **faki ja-** *– get twisted; form a tangle* : tair culo jot faki gece *– a tangle has formed in her hair* [B. pak-]
faka ['fā:χā] (adj) *hollow; empty* | faka oal *– a hollow wall* : faka rasta *– an empty street* : faka jaega *– a vacant space* [B. phaⁿka]
faka- ¹ ['fāχā] (vt) *cause to mature; cook* | katol fakaitam oimu *– we must let the jackfruit ripen* : afne kita fakaira? *– what are you cooking?* [B. paka-]
faka- ² (v) *twist; gad about* | tara dori fakar *– they are twisting fibre into twine* : caca fakaira *– uncle is moving around here and there* : **fakani** *– gadding; jaunting* : tara kuae? fakanit *– where are they? on a jaunt* [B. paka-]
fak-barot ['fāχ-bāròt] (n) *Pakistan and India*
fake ['fāχε] (adv) *on occasion* | **fake fake** *– again and again* : fake fake ou kota jikkae *– she asks that question quite frequently* < **fak** ²
faki ¹ ['fākī] (n) *purity* [P. pākī]
faki ² (n) *bird* [B. pakhi]
faki ³ ['fā:kī] (n) *evasion* | **faki de-** *– be evasive; let down; hoodwink* : he faki dice amare *– he gave me the slip; he has let me down* : **faki mar-** *– avoid duties; shirk* : betae kali faki mare *– the fellow is a slacker* [B. phaⁿki]
fakibaj ['fākībāz] (n) *shirker* = **faki + -baj**
fakibaji ['fākībāzī] (n) *shirking* | **fakibaji kor-** *– avoid duties; shirk* = **faki + -baji**
fakka ['fāk-kā] (adj) *fully developed; of a proper standard; thorough; complete* | tain fakka alim oicoin *– he's become a real Islamic scholar* : he fakka mucolman *– he's a proper Muslim* : tain fakka kam koroin *– she does a thorough job* : jaite fakka dui gonta lagce *– it took two whole hours to get there* [H. pakkā]
fakna ['fāχ-nā] (adj) *ripe; matured* | ou am fakna *– this mango is ripe* : tan fakna cul *– she's got grey hair* < **fak-** ¹

fakra- ['fāχ-rā] (vt) *grab; seize* (a person) | fulise ek curre fakraice – *the police have apprehended a thief* [H. pakaṛ-]

fakrau ['fāχ-rāu] (n) *seizure* (of a person) | **fakrau kor-** – *seize* : tara cur otare fakrau korce – *they have caught that thief* [H. pakṛā]

fak-sak ['fāχ-šāχ] (n) *cooking* = **fak** ¹

fal [fāl] (n) *leap* | **fal de-/fal di la-** – *jump; leap up* : gurae akta fal dice – *the horse suddenly capered* : **fal mar-** – *jump; leap about* : fuainte iato fal marer – *the boys are jumping about in the yard* [H. phalāŋ < O. sphāla]

fal- (v) *foster; keep as a pet* | tara ek etimre falce – *they have taken in an orphan* : tain kutta falra – *he is keeping a dog* [B. pal-]

fala- ['fālā] (vt) *throw away; get rid of; disregard; throw down; plant* | butol·ta daco falaimu – *I'll throw the bottle in the bin* : he cul falanit gece – *he's gone to get his hair cut* : falauka! – *oh, ignore it; forget it!* : tara noea karfit falaice – *they've laid down a new carpet* : tain iato hag falaita – *she wants to plant spinach in the garden* : caci cokkur fani falaicla – *auntie was shedding tears* : amare bifoto falaice – *he's put me in an awkward situation* : afnare osubidar maje falaitam cai na – *I don't want to put you in difficulties* : **falae** (impersonal) – *it lays on* (weather) : bakka tanda falaice – *it's turned very cold* : **falai de-** – *throw away; cast down; knock over; spill* : gori·ta falai dao na kene? – *why don't you throw that clock away?* : gume falai dice taire – *sleepiness has floored her; she's so sleepy she can't stand* : deko, falai dibae! – *watch out, you're going to spill it!* : **falai torak-** – *cast aside; leave unattended* : fail·ta falai torakce – *they've put the file on one side* : **falaia ja-** – *leave behind; go past* : tarar gor falaia geci – *we've overshot their house; we've gone past their house* [B. phel-]

falguin ['fālgūɪn] (n) *Phalgun (February-March)* [B. phalgun < S. phālguṇa]

falis ['fālīš] (n) *polish* | **falis de-** – *apply polish; polish* [E.]

falka ['fāl-χā] (adj) *fostered* | falka fua – *foster-son* < **fal-**

falla ['fāl-lā] (n) *leaves (of double door); scales (of weighing apparatus)* | «falla di beŋ ujon kora» – *to weigh frogs in a pair of scales; to scoop water with a sieve* : **(kar loge) falla de-** – *try to match up (with someone); compete (with someone)* : tarar loge falla dirae ni? – *are you trying to compete with them?* : **(kar) fallae for-** – *fall into the clutches (of someone)* : bad mainsor fallae force – *he's fallen in with bad people* [B. palla]

falok ['fālòχ] (adj) *fostered* = **falka**

falon ['fālòn] (n) *fostering* | **falon kor-** – *foster; keep as a pet* : tara koutor falon kore – *they keep pigeons* < **fal-**

faloŋ ['fālòŋ] (n) *wooden bed-platform* [B. palåŋ]

falt- [fālt] (vi) *be changed* | **falti ja-** – *be changed* : duinna falti gece – *the world has changed*

falta ['fāl-tā] (v adj) *alternative; different* | falta balis deuka – *please give me a different pillow* : falta ar ek·jon aiba – *someone else will come instead* < **falt-**

falta- (vt) *change* | hokol caddor faltaimu – *I'm going to change all the sheets* : **faltai de-** – *change* : keced faltai deuka – *please change the cassette* [B. palta-]

faltu ['fāl-tū] (adj) *unnecessary; useless* | faltu kota – *useless talk; nonsense* [H. faltū]

fam [fām] (n) *inflation* | cakkar maje fam nae – *there's no air in the tyre; the tyre's flat* : **fam de-/fam di la-** – *pump up; flatter* : cakkar maje fam deoa lagbo – *the tyre needs inflating* : betare fam di laici – *I buttered him up* [E. pump]

fan [fān] (n) *betel-leaf; paan* | fan-sufari – *betel-leaf and areca nut; paan* : **fan ka-** – *chew betel-leaf; take paan* : ami fan kai na – *I don't take paan* : **fan kaoa-** – *offer paan* (as an act of hospitality) : memanre fan kabaiclae ni? – *did you offer paan to the guests?* [B. pan]

fana ¹ ['fānā] (v n) *getting; acquisition* < **fa-**

fana ² (n) *annihilation* | **fana o-/fana oi ja-** – *be annihilated* : ek din dunia fana oibo – *one day the world will be destroyed; the world will end* [A. fanā']

fana ³ (n) *deliverance* | kunukano fana nae – *there's no security anywhere* : **fana de-** – *deliver; save* : alla tarare fana dito – *may God save them* [P. panāh – *protection*]

fanḍan ['fānḍān] (n) *paan salver*   [H. pāndān]
faneala ['fānɛ-ālā] (n) *recipient; addressee*   [H. pānevālā]
fani ['fānī] (n) *water; liquid* | fani kaita ni? – *would you like a drink of water?* : saḍa fani – *plain water* : kaca fani – *unboiled water* : siŋor fani – *tap water* : nariulor fani – *coconut milk* : cokkur fani – *tears* : **fani koroc kor-** – *use water; do ablutions*   [H. pānī]
fanisa ['fānīšā] (n) *furniture*   [E.]
fanja ['fān-jā] (n) *fist*   [P. panja – *hand*]
faŋgas ['fān-gāš] (n) *a species of fish rich in oil (Pangasius pangasius)*   [B. paŋgas]
faŋka ['fāŋ-χā] (n) *fan*   [B. paŋkha]
far[1] [fār] (n) *crossing over; transition* | **far o-** – *cross over; make a transition* : amra rasta far oitam kila? – *how are we to get across the road?* : tara noea goro far oice – *they've moved to their new house*   [B. par]
far[2] (n) *edge; bank; border; width* | gaŋor far – *river bank* : lal far – *a red border* : kaforor far koto? – *what is the width of the cloth?*   [B. paṛ]
far-[1] (v) *be able; be capable; be allowed; possibly do* | farba ni? – *will you manage?* : ami fartam nai! – *I can't do it!* : ami fortam fari – *I can read* : tumi jaitae gi faro – *you may go* : tain gussa korta faroin – *he may be angry* : **oito fare** – *it may happen; it may be so* : meg dibo ni? oito fare – *is it going to rain? maybe* : **fare na** – (to child) *it's not the done thing; you shouldn't say/do that!* : cii! fare na! – *tut! don't do that, it's naughty!* : **fara jae** – *it is possible* : ila fara jae na – *it just can't be done like this* : asa koro kail fara jaibo – *I hope it will be possible tomorrow*   [B. par-]
far-[2] (vt) *bring down; pick (fruit); lay (eggs)* | tain koto aefol farcoin – *she's picked a whole lot of apples* : murgi enda fare – *the hen lays eggs*   [B. paṛ-]
far-[3] (v) *tear; rip; split; get torn* | tumar fen farco – *you've ripped your trousers* : tara lakri farer – *they're splitting firewood* : kafor farce – *the cloth has got ripped* : **fari le-** – *tear; split* : tumar fen fari lico – *you've ripped your trousers* : **fari ja-** – *get torn; get split* : kagoj fari gece – *the paper's got torn*   [B. phaṛ-]
fara[1] ['fārā] (v n) *being able* | oto·ta fara muskil – *it'll be hard to manage so much* : **fara jae** – *it is possible* : jeca·ta fara jae – *anything is possible* : ḍui ḍine fara jaibo – *it will be possible to do it in two days*   < **far-**
fara[2] (n) *neighbourhood; locality*   [B. paṛa]
fara[3] (n) *fateful juncture in life*   [B. phaⁿṛa]
fara[4] (n) *section of the Quran*   cf **cifara**   [P. pāra]
fara[5] (n) *crossing over; stepping out* | **fara de-/fara di la-** – *cross over; step out* : one fara ḍio na! – *don't cross (the road) now!* : **fara di** – *across; past* : ou fara di gecoin – *he just went past*   = **fari**
fara[6] (v adj) *torn; ripped*   < **far-**[3]
farak ['fārāχ] (n) *gap; discrepancy*   [A. farq]
farc ['fārs] (n) *Persia*   [P. fārs]
farci ['fārsī] (adj) *Persian; Iranian* ¶ **farci** (n) *Persian (person); Farsi (language)* | tain farci janoin – *he can speak Farsi*   [P. fārsī]
fari ['fārī] (n) *crossing over* | **fari de-/fari di la-** – *cross over* : tara gaŋ fari ḍito – *they want to cross the river*   [B. paṛi]
fark [fār-k] (n) *park* | hurutae farko kelar – *the kids are playing in the park*   [E.]
farkiŋ ['fār-kīŋ] (n) *parking space; car park*   [E.]
faro ['fārò] (n) *pigeon*   [O. pārāvata]
fas[1] [fāš] (n) *side; breadth; thickness* | dain fas – *right side* : bam fas – *left side* : kaforor fas ek goj – *the width of the cloth is one yard* : ou karfitor fas besi – *this carpet is thicker* : **fase** – *at the side; near* : afnar fase ke? – *who's that beside you?* : amar dain fase ek fua – *there's a boy on my right* : fase ḍukan ace – *there's a shop nearby*   [B. pas < O. pārśva]
fas[2] (n) *manure; fertilizer*   [H. pāⁿs < O. pāŋśu – *ash*]
fas[3] (adj) *passed; graduated* | tain mettik fas – *he is a matriculate* : **fas o-** – *pass (an exam); win (an election)* : ileksone ke fas oice? – *who won the election?*   [E.]

fasafasi ['făsāfăsī] (adv) *side by side* < **fas** [1]
fasfut ['făsfūt] (n) *passport* | **fasfut kor-/fasfut bar kor-** – *obtain a passport* : amra fasfut kortam oimu – *we'll have to get passports* : tan furir lagi fasfut bar korra – *he's getting a passport for his daughter* [E.]
fasi ['făsī] (n) *hanging; condemnation* | tumar fasi oibo! – *you'll get it in the neck!* : **fasi o-/fasi oi ja-** – *be hanged* : **fasi de-/fasi di la-** – *hang (a person)* [B. phaⁿsi]
fassait ['făš-šāıt] (n°) *sixty-five* = **fac + sait**
fassala ['făš-šālā] (n) *elementary school* [B. pathsala]
fat [1] [făt] (n) *jute* [B. pat]
fat [2] (n) *reading; study* | **fat kor-** – *read; read out; study* : hurutae kuran fat korer – *the children are reciting the Quran* : amar fua tu fojonto fat korce – *my son has studied up to Class Two* [B. path < S. pātha]
fat- (v) *split; crack; burst; curdle* | ou lakri fate na – *this firewood won't split* : haddi fatce – *a bone has cracked* : belun fatbo – *the balloon will burst* : dud fatto fare – *the milk may curdle* : **fati ja-** – *split; crack; burst; curdle* : ruk karakara fati jae – *the wood splits easily* : tar mata fati gece – *his scalp has been split open* : amar gurda fati jar – *my heart is breaking* : cakka fati jaito fare – *the tyre may burst* : dud·ta fati gece – *the milk has curdled* [B. phat-]
fata [1] ['fătā] (n) *pounding slab* [B. pata]
fata [2] (v adj) *split; burst; curdled* < **fat-**
fata- (vt) *send* | **fatai de-** – *send* : tare goro fatai dici – *I've sent him home* [B. patha-]
fataura ['fătāurā] (n) *sender* < **fata-**
fattia ['făt-tīā] (n) *backbone* [B. pithdaⁿra]
fat [făt] (n) *place at table* [B. pat]
fata ['fătā] (n) *leaf; page; flat surface; spinach* | fata forer – *leaves are falling* : bakor fata – *coriander leaf* : boir fata – *pages of a book* : ulto fata – *the next page; the other side (of a sheet of paper)* : cokkur fata – *eyelid* : faur fata – *sole of the foot* : amra fata di kaici – *we ate our rice with spinach* [B. pata < O. pattra]
fata- (vt) *spread out* | matit caddor fataicil – *they spread a sheet on the ground* : tumar at fatao – *extend your hand; hold out your hand* : **gum fata-** – *lull to sleep* : baiccaintore gum fataira – *she's putting the children to sleep* : **fatai le-** – *spread out* : tebulo kafor fatai licoin – *he has spread a cloth on the table* [B. pat-]
fatar ['fătār] (n) *breadth* [O. prastha]
fatare ['fătārɛ] (n adv) *across; crosswise* < **fatar**
fatla ['făt-lā] (adj) *insubstantial; thin; light; shallow* | fatla kafor – *thin cloth; lightweight clothing* : fatla ledar – *a light suitcase* : fatla gum – *light sleep* : boro fatla manus – *a very shallow person* : fatla mat – *frivolous talk* : fatla ca – *weak tea* : fatla faekana – *loose stools* [B. patla]
fatri ['făt-rī] (n) *eligible girl* [B. patri < S. pātrī]
fatro ['făt-rò] (n) *receptacle; eligible boy* | matir fatro – *earthenware vessel* : batijir lagi fatro tukairam – *we're looking for a husband for our niece* [B. patrå < S. pātra]
fatta [1] (n) *current details; news* | rajar kunu fatta janoin ni? – *have you heard anything of Raja?* : tar fatta fai na – *I can't get any news of him* : tar kunu fatta-u nae – *he has disappeared without trace* [P. pata – *note; chit*]
fatta [2] (n) *leaf* [H. pattā < O. pattra]
fattoir ['făt-tòır] (n) *stone* [H. patthar < O. prasthara]
fau [fău] (n) *foot; leg* | kali fau – *bare feet* : tar fau lamfa – *his legs are long* : faur mura – *heel* : faur gonta – *ankle* : faur tol – *sole* : faur tole – *under one's feet* : tain faut duk faicoin – *he was hurt on his leg* { H. pāoⁿ]
fauar ['făuār] (n) *power rating* | ek so fauar – *100 watt (bulb); 100 mg (medicine)* : sait fauaror batti – *a sixty watt bulb* : ou daoaior fauar nae – *this medicine isn't strong enough* : afnar cosmar fauar ace – *your specs are very powerful* [E.]

fauna ['fāunā] (n) *credit* | amar ɖui so fon fauna – *I am owed £200* : amar gece afnar fauna nae – *nothing is owing to you from me* [B. paona]

faur- [fāur] (v) *forget* | **fauri le-** – *forget* : tan nam fauri lici – *I've forgotten his name*

faura ['fāurā] (n) *one who receives; recipient; addressee* | ou citir faura ke? – *to whom is this letter addressed?* < **fa-**

fec [fɛs] (n) *loop; tangle* | i fec kultam kila? – *how can I undo this tangle?* : **fec lage** – *a tangle forms; complications arise* : ulor maje fec lagce – *the wool has got tangled* : tikit loia fec lagce – *there's been a mix-up about the tickets* : **fec laga-** – *make a tangle; cause complications* : he kamor maje fec lagaice – *he's messed the job up* [P. pec]

feca- ['fɛsā] (vt) *coil; entangle* | **fecai le-/fecai de-** – *entwine; entangle; complicate* : fogeto ɖori fecai ɖici – *I've wound some string round the packet* : tain hokolti fecai licoin – *he has messed everything up* [B. peⁿca-]

fecaɖ ['fɛsāɖ] (n) *strife; trouble* | **fecaɖ kor-** – *make trouble* : tara amrar loge fecaɖ kore – *they make trouble for us; they harass us* [A. fasād – *corruptness*]

fecafeci ['fɛsāfɛsī] (n) *complications; hassle* < **fec**

fecail ['fɛsāil] (v adj) *convoluted* < **feca-**

fecfec ['fɛsfɛs] (n) *nagging; whining* | **fecfec kor-** – *nag; moan; carry on* [B. phec phec]

fecfeca ['fɛsfɛsā] (adj) *damp (weather)*

fecra ['fɛsrā] (n) *suppurating pustule; spots* [B. paⁿcɽa – *itch; scab*]

fefar ['fɛfār] (n) *newspaper* [E.]

fefarsof ['fɛfāršòf] (n) *newsagent's shop* [E.]

fegombor ['fɛgòmbòr] (n) *prophet* [P. paiġambar]

feil [féil] (n) *examination failure* | **feil mar-** – *fail (in an exam)* : he tinbar feil marce – *he failed the test three times* [E.]

fek [fɛχ] (n) *mud* [B. paⁿk]

fekal ['fɛχāl] (n) *fecal matter* [P. paiḳāl]

fekra ['fɛχrā] (n) *side-shoot; snag* [B. pheⁿkɽa]

fektri ['fɛχ-trī] (n) *factory* [E.]

fen¹ [fɛːn] (n) *froth* [B. phen]

fen² [fɛn] (n) *trousers* [E. pants]

feni ['fɛnī] (n) *penny* [E.]

fera ['fɛrā] (n) *measles* | tar fera bar oice – *he's come out in measles*

feram ['fɛrām] (n) *pram* [E.]

ferent ['fɛrɛnt] (n) *friend; parent* [E.]

feresan ['fɛrɛšān] (adj) *disturbed* | **feresan o-/feresan oi ja-** – *be disturbed* : afne feresan oi gecoin – *you've been put to a lot of trouble* [P. pirešān]

feresani ['fɛrɛšānī] (n) *disturbance; harassment* [P. pirešānī]

feresar ['fɛrɛšār] (n) *blood pressure* | amar feresar hai oi gece – *my blood pressure has got high; I've got hypertension* [E.]

feresta ['fɛrɛs-tā] (n) *angel* [P. firišta]

feront ['fɛròn̄t] (n) *front room* | feronto bouka – *please take a seat in the front room* [E.]

ferot ['fɛròt] (n) *ghost; vagabond*

fes [fɛš] (n) *pesh; dhamma ("u" sign in Arabic)* [P. peš – *front*]

fesaf ['fɛšāf] (n) *urine* | fesaf faekana – *urine and stools; bodily functions* : fesafor jaega – *urinal; urinary orifice* : **fesaf kor-** – *urinate* : (to child) fesaf kortae ni? – *do you want to go to the toilet?* : **fesaf bar oe** – *urine leaks out; signs of fear are exhibited* : betar fesaf bar oice – *that chap's dying of fright* : **fesaf bar kori le-** – *scare; terrify* : tar fesaf bar kori limu – *I'll scare the piss out of him* [P. pešāb]

fet [fɛt] (n) *belly; stomach; bowels; womb* | tan fet muta – *he has a fat belly* : tan fet kali – *his stomach is empty; he hasn't eaten* : kali feto – *on an empty stomach* : tain kali feto kam korra – *she's working on an empty stomach* : amar fet fakar – *my stomach is turning* : tan feto baicca – *she's carrying a baby; she's pregnant* : bour feto baicca toia gecoin – *he left his wife pregnant* : mar fetor bai – *uterine brother; true brother* : fetor kota – *innermost*

thoughts; private thoughts : he tar fetor kota koe na – *he never says what's on his mind* : **feto buk** – *hunger* : amar feto buk lagce – *I'm hungry* : **fet lame** – *the bowels loosen* : tar fet lamer – *he's got diarrhoea* : fet lama – *diarrhoea* [B. pet]
fetla ['fɛt-lā] (adj) *pot-bellied* [H. petal]
fetor fetor ['fɛtòr-fɛtòr] (n) *grumbling* | **fetor-fetor kor-** – *grumble*
fiaij ['fĩāɪz] (n) *onion; bulb* [P. piyāz]
fial ['fĩāl] (n) *addiction* [A. infi¿āl – *stimulation*]
fiala ['fĩāla] (n) *bowl; cup* [P. piyāla]
fiar ['fĩār] (n) *love; affection* [H. pyār]
fiara ['fĩāra] (n) *loved one; darling* [H. pyārā]
fias ['fĩāš] (n) *thirst* | fanir fias – *thirst for water* : **fias lage** – *thirst is felt* : amar fias lagce – *I feel thirsty* : **fias mite/fias miti jae** – *thirst is quenched* : amar fias miti gece – *I don't feel thirsty any more* [H. piyās < O. pipāsā]
fic[1] ['fĩs] (n) *rear; back* | gorir fic – *the back of the clock* : **ficor** – *of the rear; of the back* : ficor ɖoroja – *the back door* : **fice** – *at the back; behind* : tara fice fori gece – *they've fallen behind* : almarir fice ʈukauka – *look for it behind the cupboard* [B. pich]
fic[2] (n) *pitch; asphalt* | ficor rasta – *an asphalted road; a tarmac road* [E.]
fica- ['fĩsā] (vt) *set back; put back; postpone* | bonnae amrar hokol kam ficaice – *the floods have set back all our work* : tara tarar jaoar tarik ficaice – *they've put back their date of departure* [B. picha-]
fice ['fĩsɛ] (n adv) *behind* | fice gari ar – *there's a car coming up behind* : tara amrar bout fice – *they're far behind us* : jon fice – *per person* : jon fice bis fon – *twenty pounds per head* : **fice for-/fice fori ja-** – *fall behind* : balaʈike forasuna na korle fice fori jaibae – *if you don't study properly you'll get left behind* < **fic**[1]
ficl- ['fĩsl] (vi) *slip* | **ficli ja-** – *slip* : cakka ficli jar – *the wheel is slipping* : tain rastar maje ficli gecla – *he slipped on the road* [H. phisal-]
ficla ['fĩs-lā] (adj) *slippery; slimy* | mati ficla – *the ground is slippery* : ficla lage – *it feels slimy* ¶ **ficla** (n) *slime* | ficla bar oe – *slime oozes out* [B. pichla]
ficol ['fĩsòl] (adj) *slippery* [B. pichål]
fifra ['fĩf-rā] (n) *ant* [B. pinpra]
fiit [fĩːt] (n) *rear surface; back* | tar fiit baka – *his back is crooked* : **fitir** – *of the back* : fitir maijkano – *in the middle of the back* : **fitit** – *in the back* : amar fitit bis kore – *it hurts in my back; my back hurts* [B. pith]
filaf ['fĩlāf] (n) *filling up* | **filaf kor-** – *fill up; fill in* : forom filaf korta oiba – *you'll have to fill in the form* [E.]
fina ['fĩnā] (n) *drinking* [H. pīnā]
finɖ- [fĩnɖ] (vt) *put on; wear* | ʈumar kut̪ finɖo – *put your coat on* : amra juta finɖci – *we have put our shoes on* : tain t̪oki finɖoin – *he wears a cap* : **finɖi le-** – *put on* : juta finɖi loo – *put your shoes on* : tain kut̪ finɖi licoin – *he has put on his coat* [H. pahan-]
finɖa- ['fĩnɖā] (vt) *cause to put on (clothes); clothe* | tain baiccaintore kut̪ finɖaira – *she is getting the children to put on their coats* : et̪imre kabaita ar finɖaita – *you should feed and clothe the orphans* [H. pahnā-]
finɖon ['fĩnɖòn] (v n) *putting on of clothes; wearing* | **finɖono** – *being worn; on one's body* : tar finɖono fen – *he had trousers on* : tair finɖono seloar kamij – *she is wearing a shalwar and kameez* < **finɖ-**
finfini ['fĩnfĩnī] (adj) *small and creepy* | finfini meg – *fine rain; drizzle*
finifini ['fĩnīfĩnī] (adj) *small and creepy* = **finfini**
finjira ['fĩnjīrā] (n) *cage* [H. pinjrā]
fiŋ [fĩŋ] (n) *pin; nail* | oalo fiŋ marce – *he hammered a nail into the wall* [E.]
fiŋla ['fĩŋ-lā] (adj) *tawny; yellowish* [B. piŋgål < O. piŋga]
fion ['fĩòn] (n) *peon; postman* [E.]
fir[1] [fĩr] (adv) *again* [H. phir]
fir[2] (n) *Muslim saint; Pir* [P. pīr – *old man; sage*]

fir- (vi) *come back; return; go round* | afne kun đin fircoin? *– when did you get back?* : he gure ar fire *– he wanders about* [B. phir-]
fira ['fīrā] (n) *time round; turn* | ou fira *– this time round* : agor fira *– last time* : tumar fira! *– it's your turn!* < **fir-**
fira- (vt) *turn back; send back* | betare iarfut taki firaice *– they turned the man back from the airport* [B. phira-]
firaki ['fīrākī] (n) *treatment by a Muslim saint* | firaki bemar *– illness requiring treatment by a Pir*
firbair ['fīrbāır] (adv) *once again* = **fir + bar**
firia ['fīrīā] (v adj) *again* < **fir-**
firiti ['fīrītī] (n) *affection; love* [B. priti < S. prīti]
firon ['fīròn] (n) *shirt* [P. pairahan]
fis [fīš] (n) *fees; official charges* | fis koto lage? *– how much is the fee?* : đos fon fis lage *– there is a charge of £10* : fis đice na ebu *– he hasn't yet paid the fee* [E.]
fissab ['fīš-šāb] (n) *Muslim saint; spiritual lord; Pir* = **fir ² + sab**
fit [fīt] (n) *back* = **fiit**
fit- (vt) *beat; thrash* [B. pit-]
fita ¹ ['fītā] (v n) *beating* | **fita đe-/fita đi la-** *– give a beating; thrash* : tumare fita đi laimu! *– I'll thrash you!* : **fita ka-/fita kai le-** *– take a beating* : koeđi fita kaice *– the prisoner has taken a walloping* < **fit-**
fita ² (n) *pancake* [B. pitha]
fita- (vt) *beat; thrash* [B. pita-]
fitfat ['fīt-fāt] (adj) *neat and clean*
fiti ['fītī] (n) *back* = **fiit**
fitkiri ['fīt-kīrī] (n) *alum (aluminium-potassium sulphate)* [B. phåtkiri < O. sphatikari]
fitti ['fīt-tī] (n) *beating* = **fita ¹**
fit [fīt] (n) *gall bladder* [B. pīttå *– bile* < S. pitta]
fita ['fītā] (n) *ribbon; tape* [B. phita < Pg. fita]
fitor ['fītòr] (n) *fast-breaking* | iđul fitor *– Eid-ul-Fitr (festival after Ramadan, the month of fasting)* [A. fiṭr]
fitra ¹ ['fītrā] (n) *creation; nature; disposition* [A. fiṭra]
fitra ² (n) *alms given at Eid-ul-Fitr* < **fitor**
fitti ['fīt-tī] (n) *time round; turn* | ou fitti afnera kuae jaita? *– where do you intend to go this time?* [B. phirti]
foc- [fòs] (vi) *rot* | **foci ja-** *– rot; go bad* : foci gece *– it's gone bad* [B. påc-]
foca ['fòsā] (v adj) *rotten; no good* | foca aefol *– a rotten apple* : foca manus *– a worthless person* < **foc-**
foca- (vt) *cause to rot; allow to rot* [B. påca-]
focanobboi ['fòsānob-bòı] (n°) *ninety-five* [B. pån̄canåbbåi]
focasi ['fòsāšī] (n°) *eighty-five* [B. pån̄casi]
focattoir ['fòsāt-tòır] (n°) *seventy-five* [B. pån̄cattår]
foccim ['fòtšīm] (adj) *west; western* | foccim efrika *– West Africa* ¶ **foccim** (n) *the west* | **foccime** *– in the west; towards the west* : bajar·ta aro foccime *– the marketplace is further west* : mocjidor foccime *– west of the mosque* : **foccimor** *– of the west; western* : foccimor gor *– the west hut* [B. påscim < S. paščima]
focfanno ['fòs-fān-nò] (n°) *fifty-five* [B. pån̄cannå]
focina ['fòsīnā] (n) *perspiration; sweat* | **focina bar oe/ focina bar oi jae** *– perspiration occurs* : tar focina bar oice *– he is sweating; he is in a sweat* : **focina cute/focina cuti jae** *– copious perspiration occurs* : tar focina cuti gece *– he's drenched in sweat* [H. pasīna]
focis ['fòsīš] (n°) *twenty-five* [B. påcis]
focond ['fòsònđ] (n) *choice; liking* | **focond oe** *– a liking develops* : jaega focond oice amar *– I've taken a liking to the place* : ou ca afnar focond oibo *– you'll like this tea* : **focond kor-** *– choose; take a liking; like* : kun·ta focond korcoin? *– which one have you chosen?* :

85

lal focond kori na – *I don't like red* : **focond kori le-** – *choose* : huru·ta focond kori licoin – *she has chosen the smaller one* [P. pasand]

fodda ['fòddā] (n) *curtain* = **forda**

foeda ['fòyda] (adj) *born* | **foeda o-** – *be born; become manifest*: jura baicca foeda oice – *twins have been born* : osanti foeda oice – *unrest has appeared* : **foeda kor-** – *create; produce* : alla amrare foeda korce – *God created us* [P. paidā]

foedais ['fòydāɪš] (n) *birth; genesis* [P. paidāiš]

foedis ['fòydīš] (n) *birth; genesis* = **foedais**

foegombor ['fòygòmbòr] (n) *prophet* [P. paiġambar]

foel [fòyl] (n) *beginning* | **foel taki** – *from the first* : ami foel taki koici – *I said so from the very beginning* [H. pahl]

foela ['fòylā] (adj) *first* | foela bar – *the first time* : foela tarik – *1st (of a month)* : tair foela baicca – *her first child* ¶ **foela** (adv) *first; firstly* | tara foela gucol korce – *first they had a bath* : tain matuka foela – *let him speak first* : **foelaku** – *at first; firstly* : foelaku bujclam na – *at first I didn't understand* : foelaku jiggauka tare – *first ask him* : **foelakur** – *of the first instance; initial* : tar foelakur kam bala acil – *his initial job was a good one* : foelakur somoe kuae takta? – *where did you live originally?* [H. pahlā]

foesa ['fòyšā] (n) *small coin; money* | amar ek·ta foesa-o nae – *I haven't got a single penny* : he kali foesa cine – *money is all he understands* : tara bout foesa nosto kore – *they waste a lot of money* : foesar lagi nae – *not for money; not for financial reasons* : amar i foesae cole na – *I can't manage on this money* : baŋla foesa – *loose change* : lal foesa – *copper coin* : betae ek·ta lal foesa-o dice na – *the man didn't donate a single farthing* : **foesa oe/foesa oi jae** – *wealth is attained* : tarar bout foesa oi gece – *they have become very rich* : **foesa kor- /foesa kori le-** – *make money; get rich* : hou betae bout foesa korce – *that fellow has made stacks of money* [B. påysa]

foesaela ['fòyšā-ɛlā] (n) *moneyed person* = **foesa + -ala**

foesa-kori ['fòyšāχòrī] (n) *money* = **foesa + kori** ²

foesola ['fòyšòlā] (n) *decision; solution* [A. faiṣala]

foesotti ['fòyšòt-tī] (n°) *sixty-five* [B. påɪⁿsåtti]

foetis ['fòytīš] (n°) *thirty-five* = **foetris**

foetris ['fòytrīš] (n°) *thirty-five* [B. påɪⁿtris]

foget ¹ ['fògɛt] (n) *packet; pocket* | cigretor foget – *cigarette packet* : fogeto toici – *I've put it in my pocket* [E.]

foget ² (n) *lapse of memory* | **foget kor-/foget kori le-** – *forget* : ami tan kota foget kori liclam – *I forgot about him* [E.]

fojilot ['fòzīlòt, 'fòjīlòt] (n) *virtue* [A. faÐīla]

fojol ['fòzòl, 'fòjòl] (n) *(God's) bounteousness* | allar fojole bala aci – *by God's grace I'm quite well* [A. faÐl]

fojonto ['fòzòntò, 'fòjòntò] (post) *up to; until; as far as; as long as; even* | gola fojonto – *up to the neck* : kail fojonto – *till tomorrow* : ami cilot fojonto jaimu – *I'll go as far as Sylhet* : larai cola fojonto – *as long as the war goes on* : tara na aoa fojonto – *until they come* : caca fojonto raji oicoin – *even uncle agreed* [B. pårjåntå < S. paryanta]

fojor ['fòzòr, 'fòjòr] (n) *dawn* [A. fajr]

fokir ['fòkīr] (n) *mendicant; fakir* | **fokir o-/fokir oi ja-** – *become destitute* : amra fokir oi geci – *we've been ruined* [A. faqīr]

fokirali ['fòkīrālī] (n) *treatment by a fakir*

fokke ['fòk-kɛ́] (n adv) *on one side; on one's behalf; on one's part* | tain amrar fokke – *he's on our side* : ukile afnar fokke mati liba – *the solicitor will speak on your behalf* : amar fokke sombob oito nae – *it won't be possible on my part* < **fokko**

fokko ['fòk-kò] (n) *side* | **fokko dor-** – *take a side* : tara amrar fokko dorce – *they have taken our side* : **fokko lo-** – *take a side* [B. påkkå < S. pakśa]

fol [fòl] (n) *fruit; result* | joŋli gacor fol – *fruit of a wild tree* : gaflatir fol – *the result of carelessness* : forikkar fol – *exam result* : **fole** – *as a result* : bonnar fole – *as a result of the*

floods : gor becar fole – *as a result of selling the house* : meman aicla, fole goro roiclam – *visitors came, so we stayed at home* [B. phål]
fol- (vi) *be borne as fruit; grow* | bondo dan fole – *rice grows in the paddy fields* : gaco tometu folce – *tomatoes have grown on the plants* [B. phål-]
fola- (vt) *cause to fruit; grow; cultivate* | hono geu folae – *they grow wheat there* : iato uri folaimu – *we'll grow beans in the back yard* [B. phåla-]
folafol ['fòlāfòl] (n) *results* < **fol**
folat ['fòlāt] (n) *flat, apartment* [E.]
fol-mul ['fòl-mūl] (n) *fruit and vegetables* = **fol** + **mul**
fon [1] [fòn] (n) *pound* | dui fon cail – *two pounds of rice* : der fon – *one and a half pounds; £1.50* : koto kori fon? – *how much is it per pound?* : atar fon koto? – *how much is a pound of flour?* : asi feni fon/fone asi feni – *eighty pence a pound* : dui fone fon – *two pounds a pound* : fac fonor baŋla deuka – *please give me five pounds in small change* [E.]
fon [2] (n) *telephone; telephone call* | fonor lain anci – *we've had a telephone line installed* : afnar fon aice – *a call has come through for you* : afnar fon! – *a call for you!* : **fon dor-** – *answer the phone* : joldi fon doro! – *quick, answer the phone!* : keu fon dore na – *nobody is answering the phone* : **fon car-/fon cari de-** – *ring off; hang up* : tara fon care na – *they never stop telephoning* : fon cari dice! – *she's hung up!* : **fon kor-** – *make a phone call; telephone* : ofiso fon kora lagbo – *it will be necessary to phone the office* : tarar goro fon korclam – *I phoned their house; I phoned them* : tain afnar gece fon korcla ni? – *did he phone you?* : **fon de-/fon di la-** – *give (someone) a call* : rinare ek·ta fon dio cai – *give Rina a call, will you* : goro gia ek·ta fon di laiba – *please give us a ring when you get home* : **fon laga-** – *start a phone conversation* : one minar loge fon lagaice – *now she's started chatting on the phone with Mina* [E.]
fonc [fòns] (n) *rubber flip-flop sandals* [E. sponge]
foncait ['fòn-sāɪt] (n) *panchayet; village council* [H. pancāyat]
foncas ['fòn-sāš] (n°) *fifty* [B. påncas]
fondit ['fòn-dīt] (n) *learned person; pundit; know-all* | hial fondit – *the wise jackal* : oto boro fondit! – *such a wise guy, thinks he knows it all!* : (to child) tui fondit oi gecoc! – *you're getting too big for your boots!* [B. påndit < S. pandita – *learned*]
fondi ['fòn-dī] (n) *trick* [B. phåndi < O. pravandha]
fonti ['fòn-tī] (n) *great-grandchild* [O. prapautra]
for [1] [fòr] (n) *aftermath* | tar for? – *what is its aftermath? what next?* : **for taki** – *from afterwards; since* : bonnar for taki – *ever since the floods* : **for for** – *successively; at intervals* : tara for for tinbar jitce – *they won three times in a row* : tain tin din for for ain – *he comes here every third day* [B. pår < O. para – *further*]
for [2] (n) *duty watch; daylight* | one for deka jae – *now you can see daylight* : **for oe/for oi jae** – *it becomes light* : for oice – *daybreak has come* : bur cair·tat for oi jae – *it gets light at 4 a.m.* : **for take** – *it is light; it remains light* : rait noe·tar bade-o for take – *it's still light after 9 p.m.* : **for de-** – *keep watch; stay on guard* : tain raitku for dein – *he keeps watch at night; he's a night watchman* [B. pråhår < S. prahara – *watch; three hour period*]
for [3] (n) *feather; wing* [P. par]
for- [1] (v) *read; study; be a student* | abba fefar forra – *Dad's reading the newspaper* : caci baŋla forcoin – *my aunt has studied Bengali* : ami kolijo fortam – *I want to study at college; I want to go to college* : **nomaj for-** – *perform prescribed Muslim prayers* : tain ruj fac okt nomaj foroin – *she says her prayers five times every day* : **fori le-** – *read; study; perform (prayers)* : tumar boi fori lao – *read your book* : aij ami nomaj fori lici – *today I have performed my prayers* [B. pår- < O. patha-]
for- [2] (vi) *fall; drip; be dropped; be laid; be situated; happen* | ufor taki it force – *a brick fell from an upper floor* : tain gaŋo forcla – *he had fallen into the river* : tai bemar force – *she has fallen ill* : id sombare forbo – *Eid will fall on a Monday* : tajfur balogonjo force – *Tajpur falls within Baloganj* : kadif kunano force? – *whereabouts is Cardiff situated?* : kuasa forto fare – *fog may descend* : fani forer – *water is dripping out* : deko, kaf forbo! –

mind, you're going to drop that cup! : enda force – *an egg has been laid* : bacur force – *a calf has been born* : tarik force – *the due date has arrived* : tanda force – *cold weather has come* : **fore** – *falls to one's lot; becomes necessary* : akta kam fore – *odd jobs crop up unexpectedly* : afnar aoa forbo ni? – *will you be coming at all?* : amar ekbar jaoa forcil – *I once had to go there* : maje maje fis dena fore – *sometimes one has to pay some fees* : **boes fore** – *one's age falls in a given age-group* : tar boes faco force – *he's in his fifth year; he's aged between four and five* : tair boes sato force – *she's in her seventh year; she's six and a bit* : **fori ja-** – *fall; fall down; happen* : tain akta fori jain – *he falls down without warning* : tan jaoar tarik fori gece – *the date for her departure has arrived* : bakka gorom fori gece – *it's got really hot* : **aia for-** – *arrive* : tara istesono aia force – *they've arrived in the station* : aia foro! – *come along, now!* [B. pår- < O. pata-]

fora[1] ['fòrā] (n) *another person; someone else* | **forar** – *of other people; someone else's* : forar mal coio na – *don't touch other people's property* : forar kam – *someone else's business* : forar goro jai na besi – *I don't often go to other people's houses* : he forar buiḋḋi loia cole – *he follows the lead of others* [B. pår < S. para – *distant; other*]

fora[2] (v n) *reading; lessons; studies* | tumar fora ses kori lao – *finish your reading* : tar fora fae ni? – *does he learn his lessons well?* : tai fora cari ḋice – *she's abandoned her studies* : huruta one forat – *the children are at their lessons now* : he kamo nae, forat – *he's not working, he's studying* < **for-**[1]

fora-[1] (v) *cause to read; cause to study; teach* | amar fuare ḋi citi foraici – *I got my son to read the letter* : caci mocjiḋo ḋua foraiba – *auntie will have a prayer recited at the mosque* : tan hokol furintore foraicoin – *she got all her daughters educated* : tain baṇla forain – *he teaches Bengali* : tain one foranit – *he's teaching right now* [B. påṛa-]

fora-[2] (v) *let fall; drop* | bilaie baicca foraice – *the cat has had kittens* [B. påṛa-]

forae ['fòrāy] (adv) *a lot; often; almost* | forae mainse cinoin tare – *a lot of people know him* : tain forae london jain – *he often goes to London* : kam·ta forae ses – *the job is almost done* : forae tin mail – *nearly three miles* [B. pray < S. prāyah]

fora-leka ['fòrāleχā] (n) *reading and writing; studies* = **fora**[2] + **leka**

foramfor ['fòrām-fòr] (adv) *by hearsay* | foramfor hunci, maramari oice – *I've heard people say there's been a fight* [B. påråmpår < S. parampara – *succession*]

foramforam ['fòrām-fòrām] (adv) *by hearsay* | foramforam kobor faici – *I got news by word of mouth; I heard a rumour* = **foramfor**

foramis ['fòrāmīš] (n) *deliberation* | **foramis kor-** – *confer; discuss* : tan loge foramis korci – *I've consulted with him* : **foramis lo-** – *take advice* : afnar ek·ta foramis loitam – *I would like some advice from you* : **foramis de-/foramis ḋi la-** – *give advice* : ek·ta foramis ḋeuka amare – *please give me your advice* = **foramosso**

foramosso ['fòrāmòš-šò] (n) *deliberation* | **foramosso kor-** – *confer; discuss* : kail tarar loge foramosso kormu – *we'll talk it over with them tomorrow* : **foramosso lo-** – *take advice* : afnar foramosso loitam – *I want your advice, please* : **foramosso de-/foramosso ḋi la-** – *give advice* : cacae bala foramosso ḋicoin amare – *uncle gave me a good piece of advice* [B. påramårså < S. parāmarša]

foran ['fòrān] (n) *heart; soul; life* [B. pran < O. prāṇa]

forasuna ['fòrāšūnā] (n) *studying; study* [B. påṛasona]

forca ['fòrsā] (n) *land registry abstract* [P. parca – *note; chit*]

forḋa ['fòrḋā] (n) *curtain; screen; (eye) cataract; purdah* | forḋa tano! – *draw the curtains!* : forḋar ufre fotu ḋekaice – *they showed pictures on a screen* : tan cokkut forḋa force – *cataracts have formed in her eyes* : aijkail forae betinte forḋa mane na – *many women don't observe purdah nowadays* [P. parda]

fore ['fòrɛ] (n adv) *afterwards; after* | fore koimu ne – *I'll tell you afterwards* : tin ḋin fore – *three days later* : tain amar fore aicoin – *he came after me* < **for**[1]

forgona ['fòr-gònā] (n) *village area; pargana* [P. pargana]

forhu ['fòrhū] (n/adv) *next day but one* | tara forhu ino aicil – *they came here the day before yesterday* : amra forhu jaimu – *we'll go the day after tomorrow* : citi kail forhu aito fare –

the letter may come tomorrow or the next day : **forhu đin** – *the day before yesterday; the day after tomorrow* [B. pårsu]
fori [¹] ['fòrī] (n) *fairy* [P. parī]
fori [²] (n) *neighbour* [B. pårsi < O. pratibeśī]
foribar ['fòrībār] (n) *family; wife* | amrar foribar boro – *our family is a large one* : afnar foribaror manus koe·jon? – *how many people are there in your family?* : tan foribar aicla tan loge – *his wife came with him* [B. påribar < S. parivāra]
foribes ['fòrībéš] (n) *environment* [B. påribes < S. pariveśa – *circumference*]
foricalona [fòrī'sālònā] (n) *management; conduct* | **foricalona kor-** – *manage; administer; run* [B. påricalåna < S. paricālana – *moving*]
foricoe ['fòrīsòy] (n) *acquaintance; means of knowing; evidence* | agor foricoe – *previous acquaintance* : bout đinor foricoe – *long acquaintance* : tain amar foricoer manus – *he is one of my acquaintance; he is someone I know* : bala mainsor foricoe kita? – *how can tell whether a person is good?* : buiđđir foricoe – *signs of intelligence* : imaner foricoe – *evidence of one's faith* : **foricoer** – *of one's acquaintance; known* : tain amar foricoer manus – *he is a person belonging to my circle of acquaintance; he is someone I know* : **foricoer maje** – *in one's circle of acquaintance* : amar foricoer maje ola keu nae – *there's nobody like that in my circle of acquaintance; I don't know anybody like that* : **(keur loge) foricoe ace** – *one is acquainted (with someone)* : tan loge amar bout đinor foricoe acil – *I had been acquainted with him for a long time* : tan loge amar kolij taki foricoe – *I know him from college* : tan loge amar foricoe nae – *I don't know him* : **(keur loge) foricoe oe/foricoe oi jae** – *acquaintance is made (with someone)* : aste aste foricoe oibo tarar – *they'll gradually get to know each other* : afnarar foricoe oice ni? – *have you got acquainted? have you met each other?* : tan loge đeso foricoe oice amar – *I first met him in Bangladesh* : **(keur) foricoe fa-** – *get to know (someone)* : tan foricoe faici tan kamor maje – *it was from his deeds that I really got to know him* : tan bala foricoe faici – *I got a good impression of him* : **(keur loge) foricoe kor-/foricoe kori le-** – *make acquaintance (with someone); be introduced (to someone)* : tain afnar loge foricoe korta cain – *he would like to get to meet you* : amar bair loge foricoe korouka – *please meet my brother; let me introduce you to my brother* [B. påricåy < S. paricaya]
forikka [fòr'īk-kā] (n) *test; examination* | cokkur forikka – *eye test* : baŋla forikka – *Bengali exam* : iskulo forikka coler – *exams are in progress at the school* : **forikka kor-** – *test; try out* : fani·ta forikka korer – *they are testing the water* : **forikka kori đek-** – *find out by experiment* : amra forikka kori đekmu, ino baiŋgon oibo ni na – *we'll have a try, and see whether aubergines will grow here* : **forikka kora-** – *have tests carried out* : amar cokkur forikka koraici – *I've had my eyes tested* [B. pårikka < S. parīkśā]
foriman ['fòrīmān] (n) *amount; quantity* | boro foriman foesa – *a large amount of money* : ek foriman asa kora jae – *one can feel a certain amount of hope* : ki foriman đuđ roice? – *how much milk is left?* [B. påriman < S. parimāṇa]
foriskar [fòrīš 'χār] (adj) *clear; clean; fair (complexion)* | akas foriskar – *the sky is clear* : foriskar fani – *clear water; clean water* : tair cera foriskar – *her complexion is fair* : **foriskar kor-/foriskar kori le-** – *make clean; cleanse* : tumar at foriskar kori loo – *clean your hands* : **foriskar kori** – *clearly* : foriskar kori kouka amare – *say it to me clearly; tell it to me straight* [B. påriskar < S. pariśkāra – *cleansing*]
forja ['fòrjā] (n) *commoners; subjects; tenant farmers* | raja ar forja – *the king and his subjects* : tara amrar forja – *they are tenants on our land* [B. pråja < S. prajā – *progeny*]
forjae ['fòrjāy] (n) *stage; level* [B. pårjay < S. paryāya – *revolution; time lapse*]
forma- ['fòrmā] (vt) *ask for; order* | tain ek·ta noea gari formaicoin – *he has ordered a new vehicle* [H. farmā- < P. farmūdan – *to order*]
formais [fòr'māiš] (n) *request; command* | afnar formais kita? – *what is your command? what would you like?* [P. formāiš]
forman [fòr'mān] (n) *proof; evidence* | curir forman – *evidence of theft* : forman kita? – *what's the proof?* : tara forman đekaice – *they have produced proof* = **froman**

foroa ['fòrowā] (n) *concern; care* | **foroa kor-** – *be concerned; care* : he ekɖom foroa kore na – *he doesn't care at all; he doesn't give a damn* [P. parvāh]

foroj ['fòròz, 'fòròj] (n) *moral imperative* | nomaj fora foroj – *saying one's prayers is a moral obligation* [A. farƊ]

forom ['fòròm] (n) *form* | forom filaf korta oiba – *you'll have to fill in a form* [E.]

forsa ['fòr-šā] (adj) *fair-skinned* [B. phârsa]

fortek ['fòr-tɛχ] (adj) *each; every* | fortek afta – *every week* [B. pråttek < S. pratyeka]

forti ['fòrtī] (adj) *each; every* | forti ɖin – *every day* : amra forti maso jai – *we go there every month* = **froti**

foru ['fòrū] (n/adv) *next day but one* = **forhu**

fosol ['fòšòl] (n) *crop; crops* | bala fosol oice – *there has been a good crop* : nanan jator fosol – *various kinds of crops* : **fosol tul-** – *harvest a crop* : tara fosol tulce na ebu – *they haven't yet brought the crops in* [A. faṣl – *division; season*]

fossa ['fòš-šā] (adj) *fair-skinned* = **forsa**

fosto ['fòš-tò] (adj) *clear* | fosto leka – *clear writing* : fosto onniae – *a blatant injustice* ¶ **fosto** (adv) *clearly* | on taki boro mocjiɖ fosto ɖeka jae – *the main mosque can be seen quite clearly from here* [B. spåstå < S. spaśta]

fosu ['fòšū] (n) *beast* [B. påsu < S. pašu]

fosu-faki ['fòšūfākī] (n) *birds and beasts; animals* = **fosu + faki**

fot [fòt] (n) *pop* | **fot kor-** – *go "pop"; burst* : **fot kori** – *in a burst; suddenly* : tain fot kori gecoin gi – *he went off all of a sudden*

fotafot ['fòtāfòt] (adv) *suddenly; quickly* < **fot**

fotka ['fòtχā] (n) *exploding firework; banger* [B. phåtka]

fotok ['fòtòχ] (n) *entrance room; front part of dwelling house* [B. phåtåk – *gateway*]

fotor-fotor ['fòtòr-fòtòr] (n) *fussing* | **fotor-fotor kor-** – *fuss about*

fotti ['fòt-tī] (n) *bandage* [H. pattī]

fotu ['fòtū] (n) *photograph; picture* | afnar fotu – *a photo of you* : ikta kar fotu? – *who is this picture of?* : tai sunɖor fotu akaice – *she has drawn a beautiful picture* : **fotu tul-** – *take a photograph* : afnar fotu tultam – *I want to take a photo of you* [E.]

fot [fòt] (n) *way; journey* | fot cini – *I know the way* : hi ousuɖ faibar kunu fot ace ni? – *is there any way of obtaining that medicine?* : janbar kunu fot nae – *there's no way of knowing* : tain foesa korar fot tukaira – *he's looking for a way of making money* : tin ɖinor fot – *a three-day journey* : **foto** – *on the way (literally)* : amra foto kai limu – *we'll eat on the way* : **fote** – *on the way (figuratively)* : tain morbar fote – *he's on the way to ruin* : **fotor maje** – *on the way; in the way* : fotor maje ekbar tamclam – *we stopped once on the way* : tara amar fotor maje bera rakce – *they've put obstacles in my way* : **fot ɖe-/fot ɖi la-** – *set out; set off* : kail fot ɖimu – *we'll set off tomorrow* : tara fot ɖi laice – *they've set out on their journey* : **fot ɖor-** – *get under way; embark on a course* : kail fot ɖormu – *we'll make a start tomorrow* : ek·ta fot ɖora lagbo – *we'll have to do something* : he kunu fot ɖore na – *he doesn't get off his backside* [B. påth < S. patha]

fota ['fòtā] (n) *early morning* | amra fotar somoe ceeri kai – *we have our sehri in the early morning (before dawn)* [B. pratå < S. prātah]

fotor ['fòtòr] (n) *crack; crevice* [A. faṭr]

fotrika ['fòt-rīkā] (n) *newspaper; periodical* [B. påtrika < S. patrikā – *document*]

fotro ['fòt-rò] (n) *piece of paper* [B. påtrå < S. patra – *leaf*]

fotua ['fòtuā] (n) *legal pronouncement by Islamic scholar; fatwa* [A. fatwā]

fotur ['fòtūr] (adj) *bankrupt; penniless* [A. futūr – *slackening; dissolution*]

fouj ['fòuz, 'fòuj] (n) *army* [A. fauj]

foujɖari ['fòuzɖārī] (adj) *criminal (proceedings)* [P. faujɖārī]

fout ['fòut] (adj) *bankrupt; penniless* = **fotur**

fresani ['frešānī] (n) *disturbance; harassment* = **feresani**

frio ['frìò] (adj) *dear; favourite* | frio boin – *dear sister* : amar frio kani dail bat – *my favourite food is rice and dhal* [B. priyå < S. priya]

frista ['frīštā] (n) *lateral surface; page* [B. pristha < S. pŕstha]
friti ['frītī] (n) *affection; love* [B. priti < S. prīti]
fritibi ['frītībī] (n) *world* [B. prithibi < S. pŕthvī]
fritok ['frītòχ] (adj) *separate* [B. prithåk < S. pŕthak]
froman ['fròmān] (n) *proof; evidence* | curir froman – *evidence of theft* : he korcil, tar froman kita? – *what's the proof that he did it?* : tara gaflatir froman dekaice – *they have produced proof of negligence* [B. pråman < S. pramāṇa – *standard*]
fronam ['frònām] (n) *bow of homage and respect* (a gesture of veneration particularly associated with Hindu culture) | **fronam kor-** – *salute respectfully (with head bent and palms joined, or with a deep bow to touch the recipient's feet)* [B. prånam < S. praṇāma]
frosno ['fròšnò] (n) *question* | **frosno kor-** – *ask; enquire* : kita oice, tare frosno kortam – *I want to ask him what happened* [B. pråsnå < S. prašna]
froti ['fròtī] (adj) *each; every* | froti din – *every day* : amra froti maso jai – *we go there every month* [B. pråti < S. prati]
frotistan ['fròtīstān] (n) *institution; organization* [B. pråtisthan < S. pratisthāna – *pedestal; foundation*]
fu [fū:] (n) *blowing* | **fu de-/fu di la-** – *blow; apply a curative mantra by blowing* : bego fu di lao – *blow into the bag* : mulla sab tair matat fu dicoin – *the mullah blew a prayer over her head (to cure her)* [B. phuⁿ]
fua ['fūā] (n) *boy; son* | amar dui fua, dui furi – *I have two sons and two daughters* : **fuae** – *boy; son* (instrumental) : hou fuae korce – *that boy did it* : **fuain** – *boys; sons* : ou iskulo kali fuain – *it's boys only in this school* : **fuainte** – *boys; sons* (instrumental) : fuainte doroja baṇce – *the boys have broken the door* : **fuaintor** – *of boys; of sons* : fuaintor kafor – *boys' clothes* : **fuaintore** – *(to) boys; (to) sons* (objective) : ami fuaintore hokol kota koici – *I said it all to the boys; I told the boys everything* [H. poā < O. putra]
fua-furi ['fūāfūrī] (n) *boys and girls; children* = **fua + furi** ¹
fub [fūb] (n) *east* | **fube** – *in the east; towards the east* : bajar·ta aro fube – *the marketplace is further east* : mocjidor fube – *east of the mosque* : **fube di** – *eastwards* : fube di jauka – *proceed towards the east* : **fubor** – *of the east; eastern* : amra fubor goro taki – *we live in the east building* [B. pub < O. pūrva]
fubar ['fūbār] (n) *vacuum cleaner* = **hubar**
fuc- ¹ [fūs] (v) *wipe* | tebul fuctam oimu – *I must wipe the table* : **fuci le-** – *wipe* : gari fuci lici – *I've wiped the car* [B. poⁿch-]
fuc- ² (v) *ask* [H. pūch-]
fufa ['fūfā] (n) *father's sister's husband* [H. phūphā]
fufu ['fūfū] (n) *father's sister; father's boin* | **fufur goror** – *descended from father's sister* : fufur goror bai – *paternal cousin; father's sister's son* [H. phūphī]
fuj [fūz] (n) *pus* [B. puⁿj]
fuja ['fūzā, 'fūjā] (n) *idol worship; Hindu festival* | durga fuja – *the Durgapuja festival* : **fuja kor-** – *worship (an idol)* : tara butor fuja kore – *they worship idols* : boisnob era durgare fuja kore na – *Vaisnavas do not worship Durga* [B. puja < S. pūjā]
fuk ¹ [fūk] (n) *insect; bug* [B. poka]
fuk ² (n) *blowing* [B. phuⁿk]
fukoir ['fūkòir] (n) *reservoir; pond* [B. pukur]
fukri ['fūkrī] (n) *reservoir; pond* = **fukoir**
ful ¹ [fūl] (n) *flower; rosette; ornamentation* | amor ful – *mango blossom* : genda ful – *marigold* : gulaf ful – *rose* : joṇli ful – *wild flowers* : kaforo ful deoa – *the cloth has floral designs on it* : kanor ful – *earring* : nakor ful – *nose clove* : **ful kata** – *embroidery; embroidered* : ful kata kafor – *embroidered cloth* [B. phul]
ful ² (n) *bridge* [B. pul < P. pul]
ful ³ (n) *hole* = **hul** ²
ful- (vi) *puff up; swell* | amar at fulce – *my arm has swollen up* : tar buk fuler – *his chest is puffing up (with pride)* : **fuli ja-** – *puff up; become swollen; take offence; get shirty* : tar fau

fuli gece – *his foot has become swollen* : i kota hunia beta fuli gecoin – *in hearing this the old fellow started bristling*   [B. phul-]
fula ['fūlā] (v adj) *puffed up; swollen* | tar couk fula – *his eyes are puffy* : fula fet – *a distended stomach* : **fula fula** – *puffed up; swollen*   < **ful-**
fula- (vt) *puff up; inflate* | tain cakka fulaira – *he's inflating the tyre* : tumar gal fulao kene? – *why are you puffing out your cheeks? why are you looking so cross?* : **fulai đe-** – *puff up; inflate* : tara belun fulai đer – *they're blowing up balloons*   [B. phula-]
fulfuli ['fūl-fūlī] (n) *flea*
fulis ['fūlīš] (n) *policeman; police force* | ek·jon fulis aicla – *a policeman came* : fulis daktam ni? – *shall I call the police?* ¶ **fulis** (adj) *(of the) police* | fulis kout – *magistrate's court* : fulis difat – *police department*   [E.]
fulob [sup]1[/sup] ['fūlòb] (n) *pilaf; pulao*   = **fulou**
fulob [sup]2[/sup] (n) *filling up*   = **filaf**
fulou ['fūlôu] (n) *pilaf; pulao*   [P. pilāv, pilāw]
fulu ['fūlū] (n) *influenza* | hokolor fulu oi gece – *everyone's got the flu*   [E.]
fun [fūn] (n) *phone*   = **fon** [sup]2[/sup]
fun- (v) *hear; listen*   = **hun-**
funda ['fūndā] (n) *motorcycle*   = **hunda**
funđ ['fūnđ] (n) *vulva* [indecent]   [B. poⁿđ]
funđa ['fūnđā] (n) *arsehole; sod* [indecent]   cf **funđ**
funđro ['fūn-đrò] (nº) *fifteen*   [H. punđra]
funoro ['fūnòrò] (nº) *fifteen*   [B. pånårå]
funra ['fūn-rā] (n) *hearer; listener*   = **hunra**
fuŋga ['fūŋ-gā] (n) *bastard*
fuŋgami ['fūŋ-gāmī] (n) *malicious behaviour*
fuŋgi ['fūŋ-gī] (n) *female bastard*
fur- [sup]1[/sup] [fūr] (vi) *become filled; be completed; pass* | fuskunni furce – *the pond has filled up* : mas furer – *the month is coming to its end* : somoe fure na – *time doesn't pass* : coe afta furbo – *it'll soon be six full weeks* : tar noe bocor furce – *his nine years are completed; he's turned nine* : **furi ja-** – *be completed* : tin bocor furi gece – *three years have passed in full*   [B. pur-]
fur- [sup]2[/sup] (vi) *be fully used up; run out* | **furi ja-** – *be fully used up; run out* : cail furi gece – *the rice has run out*   [B. phura-]
fura ['fūrā] (v adj) *filled; full; whole; entire* | fura butol – *a full bottle* : afnar fura nam kouka – *tell me your full name* : fura đus tar – *the entire blame is on him* ¶ **fura** (adv) *fully; completely* | tain fura fagol – *he's completely mad* : fura ek mail – *fully one mile* : tin đin fura – *three whole days*   < **fur-** [sup]1[/sup]
fura- [sup]1[/sup] (vt) *fill up; make up to the full amount* | ami ek bosta furaici – *I've filled one sack* : tain bis fon furaicoin – *he made it up to twenty pounds* : **furai đe-** – *fill up; make up to the full amount*   [B. pura-]
fura- [sup]2[/sup] (v) *come to an end; come to terms* | cini furaice – *all the sugar is finished* : tara fac ajar fon đi furaice – *they settled for £5000* : amra bibađ furaitam cai – *we want to settle the dispute* : **furai ja-** – *come to an end; run out* : somoe furai jaibo – *time will run out* : amar foesa furai gece – *my funds are exhausted*   [B. phura-]
fura- [sup]3[/sup] (v) *sweep with a broom*   = **hura-**
furafuri ['fūrāfūrī] (adv) *completely; altogether* | furafuri bađ – *totally spoilt* : furafuri bala – *perfectly all right*   [B. purapuri]
furail ['fūrāil] (v adj) *agreed; contracted*   < **fura-** [sup]2[/sup]
furan [sup]1[/sup] ['fūrān] (adj) *old*   = **furana**
furan [sup]2[/sup] (n) *agreement; contract*   [B. phuran]
furana ['fūrānā] (adj) *old; outdated* | furana kafor – *old clothes* : furana manus – *old-timer; long-standing figure* : ou fefar furana – *this paper is out of date*   [H. purānā]

furbe ['fūr-bɛ] (n adv) *previously; before* | afnera furbe kunano takta? – *where did you live previously?* : tain furbe fulis acla – *he was formerly a policeman* : bout furbe – *a long time ago* : larair furbe – *before the war* : tain aoar furbe – *before she arrived* < **furbo**
furbo ['fūr-bò] (adj) *prior; eastern* | furbo kal – *earlier times; olden days* : furbofurus – *ancestors* : furbo baŋla – *East Bengal* ¶ **furbo** (n) *earlier time; the east* | furbo foccim – *east and west* : **furbor** – *of earlier times; previous* : furbor malik indu acla – *the previous owner was a Hindu* : **furbe** – *in earlier times; previously* : amra furbe hono taktam – *we used to live there previously* [B. purbå < S. pūrva]
furcot ['fūr-sòt] (n) *chance; opportunity* [A. furṣa – *leisure*]
furi¹ ['fūrī] (n) *girl; daughter* | amrar dui furi, dui fua – *we have two daughters and two sons* : **furie/fuire** – *girl; daughter* (instrumental) : furie malaice – *it was my daughter who made it* : **furin** – *girls; daughters* : ou iskulo kali furin – *it's girls only at this school* : **furinte** – *girls; daughters* (instrumental) : furinte fotu akar – *the girls are painting pictures* : **furintor** – *of girls; of daughters* : furintor kafor – *girls' clothes* : **furintore** – *(to) girls; (to) daughters* (objective) : ami furintore koici – *I said it to the girls; I told the girls* [O. putrī]
furi² (n) *pimple* [B. phoⁿṛa]
furkan ['fūr-χān] (n) *the Holy Quran* [A. furqān – *criterion; evidence*]
furoin ['fūròın] (n) *broom* = **huroin**
furon¹ ['fūròn] (n) *multiplication* [B. purån < S. pūrāṇa – *filling*]
furon² (n) *prawn* [E.]
furti¹ ['fūrtī] (n) *completion* [B. purti < S. pūrti – *filling*]
furti² (n) *fun* | **furti kor** – *have fun* [B. phurti < O. sfurti – *tremor; excitement*]
furtibaj ['fūrtībāz] (n) *fun-loving person; joker* = **furti**² + -**baj**
furtibaji ['fūrtībāzī] (n) *indulgence in fun* = **furti**² + -**baji**
furu ['fūrū] (adj) *small; smaller; too small; junior* | furu cear – *a small chair* : tai tumar furu – *she is smaller than you* : ita amar lagi furu – *this is too small for me* : ou fen tumar furu lagce – *these trousers are too small to fit you* : furu caca – *junior paternal uncle* : furu baisab – *least senior elder brother* : furu mon/furu dil – *faint heart; ungenerous nature* : amar mon furu oi gece – *my heart is reduced; I feel discouraged* : tar dil furu – *he is petty minded* : «furu mainsor boro mat» – *little people always talk big* : **furu kor-/furu kori le-** – *make smaller* : tar couk furu kori lice – *he's screwed up his eyes* : **furu furu** – *very small* : furu furu dana – *little tiny grains* = **huru**
furumuru ['fūrūmūrū] (adj) *very small; tiny* = **hurumuru**
furus ['fūrūš] (n) *male person; generation* | furus na moila? – *man or woman? male or female?* : furus manus – *males; men* : ino furus mainsor tolet – *this is the men's toilet* : furbofurus – *ancestors* : tin furus furbe – *three generations back* [B. purus < S. puruśa]
furutta ['fūrūt-tā] (n) *little ones; children* = **hurutta**
fus¹ [fūš] (n) *Poush (December-January)* [B. pous < S. pauśa]
fus² (n) *consciousness* = **hus**
fus- (vt) *nurture; foster* | **fuse** – *it suffices* : amrar fuse – *it's enough for us* : i foesae amar fuse na – *I can't make do with this money* [B. posa-]
fusa ['fūšā] (v adj) *fostered; kept as a pet* | fusa bilai – *pet cat* < **fus-**
fusfus ['fūš-fūš] (n) *lung; lungs* [B. phusphus]
fusiar ['fūšıār] (adj) *alert* = **husiar**
fusiari ['fūšıārī] (n) *warning* = **husiari**
fuskundi ['fūš-kūndī] (n) *reservoir; pond* = **fuskunni**
fuskunni ['fūš-kun-nī] (n) *reservoir; pond* [B. puskårini < S. puśkariṇi – *lotus pool*]
fustok ['fūštòχ] (n) *book; books* [B. puståk < S. pustaka]
fustofis ['fūštòfīš] (n) *post office* [E.]
fut¹ [fūt] (n) *foot (length)* [E.]
fut² [fū:t] (n) *pimple; boil* cf **furi**²
fut- (vi) *open out; blossom; burst; seethe* | aij ful futbo – *the flower will open today* : gorom telor maje fafra fute – *rice crackers expand in hot oil* : furir muko asi futice – *a smile*

bloomed on the girl's face : fani futer – *the water is seething; the water is boiling* : **futi ja-** – *burst; burst open* : muri futi jar – *the pop rice is bursting open* : boron futi jaibo – *the abscess will burst* : fani futi gece – *the water has come to the boil* : buma futi gecil – *a bomb had exploded*   [B. phut-]

futa [¹] ['fūtā] (n) *droplet; drop* | megor futa – *raindrops* : ruj tin futa lagaita – *you should apply three drops per day* : **ek futa** – *a drop; a small amount* : ek futa tel force na – *not one drop of oil has spilt out* : ca ek futa kaitam – *I could do with a spot of tea* : amar ek futa gum oice na – *I didn't get a wink of sleep*   [B. phota]

futa [²] (v adj) *opened out; burst; boiled* | futa gulaf – *a full-blown rose* : futa fani – *boiled water*   < **fut-**

futa- (vt) *cause to expand; blow up; bring to the boil* | belun futaitam ni? – *shall I blow up the balloon?* : tara buma futaice – *they let off a bomb* : ek ketli fani futao cai – *please boil up a kettleful of water* : **futai đe-** – *cause to expand; blow up* : fuainte cakka futai đice – *the boys pumped up the tyre*   [B. phuta-]

futani ['fūtānī] (v n) *puffing up* | **futani kor-** – *show off* : betae kali futani kore – *that fellow's always showing off*   < **futa-**

futbol ['fūtbòl] (n) *football; football pools* | amar futbolo lage jođin.. – *if I win the pools..* : **futbol kela-** – *play football; play the pools*   [E.]

futi ['fūtī] (n) *any of several species of small fish (Barbus spp)*   [B. puⁿti]

futki ['fūt-kī] (n) *dried fish*   = **hutki**

fut [fūt] (n) *son* | afnar furu fut kuae? – *where's your younger son?* ¶ **fut** (int) *sonny* | a re fut! – *come here, sonny boy!*   [B. put < O. putra]

futi ['fūtī] (n) *chap-book; ballad*   [B. puthi < O. postaka]

futra ['fūt-rā] (n) *brother of child's spouse*

futul ['fūtūl] (n) *doll; figurine*   [B. putul < O. puttala]

g

ga [gā] (n) *body; torso; lateral surface* | amar ga gorom oi gece – *my body has got hot; I'm (feeling) hot* : tar ga semla – *his body is nut-brown; he has a brown skin* : bebir ga kali – *the baby's body is bare* : tair gar maje dag ace – *she's got a birthmark on her torso* : furir gat tel makcoin – *she has rubbed her daughter's skin with oil* : garir gat joŋ lagce – *there is rust on the side of the car* : **kali gae** – *with a bare body; with the upper part of the body unclothed* : fuae kali gae kelar – *the boy is playing with his torso bared* : **gae taki** – *from one's body; from one's own resources* : tar beton ami gae taki diram – *I'm paying his wages out of my own pocket* : **gat lage** – *it hits the body; it hurts* : tar kota amar gat lagce – *what he said really wounded me* [B. ga < O. gātra]

ga [gā:] (n) *wound; sore* | **ga oe/ga oi jae** – *a sore develops* : tar ator maje ga oi gece – *he's got a sore on his hand* : tair gola ga oi gece – *she's got a sore throat* [B. gha]

ga- (v) *sing; recite information* | hurutae gan gar – *the children are singing songs* : tain cacar kota gaicoin na – *he didn't mention uncle (when supplying details of the family)* : **keic ga-** – *conduct a lawsuit* : ami tare keic gaia ou deso anci – *I went through legal proceedings in order to bring him to this country* [B. ga-]

gab [gāb] (n) *mangosteen (tree and fruit)* [B. gab]

gabi ['gābī] (n) *(milch) cow* [B. gabhi < O. garbhinī – *pregnant female*]

gabr- ['gābr] (vi) *be alarmed* | caci gabricoin – *aunt has become alarmed* : **gabri ja-** – *be alarmed* : hunia tara gabri gecil – *hearing that, they got the wind up*

gabra- ['gābrā] (v) *be alarmed* | gabraio na! – *don't be alarmed!* : gabraita kene? – *why should you be alarmed? there's no need to panic!* : **gabrai ja-** – *be alarmed* : caca gabrai gecoin – *uncle has lost his nerve* : **gabrai de-** – *alarm; scare* : afne gabrai dicoin tare – *you've put the wind up him* [B. ghabra-]

gabru ['gābrū] (n) *young bridegroom* [H. gabrū < O. garbharūpa]

gac [gās] (n) *plant; tree* | bakor gac – *coriander plant* : kola gac – *banana plant* : am gac – *mango tree* : gaco koto fol – *there's a lot of fruit on the tree* : **gac laga-** – *put a plant in the ground; plant a tree* [B. gach]

gaca ['gāsā] (n) *strand; strip* | ek gaca cul – *a strand of hair; a single hair* : tin gaca bel – *three strips of belt; three belts* : dorir gaca – *a piece of string* [B. gacha]

gac-gacra ['gās-gāsrā] (n) *vegetation* = **gac + gacra**

gacra ['gāsrā] (n) *small plant* [B. gachra]

gaddi ['gād-dī] (n) *heap; pile* | ek gaddi kafor – *a heap of clothes* : citir gaddi – *piles of letters* : amar kam ek gaddi – *I've got loads of work to do* [H. gaddī]

gada ['gādā] (n) *donkey; fool* [B. gadha < O. gardhabha]

gadda ['gād-dā] (adj) *thick-headed; unteachable* cf **gada**

gaddar ['gād-dār] (n) *traitor* [A. ġaddār]

gae [gāɛ] (n) *the body* < **ga**

gae (n adv) *in the village* < **gau**

gaeb ['gāɛb] (adj) *out of sight* | **gaeb o-/gaeb oi ja-** – *disappear* [A. ġāib – *absent*]

gae-gerame ['gāɛgɛrāmɛ] (n adv) *all over the countryside* < **gau-geram**

gae holud ['gāɛ hòlūd] (n) *turmeric ceremony* (pre-nuptial ceremony where the future bride or groom is smeared with turmeric) [B. gaye holud]

gael ['gāɛl] (adj) *wounded* [H. ghāel]

gafar ['gāfār] (n) *gaffer; boss* [E.]

gafru ['gābrū] (n) *young bridegroom* = **gabru**

gafil ['gāfīl] (adj) *careless; heedless* [A. ġāfil]

gafla ['gāflā] (n) *mess-up; disorder* [H. ghaplā]

gaflati ['gāflātī] (n) *carelessness; negligence* | ofiso bout gaflati coler – *a lot of carelessness is going on in the office* : **gaflati kor-** – *be careless; be negligent* [A. ġafla]

gai ['gāɪ] (n) *cow* [H. gāe]
gail ['gāɪl] (n) *abuse; swearing; swearword* | kora gail – *strong swearwords* : **gail đe-** – *curse; swear* : keure gail đio na – *never swear at anyone* : **gail huna-** – *regale with swearwords* : tar bocre gail hunaice – *he swore at his boss* = **gali**
gait [gāɪt] (n) *knot; bundle* | rossir maje gait đui·ta – *there are two knots in the rope* : kaforor gait – *a bundle of clothes* : **gait banđ-/gait banđi la-** – *tie a knot; tie up a bundle* : cacae gait banđi lira – *uncle is packing his bags* : tara gait banđi gece gi – *they've packed up and gone away* [B. gaⁿt]
gait-gut ['gāɪt-gūt] (n) *bag and baggage* | tara gait-gut loia gece gi – *they went, taking all their belongings with them*
gal [gāl] (n) *cheek; swearword* | gul gal – *round cheeks* : kora gal – *a bad swearword* : **gal fula-** – *puff up the cheeks; pout; show annoyance* : tare kunta koile-u he gal fulae – *if you say anything to him he gets grumpy* : **gal đe-/gal đi la-** – *use swearwords; cuss* : he koto gal đee – *he swears a lot* : amare gal đi laice – *he swore at me* [B. gal]
gal- (v) *use swearwords* | he amare galice – *he swore at me*
gala¹ ['gālā] (n) *side* | baskor gala – *the side of the box* : afne kun gala jaita? – *which side would you proceed?* *which way are you heading?* : **galat** – *at the side; beside; nearby* : hou galat – *on that side* : tumar galat – *beside you* : tebulor galat – *near the table*
gala² (n) *asphalt* | rastat gala daler – *they're laying asphalt on the road*
galabae ['gālābāɛ] (n adv) *beside; near; nearby* = **gala + bae**
galagali ['gālāgālī] (n) *swearing; verbal abuse* < **gal-**
galfula ['gāl-fūlā] (n) *swelling of the cheeks; mumps* [B. gal-phula]
gali ['gālī] (n) *abuse; swearing; swearword* | **gali đe** – *curse; swear* [B. gali]
galica ['gālīsā] (n) *(non-fitted) carpet* [P. ġālīca]
gali-golaj ['gālīgòlāz, 'gālīgòlāj] (n) *swearing; verbal abuse* [H. gālī-galoj]
gam [gām] (n) *perspiration* | tar gam cuter – *his sweat is running; he's sweating hard* : amar gam cuti gece! – *phew, I'm sweltering!* [B. gham < O. gharma]
gam- (vi) *perspire* | amra gamte gamte ses! – *we're boiling to death!* : **gami ja-** – *break out in sweat* : caca gami gecoin – *uncle has started to perspire* [B. gham-]
gama- ['gāmā] (vt) *cause to perspire* | **mata gama-** – *exert one's brain; worry* : tain kali kali mata gamaira – *he is taxing his brains unnecessarily* : ilagi mata gamain na jen – *please don't bother yourself about that* : mata gamaibar kam nae – *there's no need to worry* [B. ghama-]
gamaci ['gāmāsī] (n) *prickly heat* [B. ghamaci]
gamca ['gām-sā] (n) *body-cloth; muslin towel* [B. gamcha]
gamla ['gām-lā] (n) *tub; bowl* [B. gamla]
gan [gān] (n) *song; singing; music* | one tara gan gaibo – *now they're going to sing a song* : caca kecedor gan hunra – *uncle is listening to music on cassettes* [B. gan]
gan-bajna ['gān-bāz-nā] (n) *music* = **gan + bajna**
gandu ['gān-dū] (n) *good-for-nothing* [H. gāndū]
ganđa ['gān-đā] (adj) *putrid; dirty* [P. ganđa]
ganja ['gān-jā] (n) *cannabis* [H. gānjā]
gaoa- ['gāwā] (vt) *cause to sing; cause to declare* | tan furire đia gan gaoaicoin – *he got his daughter to sing a song* : ukile mica kota gaoaice – *the advocate got him to make a false declaration* [B. gaoa-]
gar- [gār] (vt) *drive into the ground; implant; embed* | goror samne boud garce – *they've planted a signboard in front of the house* : **gari le-** – *drive in; implant; embed* : kuti gari ler – *they are driving posts into the ground* : amar ato cui gari licil – *they stuck a needle in my arm* [B. gaɽ-]
gara ['gārā] (v adj) *driven in; implanted; embedded* < **gar-**
gari ['gārī] (n) *vehicle; car* | gurar gari – *horse-drawn vehicle* : koe·tat carbo gari? – *at what time will the bus / coach / train / tram depart?* : taintain noea gari loicoin – *they've bought a new car* : afne gari calain ni? – *do you drive?* : **gari loia** – *with a car; by car* : amra gari

loia jaimu – *we'll go by car* : **garit** – *in a car; by car* : garit takouka – *stay in the car* : kila aicla? garit – *how did you come? by car*   [B. gaṛi]
garibara ['gārībārā] (n) *(vehicle) fare*   = **gari + bara** [2]
gariola ['gārī-òlā] (n) *car-owner*   = **gari + -ala**
gas [gāš] (n) *grass*   [B. ghas]
gat [gāt] (n) *landing-stage*   [B. ghat]
gat- (vt) *drive in; implant; imbed*   = **gar-**
gatta ['gāt-tā] (adj) *thickset*   [B. ga^{n}tta]
gatti ['gāt-tī] (n) *insufficiency; shortfall*   [B. ghatti]
gat [1] [gāt] (n) *cavity; hole* | gato force – *it's fallen into a hole*   = **gorto**
gat [2] (n) *opportunity; excuse* | tara jograr gat tukar – *they're looking for an excuse to start a quarrel*   [B. ghat]
gat- (vt) *impale; pin; string* | mac borsit gata – *the fish is impaled in a hook* : kagojain fin dia gatci – *I've pinned the papers together* : cutar maje bici gatcoin – *she's strung the seeds on a thread* : tara mala gater – *they're stringing together a garland* : **gati le-** – *impale; pin; string* : katacamuco alu gati lice – *he's impaled a potato on a fork*   [B. ga^{n}th-]
gata ['gātā] (v adj) *impaled; pinned; strung*   < **gat-**
gatni ['gāt-nī] (n) *injection*   < **gat-**
gau [gāu] (n) *village* | amrar gau boro – *our village is a large one* : cearmen ducra gaur – *the council chairman is from a different village* : tara gaut take – *they live in a village; their home is in the country* : «gaut aguin lagle mocjid baki take na» – *when disaster strikes nothing is sacred any more* : **gau mar-** – *roam the villages; gad about* : haridin gau marat take – *they're out visiting friends all day*   [B. gao^n]
gauali ['gāwālī] (adj) *rustic*   < **gau**
gaue-gonje ['gāŵɛ-gònjɛ] (n adv) *all over the country*   < **gau, gonj**
gau-geram ['gāu-gɛrām] (n) *villages; countryside*   = **gau + geram**
gaura ['gāu-rā] (n) *one who sings; one who recites*   < **ga-**
gauuua ['gāŵŵā] (adj) *rustic*   < **gau**
ge- (gɛ) (vi) *have gone* | tara goro gece – *they have gone home* : ami sofo geclam – *I had gone to the shop* : tain london gecoin gi – *he has gone to London* : tumra gele amra-o gelam ne – *if you went we'd go too* : **oi ge-** – *have become; have happened* : tain buro oi gecoin – *he's become old* : rait oi gece – *it's got dark* : kam oi gece – *the job is done*   Note: This root is used in past tenses only, where it replaces **ja-** (q.v.)
gean ['gɛān] (n) *knowledge* | i somonde amar kunu gean nae – *I have no knowledge of that; I know nothing about that*   [B. gyan < S. jñāna]
geani ['gɛānī] (adj) *knowledgeable; wise* | tain geani manus – *he's a well informed, sensible person*   [B. gyani < S. jñānī]
gec [1] [gɛs] (n) *personal vicinity; personal possession* | **(keur) gece** – *in the presence (of somebody); in the hands (of somebody)* : tumar ammar gece tako – *stay with your mummy* : cafi cacar gece – *the keys are in uncle's possession* : **(keur) gec taki/gec tone** – *from the presence (of someone); from the hands (of someone)* : he amar gec taki nice – *he took it from me* : kar gec tone kobor faiclae? – *from whom did you hear the news?* : tain amrar gec taki gecoin gi – *she has gone away from us; she has left us*
gec [2] (n) *gas; gastric secretion* | haridin gec jole – *the gas fire is on all day* : gecor lain kata – *the gas supply has been cut off* : amar bukut gec ute – *I get gastric reflux*   [E.]
gece [1] ['gɛsɛ] (n adv) *in the presence (of); in the hands (of)* | he tar cacar gece take – *he lives with his uncle* : tan gece tikit ace – *he's got some tickets with him* : amar gece foesa nae – *I have no money on me* : tan gece di lauka – *hand it over to him* : nanar gece citi dimu – *I'll write a letter to grandfather* : keur gece koitam nai – *I won't tell anybody*   < **gec** [1]
gece [2] (verb as modifier) *which has passed; past; last* | gece afta – *last week*   < **ge-**
gectik ['gɛstīk] (n) *gastric ulcers; gastric illness*   [E.]
geda ['gɛdā] (n) *male infant*   [H. gedā]
gedi ['gɛdī] (n) *female infant*

gelas ['gɛlāš] (n) *glass tumbler* | fanir gelas – *drinking glass* [E.]
gelo ['gɛlò] (verb as modifier) *which has passed; past; last* | gelo budbar – *last Wednesday* < **ge-**
genda ['gɛndā] (adj) *rotten; smelly* = **ganda**
genjam ['gɛnjām] (n) *messy complication; botheration* | tarar loge kali genjam – *dealing with them is sheer hassle* : **genjam kor-** – *cause complications; cause botheration* : betae hokol somoe genjam kore – *that fellow always makes things complicated*
genji ['gɛnjī] (n) *cotton undershirt; vest* [E. Guernsey (cloth)]
gerafi ['gɛrāfī] (n) *anchor*
geram ['gɛrām] (n) *village* [B. gram < S. grāma]
geran ['gɛrān] (n) *(pleasant) smell; scent* [B. ghran < S. ghrāṇa – *smelling*]
gerau ['gɛrāu] (n) *encirclement* | **gerau kor-** – *encircle; surround* [H. gherāo]
geu [gɛu] (n) *wheat* [H. gehū]
gi [gī] (v adv) *having gone* | (as reinforcement for the verb **ja-**) ami jairam gi! – *I'm going; I'm off!* : jauka gi! – *all right, off you go!* : tara kail jaibo gi – *they will depart tomorrow* : hokole gecoin gi – *everyone has gone* : tain gele gi bala oibo – *it will be better if he does go* : tumi jaitae gi faro – *you may go* : ami jaitam gi oimu – *I shall have to go* : (adding a sense of motion to other verbs) afne one gumauka gi – *now go and get some sleep* : tara feronto boito gi – *they should go and sit in the front room* : tain cafi·ta nicoin gi – *he's gone off with the key* : amar kut ano gi cai – *please go and get my coat* : **gi ar-** – *have (already) gone* : tain gi arcoin – *he's already gone* : tumra gi arle tain koiba – *he'll tell you once you've got there* : nana mokkat gi ari morcoin – *great-uncle died after reaching Mecca* : **oi gi ar-** – *have become; have taken place* : tain sef oi gi arcoin – *he's become a chef* : kela oi gi arce – *the match is over* : **gi an-** – *go and get; fetch* : ami fefarsofo gi anci – *I went and got it from the newsagent's* : tar citi gi anto – *he should go and fetch his letters* : **gi a-** – *go and come back; get back (having gone somewhere)* : tara london gi aice – *they've been to London and come back* : afne oto joldi gi aicoin! – *how quickly you got back!* = **gia**
gia ['gīā] (v adv) *having gone; after going* | tain deso gia mara kaicoin – *he died after having gone to Bangladesh* : ami gia dekmu – *after going I shall see; I'll go and see* : sofo gia dud ano cai – *please go to the shop and get some milk* : tumar ammare gia koo – *go and tell your Mum* : **hono gia** – *(literally) having got there; (metaphorically) at that point; thereby* : amra hono gia kaimu – *we'll eat when we get there* : tain hono gia doraicoin – *having got thus far he lost his nerve* : afne hono gia morba – *at that point you're going to come to grief* : hono gia tekci – *that's where I ran into difficulties* : **tou gia** – *indeed, having got to that point; only then* : keic korce, tou gia foesa faice – *he took legal proceedings, and only then did he get his money* < **ge-**
gialle ['gīāl-lɛ́] (v adv) *once having gone* | tara gialle jaega oibo – *once they've gone there'll be room* : afne hono gialle kam faiba – *once you get there you'll find work* : **oi gialle** – *once having become; once having happened* : boro oi gialle tumra bujbae – *once you've become old enough you'll understand* : for oi gialle amra fot di laimu – *once it's got light we'll set off* = **gia + arle**
gian ['gīān] (n) *knowledge* = **gean**
giari ['gīārī] (v adv) *having gone; after going* | tara goro giari bat kaice – *having gone home they had a meal* = **gia + ari**
giani ['gīānī] (adj) *knowledgeable; wise* = **geani**
gibot ['gībòt] (n) *slander; backbiting* [A. ġība]
gil- [gīl] (v) *swallow* | tain gilta faroin na – *she can't swallow* : guc cibaia gilce – *he chewed the meat and then swallowed it* : **gili le-** – *swallow* : fuae foesa gili lice – *the boy has swallowed a coin* [B. gil-]
gila- ['gīlā] (vt) *cause to swallow* | baicca·tare tin·ta bori gilaice – *they made the child swallow three pills* [B. gila-]

ginna ['gīn-nā] (n) *loathing; disgust* | **ginna lage** – *one feels disgusted* : kirmi dekle ginna lage amar – *I feel disgusted when I see parasitic worms* : **ginna kor-** – *despise* : hokoloe ginna kore tare – *they all despise him*   [H. ghin < O. ghŕṇā]
ginna- (v) *loathe; despise* | tara amare ginnae – *they can't stand the sight of me* : **ginnae** (impersonal) – *one feels disgusted* : juk dekle ginnae – *seeing a leech makes me sick*
gir- [gīr] (vi) *fall down*   [H. gir-]
gira ['gīrā] (n) *knot*   [P. gira]
girgiri ['gīr-gīrī} (n) *gargling; growling; crackling* | **girgiri dake** – *it's making a crackling noise*
girost ['gīròst] (n) *farmer*   [B. grihåsthå < S. gŕhastha – *householder*]
girosti ['gīròstī] (n) *farming* | **girosti kor-** – *practise farming; be a farmer* : ino keu girosti koroin na – *nobody here is engaged in farming*   [B. grihåsthi < S. gŕhasthī]
git [gīt] (n) *knot* | **git band-** – *tie a knot*   [B. giⁿt]
git [gīt] (n) *song; singing*   [B. git < S. gīta]
go [gô] (int) *my dear* | kegu? ami go! – *who is it? it's me, dear* : siuli ni? na go, rina – *is that Shiuli? no, dear, it's Rina* : amar feto buk lagce go! – *I'm starving, dear mother / aunt / grandmother / sister* : aio go! – *come on, dear!* : ialla go! – *oh my goodness!*   Note: A good humoured interjection added at the end of a phrase. Principally used by women, or by men when addressing women. Informal and familiar.
gobi ['gòbī] (n) *cabbage*   [H. gobhī]
gobir ['gòbīr] (adj) *deep*   [B. gåbhir]
goc- [gòs] (vt) *take receipt of; take over; take on* | cafi gocouka – *here, take the key* : tara amar keic goce na – *they won't take on my case* : **goci le-** – *take receipt of; take over*
goca ['gòsā] (n) *fishbone*
goca- ¹ ['gòsā] (vt) *hand over* | garir cafi gocaita – *he wants to hand over the car keys* : fail·ta tan gece gocaici – *I've handed the file over to him* : **gocai de-** – *hand over* : cacar ate gocai deuka – *hand it to uncle*   [B. gåcha-]
goca- ² (vt) *loosen; open* | duar gocao! – *open the door!*   [B. ghuca-]
gocmoc ['gòs-mòs] (n) *fiddling about; wasting time* | **gocmoc kor-** – *fiddle around*
gocormocor ['gòsòr-mèsòr] (n) *fiddling about; wasting time* | **gocormocor kor-** – *fiddle around; mess about* : tain haridin kagoj loia gocormocor koroin – *he fiddles around with his papers all day long*   [B. gåṛimåsi]
goddi ['gòd-dī] (n) *cushion* | **goddit bo-** – *sit in one's seat of office* : raja goddit boin – *the king sits on his official cushion; the king sits on the throne* : dukanor malik tan goddit boicoin – *the shopkeeper is at his seat on the dais*   [H. gaddī]
goebi ['gòɛbī] (adj) *hidden; secret* | goebi mal – *hidden resources (e.g. minerals underground)*   [A. ġaibī]
goena ['gòɛnā] (n) *ornament; jewelry*   [B. gåyna]
goenagati ['gòɛnākātī] (n) *jewelry*   [B. gåynagaⁿti]
gof [gòf] (n) *chit-chat* | **gof kor-** – *chatter* : betainte gof korra – *the menfolk are having a good chinwag* : **gof huna-** – *tell stories* : dadi amare ajob gof hunaicoin – *granny told us some amazing stories*   [H. gap]
goffo ['gòp-pò] (n) *chit-chat*   [B. gåppå]
gofsof ['gòf-šòf] (n) *chit-chat*   = **gof**
goj [gòz, gòj] (n) *yard (length)*   [P. gaz]
gojob ['gòzòb, 'gòjòb] (n) *wrath of God; calamity* | amrar ufre gojob forbo – *some calamity is going to befall us*   [A. ġaDab – *anger*]
gol- [gòl] (vi) *melt; flow* | alkatra golbo – *the asphalt will melt* : cacir mon golce – *auntie's heart has melted; auntie has taken pity* : tumar nake di goler – *your nose is running* : **goli ja-** – *melt* : boraf joldi goli jaibo – *the snow will soon melt*   [B. gål-]
gola ['gòlā] (n) *throat; neck; voice* | tair golar maje goca lagce – *a fishbone has stuck in her throat* : tair golar maje sundor ar – *she's got a nice necklace round her neck* : tumar golar maf koto? – *what is your neck measurement? what is your collar size?* : cacar gola cinci – *I*

recognised uncle's voice : **gola ga** – *a sore throat* : tar gola ga oi gece – *his throat has got sore; he's developed a sore throat* : **gola baŋe** – *one's voice changes* : tar gola baŋce – *his voice has broken; he's gone hoarse* [B. gåla]

gola- ['gòlā] (vt) *cause to melt* | **golai le-/golai de-** – *cause to melt* : batar age golai louka – *melt the butter first* [B. gåla-]

golod ['gòlòd] (n) *error; fault; something wrong* [A. ġalaṭ]

golti ['gòltī] (n) *error; fault* [A. ġalṭa]

gom[1] [gòm] (n) *wheat* [B. gåm < P. gandum]

gom[2] (n) *anxiety; worry* | **gom kor-** – *worry* : afne gom koroin kitar lagi? – *why are you worrying yourself?* [P. ġam]

gombir ['gòmbīr] (adj) *solemn; grave* [B. gåmbhir < O. gambhīra – *deep*]

gomi ['gòmī] (n) *dejection; sadness* | kusi ar gomi – *joy and sorrow* [P. ġamī]

gon- [gòn] (v) *count* = **gun-**

gondogul ['gòndògūl] (n) *disruption; upset; disorder; trouble* | amar fetor maje gondogul – *I have a stomach upset* : tar matar maje gondogul – *there's something wrong with his head* : lanir maje gondogul – *there's a glitch in the (phone) line* : kail rastat gondogul oicil – *there was trouble in the street yesterday* : **gondogul lage** – *disruption occurs* : kamo tura gondogul lagce – *there has been a bit of trouble with the job* : **gondogul laga-** – *cause disruption* : beta aia gondogul lagaice – *that fellow came and messed things up* : **gondogul kor-** – *make a disturbance; make trouble* : ino gondogul korio na – *please don't disturb us* : tain gondogul koroin kali – *he just makes things worse* [B. gåndågol]

gond [gònd] (n) *smell* | **gond kore** – *it smells* : telor gond kore – *it smells of oil* : gecor gond kore - *there's a smell of gas* : **gond fa-** – *detect a smell* : modor gond faici – *I can smell alcohol* [P. gand]

gondo ['gòndò] (n) *smell* [B. gåndhå < S. gandha]

gonj [gònj] (n) *rural marketplace* [P. ganj – *hoard*]

gono ['gònò] (adj) *dense; thick* | gono kuasa – *dense fog* : gono cul – *thick hair* : gono dud – *condensed milk* : **gono gono** – *very dense; frequent* : gono gono cul – *very thick hair* : gono cutti – *frequent holidays* : tara gono gono aoa jaoa kore – *they make frequent comings and goings* [B. ghånå]

gonta[1] ['gòntā] (n) *bell; hour* | gonta bajer – *a bell is ringing* : ad gonta – *half an hour* : ek gonta bade – *one hour later* : dui gontar rasta – *a two hour journey* : gontar maje jaitam farmu – *we'll get there within the hour* : **gontat** – *in an hour; per hour* : gontat tis mail – *thirty miles per hour* : **gontae** – *on the hour; hourly* : bac gontae gontae cole – *the bus goes every hour* [B. ghånta < O. ghantā]

gonta[2] (n) *(anatomical) joint* | aŋgulor gonta – *finger joints* : faur gonta – *ankle* : amar gontar maje bis korer – *my joints are painful* [B. ga^{n}t < O. granthi]

gor [gòr] (n) *hut; building; house; household; dynasty* | sodor gor – *main hut (of a village homestead)* : deria gor – *spare house; guest hut (in homestead)* : tara gor tuler – *they are erecting a building* : tantanor gor curi oi gece – *their house has been burgled* : tin betrumor gor – *a three bedroom house* : tara noea gor loito – *they are going to buy a new house* : tain gur dulaicoin – *he has moved house* : amra ek gor – *we're one household; we're all one family* : ek goror manus – *people of the same household* : cacar gor – *paternal uncle's section of the family* : cacar goror bai – *cousin on paternal uncle's side* : codrir goror fua – *a boy from the Choudhury family* : tara coiodor goror – *they are of the house of Syed; they are Syeds* : makalor goror makal – *a loser from a race of losers; a real good-for-nothing* : **goro** – *at home* : keu nai ni goro? – *hello, is there anyone at home?* : tain goro nae – *he's not at home* : amra goro jaitam – *we want to go home* : **gor kor-/gor kori le-** – *set up home* : tara lutono gor korce – *they've set up home in Luton* [B. ghår]

gorbar ['gòr-bār] (n) *confusion* | gorbar lage – *confusion occurs* [B. gåṛbåṛ]

gorbara ['gòr-bārā] (n) *(house or apartment) rent* = **gor + bara**[2]

gorbo[1] ['gòr-bò] (n) *pride* [B. gårbå < S. garva]

gorbo[2] (n) *womb* [B. gårbhå < S. garbha]

gorboboti ['gòr-bò-bòtī] (adj) *pregnant* [B. gårbhåbåti < S. garbhavatī]
gorbonđi ['gòr-bònđī] (n) *prisoner in a house* | **gorbonđi o-/gorbonđi oi ja-** – *be confined to one's house; be a prisoner in one's own home* = **gor + bonđi**
gorcur ['gòr-sūr] (n) *house thief; burglar* = **gor + cur**
gorcuri ['gòr-sūrī] (n) *burglary* | gorcuri oi gece – *we've been burgled* = **gor + curi**
gorđona ['gòr-đònā] (n) *neck; nape* [P. gardan]
gor-đoroja ['gòr-đòròjā, 'gòr-đòròzā] (n) *four walls; house and home* | tan gor-đoroja nae – *he has no house of his own* : tara hono gor-đoroja korce – *they have set up house there* = **gor + đoroja**
gor-đuar ['gòr-đūār] (n) *four walls; house and home* = **gor + đuar**
gori ['gòrī] (n) *clock; watch; measuring instrument* | oal gori – *wall clock* : at gori – *wrist watch* : gori bae caia kam kore – *he works with an eye on the clock* : đaktor gori lagaia đekcoin tare – *the doctor examined him with an instrument* : **gorir** – *of the clock; o'clock* : gorir koe·ta oice? – *how many o'clock is it? what time is it?* [B. ghåṛi]
gorib ['gòrīb] (adj) *poor* | tar caca gorib – *his uncle is poor* : era gorib manus – *these are poor people* ¶ **gorib** (n) *poor person; pauper* | gorib hokole bikka korer – *the poor people are out begging* [A. ġarīb – *alien*]
goribaloe ['gòrībālòɛ] (n) *poor man's house* (sometimes used to refer modestly to one's own home) amar goribaloe đeki jauka – *please step inside and have a look at my humble abode* = **gorib + aloe**
goribi ['gòrībī] (n) *poverty* [P. ġarībī]
gormi ['gòr-mī] (n) *heat; venereal disease* [P. garmī]
gormil ['gòr-mīl] (n) *discrepancy; inconsistency* | isabor maje gormil oi gece – *there are discrepancies in the accounts* : tar kotar maje gormil đeka jae – *inconsistency can be seen in his words; what he says doesn't add up* [B. gårmil]
goroj ['gòròz, 'gòròj] (n) *strong motive; vested interest* | amar goroj nae kunta korbar – *I feel no urgency to do anything* : tan goroj forle tain korba – *if his interests are at stake, he'll do it* [A. ġaraĐ – *aim, purpose*]
gorom ['gòròm] (adj) *warm; hot; peevish* | aij đin·ta gorom – *today the weather's hot* : gorom fani – *hot water* : đuđ ebu gorom roice – *the milk is still warm* : gorom kafor – *warm clothing* : tan mata gorom – *he's hot-headed; he's irascible* : **gorom lage** – *it feels warm* : afnar gorom lager ni? – *are you feeling too hot?* : **gorom o-/gorom oi ja-** – *warm up; get heated; get angry* : ou rum gorom oe na – *this room never warms up* : caca gorom oi gecoin – *uncle has got annoyed* : **gorom kor-/gorom kori le-** – *warm up; heat up* : afnar at gorom kori louka – *do warm up your hands* : bat gorom korci – *I've heated up the rice* ¶ **gorom** (n) *heat; hot season* | ila gorom aŋgej koroin kila? – *how do you stand such heat?* : goromor somoe beranit jaimu – *in summer we'll go for a trip* : **gorom fore** – *the weather gets hot* : aij bakka gorom force – *it's really hot today* [P. garm]
gorto ['gòrtò] (n) *hole* [B. gårtå < S. garta – *pit*]
goru ['gòrū] (n) *cow; ox; cattle* [B. gåru]
gosa- ['gòsā] (v) *scrub; rub* | handi gosaici – *I've scrubbed the pan* : tumar đat gosao – *brush your teeth* : **gosai le-** – *scrub; rub* [B. ghås-]
got- [gòt] (vi) *happen; come to pass* | **goti ja-** – *happen* [B. ghåt-]
gota- ['gòtā] (vt) *cause to happen; give rise to; cause* [B. ghåta-]
goton ['gòtòn] (n) *construction; structure; build* | goror goton – *structure of a building* : sorilor goton – *bodily structure; build* : **goton kor-/goton kori le-** – *construct; form; set up* : bas đi kuti goton kore – *they make posts from bamboo* : amra kumiti goton korci – *we formed a committee* [B. gåthån < S. gathana]
gotona ['gòtònā] (n) *occurrence; event* | ek gotona oice – *an incident has occurred* : mosto boro gotona – *an extraordinary occurrence* [B. ghåtåna < S. ghatanā]
goti ['gòtī] (n) *recourse; way forward; way out* | icara kunu goti đeki na – *I don't see any other way out* : gor beca cara goti nae – *there's nothing to be done other than sell the house*

: **goti kor-** – *make shift; find a way* : tain kunu ek·ta goti korba – *he'll manage something somehow* [B. gåti < S. gati – *going; motion*]
gotik ['gòtīk] (n) *condition; state* | amar sorilor gotik bala nae – *my body's condition is not good; I'm in poor shape* [B. gåtik < S. gatika]
gotike ['gòtīkɛ] (n adv) *in the circumstances; therefore; so* | er gotike ami ubaici na – *because of that I didn't wait* : foesa nae gotike goro roin – *he has no money so he stays at home* < **gotik**
goto ['gòtò] (adj) *past; last* | tain goto maso aicla – *he came last month* : goto đin – *yesterday* : goto fira – *last time round* : **goto o-/goto oi ja-** – *be past; pass away* : bout đin goto oice – *a long time has passed* : janoin ni, caci goto oi gecoin – *did you know that auntie had passed away* [B. gåtå < S. gata – *gone*]
gotor ['gòtòr] (n) *body* | tair gotor ekere fatla – *her body is really thin* : amar gotoror maje bis korer – *I've got pains in my body* [B. gatrå < S. gātra]
gu [gū] (quantifier) *unit; one* | boro·gu – *the big one* : noea·gu – *the new one* : i·gu bala nae – *this one is no good* : fac·gu beta – *five men* : i furi·gu amar – *this girl is my daughter* : **guin** – *ones* : i·guin bala – *these ones are good* : afnar·guin loia jauka – *take yours with you* : ho·guintor đam koto? – *what's the price of those ones?* : noea·guintore đekci na – *I haven't seen the new ones*
gu[2] (n) *excrement* [H. guh < O. gūtha]
gua ['gūa] (n) *areca nut; betelnut* | afne gua kain ni? – *do you take betelnut? (a small hard nut customarily chewed with or without paan leaf)* [O. guvāka]
gual ['gū-al] (n) *a species of catfish (Wallago attu)* [B. boal]
guamuri ['gūa-mūrī] (n) *anise; fennel* [B. mouri]
gubor ['gūbòr] (n) *cowdung* [B. gobår]
guc [gūs] (n) *meat* = **gust**
guca ['gūsā] (n) *anger* = **gussa**
guca- (v) *arrange; put in order; tidy up* [B. gocha-]
gucari ['gūsārī] (n) *ankle* [B. goch]
gucol ['gūsòl] (n) *ablutions; bathing* | **gucol kor-/gucol kori le-** – *perform full ablutions; have a bath* : aij gucol korco ni? – *have you had a bath today?* : tain gucol kori licoin – *she has done her ablutions* [A. ġusl – *ablution*]
gucolkana ['gūsòlχānā] (n) *ablution room* [P. ġuslχāna]
guddi ['gūd-dī] (n) *paper kite* [B. ghuṛi]
gudokkor ['gūdòk-kòr] (n) *clear alphabetic script* | **gudokkore** – *in clear handwriting; in capital letters* cf **okkor**
guf [gūf] (n) *whiskers; moustache* [B. goⁿph]
gufat ['gūfāt] (n) *village path; alleyway* [B. gobat]
gufon ['gūfòn] (n) *hiding; secrecy* | **gufon kori rak-** – *keep secret* : tain kota·kan gufon kori rakcoin – *he has kept it a secret* : **gufone** – *in secret* : tara gufone cigret kaito, mođ kaito – *they used to secretly consume alcohol and smoke cigarettes* ¶ **gufon** (adj) *hidden; secret* | gufon kota – *secret words; a secret* [B. gopån < O. gopana – *guarding; protection*]
gufonio ['gūfònīò] (adj) *secret; private* [B. gopåniå]
gufoniota ['gūfònīòtā] (n) *secrecy; privacy* [B. gopåniåta]
guin [guīn] (quantifier) *units; ones* < **gu**[1]
gul[1] [gūl] (n) *sphere; ball; circle* | hurutae matir gul malaice – *the children made balls of mud* : tan furi gul akaito jane – *his daughter knows how to draw circles* ¶ **gul** (adj) *spherical; round* | gul muk – *a round face* : gul moric – *spherical peppers; black peppercorns* [B. gol < O. gola]
gul[2] (n) *bluff; empty words* | **gul mar-** – *use bluff; make empty claims; talk big* : betae kali gul mare – *he's nothing but a big mouth* : **gul ka-** – *be deceived; be disappointed* : ekbar gul kaici, ar fatta đitam nai tare – *I've been had once, now I'm not going to take any more notice of him* [P. gol – *deceit*]
gula ['gūlā] (n) *pellet; ball* [B. gola < O. gola]

gulaf ['gūlāf] (n) *rose* [P. gulāb – *rosewater*]
gulafi ['gūlāfī] (adj) *rose-coloured; pink* < **gulaf**
gulaguli ['gūlāgūlī] (n) *gunfire; gunfighting* < **gula**
gulam ['gūlām] (n) *slave; dogsbody* [A. ġulām – *young man*]
gulami ['gūlāmī] (n) *slavery* [P. ġulāmī]
gulel ['gūlɛl] (n) *catapult* [P. ġulel]
gulli ['gūl-lī] (n) *bullet; pill* | bonḍukor gulli – *rifle bullet* : nim fatar gulli – *neem-leaf pills* : **gulli mar-** – *fire bullets; shoot* : betare gulli marce – *they shot the man* : gulli maro! – *oh, to hell with it!* [H. gullī]
gulmal ['gūlmāl] (n) *noise and rowdiness; disturbance; irregularity* | bajaro gulmal coler – *a disturbance is going on in the bazaar* : tar fasfutor maje gulmal acil – *there was something wrong with his passport* : **gulmal lage** – *trouble arises* : kail gulmal lagto fare – *there may be trouble tomorrow* : **gulmal laga-/gulmal lagai de-** – *cause trouble* : jani, tain gulmal lagai diba – *I'm sure he's going to make problems* : **gulmal kor-** – *make a disturbance; cause trouble* : kamlainte majemaje gulmal kore – *the workers sometimes cause problems* [H. golmāl]
gulmul ['gūl-mūl] (adj) *round* < **gul**
gum ¹ [gūm] (n) *sleep* | bala gum – *a good sleep* : tair gumor osubida – *she has difficulty sleeping* : **gumo** – *asleep* : tara gumo – *they're asleep; they're sleeping* : **gumor maje** – *in sleep* : tain gumor maje – *he's wrapped in sleep; he isn't properly awake* : gumor maje dekci afnare – *I saw you in my sleep; I dreamed about you* : **gum oe** – *sleep takes place* : afnar gum oice ni? – *have you had enough sleep? did you sleep well?* : amar gum oe na – *I don't get enough sleep; I can't sleep properly* : **gume dore** – *sleep takes hold* : amar gume dorce – *sleep has gripped me; I'm feeling sleepy* : **gum care** – *sleep leaves off* : tumar gum carce ni? – *has your sleep left you; are you fully awake?* : tar gum care na – *his sleep won't leave him; he simply can't wake up* : **gum baŋe** – *sleep is interrupted* : amar gum baŋcil – *my sleep was broken; I woke up* : **gum de-/gum di la-** – *have a sleep* : tara bala gum dice – *they have had a decent sleep* : tura gum di laitam – *I'd like to take a nap* : **gum fata-/gum fatai de-** – *lull to sleep* : baiccaintore gum fataicoin ni? – *have you got the children to sleep?* [B. ghum]
gum ² (adj) *silent* | **gum oia ro-** – *keep silent* : tumi ola gum oia roico kitar lagi? – *why are you keeping mum like that; why don't you say something?* = **gumcum**
gum- (vi) *sleep* | tain besi gumoin – *he sleeps too much* : **gumi ja-** – *go to sleep; go to bed* : tara gumi gece – *they've gone to bed* cf **guma-**
guma- (vi) *sleep; go to sleep; go to bed* | tara haridin gumae – *they sleep all day* : tain dos·tat gumain – *he goes to bed at ten* : gumaita ni? – *do you want to retire to bed?* : **gumai ja-** – *go to sleep; go to bed* : fuae gumai gece – *the lad has fallen asleep* : **gumai for-** – *fall asleep* : gumai foro! – *go to sleep!* [B. ghuma-]
guman ['gūmān] (n) *pride* | **guman kor-** – *act proud; behave haughtily; be arrogant* [P. gumān – *idea, notion*]
gumcum ['gūm-sūm] (adj) *dumb; unspeaking; silent* | afne ekebare gumcum deki – *I see you're keeping very quiet* : **gumcum oia ro-** – *remain silent; keep quiet; be speechless* [H. gum-sum < P. gum – *lost* + A. ṣumm – *dumb*]
gun [gūn] (n) *quality; virtue; efficacy; multiplication; number of times* | cacir koto gun – *auntie has many virtues* : i ousudor gun ace – *this medicine has qualities; this medicine is effective* : gun bag – *multiplication and division* : er caite cair gun besi – *four times as much as this* : tumar taki tin gun boro – *three times bigger than you* : **(keur) gun ga-** – *recite (someone's) virtues; sing (someone's) praises* : tain afnar gun gaicoin – *he spoke highly of you* : **gun kor-/gun kori le-** – *multiply* : tin dia gun kori louka – *multiply it by three* : fac dui dia gun korle dos oe – *five multiplied by two makes ten* [B. gun < S. guṇa]
gun- (v) *count* | tai tis fojonto gunto fare – *she can count up to thirty* : **guni le-** – *count* : borton guni lici – *I've counted the plates* [B. gun-]

guna [ˈgūnā] (n) *sin* | kobira guna – *major sin* : alla amar guna maf koruk – *may God forgive me my sins* : **guna kor-** – *commit sins* [P. gunāh]

guna ² (quantifier) *(multiple) sets* | tin ɖu·guna coe – *two sets of three is six; two threes make six* : cair coe·guna cubbis – *six fours are twenty-four*

gunagar [ˈgūnāgār] (n) *sinner* [P. gunāhkār]

gunda [ˈgūndā] (n) *thug* [H. gundā]

gunda-fanda [ˈgūndāfāndā] (n) *thugs; gang of henchmen* = **gunda**

gundami [ˈgūndāmī] (n) *thuggery* | **gundami kor-** – *behave like a thug*

gungun [ˈgūn-gūn] (n) *humming* | **gungun kor-** – *hum*

guni ¹ [ˈgūnī] (quantifier) *units; ones* = **guin**

guni ² (adj) *virtuous; worthy* [B. guni < S. guṇī]

gur [gūr] (n) *raw sugar; molasses* [B. guṛ]

gur- ¹ (vi) *spin; go round; roam around* | cakka gure – *the wheel goes round and round* : he rasta gure – *he roams the streets* : **guri a-** – *go and come back again* : tain sof taki guri aicoin – *he's been to the shop and back* : ubauka, ami guri ai – *wait, I'll be back in a minute* : **guri ja-** – *come and go away again* : caca biane guri gecoin – *uncle dropped by this morning* : **guri bera-** – *wander around* [B. ghur-]

gur- ² (vt) *cover up* | tumar mata guro – *cover your head* : **guri le-** – *cover up* : handi guri lita acla – *you should have put a lid on the saucepan* : **guri rak-** – *cover up; keep covered* : mac guri rakci – *I've put a cover over the fish* [B. guṛ-]

gura ¹ [ˈgūrā] (adj) *fair-skinned* | gura beti – *a fair-skinned woman; a white woman* ¶ **gura** (n) *white person* | kala ek·jon, gura ek·jon – *one black person and one white* [B. gora]

gura ² (v adj) *covered up* | **gura tak-** – *keep oneself covered; keep in purdah* : beta manus keu goro aile tain gura takoin – *she keeps herself covered when any male person visits her house* < **gur-**²

gura ³ (n) *powder* | calir gura – *rice powder; rice flour* : moslar gura – *powdered spice* : **gura kor-/gura kori le-** – *grind to powder* [B. guⁿṛa]

gura ⁴ (n) *horse* | tai gura corto – *she wants to ride a horse* : gurar ɖour – *horse racing* : **gura kela-** – *bet on horses* : gura kelaia foesa kuaice – *he lost his money betting on horses* [B. ghoṛa]

gura- (vt) *cause to rotate; turn* | at ɖi cakka gurae – *they turn the wheel by hand* : tumar cear gurao – *turn your chair round* : gari guraibar jaega nae – *there's no room to turn the car* : **gurai le-** – *turn* : tebul gurai litam ni? – *shall I turn the table round?* : gari farkiɲo gurai licoin – *he turned the car in the car park* : **lombor gura-** – *dial a number* : tan lombor tin bar guraici – *I've tried dialling his number three times* [B. ghura-]

gurafira [ˈgūrāfīrā] (n) *wandering* < **gur-**¹, **fir-**

guraguri [ˈgūrāgūrī] (n) *wandering* < **gur-**¹

gurɖa [ˈgūrɖā] (n) *sensitive organ; heart* [P. gurda – *kidney*]

gurɖis [ˈgūrɖīš] (n) *misfortune* [P. gurdiš – *turning; twist of fate*]

gurostan [ˈgūròstān] (n) *graveyard* [P. gūristān]

guru [ˈgūrū] (n) *senior; major* | guru·jon – *senior person; elders and betters* : guru faf – *major sin* ¶ **guru** (n) *spiritual leader; guru* [B. guru < S. guru]

gurutti [ˈgūrūt-tī] (adv) *in a trice; quickly*

gurutto [ˈgūrūt-tò] (n) *importance* | itar besi gurutto nae – *it's not very important* : **gurutto ɖe-** – *attach importance (to); take seriously* : tain amar kotare kunu gurutto ɖicoin na – *he didn't take what I said at all seriously* [B. guruttå < S. gurutva]

gus [gūš] (n) *bribe* | **gus ka-** – *accept a bribe* : tara hokoloe gus kae – *all of them take bribes* : **gus kaoa-** – *offer a bribe* [B. ghus]

gusa- [ˈgūšā] (vt) *scrub; rub* = **gosa-**

gusona [ˈgūšònā] (n) *announcement* | **gusona kor-** – *announce; proclaim* : kail tara ileksonor tarik gusona korto fare – *they may announce the election date tomorrow* [B. ghosåna < S. ghośaṇā]

gussa ['gūš-šā] (n) *anger* | **gussa kor-/gussa kori le-** – *get angry; take offence* : tain hunia gussa korba – *he'll be angry when he hears about it* : afne amar ufre gussa korcoin ni? – *are you cross with me?* [A. ġuṣṣa – *choking*]

gusti ['gūštī] (n) *lineage; wider family* | amar gustir maje ota nae – *such a thing is unknown throughout my entire family* : tarar gusti-u kanjis – *they're misers, the whole clan of them* [B. gosthi < S. gośthī – *assembly*]

gust [gūst] (n) *meat; flesh* | merir gust – *mutton* : gorur gust – *beef* : tair sorilor maje gust nae – *she has no flesh on her at all* [P. gošt]

guta [¹] ['gūtā] (n) *round bead; counter* = **guti**

guta [²] (adj) *whole; entire* | guta londonor maje nae – *not in the whole of England* : guta fac din – *five whole days* [B. gota]

guti ['gūtī] (n) *pimple; bead; counter* [B. guti]

guṭa [¹] ['gūṭā] (n) *prodding* | **guṭa mar-** – *prod; poke; butt* [B. guⁿta]

guṭa [²] (quantifier) *unit; one* | bala·guṭa – *the good one* : i·guṭa – *this one* : cear·guṭa – *the (single) chair* : fac·guṭa bet – *five beds* = **gu** [¹] + **-ta** [²]

guṭi ['gūṭī] (n) *crouching posture* | **guṭi mar-** – *make oneself small and inconspicuous; hide away* [B. guṛi]

h

ha (int) *yes* | **ha na** – *yes or no* : ha na ek·ta koita – *he should either say yes or say no: one or the other* [H. ha{n}]

haai ['hā:ī] (n) *husband* [B. sami < O. swāmi]

habi ['hābī] (adj) *entire* [A. ḥāwī – *encompassing*]

habigusti ['hābīgūstī] (n) *entire clan* | habigusti loia aice – *he came, along with all his relatives and hangers-on* = **habi + gusti**

habijabi ['hābījābī] (n) *bits and pieces; mess; complication* | almarir maje bout habijabi – *there's a lot of junk in the cupboard* : bisa loite koto habijabi – *it's such a fiddlesome business getting a visa* < **habi**

habon ['hābòn] (n) *oven; cooker* [E.]

haca ['hāsā] (adj) *true* | haca na mica – *true or false* : haca ni? – *is that true? is that so?* : haca nae ni? – *isn't that true? am I not right?* : afnar kota·kan haca – *what you say is true* : **haca kota** – *true words; the truth* : haca kota hunouka – *listen to the real truth* : **haca kota ko-** – *speak the truth* : haca kota kouka – *tell me the truth* : tain haca kota koira – *he is speaking the truth* : afne haca kota koicoin – *you've said something true; you're quite right* : haca kota koitam ni? – *shall I speak the truth? shall I be frank?* ¶ **haca** (n) *truth* | haca koitam ni? – *shall I speak the truth?* : haca koite gele.. – *to speak the truth..* : **hacar** – *true; real; genuine* : tan furire hacar gori dicoin – *she's given her daughter a real watch (not a toy one)* : tain amar hacar bai – *he's a genuine brother to me* ¶ **haca** (adv) *truly; really* | ami haca geclam – *I really did go there* : tumi ota korco ni haca? – *did you really do it?* : **haca-u** – *most truly; really truly* : tain haca-u tan gari becta – *he really truly does want to sell his car* [H. saccā < O. satya]

hacil ['hāsīl] (n) *acquisition* | **hacil kor-** – *obtain; gain* : tain cuab hacil korra – *he is earning merit* [A. ḥāṣil]

hacri ['hās-rī] (n) *spreading (of contagion)* | **hacri ja-** – *(contagion) spread; get passed on* : rug hacri gece – *the disease has spread* [B. cho{n}a churi]

haddi ['hād-dī] (n) *bone* | majir haddi – *backbone* [H. haddī < O. hadda]

haddi-guddi ['hād-dī-gūd-dī] (n) *bones; skin and bones* = **haddi**

hae [hāy] (int) *alas! oh, no!* | hae hae! – *oh dear! oh no!* : hae re hae! – *oh no, for goodness' sake!* : hae re suna! – *oh, no, darling, no!*

haf[1] [hāf] (n) *snake* | caci sofnor maje haf dekoin – *aunt sees snakes in her dreams* : tare hafe kamor marce – *a snake bit him* : «haf ni beŋ, koito fare na» – *he can't tell whether it's a snake or a frog; he has no idea what to make of it* [B. sap < O. sarpa]

haf[2] (n) *puff of breath; gasp* [B. ha{n}p]

haf[3] (n) *half; half day; half price* | aij haf – *today's a half holiday* : hurutar haf – *it's half price for children* : haf haf – *half and half* : haf haf kori deuka – *make it into two halves, then give it; give them half each* [E.]

hafa- ['hāfā] (vi) *pant* | caca hafaira – *uncle is panting (with effort)* : **hafai ja-** – *become short of breath* : sirit utle ami hafai jai – *I get short of breath when I go up the stairs* : **hafai ut-** – *become short of breath* : tain hafai utcoin – *she's panting* [B. ha{n}pa-]

hafani ['hāfānī] (v n) *panting; asthma* | besi ataati korle hafani arombo oe – *if I walk about too much, panting begins (I get breathless)* : tan hafani rug – *she has asthma* < **hafa-**

haffen ['hāp-pɛn] (n) *shorts* [E. half + pants]

hafij[1] ['hāfīz] (n) *the Guardian (God)* | alla hafij / koda hafij – *God is the Guardian* (formula used by Muslims when taking leave) [A. ḥāfiẓ – *guardian*]

hafij[2] [hā'fīz, hā'fīj] (n) *one who has memorized the Holy Quran; a hafiz* [A. ḥāfiẓ]

hafiji ['hāfīzī, 'hāfījī] (n) *mnemonic study of the Quran* | tara hafiji forer – *they are studying on a course for becoming a "hafiz"* ¶ **hafiji** (adj) *relating to "hafiz"* : hafiji madrasa – *madrasa which teaches "hafiz" students* = **hafij**[2] **+ -i**[2]

hafta ['hāf-tā] (n) *week* | haftar maje – *during the week; within a week* : ḍui tin haftar bitre – *within a couple of weeks* : tin hafta baḍe – *after three weeks; three weeks later* : **haftat** – *in a week; per week* : afne haftat koto fain? – *how much do you earn per week?* : **haftae aftae** – *week by week; weekly* : tain haftae aftae ain – *he comes every week* : **hafta ḍin** – *about a week* : hafta ḍin baḍe firbair aimu – *I'll come again in about a week's time* [P. hafta]
hag [hāg, hāk] (n) *greens; spinach* [H. sāg]
hai[1] ['hāɪ] (int) *oh dear! oh no!* | **hai hai** – *oh dearie me! oh no!* : hai hai, ita kita koila! – *oh no, don't say that!*
hai[2] (adj) *at a high level* | tan sugar hai oi gece – *her blood sugar level is high* [E.]
haiat ['hāɪāt] (n) *life; time left to live* | tan haiat nae – *he hasn't long to live* : afnar haiat ace! – *you're going to have a long life!* (said when someone just mentioned by name suddenly appears in person) : **haiat mout** – *life and death* : haiat mout allar gece – *life and death are in the hands of God* : haiat mout koa jae na / haiat mout kita koita – *with life and death, you can never tell; anybody's life may end at any moment* [A. hayāh]
haja- ['hāzā, 'hājā] (vt) *decorate; arrange nicely* | biar lagi gor hajaicoin – *they've decorated the house for the wedding* [B. saja-]
hajail ['hāzāɪl, 'hājāɪl] (v adj) *decorated* < **haja-**
haji ['hāzī, 'hājī] (n) *Hajj pilgrim; one who has performed the Hajj pilgrimage* | haji sab – *Mr Pilgrim* : haji manus fecaḍ koroin na – *a person who has been on Hajj should never cause discord* [U. hājjī < A. ḥājj – *one who performs Hajj*]
hajir ['hāzīr, 'hājīr] (adj) *in attendance; present* | ami mitiɲo hajir aclam na – *I wasn't present at the meeting* : akta ḍeki caca hajir – *suddenly I noticed uncle there* : **hajir o-/hajir oi ja-** – *show up; make one's appearance* : tain ekere hese hajir oicoin – *he came at the very end* : **aia hajir o-** – *turn up* : tara raitku aia hajir oice – *they turned up at night* : **hajir kora-** – *cause to appear; produce* : tain tin·jon sakki hajir koraicoin – *he made three witnesses attend; he produced three witnesses* [A. hāḎir]
hajira ['hāzīrā, 'hājīrā] (n) *attendance; presence* | iskulor hajira kata – *school attendance register* : **hajira ḍe-** – *be in attendance* : tain kouto hajira ḍita oiba – *he'll have to attend in court* [A. haḎra]
hajom ['hāzòm, 'hājòm] (n) *surgeon-barber* [A. ḥajjām – *cupper*] **Note:** In traditional rural Bengali Muslim society, a barber who is also capable of performing circumcisions.
hal[1] [hāl] (n) *plough; ploughing; a measure of land* | beta hal jane na – *that man doesn't know how to plough a field* : «hal-o cine na, jal-o cine na» – *he's no good at any type of work* : ek hal jomin – *one haal of land* : **halor** – *of the plough; for ploughing* : halor goru – *oxen used for ploughing* : «na halor na bicor» – *fit neither for ploughing nor for breeding; useless* : **hal ba-** – *wield a plough; plough land* : jelera hal bae na – *fisherfolk don't cultivate land* [B. hal[1]]
hal[2] (n) *tiller (of boat)* | **hal car-/hal cari ḍe-/hal cari ja-** – *let go of the tiller; relinquish control; give up* : hal cari ḍicoin ni? – *have you thrown up the sponge?* [B. hal[2]]
hal[3] (n) *state; condition* [A. hāl]
hal[4] (n) *pimple* [A. ḳāl – *freckle*]
hala ['hālā] (n) *wife's younger brother; person of low status* | ḍur hala! – *get away with you, you clown!* (vulgar when used as a term of abuse) [B. sala]
halak ['hālāχ] (adj) *worn out; emaciated* | afne halak fori gecoin – *you seem to have lost condition* [A. halāk – *ruination*]
halal ['hālāl] (adj) *permitted (in Islam)* | halal gust – *halal meat* : halal foesa – *money obtained in an ethical way* : tar ruji halal nae – *his earnings are unethical* : **halal kor-/halal kori le-** – *make ritually pure; ritually slaughter* [A. ḥalāl]
halgora ['hāl-gòrā] (n) *callosity; corn*
hali[1] ['hālī] (n) *set of four* | ek hali am – *four mangoes* : tin hali enda – *a dozen eggs* : endar hali koto? – *how much do four eggs cost?* [B. hali]
hali[2] ['hālī] (n) *wife's younger sister* [B. sali]

halka ['hālχā] (adj) *light; mild; relieved* | ou bosta bes halka – *this sack is quite light* : halka kam – *light work* : halka roŋ – *a light colour* : halka kani – *light, digestible food* : halka roiđ – *soft sunshine* : halka ousuđ – *mild medicine* : halka mat – *flippant talk* : i caikel besi halka – *this cycle is too flimsy* : amar mon halka oi gece – *I feel relieved* [B. halka]

hal-obosta ['hālòbòstā] (n) *state; condition* = **hal** [3] + **obosta**

halot ['hālòt] (n) *state; condition* [A. ħāla]

halua ['hālwā] (n) *halwa; flummery* [A. ħalwā – *sweetmeat*]

hama- ['hāmā] (vi) *go in* | tara sofo hamaice – *they've gone into the shop* : tair rumo hamaitam kila? – *how am I to get into her room?* : foesa hamae na – *the money won't go in (into a coin slot)* : keur goro hamaicoin – *he's dropped in on someone*

hamesa ['hāmɛšā] (adv) *often; always* | tara hamesa ae – *they often come; they're always coming* : hamesa đeki tane – *I frequently see him* [P. hameša – *always*]

hamla ['hāmlā] (n) *attack* | **hamla kor-** – *attack* : **hamla cala-** – *conduct an attack* : tara tanar ufre hamla calaice – *they attacked the police station* [A. ħamla]

handi ['hāndī] (n) *cooking-pot* [H. hāndī]

handi-bason ['hāndī-bāšòn] (n) *pots and pans; kitchen utensils* = **handi** + **bason**

handes ['hāndɛš] (n) *rice-flour pancake* [B. sånđes – *a disc shaped sweetmeat*]

hanj [hānj] (n) *dusk; early evening* | **hanje** – *at dusk; in the early evening* : tara hanje ae – *they come at sundown* : **hanje bađe** – *after dark* : hanje bađe ain jen – *come after sundown; come in the evening* [B. sanjh < O. sandhyā]

hanjebala ['hānjɛbālā] (n/adv) *early evening time* | amra aite aite hanjebala oibo – *by the time we get back it will be evening*

haŋgama ['hāŋ-gāmā] (n) *affray; civil disturbance* [P. hangāma – *uproar*]

haoa [1] ['hāoā] (n) *air; draught; wind* | tanda haoa – *cold air* : ino haoa lagbo – *it'll be draughty here* : tanda haoa boice – *a cold wind is blowing* : **haoa ka-** – *breathe air; take a breather* : tura haoa kai – *let's take a breath of air* : **haoa đe-** – *supply air; ventilate* : rugire haoa đeuka – *fan the patient; let the patient get some air* : **haoa o-/haoa oi ja-** – *turn into thin air* : tain haoa oi gecoin – *he's vanished* [A. hawā']

haoa [2] (n) *Eve* | bibi haoa – *Eve* [A. hawā']

haoa-batas ['hāoā-bātāš] (n) *fresh air* = **haoa** + **batas**

haola ['hāolā] (n) *care; custody* | allar haola – *(we are in) God's care* [A. ħawāla]

haolat ['hāolāt] (n) *loan* [A. ħawāla]

haon ['hāòn] (n) *Shraban (July-August)* [B. srabån < S. šrāvaṇa]

haor ['hāòr] (n) *flood lake* [O. sāgara – *sea*]

har- [hār] (v) *finish* = **ar-**

hara ['hārā] (v adj) *completed; complete; whole* | hara rait – *the whole night* < **har-**

hara- (vt) *put in; push in; insert* | cafi bego haraici – *I've put the key in my bag* : hurutare goro harauka – *get the children inside the house* : betare jelo haraibo – *they're going to put the man in jail* : fasfuto tan baiccaintor nam haraita – *he wants to have his children's names entered in his passport* : kamor maje bas haraice – *he's put a spanner in the works* : **harai đe-** – *put in; push in; insert* : foesa tumar jebo harai đeo – *put the money in your pocket*

haram ['hārām] (adj) *forbidden in Islam; unlawful; evil* | haram kani – *prohibited food* : mica mata haram – *telling lies is sinful* : **haram!** – *on my faith!* : haram kortam nae ar! – *word of honour, I swear I won't do it again!* [A. ħarām]

harami ['hārāmī] (adj) *bloody-minded* < **haram**

haramjađa ['hārām-zāđā, 'hārām-jāđā] (n) *illegitimate son; bastard* (used solely as an insult) [P. harāmzāđa – *(child) born of sin*]

haramjađi ['hārām-zāđī, 'hārām-jāđī] (n) *illegitimate daughter; bitch* (used solely as an insult) cf **haramjađa**

haram sorif [hā'rām-šòr'īf] (n) *the sacred precincts in Mecca* [A. ħaram šarīf]

haridin ['hārīđīn] (adv) *all day long* = **hara** + **đin**

hasor ['hāšòr] (n) *assembly of all humans and djinns for judgment on Doomsday* | hasoror moeđan – *the assembly field* [A. ħašr]

hat [hā:t] (n) *heart* | tan hato ɗora – *he has pains in the heart; he has heart disease* [E.]
hatetek ['hātɛtɛk] (n) *heart attack* | tan hatetek oicil – *he had a heart attack* [E.]
haton ['hātòn] (n) *stepmother* | **haton ma** – *stepmother* : **hatnor goror** – *descended from a stepmother* : hatnor goror boin – *stepsister; half sister* : hatnor goror bai – *stepbrother; half brother* [O. sārthinī – *co-wife*]
hatra- ['hātrā] (vi) *swim* [O. santara- – *cross over*]
hatrani ['hātrānī] (v n) *swimming* < **hatra-**
hau [hāu] (adj) *that too* | hau cidi loin na kene – *why not buy that CD as well* : hau muja tar – *these socks are his too* = **he + -u**
hauk [hāuk] (n) *yell* | **hauk mar-** – *yell; shout* : iato hauk mare ke? – *who's that shouting in the backyard?* [B. haⁿk]
hauka- ['hāukā] (vi) *yell; shout* [B. haⁿk-]
hau-mau ['hāumāu] (n) *loud talking; yakking; fuss*
he [hɛ́] (pron) *he* | he kita koe? – *what does he say?* : **her/tar** – *of him; his* : tar nam jani – *I know his name* : **here/tare** – *to him; him* : tare ɗeo – *give it to him* : keu cine na tare – *nobody recognises him* : **hera/tara** – *they* : hera kua gece? – *where have they gone?* : **herar/tarar** – *of them; their* : tarar gor kanɗat – *their house is nearby* : **herare/tarare** – *to them; them* : herare koici na – *I haven't told them* ¶ **he** (adj) *that* | he beta ke? – *who is that fellow?* : he ɗin goro aclam – *we were at home that day* : he kota koici na – *I didn't say that word; I didn't say that* [B. se]
heɗ [hɛɗ] (n) *fomentation* [B. seɗ < S. sveda – *sweat; steam*]
heɗ- (v) *apply a fomentation; heat so as to cause sweating* cf **heɗ**
heɗaet ['hɛɗāɛt] (n) *divine guidance* | alla heɗaet ɗeuka amrare – *may God guide us on the right path* [A. hidāya]
heɗin ['hɛɗīn] (n/adv) *that day* | **heɗinku** – *that day; the other day* : heɗinku london geclam – *the other day I went to London* : **heɗinkur** – *of that day* : heɗinkur kela mojar acil – *that day's game was good fun* : aij heɗinkur lakan nae – *today isn't like that other day* = **he + ɗin**
hefajot ['hɛfāzòt, 'hɛfājòt] (n) *custody; safe keeping* | alla hefajote rakta tane – *may God keep her in safety* [A. hifāźa]
hefibar ['hɛfībār] (n) *hay fever* [E.]
hei [hɛɪ] (pron) *she* cf **tai**
hein [hɛɪn] (pron) *that person; he; she* | hein ke? – *who is that person?* : **hen** – *of that person; his; her* : hen nam jani na – *I don't know his name* cf **tain**
heintain ['hɛɪntāɪn] (pron) *those people; they* cf **hein**
hekarot ['hɛχāròt] (n) *contempt* [A. hiqāra]
hekim ['hɛkīm] (n) *judge* | «hekim lore, hukum lore na» – *a judge may bend but the law is immutable* [A. ḥākim]
hekimi ['hɛkīmī] (adj) *of a judge* | hekimi kout – *judge court; crown court* < **hekim**
hekmot ['hɛkmòt] (n) *wisdom* = **hikmot**
helan ['hɛlān] (n) *physical inclination; leaning* | helan ɗe – *lean (against)* : he oalo helan ɗice – *he leaned against the wall* [B. helan]
heman ['hɛmān] (n) *animal; beast* [A. hayawān]
hemne ['hɛm-nɛ] (adv) *that way; in some way; thus* < **hemon**
hemon ['hɛmòn] (adj) *like that; such* [B. temån]
hen [hɛn] (pron adj) *of that person; his; her* < **hein**
hen-ten ['hɛn-tɛn] (pron) *this and that* | ranɗa, caf kora, hen-ten – *cooking, cleaning and all that stuff*
hentain ['hɛntāɪn] (pron) *those people; they* | hentain amrar aittio – *they are relatives of ours* : **hentan** – *of those people; their* : hentan bari catok – *their original home is in Chatak* = **heintain**
heŋgais ['hɛŋgāɪš] (n) *snot; catarrh*
her[1] [hɛr] (pron adj) *of him; his* < **he**

her² (n) *seer (measure of weight, approximately one kilogram)* [B. ser]
her³ (n) *narrow space*
hera ['hɛrā] (pron) *they* < **he**
heran ['hɛrān] (adj) *bothered; put out* | **heran o-/heran oi ja-** – *be bothered; be put to trouble; be put out* : afne heran oi gecoin – *you've been bothered; I'm sorry to have put you to so much trouble* [A. hayrān – *perplexed*]
herani ['hɛrānī] (n) *disturbance; harassment* < **heran**
hes [hɛš] (n) *end* | **hese** – *in the end; finally* : tumi hese kita korclae? – *what did you do in the end?* : **hesor** – *final* : hesor gan·ta bala acil – *the last song was the best* = **ses**
heskal ['hɛšχāl] (n) *the end* | **heskalo** – *in the end; finally* : heskalo amra ar geci na – *in the end we didn't go after all* = **hes + kal¹**
heta ['hɛtā] (pron) *he* = **he + -ta²**
hetai ['hɛtāɪ] (pron) *she* = **tai**
hi [hī] (adj) *that* cf **he**
hia- ['hīā] (vi) *wheeze*
hial ['hīāl] (n) *jackal* | «bag nae, hial raja»– *where there's no tiger, the jackal is king* : hial fondit – *the wise jackal* [B. siyal < O. šṛigāla]
hiani ['hīānī] (v n) *wheezing; asthma* < **hia-**
hibbair ['hīb-bāɪr] (adv) *again* = **firbar**
hibijibi ['hībījībī] (n) *small fiddly things; scribblings*
hifajot ['hīfāzòt, 'hīfājòt] (n) *custody; safe keeping* [A. hifāźa]
hija- ['hīzā, 'hījā] (vt) *boil* | tura fani hijaici – *I've boiled some water* [H. sijhā-]
hijail ['hīzāɪl, 'hījāɪl] (v adj) *boiled* < **hija-**
hijra ['hīzrā, 'hījrā] (n) *the Prophet's move from Mecca to Medina in 622 A.D.; the Hegira* [A. hijra – *migration*]
hijri ['hīzrī, 'hījrī] (adj) *of the Hegira* | cuďďo so hijri – *1400 A.H.; year 1400 after the Hegira (in the Muslim system of dating)* [A. hijri]
hik- [hīk] (v) *learn* | afnarar mat hikram – *I'm learning your language* : tain gari calani hikta – *she wants to learn to drive a car* : hiki **le-** – *learn* : tara arbi hiki lice – *they've learned Arabic* : iŋlis hiki louka! – *learn English!* [B. sikh-]
hika- ['hīkā] (vt) *teach* | tain iŋlis hikain – *she teaches English* : tumare ful kata hikaimu – *I'll teach you how to do embroidery* : **hikai de-** – *teach* : tare oŋko hikai ďeuka – *please teach him some maths* : amare ranďa hikai ďira – *she's teaching me to cook* [B. sekha-]
hikmot ['hīkmòt] (n) *wisdom* [A. ḥikma]
hikta ['hīktā] (pron) *that (thing)*
hil [hīl] (n) *hailstone* [O. šilā – *stone*]
hin [hīn] (n) *that place* | **hino** – *at that place; there* : hino sof nae – *there are no shops there* : **hinor** – *of that place* : hinor manus beŋ kae hunci – *I've heard that the people there eat frogs* [B. sekhan]
hiŋgi ['hīŋ-gī] (n) *catfish* | «hiŋgi kae na, hiŋgir sira kae» – *he may not eat catfish, but he does drink catfish gravy; he isn't as strictly principled as he pretends to be* [B. siŋ]
hir- [hīr] (vi) *come back; return; go round* | **hiria ca-** – *look back* = **fir-**
hira- ['hīrā] (vt) *turn back; send back* = **fira-**
hiraia ['hīrāɪā] (v adv) *again* < **fira-**
hirbair ['hīr-bāɪr] (adv) *once again* = **firbair**
hiria ['hīriā] (v adv) *again* < **hir-**
hirok ['hīròχ] (n) *diamond* [B. hiråk < S. hīraka]
hita ['hītā] (pron) *that (thing); it* = **hi + -ta²**
ho+ [hò, hô] (adj prefix) *that* = **hou**
hobae ['hòbāɛ] (adv) *that side; over there; that way* | hobae cauka – *look over there* : tain hobae gecoin gi – *he went that way* = **ho + bae**
hobaeďi ['hòbāɛďī] (adv) *that way; over there* = **ho + bae + dia**

hobaju ['hòbājū] (n) *that side* | **hobajut** – *on that side; over there* : ibajut nae, hobajut – *not on this side, on that side* : hobajut jauka – *go that way* = **ho + baju**
hobala ['hòbālā] (adv) *at that time; then* = **ho + bala** ¹
hoɗdo ['hòd-dò] (n) *boundary* [A. ḥadd]
hoɗic ['hòdīs] (n) *news* | **hoɗic fa-** – *get news; discover the whereabouts* : tan kunu hoɗic fairam na – *I find no trace of him; I've lost track of him* [A. ḥadīθ]
hogu ['hògū] (pron) *that (thing); that (person)* (discourteous when used in respect of a person) | hogu kita? – *what's that?* : hogu tan batija – *that's his nephew* : **hoguin** – *those ones; those* : hoguin amrar – *those ones are ours* = **ho + gu** ¹
hoguta ['hògūtā] (pron) *that (thing)* = **ho + guta** ²
hoj [hòz, hòj] (n) *the pilgrimage to Mecca; Hajj* | akbori hoj – *pilgrimage whose climax falls on a Friday* : umrau hoj – *off-season pilgrimage* : **hojo** – *on the pilgrimage* : caca hojɔ – *uncle is away doing Hajj* : **hoj kor** – *perform Hajj* [A. ḥajj]
hojag ['hòzāk, 'hòjāg] (adj) *awake; alert* | afne hojag ni? – *are you awake?* : **hojag o-/hojag oi ja-** – *wake up* : bur fac·tat hojag oici – *I woke at five a.m.* : **hojag tak-** – *stay awake; remain vigilant* : afne hojag takba – *do keep vigilant* [B. sâjag]
hojom ['hòzòm, 'hòjòm] (n) *digestion* | **hojom kor-/hojom kori le-** – *digest; stomach* : kani hojom kori liram – *I'm digesting my meal* : tan ɗuk hojom korta oiba – *he will have to stomach his disappointment* : **hojom o-/hojom oi ja-** – *get digested* : ɗoi jolɗi hojom oi jae – *yogurt quickly gets digested* [A. haÐm]
hojor ['hòzòr] (n) *dawn* = **fojor**
hojrot ['hòz-ròt] (n) *revered person; His Reverence; His Holiness* (a title of respect for a spiritual leader or prophet) [A. ḥaÐra – *presence*]
hok [hòχ] (adj) *true; righteous; fair* = **hokk**
hokan ¹ ['hòχān] (pron) *that (thing)* | hokan ano cai – *bring me that one, will you please* : **hoknain/hoknin** – *those (things)* : hoknain lagto nae – *those ones won't be needed* : hoknin kamalor – *those ones are Kamal's* = **ho + kan** ²
hokan ² (n) *that place; there* | hokan fojonto – *up to there* : **hokano** – *in that place; there* : **hokanor** – *of that place* = **ho + kan** ³
hokano ['hòχānò] (n adv) *there* < **hokan** ²
hokanta ['hòχān-tā] (pron) *that (thing)* = **hokan** ¹ + **-ta** ²
hokigot ['hòkīgòt] (n) *true account* [A. ḥaqīqa – *reality; fact*]
hokir ['hòkīr] (n) *mendicant; fakir* = **fokir**
hokk [hòk] (adj) *true; righteous; fair* | hokk kota – *true words* : hokk manus – *righteous person* : hokk bicar – *fair trial; fair judgment* ¶ **hokk** (n) *truth; right* | hokk tukaita – *you should seek the truth* : afnar hokk ota – *it's your right; you have a right to it* : **hokk aɗae kor-** – *obtain one's rights* [A. ḥaqq]
hokkani ['hòk-kānī] (adj) *righteous* [A. ḥaqqānī]
hokki ['hòk-kī] (adj) *righteous* = **hokkani**
hokol ['hòχòl] (adj) *all* | hokol foesa tumar – *all the money is yours; the money is all yours* : tar hokol kam bala – *all his work is good* : (used after a noun as a sign of plurality) borton hokol fuco – *give the plates a wipe* : afnar kagoj hokol tik korci – *I've sorted your documents* : **hokol somoe** – *all the time; always* : amra hokol somoe ca kai – *we're always drinking tea* : **hokol jaegae/hokol jagae** – *in all places; everywhere* : hokol jagae baɗa – *there's litter all over the place* ¶ **hokol** (pron) *everything; everyone* | hokol bala – *everything's all right; everyone is well* [B. sâkâl < S. sakala]
hokole ['hòχòlέ] (pron) *everyone* = **hokoloe**
hokolgae ['hòχòl-gāε] (adv) *everywhere* = **hokol + gae** ²
hokolguin ['hòχòl-gūın] (pron) *all of them* = **hokol + guin**
hokolguni ['hòχòl-gūnī] (pron) *all of them* = **hokol + guni** ¹
hokolkano ['hòχòl-χānò] (adv) *everywhere* = **hokol + -kano**
hokoloe ['hòχòlòε] (pron) *everyone* | hokoloe koira bala – *everyone's saying how good it is* : hokoloe cincoin afnare – *everyone has recognized you* : tara hokoloe mucolman – *they are*

all Muslims; all of them are Muslims : **hokolor/hoklor** – *of everyone; everyone's* : tain hokolor nam janoin – *he knows everybody's name* : hoklor lagi kani ace – *there's food for everyone* : **hokolere/hokolre** – *(to) everyone* (objective) : ami hokolere dici – *I've given some to everyone* : tain hokolre bala fain – *he likes everybody*   < **hokol**
hokolou ['hòχòlôu] (adj) *all* (emphatic)   = **hokol + -u**
hokolta ['hòχòl-tā] (pron) *all of it*   = **hokol + -ta** ²
hokolti ['hòχòl-tī] (pron) *all of it* | hokolti bad – *all of it is spoilt* : tara hokolti kai lice – *they've eaten the whole lot* : hokoltir ujon koto oibo? – *what would be the weight of it all?* : **hokoltit** – *in all; altogether* : hokoltit dos fon oice – *it comes to ten pounds altogether* = **hokol + -ti**
hokta ['hòχtā] (pron) *that (thing)*
hoktata ['hòχtātā] (pron) *that (thing)*   = **hokta + -ta** ²
hokto ['hòktò] (adj) *hard*   = **sokto**
hokun ['hòkūn] (n) *vulture*   [B. såkun < S. šakuna]
holid ['hòlīd] (n) *holiday* | coe aftar holid – *the six week holiday; the summer holidays* : **holid kor-** – *go on holiday* : tara italit holid korer – *they're on holiday in Italy*   [E.]
homan ['hòmān] (adj) *same; equal* | hota ar ita homan – *that one and this one are the same* : ek dorjon tin 'ali homan – *one dozen is the same as three "hali"* : tin cair·guna homan baro – *four threes equal twelve* : tan homan afne – *you are equal to him* : **homan homan** – *just the same; equal* : tara dui bai homan homan – *they two brothers are exactly the same* = **soman**
homane ['hòmānɛ] (adv) *steadily; continually*   = **somane**
homar ['hòmār] (adj) *even; level*   [P. hamwār]
homdi ['hòmdī] (adv) *that way*   = **homon + dia**
homola ['hòmòlā] (adv) *like that*   = **homon + lakan**
homon ['hòmòn] (adj) *such*   = **hemon**
homuka ['hòmūkā] (adv) *in that direction*   = **ho + muka** ²
hon [hòn] (n) *that place* | **hon taki/hon tone** – *from that place; from there* : tara hon taki hori gece – *they have moved from there* : **honor** – *of that place; of there* : honor am bout bala – *the mangoes of that locality are very good* : **hono** – *at that place; there* : tara hono take – *they stay in that place; they live there* : malik sabor hono – *over there at Mr Malik's place* : afnar hono tibi ace ni? – *is there a TV at your place?*   = **hokan** ²
hone ['hònɛ] (post) *from*   = **tone**
hono ['hònò] (adv) *there*   < **hon**
hor+ [hòr] (adj prefix) *every; all*   [P. har – *each*]
hor- (vi) *move away; get out of the way* | horo be! – *out of my way, child!* : hor okan taki! – *scram!* : **hori ja-** – *move away* : taintain i jaga taki hori gecoin – *they have moved out of this area* : tura hori jauka – *please move away a little bit*   [B. sår-]
hora- ['hòrā] (vt) *displace; remove; put out of the way* | amar cear ke horaice? – *who's shifted my chair?* : hou tebul kail horaimu – *I'll get rid of that table tomorrow* : tumar fau horao – *get your feet out of the way* : **horai le-/horai de-** – *shift; move out of the way* : tara gari horai lice – *they've moved the car out of the way*   [B. såra-]
hordom ['hòr-dòm] (adv) *all the time*   [P. hardam]
hor-hamesa ['hòr-hāmɛšā] (adv) *always*   = **hor + hamesa**
hori ['hòrī] (n) *mother-in-law*   [B. sasurī < O. švašrū]
horiŋ ['hòrīŋ] (n) *deer*   [B. hårin < S. hariṇa]
hosta ['hòs-tā] (adj) *cheap*   = **sosta**
hota ['hòtā] (pron) *that*
hota ['hòtā] (pron) *that*
hoti ['hòtī] (adj) *related through a co-wife* | hoti furi – *stepdaughter* : hoti fua – *stepson*
hotin ['hòtīn] (n) *co-wife*   [B. såtin < O. sapatnī]
hou [hôu] (adj) *that* | hou cearo bouka – *do take a seat in that chair* : tara hou gor rakto – *they want to buy that house there*

houmuka ['hôu-mūkā] (adv) *in that direction* = **hou** + **muka** ²
hour ['hôur] (n) *father-in-law* [B. såsur < O. švašura]
hubar ['hūbār] (n) *vacuum cleaner* | **hubar mar-** – *do vacuum cleaning* : tain asto goro hubar marcoin – *she has vacuumed the whole house* [E. Hoover]
hubuhu ['hūbūhū] (adj) *exactly alike* | hubuhu nokol – *an exact replica* [P. hū ba hū]
huđa ['hūđā] (adv) *purely and simply; for no reason* | tain huđa koicoin ita – *he just said that for no good reason* [O. šuđđha – *pure*]
huđa- ['hūđā] (vi) *disappear*
huđahuđi ['hūđā-hūđī] (adv) *for no reason; without need* | kam·ta huđahuđi korce – *he did it for no good reason* : tumi huđahuđi koico i kota – *there was no need for you to say that* = **huđa**
hufu ['hūfū] (n) *father's sister* = **fufu**
hujur ['hūzūr, 'hūjūr] (n) *spiritual master* [A. ḥuÐūr – *presence*]
huk- ¹ [hūk] (vi) *become dry* | cađđor huker na – *the sheets aren't drying* : **huki ja-** – *get dry; dry up* : kafor jolđi huki jaibo – *the clothes will soon dry*
huk- ² (vt) *sniff a scent; smell* | ou fulor geran huko – *just smell this flower* [B. suⁿk-]
huka- ['hūkā] (v) *become dry; cause to dry* | bija karfit hukaitam kila? – *how am I to get the wet carpet to dry?* : **hukai ja-** – *dry up; get shrivelled; get emaciated* : gaŋ hukai gece – *the river has dried up* : afne hukai gecoin – *you have lost weight* [B. suka-]
hukail ['hūkāıl] (v adj) *dried; desiccated* < **huka-**
hukka ['hūk-kā] (n) *hookah* [A. ḥuqqa – *small pot*]
hukna ['hūk-nā] (adj) *dry* [B. sukna]
hukoin ['hūkòın] (n) *dried fish* cf **hukna**
hukum ['hūkūm] (n) *command* | allar hukum – *God's command; whatever God ordains* : allar hukum oile.. – *if God so wills.* : allar hukum kail jaimu – *God willing I shall go tomorrow* : **hukum đe-** – *give a command* : **hukum jana-** – *issue a command* : **hukum man-** – *accept a commandment; obey an order* : afne allar hukum manta oiba – *you have to accept what God ordains* [A. ḥukm]
hul ¹ [hūl] *(insect's) sting* [B. hul]
hul ² (n) *hole* [E.]
hun- [hūn] (v) *listen; hear* | hunouka! – *please listen; please hear me out* : huni! – *let me listen; let me hear this* : huni jauka – *listen to me a moment; a word in your ear before you go* : ami kunta huni na – *I can't hear anything* : tara gan huner – *they're listening to some music* : amra cacar mat hunram – *we're listening to uncle* : tain kane hunoin na – *he can't hear with his ears; he is deaf* : **huna jae-** – *(it) can be heard* : aoaj huna jar – *a noise is being heard; a noise is audible* : tan mat huna jae – *his talking can be heard; one can hear him speak* : tarar kota huna gece na – *it was impossible to catch what they were saying* : huna jae, tain aiba – *people say he's going to come* : tan foesa ace huna jae – *apparently he's got loads of money* : **huni le-** – *listen; hear* : huni louka! – *listen!* : ke huni libo – *someone may hear* : tain huni licoin – *he has heard; he has overheard (what we said)* : **kota hun-** – *heed what is said; be obedient* : hurutae kota hune na – *the children don't do as they're told* [B. sun-]
huna ['hūnā] (v adj) *heard; overheard* | huna kota – *words which have been heard; overheard talk; hearsay* < **hun-**
huna- (vt) *allow to hear; cause to listen; tell; recite (so that others may hear)* | i kota hunaitam nai keure – *I won't let anybody hear of this* : tain cacire redio hunain – *she gets auntie to listen to the radio* : baiccaintore hunaici na ebu – *I haven't told the children yet* : natine gan hunaibo amrare – *grand-daughter is going to sing us a song* : tain hurutare kicca hunain – *she tells the children stories* : betae bason hunaicoin – *the man gave a speech* : caca kotota hunaira tare – *uncle is giving him a long lecture* : **hunai đe-** – *allow to hear; cause to listen* : oajor keced hunai đicoin amrare – *he made us listen to cassettes of sermons* [B. suna-]
hunda ['hūndā] (n) *motorcycle* [E. Honda]

hunia ['huɪnɪā] (v adv) *having heard; on hearing* | i kota hunia tain rag korcoin – *on hearing this he got angry* : hunia ami kusi – *I'm glad to hear that*   < **hun-**
hunra ['hūn-rā] (n) *listener*   < **hun-**
huŋga ['hūŋ-gā] (n) *bastard*   = **fuŋga**
huŋgi ['hūŋ-gī] (n) *female bastard*   = **fuŋgi**
huo ['hūò] (n) *porpoise*   [B. susuk]
huor ['hūòr] (n) *pig; swine*   [O. šūkara – *wild boar*]
hur- [hūr] (v) *sweep with a broom*
huroin ['hūròɪn] (n) *broom*
huru ['hūrū] (adj) *small; smaller; too small; junior* | huru camuc – *a small spoon* : he tumar huru – *he is smaller than you* : ita amar lagi huru – *this is too small for me* : ou fen tumar huru lagce – *these trousers are too small to fit you* : huru caca – *junior paternal uncle* : huru baisab – *least senior elder brother* : huru mon/huru ɖil – *faint heart; ungenerous nature* : amar mon huru oi gece – *my heart is reduced; I feel discouraged* : tar ɖil huru – *he is petty minded* : «huru mainsor boro mat» – *little people always talk big* : **huru kor-/huru kori le-** – *make smaller* : tar couk huru kori lice – *he's screwed up his eyes* : **huru huru** – *very small* : huru huru ɖana – *little tiny grains*
hurumanus ['hūrūmānūš] (n) *child; children*   = **huru + manus**
hurumuru ['hūrū-mūrū] (adj) *very small; wee*   = **huru**
huruta ['hūrūtā] (n) *little one; child; children* | tain ek hurutare ancoin – *she brought one child* : afnar huruta koe·gu? – *how many children have you?* : hurutae farko kelar – *the children are playing in the park*   = **huru + -ta** [2]
hurutta ['hūrūt-tā] (n) *children*   = **huruta**
hus [hūš] (n) *consciousness; awareness* | tar hus roice – *his consciousness has remained; he is still conscious* : tar hus nae – *he is unconscious* : tar hus gece gi – *he has lost consciousness* : foesar bae hus nae tar – *he is oblivious to money matters*   [P. hoš]
hus-buɖɖi ['hūš-būɪɖ-dī] (n) *consciousness; senses* | tar hus-buɖɖi tik nae – *he's not in his right senses*   = **hus + buɖɖi**
husiar ['hūšɪār] (adj) *alert* | **husiar o-/husiar oi ja-** – *become cautious* : i kobor faia tara husiar oi gece – *after hearing this they've become quite wary* : **(kare) husiar kor-** – *warn (someone) to be cautious* : cacare husiar kortam oimu – *we must warn uncle to be on his guard* ¶ **husiar** (int) *beware!*   [P. hošyār]
husiari ['hūšɪārī] (n) *caution* | **husiari ɖe-/husiari ɖi la-** – *give a warning* : fulise tare husiari ɖice – *the police have given him a caution*   [P. hošyārī]
hutki ['hūt-kī] (n) *dried fish*   [B. sutki]
hut- [hūt] (vi) *lie down; go to bed* | afne hutita ni? – *do you want to lie down?* : amma huticoin – *Mum has gone to bed; Mum is having a lie-down* : **huti ja-** – *go to lie down; go to bed* : tain huti gecoin – *she has gone to bed* : **huti ro-** – *be lying down; be in bed* : hurutae huti roice – *the children are in bed*   [B. su-]
huta- ['hūtā] (vt) *lay down; put to bed* | tare beto hutauka – *lay him down on the bed* : nati hokolre hutaici – *I've put the grandchildren to bed* : **hutai ɖe-** – *lay down; put to bed* : baiccaintore hutai ɖita ni? – *are you going to put the children to bed?*   [B. soa-]
huton ['hūtòn] (v n) *act of lying; state of lying* | **hutno** – *in a reclining state; lying down* : caca hutno – *uncle is lying down* : **hutnor maje** – *in a reclining state; lying down* : tara hutnor maje – *they are in bed*   < **hut-**

i

i¹ [ī] (adj) *this* | i kolom bala – *this pen is good* : i·ta tumar – *this one is yours* ¶ **i** (pron) *this* | i kita? – *what is this? what's all this?* : i kene? – *why all this?* [B. e]

i² (int) *indeed* | i oibo – *yes, indeed it will be so* : i faiba – *indeed you will find something*

-i¹ (noun suffix) *-ness; characteristic behaviour* | nek, neki – *good, goodness* : calak, calaki – *crafty, craftiness* : mastor, mastori – *teacher, teaching* : colicitar, colicitari – *solicitor, the work of a solicitor* [P.]

-i² (adj suffix) *-ish; -al; -ese; redolent of; pertinant to* | gulaf, gulafi – *rose, pinkish* : keal, keali – *whim, whimsical* : jafan, jafani – *Japan, Japanese*

-i³ (noun suffix) *-er; practicant or exponent of* | jaaj, jaaji – *ship, ship's crewman* < **-i²**

iaa [ɪā:] (int) *o* | iaa koda! – *o God! oh goodness!* : iaa mabud! – *good Lord!* [A. yā]

iadra ['ɪād-rā] (adv) *now; recently*

iaid ['ɪāɪd] (n) *recollection; memory* | **(kar) iaid ace** – *(someone) has a recollection; one remembers* : he kita koicil, afnar iaid ace? – *do you remember what he said?* : amar iaid nae – *I have no recollection* : tan kota amar iaid acil na – *I was forgetting about him* : tan iaid take hokolta – *he remembers everything* : tumar iaid takbo ni? – *are you sure you'll remember?* : i kota ebu iaid roice tarar – *they still remember this matter* : **(kar) iaid oe** – *(someone) gets a recollection; one recalls* : ke ancla tan iaid oito fare – *he may be able to recall who brought it* : akta amar iaid oicil, cafi kunano – *I suddenly remembered where the key was* : tan kota amar iaid or na – *I can't recollect him* : **iaid kor-** – *remember* : tan nam iaid kortam farci na – *I haven't been able to recall his name* : **iaid rak-** – *keep in mind* : otota iaid raktam kila? – *how am I to remember all that?* [P. yād – *memory*]

iakub ['ɪākūb] (n) *Jacob; James* [A. ya¿qūb]

ialla ['ɪāl-lā] (int) *o God!* [A. yā l-lāh]

ian [ɪān] (n) *north east; north-eastern pillar* | ian kuna – *the north east compass point* : **ian tul-** – *erect the north-eastern post* (to inaugurate a new construction) [B. isan < S. īšāna]

iar [ɪār] (n) *friend* [P. yār]

iarfut ['ɪār-fūt] (n) *airport* [E.]

iat [ɪāt] (n) *backyard* | **iato** – *in the yard; in the back garden* : tumra iato gia kelao – *go and play in the back garden, you lot*: amra iato uri falaici – *we've planted beans in the back yard* [E.]

ibadot ['ībādòt] (n) *worship* [A. ¿ibāda]

ibae ['ībāɛ] (adv) *this side; over here; this way* | tara ibae ae na besi – *they don't often come over here* : ibae cauka – *look this way* : amrar ibae sof nae – *there aren't any shops over here, round our way* = **i¹ + bae**

ibaedi ['ībāɛdī] (adv) *this way; over here* = **i¹ + bae + dia**

ibae-hobae ['ībāɛ-hòbāɛ] (adv) *this way and that* = **ibae + hobae**

ibaju ['ībāzū, 'ībājū] (n) *this side* | ibaju amrar, hobaju tarar – *this side is ours and the other side is theirs* : **ibajut** – *on this side; over here* : ibajut kunu cear nae – *there aren't any chairs over here* = **i¹ + baju**

ibala ['ībālā] (adv) *at this time; now* = **i¹ + bala¹**

ibla ['īb-lā] (adv) *now* | ibla meg der – *now it's raining* : **iblaku** – *now* : iblaku goro jaitam oimu – *I must go home now* : **iblakur** – *of now; present* : iblakur somoe – *the present time* = **ibala**

ibraim ['ībrāɪm] (n) *Abraham* [A. ibrāhīm]

ica¹ ['īsā] (n) *shrimp; prawn* | ica mac – *shrimp; prawn*

ica² (n) *Jesus* | ica-ul-islam – *Jesus* [A. ¿īsā]

icara ['īsārā] (adv) *apart from that; otherwise* = **i¹ + cara**

icca ['ītšɪa] (n) *wish; desire* | afnar icca – *as you will* [B. iccha < S. icchā]

icub ['īsūb] (n) *Joseph* [A. yūsuf]

id [īd] (n) *Muslim festival; Eid* | rujar id *– festival after Ramadan; Eid ul Fitr* : kurbanir id *– festival of the sacrifice; Eid ul Adha* : **id kor-** *– have a festival; celebrate Eid* : amra kail id kormu *– we're going to have Eid tomorrow* [A. ¿īd]
idga ['īd-gā] (n) *Eid prayer ground* [P. īdgāh]
igca ['īk-sā] (pron) *this (thing)* | igca sundor *– this one is pretty* : **igcain/igcin** *– these (things)* : igcin ke ance? *– who bought these?* = **i¹ + gaca**
igu ['īgū] (pron) *this (thing); this (person)* (discourteous when used in respect of a person) | igu kita? *– what's this?* : igu tarar fua *– this is their son* : **igue** *– this (person)* (instrumental) : mic, igue galice amare *– this boy swore at me, Miss* : **igur** *– of this (one)* : igur nam jani na *– I don't know the name of this one* : **igure** *– this (one)* (objective) : igure loia jao *– take this one away* : **iguin** *– these (ones)* : iguin afnar lagi *– these are for you* : **iguinte** *– these (ones)* (instrumental) : iguinte kam kore na *– these ones don't work* : **iguintor** *– of these (ones)* : iguintor dam ek fon *– the price of these is one pound* : **iguintore** *– these (ones)* (objective) : iguintore falai dimu *– I'm going to throw these away* = **i¹ + gu¹**
iguta ['īgūtā] (pron) *this (thing)* | iguta cai na *– I don't want this* : **iguinta** *– these (ones)* : iguinta afnar lagi *– these are for you* = **i¹ + guta²**
ihudi ['īhūdī] (adj) *Jewish* ¶ **ihudi** (n) *Jew* [A. yahūdī]
ijjot ['īj-jòt] (n) *honour; dignity; prestige* | ijjotor befar *– a matter of honour* : tumar ijjot nae ni? *– don't you have any pride?* : tan ijjote lagce *– his prestige is at stake* : tara amrar ijjote marce *– they have impugned our honour* [A. ¿izza]
ikan¹ ['īχān] (pron) *this (thing)* | ikan kar? *– whose is this?* : **iknain/iknin** *– these (things)* : iknain kamor *– these are useful* = **i¹ + kan²**
ikan² (n) *this place; here* | ikan taki koto dur oibo? *– how far would it be from here?* : **ikano** *– in this place; here* : **ikanor** *– of this place; of here* = **i¹ + kan³**
ikano ['īχānò] (n adv) *here* < **ikan²**
ikanta ['īχāntā] (pron) *this (thing)* = **ikan¹ + -ta²**
ikta ['īχtā] (pron) *this (thing)*
iktata ['īχtātā] (pron) *this (thing)* = **ikta + -ta²**
iktiar ['īχtıār] (n) *(divine) authority* [A. iḵtiyār]
ila ['īlā] (adv) *like this; thus; so; such* | ila korouka *– do it like this* : ola nae, ila! *– not like that, like this!* : ila calaile morba *– if you drive like this you'll be killed* : ila sundor lage! *– oh, it's so pretty!* : ila faji beta *– he's such a tiresome man* : ila manus ami ar dekci na *– I've never seen such a character* = **ilakan**
ilagi ['īlāgī] (adv) *for this reason; so* | bemar aclam, ilagi geci na *– I was ill, that's why I didn't go* : tain naraj, kunta koico na ilagi *– he's annoyed because you didn't say anything* : ilagi bada nae *– there's no objection on account of that; that's no problem* : ilagi kita oilo? *– what of that? so what?* = **i¹ + lagi**
ilaj ['īlāz] (n) *treatment* [A. ¿ilāj]
ilakan ['īlāχān] (adv) *like this; thus; so; such* | ilakan coltam kila? *– how can we carry on like this?* : ilakan kaca tometu ar anio na *– don't get such unripe tomatoes next time* : ilakan gori kunano mile? *– where can one get a clock like this?* = **i¹ + lakan**
ilan ['īlān] (adv) *like this; thus; so; such* | ilan koro *– do it like this* : tain ilan maticla *– he spoke thus* : ilan boro *– so big* : ilan huruta *– such children* = **ilakan**
ilekson ['īlεkšòn] (n) *election; elections* | o maso ilekson oibo *– elections will be held this month* : tain ileksono kara oicoin *– he is standing in the elections* [E.]
ilektik ['īlεktīk] (n) *electricity; electricity supply* | ilektikor lain *– electric supply cable* : ino ilektikor lain nae *– there is no electricity supply here* : ilektik joler *– electricity is being consumed* : ilektikor bil *– electricity bill* [E.]
ilim ['īlīm] (n) *(Islamic) learning* | tan ilim ace boutta *– he is very well versed in Islamic knowledge* [A. ¿ilm *– knowledge*]
ilisa ['īlīšā] (n) *hilsa; a species of fish prized as food (Hilsa ilisha)* [B. ilis]
imam ['īmām] (n) *prayer leader; imam* [A. imām]
imamoti ['īmāmòtī] (n) *leadership of prayers; function of an imam* [A. imāma]

iman ['īmān] (n) *belief; faith; integrity* | tain iman ancoin – *he has embraced the faith* : iman tik raka lage – *one has to preserve one's faith by practising one's beliefs* : tar iman nae – *he has no integrity* [A. īmān]

imanḍar ['īmānḍār] (adj) *possessed of faith* | tain boro imanḍar manus – *he's a sincere, devout person* [P. imāndār]

in [īn] (n) *this place; here* | in taki ek mail ḍuroe – *one mile away from here* : **ino** – *in this place; here* : tara ino nae – *they aren't here* : **inor** – *of this place; of here* : inor abaoa bala – *the climate of this place is good* : inor maje kunta nae – *there's nothing inside here* = **ikan** ²

inain ['īnāın] (pron) *these people; they* | inain amar kutum – *these are my relatives* : inain london taki aicoin – *they have come from London* : **inaintor** – *of these people; their* : inaintor bari silot – *their home is in Sylhet* : **inaintore** – *these people; them* (instrumental) : inaintore ḍaot ḍici – *I have given them an invitation* = **enain**

incab ['īnsāb] (n) *fairness* | cacar incab ace – *uncle is fair-minded* : tan incab nae – *he's unfair* : ila incab oe na – *it's not fair like that* : **incabor** – *fair; equitable* : tain incabor manus – *she's a fair-minded person* = **incaf**

incaf ['īnsāf] (n) *fairness* [A. inṣāf – *equity*]

inci ['īntšī] (n) *inch* [E.]

inḍu ['īnḍū] (adj) *Hindu* | inḍu ḍormo – *Hindu religion; Hinduism* ¶ **inḍu** (n) *Hindu person* [B. hinḍu]

injil ¹ [īn'jīl] (n) *Christian gospel* [A. injīl]

injil ² ['īnjīl] (n) *engine* [E.]

ino ['īnò] (n adv) *here* | ino ao! – *come here!* : tain ino nae – *he isn't here* : amar ino roita faroin – *you can stay at my place here* < **in**

insalla ['īn-šāl-lā] (int) *God willing* [A. in šā'a l-lāhu – *if God wishes*]

inuc [īn'ūs] (n) *Jonah* [A. yūnus]

iŋblaf ['īŋblāf] (n) *envelope* [E.]

iŋgej ['īŋgɛz, 'īŋgɛj] (n) *engaged tone (of telephone)* | **iŋgej mare** – *it gives the engaged tone* : kali iŋgej mare – *it's giving the engaged tone all the time* [E.]

iŋgrej ['īŋgrɛz, 'īŋgrɛj] (n) *English person* [Pg. inglês]

iŋgreji ['īŋgrɛzī, 'īŋgrɛjī] (a) *English* | ami iŋgreji mat buji na – *I don't understand English speech* ¶ **iŋgreji** (n) *English language; date (A.D.)* | tara iŋgreji matto fare – *they can speak English* : tain bala iŋgreji janoin – *she knows good English* : ḍui ajar ḍos iŋgreji – *2010 A.D.* : aij koto iŋgreji? – *what date is it today?* [P. inglesī]

iŋlend ['īŋlɛnd] (n) *England* [E.]

iŋsa ['īŋšā] (n) *ill-will; jealousy* | tan maje iŋsa nae – *she is free of malice* : **iŋsa kor-** – *be ill-disposed (to); be resentful (of)* : gaur mainse amrare iŋsa kore – *the villagers are ill-disposed towards us* [B. hiŋsa < S. hiŋsa – *violence*]

iŋsalla ['īŋšāl-lā] (int) *God willing* = **insalla**

io [ıò] (n) *thingummy* | amar io kunano? – *where's my thingummy-jig?* : ebu iot roice – *it's still in the what-you-may-call-it*

iraḍa ['īrāḍā] (n) *idea; intention* | **(kar) iraḍa ace** – *one has a mind; one intends* : amar emrika jaibar iraḍa acil – *I had a mind to go to America* : tarar gari loar iraḍa nae – *they have no intention of buying a car* [A. irāḍa – *wish*]

irsa ['īršā] (n) *jealousy* | **(kar) irsa lage** – *one feels jealous; one feels resentful* : amar gori ḍeki tar irsa lagce – *seeing my watch he felt jealous* : **irsa kor-** – *envy; resent* : tara afnare irsa kore – *they are envious of you* [B. irsa < S. īrṣā]

is [īs] (int) *oh! oh dear! ouch!* | is, fori gece! – *oh dear, it's fallen!* : is! ḍuk faici! – *ow! that hurt!* : is, mica mat! – *oh, what a fib!*

isab ['īšāb] (n) *calculation; reckoning; account* | tain isab janoin na – *he can't do arithmetic* : koto manus morcoin, isab nae – *there's no reckoning how many people died* : isabor maje gondogul ace – *there's a discrepancy in the accounts* : **isabe** – *by calculation; on a specific basis* : isabe ḍeka jae, asi fon lab – *if you work it out, that's £80 profit* : masik isabe foncas

117

fon – *fifty pounds on a monthly basis; fifty pounds per month* : tain caca isabe matcoin – *he spoke in his capacity as an uncle* : afne kun isabe koira? – *on what basis are you saying that?* : **isab kor-** – *calculate; reckon; esteem* : isab korouka, koto oice – *calculate how much it's come to* : tara afnare isab kore – *they have respect for you* : **isab kori le-** – *calculate; work out* : labor isab kori litam ni? – *shall I work out the profit?* : **isab kori dek-** – *work out (for oneself)* : mut koto, isab kori deki – *let's work out what the total is* : **isab rak-** – *keep an account* : korocfatir isab rakcoin ni? – *have you kept an account of expenses?* [A. hisāb – *accounting*]
isabi ['īšābī] (adj) *calculating; miserly*   = **isab** + **-i** ²
isaf ['īšāf] (n) *calculation*   = **isab**
isan ['īšān] (n) *north east* | isan kuna – *north east compass point*   [B. isan < S. īšāna]
ise ['īšέ] (int) *um; whatsit*
islam [īss-'lām] (n) *Islam*   [A. islām]
islami ['īss-lāmī] (adj) *Islamic*   [A. islāmī]
istem [īs'tεm] (n) *postage stamp; National Insurance contribution* | citit istem koto lagbo? – *how much postage will be needed on the letter?* : tan istem kom – *he hasn't got a full contribution record* : **istem laga-** – *affix a postage stamp* : **istem mar-** – *affix a stamp; pay National Insurance contributions* : tair boce istem lagaice na – *her employer hasn't paid her National Insurance contributions*   [E.]
isteson [īs'tεšòn] (n) *(rail) station*   [E.]
istaii [īs'tāī] (adj) *permanent*   = **staii**
istan [īs'tān] (n) *place*   = **stan**
istari ['īstārī] (n) *food to break the ritual fast in Ramadan* | **istari kor-** – *break the fast by eating a specially prepared snack*   [A. ifṭār]
istiri ¹ ['īstīrī] (n) *woman; wife*   [B. stri < S. strī]
istiri ² (n) *(smoothing) iron*   = **istori**
istori ['īstòrī] (n) *(smoothing) iron* | **istori kor-** – *iron* : amar sat istori korci na – *I haven't ironed my shirt*   [H. istrī]
istogit [īs'tògīt] (adj) *postponed*   = **stogit**
it [īt] (n) *brick* | it dia gor malaira – *they're building a house out of bricks* : itor gor – *a brick house*   [B. it < O. iśtaka]
ita ¹ ['ītā] (pron) *this (thing)*   [B. eta]
ita ² (n) *clod; brick* | fuainte ita marer – *the boys are throwing brickbats* : «it bijaile-o gole na» – *even if you soak a brick in water, it won't melt; a leopard can't change his spots* : **itar** – *(made) of brick* : itar gor – *a house of brick*   = **it**
ita- (v) *throw brickbats* | tare amare itaice – *they threw stones at me*   < **it**
ita ['ītā] (pron) *this (thing)* | ita kita? – *what's this?* : ita tumar nae ni? – *this is yours, isn't it?* : ita kene? – *what's all this fuss about?*   = **i** ¹ + **-ta** ²
ita-ota ['ītā-òtā] (pron) *this and that*   = **ita** + **ota**
itor ['ītòr] (adj) *inferior; vile; mean*   [B. itår < S. itara – *other*]
itrami ['ītrāmī] (n) *mean mindedness*   = **itor** + **ami** ²

j

ja [jā] (pron) *whatever* | afne ja bala mone koroin – *whatever you think best* : ja cae ta dimu – *whatever he wants, that I shall give; I'll give him whatever he wants* : ja oibar oibo – *whatever shall be shall be* : **ja-u** – *whatever* (emphatic) : ja-u oe – *whatever happens; in any case* ¶ **ja** (adv) *so much; so very* | afne ja kaoiaicoin! – *you have provided so much to eat!* : ja sundor oice! – *it's so beautiful!* [B. ja]

ja- (vi) *go; go away; carry on; be in the process* | afne bara jaita ni? – *are you going to go out?* : tain ruj sofo jain gi – *he goes to the shop every day* : jai gi? – *may I go now?* : jauka gi – *all right, off you go* : boia jauka – *sit for a while, then you can go* : ca kaia jaiba gi – *you must have tea before you go* : bedna jae na – *the pain doesn't go away* : ami kam kori jairam – *I'm carrying on doing my job* : fua bari jar – *the boy is in the process of growing* : aefol foci jar gi – *the apples are rotting away* : boraf goli jar – *the ice is melting* : ola koto din jaibo? – *how long can it continue like this?* : te jao! – *in that case just carry on; oh well, all right then* : **(kora) jae** – *can be (done)* : kunta kora jae – *something can be done* : ola banga jae – *it can be folded like this* : cand deka jae ni? – *is the moon visible?* : ono taka jaito nae – *it won't be possible to remain here* : koa jae na – *it cannot be said; one can't say for sure* : jaoa jaito fare – *it may be possible to go* [B. ja-] Note: **ja-** is usually replaced by **ge-** (q.v.) in past tenses. This verb is used as an auxiliary in many verbal compounds, e.g. **oi ja-, fori ja-** ; these are listed under the relevant verb root. The past participle **gi** (q.v.) is often appended to parts of the verb **ja-**.

jaaj ['jā-āz, 'jā-āj, jā:z, jā:j] (n) *ship* | bitisor jaaj – *a British ship* : tain jaajo kam korta – *he used to work on ships (as a seaman)* [H. jahāz < A. jahāz – *equipment*]

jaaji ['jā-āzī, 'jā-ājī, jā:zī, jā:jī] (n) *seaman* = **jaaj + -i** [3]

jac- ['jās] (vt) *ask for* [B. jac- < O. yāc-]

jacai ['jāsāı] (n) *testing* [B. jacai < O. yācnā]

jacia ['jāısıā] (v adv) *deliberately; on close examination* | tain jacia korcoin – *he did it deliberately* : jacia kouka – *think it over and say; give a considered reply* : **jacia dek-** – *test; examine critically* : bisoe·ta jacia dekouka – *think the matter over* < **jac-**

-jada ['jādā] (noun suffix) *son (of)* [P. zāda – *born (of)*]

-jadi ['jādī] (noun suffix) *daughter (of)* [P. zādī]

jadu ['jādū] (n) *magic* | **jadu kor-/jadu kori le-** – *perform magic; bewitch* : taire ke jadu kori lice – *someone has cast a spell on her* [P. jādū]

jaega ['jāɛgā] (n) *place· space; land* | sundor jaega – *a beautiful place* : amrar goro jaega nae – *there's no room in our house* : ibae codri sabor jaega – *on this side it's Mr Choudhury's land* [P. jāygāh]

jaej ['jāɛz, 'jāɛj] (adj) *permissible* [A. jā'iz]

jaenomaj ['jāɛnòmāz, 'jāɛnòmāj] (n) *prayer mat* [P. jā-namāz]

jag- [jāg] (vi) *wake; stay awake* | tain dos·tat jagcoin – *she woke up at ten o'clock* : ami hara rait jagci – *I stayed awake all night* : **jagi ja-** – *wake up* : tain sokal sokal jagi jain – *he wakes early* : hurutae jagi gece – *the children have woken up* [B. jag-]

jaga ['jāgā] (n) *place; space; land* | ek jaga – *some place; somewhere* : ino bout jaga – *there's plenty of room here* : ino amrar jaga – *this here is our land* : tain bout jagar malik – *he is the owner of much land* : **jagae** – *in a place; instead* : kun jagae? – *in which place? where?* : bout jagae – *in many places* : hokol jagae – *everywhere* : tumar jagae ami korlam ne na – *in your place I wouldn't have done it* : tain ekor jagae egaro lekcoin – *he wrote eleven in place of one* : garir jagae ben loimu – *instead of a car I'll get a van* : **jagae jagae** – *here and there; all over the place* : jagae jagae fani – *there's water all over the place* : **jagat** – *in a place; in place; instead* : kun jagat? – *in which place?* : cear·kan jagat rako – *put the chair in its proper place* : tan kam jagat roice – *his job is still there* : tan jagat ke takbo? – *who will be there in his stead?* : **jaga oe/jaga oi jae** – *space is available* : i goro jaga oe na – *there isn't enough space in this house* : amrar tin·jonor jaga oibo ni? – *will*

there be room for the three of us? : **jaga kor-/jaga kori le-/jaga kori de-** – *make room* : huru rumo jaga kori lici – *I've made space in the boxroom* : cacir lagi jaga kori deuka – *make some space for auntie* : **jaga rak-/jaga raki le-** – *buy land* : tara bout jaga raki ler – *they're buying up lots of land* : **jagat a-** – *return to the right place; get back to normal* : caka one jagat aice – *the cog has got back into its correct position* : dui dinor maje afnar befsa jagat aibo – *your business will recover in a day or two* : tan hus-buddi ebu jagat aice na – *he hasn't yet come back to his senses* = **jaega**
jaga- (vt) *waken; cause to wake* | hurutare jagaitam cai na – *I don't want to wake the children* : **jagai de-** – *waken; arouse* : afnare coe·tat jagai dimu – *I'll wake you at six o'clock* [B. jaga-]
jaga-jomin [ˈjāgā-jòmīn] (n) *landed property* = **jaega + jomin**
jag-ge [ˈjāg-gɛ] (int) *let it pass; never mind* = **jauk + gi** < **ja-**
jagir [ˈjāgīr] (n) *freeholding* = **jaigir**
jagran [ˈjāgrān] (n) *staying awake; vigil* [O. jāgaraṇa]
jaigir [ˈjāɪgīr] (n) *freeholding (originally, a freehold feudal estate granted by a superior to a subordinate)* | **jaigir tak-** – *live as a free tenant on someone else's property* : tara amrar barit jaigir take – *they are guest tenants at our homestead* [P. jaegīr]
jaigirdar [ˈjāɪgīrdār] (n) *holder of a feudal estate* [P. jaegīrdār]
jail [ˈjā-īl] (adj) *boorish; cruel* [A. jāhil – *ignorant*]
jak- [jāχ] (vi) *shake* [B. jhaⁿk-]
jaka- [ˈjāχā] (vt) *shake* [B. jhaⁿka-]
jakat [jāˈχāt] (n) *prescribed almsgiving* [A. zakāh]
jakni [ˈjāχ-nī] (n) *jolting; shaking* [B. jhaⁿkni]
jal¹ [jāl] (n) *net; web* | mac dorar jal – *fishing net* : jal dia mac dore – *they catch fish with a net* : makoror jal – *spider's web* : **jal ba-** – *ply a net; fish with a net* : tara jal bae – *they are fishermen by trade* [B. jal < O. jāla]
jal² (n) *husband's brother's wife* [B. ja]
jal³ (n) *forgery* | he jale dora force – *he was caught doing forgery* : **jal kor-** – *do forgery; forge* : tara foesa jal kore – *they forge money* ¶ **jal** (adj) *forged* | jal fasfut – *a forged passport* : ou keala jal – *this land deed is forged* [A. jaɂl – *fabrication*]
jal⁴ (n) *heat* | **jal de-** – *apply heat (to); heat up* : handit jal dici – *I've put the pan to heat up* : car fani jal ditam ni? – *shall I heat up some water for tea?* [B. jal < O. jvāla]
jal⁵ (adj) *piquant; hot* | jal lage – *it tastes hot* : jal oice ni? – *is (the food) hot enough? is it too hot?* ¶ **jal** (n) *piquancy; hotness* | afne jal kain ni? – *do you eat spicy-hot food?* : besi jal dici na – *I haven't put too much hot spice* [B. jhal]
jala [ˈjālā] (n) *torment; annoyance* | ki jala! – *what a pain! how annoying!* : **jala kore** – *it causes torment; it hurts to distraction* : borone jala kore – *the boil is hurting a lot* : **jalae** – *on account of torment; on account of annoyance* : tar jalae kam kortam fari na – *thanks to his pestering I can't work* : **jala de-** – *torment; annoy* : tumar hurutae jala der amare – *your children are driving me mad* [B. jala < O. jvālā]
jala- (vt) *set alight; burn; switch on; annoy* | fuainte gerij jalaice – *the boys set fire to the garage* : tara hokol somoe agorbatti jalae – *they burn incense sticks all the time* : aguin jalaitam ni? – *shall I light the fire?* : mumbatti jalaicoin – *she has lit a candle* : batti jalao – *turn on the light* : tibi jalaitam nai – *I'm not going to switch the TV on* : he ana kame aia jalae amrare – *he comes for no reason and bothers us* : **jalai de-** – *set alight; switch on* : hitar jalai dici – *I've turned on the heater* [B. jala-]
jala-jontrona [ˈjālājòntrònā] (n) *tormentation* = **jala + jontrona**
jalim [ˈjālīm] (adj) *bullying; cruel* [A. źālim – *tyrannical*]
jam¹ [jām] (n) *jamun tree (Syzygium cuminii); jamun fruit* [B. jam]
jam² (n) *drinking bowl* [P. jām]
jam³ (n) *congestion; jamming* | jam oe/jam oi jae – *congestion occurs* : rasta jam oi gece – *the street is choked with traffic* : baco besi jam oe – *there's too much crowding in the buses* [E.]

jama ['jāmā] (n) *sleeved garment; shirt* [P. jāma – *garment*]
jamai ['jāmāɪ] (n) *son-in-law; bridegroom; husband* [B. jamai < O. jāmātŕ]
jamai-bou ['jāmāɪbòu] (n) *husband and wife* | jamai-boue jograjati koroin – *the couple quarrel with each other* = **jamai + bou**
jama-kafor ['jāmāχāfòr] (n) *clothes; clothing* = **jama + kafor**
jambura ['jāmbūrā] (n) *pliers* [H. jambūr < P. zunbūr – *wasp; bee*]
jamela ['jāmɛlā] (n) *bother; hassle* | besi jamela lage – *it's too much of a hassle* : **jamela kor-** – *cause hassle; take trouble* : fulise jamela korce – *the police gave some hassle* : tain bout jamela korcoin amrar lagi – *he's gone to great pains for us* [B. jhamela]
jami[1] ['jāmī] (n) *gums (of teeth)* [O. jambha – *tooth; set of teeth*]
jami[2] ['jāmī] (adj) *principal; main (mosque)* | jami mocjid – *principal mosque (of a locality)* [A. jāmiɂ - *comprehensive*]
jamir ['jāmīr] (n) *orange; tangerine* [O. jambīra – *lime*]
jan [jān] (n) *life; soul; heart; darling* | jan boro na man boro? – *which is more important, one's life or one's honour?* : tar jan·kan huru – *his soul is small; he is faint hearted* : tumi amar janor jan – *you are my heart's dearest* : abba jan – *dearest father* : **jan take** – *life is there; one is alive* : tar jan ebu roice – *he is still alive* : **jan takte** – *while life is there; while one is alive* : jan takte nekir kam korta – *you should do good deeds while you're still alive* : **jan bace** – *life persists; one survives* : tar jan bacce – *he has survived* : amar jan bacer na – *I'm not surviving; it's just too much for me to bear* : **jan jae** – *the soul departs; one expires* : tar jan jar – *he is dying; he's had as much as he can take* : afnare ɖekbar lagi amar jan jar – *I'm dying to see you* : **jan bar oe/jan bar oi jae** – *the soul slips out; one dies* : amra takte takte tan jan bar oi gecil – *he breathed his last whilst we were there* : amar jan bar or – *I'm dying; I've had all I can take* : **jan loia bac-** – *get away with one's life; survive* : tain kunumote jan loia baccoin – *somehow he came out of it alive* : **jan baca-** – *save a life; stay alive* : amar jan bacaicoin afne – *you have saved my life* : ila jan bacaita kila? – *how is one to survive in these circumstances?* : **jan ɖe-/jan ɖi la-** – *give one's life; apply one's heart; devote oneself* : tara ɖesor lagi jan ɖi laicil – *they gave their lives for their country* : tain mocjiɖor lagi jan ɖein – *he works whole-heartedly for the mosque* : hurutae jaibar lagi jan ɖer – *the children are pining to go* : **jan ɖia** – *with all one's heart* : taire jan ɖia bala fai – *I love her with all my heart* : tain jan ɖia kam korra – *he is putting heart and soul into his work* : **jan ka-/jan kai le-** – *consume (another's) life; importune; pester* : ruge bearame tar jan kai licil – *illness ruined his life* : nati amar jan kai ler – *my grandson is giving me no peace* : betae foesar lagi amar jan kar – *that fellow keeps pestering me for money* : **jan kua-/jan kuai le-** – *lose one's life* : tain larit jan kuaicla – *he lost his life in the war* : jan kuaia lab kita? – *what's the point in risking one's life?* : **jane** – *in respect of life; with the heart* (instrumental) : **jane ɖile** – *with heart and soul* : ami jane ɖile bissas kori – *I believe with all my heart* : **jane mane na** – *one's heart will not accept it* : tar nani mara kaicoin kori tar jane manto cae na – *he can hardly bear the thought that his grandmother has died* : oto bokbok, amar jane mane na – *I can't bear all this idle talk* : **jane bac-** – *go on living; survive* : mone loe, tain jane bacta nae – *I fear he's not going to survive* : **jane mar-/jane mari le-** – *assault fatally; murder; kill* : amare jane marto acil – *they were going to kill me* : tar nijor bafre jane mari lice – *he murdered his own father* [P. jān]
jan- (v) *know; ascertain; deem* | ami jani na – *I don't know* : ami janram na – *I'm not knowing; I don't know* : ami tar nam jani – *I know his name* : tai arbi mat jane – *she knows Arabic* : tain gari calaita janoin – *he knows how to drive a car* : tain mac ranɖa janoin na – *he doesn't know how to cook fish* : tain coli gecoin ami jani – *I know he's gone away* : kitar lagi janoin ni? – *and do you know why that is?* : ami jani kitar lagi – *I know why* : kita oice ke jane – *who knows what's happened* : caca janta faroin – *uncle may know (the answer)* : ami ebu jantam farci na – *I haven't yet been able to find out* : tumi balatike janco ni? – *have you ascertained properly? are you sure?* : tare bala manus jani – *I take him to be a decent person* : hou betare jani – *I know what that man's like* : «cur firre-o cur jane» – *a thief views everyone as a thief, even a saint* : **ki jani** – *what do I know; I wonder; just supposing*

: ki jani buli lein – *supposing he forgets?* : ki jani ari jae – *just think, it might get lost* : **jana jae** – *it can be known; it can be found out* : tar tikana jana gece na – *his address couldn't be ascertained* : cacar gece jana jaibo – *one can always find out from uncle* : kunu din jana jaito nae – *it will never be possible to know (the answer)* : **jani le-** – *find out* : tara tumar nam jani lice – *they have found out your name* : **jania rak-** – *inform oneself* : bacor taim jania rako – *find out the times of the buses* [B. jan-]

jana[1] (v adj) *known; acquainted* | jana kota – *a known fact* : tumar jana keu aicoin ni? – *has anybody you know come here?* : **(kar) jana ace** – *it is known (by someone); one knows* : hou kota amar jana ace – *that fact is known by me; I know that* : tar dus hokolor jana – *his faults are known to all* : okta amar jana nae – *I don't know about that* : cacar jana takto fare – *it may be known to uncle; uncle may know* : afnare jana takle koiba – *tell me if you happen to know* : tar jana takar kota – *he might be expected to know* : **(kar) jana oe/jana oi jae** – *it becomes known (to someone)* : amrar lombor hokolor jana oi gece – *our number has become known to all and sundry* : **(kar) janar maje** – *within (one's) knowledge; within (one's) acquaintance* : amar janar maje kunu jogra oice na – *as far as I know, no argument took place* : amar janar maje keure deki na – *I can't think of anybody I know* < **jan-**

jana[2] (v n) *going* < **ja-**

jana- (vt) *let know; inform; tell (of)* | runare kobor·kan janaici – *I've let Runa know the news* : kita oe, amare janain jen – *please do let me know what happens* : afnare janaitam kila? – *how am I to let you know?* : he amare kunta janae na – *he never tells me anything* : tair tikana janaito acil – *she should have told me her address* : cacire amar colam janaibae – *you must convey my salaams to auntie* : tara amrare daot janaice – *they have extended us an invitation* : **janai de-** – *inform; tell* : tantanre kobor·ta janai deuka – *do let them know the news* : amra kauncilre janai dici – *we have informed the Council* [B. jana-]

janaja ['jānāzā, 'jānājā] (n) *Muslim funeral* [A. janāza]

janajani ['jānājānī] (v n) *knowledge; awareness* | **janajani oe/janajani oi jae** – *it becomes generally known* : tarar bibador kota hokolor janajani oi gece – *the fact of their dispute has become widely known* < **jan-**

janauna ['jānā-ūnā] (v n) *acquaintance* | **(kar) loge (kar) janauna ace** – *(someone) is acquainted with (someone else)* : tantanor loge amar janauna nae – *I'm not acquainted with them* = **jana**[1] + **huna**

janda ['jāndā] (adj) *cool*

jania ['jāmā] (v adv) *having come to know; knowingly* < **jan-**

janiuni ['jānī-ūnī] (v adv) *knowingly; deliberately* | tain janiuni bera lagaicoin – *he made a muddle on purpose* = **jania + hunia** < **jan-, hun-**

janla ['jān-lā] (n) *window* | janla kultam ni? – *shall I open the window?* : janla lagao – *shut the window* : tai janla di car – *she is looking out of the window* [B. janala < Pg. janela]

janoar ['jānwār] (n) *beast; brute* [P. jānvar]

janra ['jān-rā] (n) *one who knows* < **jan-**

janra-hunra ['jānrā hūnrā] (adj) *knowing; well informed* | janra-hunra manusre jikauka – *ask somebody who is well informed* = **janra + hunra**

janu[1] ['jānū] (adj) *cunning; crafty* [B. jhanu]

janu[2] (n) *knee* [P. zānū]

jaoa ['jāŵā] (v n) *going* < **ja-**

jaoa-aoa ['jāŵā āŵā] (n) *going and coming; return trip* = **jaoa + aoa**

jar[1] [jār] (pron adj) *of whomsoever; whose* < **je**

jar[2] (n) *cold* | jar lage – *it feels chilly; it's cold* [B. jar]

jar- (vt) *shake out; shake off; dispel; exorcise* | caddor jara lagbo – *the sheets will need shaking out* : kafor taki dula jarci – *I've shaken the dust from the clothes* : tumar nak jaro – *blow your nose* : gorol jartam kila? – *how can we get rid of the poisoning?* : mulla sabe deu-but jaroin – *the mullah exorcises evil spirits* : deki, tar sorile jare ni na – *we'll see whether his body shakes it off; we'll see whether he gets over it* [B. jhar-]

jara[1] ['jārā] (pron) *whoever; who* (plural) < **je**

jara² (n) *small amount* | ek jara lobon deoa lage – *one has to add a tiny bit of salt* : ami ek jara dukko kori na – *I'm not in the least bit disappointed* : bouka ek jara – *please do sit down for a while* [A. ðarra – *tiny particle*]
jara- (vt) *exorcise* | moulana sab but jaraicoin – *the Moulana exorcised a spirit* [B. jhaṛa-]
jare ['jārɛ́] (pron) *(to) whomever* < **je**
jar-fuk ['jārfūk] (n) *exorcism* [B. jhaṛ-phuⁿk]
jari ['jārī] (adj) *current; in force* | jari o-/jari oi ja- – *come into force* : noea ain jari oice – *a new law has come into effect* : **jari kor-** – *enact; put into effect* : sorkar noea ain jari korer – *the government are bringing out a new law* : coucallis dara jari korce – *they have imposed Section 44* [A. jārī – *flowing; current*]
jarjir ['jār-jīr] (pron adj) *each one's* | taintain jarjir goro gecoin – *they've gone, each to his own home* : amra jarjir camus dia kai – *we each eat with our own spoon* : tumra jarjir jagat taktae oibae – *each of you must remain in her own place* = **jar + jar**
jarman ['jār-mān] (n) *Germany* [E.]
jarmoni ['jārmònī] (n) *water hyacinth*
jata ['jātā] (n) *broom* | jata mar- – *beat with a broom* [B. jhaⁿta]
jata- (v) *thrash (with a broom)* < **jata**
jat [jāt] (n) *class; caste; race; nationality; species* | komin jat – *low caste* : bala jator manus – *people of high class* : hokol jator manus – *people of all races* : tara kun jat? – *what nationality are they?* : bitisor jat – *the British people* : kok jator faki – *birds of several species* : **ki jat** – *of what kind* : ota ki jat gari? – *what kind of car is it?* : ki jat kanjis beta! – *what a miser!* : **jator** – *of a type; kinds of* : nanan jator kolom – *various kinds of pen* : amar borton hokol ekoi jator – *all my plates are of the same kind* : **jate** – *by caste; by nature* : tara jate kumar – *they are potters by caste* : hogu jate soetan – *that fellow is evil by nature* : **jate jate** – *in separate classes; by type* : bici jate jate alada kori rakci – *I've separated the beans according to type* [O. jāta - *born* × A. ðāt – *essence; nature*]
jata ['jātā] *heavy weight* | **jata mar-** – *apply heavy pressure* [B. jaⁿta – *millstone*]
ja-ta (pron) *anything imaginable; any old thing* | betae ja-ta kae – *he eats any old thing* : he ja-ta galice amare – *he swore at me in all sorts of bad language* : goror ja-ta obosta – *the house is in an unspeakable state* = **ja + ta**
jati ['jātī] (n) *nation; species; kind* | baŋgali jati – *the Bengali nation; the people of Bengal* : koto jati kafor – *so many kinds of cloth* : ino hokol jati fol-mul mile – *all sorts of fruit and vegetables are available here* [B. jati < S. jātī]
jatio ['jātīò] (adj) *national; of a kind* | amrar desor jatio soŋgit – *our national anthem* : kurta jatio sat – *a shirt rather like a caftan* : ek jatio luar cear malaice – *they've constructed a sort of chair made out of iron* [B. jatiå < S. jātīya]
jatra ['jāt-rā] (n) *traditional Hindu theatrical festival* [B. jatra < S. yātrā – *procession*]
jau [jāu] (n) *rice gruel* [B. jau]
je [jɛ́] (pron) *whoever; the person who* | je jane he koito – *whoever knows should speak up* : je caibo tare di laimu – *whoever asks for it, I'll give it to them; I'll give it to whoever wants it* : afnar gari je loice, he ke? – *the person who bought your car, who is he?* : **jar** – *of whomever; the person whose* : jar kutta tar dus – *whoever's dog it is, it's their fault* : jar nam koila tare cini na – *I don't know the person whose name you mentioned* : «jur jar mulluk tar» – *whoever has the power wins the kingdom* : **jare** – *(to) whomever; the person whom* : jare cao tare di lao – *give it to whomever you please* : jare dekclam tar nam kita? – *what's the name of that person we saw?* : **jara** – *whoever* (plural); *the people who* : jara roice tara amar kutum – *the ones who have stayed are relations of mine* : jara jara jaito at tulto – *all those who want to go should put up their hands* ¶ **je** (adj) *which; such* | je furi ae – *which girl comes; the girl who comes* : je kolom caicoin – *which pen you wanted; the pen which you wanted* : je beta aicla he ke? – *the man who came, who is he?* : je citi cartam, ho·kan di lauka – *give me the letter which I'm to post* : je lakan fari – *in such a way as I'm able* : je somoe cain – *at such a time as you wish* : je·kan dorkar ta ino nae – *the one that's needed isn't here* : **je keu** – *anyone* : je keu aito fare – *anyone may come* : je keure di

lauka – *give it to anybody* : **je kunu** – *any; some or other* : je kunu jaega – *any place* : je kunu beti – *any woman* : je kunu ɗin – *any day* : afne je kunu somoe aita faroin – *you can come any time* ¶ **je** (adv) *so; so very; so much; such* : je sunɗor! – *it's so pretty!* : je bala lage – *how nice it feels* : afne je katni korcoin – *you've put in so much hard work* : beta je lamfa – *he's so tall* ¶ **je** (conj) *but; yet; so* (cf **jen**) | tare cini na je – *but I don't know him* : meg ɗer je – *but it's raining* : tara ailo na je – *so they haven't turned up* [B. je]

jeb [jɛb] (n) *pocket* | amar jeb kali – *my pockets are empty* : tumar jebo too – *put it in your pocket* [A. jaib]

jebae ['jébāɛ] (adv) *whichever way; whichever side* | jebae cain kali gari ar gari – *whichever way you look there are cars and more cars* : tain jebae atira hobae sof nae – *the direction he's walking, there aren't any shops around* = **je** + **bae**

jebaju ['jébāzū] (adv) *whichever side* = **je** + **baju**

jebla ['jɛblā] (adv) *at whatever time; when; since* | ami jebla jaimu cafi ɗi laimu – *when I go I'll hand over the keys* : tain jebla nae ami-u kulmu – *since he's not here I'll open it myself* : afne koicoin jebla.. – *well, since you say that..* = **je** + **bala** ¹

jeca ['jésā] (adj) *any* | jeca kolom ɗeuka – *give me any old pen* : tain jeca ɗin aita faroin – *he may come any day* : jeca beta koibo – *anybody will tell you* : jeca·ta kaimu – *I'll eat anything* : jeca ɗui·ta loita – *he wants to buy any two of them* = **je** + **cai**

jecakano ['jésāɣānò] (adv) *anywhere* = **jeca** + **-kano**

jecata ['jésātā] (pron) *anything* = **jeca** + **-ta** ²

jeɗik ['jéɗīk, 'jéɗīg] (n) *whichever direction* | jeɗik taki ae na kene – *whichever direction it comes from* : **jeɗike** – *in whichever direction* : ami jeɗike cai kali kuasa ɗeki – *whichever way I look I see nothing but fog* = **je** + **ɗik**

jega ['jɛgā] (n) *place* = **jaga**

jegu ['jɛgū] (pron) *whichever one; the one which* | jegu caici hogu kuae? – *where's the one I asked for?* : jegur nam jani na he gece gi – *the one whose name I don't know has gone* : **jeguin** – *the ones which* : jeguin ɗorkar hoguin neuka gi – *take the ones which you need* : kali jeguintor roŋ sunɗor – *only the ones whose colour is nice* = **je** + **gu** ¹

jein [jéɪn] (pron) *whoever; the person who* (respectful) | jein aiba tane jikaimu – *whoever comes, I'll ask them* : mitiŋo jein matcla tain ke? – *who was that person who was speaking at the meeting?* [B. jini] **Note:** **jein** is the respectful form of **je**.

jekan ¹ ['jɛɣān] (pron) *whichever (thing); the one which* | louka, jekan kusi – *take whichever one you please* : tain jekan cain hokan nae – *the one she wants isn't available* : ami jekan koici bujco ni? – *did you get what I said?* : **jeknain** – *the ones which* : jeknain kamor nae falai ɗiram – *I'm throwing out the ones that are no use* = **je** + **kan** ²

jekan ² (n) *whichever place; the place which* | tara jekan taki aice – *the place from which they came* : **jekano** – *wherever; the place where* : afne jekano cain – *wherever you wish* : tain jekano takoin – *the place where he lives* = **je** + **kan** ³

jekta ['jɛɣ-tā] (pron) *whatever; the one which* | afne jekta koiba hokta kormu – *I shall do whatever you say* : tain jekta caicoin hokta fairam na – *I can't find the one he wants* : jekta koiclam afne bujcoin ni? – *did you understand what I was saying?* : jekta oibar oibo – *whatever's to be shall be*

jel [jɛl] (n) *jail; imprisonment* | **jelo** – *to jail; in jail* : tare jelo haraice – *they've bunged him in jail* : bicara jelo – *the poor chap's in prison* : **(kar) jel oe** – *(someone) gets sent to prison* : betar tin bocoror jel oice – *he's been sent down for three years* : ek ɗin na ek ɗin tar jel oibo – *sooner or later he'll find himself behind bars* : **jel kat-** – *spend time in jail* : tara ɗui bocor jel katce – *they served two years in prison* [E.]

jela ['jɛlā] (adv) *just as; in whatever manner; in such a way that* | afne jela koiba ola kormu – *I shall do just as you say* : amra jela tara-u ola – *they are just like we are* : jela bala oe – *in whatever way is best* : jela ɗua rakcoin – *in accordance with your prayers* : ola guro, jela gorom take – *cover it like that, so that it'll stay warm* : tain aita nae jela, te jai gi – *since he's not going to show up, I'll be off* = **jelakan**

jelakan ['jɛlāɣān] (adv) *just as* = **je** + **lakan**

124

jelan ['jɛlān] (adv) *just as* | «jelan des olan raja» – *just as the country, so the king; people get the riler they deserve* = **jelakan**
jeli ['jɛlī] (n) *jam* [E.]
jelkana ['jɛl-χānā] (n) *prison building* = **jel + kana** [3]
jem [jɛm] (n) *jamming* | **jem o-/jem oi ja-** – *get jammed; be jam-packed* : rasta jem oi gece – *the street is jammed with traffic* [E.]
jemne ['jɛm-nɛ] (adv) *just as* | jemne baf, omne beta – *just as the father, so the son* : jemne subida omne korouka – *do it just as convenient; do it however is convenient* : jemne hamaici, bar oicoin tain – *just as I went in, he came out* < **jemon**
jemola ['jɛmòlā] (adv) *just as* | tain jemola, tan fua-u omola – *his son is just the same as he is* : kori louka, jemola faroin – *do it as best you can* = **jemon + lakan** cf **jela**
jemon ['jɛmòn] (adv) *just as; as if; as it seems* | jemon mestri omon kam – *as the workman, so the work* : tain jemon lamfa afne-o lamfa – *just as he is tall, so are you* : age jemon fartam one ar fari na – *I can no longer do it like I used to do* : tain jemon bujcoin na – *it's as if he hasn't realised* : tara bara gece jemon – *they've gone out, it seems* : afnar gece acil jemon – *I'm pretty sure you had it with you* [B. jemån]
jen [jɛn] (conj) *that; so that* | jain jen – *(make sure) that you go* : kain jen – *(be sure) that you eat* : buloin na jen – *be sure you don't forget* : hokoloe take jen – *make sure everyone is there* : samnor aftat ain jen – *do come next week* : amra luton geclam jen – *you know, that time we went to Luton* : afne karakkara aila jen? – *how come you returned so soon?* [B. jenå]   Note: Used in elliptical constructions where the main clause (conveying a sense of *"be sure"* or *"you know"*) is missing. **jen** with the simple present tense is used to form the future imperative and negative imperative. **jen** with a past tense is used to refer to events in such a manner as to invite comment. **jen** always follows the verb.
jene ['jɛnɛ] (conj) *that; so that* | ain jene – *make sure that you come* : kail fon koroin jene – *do phone me tomorrow* : kunta dorkar oile amare koin jene – *do tell me if you need anything* : afne ek bidio loicla jene – *you know, that video you bought* : tara hokolta nilo jene? – *how come they took the whole lot?* Note: Used in the same way as **jen** above.
jeno[1] ['jɛnò] (conj) *that* = **jen**
jeno[2] (adv) *wherever; the place where* | jao, jeno kusi – *go wherever you please* : tain jeno jaiba ami-o jaimu – *I shall go wherever he goes* : jeno kam kori hono gori nae – *there are no clocks in the place where I work* : «jeno duma hono aguin» – *where there's smoke, there's fire* = **jekano**
jeŋ [jɛŋ] (n) *pungency; fizz* | jeŋ lage – *this tastes effervescent* : o jusor maje jeŋ nae – *this juice has no fizz in it*
jer [jɛr, 'zɛr] (n) *lower section; zer; kasra (the "i" sign in Arabic writing)* | jobor, jer, fes – *fatha, kasra, dhamma, the "a", "i", "u" signs in Arabic* : **jer tan-** – *carry down (an item in accounting)* [P. zer – *lower part*]
jerokom ['jɛròχòm] (adv) *in whatever manner* = **je + rokom**
jerom ['jɛròm] (adv) *in whatever manner; in the way that* | afne jerom koiba olan kormu – *I'll do it in whatever way you suggest* : aci, jerom dua rakcoin – *I'm as well as you have prayed for me to be* = **jerokom**
jesmoe ['jɛšmòɛ] (adv) *at whatever time; when* | jesmoe buk lagbo ho somoe kaiba – *whenever you feel hungry, have something to eat* : caca jesmoe utba koimu tane – *when uncle wakes up I'll tell him* = **je + somoe**
jeta ['jɛtā] (pron) *whatever; the one which* | afne jeta cain – *whatever you want* : jeta oice oice – *whatever's happened, has happened; it's no use crying over spilt milk* : aicca, jeta kori kormu – *anyway, I shall do whatever I do; I shall take some kind of action* : age jeta dekclam hota kuae? – *where's that one which I saw earlier?* [B. jeta]
jetuk ['jɛtūk] (pron) *whatever amount* = **je + tuk**
jetuku ['jɛtūkū] (pron) *whatever amount; the amount which* | kauka, jetuku faroin – *please do eat whatever amount you can* : jetuku roice, hotuku rakia lab nae – *the bit that's left is not worth keeping* = **je + tuku**

ji¹ [jī] (int) *sir; madam; yes* | ei raju! .. ji? – *oy, Raju! .. yes, sir?* : afne london jaira? .. ji! – *you're going to London? .. yes!* : tik ace? .. ji ji ji! – *all right? .. oh yes, yes, indeed!* : **ji oe** – *yes* : afne bujcoin ni? .. ji oe – *have you understood? .. yes* : **ji na** – *no* : afne ca kain ni? .. ji na – *do you drink tea? .. no* ¶ **ji** (noun suffix) *honourable* (an indication of respect) | bala acoin ni caca-ji? – *are you in good health, honourable uncle?* : ustađ-ji koicoin amare – *my honourable teacher told me so* [H. jī]
ji² (n) *daughter* [B. jhi]
jian¹ ['jīān] (pron) *whichever (thing)* = **jekan¹**
jian² (n) *whichever place* = **jekan²**
jiano ['jīānò] (n adv) *wherever* < **jian²**
jiar ['jīār] (n) *enquiry* = **jigar**
jiarot ['jīāròt] (n) *attendance at a grave* [A. ziyāra – *visiting*]
jib [jīb] (n) *living creature* [B. jib < O. jīva]
jibba ['jīb-bā] (n) *tongue* | **jibba bar kor-** – *put out one's tongue* [O. jihvā]
jib-janoar ['jīb-jānwār] (n) *creatures; animals* = **jib** + **janoar**
jibjontu ['jīb-jòntū] (n) *living creature* [B. jibjåntu]
jibon ['jībòn] (n) *life* [B. jibån < S. jīvana]
jibra ['jīb-rā] (n) *tongue* = **jibba**
jibril ['jīb-rīl] (n) *(angel) Gabriel* [A. jibrīl]
jiđ [jīđ] (n) *contrariness; enmity; feuding; obstinacy* | cacar jiđ besi – *uncle is very obstinate* : «mege nosto lau, jiđe nosto gau» – *a gourd is spoilt by rain, but a whole village is spoilt by feuding* : **jiđ kor-** – *be contrary; be stubborn* : tain jiđ korcoin – *he has dug his heels in* : **jiđ kori** – *out of contrariness; out of obstinacy* : he jiđ kori đee na – *he refuses to hand it over, out of sheer cussedness* : **jiđ dor-** – *adopt a contrary stance* : amrar goroj đeki tara jiđ đorce – *seeing our interest in the matter, they've dug their heels in* [A. Đidd – *opposite*]
jidi ['jīđī] (adj) *contrary; obstinate* < **jiđ**
jiđkur ['jīđ-kūr] (n) *contrary person* < **jiđ**
jiga- ['jīgā] (v) *enquire* = **jigga-**
jigar ['jīgār] (n) *enquiry* | **jigar kor-** – *enquire; ask* : tikana jigar korouka – *ask what the address is* : kita oice, tane jigar kormu – *I'll ask him what's happened* : tumar cacare jigar koro, kun somoe jaita – *ask your uncle when he's going to leave* = **jiggasa**
jigga- ['jīg-gā] (v) *enquire; ask* | jiggaitam oimu – *I'll have to enquire* : tumar ammare jiggao cai – *please ask your Mum* : tar nam jiggaicla ni? – *did you ask what his name was?* : koe·ta baje, jiggauka cain – *ask what time it is* cf **jiggasa**
jiggas ['jīg-gāš] (n) *enquiry* = **jiggasa**
jiggasa ['jīg-gāsā] (n) *enquiry; question* | amar ek·ta jiggasa ace – *I have a question (to ask)* : **jiggasa kor-** – *enquire; ask* : cacare jiggasa koro gi, taim koto – *go and ask uncle what the time is* [B. jiggasa < S. jijñāsā – *desire to know*]
jigor ['jīgòr] (n) *liver* [P. jigar]
jihađ ['jīhād] (n) *efforts in the cause of religion; moral strife* [A. jihād]
jika- ['jīkā] (v) *enquire* = **jigga-**
jikan ['jīkān] (pron) *whichever (thing)* = **jekan¹**
jikar ['jīkār] (n) *enquiry* = **jigar**
jikir ['jīkīr, zīkīr] (n) *incantation of God's name* [A. ðikr – *remembrance*]
jikta ['jīktā] (pron) *whatever* = **jekta**
jila ['jīlā] (n) *administrative district* [A. Đila¿ - *side*]
jilka- ['jīl-χā] (vi) *flash; twinge* | **jilkae** – *it flashes; it twinges* : asmane jilkar – *the sky is flashing* : amar faur maje jilkae – *there are sharp twinges in my leg* [B. jhålka-]
jilkani ['jīl-χānī] (v n) *flashing; twingeing* < **jilka-**
jilki ['jīlkī] (n) *flashing* | jilki mare – *it flashes* : hara rait kali jilki marce – *it was flashing (with lightning) all night long* [B. jhilik]
jilkoj ['jīl-χòz] (n) *the month of Hajj* = **julhoj**

jim [jīm] (n) *drowsiness* | **jime ɖore** – *drowsiness overtakes one* : jime ɖorce taire – *she's getting drowsy* [B. jhim]
jima- ['jīmā] (vi) *drowse; doze* | tain hariɖin jimaita – *he used to doze all day* : **jimai ja-** – *doze off* : baco hurutae jimai gecil – *the children dozed off in the bus* [B. jhima-]
jin [jīn] (n) *genie; djinn* [A. jinn]
jinɖa ['jīnɖā] (adj) *alive* | **jinɖa o-** – *come alive* [P. zinda]
jinɖegi ['jīnɖɛgī] (n) *life; lifetime* | tan jinɖegi hono kataicoin – *he's spent his life there* : amar jinɖegir maje ɖekci na ola kunta – *I've never seen such a thing in my life* : asta jinɖegit ekbar oito fare – *it might happen once in a whole lifetime* [P. zindegī]
jine ['jīnɛ] (n) *firefly* [B. jånaki]
jinis ['jīnīš] (n) *thing; object* | sunɖor jinis – *a beautiful object* : kamor jinis – *a useful thing* : bout jinis – *lots of things* [A. jins – *type, category*]
jinjin ['jīn-jīn] (n) *tingling* | **jinjin kore** – *it tingles* : amar ato jinjin korer – *I've got pins and needles in my hand* [B. jhinjhin]
jino ['jīnò] (adv) *wherever; the place where* | tai jino take hono bac nae – *there are no buses where she lives* = **jeno** ²
jion ['jīòn] (n) *living; life* [O. jīvana]
jion-moron ['jīòn-mòròn] (n) *living and dying; life and death* = **jion + moron**
jior ['jīòr] (n) *liver* = **jigor**
jir [jīr] (n) *earthworm*
jira- ['jīrā] (v) *relax; rest* | tura jiraitam – *I want to relax a bit* : afnar soril jirauka, baɖe jaiba ne – *rest yourself a while, you can depart later on* [B. jira-]
jirat ['jīrāt] (n) *cultivation; farming* [A. zirā¿a]
jita ['jītā] (pron) *whatever* = **jeta**
jit- [jīt] (v) *win* | ke jitcoin? – *who won?* : amra kelat jitci – *we won the match* : **jiti ja-** – *win* : taigar jiti gecoin – *the Tigers won* [B. jit-]
jita ['jītā] (adj) *alive* | jita mac – *live fish* : ota jita ni mora? – *is it alive or dead?* [H. jītā]
jo ¹ [jò] (int) *um; er; you know what I mean*
jo ² (adj) *however many; as many* = **joe** ¹
jobai ['jòbāī] (n) *ritual slaughter* | **jobai kor-** – *slaughter ritually* [A. ðabh]
joban [jò'bān] (n) *speech; power of speech; word of honour* | tar joban ace – *he possesses the power of speech; he can talk* : tar joban bonɖ – *he is unable to speak* : tar joban bala – *he speaks well* : tar joban tik ace – *his word is good; he is as good as his word* : **joban kule** – *the faculty of speech develops* : geɖar joban kulce na ebu – *the baby can't talk yet* : **joban ɖe-/joban ɖi la-** – *give one's word* : tain gori·ta kail anba, joban ɖi laicoin – *he has promised he will bring the clock tomorrow* [P. zabān – *tongue*]
jobanbonɖi ['jòbān-bònɖī] *(formal) statement* [B. jåbanbåndi]
jobor ¹ ['jòbòr] (n) *zabar; fatha (the "a" sign in Arabic)* [P. zabar – *upper*]
jobor ² (adj) *tremendous; great* | jobor beta – *a great fellow* : kani jobor oice – *this food's terrific* ¶ **jobor** (adv) *tremendously; very* | kam·ta jobor kotin – *the job is terribly difficult* : ou ful jobor sunɖor – *this flower is awfully pretty* : ɖin·ta jobor bala – *it's a wonderfully fine day* : tain jobor katni koroin – *he works extremely hard* cf **joborɖost**
joborɖost ['jòbòr-ɖòst] (adj) *terrific; terrible; dangerous* [P. zabardast – *upper-handed*]
joborɖosti ['jòbòr-ɖòstī] (n) *force; coercion* | **joborɖosti kor-** – *use force; behave oppressively* [P. zabardastī]
jobur ['jòbūr] (n) *the Psalms* [A. zabūr]
joɖɖa ['jòd-ɖā] (n) *chewing tobacco* [P. zarda]
joe ¹ [jòy] (adj) *however many; as many* | tara joe bar ae, kani loia ae – *however many times they come, they bring food* : bouka, joe·jone faroin – *sit down, as many of you as can* : joe·kan ɖorkar ani limu – *I shall bring as many as are needed* cf **joto**
joe ² [jòy] (n) *victory* | joe baŋla – *victory to Bengal; may Bangladesh rule* (nationalist slogan) [B. jåy < S. jaya]

jogra ['jòg-rā] (n) *quarrel; dispute* | tarar maje jogra coler – *a dispute is going on between them* : **jogra lage/jogra lagi jae** – *a quarrel starts* : tarar maje jogra lagi gece – *a quarrel has broken out among them* : **jogra kor-** – *quarrel* : jarjir loge jogra koro kene? – *why do you quarrel with one another?* [B. jhâgṛa]

jogra-fecad ['jòg-rā-fɛsād] (n) *quarreling; strife* = **jogra + fecad**

jograjati ['jòg-rā-jātī] (n) *quarreling; strife* [B. jhâgṛa-jhaⁿti]

joif [jòıf] (adj) *old and decrepit* [A. Ða¿īf]

joini ['jòınī] (adj) *of joining; pertaining to enrolment* | joini ɖaktor – *doctor of enrolment; registered practitioner; G.P.* [E.]

joit [jòıt] (n) *Jyaistha (May-June)* [B. joisthå < S. jyaiśtha]

joitun ['jòıtūn] (n) *olive* [A. zaitūn]

joj [jòz] (n) *judge* [E.]

jo·jon ['jòjòn] (pron) *however many (people); as many (people)* | jo·jonre ataitam farmu – *as many people as we can fit in* = **jo² + jon**

jokka ['jòk-kā] (n) *tuberculosis* [B. jåkka < S. yakśmā]

jokom ['jòχòm] (n) *wound* | **jokom o-/jokom oi ja-** – *get wounded* : bout manus jokom oice – *many people have been wounded* : **jokom kor-/jokom kori le-** – *wound* : dakaite tin·jonre jokom korce – *the robbers wounded three people* [P. zaḵm]

jokon ['jòχòn] (adv) *whenever; when* [B. jåkhån]

jol [jòl] (n) *water* [B. jål]

jol- (vi) *burn; get burnt; light up* | kita joler – *something's burning* : ek baicca jolce – *one child got burnt* : batti jole na kene? – *why won't the lamp go on?* : hara rait tibi jolce – *the television was on all night* : beta joler – *he's fuming (with anger)* : **joli ja-** – *catch fire; burn; be burnt* : laga gor joli jaibo – *the house next door will catch fire* : calon joli gece – *the curry has got burnt* [B. jål-]

jolɖi ['jòlɖī] (n) *haste* | **jolɖi kor-** – *make haste; be quick* : jolɖi koro, bac aice! – *hurry up, the bus is coming!* ¶ **jolɖi** (adv) *quickly; soon; readily* | kamlainte jolɖi kam korer – *the labourers are working fast* : amra jolɖi aimu – *we'll come back soon* : rasta jolɖi tik oito nae – *the road won't be repaired in a hurry* : oto jolɖi baɖ ɖitam nae – *I'm not going to give up that easily* [P. jaldī – *quickness*]

jom- [jòm] (vi) *gather; assemble; congeal* | bir jomce – *a crowd has assembled* : bout foesa jomce – *a lot of money has accumulated* : gi jomce – *the ghee has congealed* : **jome** – *(a gathering) gets into its swing* : aij bes jomce – *today's get-together is going well* : **jomi ja-** – *get assembled; congeal; freeze* : beŋko foesa jomi jar – *money is piling up in the bank* : fukrir fani jomi gece – *the water in the pond has frozen over* [B. jåm-]

joma ['jòmā] (v adj) *collected* | joma foesa – *accumulated money; savings* : **joma o-/joma oi ja-** – *gather; accumulate* : manus joma oira – *people are gathering (into a crowd)* : bout kam joma oi gece – *a lot of work has accumulated; a backlog of work has built up* : **joma ɖe-/joma ɖi la-** – *deposit* : ɖui so fon beŋko joma ɖi laici – *I've deposited two hundred pounds in the bank* < **jom-**

joma- (vt) *collect; save up* | Mina istem jomae – *Mina collects stamps* : tain bout foesa jomaicoin – *he's saved loads of money* : **jomai rak-** – *save up; hoard* : tara koto furan jinis jomai rake – *they hoard all kinds of old stuff* [B. jåma-]

jomi ['jòmī] (n) *land* = **jomin**

jomiɖar ['jòmīɖār] (n) *landowner* [P. zamīndār]

jomiɖari ['jòmīɖārī] (n) *land ownership; land estate* [P. zamīndārī]

jomijoma ['jòmījòmā] (n) *land property* = **jomi**

jomin ['jòmīn] (n) *land* [P. zamīn]

jomjom ['jòmjòm, 'zòmzòm] (n) *the sacred well at Mecca* [A. zamzam]

jomjoma ['jòmjòmā] (adj) *splendid* [B. jåmjåma]

jon [jòn, zòn] (n) *person* | lok-jon – *people* : jon-manus – *people* : koto jon – *so many people* : **jon fice** – *per person* : jon fice fac fon – *five pounds per head* : **jone** – *per person* : jone ɖui butol – *two bottles per person* ¶ **jon** (quantifier) *one (person); head (of*

population) | ek-jon manus – *one person* : tin-jon ticar – *three teachers* : tara koe-jon? – *how many of them are there?* : boro-jon aicoin na – *the elder one hasn't arrived* : ino fac-jonor jaega ace – *there's space for five (people) here*   [B. jån]
jonaja ['jònāzā, 'jònājā] (n) *Muslim funeral*   [A. janāza]
jon-bosoti ['jòn-bòšotī] (n) *inhabitants; habitation*   = **jon** + **bosoti**
jonjal ['jònjāl] (n) *hassle*   [H. janjāl – *encumbrance*]
jonjali ['jònjālī] (adj) *troublesome; quarrelsome*   [H. janjālī]
jonm- ['jòn-m] (vi) *be born* | ek baicca jonmice – *a child has been born* : **jonmi ja-** – *be born* : tai kun din jonmi gecil? – *which day was she born?*   [B. jånm-]
jonma- ['jòn-mā] (vt) *give birth to*   [B. jånma-]
jonmo ['jòn-mò] (n) *birth*   [B. jånmå < S. janma]
jonmotarik ['jònmò-tārīk] (n) *date of birth*   = **jonmo** + **tarik**
jonogon ['jònògòn] (n) *people; the public*   [B. jånågån]
jonom ['jònòm] (n) *birth; life; incarnation* | tin jonom – *three lives; three incarnations* : **jonomor/jonmor** – *of birth; of life* : tumar jonomor age – *before your birth; before you were born* : tai jonomor lagi leŋra – *she will be lame for life* : **jonome** – *by birth; in life* : he jonome dukki – *he's unlucky by birth* : **jonom o-/jonom oi ja-** – *be born* : jura baicca jonom oice – *twins have been born*   = **jonom**
jonom-moron ['jònòm-mòròn] (n) *life and death*   = **jonom** + **moron**
jontro ['jònt-rò] (n) *contraption*   [B. jåntrå < S. yantra]
jontrofati ['jònt-rò-fātī] (n) *equipment*   [B. jåntråpati]
jontrona ['jònt-rònā] (n) *torment; botheration* | hae re jontrona! – *oh, for goodness' sake!* : **jontrona kor-** – *torment; bother* : amar date boro jontrona korer – *my tooth is killing me* : **jontrona de-** – *torment; bother* : raitku mosae jontrona dee – *the mosquitoes torment us at night*   [B. jåntråna < S. yantranā]
joŋ [jòŋ] (n) *rust*   [P. zang]
joŋgi ['jòŋ-gī] (adj) *warlike; martial* ¶ **joŋgi** (n) *combatant; fighter*   [P. jangī]
joŋgol ['jòŋ-gòl] (n) *wilderness*   [P. jangal]
joŋli ['jòŋ-lī] (adj) *wild*   [P. jangalī]
jor [1] [jòr] (n) *fever* | **jor oe/jor oi jae** – *fever sets in* : cacir jor oi gece – *aunt has got a fever* : **jor ute** – *fever sets in* : raitku tan jor utcil – *she got a fever during the night* : **jor maf-** – *measure a fever; take someone's temperature* : daktore tan jor mafce, tan ek so jor – *the doctor took her temperature, she's got a temperature of 100°*   [B. jår < S. jvara]
jor [2] (n) *storm* | **jor boe** – *a storm brews; the weather gets stormy* : aij jor boice – *a storm is blowing today*   [B. jhår]
jor- [1] (vi) *get involved* | **jori ja-** – *get involved* : he kelat jori gece – *he's got caught up in the game*   [B. jår-]
jor- [2] (vi) *be shed; fall; pour* | gac taki fata jorer – *leaves are falling from the trees* : siŋ taki fani jorer – *water is pouring from the tap* : tumar nak jorer – *your nose is running* : **jori ja-** – *fall; pour down* : cat taki fani jori jar – *water is pouring off the roof*   [B. jhår-]
jora ['jòrā] (v adj) *fallen* | jora fata – *fallen leaves*   < **jor-**
jora- (vt) *clutch; hug* | tain amar at joraia kandicoin – *he clutched my hand and wept* : **joraia dor-** – *clutch; hug* : tar mare joraia dorce – *he clung onto his mother; he hugged his mother tight*   [B. jåṛa-]
jorajori ['jòrājòrī] (n) *mutual clutching; hugging* | **jorajori kor-** – *clutch one another; hug one another; cling together*   < **jora-**
jorif ['jòrīf] (n) *government land survey* | jorif coler – *the official land survey is going on* : amrar gaut jorif aice – *the survey has reached our village*   [A. jarīb – *plot of land*]
jorimana ['jòrīmānā] (n) *fine* | ek so fon jorimana – *a fine of £100*   [P. jarmānah]
jorito ['jòrītò] (adj) *involved* | tain befsar maje jorito – *he's involved in some business* : **jorito o-/jorito oi ja-** – *get involved*   [B. jåṛitå]
jormo ['jòr-mò] (n) *birth*   = **jonmo**
jorna ['jòr-nā] (n) *waterfall*   [B. jhårna]

jor-tufan ['jòr-tūfān] (n) *storms; stormy weather* = **jor** + **tufan**
jorur ['jòrūr] (adv) *of necessity; surely; of course* | tain jorur fon korba – *he will surely telephone* : jorur meg đibo – *it will certainly rain* : kail aiba ni? jorur! – *will you come tomorrow? of course!* [A. Ɖarūr – *necessity*]
joruri ['jòrūrī] (adj) *necessary; important; urgent* | joruri jinis – *necessary things* : ou kagjain bout joruri – *these papers are most important* : amar kub joruri kam – *I've got some very urgent work to do* : one joruri obosta – *now there's an emergency situation* : kam·ta joruri mone korba – *treat the job as urgent* [A. Ɖarūrī]
jorurot ['jòrūròt] (n) *necessity; urgency* | kunu jorurot nae – *there's no urgency; there's no real need* : tan nam koibar jorurot nae – *there's no need to mention his name* : afnar jorurot takle jauka gi – *if you need to do so, please do go* [A. Ɖarūra]
josti ['jòštī] (n) *Jyaistha (May-June)* [B. joisthå < S. jyaiśtha]
jot [jòt] (n) *tangle* | tumar culo jot lagce – *your hair has got into a tangle* : ulor maje jot faki gece – *a tangle has formed in the wool* : jot kule na – *the tangle won't undo* : ila jot kultam kila? – *how can I undo such a tangle?* [B. jåt < O. jatā]
jotil ['jòtīl] (adj) *tangled; complicated* [B. jåtil < O. jatila]
jotesto ['jòtɛštò] (adv) *enough; in considerable quantity* | tara jotesto foesa nosto kore – *they waste a great deal of money* [B. jåthestå < S. yatheśta – *agreeable*]
jotno ['jòtnò] (n) *care* | **jotno kor-** – *take care* : tumar bonire jotno koro – *take care of your sister* : **jotno kori** – *carefully* : jotno kori rakci – *I've kept it carefully* : jotno kori colouka – *careful how you go* [B. jåtnå < S. yatna – *effort*]
joto ['jòtò] (adj) *however much; as much; as many; so much; so many* | joto foesa lage – *as much money as is needed* : joto bar sombob – *as many times as possible* : amar joto kam – *I've got so much work to do* : tara joto·ta koice oto·ta nae – *it's not as much as they said* : joto·jon aicoin toto·jon gecoin – *as many people have left as have arrived* : tan gece joto·gula jinis – *he has so many things* : louka joto·kan đorkar – *take as much as you need*
¶ **joto** (adv) *as much; as; so* | he joto bare toto buje – *as much he grows, so much he understands; the older he gets the more he understands* : tai joto lamfa he oto lamfa nae – *he isn't as tall as she is* : ful·ta joto sunđor! – *the flower is so pretty!* : **joto-u** – *however much; however* : joto-u kam koroin – *however much you work* : joto-u koin na kene – *however much you may object* : joto-u đami oe – *however expensive it is* [B. jåtå]
jotobar ['jòtòbār] (adv) *however many times; as many times; as often* | jotobar jai, đeki taire – *every time I go, I see her* : tain jotobar faroin mac anoin – *he buys fish as often as he can* = **joto** + **bar** [1]
jotokan ['jòtòχān] (pron) *however much; as much; the amount which* | jotokan cain, neuka gi – *take as much as you want* : jotokan faroin, koroin jen – *please do as much as you can* : ami jotokan jani – *the bit that I know; as far as I know* = **joto** + **kan** [2]
jotokon ['jòtòχòn] (adv) *for however long; as long (in time)* | jotokon lage – *as long as it takes* : tain jotokon faroin takba – *she will stay as long as she can* = **joto** + **kon**
joton ['jòtòn] (n) *care* = **jotno**
jototuk ['jòtòtūk] (pron) *however much; as much; the amount which* | tain jototuk faroin, đein – *he gives as much as he can* : ami jototuk buji.. – *the little amount I understand; as far as I can understand..* = **joto** + **tuk**
jototuku ['jòtòtūkū] (pron) *however much; as much; the amount which* = **jototuk**
jotota ['jòtòtā] (pron) *however much; as much; the amount which* | tara jotota cae, kaito – *they are to eat as much as they want* : amra jotota fari kormu – *we will do whatever we can* : tain jotota koicoin, haca – *all that he has said is true* = **joto** + **-ta** [2]
jou [jôu] (n) *whatever-it-is; thingummy* | jou·ta ano cai – *please bring me the whatsit* : jour maje faibae – *you'll find it in the what-you-may-call-it*
jua ['jūā] (n) *gambling* | **jua kela-** – *gamble* [B. jua < O. đyūta]
juab ['jūāb] (n) *reply* [A. jawāb]
juaf ['jūāf] (n) *reply* | kunu juaf aice na – *no reply has come; I haven't received any reply* : afne kail juaf faiba – *you will get a reply tomorrow* : **juaf đe-/juaf đi la-** – *give an answer;*

reply : đeki tain kita juaf đein – *let's see what he says in reply* : tara loge loge juaf đi laice - *they replied straight away* = **juab**

juait ['jūāit] (adj) *cultured* [A. ðawātī – *of high class*]

juan ['jūān] (n) *young man* | juan budda hokoloe aicoin – *young men, old fogeys, all of them came* ¶ **juan** (adj) *young; in the prime of life* | juan beta – *young man* : tain juan manus – *he's still in his prime* [P. javān]

jubba ['jūb-bā] (n) *tunic; gown* [A. jubba]

jubok ['jūbòχ] (n) *young man* [B. jubåk < S. yuvaka]

juboti ['jūbòtī] (n) *young woman* [B. jubåti < S. yuvatī]

jug [jūg] (n) *era; age; twelve-year period* | ađi jug – *primeval era; prehistoric times* : bout jug age – *ages ago* : jug jug đori – *for ages and ages* : ek jug – *twelve years* : amra aici đuː jug oice – *it's twenty-four years since we came* [B. jug < S. yuga]

jug² (n) *joining; addition* | tai jug big jane – *she can do addition and subtraction* : đui jug tin homan fac – *two plus three equals five* : **jug đe-/jug đi la-** – *join; join in* : tain somitit jug đi laicoin – *he has joined the association* : ami tarar loge jug đimu – *I shall join up with them* : **jug kor-** – *add* : facor loge tin jug koro – *add three to five* [B. jog < S. yoga]

juga- ['jūgā] (vt) *provide; obtain* | tara kani jugaibo – *they're going to provide food* : lakri kuae tone jugaitam? – *where am I to get the wood from?* [B. joga-]

jugajug ['jūgājūg] (n) *communication* | **(kar loge) jugajug take** – *communication exists (with someone)* : tarar loge amar jugajug ace – *I'm in touch with them* : cacar loge hokol somoe jugajug oe – *we always keep in touch with uncle* : tan loge amar jugajug nae – *I don't have any contact with him* : **jugajug kor-** – *communicate; get in touch* : tarar loge jugajug kormu – *I shall get in touch with them* [B. jogajog]

jugali ['jūgālī] (n) *workman's assistant* [B. jogali]

jugar ['jūgār] (n) *provision* | jugar oe/jugar oi jae – *is obtained* : foesa kila jugar oito? – *how is the money to be raised?* : cail jugar oi gece – *rice has been obtained* : **jugar kor-** – *obtain; get hold of* : tara gari jugar korce – *they've arranged a vehicle* : rossi kila jugar kortam? – *how can I get hold of some rope?* [B. jogaṛ]

juggo ['jūg-gò] (adj) *deserving; fit* | tain juggo manus – *he's a worthy person* : ita kanir juggo nae – *this is not fit to eat* [B. joggå < S. yogya]

juggota ['jūg-gòtā] (n) *worthiness; fitness; qualification* | i kamor lage tar juggota nae – *he isn't fit for this job* : tan lekaforar juggota kotokani? – *how far is he qualified in study; what are his educational qualifications?* [B. joggåta < S. yogyatā]

juha ['jūhā] (n) *forenoon; forenoon prayer time* [A. Đuhā]

juhor ['jūhòr] (n) *noon; noon prayer time* [A. źuhr]

juit ['jūīt] (n) *suitability; scope* | aij kanir juit nae – *today the food is not up to much* : kunta korbar juit nae – *there's no scope for doing anything* : tan cokkur juit ace – *his eyes possess efficacy; he has good eyesight* : **juit lage** – *things feel right* : ino juit lage na – *it doesn't feel good here* : afnar hou cearo juit lagbo – *you'll feel more at ease in that other chair* : **jutir maje** – *in a suitable arrangement; in a good setup* : ek jutir maje kam korta – *you need to work in suitable conditions* : tara bakka jutir maje – *they are in very favourable circumstances* : **juit kor-/juit kori le-/juit kori đe-** – *arrange things suitably* : amrar lagi ek juit kori đeuka – *please make things convenient for us* [B. jut]

juk¹ [jūk] (n) *leech* [B. joⁿk]

juk² (n) *measuring* < **juk-**

juk- (v) *measure* [B. jukh-]

juki ['jūkī] (n) *risk* | **juki lo-** – *take a risk* [B. jhūki]

jukti ['jūk-tī] (n) *reason; logic* | tain jukti cara kam koroin na – *he doesn't act without some reason* : tar kotar maje kunu jukti nae – *there is no logic in what he says* : **jukti đeka-** – *show reasons; present an argument* : tara koto jukti đekae – *they come up with a host of arguments* : **jukti đe-/jukti đi la-** – *suggest arguments; give advice* : tain amare jukti đi laicoin – *he's given me an idea of what to do* [B. jukti < S. yukti – *connection*]

julhoj ['jūl-hòz, 'jūl-hòj] (n) *Dhul Hijja; the Islamic month in which the Hajj pilgrimage is performed* [A. ðū l-hijja]

julum ['jūlūm] (n) *tyranny; bullying; undue pressure* | afnar ufre julum ita – *sorry, this is a gross imposition on you* : betintor ufre julum coler – *women are being subjected to bullying* : tar bour ufre julum calaito – *he used to tyrannise his wife* : **julum kor-** – *practise bullying; be importunate* : tar mar loge julum kore – *he bullies his mother* [A. źulm]

jum [jūm] (n) *ecstasy; trance* [H. jhūm]

jumana ['jūmānā] (n) *era; epoch; world* | agor jumana – *the olden days* : aijkur jumana – *the present era; today's world* : aijkailkur jumana bes bala nae – *the world today is not very good* [P. zamāna]

jumma ['jūm-mā] (n) *Friday congregational prayer meeting* | jumma bar – *Friday* : jummar din – *Friday* : jummar nomaj – *the Friday congregational prayer* : tain jummat gecoin – *he's gone to the Friday prayers* : jummar bade deka kormu – *I'll come and see you after Friday prayers* [A. jum¿a]

junab ['jūnāb] (n) *mister; sir* [A. janāb – *his honour*]

juor ['jùòr] (n) *noon prayer time* = **juhor**

jur [jūr] (n) *strength; force* | tar jur nae – *he has no strength* : «jur jar, mulluk tar» – *he who has the force, has the country* : **jur de-** – *apply force; emphasise* : beltifo jur deuka – *press the doorbell firmly* : tain ek kotar ufre jur dicla – *he emphasised one point* : **jur dia** – *with force; emphatically* : tara jur dia koice jaibar lagi – *they emphatically requested us to go* : **jur kor-** – *use force; insist* : amra kaibar lagi jur korra – *she's insisting that we should eat*: jur koroin na jen – *please don't insist* : **jur kori** – *by force; insistantly* : fua·tare jur kori nice gi – *they forcibly abducted the boy* : **jure** – *strongly; forcefully* : jure tan deuka – *pull hard* : duar jure lagaice – *he slammed the door shut* : tain jure matoin – *he speaks loudly* : jure kouka! – *please speak up!* [P. zor]

jur- [1] (vt) *join together* | tumar at juro – *clasp your hands* : **juri le-** – *take over; occupy* : cear·kan bout jaega juri loe – *the chair takes up a lot of room* [B. joɽ-]

jur- [2] (vi) *grow cold; cool off* | **juri ja-** – *grow cold* : afnar ca juri jar – *your tea is getting cold* [B. juɽ-]

jura ['jūrā] (n) *joining; pair; other one of a pair; equivalent; even number* | jura·ta deka jae – *the join is visible* : ek jura juta – *a pair of shoes* : mujar jura kuae? – *where's the other sock?* : tan jura nae – *there's nobody like him* : egaro, jura na bejuita? – *is eleven an even or an odd number?* : **jura lage** – *pairing occurs; adhesion occurs* : kafe firice jura lagce – *the cup and saucer have stuck together* : **jura kor-** – *bring together; join* : tar at jura korce – *he held his hands together; he clasped his hands* : tara injilor loge gari jura korto oibo – *they will have to couple the carriages to the engine* [B. juɽa]

jura- (v) *gather* [B. juɽ-]

jure ['jūrɛ] (n adv) *forcibly; vigorously; loudly* | tain fua·tare jure marcoin – *he hit the boy hard* : jure matouka – *you must speak a bit louder* < **jur**

jurimana ['jūrīmānā] (n) *fine* | tar ufre tin so fonor jurimana falaice – *they have imposed a fine of £300 on him* [P. jurmāna]

jur-jobordosti ['jūr-jòbòr-dòstī] (n) *force; coercion* = **jur + jobordosti**

jus [jūš] (n) *enthusiasm; excitement* | i kamor lage jus nae tar – *he has no enthusiasm for this job* : tar jus utce – *he's got excited* : **juse** – *with enthusiasm; excitedly* : tara juse kam kori lice – *they did the work enthusiastically* : tain juse matoin – *he talks in an excitable way* : **jus de-/jus di la-** – *heat up; put on the boil* [P. još – *ardour*]

jut [jūt] (n) *untruth; lie* | jut kota – *a lie* : he jut mate – *he tells lies* [H. jhūt]

jut- (vi) *come to hand; be obtainable* | ino akta am jute – *occasionally mangoes are available here* : tarar kani jute na – *they don't get enough to eat properly* [B. jut-]

juta ['jūtā] (n) *shoe* | ek jura juta – *a pair of shoes* : goror juta – *indoor shoes* : barar juta – *outdoor shoes* : juta takuk! – *let the shoes remain; please don't bother to remove your footwear* : he juta rakia mocjido hamaice – *he came into the mosque with his shoes on* : **juta lage** – *a shoe fits* : ou juta afnar lagbo ni? – *will these shoes fit you?* : **juta laga-/juta**

lagai de- – *put on shoes* : tumar juta lagao be! – *put your shoes on, child!* : **juta kul-/juta kuli le-** – *take shoes off* : juta kuloin na jen – *please don't take your shoes off* : one juta kuli licoin – *now he's taken his shoes off* [B. juta < O. yuktaka]

k

ka- [χā] (v) *eat; drink; consume; endure* | tara beret kaice : *they have eaten some bread* : afne fani kaita ni? – *would you like to have a drink of water?* : kaibar lagi kunta ɖeuka – *please give us something to eat and drink* : ami cigret kai na – *I don't smoke cigarettes* : tumar ousuɖ kaico ni? – *have you taken your medicine?* : amar gari besi tel kae – *my car consumes too much petrol* : tara gus kae – *they take bribes* : he tar bafor somfotti kar – *he's using up his patrimony* : tara mair kaibo – *they're going to take a beating* : fulise tin·ta guli kaicil – *the policeman suffered three bullet wounds* : ami toga kaici – *I've been cheated* : afne meg kaicoin – *you've got wet from the rain* : fasfute sil kaice – *the passport has been stamped* : **kai le-** – *eat; eat up; consume; devour* : kai louka – *go on, have your food; eat up, don't be shy* : gaŋge amrar jaega kai ler – *the river is eroding our land* : tane ruge kai lice – *disease has ravaged him* : amrar foesa kai lito – *they would like to embezzle our money* : amar atti kai licoin! – *oh, you've taken my bishop!*   [B. kha-]

kaa- [χā:] (vi) *cough*   [B. kas-]
kaal [χāl] (adj) *deaf*   [B. kala]
kaani ['χānī] (v n) *coughing*   < **kaa-**
kab [χāb] (n) *dream*   = **kuab**
kaba ['χābā] (n) *the Ka'ba at Mecca*   [A. al-ka¿ba]
kaba- (vt) *give to eat; give to drink; feed; administer* | tain amare fol kabaicoin – *she gave me some fruit to eat* : tara ɖuɖ kabaito – *they used to give us milk to drink* : bebire ousuɖ kabaitam kila? – *how can I get the baby to take the medicine?*   = **kaoa-**
kabin ['χābīn] (n) *marriage deed*   [P. kābīn nāma]
kac¹ [χās] (n) *bracelet*   [B. kac]
kac² (n) *proximity* | **(keur) kac taki** – *from (someone)* : nanar kac taki faici – *I got it from great-uncle* : **kace** – *near; in the hands of* : tara kace take – *they live close by* : bajaror kace – *near the marketplace* : tan kace cafi ace – *he has a key with him*   [B. kach]
kaca ['χāsā] (adj) *raw; uncooked; unripe; immature; makeshift* | tain kaca fiaij bala fain – *he loves raw onions* : kaca am kaite teŋga lage – *unripe mangoes taste sour* : kaca moric – *green chillies* : tain calanit kaca roicoin – *he's still inexperienced at driving* : kaca uetar – *novice waiter* : kaca rasta – *unmade road* : kaca gor – *hut made of impermanent materials* : kaca roŋ – *impermanent dye* : kaca kam – *amateurish, poor quality work*   [B. kaⁿca]
kaca- (vi) *approach* | beta kacar – *the man is coming nearer* : somoe kacaice – *the time has drawn near*   [B. kacha-]
kacari ['χāsārī] (n) *office; law court* | kout-kacari – *courts and offices; government offices* : **kacari gor** – *business room; reception hut; outer building for reception of visitors (in a village homestead)*   [B. kachari < O. kŕtyagŕha – *business chamber*]
kacat ['χāsāt] (n adv) *nearby; near* | tain kacat takoin – *he lives nearby* : kacat ɖukan nae – *there are no shops in the vicinity* : auka amar kacat – *come here, near me*   < **kac²**
kace ['χāsɛ] (n adv) *nearby; near*   < **kac²**
kacra ['χāsrā] (n) *dirt; trash; disreputable person* | i rumo kacra besi – *there's too much dirt in this room* : kacra kunano falaitam? – *where shall I throw the rubbish?* : ek·jon kacra take hou goro – *an anti-social man lives in that house* : raitku kacrain aia gondogul korce – *ruffians came at night and disturbed the peace* : **kacra lage/kacra lagi jae** – *dirt gets on* : ɖekouka, kacra lagbo kuto – *mind out, dirt will get on your coat; you'll get your coat dirty* : is, kacra lagi gece – *oh dear, it's all filthy* ¶ **kacra** (adj) *dirty; disreputable* | tumar at kacra – *your hands are dirty* : kacra kafor – *dirty clothes* : kacra manus – *low-class people* : **kacra kor-/kacra kori le-** – *make dirty; soil* : tumar kafor kacra kori lico – *you've dirtied your clothes* : **kacra kela-** – *play dirty; play foul*   [H. kacrā < O. kaccara]
kacrami ['χāsrāmī] (n) *foul play*   = **kacra + -ami**
kaeɖa ['χāɛɖā] (n) *method; way; Quranic primer* | kam korbar kaeɖa – *a way of doing things* : bat ranɖibar kotogula kaeɖa ace – *there are various methods of cooking rice* : katol

kanir kaeđa janoin ni? – *do you know the way to eat a jackfruit?* : bagđađi kaeđa – *the Baghdad Qaida (Quran reading primer)* : tara ebu kaeđa forer – *they are still on the Qaida (i.e. not yet ready to start reading the Quran)*   [A. qā¿ida – *basis; method*]

kae-karbar ['χāɛ-χār-bār] (n) *trade; business* = **karbar**

kaes ['χāɛš] (n) *fancy; whim* | afnar kunu kaes ace ni? – *is there anything you fancy?* : tan am kaibar kaes – *she's longing to eat some mangoes* : amar kunta kaibar kaes nae – *I don't feel like eating anything*   [P. ḳāhiš]

kaf [χāf] (n) *cup* | đui kaf ca – *two cups of tea* : car kaf – *teacup* : **kafo** – *in a cup; from a cup* : tain kafo sira kain – *he drinks gravy from a cup*   [E.]

kaf- (vi) *tremble; shake* | cacar at kafe – *uncle's hand is shaky*   [B. kaⁿp-]

kafa- ['χāfā] (v) *tremble; cause to tremble* | tan ate kafae – *his hand shakes* : buisal gor kafaicil – *the earthquake made the house tremble*   [B. kaⁿpa-]

kafani ['χāfānī] (v n) *trembling; palsy* < **kafa-**

kafer ['χāfɛr] (n) *non-believer; infidel; polytheist*   [A. kāfir]

kafor ['χāfòr] (n) *cloth; clothes; sari* | tin at kafor – *three cubits of cloth* : cutir kafor – *cotton cloth* : tumar kafor gucao – *tidy up your clothes* : furie kafor finđce – *the girl has put on a sari* : **kafror** – *of cloth; of clothes* : kafror beg – *bag made of cloth*   [B. kapåṛ]

kafor-cufor ['χāfòr-sūfòr] (n) *clothing* = **kafor**

kagoj ['χāgòz, 'kāgòj] (n) *paper; piece of paper; document* | sađa kagoj – *plain paper* : rul kora kagoj – *lined paper* : citi lekar kagoj – *writing paper* : ek·kan kagoj – *a sheet of paper* : aijkur kagoj kunano? – *where is today's paper?* : ou kagoj·kan foria đekouka – *please read this document and see what it says* : **kagjor** – *of paper* : kagjor nau – *paper boat* : ou kaf kagjor – *this cup is made of paper*   [P. kāġað]

kagoj-fotro ['χāgòzfòtrò] (n) *papers* = **kagoj + fotro**

kaice ['χāısɛ́] (int) *touché! uh-oh! that's done it!* | is! kaise! – *uh-oh, that's torn it!* : kaice amare! – *I've had it! I'm done for!* < **ka-**

kaiclot ['χāıslòt] (n) *character* | tar kaiclot karaf – *he has a bad character* : tar kaiclotor đus – *he's imperfect by nature*   [A. ḳaşla – *quality; temperament*]

kaiil [χāʾīl] (adj) *weakened* | **kaiil o-/kaiil oi ja-** – *become weakened* : tara kam kori kaiil oi gece – *they've got worn out from working*   [H. kāhil < A. kāsil – *indolent*]

kail [χāıl] (n/adv) *yesterday; tomorrow* | goto kail – *yesterday* : gelo kail – *yesterday* : agami kail – *tomorrow* : samnor kail – *tomorrow* : kail sombar acil – *yesterday was Monday* : kail buđbar oibo – *tomorrow will be Wednesday* : kail cutti – *tomorrow there will be a holiday* : kail london geclam – *yesterday we went to London* : kail taki – *since yesterday* : kail bađe – *after tomorrow* : **kailku** – *yesterday; tomorrow* : kunano jaiba kailku? – *where are you going tomorrow?* : kailku goro aclam na – *I wasn't at home yesterday* : **kailkur** – *of yesterday; of tomorrow* : kailkur kagoj – *yesterday's paper; tomorrow's paper* : kailkur đin – *yesterday; tomorrow* : kailkur đinor agor đin – *the day before yesterday*   [B. kal]

kainci ['χāıntšī] (n) *scissors; pair of scissors* | kainci đia fita katce – *she cut the ribbon with scissors* : ek·ta kaincī loimu – *I'll buy a pair of scissors*   [P. qaincī < T.]

kaini ['χāınī] (n) *story; yarn* | ajob kaini – *an extraordinary tale* : ita boro lamfa kaini – *it's a very long story*   [H. kahānī]

kait [χāıt] (adj) *inclined; lying down* | «jeno rait, hono kait» – *wherever night finds you, lie down and sleep there* : **kait o-/kait oi ja-** – *become tilted; recline* : kuti kait oi gece – *the post is leaning sideways* : tura kait oimu – *I'm going to lie down for a bit* : **kait kor-/kait kori le-** – *tilt; tip sideways* : kait kori haraitam oimu – *we'll have to tilt it to get it through*   [B. kat]

kaite ['χāıtɛ] (v adv) *for eating; in taste* | kaite moja – *nice to eat* : kaite teŋga – *sour in taste* : moric kaite jal lage – *chillies taste hot* < **ka-**

kaj ¹ [χāz, kāj] (n) *work; occupation* | afnar kaj kita? – *what is your job?* : tar kaj nae, kam nae, kali bokbok kore – *he has nothing to do, he just chatters*   [B. kaj < O. kārya]

kaj² (n) *coaxing manner* | **kaj kori ko-** – *say in a coaxing manner; wheedle; entreat* : tain kaj kori koicoin jaita – *he has earnestly begged you to go*   [B. kac]
kaja ['χāzā, 'kājā] (n) *late performance of prescribed prayer* | **kaja o-/kaja oi ja-** – *(scheduled prayer) become overdue* : mugribor nomaj kaja oi gece – *the time for Maghrib prayers is past* : **kaja kor-** – *make up (missed scheduled prayers) later* : acoror nomaj kaja kora lagbo – *I'll have to say the Asr prayers late*   [A. qaÐā' – *settling; discharge*]
kaji ['χāzī, 'kājī] (n) *Muslim marriage registrar*   [A. qāÐī – *judge*]
kaj-kormo ['χāz-χòrmò] (n) *activities; deeds; work*   = **kaj¹ + kormo**
kajli ['χāzlī, 'kājlī] (n) *itching; impetigo*   [H. khajlī]
kajna ['χāznā, 'kājnā] (n) *land revenue; rates*   [A. ķizāna – *treasury*]
kajol ['χāzòl, 'kājòl] (n) *stibium; antimony; eye-black*   [B. kajål]
kajur ['χāzūr] (n) *date; date palm*   [H. khajūr]
kakai ['χāχāi] (n) *hobgoblin*
kakra ['χāχrā] (n) *crab* | «tara đol tania kakra kae» – *they pull up water weeds and eat crabs; they struggle to make ends meet*   [B. kakṛa]
kal¹ [χāl] (n) *time; period; season* | bout kal – *a long time* : burakir kal – *the time of old age* : sukir kal – *good times* : gorom kal – *the hot season* : **kalo** – *at some time* : ek kalo – *at one time; once upon a time* : hes kalo – *at last; finally* : bifotor kalo – *in times of danger* : anir kalo – *at the time of coming; when one comes* : **kalor** – *of time* : agor kalor manus – *people of olden times*   [B. kal]
kal² (n) *skin*   [H. khāl]
kal³ (n) *watercourse; canal*   [B. khal]
kala¹ ['χālā] (adj) *black; dark* | kala cul – *black hair* : kala manus – *dark-skinned person* : kala muk – *dark face; glowering expression* : **kala o-/kala oi ja-** – *become black; cloud over* : cacar muk kala oi gece – *uncle is looking displeased* : **kala kor-** – *blacken; darken* : tumar muk kala korco killagi? – *why are you looking so cross?*   [H. kālā]
kala² (n) *mother's (younger) sister; mother's boin*   [A. ķāla]
kala- (v) *play*   = **kela-**
kalac ['χālās] (n) *expiry; ending* | **kalac o-/kalac oi ja-** – *be at an end; be finished* : caul kalac oi gece – *the rice supply has run out* : tumar iskul kalac ni? – *have you left school?* : bac, kalac! – *and that's all; and that's it!*   [A. ķalāş – *discharge; riddance*]
kala-đola ['χālāđòlā] (adj) *black and white*   = **kala¹ + đola¹**
kalam ['χālām] (n) *words; scriptural phrases*   [A. kalām – *utterance*]
kalamma ['χālām-mā] (n) *mother's sister; auntie* (affectionate mode of address for a woman of the same generation as one's parents)   = **kala² + amma**
kalasi ['χālāšī] (n) *hired deck-hand; seaman*   [P. ķalāşī – *discharged one*]
kali¹ ['χālī] (n) *ink*   [B. kali]
kali² (adj) *empty; bare* | kali basko – *empty box* : gor kali – *the house is empty* : kali feto – *on an empty stomach* : kali fau – *bare feet* : kali gae – *with bare torso; half-dressed* : betaintor mata kali – *the men have their heads uncovered* : rum·ta kali lage – *the room feels bare* : **kali kor-/kali kori le-** – *make empty; make bare* : tan leđar kali korra – *he is emptying his suitcase* : ek rum kali kori lici – *I've cleared out one room* : tumrar mata kali koro – *bare your heads*   ¶ **kali** (adv) *only; just; endlessly* | ou rum kali betintor lagi – *this room is for women only* : amra kali jani – *only we know* : ein kali kofi kain – *he only drinks coffee* : kali balu ar balu – *just sand, endless sand* : tai gumae kali – *she just sleeps all the time* : kali ketket koro kene? – *why do you keep fussing all the time?* : **kali kali** – *needlessly; uselessly* : tain kali kali rag koroin – *he gets angry for no reason* : betae kali kali torko kore – *he argues for the sake of it*   [A. ķālī – *vacant*]
kaliana ['χālīānā] (n) *dark-skinned person*   < **kala¹**
kalo ['χālò] (n adv) *at the time* | jaibar kalo – *at the time of going; while going* : ami jai kalo – *at the time when I went* : morbar kalo tain london acla – *he was in England when he died* : hes kalo – *at last; finally*   < **kal¹**
kalua ['χāluā] (n) *deaf man*   < **kaal**

kam¹ [χām] (n) *work; job; handiwork; business* | tara kam tukar – *they're looking for work* : kam mile na – *jobs are unavailable* : tain kam faicoin – *he has found a job* : tain kam dorcoin – *he has taken a job* : tain kam carcoin – *he has left his job* : tan kam gece gi – *he's lost his job* : tain kam cara – *he's without a job; he's unemployed* : tai bala kam jane – *she knows how to do a good job; she is a skilled worker* : ino tumar kam kita? – *what business have you coming here?* : ek kam korouka – *do this one thing; here's what I advise you to do* : **kam ace** – *there is some business; there is a need* : afnar loge amar kam ace – *I have some business (to discuss) with you* : tura foesar kam acil – *we are in need of some money* : one bujbar kam – *we need to find out now* : kam nae jaibar – *there's no need to go; there's no point in going* : **kam oe/kam oi jae** – *a purpose is achieved; things work out* : kam oi gece, tara mani lice – *everything's all right, they've agreed* : ila kam oito nae – *it won't work like that; that approach will not be successful* : **kam ae** – *a useful purpose is served* : gari takle kam ae – *it's useful to have a car* : afnar catti dia koto kam aice – *your umbrella has been so useful* : na, kam aito nae – *no, this isn't going to work out* : **kam bone/kam boni jae** – *a purpose is achieved; things work out* : amrar kam boni gece – *our task is done; we've achieved what we set out to do* : **kam cole** – *things work tolerably* : kunu lakan kam coler – *we're getting along somehow* : i kolom di afnar kam colbo ni? – *will you be able to make do with this pen?* : **kam kor-** – *do work; work* : tai fektrit kam kore – *she works in a factory* : mesine kam kore na – *the machine doesn't work* : amar matae kam korer na – *my brain isn't functioning properly* : **kamo** – *at work; to work; to good use* : tain kamo gecoin – *he's gone to work* : he kamo lora dee – *he often skips work* : tai kamo bala – *she's good at her job* : beg·ta kamo lagce – *the bag came in useful* : ota kamo lagaimu – *I'll put it to good use* : **kamor** – *of work; of use* : kamor manus – *an efficient person* : kamor jinis – *a useful thing* : i juta kamor nae – *these shoes are of no use* : **kame** – *for a job; for a purpose* : afne kunu kame aicoin ni? – *have you come for any particular purpose?* : **ana kame** – *without a job; for no purpose* : he ana kame aoa-jaoa kore – *he comes and goes for no particular reason* [H. kām < O. karma]

kam² [χā:m] (n) *envelope* [B. kham < P. k̤ām – *fold*]

kama- ['χāmā] (v) *earn (wages)* [B. khama-]

kamai ['χāmāɪ] (n) *earnings* | **kamai kor-** – *earn* : tara bout foesa kamai korer – *they are earning lots of money* < **kama-**

kamar ['χāmār] (n) *farm* [B. khamar]

kamcur ['χām-sūr] (n) *shirker* = **kam¹ + cur**

kamcuri ['χām-sūrī] (n) *skiving; shirking; failure to do a good job* = **kam¹ + curi¹**

kamiab ['χāmɪāb] (adj) *successful* [P. kāmyāb]

kamiabi ['χāmɪābī] (adj) *successful* ¶ **kamiabi** (n) *success* = **kamiab + -i¹**

kamij ['χāmīz] (n) *tunic* [A. qamīṣ]

kam-kaj ['χāmχāz, 'χāmχāj] (n) *work; occupation* | amar kunu kam-kaj nae – *I've got nothing to do* = **kam¹ + kaj¹**

kamkeal ['χāmχɛāl] (n) *idle thought; vain notion* [P. k̤ām k̤eyāl]

kamkeali ['χāmχɛālī] (adj) *whimsical; capricious* ¶ **kamkeali** (n) *caprice; capriciousness* < **kamkeal**

kamla ['χāmlā] (n) *worker; employee* | amrar ek·jon kamla dorkar – *we need someone to work for us* : tan kamla ataro·jon – *he has eighteen employees* ¶ **kamla** (adj) *working; hardworking* | kamla beti – *working woman; female servant* : tain boro kamla manus – *he's a very hardworking person* [B. kamla]

kamoka ['χāmòχā] (adv) *needlessly* | tain kamoka torko koroin – *he argues for no reason* : afne kamoka kosto korra – *you're going to unnecessary trouble* = **kanoka**

kamona ['χāmònā] (n) *desire* | **kamona kor-** – *wish* : afnar mongol kamona kori – *I wish you prosperity* [B. kamånå < S. kāmanā]

kamor¹ ['χāmòr] (n adj) *of use; useful; worthwhile* | iguin kamor nae – *these are of no use* : ita afnar kamor ni? – *is this of any use to you?* : kamor jinis falaio na – *don't throw away*

things which have some use : kamor kam – *important business* : kamor kota – *apposite talk; important subject* < **kam** [1]
kamor [2] (n) *nip; bite; sting* | mosar kamor – *mosquito bite* : ek kamore kai lice – *he ate it in one bite* : **kamor đe-** – *bite; sting* : kuttae kamor đice tare – *a dog bit him* : amare ekbar bolae kamor đicil – *a wasp once stung me* : **kamor mar-** – *bite; sting* : mosae kamor marer – *the mosquitoes are biting* [B. kamå̄ɽ]
kan [1] [χān] (n) *ear; hearing; fin* | amar kan bonđ oi gece – *my ears are blocked* : afnar kan bala – *you have good hearing* : macor kan – *fish's fin* : kanor đul – *ear-ring* : kanor forđa – *eardrum* : kanor đus – *hearing defect* : **kane** – *in the ear; by the ear* : tair kane fani hamaice – *water has got into her ear* : ricibar kane lagauka – *hold the receiver to your ear* : amar kota tar kane hamae na – *my remarks don't get through to him* : **kane kane** – *(whispered) in the ear* : cacire kana kane kita koicoin – *she whispered something in aunt's ear* : **kane hun-** – *be able to hear* : tain kane hunoin na – *she can't hear; she is deaf* : kane huno na ni? – *don't you have any ears?* : **kan fake/kan faki jae** – *an ear gets an infection* : milir kan faki gece – *Mili's got an ear infection* : **kan fate/kan fati jae** – *one's ears split; one is deafened* : caunđ komao, amar kan fati jar – *turn down the volume, I'm being deafened* : **kan đe-** – *lend an ear; pay attention* : tura kan đeuka! – *please listen a moment!* : tar kotae kan đein na jen – *don't pay any attention to what he says* : kan đia huner – *he's listening attentively* : **kan đor-** – *hold one's ears; demonstrate contrition* : he kan đori cori koice – *he has humbly apologised* : **kan kara kor-** – *prick up one's ears* : tara kan kara kori huner – *they're listening agog* [B. kan < O. karṇa]
kan [2] (quantifier) *item; unit* | tin·kan cear – *three units of chair; three chairs* : ou kata·kan amar – *this particular notebook is mine* : hou·kan tumar – *that one is yours* : lal·kan sunđor – *the red one is pretty* [B. khana < O. khaṇḍa]
kan [3] (n) *place* | i kan – *this place* : hou kan – *that place* : ek kan – *some place* cf **kana** [3]
kana [1] ['χānā] (adj) *one-eyed; defective* ¶ **kana** (n) *one-eyed man* [B. kana < O. kāṇa]
kana [2] (n) *food; meal* | ino bala kana mile – *you can get good food here* : kana kaicoin ni? – *have you had your meal?* [H. khānā – *eating; food*]
-kana [3] (noun suffix) *house; locale* | goribkana – *poor man's home* : jelkana – *jailhouse* : etimkana – *orphanage* [P. k̲āna – *house*]
kanakani ['χānāχānī] (n) *whispering* cf **kan** [1]
kanci ['χāntšī] (n) *scissors* = **kainci**
kando ['χānđò] (n) *affair* | birat kando – *a huge affair; a major event* : bejali kando – *a messy business* [B. kanđå̄ < S. kānda]
kanđ [χānđ] (n) *shoulder* | amar kanđe bis korer – *my shoulder is hurting* : tan fua·tare kanđo loicoin – *he lifted his son onto his shoulders* [B. ka[n]đh < O. skanđha]
kanđ- (vi) *weep; cry* | kitar lagi kanđirae? – *why are you weeping?* : kanđio na – *don't cry* : tai kanđte kanđte ses – *she's been crying her heart out* [B. ka[n]đ-]
kanđa ['χānđā] (n) *vicinity* | kanđar manus – *people of the locality* : i kanđar maje sof nae – *there are no shops in this area* : **kanđat** – *in the vicinity; near; around* : kanđat fark ace – *there's a park nearby* : goror kanđat – *near the house* : tan boes asir kanđat oibo – *his age must be around eighty* [O. skandha]
kanđa- (vt) *cause to weep; goad to tears* | oice, kanđaio na tare – *that's enough now, don't make him cry* [B. ka[n]đa-]
kanđabae ['χānđābāɛ] (adv) *nearby* = **kanđa + bae**
kanđa-kace ['χānđāχāsɛ] (adv) *in the vicinity; anywhere near* = **kanđa + kace**
kanđan ['χānđān] (n) *lineage; family* [P. k̲ānđān – *family*]
kanđani ['χānđānī] (adj) *of good pedigree* = **kanđan + -i** [2]
kanđat ['χānđāt] (n adv) *in the vicinity; nearby; around* | kanđat sof ace – *there's a shop nearby* : mocjid kanđat – *the mosque is nearby* : tain amar kanđat takoin – *he lives near me* : agunor kanđat bouka – *sit near the fire* : dui ajaror kanđat – *about two thousand* < **kanđa**
kanđon ['χānđòn] (v n) *weeping* | tumar kanđon bonđ koro – *stop your crying* : furi kanđon đorce – *the girl has started crying* < **kanđ-**

kani [1] (n) *one-eyed woman* cf **kana** [1]
kani [2] ['χānī] (v n) *eating; food; meal* | tan kani bond – *she's stopped eating* : besi kani bala nae – *too much eating is no good* : aij bala kani ace – *there's some good food on the menu today* < **ka-**
kanibuni ['χānībūnī] (n) *eating; food* = **kani** [2]
kanjis ['χānjīš] (adj) *miserly* [H. kanjūs]
kano ['χānò] (adv) *where* | afne kano jaira? – *where are you going?* : tain kano takoin jano na? – *don't you know where he lives?* = **kunano**
-kano (adv suffix) *at a place* | oukano – *at this place; here* : hokolkano – *at every place; everywhere* : kurukano – *at some place; somewhere* < **kan** [3]
kanoka ['χānòχā] (adv) *needlessly; for no reason* | tain kanoka ketket koroin – *he fusses for no reason* : afne kanoka kosto korcoin – *you have gone to unnecessary trouble* : amra kanoka urauri korci – *we hurried, but it was all in vain* : tara kanoka ita kore – *there's no call for them to do these things* [P. ḳvāh na ḳvāh – *willy-nilly*]
kanta ['χāntā] (quantifier) *item; unit* = **kan** [2] + **-ta** [2]
kanun ['χānūn] (n) *rule; law* [A. qānūn]
kaŋki ['χāŋ-kī] (n) *whore* [P. ḳānahgī]
kaoa ['χāwā] (v n) *eating* < **ka-**
kaoa- (vt) *give to eat; give to drink; feed; administer* | tain amare fol kaoaicin – *she gave me some fruit to eat* : tara duḍ kaoaito – *they used to give us milk to drink* : koutorre beret kaoaimu – *I'll feed the pigeon on bread* : bebire ousuḍ kaoaitam kila? – *how can I get the baby to take the medicine?* : he fulisre foesa kaoaito acil – *he tried to give the policeman a bribe* : memanre kunta kaoao! – *offer our guests some refreshments!* : afne ja kaoaicoin! – *you have given us such a feast!* : **kaoai ḍe-** – *give to eat; give to drink; administer by mouth* : tai geḍare cini kaoai ḍicil – *she gave the baby some sugar to eat* [B. khaoa-]
kaoaḍaoa ['χāwāḍāwā] (n) *eating; meal* | kaoaḍaoa ses ni? – *have you finished your meal?* : **kaoaḍaoa kor-** – *have a meal* : kaoaḍaoa korcoin ni? – *have you had your dinner?* : afne kaoaḍaoa kori jaiba – *have some dinner before you go* = **kaoa**
kar [χār] (pron) *someone's; whose?* | kar kolom ita? – *whose pen is this?* : hou gari·ta kar? – *whose car is that?* : kar rumal matit – *someone's hanky is on the floor* : **kar kar** – *whose?* (plural) : kar kar kad ace? – *which people have got cards?* : **kar-o kar-o** – *some people's* : kar-o kar-o cul lal – *some people's hair is red* : kar-o kar-o tibi-u nae – *some people don't even have TV* < **ke**
kara [1] ['χārā] (adj) *standing upright; steep; stationary* | kara kuti – *an upright post* : kara ḍag – *a vertical penstroke* : kara faar – *a steep hill* : kara gari – *a stationary car* : **kara o-** – *stand up; make a stand* : caca kara oicoin – *uncle has stood up* : tain ilekεono kara oita – *he wants to stand in the elections* : ami ebu kara oitam farci na – *I haven't found my feet yet* : **kara oi ja-** – *stand up; get to one's feet* : **kara ro-** – *stay standing* : tain rastar maje kara roicoin – *he's standing in the roadway* : gari kara roice – *the taxi is standing waiting* : **kara kor-/kara kori le-** – *set up; set upright* : cear·kan kara kori lao – *stand the chair upright* : amra kumiti kara korci – *we have set up a committee* : tara kan kara korce – *they have pricked up their ears* [H. khaṛā]
kara [2] (pron) *some people; who?* (plural) | kara aicoin – *some people have come* : kara aicoin? – *who have come?* era kara? – *who are these people?* : **karar** – *some people's; whose?* : karar caikel oguin? – *whose bikes are these?* : **karare** – *(to) some people; (to) whom?* : karare faicla mocjiḍo? – *whom did you meet at the mosque?* < **ke**
karabi ['χārābī] (n) *evil doings* [P. ḳarābī < A. ḳarāb – *bad*]
karaf ['χārāf] (adj) *bad; inauspicious; unpleasant; evil* | karaf kobor – *bad news* : ḍin·ta karaf – *the weather's lousy* : tar motlob karaf – *his intentions are evil* : karaf nae – *not bad; all right* : tan soril karaf – *her health is bad; she is ill* : tar mata karaf – *his head is deranged; he is crazy* : amar mon karaf – *my spirits are bad; I feel depressed* : aij tan mijaj karaf – *her mood is bad today* : **karaf lage** – *it feels bad* : tair karaf lager – *she is feeling lousy* : tumar karaf lagto fare – *you may feel bad; you may not like it* : **karaf o-/karaf oi ja-**

– *get bad; turn out badly* : fua·ta karaf oi gece – *the boy's turned out bad* : fotu karaf oice na – *the photo hasn't come out badly* : **karaf kor-/karaf kori le-** – *do badly; get bad* : he iŋliso karaf korto fare – *he may do badly in English* : tan soril karaf kori lice – *she has fallen ill* : amar mon karaf korer – *I'm feeling downhearted* : **karaf kori le-/karaf kori de-** – *make bad; spoil* : afnar soril karaf kori liba – *you'll make yourself ill* : tan mijaj karaf kori diba – *you'll put him in a bad mood* : **karaf ko-** – *speak ill* : mainse afnar karaf koibo – *people will speak ill of you*   [A. ḳarāb]
karakara ['χārāχārā] (adv) *while you wait; at once; speedily* | afne karakara aicoin je! – *you've come back very quickly!* : karakara ses oibo – *it will be finished in a jiffy*
karakkara ['χārāk-kārā] (adv) *at once; speedily* = **karakara**
karbar ['χār-bār] (n) *trading; business; matter* | tara karbar kore – *they are engaged in trading*: calir karbar – *dealing in rice; rice trade* : ajob karbar – *an extraordinary affair* : karbar kita? – *what's the deal? what's up?*   [P. kārobār]
karbari ['χār-bārī] (n) *dealer; meddler* | tain calir karbari – *he's a rice dealer* : koto boro karbari! – *what a meddlesome person!* = **karbar + -i** ³
karen ['χārɛn] (n) *electric current; electricity supply* | karen gece – *the electricity supply has failed*   [E.]
karfit ['χār-fīt] (n) *carpet* | **karfit bica-** – *lay a carpet* : **karfit fala-** – *lay a carpet*   [E.]
kari ['kārī] (n) *expert reader of the Quran*   [A. qāri']
karigor ['χārīgòr] (n) *worker; tradesman*   [P. kārigar]
karigori ['χārīgòrī] (n) *workmanship; skill*   [P. kārigarī]
karkana ['χār-χānā] (n) *workshop; factory*   [P. karḳāna]
kar-o ['χārò] (pron) *someone's*   see **kar**
karon ['χāròn] (n) *causation; reason* | hokol jinisor karon ace – *there's a reason for everything* : afnar derir karon kita? – *what is the reason for your delay?* : tan dukkit oibar kunu karon deki na – *I can see no reason for his being offended* : cintar karon nae – *there's no cause for concern* : **karone** – *for a reason* : afne kun karone london gecla? – *for what reason did you go to London?* : **ana karone/bina karone** – *without any reason* : tain ana karone rag korcla – *he got angry for no reason* : afne bina karone cinta koroin – *you worry for no reason* ¶ **karon** (conj) *because* | goro roimu, karon caci aita faroin – *I'll stay at home, because auntie may come*   [B. karån < S. kāraṇa – *cause*]
kas [χāš] (adj) *special; particular* | tara kas london taki aice – *they have come from London itself* : kas jomin – *land farmed by its owner; untenanted land* : **kas kori** – *specially* : tan lagi kas kori dua kormu – *I'll say a special prayer for her*   [A. ḳāṣṣ]
kasi ['χāšī] (n) *cough* | amar kasi lagce – *I've got a cough* : ke kasi mare? – *who's that coughing?*   [B. kasi]
kat ¹ [χāt] (n) *wood*   [B. kath < O. kāśtha]
kat ² (n) *bedstead*   [B. khat < O. khatvā]
kat- ¹ (vt) *cut; cut off; deduct; slaughter; dissect; dig; bite; close* (vi) *get cut; pass* | tar nouk katce – *he's cut his fingernails* : tar cul katce – *he's had his hair cut* : fanir lain katce – *they've cut off the water supply* : bil taki dos fon katce – *they've deducted ten pounds from the bill* : tara ek·ta murgi katce – *they have slaughtered a chicken* : rugire katia fattoir bar korce – *they incised the patient and removed a stone* : tara fuskunni katce – *they have dug a pond* : tare hafe katce – *a snake bit him* : duar kato! – *close the door!* : muk kato! – *shut your mouth!* (impolite) : somoe kate na – *the time won't pass* : **kati le-** – *cut; cut out; kill* : tan at kati licoin – *he's cut his hand* : tan nam kati louka – *cross out his name* : tumare kati limu! – *I'll kill you!* : **kati rak-** – *cut and keep; deduct* : tara fac fon kati rakce – *they've deducted five pounds* : **kati ja-** – *get cut; pass* : fonor lain kati gece – *the phone line has been cut off* : ek gonta joldi kati jaibo – *one hour will soon pass* : tar dor kati gece – *his fear has been overcome*   [B. kat-]
kat- ² (vi) *work; be suitable* | tain bejan katoin – *he works very hard* : afnar gae lal kate na – *red doesn't suit you* : gulafir maje ou lal kate na – *this red doesn't go well with pink* : afnar hou kota kate na – *what you said is not apposite*   [B. khat-]

140

kata [¹] ['χātā] (v adj) *cut off* | tar ek aŋgul kata – *he's had one finger amputated* : gecor lain kata – *the gas supply is cut off* < **kat-**
kata [²] (n) *thorn; spike; fishbone* [B. kaⁿta < O. kaṇtaka]
kata [³] (n) *rood; twentieth of a kedar* (land measurement) [B. katha]
kata- [¹] (vt) *cause to be cut; spend (time)* | amar cul kataitam – *I want to get my hair cut* : tarar fonor lain kataice – *they've had their telephone line cut off* : tan lombor kataicoin – *he's had his number deleted* : hono ek rait kataimu – *I'll spend one night there* : **katai le-** – *cause to be cut; spend* : tara gac katai lito – *they want to have a tree cut down* : tain bian·ta goro katai lein – *she spends the morning at home* : **katai de-** – *spend* : tarar cutti ḍeso katai dice – *they spent their holidays in Bangladesh* [B. kata-]
kata- [²] (vt) *cause to work; force to work* | furintore besi katain na jen – *please don't make the girls overwork* : boce tan ḍamanḍre begar katain – *the boss makes his son-in-law work for nothing* [B. khata-]
katacamuc ['χātāsāmūs] (n) *spiked spoon; (table) fork* = **kata** [²] + **camuc**
katakati ['χātāχātī] (n) *cutting; crossing out* | ḍolilo katakati cole na – *crossings out are not permissible on legal documents* : **kotar katakati** – *verbal slashing; altercation* : tarar maje kotar katakati oice – *a heated argument took place between them* < **kat-** [¹]
katatar ['χātā-tār] (n) *barbed wire* = **kata** [²] + **tar** [²]
kati ['χātī] (adj) *pure; genuine* | kati ḍuḍ – *pure milk* : kati hirok – *a genuine diamond* : kati manus – *a sincere person* [B. khaⁿti]
katikuti ['χātīkūtī] (v adv) *after cutting; nett* | tain katikuti ḍui so fon tolof fain – *he gets £200 wages after deductions* < **kat-** [¹]
katmistri ['χāt-mistrī] (n) *carpenter; joiner* = **kat** [¹] + **mistri**
katni [¹] ['χātnī] (n) *cutting tool; cutter* cf **kat-** [¹]
katni [²] (n) *hard work* | katnir fol – *the fruits of hard work* : **katni kor-** – *work hard* : tain jobor katni koroin – *she works terribly hard* cf **kat-** [²]
katol ['χātòl] (n) *jackfruit* [B. kaⁿthal < O. kaṇtaki]
katta ['χāt-tā] (adj) *sour* [H. khattā < O. khatta]
katua ['χātuā] (n) *turtle* [H. kachuā < O. kaccapa]
kata ['χātā] (n) *writing pad; exercise book* [B. khata < O. kśatra]
katir ['χātīr] (n) *esteem* | (**kar loge**) **katir ace** – *cordial relations exist (with someone)* : tan loge afnar katir ace ni? – *are you on good terms with him?* : tan loge amar kub katir – *I get on very well with him* : **katir kor-** – *respect; lavish attention on* : tara mare kub katir korce – *they made a fuss of me* : **katire** – *for the sake (of)* : afnar katire ilisa mac ranḍci – *for your sake I've cooked some hilsa fish* : ḍustir katire – *for the sake of friendship* : foesar katire – *for the sake of money* [A. ḳāṭir – *notion; inclination*]
katla ['χāt-lā] (n) *a carp-like species of fish (Catla catla)* [B. katla]
katti ['χāt-tī] (n) *Kartik (October-November)* [B. kartik < S. kārttika]
kaujra- ['χāuz-rā] (vi) *itch* [H. khijla-]
kaujrani ['χāuz-rānī] (v n) *itching* < **kaujra-**
kauni ['χāunī] (n) *coughing* = **kaani**
kaura ['χāurā] (n) *one who eats* | amra aij at·jon kaura – *there are eight of us eating today* : ami kaura nai – *I'm not going to eat* : fan kaura keu acoin ni? – *is there anyone here who wants to chew paan?* : cigret kaura – *a smoker* : moḍ kaura – *a drinker* < **ka-**
kauua ['χāw-wā] (n) *crow* [H. kauvā < O. kāka]
ke [χέ] (pron) *someone; who?* | ke aicoin mone loe – *I think someone has come* : iato ke kacra falaice – *somebody has dumped rubbish in the yard* : ke aicoin? – *who has come?* : i kota koilo ke? – *whoever said that?* : **ke ke** – *who?* (plural) : ke ke jaitae, at tulo – *hands up who wants to go* : **kar** – *someone's; whose?* : fulise kar gari ner gi – *the police are towing away somebody's car* : i kut kar? – *whose coat is this?* : **kar kar** – *whose?* (plural) : afnerar kar kar mubail ace? – *which of you have mobile phones?* : **kare** – *(to) someone; (to) whom?* : hono kare faicla? – *whom did you meet there?* : **kera/kara** – *some people; which people?* : era kera? – *who are they?* : kara jaiba? – *which people are going to go?* : **kerar/karar** –

141

of some people; of which people? : kerar juta ino – *some people's shoes are here* : karar loge acla? – *in whose company were you?* : **kerare/karare** – *(to) some people; (to) which people?* : kerare koicla? – *which people did you tell?* [B. ke]

keal ['χɛāl] (n) *idea; notion; mind* | ođbut keal – *an extraordinary idea* : afnar kealor maje kita? – *what is in your mind? what do you have in mind?* : amar kealor maje acil, london jaitam – *I had a mind to go to London* : **(kar) keal ace** – *one is aware; one remembers* : amar fura keal ace – *I'm fully aware; I remember clearly* : tumar keal take na – *you never notice things* : amar keal nae – *I'm not sure* : tai kita koicil amar keal nae – *I don't recall what she said* : tan keal-u nae – *he's totally unaware* : **(kunta korbar) keal ace** – *one has a mind (to do something)* : tan befsa korbar keal – *he's thinking of going into business* : amar aibar keal acil na – *I had no intention of coming* : **keal kor-** – *take notice; pay attention* : ami keal korci na – *I didn't notice* : amar kota keal koroin jen – *please note what I'm saying* : **keal rak-** – *pay heed; take care* : hurutar bae keal rakta oiba – *you must attend to the children* [A. ḳayāl – *phantom; imagination*]

keali ['χɛālī] (adj) *whimsical* < **keal**

keal-kusi ['χɛāl-kūšī] (n) *whim* | he tar keal-kusi moto kam kore – *he works as and when he feels like it* = **keal + kusi** [1]

kear [1] ['χɛār] (n) *kedar (≈ ⅓ acre)* [O. keđāra – *cultivated field*]

kear [2] (n) *care; heed* | **kear kor-** – *care; pay attention* : keu kear kore na – *nobody can be bothered* [E.]

kebol ['χɛbòl] (n) *cable TV* [E.]

kec- [1] [χɛs] (v) *tug; jam* [B. khe^{n}c-]

kec- [2] (vt) *stuff; fill very full*

keced ['χɛsɛd] (n) *cassette; cassette player* [E.]

kecia ['χɛsīā, 'χɛis-sīā] (v adv) *in full measure; heavily* | kecia meg đer – *it's raining heavily* : kecia kauka! – *eat as much as you can!* < **kec-** [2]

kecua ['χɛsuā] (n) *worm* [H. ke^{n}cuā < O. kencuka]

keđa- ['χɛđā] (vt) *chase away* [B. kheđa-]

keđmot ['χɛđmòt] (n) *service* | **(kar) keđmot kor-** – *render service; serve (someone)* : tumar mabafor keđmot kortae – *you should be of service to your parents* : mumine allar keđmot koroin – *true believers serve God* [A. ḳidma]

kef [χɛf] (n) *throw; turn; trip* | tumar kef! – *it's your go!* : đui kefe oibo – *it can be done in two separate trips* : **kef de-/kef đi la-** – *have a throw; do a trip* : ben đi ek kef đi laimu – *we'll make one trip with the van* [B. khep < O. kśepa]

kef- (vi) *get annoyed* | tain kefcoin mone loe – *I think he's lost his cool* : **kefi ja-** – *get annoyed* : caca akta kefi jain – *uncle suddenly loses his temper* [B. khep-]

kefa ['χɛfā] (v adj) *annoyed* | tain amar ufre kefa – *he's annoyed with me* < **kef-**

kefa- (vt) *annoy* | kuttare kefaio na – *don't make the dog angry* : **kefai đe-** – *annoy* : tara buddare kefai đice – *they've annoyed the old man* [B. khepa-]

kegu ['χɛgū] (pron) *someone; who?* | kegu re? – *who is it?* : kegu koice tumare? – *who was it who told you that?* : kegu mater – *someone is talking* : kegue fulisre gia janaice – *somebody went and told the police* = **ke + gu** [1]

keic ['kɛis] (n) *lawsuit; case* | keic coler – *legal proceedings are going on* : amrar keic boice – *our lawsuit has been instituted* : tarar maje keic lagce – *a legal battle has started between them* : tain kecir maje forcoin – *he's got embroiled in litigation* : tain kecit jori gecoin – *he's got involved in a lawsuit* : **keic kor-/keic kori le-** – *start legal proceedings; sue* : tara amrar ufre keic korce – *they have started a lawsuit against us* : **keic boa-/keic boai đe-** – *lodge a case* : tain cilot gia cearmenor ufre keic boaicoin – *he went to Sylhet and lodged a case against the chairman* : **keic ga-** – *go ahead with a lawsuit; appear in court* : tara keic gaito nae – *they aren't going to take their suit to court* : **keic cala-** – *conduct a lawsuit* : bala ukilre đia keic calain jen – *make sure you get a good lawyer to deal with your case* : **keic fa-/keic fai le-** – *win a lawsuit* : tain keic faita nae – *he won't win his case* : keic fai lici! – *we've won!* [E.]

kejmot ['χɛzmòt] (n) *service* = **kedmot**
kela ['χɛlā] (n) *game; play; sport; match* | futbol kela – *the game of football* : daba kela janoin ni? – *do you know the game of chess?* : hurutar kela – *child's play* : hokol jat kela bala fai – *I like all kinds of sport* : aijkur kela ses – *today's match is over* : **kela kor-** – *play* : fuainte haridin kela kore – *the boys play all day* : tumra kela koro gi jao – *go away and play, all of you* [B. khela]
kela- (v) *play (games)* | amra futbol kelai – *we play football* : fuainte bol kelaibo – *the boys will play with a ball* [B. khel-]
keladula ['χɛlādūlā] (n) *playing; sports* = **kela**
kelani ['χɛlānī] (v n) *playing; play* | bara kelani bala – *playing out of doors is better* : tai iato kelanit – *she's playing in the garden* < **kela-**
kelanto ['χɛlān-tò] (adj) *tired* [B. klantå < S. klānta]
kelatifat ['χɛlātīfāt] (n) *passing of time* [B. kalatipat < S. kāla + atipāta]
kelaura ['χɛlāurā] (n) *player* < **kela-**
kelenkeri ['χɛlɛŋ-χɛrī] (n) *scandal* ¶ **kelenkeri** (adj) *outrageous; scandalous* | boro kelenkeri befar ita – *it's a real scandal* [B. kelenkari – *scandal* < S. kalankakara – *causing a blot or blemish*]
kemne ['χɛmnɛ] (adv) *how?* | kemne koitam? – *how am I to say?* : afne ufre anla kemne? – *how did you get it upstairs?* = **ki + mone**
kemon ['χɛmòn] (adv) *how? how much? what sort?* | tumar ammar soril kemon? – *how is your Mum's health?* : ota kaite kemon? – *what's that like to eat?* : dud kemon roice? – *how much milk is left?* : kemon manus oicil daktor sabor jonajat? – *were there many people at the doctor's funeral?* [B. kemån]
kemota ['χɛmòtā] (n) *power; capacity* | jonogonor kemota ace – *the people have power* : tar bujbar kemota nae – *he hasn't got the capacity to understand* : kam ota tan kemotar bitre – *that job is within his capability* [B. khåmåta < S. kśamatā – *ability*]
kemte ['χɛm-tɛ] (adv) *how?* = **ki + mote**
ken [χɛn] (adv) *why?* = **kene**
kenci ['χɛntšī] (n) *scissors* = **kainci**
kene ['χɛnɛ] (adv) *why?* | tara buje na kene? – *why don't they understand?* : ousud kani carcoin kene? – *why have you stopped taking the medicine?* : jao na kene? – *why don't you go?* : oto gussa kene? – *why are you so cross?* : kene, ami-u dekci – *but listen, I've seen it myself* : **na kene** – *(now)ever; (what)ever* : afne joto-u koin na kene, tain janta acla – *however much you may argue about it, he should have known* : ja-u kore na kene, ami cartam nai – *whatever he does, I won't give in* [B. kenå] Note: Usually conveys an element of reproach or contradiction.
keoala ['χɛòālā] (n) *land deed* [A. qabāla – *guarantee*]
ker [¹] [χɛr] (pron) *of what; of what kind* | ita ker kafor? – *of what is this cloth made? what kind of cloth is this?* : ker mestur hogu! – *what sort of craftsman is he, then!* < **ki**
ker [²] (n) *straw* [B. khår]
kera ['χɛrā] (pron) *who? which people?* < **ke**
keramot ['χɛrāmòt] (n) *miracle* [A. karāma]
keramoti ['χɛrāmòtī] (n) *conjuring; performance of tricks* = **keramot + -i** [¹]
kerani ['χɛrānī] (n) *clerk* [B. kerani]
kerej ['χɛrɛz, 'χɛrɛj] (n) *kerosene* [E.]
kerela ['χɛrɛlā] (n) *bitter-gourd* [B. kåråla]
kereti ['χɛrɛtī] (n) *knack* [B. kriti < O. kŕti – *action*]
kes [¹] [χɛš] (n) *kinsman* [P. ķīš]
kes [²] (n) *cash; encashment* | **kes o-/kes oi ja-** – *get cashed* : ceg kes oice na – *the cheque hasn't been cashed* : **kes kor-/kes kori le-** – *cash* : ceg·kan joldi kes kori louka – *cash the cheque quickly* [E.]
kes-foesa ['χɛšfòɛšā] (n) *cash* = **kes** [²] + **foesa**
kes-kutum ['χɛškūtūm] (n) *relatives* = **kes** [¹] + **kutum**

keta ['χɛtā] (pron) *who?* | keta korce? – *who did it?* : ɖeko, keta aice – *go and see who's come* : batrumo keta? – *who's that in the bathroom?* = **ke**

ketket ['χɛtχɛt] (n) *grumbling* | **ketket kor-** – *grumble; grouse* : caci kali ketket koroin – *aunt is always grousing about something* [B. kåtkåt]

ketketi ['χɛtχɛtī] (n) *tickling* | **ketketi kore** – *it tickles* : is! ketketi korer! – *oh, I feel a tickling feeling!*

ket [χɛt] (n) *cultivated field* [B. khet < O. kśetra]

keti ['χɛtī] (n) *damage; loss; harm* | fac ajar fon keti – *a loss of five thousand pounds* : kunu keti nae – *no harm; it doesn't matter* : **keti oe/keti oi jae** – *damage is caused; loss is sustained* : tar befsar maje keti or – *damage is being done to his business* : amrar bakka keti oi gece – *we have suffered considerable losses* : **keti kor-** – *cause loss; damage; harm* : bonnae amrar bout keti korce – *the floods have done us much harm* [B. khåti < S. kśati]

ket-kamar ['χɛtχāmār] (n) *farm; farmland* = **ket + kamar**

keu ['χɛu] (pron) *somebody; anybody* | afnare keu dakcoin – *somebody called you* : keu acoin ni goro? – *is anybody at home?* : **keu nae/keu na** – *nobody* : ino keu nae – *there's no-one here* : keu aicoin na – *nobody has come* : keu hamaito farto nae – *nobody will be able to get in* : **keur** – *of somebody; of anybody* : ein kaur kutum oiba – *he must be a relative of someone* : keur loge matcoin ni? – *have you discussed it with anybody?* : **keure** – *(to) somebody; (to) anybody* : citi·kan keure ɖekaita acla – *you should have shown the letter to someone* : keure koin na jen – *don't tell anybody* : **keu keu** – *some people* : keu keu koin .. – *some people say ..* : keur keur tikit ace – *some people have got tickets* : **keu .. keu ..** – *some people .. other people ..* : keu gecoin gi, keu roicoin – *some people have gone, some are still here* : **keu na keu** – *one person or another; somebody or other* : keu na keu bala faito fare – *some people may possibly like it* = **ke + -u**

keun ['χɛun] (n) *millet* [B. kaun]

ki¹ [kī] (adj) *which?* | ki jat gac ota? – *which species of tree is this?* : afne ki rokom kafor cain? – *which kind of cloth do you want?* : tai ki lakan kam kore? – *what manner of work does she do? how is her work?* : aij ki bar? – *what day is it today?* ¶ **ki** (adv) *so (much); how (much)* | ki sundor! – *how beautiful!* : beta ki calak – *how crafty that fellow is* : ki osombob! – *how preposterous!* : ki muskil! : *what a nuisance!* ¶ **ki** (pron) *what(ever); what?* | ki koin afne! – *whatever are you suggesting!* : ki ota? – *what is this?* : **kior** – *of what; made of what; of which kind* : ita kior tel? – *this oil, what's it made from?* : kior gan ota? – *what sort of music is that?* : kior sef tain! – *what kind of a chef is he, may I ask!* : **ker** – *of what; made of what; of which kind* : ker gari ita! – *and what kind of a car is this meant to be!* : **ki kori** – *by what means? how?* : tara janlo ki kori? – *how did they find out?* [B. ki]

ki² (conj) *or* | janram na, tik ki na – *I don't know whether it's correct or not* [B. ki]

kiamot ['kīāmòt] (n) *doomsday* [A. qiyāma – *resurrection*]

kiba ['kībā] (conj) *or; or maybe; or else* | aij kiba kail – *today or tomorrow* : ek·jon kiba ɖui·jon – *one person, or maybe two* : gari loiba kiba ben loiba – *he will buy either a car or a van* ¶ **kiba** (adv) *perhaps; maybe* | kiba goro gecoin gi – *maybe he's gone home* : tain buli licoin kiba – *perhaps she's forgotten* [B. kimba < O. kiŋvā]

kiban ['kībān] (conj) *maybe* | kiban aita faroin – *maybe he will come* : tara kiban gussa korce – *maybe they are angry* cf **kiba**

kibarɖin ['kībār-ɖīn] (adv) *which day of the week* | aij kibarɖin? – *what day is it today?* = **ki¹ + bar¹ + din¹**

kibla ['kīblā] (n) *direction of Mecca* [A. qibla – *front*]

kic¹ [kīs] (n) *instalment* | tin kic ɖi arci – *I've already paid three instalments* = **kisti**

kic² (n) *paper bag* [A. kīs – *bag*]

kica ['kīsā] (n) *small envelope* [A. kīsa]

kicca ['kītšā] (n) *story; tale* [A. qişşa]

kicim ['kīsīm] (n) *sort; kind* | ek kicim toki – *a kind of cap* : **kicimor** – *of kinds; varieties of* : nana kicimor juta – *shoes of various kinds* : tin kicimor beg – *bags of three kinds; three*

144

sorts of bag : koto kicimor fol – *so many kinds of fruit* : **kicim kicim** – *various kinds* : hono kicim kicim uri mile – *various kinds of beans are available there* [A. qism – *sort*]
kicin ['kīsīn] (n) *kitchen* [E.]
kicin faudar ['kīsīn faudār] (n) *kitchen porter; cook's assistant* [E.]
kicirmicir ['kīsīr-mīsīr] (n) *twittering; chirruping; chattering* [B. kicirmicir]
kicmot ['kīsmòt] (n) *fate; fortune* | kicmot, kita koita – *it's fate, there's nothing more to say* : amar kicmotor dus – *my luck is at fault; I'm just unlucky* : kicmotor mair – *blows of fate; ill fortune* [A. qisma – *apportionment*]
kicu ['kīsū] (adj) *some; a few* | kicu kagoj – *some paper* : kicu enda – *some eggs* ¶ **kicu** (pron) *something* | kicu roice – *something is left over* : kicu kauka – *please have something to eat* : **kicu nae/kicu na** – *not anything; nothing* : ino kicu nae – *there's nothing here* : tain kicu cinoin na – *he doesn't know anything* ¶ **kicu** (adv) *somewhat; a little* | meg kicu komce – *the rain has eased off a little* : cuetar kicu boro oi gece – *the sweater's turned out a bit too big* : **kicu kicu** – *a little bit* : kicu kicu atta faroin – *he can walk a little bit* [B. kichu < O. kińcit]
kicuri ['kīsūrī] (n) *rice and lentil pottage; a mish-mash* | hokolti kicuri oi gece – *its all a big muddle* [B. khichuri]
kida ['kīdā] (n) *hunger* | amar feto kida – *there is hunger in my belly; I feel hungry* : **kida lage/kida lagi jae** – *hunger is felt* : tumar kida lagce ni? – *do you feel hungry?* : tar kida lage na – *he never has any appetite* [B. khida < O. kśudā]
kigu ['kīgū] (pron) *somebody; who?* | kigu re? – *who is it?* : kigu aice deko cai – *go and see who's come* : kigu camuc loia gece gi – *someone's gone off with the spoon* = **kegu**
kijat ['kīzāt, 'kījāt] (adv) *of what kind; such; how* | kijat manus era? – *what kind of people are they?* : tain kijat kosto korcoin – *she's gone to such a lot of trouble* : kijat sokto ita! – *how hard this thing is!* = **ki¹ + jat**
kila ['kīlā] (adv) *how?* | afne kila acoin? – *how are you?* : tain kila janla? – *how did he find out?* : ami koitam kila? – *how am I to say?* : deki kila kita kore – *lets see how he acts* : kila gari ota – *what kind of car is that; that's not much of a car* : **kila kila** – *so-so; not quite right* : kila kila lage – *it seems rather dubious* = **kilakan**
kilagi ['kīlāgī] (adv) *why?* = **killagi**
kilail ['kīlāīl] (n) *toothpick* [A. ķilāl]
kilakan ['kīlāχān] (adv) *how?* | afne kilakan korcoin ita? – *how did you do it?* : tan soril kilakan? – *how is her health?* = **ki¹ + lakan** cf **kila**
kilan ['kīlān] (adv) *how? so-so; not quite right* | kilan coler afnar? – *how are you doing?* : hou kafor kilan lage – *that sari looks a bit odd* : **kilan kilan** – *so-so; not quite right* : tare kilan kilan lage – *he looks a bit strange* = **kila**
killa ['kīl-lā] (n) *fortress; stronghold* [A. qal¿a]
killagi ['kīl-lāgī] (adv) *for what? why?* | afne ketket koroin killagi? – *what are you grumbling for?* : tara jaito killagi? – *why do they want to go?* : age koila na killagi? – *why didn't you say so before?* : jikai killagi .. – *the reason I'm asking is ..* = **kior + lagi**
killai ['kīl-lāi] (adv) *for what? why?* = **killagi**
kima ['kīmā] (n) *mincemeat* [P. qīma]
kin- [kīn] (v) *buy* | tara cail kinto – *they want to buy rice* : ami fefarsofo kiric kinci – *I bought some crisps at the newsagent's* : **kini le-** – *buy; buy up; buy off* : tara asto gau kini lito – *they'd like to buy up the whole village* : cearmen kini lice tare – *the Chairman has bought his support with money* [B. kin-]
kinakati ['kīnākātī] (n) *purchasing activity; shopping* | **kinakati kor-** – *do shopping* : tara tauno gia bout kinakati korce – *they went to town and did a lot of shopping*
kinar ['kīnār] (n) *edge* | **kinare** – *on the edge; beside* : amrar gaur kinare – *at the edge of our village* : aguinor kinare – *beside the fire* [P. kanār]
kinara ['kīnārā] (n) *edge; bank* | gaŋgor kinara – *river bank* [P. kanāra]

kintuk ['kīntūk] (conj) *but; however* | ami jaitam cai, kintuk era jaito cae na – *I want to go, but they don't* ¶ **kintuk** (adv) *however; in any case* : tara manto nae kintuk – *they won't agree, though* [B. kintu < S. kintu]
kior ['kīòr] (pron) *of what? made of what?* < **ki**[1]
kir [kīːr] (n) *thickened cream* [B. khir < O. kśīra – *milk*]
kira ['kīrā] (n) *gherkin* [H. khīrā]
kira- (v) *milk* | nani gabi kiraita – *grandmother used to milk cows* cf **kir**
kiraia ['kīrāıā] (n) *rent* [U. kirāya < A. kirā']
kiran ['kīrān] (n) *farmer* [O. kŕśāṇa]
kiric ['kīrīs] (n) *crisps* [E.]
kirmi ['kīrmī] (n) *intestinal worms* [B. krimi < S. kŕmi]
kirom ['kīròm] (adv) *of such a kind; of what kind? how?* | afne kirom juta cain? – *what kind of shoes do you want?* : afnar soril kirom? – *what's your health like?* : tain kirom janla? – *how did he find out?* : kirom buḍḍi! – *such ingenuity!* = **ki**[1] + **rokom**
kismis ['kīšmīš] (n) *sultanas; raisins* [P. kišmiš]
kistan ['kīštān] (n) *Christian* [E.]
kisti ['kīstī] (n) *instalment* [A. qisṭ]
kita ['kītā] (pron) *something; what?* | ino kita ace – *there's something here* : ita kita? – *what's this?* : kita koila? – *what did you say?* : faeḍa kita? – *what's the use?* : kita oito? – *so what?* : korta kita? – *but what can you do about it?* : i kita koin! – *what are you saying! come off it!* : farle kita! – *what do you mean, "if possible"!* : tain kita cain ami buji na – *I don't understand what it is he wants* : **kita kita** – *what* (plural) : kita kita lagbo? – *what things will be required?* = **ki**[1] + **-ta**[2]
kitakiti ['kītākītī] (n) *this and that*
kiu [kīu] (n) *queue* | **kiut** – *in a queue* : amra kiut – *we're in the queue* : **kiu ḍora-** – *join a queue* : kiu ḍora lagbo – *we'll have to stand in line* [E.]
ko [χò] (adj) *some; how many?* | ko gonta lagbo? – *how many hours will it take?* : manus ko·jon aicla? – *how many people came?* : ko·ta baje? – *how many does it strike? what time is it?* : afne ko·tat utba? – *at what time will you get up?* : ko ḍinor maje ḍekci na tane – *I haven't seen him for several says* = **koe**
ko- (v) *say; tell; be able to tell; allege; call* | kouka – *now, say what you want to say* : ami kunta koitam nai – *I won't say anything* : koiclam na ni? – *didn't I say so?* : he koito koe .. – *what he says is ..* : na, koici .. – *no, what I meant was ..* : tain jaita koira – *he's saying he has to go* : tumar ammare koo aita – *tell your mum she's to come here* : tare koo jaibar lagi – *tell him to go* : kila koitam? – *how should I know?* : tain hunra, ami koitam fari na – *I didn't realise he was listening* : rait oice, tain koita farcoin na – *he didn't notice night had fallen* : ami koici tumi ino nae – *I thought you weren't here* : ḍibo ni koin? – *do you really think he'll pay up?* : ami koitam fartam nai – *I really couldn't tell you* : ita koibar moton nae – *it's not such a thing as can be expressed* : aicca, kouka cain! – *well, I ask you!* : koe kita! – *what's he on about!* : ami koe bul korci! – *so it's me who made the mistake, is it!* : koe aito! – *he'll come, says he .. come? him? not likely!* : aine koe .. – *the law says; according to the law ..* : koa jae na – *it's impossible to say* : koa muskil – *it's hard to tell* : koite gele – *if the truth be told* : micabaḍi kare koira? – *whom are you calling a liar?* : fekc kare koe, ami jani na – *I don't know what is meant by "fax"* : **koe bule** – *they say; apparently* : koe bule cearmen mair kaicoin – *people are saying the chairman was beaten up* : **koi bule** – *I was just saying; I was just thinking* : koi bule afnare jikaimu – *I was just thinking I should ask you* : **koi le-** – *say; utter; speak out* : koi lao! – *come on, out with it!* : tair houror nam koi lice – *she blurted out the name of her father in law* : **koia ḍe-** – *divulge; pass on (information)* : ke cacire koia ḍice – *someone must have told auntie* : koia ḍeuka! – *please tell me the answer!* : **koia ja-** – *take one's leave; say goodbye* : kioa jaita – *you should tell them you're leaving* : tara ana koia gece gi – *they went without saying goodbye* [B. kå-]

koa- ['χòā] (vt) *cause to say; get to say* | caca bicmilla koaicoin – *uncle got everyone to say "bismillah"* : amar fuare dia koiamu – *I'll get my son to tell them*
kob ['χòb] (n) *cup* [E.]
kobar [1] ['χòbār] (adv) *several times* = **ko + bar** [1]
kobar [2] (n) *cover* [E.]
kobic ['χòbīs] (adj) *depraved* [A. ḳabīθ – *evil*]
kobira ['χòbīrā] (adj) *great; major* | kobira guna – *major sin* [A. kabīra]
kobirej ['χòbīrɛz, 'χòbīrɛj] (n) *ayurvedic healer* [B. kåbiraj]
kobireji ['χòbīrɛzī, 'χòbīrɛjī] (n) *ayurvedic treatment* = **kobirej + -i** [1]
kobja ['χòbzā, 'χòbjā] (n) *hinge; joint* | ator kobja – *wrist* : dorojar kobja – *hinge of a door* [A. qabÐa – *handle; hilt*]
kobor ['χòbòr] (n) *tidings; news* | kobor kita? – *what's the news?* : bala kobor ace – *there's good news* : minar kobor janoin ni? – *do you know what happened to Mina?* : afnar kobor hunci – *I heard about you* : tan kunu kobor-u nae – *he's disappeared off the radar* : **kobror** – *of news* : kobror kagoj – *newspaper* : **kobor fa-** – *get news* : cacar kobor faicoin ni? – *have you received any news of uncle?* : kobor faia cintar maje forci – *since getting the news I've got worried* : **kobor kor-** – *enquire (after someone)* : cacir kobor koroin jen – *please enquire after auntie* : tain afnar kobor korcoin – *he asked after you* : **kobor lo-** – *make enquiries* : amra kobor loici – *we've made enquiries* : fulise marir befare kobor lor – *the police are investigating the fight* : **kobor rak-** – *keep informed; follow up* : tara tumar kobor rake – *they follow your progress* [A. ḳabar]
kobordar ['χòbòr-dār] (int) *beware* | kobordar, bara jaio na tumra! – *watch it, children, and don't you dare to go out of doors!* [P. ḳabardār – *aware; at attention*]
kobul ['χòbūl] (n) *agreement* | **kobul o-/kobul oi ja-** – *agree; accept* : afne kobul ni? – *do you agree?* : tain kobul oicoin na – *he hasn't given his agreement* : **kobul kor-** – *state one's acceptance* : hese tara kobul korce – *in the end they said yes* [A. qabūl]
koci ['χòsī] (adj) *tender; young and green* | koci am – *baby green mango* : koci baicca – *a tender child* [B. kåci]
kocit ['χòsīt] (adv) *seldom; occasionally* [B. kåcit < S. kvacit]
kocla- ['χòslā] (v) *rub; mess with; fidget* | tumar bat koclaio na – *don't mess about with your food* : koclao kene! – *why are you fidgeting!* [B. kåcla-]
kocom ['χòsòm] (n) *oath* | kodar kocom! – *I swear to God!* : **kocom ka-** – *take an oath; swear* : ar kortae nae, kocom kao – *swear that you'll never do it again* : **kocom kaia ko-/kocom kori ko-** – *vow; swear* : he kocom kori koice afnare dito – *he vowed that he would hand it over to you* [A. qasam]
kocu ['χòsū] (n) *edible arum tuber; taro (Colocasia esculenta)* [B. kocu]
kocua ['χòsuā] (adj) *green; blue-green* cf **koci**
kocur ['χòsūr] (n) *misdemeanour; fault; crime* | jani, amar kocur oice – *I know, I've been at fault* : **kocur kor-/kocur kori le-** – *do wrong* : kene, ami kunu kocur korci ni? – *why, have I done anything wrong?* [A. quṣūr – *shortcoming*]
kocuri ['χòsūrī] (n) *wrongdoing* | **kocurit for-** – *stray into wrong; get in a false position* : jela kocurit fortam nai – *just so long as we don't end up in the wrong* = **kocur**
koda ['χòdā] (n) *God* | koda tala – *God the Most High* : iaa koda! – *oh goodness!* : kodar ukum oile kail deka oibo – *if God permits we'll see one another tomorrow* : koda hafej! – *God is our keeper! goodbye!* [P. ḳodā]
kodom ['χòdòm] (n) *footstep* [A. qadam]
kodombusi ['χòdòmbūšī] (n) *obeisance; homage* | **kodombusi kor-** – *pay respects by touching a person's feet* : cacare kodombusi koro gi suna – *go and touch your uncle's feet like a good boy* [P. qadam bosi]
koe [1] [χòy] (adj) *several; so many; how many?* | koe gonta lagbo? – *how many hours will it take?* : tumar koe bai koe boin? – *how many brothers and sisters have you?* : koe fut koe inci – *so many feet and so many inches* : tain koe din bade aiba – *she'll come after a few days* : koe·ta – *a few; how many (things)* : koe·ta roice? – *how many are left?* : koe·ta roice

147

suɖu – *only a few are left* : koe·gu – *a few; how many (things or people)* : koe·jon – *a few; how many (people)* : koe·jon morcoin – *several people have died* : koe·jon jaita? – *how many (people) wish to go?* [B. kåy]
koe ² (adv) *where?* | afne koe jaira? – *where are you off to?* : lilu era koe? – *where are Lilu and the others?* = **kuae**
koe ³ (v) *they say* | amra koe doraici! – *we're scared, that's what they think!* : afne koe gari loicoin? – *I hear you've bought a car?* : **koe bule** – *they say* : koe bule mair lagbo – *they say a war is going to break out* < **ko-**
koe ⁴ (n) *wear and tear* | **koe o-/koe oi ja-** – *get worn down* : curi·ta koe oi gece – *the knife has got worn* [B. khåy < S. kśaya – *decline*]
koeɖi ['χòɛɖī] (n) *prisoner; convict* [U. qaiɗī < A. qaiɗ – *chain, shackle*]
koefol ['χòɛfòl] (n) *papaya*
koe-koti ['χòɛχòtī] (n) *damage* = **koe** + **koti**
koela ['χòɛlā] (n) *coal* [B. kåyla < O. kokila]
koer ['χòɛr] (n) *catechu* [B. khåyer]
koeri ['χòɛrī] (adj) *dark brown* = **koer** + **-i** ²
kof [χòf] (n) *cup* [E.]
kofal ['χòfāl] (n) *brow; forehead; fate* | tain kofal mucra – *she's wiping her brow* : kofalo leka – *written on one's forehead; part of one's destiny* : ita amar kofalo leka acil – *it was in my stars; it was just my fate* : kofalor ɖus – *a fault of fate; bad luck* : hae kofal! – *oh my goodness! darn it!* [B. kåpal < S. kapāla]
kofalkuc ['χòfāl-kūs] (n) *creasing of the brow; frowning expression* = **kofal** + **kuca** ¹
koi [χòɪ] (n) *a species of fish* (Anabas testudineus) [B. kåi]
koibor ['χòɪbòr] (n) *tomb; grave* | **koiboro ɖe-/koiboro ɖi la-** – *place in a grave; inter* : aij ɖaɖare koiboro ɖi laici – *we buried grandfather today* : **koibor jiarot kor-** – *visit a grave (as a religious observance)* [A. qabr]
koifiot ['χòɪfɪòt] (n) *explanation; excuse* [A. kaifiya – *particulars*]
koilja ['χòɪljā] (n) *liver* = **kolija**
koin [χòɪn] (n) *elbow* [B. kånui]
koirat ['χòɪrāt] (n) *good deeds; charity* [A. k̠aira – *good deed*]
koirati ['χòɪrātī] (adj) *charitable* = **koirat** + **-i** ²
koitor ['χòɪtòr] (n) *pigeon* = **koutor**
koja ['χòjā] (n) *late performance of prescribed prayer* = **kaja**
kok [χòχ] (adj) *several; a few* | kok ɖin – *several days* : kok bar – *a few times* : kok·ta – *several (things)* : kok·ta nao gi – *do take a few* : kok·ta aefol roice – *a few apples are left* : kok·jon – *several (people)* : kok·jon gecoin – *several people went* : kok·jon beti ino kam koroin – *several women work here* = **ko** + **ek**
kokon ['χòχòn] (adv) *when?* [B. kåkhån]
kol [χòl] (n) *machine; device; trick* [B. kål]
kola ['χòlā] (n) *banana* [B. kåla]
kole ['χòlɛ] (n adv) *by some means* < **kol**
kolekole ['χòlɛ-χòlɛ] (adv) *surreptitiously* < **kole**
kolfona ['χòl-fònā] (n) *idea; plan; conception* | kolfonar baire – *beyond conception; unimaginable* : **kolfona kor-** – *imagine* [B. kålpåna < S. kalpanā – *formation*]
kolija ['χòlīzā, 'χòlījā] (n) *liver; heart* | ami kolija kai na – *I don't eat liver* : tair kolija fati jar – *her heart is breaking* : amar kolijar tukra – *my dearest* [B. kålija]
kolima ['χòlīmā] (n) *Muslim declaration of faith* [A. kalima]
kol-karkana ['χòl-χārχānā] (n) *factories; industry* = **kol** + **karkana**
kolla ['χòl-lā] (n) *head* [P. kala]
kolol ['χòlòl] (n) *disruption* [A. k̠alal]
kolom ['χòlòm] (n) *pen; stroke of the pen; grafted shoot* | kalir kolom – *ink pen* : sis kolom – *ballpoint pen* : ɖui kolom lekouka – *please write a few lines* : gaco kolom lagaici – *I've grafted a shoot onto the tree* : kolomor ɖag – *pen mark* : kolomor jur – *the power of the pen*

: **kolom fire** – *the pen backtracks; a deletion is made* : tan kolom fire na – *he doesn't have to make revisions; his writing is effective* : **kolom mar-** – *make a mark with a pen; start writing* : **kolom cala-** – *write; keep writing* [A. qalam]
kolomjaɗa ['χòlòmjāɗā] (adj) *(writing) crossed out* [P. qalam zada]
kolomtoras ['χòlòmtòrāš] (n) *penknife* [P. qalamtarāš]
kom [χòm] (adj) *little; less; few* | tar foesa kom – *he has little money* : afnar caite kom foesa faice – *he received less money than you* : kub kom manus janoin – *very few people know* : somoe kom – *time is short* ¶ **kom** (adv) *in small degree; less* | kom sunɗor – *not very pretty; less beautiful* : kom ɗorkari – *not very useful; hardly necessary* : hokol caite kom ɗami – *least expensive of all* : fac fon kom ek so – *just £5 short of £100* ¶ **kom** (pron) *a limited amount; little; less* | he kom buje – *he understands little* : tara kom mane na – *they won't settle for less* : bout kom – *a very small amount* : **kom kori** – *in small measure; less* : amare kom kori bat ɗeuka – *please don't give me too much rice* : **komor maje** – *at the lower end of the scale* : komor maje ek ajar – *at least one thousand* : **kom fore/kom fori jae** – *a shortfall occurs* : calir kom fori gece – *there isn't enough rice; we're short of rice* [P. kam]
kom- (vi) *get less; decrease* | meg komce – *the rain has eased off* : endar ɗor kombo – *the price of eggs will go down* : **komi ja-** – *get less; decrease* : gorom komi jar – *the heat is getting less* : manus komi gece – *there are fewer people around* [B. kåm-]
koma- ['χòmā] (vt) *make less; make fewer; reduce* | caund komao – *turn down the volume* : amar ujon komaitam oimu – *I'll have to reduce my weight* : tara kamla komar – *they're cutting the workforce* : **komai de-** – *make less; make fewer; reduce* : amar beton komai dice – *they've reduced my wages* [B. kåma-]
kombes ['χòm-bɛš] (n) *variance; discrepancy* | tura kombes oito fare – *there may be some discrepancy* = **kom + bes** cf **beskom**
kombli ['χòmblī] (n) *blanket* [B. kåmbål]
kombokt ['χòmbòχt] (n) *hapless wretch* [P. kambaḳt]
kombol ['χòmbòl] (n) *backside; bum*
komcekom ['χòm-sɛχòm] (adv) *at least* [H. kam se kam]
komi ['χòmī] (n) *shortage* [P. kamī]
komibesi ['χòmībɛšī] (adv) *more or less* | komibesi fac fon – *five pounds, more or less* = **komi + besi** [1]
komin ['χòmīn] (adj) *mean; vile; low class* ¶ **komin** (n) *vile person* | «komine komin cine, momine momin cine» – *a scoundrel understands another scoundrel, an honest man understands another honest fellow* [P. kamīn – *least*]
komjat ['χòmjāt] (adj) *low class* [P. kamzāt]
komjur ['χòmjūr] (adj) *weak* [P. kamzor]
komjuri ['χòmjūrī] (n) *weakness* [P. kamzorī]
komola ['χòmòlā] (n) *orange* [B. kåmåla lebu]
komon ['χòmòn] (v n) *decrease* | bolon komon – *increase and decrease* < **kom-**
komor ['χòmòr] (n) *loins; hips; waist* | komoror maf / komror maf – *waist measurement* : amar komror maje bis kore – *I have lumbar pains* : **komor band-/komor banɗi le-** – *gird up one's loins (ready for action)* [P. kamar]
komti ['χòmtī] (n) *shortfall* < **kom**
kon [χòn] (n) *moment; while; time* | kicu kon age – *a little while ago* : koto kon lagbo? – *how long will it take?* : **kone** – *at times* : kone roiɗ ute – *at moments the sun comes out* : kone asi, kone kanɗi – *sometimes I laugh and sometimes I cry* [B. khån < S. kśaṇa]
koni [1] ['χònī] (n) *elbow* [B. kånui]
koni [2] (n) *excavation; mine; oil well* [B. khåni]
konjilka ['χònjīlχā] (n) *slug* [B. kånculika]
kor [1] [χòr] (n) *rear* | tara kor taki samne aice – *they came from the rear to the front* : **kore** – *at the rear; behind* : tara kore roice – *they've been left behind* : tan gari amar garir kore – *his car is behind mine* : **kore di** – *behind; in future* : huruta amrar kore di ater – *the*

children are walking behind us : kore ɗi osubiɗa oibo – *there'll be problems in the future* : **koror** – *of the rear; previous* : koror gari – *the car behind* : koror tolob faice na – *he hasn't received his back pay* : **kor lam-/kor lami ja-** – *back down; retreat* : tara one kor lamto oibo – *now they'll have to back down*   [B. pår]

kor[2] (n) *another; a stranger* | amare kor lage ni? – *do I seem like a stranger (to you)?* :
koror – *of another; someone else's* : koror citi forio na – *don't read other people's letters*   [B. pår]

kor- (v) *do; make* | afne kita korra? – *what are you doing?* : ami beam korram – *I am doing exercises* : caca kam koroin – *uncle does work; uncle works* : tara gori tik kore – *they make clocks right; they mend clocks* : tain somoe nosto korra – *he's making time spoilt; he's wasting time* : ami imel kormu – *I will do some emails* : afne teks korta ni? – *do you want to do a text message?* : hurutae farko fiknik korce – *the children had a picnic in the park* : **kora/korna/koron** – *doing; to do* (verbal noun) : ekcarcaij kora bala – *doing exercise is good* : one kita korna? – *what to do now?* : **korbar** – *of doing; in respect of doing* (possessive verbal noun) : kam korbar somoe – *at the time of doing work; while working* : tain kam korbar lagi aicoin – *he has come for the purpose of doing work* : **korat** – *in doing; in the process of doing* (oblique verbal noun) : tain gucol korat – *he's in the process of doing his ablutions* : tara koroc korat moja fae – *they find enjoyment in doing shopping* : **koria/kori** – *having done; by virtue of having done* (perfect participle) : tain bajar koria goro aicoin – *having done the shopping he came home* : tain befsa kori boro oita – *he hopes to get rich by doing business* : **korte** – *by habitually doing; in doing* (temporal participle) : amar ita korte osubiɗa – *there are problems in my doing it* : **korte korte** – *by dint of doing* : tain oibbas korte korte ustaɗ oi gecoin – *by constantly doing practice he has become an expert* : **korle** – *in case of doing; if one does* (historic participle) : ila korle suja oe – *if one does it like this it's easy* : amra ɗiroŋ korle gari faitam nai – *if we delay, we won't get the bus* : tumra bala korle ami kusi oimu – *if you do well, I'll be pleased* : **kora** – *done* (passive participle) : amar hokol kam kora – *all my work is done* : noksa kora rajai – *quilt with decorations done on it* : hul kora kagoj – *paper with holes made in it* : **kora oe** – *is done* : ino fotokofi kora oe – *photocopies are done here* : **kora jae** – *can be done* : ou rumo ranna kora jae na – *cooking can't be done in this room* : ino bala befsa kora jaibo – *good business could be done here* : **korra** – *one who does* : ami gan korra nai – *I'm not someone who does songs* : tara tin·jon beam korra – *there are three of them who do exercises* : **korneala** – *one who does* : tain bala doŋ korneala – *he's a great one for doing jokes* : **kori le-/kori la-** – *do; accomplish* : amar humak kori laici – *I've done my homework* : tain ranna kori lita – *she wants to get the cooking done* : tara kam·ta suja kori lice – *they've made the job easy* : **kori de-** – *do as a service; do for someone* : amar gori tik kori ɗeuka – *please mend my watch for me* : afnar kani gorom kori ɗici – *I've warmed up your food* : **kori rak-** – *do in readiness* : amra hokolta ranna kori rakci – *we've got all the cooking done*   [B. kår-]   Note: Can be used to make a verbal compound from virtually any noun or adjective, including ones borrowed from English.

kora[1] ['xòrā] (v adj) *done; made* | hokol ranna kora – *all the cooking is done* : taiar kora kafor – *ready made clothes* : baug kora gari – *a repaired car* : noksa kora kafor – *cloth with decorations made on it*   < **kor-**

kora[2] (adj) *pungent; strong; severe* | kora roiɗ – *fierce sunshine* : kora jal – *acute pungency* : kora roŋ – *a loud colour* : kora manus – *a severe person*   [B. kåṛa]

kora[3] (n) *drought*   [B. khåra]

kora- (vt) *cause to do; get (someone) to do* | caca bout kam koraicoin – *uncle has had a lot of work done* : tain minare ɗia ranna koraiba – *she's going to get Mina to do the cooking* : amra gori·ta tik koraici – *we've had the clock put right* : **korani** – *getting (someone) to do* (verbal noun) : hurutare kicu kam korani bala – *it's good to get the children to do some work* : **koraibar** – *(in respect of) getting (someone) to do* (possessive verbal noun) : kam koraibar age kamla ɗeka lagbo – *we'll have to choose some workmen prior to getting the work done* : **koranit** – *in the process of getting (someone) to do* (oblique verbal noun) : amra kam koranit - *we're in the process of having work done* : **koraia** – *having got (someone) to do* (perfect participle) : tain ranna koraia memanre dakba – *after getting people to do the cooking he'll call the guests* : **koraite** – *in getting (someone) to do* (temporal participle) : roŋ koraite somoe lagbo – *it will take time to get all the painting done* : **koraile** – *in case of getting (someone) to do* (historic participle) : cauni tik koraile goro takta farba – *if you get someone to fix the roof you'll be able to stay in the house* : **korail** – *done (by someone else)* (passive participle) : hokol meramotor kam korail – *all the repair work has been carried out*   [B. kåra-]

koraf ['χòrāf] (adj) *bad* = **karaf**

korat¹ ['χòrāt] (v adv) *in the process of doing* | amra ranna korat – *we're just doing the cooking* : tain uju korat – *she's doing her ablutions*   < **kor-**

korat² (n) *saw; jacksaw*   [B. kårat]

korc- ['χòrs] (v) *spend* | kali fac fon korcimu – *I'm only going to spend five pounds* : **korci le-** – *spend* : tara raijjir foesa korci lice – *they've spent a huge amount* : hurutae kali korci lee – *the children keep spending money*   [H. kharc-]

korca- ['χòrsā] (v) *spend* | he tar bafor foesa korcae – *he spends his father's money* : **korcai le-** – *spend* : tarar hokol foesa korcai lice – *they've spent all their money*   = **korc-**

korcco ['χòrtšò] (n) *expense*   [P. karca]

kore ['χòrɛ] (n adv) *to the rear; behind* | tara bout kore roice – *they are far behind* : tumar kore deko! – *look behind you!* : **kore di** – *in the rear; in future* : huruta kore di ar – *the children are following behind* : kore di kita oibo ke jane – *who knows what will happen in the future*   < **kor¹**

korfura ['χòrfūrā] (n) *camphor*   [B. kårpur < S. karpūr]

korgus ['χòrgūš] (n) *hare; rabbit*   [P. kargoš]

kori¹ ['χòrī] (v adv) *having done; after doing; while doing; in a manner* | tain ofis kori aiba – *he'll come after doing his office job* : jotno kori likci – *I've written it having taken care; I've written it carefully* : keal kori huno – *listen while paying attention; listen attentively* : (with an adjective, to enable it to be used adverbially) tik kori kouka – *say it in a correct manner; say it correctly* : tai sundor kori leke – *she writes in a beautiful manner; she writes beautifully* : bala kori hikco ni? – *have you learned it well?* : (with an adverb, for emphasis) joldi kori ao – *come quickly* : aste kori calauka – *drive slowly* : afnar kad loge kori rakoin jen – *keep your card along with you* : **(oito) kori** – *in such a way that (something happens)* : moja oito kori makao – *make it so that it'll be tasty* : tara bujto kori bujain jen – *do explain in a way they'll understand* : foesa bacto kori kom ance – *she bought less, so that money would be saved*   < **kor-**

kori² (n) *cowrie; groat* | amar ek·ta kori-o nae – *I haven't got a single penny*   [B. kåṛi]

korid ['χòrīd] (n) *purchase* | **korid kor-** – *purchase; buy* : tara noea citi-cear korid korce – *they've bought a new settee*   [P. karīd]

koriddar ['χòrīd-dār] (n) *purchaser; customer*   [P. karīddār]

korjo ['χòrjò] (n) *loan; debt* | tin ajar fon korjo – *a loan of three thousand pounds* : amrar bout korjo oi gece – *we've acquired a lot of debts* : **korjo an-** – *take out a loan* : tain fac so fon korjo ancoin – *he's taken a loan of five hundred pounds* : **korjo kor-** – *borrow; run up debts* : tain korjo kori gari anba – *he's going to borrow money and buy a car* : **korjo mar- /korjo mari le-** – *pay off debts* : amrar hokol korjo mari lici – *we've paid off all our debts*   [A. qarD]

kormi ['χòrmī] (n) *worker*   [B. kårmi < S. karmī]

kormo ['χòrmò] (n) *work*   [B. kårmå < S. karman – *action; performance*]

kormofol ['χòrmò-fòl] (n) *outcome of one's deeds; deserved fate*   [B. kårmåphål]

kormot ['χòrmòt] (adj) *hard-working*   [B. kårmåt]

korneala ['χòrnɛ-ālā] (n) *one who does* | kam korneala – *one who works* : gari meramot korneala – *man who repairs cars*   = **koron + -ala**

koroc ['χòròs] (n) *expenditure; purchases* | koroc ses oe na – *expenses never end* : tain koroc loia goro jaira – *she's going home with the shopping* : **koroc oe** – *is spent; is used* : bout foesa koroc oice – *much money has been spent* : **koroc kor-** – *spend; use; make purchases* : tara besi foesa koroc kore – *they spend too much money* : batrumo ke fani

151

koroc korer – *somebody's running the water in the bathroom* : tain bar oicoin koroc korta – *he's gone out to do some shopping* : tara koroc korat – *they're shopping* : **koroc kori le-** – *spend; use up* : asto butol koroc kori lice – *she's used up the entire bottle*   [P. ḳarc]
korocfati ['χòròsfātī] (n) *expenditure; purchases*   = **koroc**
koroj ['χòròz, 'χòròj] (n) *loan; debt*   = **korjo**
korojđar ['χòròzđār] (n) *borrower; person in debt* | korojđar oio na – *don't become a borrower* : he fac so fon korojđar – *he's in debt to the tune of £500*   [P. qarzdār]
koron ['χòròn] (v n) *doing; act of doing*   < **kor-**
kosai ['χòšāı] (n) *butcher*   [U. qasāī < A. qaṣṣāb]
kosi ['χòsī] (n) *neutered male goat*   [A. ḳaṣī]
koskos ['χòš-χòš] (n) *sensation of coarseness* | **koskos kore** – *it feels rough* : kombli·ta koskos kore – *the blanket feels scratchy*   [B. khåskhås]
koskose ['χòš-χòšɛ] (adj) *rough to the touch*   [B. khåskhåse]
kosra ['χòsrā] (n) *rough draft* | kosra kofi – *a rough copy*   [B. khåsṛa]
kosrot ['χòsròt] (n) *practice*   [A. kasra]
kosto ['χòštò] (n) *pain; pains; trouble* | kostor sima nae – *no end of trouble* : kunu kosto nae – *no trouble at all* : **kosto oe/kosto oi jae** – *trouble is experienced* : tan atat kosto oe – *she has difficulty in walking* : afnar bout kosto oi jar – *you're being put to a lot of trouble* : **kosto kor-** – *take pains; undergo difficulties* : tara kosto korer – *they're having a tough time* : afne bes kosto korcoin – *you've gone to a lot of trouble* : **kosto kori** – *while taking pains; with difficulty* : bout kosto kori jugar korci – *I obtained it with great difficulty* : kosto kori ain jen – *please do come, despite the inconvenience* : **kosto fa-** – *experience pain; undergo trouble* : bicari jobor kosto far – *the poor girl is in great pain* : **kosto đe-/kosto đi la-** – *cause pain; give trouble* : afnare kosto đitam cai na – *I don't want to give you any trouble*   [B. kåstå < S. kaśta]
kota ['χòtā] (n) *lower jaw; chin*
kotin ['χòtīn] (adj) *harsh; severe; hard; difficult* | kotin kota – *harsh words* : boro kotin manus – *a very severe person* : kotin mati – *hard earth; hard ground* : kotin kam – *hard work; difficult work* : buja kotin – *it's difficult to understand*   [B. kåthin]
kotti ['χòt-tī] (n) *hip*   [B. kåti]
kota[1] ['χòtā] (n) *word; words; talk; matter; thing; topic* | đui·ta kota – *a few words* : baje kota – *idle talk; balderdash* : bala kota – *a good point* : haca kota – *the truth* : suja kota – *a simple matter* : kamor kota – *an important matter* : arok kota .. – *and another thing ..* : tarar kotar maje beskom – *there are discrepancies in what they say* : tar kotar đam nae – *his word is worth nothing* : tar fetor kota koe na – *he doesn't say what's in his mind* : ek·ta kota jikaitam – *I'd like to ask you something* : foesar kota utcil – *the subject of money cropped up* : cacar kota buji na – *I don't understand about uncle* : tar kota oilo, bala kam jane – *the thing about him is that he's good at his job* : kota·ta bujcoin ni? – *have you got my point?* : kota·ta bar oe na jen – *make sure the matter doesn't leak out* : kota oilo, .. – *the thing is, ..* : ita kunu kota oilo ni? – *that's not an issue; that's no reason* : **kota ace** – *there is some kind of agenda* : afnar loge amar kota ace – *there's something I want to discuss with you* : aij tan aoar kota acil – *it was understood he would come today* : tan fauribar kota nae – *there's no question of his forgetting* : **kota oe** – *words are spoken* : tan loge amar kota oice – *I've had a word with him; I've spoken to him* : kail ticaror loge kota oibo – *I'll be talking to the teacher tomorrow* : **kota ko-** – *speak; talk; say* : he kota koito fare na – *he can't speak* : tara kali kota koe – *they keep talking* : ar koitam nai kota – *I shall say no more* : afne bala kota koicoin – *you've made a good point* : **kota hun-** – *hear what is said; do as one is told* : amar kota hunouka – *listen to me* : fuae kota hune na – *the boy doesn't do as he's told* : **kota đe-/kota đi la-** – *give one's word* : kota đeuka! – *promise!* : tain aiba, kota đi laicoin – *he has promised he'll come* : **kota rak-** – *keep one's word; do as someone else suggests* : tan kota rakcoin – *he has kept his word* : tan kota rakci – *I've done as he suggested* : **kota fala-** – *disregard what is said* : tan kota falaitam kila? – *how could I ignore what he said?* : **kota tul-** – *bring up a subject* : tara iskulor kota tulce – *they raised*

the subject of the school : **kota ɖor-** – *catch what is said; make a supposition* : tan kota ɖortam farci na – *I couldn't catch what he said* : aicca, cearmenor kota ɖorouka .. – *now, take the chairman for example* .. : **(kar) kotae** – *on the basis of what was said (by someone)* : cacar kotae goro roiclam – *in view of what uncle said we stayed at home* : kar kotae kagoj·kan falaicil? – *on whose authority did he throw the paper away?* : kar kotae ita korlae? – *who told you to do it?* : **kotae kotae** – *at every word; on every possible occasion* : tain kotae kotae torko koroin – *he argues about every single thing* : kotae kotae doŋ kore – *he clowns about at the drop of a hat* [B. kåtha < S. kathā]
kota² (n) *defect; fault* [A. ḳaṭā']
kotabatra ['χòtābātrā] (n) *words; talk* [B. kåtha-barta < S. kathā-vārtā]
kotek ['χòtɛχ] (adj) *a few* = **koto + ek** cf **kok**
koti ['χòtī] (n) *damage; loss* | **koti kor-** – *cause damage; cause loss* [B. khåti < S. kśati]
kotka ['χòt-kā] (n) *snag; hesitation; doubt* | **kotka lage** – *one has reservations or doubts; one feels uncertain* [B. khåtka]
koto ['χòtò] (adj) *so much; so many; some; how much? how many?* | koto foesa? – *how much money?* : koto ɖin? – *how many days?* : itar ɖam koto? – *the price of this is how much?* : tan koto kam – *she has so much work to do* : ino koto manus! – *there are so many people here!* : tara koto somoe gurafera korce – *they wandered around for some time* : **koto·ta** – *so much; how much* : ar koto·ta soitam? – *how much more must I put up with?* : **koto·tuk** – *so much; how much* : afne koto·tuk cain? – *how much do you want?* : **koto·guin** – *some; so many; how many* : afne koto·guin loita? – *how many do you wish to buy?* : **koto·gula** – *some; so many; how many* : koto·gula roice – *quite a few are left* : **koto·jon** – *some people; so many (people); how many (people)* : aij koto·jon aicoin – *quite a few people have come today* : **koto kori** – *for how much; at what rate* : cail koto kori becra? – *at what price are you selling rice?* : katol koto kori? – *how much are the jackfruit?* ¶ **koto** (adv) *how much; how; so; such* | bicara koto mate! – *how much that fellow talks!* : afnar furi koto boro? – *how old is your daughter?* : tain koto suja – *he's so simple-minded* : afne koto boro bul korcoin – *you've made such a great mistake* [B. kåtå]
kotobar ['χòtòbār] (adv) *so many times; how many times* = **koto + bar** ¹
kotobul ['χòtòbūl] (adv) *for a while; for so long; for how long* = **koto + bul** ²
kotokan ['χòtòχān] (adv) *so much; how much (quantity)* | kafor kotokan ɖorkar afnar? – *what amount of cloth do you need?* = **koto + kan** ²
kotokon ['χòtòχòn] (adv) *for a while; for so long; for how long* = **koto + kon**
kotom ['χòtòm] (n) *completion; end* | **kotom o-/kotom oi ja-** – *be completed; come to an end* : kicca kotom oi gelo / kicca kotom – *that's the end of the story* : **kotom kor-/kotom kori le-** – *finish off* : afnar kani kotom kori louka – *please do finish your meal* : **kotom fora-** – *commission a complete reading of the Quran* : tain ɖui·ta kotom foraicoin – *she's had two full readings of the Quran recited* [A. ḳatm – *sealing*]
kototuk ['χòtòtūk] *so much; how much (quantity)* = **koto + tuk**
kototuku ['χòtòtūkū] *so much; how much (quantity)* = **koto + tuku**
kotota ['χòtòtā] *so much; how much (quantity)* = **koto + -ta** ²
kototi ['χòtòtī] *so much; how much (quantity)* = **kotota**
kousol ['χôušòl] *skill* [B. kousål < S. kaušala]
kout [χôut] (n) *law court* | fulis kout – *magistrate's court* : joj kout – *judge court; crown court* : hekimi kout – *judge court; crown court* : **kout kor-** – *go to court; take legal action* : sorkar tar ufre kout korce – *the government has taken him to court* [E.]
kout-kacari ['χôut-χāsārī] (n) *law courts* = **kout + kacari**
koutor ['χôutòr] (n) *pigeon* [P. kabūtar]
-ku [kū] (noun suffix) *point in time* | raitku – *(at) night time* : sombarku – *(on) Monday* : aijku – *today* : **-kur** – *belonging to a time* : biankur faikkia – *a bird of morning time* : buɖbarkur kagoj – *Wednesday's paper* : aijkur kobor – *today's news*
kua¹ ['kūā] (n) *mist* [B. kuha]
kua² (n) *well* [B. kua]

kua-[1] (vt) *lose* | amar cafi kuaici – *I've lost my key* : ek beta jan kuaice – *one man lost his life* : **kuai le-** – *lose* : tumar foesa kuai libae – *you're going to lose your money* [H. kho-]
kua-[2] (vt) *open* | janla kuao – *open the window*
kuab ['kūāb] (n) *dream* | kuabor maje tumare ḍekclam – *I saw you in my dreams* : **kuab ḍek-** – *dream* : maje maje kuab ḍeki – *sometimes I have dreams* [P. ḳāb]
kuae ['kūāɛ] (adv) *where?* | amar gori kuae? – *where's my watch?* : tain kuae rakcoin jani na – *I don't know where he put it* : afne kuae acla? – *where were you?* : he raitku kuae jae – *at night he goes goodness knows where* : **kuae taki/kuae tone** – *from where* : tara kuae taki aice? – *where have they come from?* : kuae tone kuae – *from one state to another quite different one* = **kubae**
kub [kūb] (adv) *very; much* | kub bala – *very good* : kub boro – *very big* : kub sunḍor – *very pretty* : kub besi – *very much* : kub kom – *very little* : kub kosto – *much trouble* : kub subiḍa – *much convenience* : he kub kate – *he works very hard* [P. ḳūb – *well*]
kubae ['kūbāɛ] (adv) *where?* = **kun**[1] + **bae** cf **kuae**
kubala ['kūbālā] (adv) *at what time; when?* | afne kubala ruana ḍita? – *at what time do you intend to set off?* : tara kubala aice? – *when did they arrive?* = **kun**[1] + **bala**[1]
kubcurot ['kūbsūròt] (adj) *good-looking* [P. ḳūbsūrat]
kuca[1] ['kūsā] (n) *pleat; fold; crease* | **kuca lage** – *creasing occurs* : tumar sator maje kuca lagce – *your shirt has got creased* [B. koⁿca]
kuca[2] (n) *goad* | **kuca ḍe-** – *goad; prod; stir into action* : tarare kuca ḍitam oimu – *I'll have to give them a poke* [B. khoⁿca]
kuca-[1] (vt) *pleat; crease* [B. koⁿca-]
kuca-[2] (vt) *goad; prod; irritate* [B. khoⁿca-]
kucni ['kūs-nī] (n) *tuck; pleat* | **kucni ḍe-** – *make pleats; pleat* [B. koⁿc]
kucta ['kūs-tā] (pron) *something* | bitre kucta ace – *there is something inside* : **kucta na/kucta nae** – *nothing* : kita koila? kucta nae! – *what did you say? nothing!* : he kucta buje na – *he doesn't understand anything* [H. kuch]
kuḍ [kūḍ] (pron) *oneself* | kuḍ moulana sab koicoin – *the Moulana himself said so* : tain kuḍ aia ḍekcoin – *she came herself and had a look* [P. ḳvud]
kuḍa ['kūḍā] (n) *God* = **koḍa**
kuḍa- (vt) *goad; taunt* | kuttare kuḍaio na – *don't annoy the dog* : he amare kuḍae kali – *he keeps winding me up* [B. koⁿḍa-]
kuḍrot ['kūḍròt] (n) *power; ability* | allar kuḍrot – *the power of God* : amar kuḍrot nae ita korbar – *it's not in my power to do that* [A. qudra]
kuḍroti ['kūḍròtī] (n) *(divine) creative power* = **kuḍrot**
kufri ['kūfrī] (n) *non-belief* [A. kufr]
kufri kalam ['kūfrī kālām] (n) *infidel words; words of unbelief; blasphemous utterances* [A. kalāmu l-kufr]
kufur ['kūfūr] (n) *non-belief* [A. kufr]
kuj [kūz, kūj] (n) *enquiry; news (of someone)* | **kuj take** – *there is news (of someone)* : **kuj nae** – *there is no news (of someone)* : koe afta ḍori kuj nae tan – *nothing has been heard from him for weeks* : baro·ta baje, betar kuj nae – *it's twelve o'clock, and still no sign of him* : **kuj mile** – *news (of someone) becomes available* : kail betir kuj milce – *they got some news of her yesterday* : **kuj kor-** – *make enquiries; ask after (someone)* : tain afnar kuj korcoin – *he asked after you* : cacar kuj kortam oimu – *I'll have to enquire about uncle* : **kuj fa-** – *get news (of someone)* : hese tan kuj faici – *in the end I found out where he was* [B. khoⁿj]
kuj- (v) *search; look for; ask for* | citi·ta kujram – *I'm looking for the letter* : tara afnare kujer – *they're asking for you* : he foesa kujce – *he asked for some money* [B. khuⁿj-]
kuj-kobor ['kūzχòbòr] (n) *news (of someone)* = **kuj + kobor**
kukra ['kūkrā] (adj) *curly* | kukra cul – *curly hair* [B. koⁿkṛa]
kul[1] (n) *lineage* [B. kul < O. kula]

kul² [kūl] (n) *shore; bank* | kul nae, kinar nae – *there is no shore in sight; there is no prospect of relief* [B. kul < O. kūla]

kul³ (n) *carrying position; arm embrace* | kulor geđa – *a babe in arms* : **kulo lo-** – *take up (a child) in one's arms* : oto boro fua, kulo loitam kila? – *(you're) such a big boy, how am I to carry you?* [B. kol]

kul⁴ (n) *the whole* | **kule** – *in all; in total* : kule đos·jon – *ten people altogether* : kule đui·ta roice – *only two are left* [A. kull]

kul⁵ (n) *Quranic chapter starting with the word "qul"* | **cair kul** – *the four short suras which start with "qul"* (nos. 109, 112, 113, 114) [A. qul – "speak!"]

kul- (v) *open; take off; be untied* | akta đoroja kulce – *suddenly the door swung open* : đuar kulouka cain! – *open the door, please!* : basko kula jae na – *the box can't be opened; the box won't open* : tara noea đukan kulce - *they've opened a new shop* : caci ekaunt kulta – *auntie wants to open an account* : afnar kut kulouka – *please do take your coat off* : juta nae kula lagto nae – *there's no need to take off your shoes* : git kulce – *the knot has come undone* : bebir joban kulce – *the baby's tongue has been untied; baby has started to talk* : mon kuli kota kouka – *untie your mind and speak; speak freely* : **kuli le-** – *open; take off* : sonđuk kuli lici – *we've opened the chest* : kut kuli lei? – *may I take my coat off?* : **kuli đe-** – *open (for someone)* : dibi kuli đeuka – *please open the jar for me* : đuar kuli đici – *I've opened the door for everyone* : **kuli ja-** – *become opened; get detached* : janla kuli gece – *the window has blown open* : fogeto istem kuli jar – *the stamps on the packet are coming unstuck* [B. khul-]

kula¹ ['kūlā] (v adj) *opened; open; clear; free* | đoroja kula kene? – *why is the door open?* : kula asman – *a clear sky* : kula rasta – *a clear road* : tair mon kula – *her heart is open; she is straightforward* : tar juta kula – *his shoes are off his feet* < **kul-**

kula² (n) *divorce initiated by the wife* [A. k̠ulʕ]

kula- (vt) *cause to open; get (someone) to open* [B. khola-]

kula-mela ['kūlāmɛlā] (adj) *wide open* = **kula¹ + mela²**

kule ['kūlɛ] (n adv) *in all; altogether; only* | kule fac·ta faici – *I got five in all* : amra kule baro·jon – *there are twelve of us altogether* : tan kule đui fua – *he has only two sons* : kule? – *is that all?* < **kul⁴**

kulli ['kūl-lī] (n) *mouthwashing* | **kulli kor-** – *rinse out one's mouth* [B. kulli]

kumir ['kūmīr] (n) *crocodile* [B. kumir]

kumiti ['kūmītī] (n) *committee* [E.]

kumra ['kūm-rā] (n) *gourd* [B. kumṛa]

kun¹ [kūn] (adj) *some or other; which?* | kun furi? – *which girl?* : kun·gu? – *which one?* : kun somoe? – *which time? when?* : kun din? – *which day? when?* : kun đike? – *in which direction?* : kun karone? – *for what reason?* : kun fojonto? – *up to what point? how far?* : kun betae koice afnare? – *whoever told you that?* : kun huŋgae amar gori nice gi – *some bastard has taken my watch* [B. kon]

kun² [kū:n] (n) *blood* | kaforor maje kun force – *blood has got onto the cloth* : **kun oe** – *blood is shed; murder is committed* : ino đui betar kun oice – *two men have been murdered here* : **kun kor-/kun kori le-** – *murder* : dakaitor đol cearmenre kun korce – *a gang of robbers have killed the chairman* [P. k̠ūn]

kuna ['kūnā] (n) *corner; intermediate compass point* | agun kuna – *south east* : ari kuna – *north west* : ian kuna – *north east* : sagor kuna – *south west* : **kunat** – *in a corner* : rumor kunat – *in a corner of the room* : kunat huroin ace – *there's a broom in the corner* : **kunar maje** – *in a corner* : ek kunar maje tebul – *there's a table in one corner* [B. kon]

-kuna (adj suffix) *cornered* | tinkuna sal – *a three-cornered scarf; a triangular scarf* : coekuna tebul – *a six-cornered table; a hexagonal table* < **kuna**

kunabae ['kūnābāɛ] (adv) *in the corner* = **kuna + bae**

kunan¹ ['kūnān] (pron) *which one?* = **kun¹ + kan²**

kunan² (adv) *which place?* | tain kunan tone aicoin? – *where has he come from?* : **kunano** – *in which place? where?* = **kun¹ + kan³**

kunano[1] ['kūnānò] (adv) *where?* | kunano jaita? *– where are you off to?* : amar catti kunano? *– where is my umbrella?* < **kunan**
kunano[2] (adv) *somewhere; anywhere* | cafi·ta kunano toiclam *– I put that key somewhere* : tain kunano roita bala fain na *– he doesn't like staying anywhere* = **kunukano**
kun-karabi ['kūn-χārābī] (n) *foul deeds* = **kun**[2] + **karabi**
kunta ['kūntā] (pron) *which one?* | kunta afnar, kunta amar? *– which one is yours and which is mine?* : ami kunta antam? *– which one shall I get?* = **kun**[1] + **ta**
kunta ['kūntā] (pron) *something; anything* | tair monor maje kunta ace *– there's something on her mind* : kunta kauka! *– please have something to eat!* : afne kunta loita ni? *– do you want to buy anything?* : **kunta na/kunta nae** *– not anything; nothing* : he kunta koice na *– he didn't say anything* : iŋblafor maje kunta nae *– there's nothing in the envelope* : ita besi kunta nae *– it's nothing much* = **kun**[1] + **-ta**[2]
kunu ['kūnū] (adj) *some; any* | kunu somoe *– sometime* : kunu din *– some day* : kunu lakan *– somehow* : kunu kicu *– something* : tan kunu bearam takto fare *– he may have some kind of disease* : afne kunu mac dorcoin ni? *– have you caught any fish at all?* : tara kunu bae gece gi *– they've gone off somewhere* : kunu rokom coler *– it's going along somehow* : **je kunu** *– any* : afne je kunu din aita faroin *– you can come any day* : **ar kunu** *– some other; any other* : ar kunu beta oibo *– it must be some other fellow* : ar kunu sobji ace ni? *– are there any other vegetables?* : **kunu .. na/kunu .. nae** *– not any; no* : tain kunu foesa faicoin na *– she hasn't received any money* : ino kunu jaega nae *– there isn't any room here* : tarar kunu huruta nae *– they have no children* : ami kunu somoe jai na *– I don't go there at any time; I never go there* ¶ **kunu** (adv) *in any respect; at all* (in rhetorical questions) | hera amare koice ni kunu? *– and did they tell me at all? not a bit of it!* : tain kunu kusi ni? *– and is he at all happy about it? not likely!* = **kun**[1] + **-u**
kunukano ['kūnūχānò] (adv) *somewhere; anywhere* | tara kunukano gece *– they've gone somewhere* : ami kunukano fairam na *– I can't find it anywhere* = **kunu** + **-kano**
kunulakan ['kūnūlāχān] *of some kind; of any kind* | tan matat kunulakan buddi takto fare *– he may have some sort of plan in mind* ¶ **kunulakan** (adv) *somehow; by any means* | amra kunulakan jaimu gi *– we'll get there somehow* = **kunu** + **lakan**
kunulan ['kūnūlān] (adj) *of some kind; of any kind* ¶ **kunulan** (adv) *somehow; by any means* = **kunulakan**
kunumote ['kūnūmòtɛ] (adv) *somehow; by any means* | amra kunumote kam calairam *– we are managing somehow* : tara kunumote goro gece *– somehow they got back home* : afne kunumote faita nae tare *– you won't be able to find him by any means* = **kunu** + **mote**
kunumonte ['kūnūmòntɛ] (adv) *somehow; by any means* = **kunumote**
kunurokom ['kūnūròχòm] (adj) *of some kind; of any kind* | amrar ino kunurokom ousud nae *– we don't have any type of medicine here* ¶ **kunurokom** (adv) *somehow; by any means* | tara kunurokom baci gece *– they survived somehow* = **kunu** + **rokom**
kunurom ['kūnūròm] (adj) *of some kind; of any kind* ¶ **kunurom** (adv) *somehow; by any means* = **kunurokom**
-kur [kūr] (noun suffix) *eater; consumer* | afiŋkur *– opium eater* : modkur *– one who drinks alcohol* : haramkur *– one who consumes forbidden things* : sudkur *– one who makes a living from usury* [P. ḳor]
kur- (v) *glean; pick up; scrape up* | kuri le- *– pick up* : **kuria ka-** *– live on gleanings; scrape a living* [B. kuṛa-]
kurak ['kūrāχ] (n) *alimentation; food* [P. ḳūrāk]
kuran[1] ['kūrān] (n) *Quran* | kuran sorif *– the Holy Quran* : kuran tilaot *– recitation from the Quran* : kuran kotom *– complete reading of the Quran* [A. qurān]
kuran[2] (n) *scraper* < **kur-**
kuri ['kūrī] (n°) *a score; twenty* [B. kuṛi]
kurta ['kūrtā] (n) *kaftan* [P. kurta]
kus [kūš] (adj) *pleased* | **kus o-** *– be pleased; be happy* : afne aicoin boro kus oici *– I'm very glad you came* [P. ḳoš]

kusboe ['kūšbòɛ] (n) *pleasant aroma* [P. ḳoš bū]
kusi[1] ['kūšī] (n) *pleasure; happiness* | kusi ar gomi – *joy and sadness* : kusir sima nae – *no end of happiness* : kusir kota – *a matter for rejoicing* : afnar kusi – *just as you like* : **kusi moto** – *according to one's pleasure* : afnar kusi moto korouka – *do it how you like* : he ta‾ kusi moto cole – *he does whatever he feels like* : **kusi kor-** – *be happy; rejoice* : aij tara kusi korer – *today they're rejoicing* [P. ḳošī]
kusi[2] (adj) *pleased* | **kusi o-** – *be pleased* : tain kobor faia kusi oicoin – *she became very happy after receiving the news* : tara bes kusi nae – *they're not particularly pleased* : kusi ni? – *are you glad?* [B. khusi < P. ḳoš]
kusibasi ['kūšībāšī] (n) *rejoicing* | **kusibasi kor-** – *rejoice; have fun* : hokoloe kusibasi korra – *everyone is making merry* [P. ḳoš bāšī – *being happy*]
kusiđ ['kūšīđ] (n) *usury; interest* [B. kusiđ]
kusis ['kūšīš] (n) *endeavour* | **kusis kor-** – *try; make an attempt* [P. košiš]
kuskobor ['kūšχòbòr] (n) *good news* [P. ḳoš ḳabar]
kusol ['kūšòl] (n) *prosperity; well-being* [B. kusål < S. kušala]
kustar ['kūštār] (n) *minibus* [E. coaster]
kustorug ['kūštò-rūg] (n) *leprosy* [B. kusthå < S. kuśtha]
kusti ['kūstī] (n) *wrestling* [P. kuštī]
kut [kūt] (n) *coat* [E.]
kut- (v) *peck; pick at* [B. khuⁿt-]
kuta[1] ['kūtā] (n) *chamber; room* [B. kotha]
kuta[2] (n) *pole; post* [B. khuta]
kuti[1] ['kūtī] (adj) *small; little* | kuti aŋgul – *little finger* : kuti baicca – *little child*
kuti[2] (n°) *ten million* | fac kuti teka – *fifty million taka* : coe kuti basinđa – *sixty million inhabitants* [B. koti]
kutimuti ['kūtīmūtī] (adj) *small; tiny; wee* = **kuti**[1]
kutum ['kūtūm] (n) *relative by marriage; in-law* | era barir manus na kutum? – *are they family members or in-laws?* : goro kutum aicoin – *in-laws have come visiting* : tain kutum đekat gecoin – *he's gone to visit his in-laws* [B. kutum < O. kutumba]
kutumbari ['kūtūm-bārī] (n) *home of in-laws* | tain kutumbari gecoin – *he's gone to visit his in-laws* = **kutum + bari**[1]
kutumitta ['kūtūmīt-tā] (n) *kinship* | **kutumitta kor-** – *establish kinship (through marriage)* [B. kutumbita]
kutta ['kūt-tā] (n) *dog* | kuttar gor – *dog kennel* : kuttar ca – *puppy* : kuttar baicca! – *son of a bitch!* [H. kuttā]

l

la (quantifier) *unit* | ɗui·la – *two (of something)* : coe·la – *six ones*

la- (v) *proceed (to do)* | kori la- – *(go and) do* : gori·ta tare ɗi laimu – *I'll (go and) give him the clock* : caci ranna kori laicoin – *aunt has (gone and) done the cooking* : hurutare daki lauka – *call the children*   cf **le-**   Note: Used only as an auxiliary verb. It contributes very little to the meaning, but may add a sense of completeness to the action described. **le-** is much more common, but **la-** is always used with **ɗi** .

lab [lāb] (n) *profit* | **lab oe/lab bar oe** – *profit is made* : befsa taki tura lab bar oice – *some profit has come out of the business* : lab or na – *no profit is being made* : lab cara luskan oito fare – *there may be a loss rather than any profit* : **lab ace/lab oe** – *it is worthwhile; there is a point* : forat lab ace – *there are benefits in studying* : lab nae ɗeri korat – *there's no point in making delay* : jaia lab oice – *it was worth going* : ubaia lab oito nae – *it'll be no use waiting* : lab kita? – *what's the use?* : **lab kor-** – *make a profit* : amra kule fac so fon lab korci – *in all we made just five hundred pounds profit*   [B. labh < S. lābha]

labra ['lābrā] (n) *mixed vegetable dish; hotch-potch*

laca- ['lāsā] (v) *cause to dance; engage in dancing*   cf **naca-**

lacar ['lāsār] (adj) *destitute*   = **nacar**

lacari ['lāsārī] (n) *destitution*   = **nacari**

lae [lāɛ] (adv) *quietly; gently* | lae matouka! – *please talk quietly; please lower your voice!* : **lae lae** – *quietly; slowly* : tara lae lae kam kori ler – *they're quietly getting on with their work*

laek [lāɛχ] (adj) *able; suitable*   [A. lā'iq – *befitting*]

lafa- ['lāfā] (vi) *leap; leap about*   [B. lapha-]

lafalafi ['lāfālāfī] (n) *leaping about*   < **lafa-**

lag [lāg] (n) *conflict; clash* | runar loge minar lag – *Mina and Runa don't get on together* : keur loge lag nae amrar – *we aren't on bad terms with anyone*   [B. lag]

lag- (vi) *be attached; adhere; get involved; come into conflict; be effective* | cuiŋgom karfito lagce – *the chewing gum has stuck to the carpet* : betainte gofo lagcoin – *the men have got absorbed in conversation* : caca tarar loge lagcoin – *uncle has crossed swords with them* : he kunu kamo lage na – *he's no use for anything* : **lage** – *strikes; affects; erupts; fits; seems; feels* : bol·ta amar matat lagcil – *the ball struck my head* : is! lagce! – *touché! ow, that hurt me!* : fektrit aguin lagcil – *fire broke out at the factory* : kelat mair lagcil – *fighting broke out at the match* : ɗoroja lage na – *the door doesn't fit; the door doesn't shut properly* : hou iskruf ino lage na – *that screw doesn't belong here* : ino anɗair lage – *it seems dark in here* : kila lage? – *how does it feel?* : bala lage – *it feels good; it's nice* : kila lage – *it feels a bit odd* : lage, tain ɗorbar kori aicoin – *it looks as if he's just been involved in a quarrel* : **(kar) lage** – *affects; concerns; hurts; fits (someone)* : tumar tanda lagbo – *cold will affect you; you'll get cold* : amar feto buk lagce – *hunger has affected me in the stomach; I feel hungry* : afnar gorom lager ni? – *are you feeling too hot?* : amar bala lage na – *I don't like it; I'm fed up* : ou cuetar tumar lagbo ni? – *will this sweater fit you?* : amar boro lage – *it's too big for me* : **(kar) (kita) lage** – *(something) is necessary (to someone)* : tair ousuɗ lage – *she needs medication* : tarar bout foesa lagbo – *they'll need lots of money* : fij ɗena lage – *paying fees is necessary; payment of fees is required* : ruj jana lagcil – *we had to go every day* : **(kare) lage** – *(someone) seems* : cacare lage bala – *uncle seems to be all right* : afnare boro heran lager – *you seem quite stressed* : **(kar) (keure) (attio) lage** – *(someone) is related (to someone)* : taire afnar kita lage? – *what is she to you? how are you related to her?* : taire boin lage amar – *she's a cousin of mine* : **lagi ja-** – *adhere; have effect; get involved; come into conflict* : handit bat lagi jaibo – *the rice will get stuck to the pan* : tara kelanit lagi gece – *they've got stuck into their games* : era cearmenor loge lagi gece – *they've come into conflict with the chairman* : **lagi jae** – *affects; erupts; fits; is necessary* : tumar tanda lagi jaibo – *you'll start feeling cold* : maramari lagi jar – *fighting is*

158

breaking out : juta amar lagi gece – *the shoes have fitted me* : lotarit lagi gece ni afnar? – *have you struck lucky in the lottery?* : dui beg ciment lagi jaibo – *two bags of cement will be necessary* [B. lag-]   Note: Used impersonally in a wide range of common idiomatic expressions, loosely connected with the basic meaning of "touch" or "affect".

laga (v adj) *adhering; touching; adjacent* | tarar bari amrar barir laga – *their homestead is next to ours* : laga gor – *adjacent house; the house next door* : laga sofo noea manus aicoin – *new people have taken over the shop next door* ¶ **laga** (v n) *contact; adhesion; vicinity* | **lagar** – *of the vicinity* : lagar gorain – *the adjacent houses; the houses nearby* : **lagat** – *in the vicinity; nearby* : tarar gor lagat – *their house is in close proximity* : tara lagat take – *they live close by* < **lag-**

laga- (vt) *attach; fasten; plant; cause; start* | citit istem lagaitam ni? – *shall I stick a stamp on the letter?* : tara oalo kagoj lagar – *they're papering the walls* : tain matat toki lagain – *he puts a hat on his head; he wears a hat* : duar lagauka – *fasten the door; close the door* : tumar kut lagao – *put on your coat; do up your coat* : tain iato uri lagaira – *she is planting beans in the yard* : tumar sordi lagaibae – *you'll make yourself get a cold* : he dorbar lagaito – *he wants to stoke up a quarrel* : fuainte gerijo aguin lagaicil – *the boys had set fire to the garage* : banla gan lagain na kene? – *why don't you put on a Bengali song?* : kani lagao! – *serve up some food!* : he amare taffur lagaito acil – *he was about to give me a slap*: tara don lagaice – *they've started playing the fool* : **lagai de-** – *affix; fasten; put on; start* : tumar ato bendij lagai dimu – *I'll stick a bandage on your hand* : rajur jekit lagai deuka – *please do up Raju's coat for him* : tara mair lagai dice – *they have started a fight* : **lagai rak-** – *affix; fasten; keep on* : tumar kut lagai rako – *put your coat on and keep it on* : dorojat tala lagai rakcoin – *they've padlocked the door* [B. laga-]

lagaia ['lāgāıā] (v adv) *attaching; applying; expending* | daktor gori lagaia dekce tare – *the doctor examined him by applying a special instrument* : aro foesa lagaia gor·ta boro kormu – *we'll spend some additional money and enlarge the house* : he tin din lagaia goro gece – *he went home, taking three days to do so* : tara kamla lagaia rasta tik korce – *putting men to work they got the road repaired* < **laga-**

lagail ['lāgāıl] (v adj) *affixed; stuck on* | oalo fustar lagail – *there's a poster affixed to he wall* : goro gerij lagail – *the house has a garage attached* : lagail kagoj – *paper stuck on* : lagail cul – *artificial hair* < **laga-**

lagal ['lāgāl] (n) *contact* | lagal fa- – *be able to reach* : cuicor lagal fai na – *I can't reach the switch* : tain afnar lagal faicoin na – *he hasn't been able to get hold of you* : cacar lagal faitam kila? – *how can I get in touch with uncle?* [B. nagal]

lagat¹ ['lāgāt] (v adv) *in the vicinity; nearby* | tain lagat takoin – *he lives nearby* : tarar bari amrar barir lagat – *their homestead is next to ours* < **laga**

lagat² (post) *up to; by* | tain dos·ta lagat aiba – *he'll come by ten* : afne budbar lagat faiba – *you'll get it by Wednesday* [A. li ğāya – *to an extreme*]

lagi ['lāgī] (v adv) *because of; for the sake of; for the purpose of; for* | tain tandar lagi bar oin na – *because of the cold she doesn't go out* : gedar lagi fari na – *I can't do it on account of the baby* : tain desor lagi katra – *he's working for the sake of the country* : tara afnar lagi malaice – *they made it for you* : hokolor lagi bala oibo – *it will be best for everyone* : tara kok dinor lagi jar – *they're going for a few days* : he futbolor lagi fagol – *he's crazy on football* : tara jaibar lagi beus – *they're desperate to go* : tain takbar lagi koira – *she's asking us to stay* : ami kaibar lagi kunta dici na – *(I'm sorry) I haven't offered you anything to eat* : **kitar lagi?** – *because of what? why?* : london jaita kitar lagi? – *why do you want to go to London?* : koitam ni kitar lagi? – *shall I tell you why?* < **lag-**

lai [lāı] (n) *mustard (plant); rape (plant)* [B. rai]

lain ['lāın] (n) *line; queue; supply line* | tin lain leka – *three lines of writing* : lain ace – *there's a queue* : amrar gecor lain kata – *our gas supply has been cut off* : tain ilektikor lain anta – *he wants to get an electricity supply laid on* : **lanir** – *of the line* : lanir ufre dostokot deuka – *please sign on top of the line* : **lanit** – *on the line; in the queue* : lanit soi deuka – *put your signature on the line* : lanit takouka – *stay in the queue;* (on the telephone) *hold the* *line* : **lain kor-** – *form a queue; stand in line* : ino lain kora lage – *one has to queue here* : **lain dor-** – *join a queue; queue up* : amra lain dortam ni? – *shall we join the queue?* [E.]

lair ['lāır] (n) *butt; bottom* | amar tokit boico, lair tulo – *raise your butt, you're sitting on my hat* : **larit** – *on the buttocks* : fuar larit taba dice – *she smacked her son on the bottom*

laittia ['lāıt-tıā] (n) *lout*

lak [lāχ] (n°) *a hundred thousand* | tin lak – *three hundred thousand* : dos lak – *one million* : «lak kotae bia, tin kotae ses» – *it takes thousands of words to arrange a marriage, but only a few to break it* : **lak lak** – *thousands and thousands* : lak lak manus bagce – *thousands of people fled* : **lake lake** – *in their thousands* : faikkia lamce lake lake – *birds came down in their thousands* [B. lakh]

lakan ['lāχān] (n adv) *in a manner; in a way; as; like; resembling* | amra kunu lakan tik kormu – *we'll repair it some way or other* : tara jeca lakan koruk- *let them do it any way they like* : afne je lakan koiba – *just as you say* : ota ki lakan dekte? – *what does it look like?* : i lakan koro – *do it like this* : tain afnar lakan – *he is like you* : murgir lakan faikkia – *a bird like a chicken* : agor lakan oito nae – *it will never be as before* : huru lakan gor – *a fairly small house* : tain fetla lakan – *he's what you might call fat* : tain fauribar lakan manus nae – *he's not the kind of person who'd forget*

lakri ['lāχrī] (n) *wood; firewood* | undalo lakri jalai – *we burn wood in the stove* : **lakrir** – *of wood; made of wood; wooden* : lakrir basko – *a wooden box* : ou tebul lakrir – *this table is made of wood* [B. lakṛi]

lal[1] [lāl] (adj) *red* | lal sari – *a red sari* : lal sag – *red spinach (amaranthus)* : lal batti – *red light* : lal cul – *red hair; brown hair* : lal datu – *red metal; copper; bronze* : tar couk lal oi gece – *his eyes have become red; he's got angry* : ek·ta lal foesa-o dilo na tare – *he didn't give him a brass farthing* [B. lal < P. lāl]

lal[2] (adj) *dear; beloved; favourite* | lal afa – *dear elder sister* [B. lal]

lal[3] (n) *ruby* [A. laʿl]

lal- (vt) *nurture; foster* | bilair baicca lalto – *she wants to look after the kitten* : tara ek etimre lalce – *they have fostered an orphan* cf **fal-**

lala[1] ['lālā] (n) *saliva* | lala fore – *saliva flows; one drools* : bebir lala forer – *the baby is dribbling* [B. lala]

lala[2] (v adj) *fostered* | lala kutta – *a pet dog* < **lal-**

laloc ['lālòs] (n) *greed* | **laloc kor-** – *be greedy* [H. lālac]

lalon ['lālòn] (v n) *fostering* < **lal-**

lalon-falon ['lālòn-fālòn] (v n) *fostering* | **lalon-falon kor-** - *foster* : tair boinjire lalon-falon korer – *she is fostering her sister's daughter* = **lalon**

lam- [lām] (vi) *come down; get down; land; get off (a vehicle)* | tebul taki lamo! – *get down off the table!* : meg lamer – *rain is coming down* : tain nice lamta – *she wants to go downstairs* : gangor fani lamer – *the river water's going down* : felen aia lamce – *the plane has arrived and landed* : amra ino lamtam – *we want to get off here* : tar fet lamce – *his belly contents have moved down; he has got diarrhoea* : **lami ja-** – *come down; get down; get off* : amra lifto lami jai – *let's go down in the lift* : tara gari tone lami gece – *they've got off the train* [B. nam-]

lama[1] ['lāmā] (v n) *coming down* | fet lama – *diarrhoea* < **lam-**

lama[2] (v adj) *low; lower* | lama jaega – *a low-lying place* : lama bae – *on the lower side; lower down* : lama tajfur – *Lower Tajpur* ¶ **lama** (n) *lower place; lowland* | **lamar** – *of below; of the lowlands* : tara lamar manus – *they are people from low-lying areas* : **lamat** – *below; downstairs* : lamat gecoin – *he's gone downstairs* : tarar bari lamat – *their home is in the lowlands* < **lam-**

lama- (vt) *take down; bring down; put down; lower* | fotu lamaici – *I've taken the picture down* : ufor taki bet lamaira – *they're bringing the bed downstairs* : tumar at lamao – *put your hand down* : gari taki mal lamaitam oimu – *we must unload the stuff from the car* : baiccaintore cinemat lamaici – *I dropped the children at the cinema* : **lamai de-** – *lower; put down* : nisan lamai der – *they're lowering the flag* : amare sofo lamai deuka – *please* *drop me off at the shop* : **lamai torak-** – *set down and leave* : ricibar lamai torakce – *they've left the receiver off the hook* [B. nama-]

lamabae ['lāmābāɛ] (adv) *on the lower side; lower down* = **lama ² + bae**

lamat ['lāmāt] (n adv) *below; downstairs* | lamat ke take? – *who lives down below?* : lamat auka – *come downstairs* : amrar gaur lamat gaŋ ace – *there's a river below our village* < **lama ²**

lamfa ['lāmpā] (adj) *long; tall; extensive* | lamfa rasta – *a long road* : lamfa beta – *a tall man* : tain lamfa beton fain – *he earns a fat salary* : **lamfa o-/lamfa oi ja-** – *become longer; become taller* : goromor somoe din lamfa oe – *in summer the days get longer* : fua·ta lamfa oi jar – *the boy is getting taller* : **lamfa o-/lamfa oi ro-** – *stretch oneself out; lie down flat* : caci lamfa oi roicoin – *aunt has lain down (for a rest)* [B. lâmba]

lani ['lānī] (n) *line* = **lain**

lanot ['lānòt] (n) *curse* [A. la¿na]

lar- [lār] (v) *move* | laric na be! – *don't move, child! stay still!* : nice ke lare? – *who's moving about downstairs?* cf **lor-**

lara ['lārā] (v n) *movement* | **lara de-** – *make some movement; give a prod* : tain gumo nae, lara ɖira – *he's not asleep, he's moving* : fon kori lara ɖitam oimu – *I'll have to phone them and give them a prod* : **lara fa-** – *detect movement* : raitku lara faiclam – *I heard someone moving about in the night* < **lar-**

lara- (vt) *move; cause to move; displace* | cear larac na be! – *stop wobbling your chair, child!* : amar kagoj laraice ke? – *who's been moving my papers?* cf **lar-**

laracara ['lārāsārā] (n) *moving about; movement* | **laracara kor-** – *move; move about* : laracara koro kene? – *why are you fidgeting?* = **lara**

larai ['lārāī] (n) *fighting; battle; war* | larai coler – *a battle is going on* : boro larair somoe jajo aclam – *at the time of the world war I was on a ship* : **larai kor-** – *do battle; fight* : juan hokoloe larai korra – *all the young men are fighting in the war* [H. laṛāi]

las [lāš] (n) *corpse* [P. lāš]

lata ['lātā] (n) *stickiness; glue* | lata lage – *it feels sticky* : fotu lata ɖia lagaici – *I've stuck the picture on with glue*

lat [lāt] (n) *kick* | **lat mar-** – *give a kick; kick* : fuae tar baire lat marce – *the boy kicked his brother* [B. lath]

lau [lāu] (n) *gourd* [B. lau]

le- ¹ [lɛ] (v) *take; proceed (to do)* | litam ni? – *shall I take it?* : louka – *do take it* : tain cutti licoin – *he has taken leave* : **kori le-** – *(go and) do* : tain hokolti kori licoin – *she has got everything done* : tara befsa·ta kini lito – *they want to buy up the business* : afnar ca kai louka – *drink up your tea* : amrar mat huni lice – *he's overheard what we were saying* : taintain iŋlis mat hiki lira – *they're mastering the English language* : one buji lici! – *ah, I've got it now!* cf **ne-, lo-** Note: Used only as an auxiliary verb. It contributes very little to the meaning, but may add a sense of completeness to the action described.

le- ² (v) *lick; wipe* [B. leh-]

lecu ['lɛsū] (n) *lychee* [C.]

leda ['lɛɖā] (n) *gent* | ledar gori – *a gents' watch* cf **ledi**

ledar ['lɛɖār] (n) *ladder* [E.]

ledi ['lɛɖī] (n) *lady* | ledir gori – *a ladies' watch* [E.]

ledic ['lɛɖīs] (n) *lettuce* [E.]

leɖar ['lɛɖār] (n) *suitcase* [E. leather]

lef [lɛf] (n) *quilt* [B. lep]

lef- (vt) *coat (with emulsion)* | tara cun ɖia oal hokol lefer – *they're coating all the walls with whitewash* [B. lep-]

lei [lɛɪ] (n) *paste; gruel* [B. lei]

leia ['lɛɪā] (v adv) *having licked; having wiped* | tara leia fucia arce – *they've wiped it totally clean* < **le- ²**

lejur ['lɛzūr, 'lɛjūr] (n) *tail (of an animal)* [B. lejuṛ]

lek [lɛχ] (n) *mark; written sign* [B. rekh]
lek- (v) *write* | tain citi lekra – *she's writing a letter* : ami baŋla lektam cini na – *I don't know how to write Bengali* : tain at dia lekoin – *he writes by hand* : afne baŋlae lekba na iŋrejit? – *will you write it in Bengali or English?* : **leki le-** – *write down; note down* : amar lombor leki louka – *make a note of my number* : tikana leki lici – *I've written down the address* : **leki de-** – *write down (for someone)* : afnar tikana leki deuka – *please write out your address for me* [B. likh-]
leka ['lɛχā] (v n) *writing* | iŋlis leka suja – *writing English is easy* : tan leka fortam fari na – *I can't read his writing* : ator leka – *handwriting* : mesinor leka – *typewriting* : tair ator leka sundor – *her handwriting is beautiful* ¶ **leka** (v adj) *written* | ino kita leka? – *what's written here?* : afnar lombor amar boit leka – *your number is written in my book* : tair nijor ator leka citi – *a letter written in her own hand* < **lek-**
leka- (vt) *cause to write; get to write* | ami runare dia citi lekaici – *I got Runa to write a letter for me* [B. lekha-]
lekafora ['lɛχāfòrā] (n) *writing and reading* | tain lekafora janoin na – *he doesn't know how to read or write* : **lekafora hik-** – *learn to read and write; become educated* : **lekafora kor-** – *read and write; study* : hurutae lekafora korer – *the children are studying* : tain lekafora korcoin – *he has studied; he is educated* = **leka + fora** ²
lekaleki ['lɛχālɛki] (n) *writing* = **leka**
lembu ['lɛmbū] (n) *citrus; lemon* [B. lebu]
lemta ['lɛmtā] (adj) *naked* = **leŋta**
len [lɛn] (v n) *taking; loan* | fac ajar teka len ancoin – *he has borrowed five thousand taka* < **le-**
lenden ['lɛndɛn] (n) *transactions; trade; borrowing* | tarar loge amrar lenden oe – *we do some business with them* : amar tura lenden roice – *I do have some loans outstanding* = **len + den**
leŋgur ['lɛŋ-gūr] (n) *tail (of an animal)* [B. leŋguṛ]
leŋlud ['lɛŋ-lūd] (n) *landlord* [E.]
leŋra ['lɛŋ-rā] (adj) *lame* ¶ **leŋra** (n) *lame man* [B. leŋṛa]
leŋra- (vi) *limp* | tain leŋraia atoin – *he walks with a limp* cf **leŋra**
leŋta ['lɛŋ-tā] (adj) *naked* [B. leŋta]
lifsa ['līfšā] (n) *covetousness* | **lifsa kor-** – *be greedy (for); covet* : he besi lifsa kore – *he's too greedy* : tara foesar lifsa kore – *they hanker after money* [B. lipsa < S. lipsā]
ligel ['līgɛl] (adj) *legal; legally settled* | tain ligel nae – *he doesn't have official permission to stay* : **ligel o-/ligel oi ja-** – *become legally settled* : tara ligel oi gece – *they've acquired the right of settlement* [E.]
lik [līk] (n) *track; path* [B. lekh]
likit-forit (adj) *put in writing* | kota·ta likit-forit oito – *the agreement should be put in writing* = **likito**
likito ['līkītò] (adj) *written* [B. likhitå < S. likhita]
lilla ['līl-lā] (adv) *for God* | kam·ta lilla korce – *they did the job free, in God's name* : tain dos fon lilla dicoin – *he's donated ten pounds for God's work* ¶ **lilla** (n) *charitable donation in God's name* | lillar foesa – *portion of business takings set aside for charity* : lillar basko – *collecting box for donations* [A. li l-lāh – *for the Deity*]
lilua ['līluā] (adj) *blue* [B. nil]
lo- [lò] (v) *take; buy* | cafi louka – *here, take the key* : tara gari loice – *they have purchased a car* : ami kafor loitam – *I want to buy some clothes* : gedare kulo loicil – *she gathered the baby in her arms* : tain kagoj·kan ato loicoin – *he picked up the document* : dom louka! – *take a breather; wait a moment!* : tain ek aftar cutti loita – *he wants to take one week's leave* : ukile aro somoe loicoin – *the lawyer has obtained a time extension* : allar nam loia suru kori – *let us take God's name and begin* : loia kouka – *take (food) and eat; please help yourself* : **loi le-** – *take; take up; buy up; set off* : tumar kut loi lao – *take your coat with you* : tar gari asta jaga loi lice – *his car has taken up all the space* : tara amrar befsa loi lito –

they want to buy up our business : loi louka! – *come on, take it / come on, let's get going!* : **loia ɖe-** – *buy (for someone)* : cacare gori loia ɖicoin – *he has bought uncle a watch* : **loia ja-** – *take away* : tain natire loia gecoin – *she has taken her grandson away with her* : amɛr catti loia jauka – *you can take my umbrella with you*   [B. lå-]
loa¹ ['lòā] (v n) *taking; bringing; buying*   < **lo-**
loa² (v adj) *purchased; bought* | ita afnar goro banail na loa? – *is this home-made or bought?* : loa camana – *purchased equipment*   < **lo-**
lobon ['lòbòn] (n) *salt*   [B. låbån < S. lavaṇa]
loe [lòy] (n) *rhythm; habit; custom* | ganor loe – *rhythm in music* : cacir fan kanir loe – *aunt has the habit of chewing paan* : amrar nacor loe nae – *we don't have the custom of dancing; we don't dance* ¶ **loe** ['lòɛ] (n adv) *by custom; by kinship* | i bia·ta loe oe na – *such a marriage is not allowed by custom* : tain loe amar mama oin – *in kinship terms he's my maternal uncle*   [B. låy < O. laya]
log [lòg] (n) *attachment* | **(kar) log·kan** – *(somebody's) company* : **(kar) log·kano** – *in (somebody's) company; with (somebody)* : amar log·kano takouka – *please stay with me* : tan log·kano ke jaiba? – *who will go with her?* : **(loge) log ace** – *there is a link (with)* : kanir loge saistor log take – *there's a link between diet and health* : amrar loge log nae tar – *he has no truck with us* : log nae, lag nae – *no contact and no conflict* : kuntar loge log nae – *it doesn't fit in with anything; it's an anomaly* : **log oia** – *together; straight away* : ami log oia fon korclam – *I phoned straight away* : **(kar) log lo-/log loi le-** – *accompany (someone); attach oneself (to someone)* : he afnar log loito – *he wants to go with you* : tara amar log loi lice – *they've attached themselves to me* : **(kar) log ɖor-/log ɖori le-** – *attach oneself (to someone)* : hurutae tan log ɖorce – *the children have become his hangers-on* : **(kar) log car-/log cari ɖe-** – *stop accompanying (someone); leave (someone) alone* : he amar log care na – *he just won't leave me alone* : tain amrar log cari ɖicoin – *he's stopped keeping in touch with us*   [H. lagan]
logalog ['lògālòg] (adv) *at once* | amra logalog fulis dakci – *we called the police immediately*   cf **logeloge**
loge ['lògɛ] (n adv) *in company; with* | afnar loge ke jaiba? – *who will go with you?* : tain rutir loge jeli kain – *she eats jam with her bread* : tara amrar loge ɖorbar korce – *they have fallen out with us* : tan loge matmu – *I shall speak with him* : cacar loge bujo – *discuss it with uncle* : tar loge amar bone na – *I don't get on well with him* : tarar loge log nae amar – *I have nothing to do with them* : **loge kori** – *in company; along with* : tan natire loge kori nicoin – *he took his grandson along with him*   < **log**
logeloge ['lògɛlògɛ] (adv) *together; simultaneously; at once; immediately* | tain amrar logeloge aicoin – *he came together with us* : runar logeloge minar jor utce – *Mina got a fever at the same time as Runa* : kobor faoar logeloge fon kormu – *I'll phone immediately on receiving news* : tara logeloge gece gi – *they went off straight away*   < **log**
loggi ['lòg-gī] (n) *staff; rod*   [H. laggī]
log·kano ['lòg-χānò] (n adv) *in company; with* | tan log·kano – *with him*   < **log**
loia ['lòiā] (v adv) *taking along; with; including; about* | mama catti loia bar oicoin – *uncle has gone out, taking his umbrella with him* : tumare loia jaimu – *I'll take you with me* : afne ranare loia kunano jain? – *where are you off to with Rana?* : tain koroc loia goro jaira – *she is going home with her shopping* : amra cacare loia tin·jon – *there are three of us including uncle* : nanire loia amar boro cinta – *I'm very much concerned about granny* : tara bia loia besto – *they're busy with the wedding* : ami loia colram – *I'm putting up with it* < **lo-**
loijja ['lòij-jiā] (n) *shame* | tar loijja sorom nae – *he has no shame; he is quite shameless* : loijjar bisoe – *a matter for shame* : loijjar kunta nae – *nothing of shame; nothing to be ashamed of* : **loijja kore** – *shame is felt; one is ashamed* : tumar loijja kore na? – *aren't you ashamed?* : **loijja kor-** – *act demurely; be bashful* : afne loijja koroin kene? – *why are you so shy; why are you holding back?* : **loijja fa-** – *be put to shame; be embarrassed* : fua·ta loijja faice – *the boy has got embarrassed*   [B. låjja < S. lajjā]
loikko¹ ['lòik-kiò] (nº) *a hundred thousand*   [B. låkkå < S. lakśa]

loikko ² (n) *attention* | **loikko kor-** – *pay attention; notice* : loikko korcoin ni? – *did you notice that?* [B. låkkå < S. lakśya]

lojar ['lòzār, 'lòjār] (n) *lodger; tenant* | goro lojar ace – *the house is tenanted* [E.]

lok ¹ [lòk] (n) *companionship* cf **log**

lok ² (n) *lock* | **lok laga-** – *put a lock on; lock* : ɖorojat lok lagaicoin ni? – *have you locked the door?* [E.]

lok ³ (n) *knock* | **lok kor-** – *knock at the door* : ke lok korer – *somebody is knocking* [E.]

lokbik ['lòk-bik] (n) *companionship* | tarar kunu lokbik nae – *they have nobody to stand by them* = **lok** ¹

lombor ['lòm-bòr] (n) *number; score* | koto lombor? – *what number is it?* : ek so fac lombor (gor) – *(house) number 105* : egaro lombor bac – *a number 11 bus* : tara teis lomboro take – *they live at number 23* : afnar mubailor lombor ɖeuka – *please give me your mobile phone number* : rina iskulo bala lombor faice – *Rina has got good marks at school* : **ek lombor** – *number one; first rate* : tain ek lombor sef – *he's a first class cook* : caci selait ek lombor – *aunt is first class at sewing* : **ɖui lombor** – *second rate; alternative* : ɖui lombor karbar – *illicit or unofficial dealings* : **lombor gura-** – *dial a number; ring up* : tair lombor guraici, te faici na taire – *I called her number but didn't get her* : kar lombor guraira? – *whom are you ringing up?* [E.]

lombori ['lòm-bòrī] (adj) *of a given number* | ek lombori – *first class* = **lombor + -i** ²

lonc [lòns] (n) *river launch; river bus* [E.]

london ['lòn-dòn] (n) *London; England* | tara londonor kanɖat take – *they live near London* : ɖes caria london gecil gi – *he left the homeland and went to England* : asta londonor maje ila kunta nae – *there's nothing like it in all England* [E.]

londoni ['lòn-dònī] (n) *person settled in England* = **london + -i** ³

loŋ [lòŋ] (n) *clove (spice)* [B. låbåŋgå < S. lavaŋga]

loŋgi ['lòŋ-gī] (n) *sarong; lungi* [P. lungī]

loŋgor ['lòŋ-gòr] (n) *anchor* [P. langar]

loŋgorkana ['lòŋ-gòr-χānā] (n) *relief food station; soup kitchen* [P. langarḳāna]

loŋka ¹ ['lòŋ-kā] (n) *chilli pepper*

loŋka ² (n) *Ceylon; Sri Lanka* [B. låŋka < S. laŋkā]

lor- (vi) *move; be moved; take action* | tebul lorer – *the table is moving* : ufre ke lorer – *somebody is moving about upstairs* : amra okan taki lortam nae – *we won't move from here* : tara keu lore na – *none of them are doing anything about it* : tara lorto nae – *they're never going to budge* : «hakim lore, hukum lore na» – *a judge may be moved, but the law is immutable* : **lori ja-** – *shift; change position* : faar lori gece – *the mountain has shifted* : amar ek·ta ɖat lori gece – *one of my teeth has got loose* [B. når-]

lora ['lòrā] (v n) *movement* | **lora ɖe-** – *make movement; move out of place; play truant* : ufre ke lora ɖer – *somebody is moving about upstairs* : tain forae kamo lora ɖein – *he frequently skips work* : **lora fa-** – *detect movement* : raitku afnar lora faici – *I heard you moving about at night* < **lor-**

loracora ['lòrāsòrā] (n) *movement* | loracora nae – *there is no movement; everything is still; nobody is stirring* : **loracora kor-** – *move about; make a move* : sara rait loracora kore – *they keep moving around all night* : tain loracora korra na – *he's not budging; he's not taking any action* = **lora**

loskor ['lòš-χòr] (n) *seaman; lascar* [P. laškar – *army*]

lota ['lòtā] (n) *spouted pot* [H. lota]

lotk- (vi) *hang; dangle* | **lotki ja-** – *hang; be hung* : he gaco lotki gecil – *he was dangling from a tree*

lotka- ['lòt-χā] (vt) *hang up* | jaenomaj oalo lotkaicoin – *they've hung the prayer mat on the wall* : **lotkai ɖe-** – *hang up* : bija kafor hokol rossit lotkai ɖicoin – *she's hung all the wet clothes on a rope* [B. låtka-]

lotkail ['lòt-χāil] (v adj) *hung up; suspended* < **lotka-**

lot [lòt] (n) *vine; electric lead* | telifonor lot – *telephone cord* = **lota**

lota ['lòtā] (n) *vine; creeper* [B.låta < S. latā]
lota-fata (n) *vegetation* = **lota + fata**
lou [lôu] (n) *blood* [H. lahū < O. lohita]
loura ['lôurā] (n) *one who takes; receiver; buyer* < **lo-**
lua [luā] (n) *iron (metal)* [B. loha]
luari ['luārī] (n) *iron cooking pan*
lub [lūb] (n) *greed* | tan kanir lub nae – *she has no greed for food* : **lub lage** – *temptation is felt* : kani dekle lub lage – *when one sees food one feels like eating* : **lub oe/lub oi jae** – *greed is aroused* : tar foesar lub oi gece – *he has got greedy for money* : **lub kor-** – *be greedy* : tain lub kori bifoto forcoin – *by being greedy he got into trouble* : **lub deka-** – *appeal to another's greed; tempt* : tane foesar lub dekaice – *they tempted him with a vision of money* [B. lobh < S. lobha]
lubi ['lūbī] (adj) *greedy* [B. lobhi]
luk [lūk] (n) *man; people* | afnar lagi ek·jon luk aicoin – *a man has come to see you* : koto luk – *so many people* [B. lok < S. loka]
luka- ['lukā] (v) *hide* | he kuae gia lukaice – *he's gone and hidden somewhere* : amar gori ke lukaice? – *who's hidden my watch?* : **lukai rak-** – *conceal; keep hidden* : hurutae cafi lukai rakce – *the children have hidden the key* : **lukai de-/lukai le-** – *conceal; hide* : kiric lukai diram – *I'm going to hide the crisps* : tain deslai kunano lukai licoin – *she's hidden the matches away somewhere* [B. luka-]
luksan ['luk-šān] (n) *loss* | **luksan oe/luksan oi jae** – *loss is sustained* : one becle tarar bout luksan oibo – *if they sell now they'll lose heavily* : lab taki luksan besi oi gece – *there's been more loss than gain* [A. nuqṣān – *deficiency*]
lul [lūl] (n) *saliva* = **lala**
lun [lūn] (n) *loan* | **lun an-** – *take out a loan* : tain fac ajar fon lun ancoin – *he has borrowed five thousand pounds* [E.]
lura- ['lurā] (v) *glean*
luskan ['luš-χān] (n) *loss* = **luksan**
lut [lut] (n) *looting* [B. lut]
lut- (vt) *grab; acquire* | dakaite bajar tone mal lutce – *the robbers seized goods from the bazaar* : tain bout neki lutra – *she is acquiring a lot of (religious) merit* [B. lut-]
lutfat ['lut-fāt] (n) *looting* = **lut**
lut-toraj ['lut-tòrāz, 'lut-tòrāj] (n) *looting* = **lut + toraj**

m

ma [mā] (n) *mother* | haton ma – *stepmother* : boro ma – *great grandmother* : **mar fetor** – *uterine; born of the same mother* : amar mar fetor bai – *my full brother* [B. ma]

mabaf ['mābāf] (n) *mother and father; parents* | tumar mabaf kuae? – *where are your Mum and Dad?* : tar mabaf nae – *his parents are dead* = **ma + baf**

mabud ['mābūd] (n) *God* [A. ma¿būd – *object of worship*]

mac [mās] (n) *fish* | rou mac – *carp* : hiŋgi mac – *catfish* : baim mac – *eel* : ica mac – *shrimp; prawn* : macor enda – *fish roe* : macor mura – *fish head* : macor kan – *fin* : mac dora – *catching fish; fishing* [B. mach < O. matsya]

maci ['māsī] (n) *fly* | mou maci – *bee* [B. machi]

madani ['mādānī] (n) *noon* | madani bala – *midday* [B. måddhannå < S. madhyāhna]

madrasa ['mād-rāšā] (n) *Islamic primary school* [A. madrasa – *place of study*]

maea ['māyā] (n) *affection* | (**kar lagi**) **maea ace** – *affection exists (for someone)* : natir lagi tan koto maea acil – *she had such a fondness for her grandson* : tair lagi afnar maea nae ni? – *don't you feel any affection at all for her?* : (**kar lagi**) **maea lage** – *tenderness is felt (for someone)* : hou fuar lagi maea lage – *one feels sympathy for that boy* : **maea kor-** – *show affection; dote* : tan furire besi maea korta – *he used to dote on his daughter* : hou baicca·tare keu maea kore na – *nobody gives that child any affection* : **maea de-/maea di la-** – *give a kiss; give a nose-rub* : maea di lao! – *give us a kiss!* [B. maya < S. māyā]

maea-doea ['māyādòyā] (n) *compassion* = **maea + doea**

maea-mobbot ['māyā-mob-bòt] (n) *affection* = **maea + mobbot**

maf[1] [māf] (n) *measurement; dimensions; size* | ou jagar maf koto? – *what are the measurements of this plot?* : tumar maf koto? – *how tall are you?* : tair komror maf tis – *her waist measurement is thirty; she has a 30" waist* : tar golar maf couddo – *his neck measurement is fourteen; he has a size fourteen collar* : **maf lo-** – *take measurements* : afnar maf loitam oimu – *I'll have to measure you* [B. map]

maf[2] (adj) *forgiven; excused* | tar bul maf oi gece – *his mistakes have been forgiven* : tar sat kun maf – *he gets away with murder* : aij tarar iskul maf – *today they've been let off school* ¶ **maf** (n) *pardon; excusal* | tar maf oito fare – *he may receive a pardon* : ou fira maf nae tumar – *you're not getting away with it this time* : **maf kor-/maf kori de-** – *forgive; pardon; excuse* : alla maf koruka – *may God forgive me* : boce maf korce tare – *the boss has forgiven him* : tara curi maf korto nae – *they won't ever pardon theft* : amare maf koroin jen – *please excuse me; please count me out* : beadobi maf korouka – *excuse me if I seem impertinent* : **maf ca-** – *ask for forgiveness; ask to be excused* : garir draibar maf caice – *the driver of the car apologized* : maf cai – *I wish to be excused; please count me out* [A. mu¿āfa – *absolved*]

maf- (vt) *measure* | tebul maftam oimu – *I'll have to measure the table* [B. map-]

mafik ['māfīk] (adj) *concordant; appropriate* ¶ **mafik** (post) *in accordance (with)* : niom mafik – *in accordance with the rules* : tan ain mafik bicar oibo – *he will be tried according to law* [A. muwāfiq]

maf-juk ['māf-jūk] (n) *measuring* = **maf**[1] + **juk**[2]

maflar ['māf-lār] (n) *scarf* [E. muffler]

mag [māg] (n) *Magh (January-February)* [B. magh < S. māgha]

mag- (vt) *demand; ask for* | he kali foesa mage – *he keeps asking for money* [B. mag-]

magi ['māgī] (n) *female animal; woman* | magi hial – *female jackal* : bilai·ta magi na murda? – *is that cat a female or a male?* : betae kali magi tukae – *that fellow is forever chasing a skirt* [B. magi]

magna ['māg-nā] (v adj) *begged for; obtained free* | magna kani – *free food* : **magna fa-** – *obtain for free* : i kolom magna faici – *I got this pen free* : «magna faile bicmilla, foesa lagle aujubilla» – *if it's free, we say "yes, in the name of God!", but if it requires money, we say "God forbid!"* < **mag-**

mah [māh] (n) *month* | **mahe mahe** – *every month* [P. māh]
mai [māɪ] (n) *mother* = **ma**
maia ['māɪā] (adj) *pertaining to a month* | agon maia ɖan – *rice of the month of Agrahayan* : mag maia jamir – *tangerines of the month of Magh* < **mah**
maiɖɖom ['māɪɖɖòm] (n) *medium; means* | **maiɖɖome** – *by means (of); through* : kostor maiɖɖome suk faiba – *you will attain bliss through suffering* : ami redior maiɖɖome hunci – *I heard it over the radio* [B. maɖɖhåm < S. mādhyama]
maiggo ['māɪg-gò] (int) *oh, mother; mama mia!* = **maigo**
maigo ['māɪgò] (int) *oh, mother; mama mia!* = **mai + go**
maij ['māɪz] (n) *midst* = **maj**
maiji ['māɪzī, 'māɪjī] (n) (vocative) *Mother* = **mai + ji**
maijkan ['māɪz-χān] (n) *middle; centre* | tebulor maijkan – *the middle of the table* : aefolor maijkan baɖ oi gece – *the centre of the apple has gone bad* : gari maijkan taki horaitam ni? – *shall I move the car away from the middle?* : **maijkanor** – *of the middle; central* : maijkanor gor kali – *the middle house is empty* : **maijkano** – *in the middle; in between* : bati tebulor maijkano rakouka – *put the bowl in the middle of the table* : maijkano fulor gac lagaimu – *I'm going to plant some flowers in the centre* : ɖui goror maijkano oal ɖeoa – *a wall has been put between the two houses* : tara maijkano london gecil – *in the meantime they had been to London* : **maijkan dia/maijkan di** – *via the middle; through* : amra sooror maijkan ɖi jaitam oimu – *we'll have to go through the town* = **maij + kan** ³
maijkanta ['māɪz-χān-tā] (n) *middle* = **maijkan + -ta** ²
maijla ['māɪz-lā] (adj) *middle; second in seniority* | maijla fua – *the middle son; the second oldest son* < **maij**
maijom ['māɪzòm, 'māɪjòm] (adj) *middle; second in seniority* | maijom furi – *the middle daughter; the second oldest daughter* : maijom afa – *second of the elder sisters* : maijom caca – *second paternal uncle; uncle number two* < **maij**
maine ['māɪnɛ] (n) *monthly pay* [P. māhyāna]
mair [māɪr] (n) *fighting; battle; war; stroke* | farko mair coler – *a fight is going on in the park* : gaue gaue mair oicil – *there was a battle between the two villages* : jafanor loge mair – *the war with Japan* : kicmotor mair – *a stroke of bad luck* : **marir** – *of fighting; of war* : marir somoe – *in time of war* : **marit** – *in a fight; in war* : tain marit jokom oicla – *he was wounded in the battle* : **maire** – *in the throes (of)* : kusir maire fal ɖice – *she leapt for joy* : **mair lage/mair lagi jae** – *fighting breaks out* : akta mair lagi jaibo, ɖekba – *suddenly violence will erupt, just wait and see* : irake irane mair lagcil – *war broke out between Iraq and Iran* : **mair kor-** – *engage in fighting* : tara tara mair korce – *they fought among themselves* : **mair ɖe-/mair laga-** – *give a thrashing* : ɖusmonre bala mair ɖice – *they gave their enemy a good beating* : **mair ka-** – *receive a thrashing; be beaten* : gundae mair kaibo – *the thug will get a beating* : amrar ɖol mair kaice – *our team was beaten* [B. mar]
mair-ɖaŋga ['māɪr-ɖāŋ-gā] (n) *fighting; violence* = **mair + ɖaŋga**
mair-dor ['māɪr-dòr] (n) *fighting* = **mair**
maj [māz, māj] (n) *middle; midst* [B. majh]
maj- (vt) *scrub* | tebul maja lagbo – *the table needs scrubbing* : tumar ɖat majo – *brush your teeth* [B. maj-]
maja ['māzā, mājā] (n) *waist* [B. maja]
majar ['māzār, 'mājār] (n) *Muslim shrine* [A. mazār – *place of visit*]
maje ['māzɛ, 'mājɛ] (n adv) *in the midst; inside; within; among; between* | ou rumor maje gorom ace – *it's warm inside this room* : tumar mukor maje kita? – *what's in your mouth?* : gumor maje ɖekci tumare – *I saw you in my sleep* : amra bakka osubiɖar maje – *we are in considerable difficulties* : tan ɖilor maje kita buji na – *I don't understand what's in his mind* : itar maje ami nai – *I refuse to get mixed up in all that* : tara ek aftar maje ɖito koice – *they said they'd pay within a week* : amar janar maje kunta oice na – *nothing has happened within my knowledge* : tain kamor maje ɖistab ɖein – *he bothers us in the middle of our work* : tumra hokolor maje batmu – *I'll share it among all of you* : jaga-ta ɖui bair

maje bag oibo – *the land will be split between the two brothers* : he fakar maje forcil – *he fell onto a hard surface* : lalor maje nil – *blue on red* : ek·tar maje ar ek·ta – *one thing on top of another* : tain maje ekbar aicla – *she came once in the interim* : **er maje** – *in the meantime; up to now* : er maje kuae acla? – *where were you up till now?* : er maje kotota gotce – *so many things have happened in the meantime* < **maj**
majemaje ['māzɛmāzɛ, 'mājɛmājɛ] (adv) *sometimes* = **maje**
majemoidde ['māzɛmòiddɛ] (adv) *sometimes* = **maje + moidde**
maji ['māzī, 'mājī] (n) *boatman* [B. majhi]
majon ['māzòn, 'mājòn] (n) *merchant* [B. måhajån < S. mahājana – *man of substance*]
mak- (v) *rub; spread; squidge* | tan fitir maje bik makce – *she rubbed embrocation on his back* : bereto batar makra – *he's spreading butter on the bread* : hurutar bat maka lage – *the children's food has to be squidged by hand (to make it easier to eat)* [B. makh-]
makal ['māχāl] (n) *good-for-nothing* [B. makal]
makor ['māχòr] (n) *spider* [B. makâr̯]
mal [māl] (n) *property; goods; stuff* | kaca mal – *perishable goods* : curir mal – *stolen property* : kora mal – *hot stuff* [A. māl – *property; money*]
mala ['mālā] (n) *garland* [B. mala < S. mālā]
mala- (vt) *make; make into* | afne guddi mailata janoin ni? – *do you know how to make a kite?* : tain nijor ate malaicoin – *she made it with her own hands* : fua·ta ca malar – *the boy is making tea* : otare balis malaici – *I've made that into a cushion* : tain hacare mica malain – *he makes true into false; he twists the truth* cf **bana-**
malamal ['mālāmāl] (n) *goods; merchandise* < **mal**
mal-besat ['māl-bɛšāt] (n) *goods* = **mal + besat**
mal-camana ['māl-sāmānā] (n) *goods and chattels* = **mal + camana**
malik ['mālīk] (n) *owner; guardian* | ou garir malik ke? – *who is the owner of this car?* : tain restonor malik – *he is the owner of a restaurant* : hou fuar malik nae – *that boy has nobody in charge of him* : iaa malik! – *O Lord!* [A. mālik]
malikana ['mālīkānā] (n) *ownership* [P. mālikāna]
malis ['mālīš] (n) *massage* | **malis de-** – *perform massage* : cacar fitit malis dira – *she is massaging uncle's back* [P. māliš]
malla ['māl-lā] (n) *crewman* [A. mallāh – *sailor*]
malum ['mālūm] (adj) *known* | amar malum nae – *it isn't known to me; I don't know* : kar malum ace? – *who knows?* [A. ma¿lūm]
mama ['māmā] (n) *mother's brother; mother's bai* | **mamar goror** – *descended from mother's brother* : mamar goror bai-bun – *maternal cousins; cousins on one's mother's brother's side* [B. mama]
mami ['māmī] (n) *wife of mother's brother; wife of* mama [B. mami]
mamla ['māmlā] (n) *lawsuit* | tarar mamla coler – *their lawsuit is going on* : tara mamla faice – *they have won their action* : **mamla kor-** – *bring a lawsuit* : he afnar ufre mamla korto fare – *he may take legal action against you* [A. mu¿āmala – *affair*]
mamla-mokodma ['māmlāmòχòdmā] (n) *legal proceedings* = **mamla + mokodma**
mamoni ['māmònī] (n) *mother's brother's wife* = **mami**
mamu ['māmū] (n) *mother's brother* = **mama**
mamuli ['māmūlī] (adj) *ordinary; trivial* [A. ma¿mūl – *done, practised*]
man [mān] (n) *dignity; pride* | hokoloe man loia bacta cain – *everybody hopes to survive with their dignity intact* : **(kar) mane lage** – *it touches (someone's) pride* : cacar mane lagce – *uncle's pride has been wounded* [B. man < S. māna]
man-¹ (vt) *acknowledge; accept; agree to; obey; tolerate; respect* | hou kota manoin ni? – *do you accept that point?* : afne allare manoin ni? – *do you believe in God?* : tara afnar kota mance – *they have agreed to your proposal* : hukum mana lage – *one has to obey orders* : oto boro oinniae mantam kila? – *how can I put up with such an injustice?* : murobbire mane na he – *he shows no respect for elders* : **mani le-** – *agree to; submit to* : tara noea niom mani lice – *they have accepted the new rules* [B. man-]

man-² (vt) *solemnly intend; vow* | kuran kotom mancoin – *she has vowed to perform a full recitation of the Quran* : ek·ta goru mancoin – *he has vowed to sacrifice a cow* cf **manos**
mana ['mānā] (n) *prohibition* | **mana kor-** – *make a prohibition; forbid* : amra jaitam tain mana korcoin – *he has forbidden us to go* ¶ **mana** (adj) *forbidden* | amrar moɖ kaoa mana – *drinking alcohol is forbidden for us* : hurutar sofo jaoa mana acil – *the children had been barred from going to the shop* [A. man¿ - *prohibition*]
mana- (vt) *oblige to accept; get to agree* | tarare manaitam farci na – *we couldn't get them to agree* : **(kar) manae** – *suits (somebody)* : ou kafor taire manae – *this sari suits her* : galagali afnare manae na – *swearing doesn't become you* [B. mana-]
-mana (noun suffix) *habitual quality; -ness* | (sometimes used to form nouns from English adjectives describing behaviour) notimana – *naughtiness* : cilimana - *silliness*
mane ['mānɛ] (n) *meaning* | er mane kita? – *what is the meaning of this? what does it mean?* : fekc mane kita? – *what does "fax" mean?* : itar mane buji na – *I don't understand the meaning of this* : tar kotar kunu mane nae – *his words have no significance* : **mane oe** – *it makes sense* : kunu mane oe na – *it makes no sense* : ino takar kunu mane oe na – *there's no sense in staying here* [A. ma¿nā]
man-ijjot ['mānīj-jòt] (n) *honour; dignity; prestige* = **man + ijjot**
manik ['mānīk] (n) *jewel* [B. manik < O. mānikya]
manob ['mānòb] (n) *human being* | manob jati – *the human race* [B. manåb]
manobota ['mānòbòtā] (n) *humanity* [B. manåbåta < S. mānavatā]
manos ['mānòš] (n) *intention* | **manos kor-** – *form an intention; resolve* : jaitam manos korci – *I've made up my mind to go* [B. manås < S. mānasa – *mind*]
manot ['mānòt] (n) *vow* | **manot kor-** – *make a pledge for a ritual sacrifice* : tain ek·ta goru manot korcoin – *he has vowed to sacrifice an ox* [B. manåt < O. mānyatā]
mante ['māntɛ] (post) *from; since* | suru mante – *from the beginning* : kail mante – *since yesterday* : tain aicoin mante – *ever since he arrived*
manu ['mānū] (n) *human being* = **manus**
manus ['mānūš] (n) *human being; person; people* | era manus na janoar? – *are they human beings or wild beasts?* : caci bala manus – *aunt is a good person* : tain manus bala – *he's all right (as a person)* : beti manus – *a woman; womenfolk* : beta manus – *a man; men* : koto manus! – *so many people!* : ek·jon manus ɖorkar – *we could do with another pair of hands* : ɖui·jon manus aicla – *two people came* : inor hokol manusre cini – *I know everybody around here* : **mainse** – *people* (instrumental) : mainse kita koibo? – *what will people say?* : hokol mainse ɖekce – *everyone saw* : couɖir mainse arbi matoin – *the people of Saudi Arabia speak Arabic* : **mainsor** – *of people* : mainsor samne ita koio na – *don't say that in front of other people* : mainsor goro jai na besi – *I don't visit other people's houses much* : igu mainsor jat nae – *he can't be classified as human; he's a lousy specimen* [B. manus < S. mānuśa]
maŋso ['māŋšò] (n) *meat; flesh* [B. maŋså]
mar- [mār] (v) *beat; hit; throw; swipe; turn off; pay off; do* | igu marce amare! – *he hit me!* : gundae tare bukut marcil – *the thug hit him in the chest* : tane ijjote marce – *they struck a blow to his self-respect* : tane jane marce – *they struck him fatally; they killed him* : fuae ita marer – *the boy is throwing stones* : tumi amar kolom marco! – *you've swiped my pen!* : tara bout foesa marer – *they're embezzling a lot of money* : batti martam ni? – *shall I turn off the light?* : amar korjo marci – *I've paid off my debts* : fuainte fal marer – *the boys are practising leaps* : cik marlo ke? – *who just gave a shriek?* : bol aice, kik maro! – *here comes the ball, give it a kick!* : tain betrumo hubar marra – *he's vacuum-cleaning the bedroom* : tara fasfuto sil marce – *they've put their stamp on the passport* : jilu london marer – *Jilu is gadding around London* : **mari le-** – *strike; knock out; kill* : betare jane mari lice – *they've killed that man* : gec mari louka – *turn off the gas* : amar rin mari lici – *I've wiped out my debts* : is, mari licoin! – *oh dear, you've got me there!* [B. mar-]
mara ['mārā] (v n) *beating; swiping; doing* | tare je mara marce! – *they gave him such a thrashing!* : foesa mara bala nae – *embezzling money is not good* : **mara ka-** – *die* : bicara

kail mara kaicoin – *the poor fellow died yesterday* : **mara ja-** – *die* : ɖaɖi bout age mara gecoin – *grandmother died a long time ago* ¶ **mara** (v adj) *beaten; afflicted; done* | kicmotor mara – *afflicted by fate; doomed* : kaiclotor mara – *endowed with a bad character* : sil mara kagoj – *paper stamped with a seal* < **mar-**
mara- (vt) *cause to beat; cause to kill; get to stamp; get to put out* | tara cearmenre maraice – *they got someone to beat up the chairman* : tain fasfuto sil maraicoin – *he got them to put a stamp in the passport* : ek til baɖe batti maraimu – *in a moment I'll get them to extinguish the lights* [B. mara-]
maramari ['mārāmārī] (n) *fighting* < **mar-**
marattok ['mārāt-tòk] (adj) *terrible; dire; dangerous* [B. marattåk < S. mārātmaka – *murderous by nature*]
mar-fit ['mārfīt] (n) *fighting* = **mair** + **fita** [1]
marfot ['mārfòt] (n) *medium* | **marfote** – *through; via* : cacar marfote kobor faici – *I got the news through uncle* [A. ma¿rifa]
mari ['mārī] (v adv) *having beaten; having done* | **ɖin mari** – *after completing a day; following a day* : sombar ɖin mari rait – *the night following the hours of daylight on Monday; Monday night* < **mar-**
maria ['mārīā] (v adv) *having beaten; having fought* | maria mormu – *after fighting I shall die; I shall fight to the death* < **mar**
marifoti ['mārīfòtī] (n) *mystic knowledge of God* [A. ma¿rifa – *knowledge; gnosis*]
mas [māš] (n) *month* | fus mas – *the month of Poush* : jun mas – *the month of June* : ek mas baɖe – *one month later* : **maso** – *in a month* : tain maso ekbar jain – *he goes once a month* : **mase** – *in a month; in each month* : mase foncas fon – *fifty pounds a month* : **mase mase** – *month by month; every month* : tara mase mase london jae – *they go to London every month* : geɖae mase mase barer – *the baby is getting bigger by the month* : **masor** – *of a month; monthly* : tin masor baicca – *a baby of three months* : ou masor beton – *this month's salary* : masor hese – *at the end of the month* [B. mas < S. māsa]
masik ['māšīk] (adj) *monthly* | masik beton – *monthly wages; salary* : masik bemar – *monthly illness; menstruation* [B. masik]
mastor ['māštòr] (n) *teacher; literate person* | jalal mastor afnar lagi forom filaf korba – *Mr Jalal will fill in the form for you* [E.]
mastori ['māštòrī] (n) *teaching* | **mastori kor-** – *do teaching; do coaching* : tain mainsor goro mastori koroin – *he does private tuition at people's homes* = **mastor** + **-i** [3]
mastorni ['māštòrnī] (n) *lady teacher* = **mastor** + **-ni**
mat [māt] (n) *open field* [B. math]
mati ['mātī] (n) *earth; clay* | ou jagar mati bala – *the soil of this place is good* : tara mati ɖia kaf malae – *they make cups from clay* : **matir** – *of earth; of clay* : matir futul – *clay dolls* : matir manus – *son of the soil; person of good peasant stock* : matir ɖam – *the price of soil; a very low price* : matir roŋ – *the colour of earth; brown* : **matit** – *on the ground; on the floor* : bicari matit forcla – *the poor woman fell to the ground* : afnar cosma matit – *your spectacles are on the floor* : **mati oi jae** – *turns to dust; is ruined* : amrar befsa mati oi jaibo – *our business will go to ruin* : tar boisotor asa mati oi gece – *his hopes for the future have turned to ashes* : **mati o-/mati oi ja-** – *be buried* : tain london mati oicoin – *he was buried in London* : **mati ɖe-/mati ɖi la-** – *bury* : buɖbare tane mati ɖi laici – *we buried him on Wednesday* [B. mati]
matia ['mātīā] (adj) *earthy brown* < **mati**
mat [māt] (n) *speech; talking; language; discussion* | mainsor mat hunram – *I can hear people talking* : afnarar mat iŋreji nae ni? – *your language is English, isn't it?* : amra ciloti mat jani – *we know the Sylheti dialect* : tain cin ɖesor mat bujoin – *she understands Chinese* : he kilan mat mate – *he says strange things* : biar mat coler – *wedding negotiations are under way* : biar mat ar na – *we aren't receiving any marriage enquiries* : **mato** – *in conversation; in discussion* : cacir loge mato aclam – *I was having a chat with auntie* [H. bāt]

mat- (v) *speak; talk; say things* | tara baŋla mate – *they speak Bengali* : tain arbi matta faroin – *he can speak Arabic* : fuae mate na – *the boy won't say anything* : amra bade matmu – *we'll talk later* : cacar loge matici – *I have talked to uncle* : tarar loge matia dekmu – *I'll speak to them and see what they say* : tain nananta maticoin – *he said all sorts of things* : he kijat mat mate! – *what extraordinary things he is saying!* : ek·kan taki arok·kan mate – *he strays from the point; there's no logic to his arguments* : matia lab nae – *it's no use saying anything* : **mati le-** – *speak out; have one's say* : mati louka! – *go on, out with it; have your say!*

mata ['mātā] (n) *head; brain; end* | tumar mata guro – *cover your head* : amar matar bis – *my head has a pain; I have a headache* : amar matae bis kore – *my head is aching* : amar mata gurer – *my head is spinning; I feel dizzy* : tar mata bala – *he has a good brain; he is intelligent* : tar mata karaf – *his brain is defective; he's crazy* : tar matar dus – *his brain has a defect; he's crazy* : beta boro mata dekae – *he displays a big head; he is pretentious* : fiŋor mata – *head of a nail* : rastar mata – *head of a road* : ek mata taki arok mata – *from one end to the other* : **matat** – *at the beginning; at either end* : bocoror matat – *at the beginning of the year* : sorokor matat – *at the head of the road* : rastar hou matat – *at the far end of the street* : **matae** – *at the beginning* : dui bocoror matae – *at the beginning of the second year* [B. matha]

mata- (vt) *cause to speak; engage in talk* | taire mataitam farci na – *I haven't been able to get her to talk* : amar furi murobbi hokolre matae – *my daughter draws all the adults into conversation* : memanre mataio na – *don't bother the guests with your chatter*

matal ['mātāl] (n) *drinker of alcohol* [B. matal]

matamati ['mātāmātī] (n) *(excessive) talking* < **mat-**

matbor ['mātbòr] (n) *local dignitary; community leader* [A. mu¿tabar – *honoured*]

matbori ['mātbòrī] (n) *acting like an important person* = **matbor + -i** [1]

mat-kota ['māt-χòtā] (n) *talking; speech; discussion* | bebie mat-kota jane na ebu – *the baby can't talk yet* : buddae mat-kota buli gecoin – *the old man has forgotten how to speak* : ofiso mat-kota coler – *discussion is going on in the office* = **mat + kota**

matobbor ['mātòb-bòr] (n) *local dignitary* = **matbor**

matobbori ['mātòb-bòrī] (n) *acting like an important person* = **matobbor + -i** [1]

maton ['mātòn] (v n) *talking; talk* | **maton dor-** – *start talking* : tain je maton dorcoin, ar bondo korcoin na – *once she'd started talking she wouldn't stop* < **mat-**

matra [1] ['mātrā] (n) *extent; level; degree* | tain matra caria gecoin – *he's gone over the limit; he's gone a bit too far* [B. matra < S. mātrā]

matra [2] (n) *one who speaks; speaker* | ino farci matra keu acoin ni? – *is there anyone here who speaks Persian?* : mitiŋo matra besi acla – *there were too many people speaking at the meeting* < **mat-**

matro ['mātrò] (adv) *merely; only* | tin fon matro – *only three pounds* : dos·jon aicoin matro – *only ten people came* : amra matro aici – *we've only just come* : matro fac din lagce – *it took only five days* : koe bar gecla? ek bar? matro! – *how many times did you go? once? is that all!* [B. matrå < S. mātrā]

maug [māug] (n) *female* cf **magi**

maui ['māŵī] (n) *mother of sibling's spouse* [B. maui]

medi ['mɛdī] (n) *female animal* | medi cora – *female sparrow* : medi undur – *female mouse* : ita nor na medi? – *is it a male or a female?* [P. māda]

mee ['mɛ-ɛ] (n) *girl* [B. meye]

meer ['mɛ-ɛr] (n) *kindness* [P. mehr – *affection*]

meerban ['mɛ-ɛr-bān] (adj) *kind* [P. mehrbān]

meerbani ['mɛ-ɛr-bānī] (n) *kindness* | allar meerbani! – *such is God's mercy!* : afnar meerbani – *your kindness; if you'll be so kind; if you insist* : **meerbani kor-** – *be kind; do a favour* : afne bout meerbani korcoin – *you have been most kind* : **meerbani kori** – *as a kindness; kindly; if you please* : meerbani kori duar lagai diba – *would you kindly close the* *door* ¶ **meerbani** (int) *so kind of you! thankyou!* | bout meerbani – *thank you very much* [P. mehrbānī]

meg [mɛg] (n) *rain* | meg lamer – *rain is coming down* : megor ɖin – *a rainy day* : ou megor maje kuae jaita? – *where do you hope to go in all this rain?* : **meg ɖee** – *it rains* : one meg ɖer – *now it's raining* : kail bakka meg dicil – *it rained a lot yesterday* : **mege bij-** – *get wet in the rain* : tain mege bijcoin – *he's wet from the rain* [B. megh < S. megha – *cloud*]

megla ['mɛg-lā] (adj) *rainy* [B. meghla]

mein [mɛin] (n) *(skin) mole*

mejaj ['mɛzāz, 'mɛjāz, 'mɛjāj] (n) *disposition; temper; mood* | tan mejaj bala – *she has a mild disposition* : tan mejaj gorom – *he has a hot temper* : aij tan mejaj bala nae – *today he's in a bad mood* : tan mejaj ola – *his constitution is thus; he's like that* : amar mejaj karaf oi gece – *I'm in a bad mood; I'm fed up* : amar mejaj karaf kori licoin – *you've spoilt my mood; you've put me in a bad mood* : **mejaj ɖeka-** – *display bad temper; be peevish* [A. mizāj – *blend*]

mejaji ['mɛzāzī, 'mɛjāzī, 'mɛjājī] (adj) *moody; bad tempered* = **mejaj + -i** ²

mejik ['mɛzīk, 'mɛjīk] (n) *conjuring tricks* | **mejik ɖeka-** – *do conjuring tricks* [E.]

mekrul ['mɛx-rūl] (n) *mackerel* [E.]

mekur ['mɛkūr] (n) *cat* [B. mekur]

mel- [mɛl] (vi) *become open; open out* [B. mel-]

mela ¹ ['mɛlā] (n) *country fair* [B. mela]

mela ² (v adj) *wide open* < **mel-**

mela- (vt) *open; spread open* | tain iato kafor melaira – *she's hanging out the clothes in the garden* [B. mela-]

meman ['mɛmān] (n) *guest; visitor* | afne amar meman – *you are my honoured guest* : meman aicoin – *visitors have come* : amrar goro meman – *we've got visitors* : memanor lagi kunta ɖao – *serve up some refreshment for the visitors* [P. mehmān]

memanɖari ['mɛmānɖārī] (n) *having guests; hospitality* | **memanɖari kor-** – *play the host; look after guests* [P. mehmāndārī – *hospitality*]

membar ['mɛmbār] (n) *Union Council Member* [E.]

menda ['mɛnɖā] (n) *naïve fool; chump; idiot* [H. meⁿṛhā – *sheep*]

menɖi ['mɛnɖī] (n) *henna; henna paste* | tara menɖi bater – *they are grinding henna into paste* : tair ato menɖi lagaice – *she has applied henna paste on her palms* [H. mehaⁿdī]

menot ['mɛnòt] (n) *hard work* | **menot kor-** – *labour; toil* [A. mihna – *ordeal*]

menoti ['mɛnòtī] (adj) *hard-working* = **menot + -i** ²

mera ['mɛrā] (n) *ram* [H. meⁿṛhā]

meramot ['mɛrāmòt] (n) *repair* | **meramot o-/meramot oi ja-** – *get repaired* : afnar gari meramot oice ni? – *has your car been fixed?* : **meramot kor-** – *repair* : tara gori meramot kore – *they repair clocks* : **meramot kora-** – *cause to repair; get fixed* : bidio meramot koraitam oimu – *I'll have to get the VCR repaired* [A. maramma]

merban ['mɛrbān] (adj) *kind* = **meerban**

merbani ['mɛrbānī] (n) *kindness* = **meerbani**

meri ['mɛrī] (n) *ewe; sheep* [H. meⁿṛī]

mesab ['mɛšāb] (n) *reverend gentleman* = **miasab**

mesin ['mɛsīn] (n) *machine* | selair mesin – *sewing machine* : taif mesin – *typewriter* : mesinor leka – *typed text* : mesino toiri – *machine made* : **mesin cala-** – *operate a machine* [E.]

mestoir ['mɛštòır] (n) *skilled tradesman* [B. mistri < Pg. mestre]

mettik ['mɛt-tīk] (n) *Matriculation; S.S.C. examination* | mettik fas – *(someone) who has passed their Matric exam* : tain mettik fas – *he's a matriculate* [E.]

meti ['mɛtī] (n) *fenugreek* [B. methi]

mia ['mīā] (n) *mister; fellow; lad* | raja mia – *Mr Raja / that fellow Raja / dear old Raja* : na mia! – *no sir! not likely, mate!* [U. miyāⁿ - *gentleman*]

miaid ['mīaɩd] (n) *period of validity* | amar fasfutor miaiđ ace – *my passport is still valid* : amar tikitor miaiđ gece gi – *my ticket has run out of time* : ou kador miaiđ kail ses oibo – *this card will expire tomorrow*   [A. miżād – *promise; appointed time*]
miasab ['mīāšāb] (n) *reverend gentleman; Islamic teacher* | miasab amrare kaeđa foraira – *the respected mullah is teaching us basic Arabic*   = **mia + sab**
mic [1] [mīs] (n) *lady teacher* | amrar mic acoin – *we have a woman teacher* : ke koice? mice koicoin – *who told you? teacher did*   [E.]
mic [2] (adj) *missed* | **mic oe/mic oi jae** – *gets missed* : afnar asfatalor tarik mic oi gece – *your hospital appointment has been missed* : **mic kor-/mic kori le-** – *miss* : afnar bac mic kori liba – *you're going to miss your bus* : tain tarik mic korcoin – *he's missed his appointment*   [E.]
mica ['mīsā] (n) *untrue; false; pointless* | kota·kan haca na mica? – *is that true or not?* : mica mat – *untrue words; lies* : mica asa – *false hopes* : mica torkatorki – *fruitless argument* ¶ **mica** (n) *untruth; falsehood* | tar lagi haca mica soman – *truth and falsehood are all the same to him* : he micat đora force – *he was caught out lying* : **mica mat-** – *tell lies* : tumi mica matclae kene? – *why did you tell a lie?*   [B. micha]
micabadi ['mīsābādī] (adj) *mendacious; untruthful*   = **mica + -bađi**
micakur ['mīsākūr] (n) *liar*   = **mica + kur**
mical ['mīsāl] (n) *metaphor; simile*   [A. miθāl]
micamici ['mīsāmīsī] (n) *being untruthful; being false*   = **mica**
micil ['mīsīl] (n) *(political) demonstration; protest march*   [A. muθūl – *appearance before a king or ruler*]
micor ['mīsòr] (n) *Egypt*   [A. miṣr]
micri ['mīsrī] (adj) *Egyptian*   [A. miṣrī]
mijaj ['mīzāz, 'mīzāj, 'mījāj] (n) *disposition; temper; mood* | tan mijaj bala – *she has a mild disposition* : tan mijaj gorom – *he has a hot temper* : aij tan mijaj bala nae – *today he's in a bad mood* : tan mijaj ola – *his constitution is thus; he's like that* : amar mijaj karaf oi gece – *I'm in a bad mood; I'm fed up* : tain amar mijaj karaf kori licoin – *he has spoilt my mood; he has put me in a bad mood* : **mijaj đeka-** – *display bad temper; be peevish*   = **mejaj**   [A. mizāj – *blend*]
mil [1] [mīl] (n) *similarity; connection* | tarar maje mil tukaiclam – *I looked for any similarity between them* : one mil faici – *now I can see the connection* : **mil ace** – *similarity / connection / equivalence exists* : tarar cearar mil ace – *their faces bear a resemblance* : tarar namor mil nae – *there is no similarity in their names* : hou roŋgor loge ou roŋgor mil ace – *this colour matches that one* : tan kotar maje mil nae – *his words don't add up* : **mil oe/mil oi jae** – *harmonization is achieved* : ou đui kafore mil oi gece – *these two cloths have been well matched* : **mil ka-** – *match; correspond; agree* : roŋge roŋge mil kae – *the colours match each other* : tara mil kae na – *they don't get on together* : **mil kaoa-** – *render compatible*   [B. mil < O. milana – *joining*]
mil [2] (n) *quota; requisite amount* | ek so fonor mil – *the full equivalent of £100* : ek ajar fonor mil oito – *the money must be made up to £1000*   [A. mil' – *amount to fill*]
mil- (vi) *come together; get together; meet* | hese tara milce – *in the end they got together* : tan loge miltam oimu – *I'll have to meet with him* : **mile** – *is encountered; is available* : baŋlađeso bala ananac mile – *good pineapples are found in Bangladesh* : đeslai sofo milbo – *matches will be available at the shop* : đuđ milto nae – *milk won't be available* : cui milce na – *the needle couldn't be found* : cacare mile na – *uncle is hard to find* : afnare kun somoe milbo? – *when will it be possible to get hold of you?* : **mili ja-** – *meet; converge; become one; become indistiguishable* : taintain kail mili jaiba – *they will get together tomorrow* : hono gia đui rasta mili jae – *there the two roads converge* : fanir loge cini mili gece – *the sugar has dissolved into the water* : leka mili gece – *the writing has fade away*   [B. mil-]
mila ['mīlā] (v n) *coming together*   < **mil-**

mila- (vt) *bring together; cause to meet; get to match; make equal; make even* | tain forḍa milaicoin – *she has drawn the curtains together* : amar loge at milauka – *shake hands with me* : taire runar loge milaimu – *I'll introduce her to Runa* : roŋ milaitam oimu – *we must get the colours to match* : fotur loge nam milaira – *he's matching the names to the pictures* : isab milaito farce na – *they haven't been able to balance the books* : tara rastar mati milar – *they're making the road surface even* : **milai ḍe-** – *bring together; match up; make even* : sarir loge blauj milai ḍira – *she's matching the blouses with the saris* : **milaia ḍek-** – *compare* : ou ḍui·ta milaia ḍekouka – *just compare these two* [B. mila-]

milaḍ ['mīlāḍ] (n) *Muslim social celebration* | milaḍ-un-nobi – *celebration of the Prophet's birthday* : **milad kor-** – *hold a party (as a formal religious celebration of a birth or similar event)* [A. mīlād – *birth*]

milamisa ['mīlāmīšā] (n) *social mixing* | **milamisa oe** – *social relations are maintained* : tan loge amar milamisa oe – *I see him socially (and get on well with him)* : tarar maje milamisa nae – *they don't socialize; they aren't on friendly terms* : **milamisa kor-** – *mix socially* : tain hokolor loge milamisa koroin – *he gets on well with everyone* = mila + misa

milon ['mīlòn] (n) *meeting; union* [B. milân < S. milana]

mimaŋsa ['mīmāŋšā] (n) *resolution (of a matter)* | **mimaŋsa oe/ mimaŋsa oi jae** – *(a matter) is resolved* : rastar befare hokolor mon moto mimaŋsa oi gece – *a decision about the road has been reached to everyone's satisfaction* [B. mimaŋsa < S. mīmāŋsā]

mimbor ['mīm-bòr] (n) *preacher's platform* [A. minbar]

minar ['mīnār] (n) *minaret* [A. manār – *lighthouse*]

minit ['mīnīt] (n) *minute* | ek minit! – *just a minute!* : ami tin minit baḍe aimu – *I'll come in three minutes' time* : fani minite minite barer – *the water is rising higher by the minute* : ek minitor maje kam ses oibo – *the job will be done in one minute* [E.]

miras ['mīrāš] (n) *family land* [A. mīrāθ – *inheritance*]

mirgi ['mīrgī] (n) *epilepsy* [B. mrigi < O. mŕgī]

mis- [mīš] (v) *mingle; mix socially* | tain mainsor loge besi misoin na – *he doesn't mix much with other people* : tarar loge ami mistam cai na – *I don't wish to have anything to do with them* : **misi ja-** – *intermingle; get mixed* : ino ḍui gaŋgor fani misi jae – *here the waters of two rivers mingle together* : bego cail dail misi gece – *rice and lentils got mixed up in the bag* [B. mis-]

misa ['mīšā] (v n) *mixing together* < **mis-**

misa- (vt) *cause to mix; mix together* | moeḍar loge ḍuḍ misauka – *mix the milk with the flour* : tas misaicoin ni? – *have you shuffled the cards?* : **misai ḍe-** – *cause to mix; mix together* : cinir loge enda misai ḍici – *I've blended the sugar with the eggs* [B. misa-]

miskar ['mīšχār] (n) *mixture* [E.]

miskin ['mīs-kīn] (n) *pauper* [A. miskīn]

misor ['mīšòr] (n) *Egypt* = **micor**

misti ['mīš-tī] (adj) *sweet* ¶ **misti** (n) *sweetmeat* [B. misti]

mistri ['mīs-trī] (n) *skilled tradesman* [B. mistri < Pg. mestre]

mit- [mīt] (vi) *be erased; be expunged* | kolomor ḍag mite na – *the pen mark can't be erased* : tan ḍukko mitto nae – *her pain will never be smoothed over* : **miti ja-** – *be erased; be expunged* : tumar fetor buk jolḍi miti jaibo – *your hunger will soon be assuaged* : leka miti gece – *the writing has got rubbed out* [B. mit-]

mita ['mītā] (adj) *sweet* | ou aefol mita nae – *this apple isn't sweet* : mita ca – *sweet tea* : mita oice ni? – *is it sweet enough?* ¶ **mita** (n) *sweetening; sweetmeat* | mita ḍici na – *I haven't put any sugar in* : afnar kofīr maje mita ḍeoa – *your coffee has had sweetening put in it; your coffee is sugared* : mita kauka – *do have some sweetmeats* [B. mitha]

mita- (vt) *erase; expunge* | leka mitaitam kila? – *how can I erase the writing?* : amar afcuc mitail jae na – *my regrets cannot be wiped away* : **mitai ḍe-** – *erase; expunge* : he ek·ta oŋko mitai ḍicil – *he had erased one of the figures* [B. mita-]

mitai ['mītāī] (n) *sweetmeats* [H. mithāī]

mitiŋ ['mītīŋ] (n) *meeting* | mitiŋ coler – *a meeting is in progress* : mitiŋ fac·tat baŋce – *the meeting broke up at five o'clock* : **mitiŋ kor-** – *hold a meeting* : aij tara mitiŋ korbo – *today they're going to have a meeting* [E.]
mitmat ['mīt-māt] (n) *reconciliation* | tarar maje mitmat oi gece – *they've been reconciled* < **mit-**
mita ['mītā] (n) *special friend* [B. mita < O. mitra]
moa ['mòā] (adj) *great; enormous* | moa kanɖo – *a tremendous affair* : moa muskil – *extreme awkwardness* [B. måha < S. mahā]
moaji ['mòāzī, 'mòājī] (n) *amount* [A. muwāzi – *equivalent*]
moalu ['mòālū] (n) *dropout; hippie; pariah* [? A. muwāli – *sect follower*]
moan ['mòān] (adj) *great* [B. måhan]
mobalu ['mòbālū] (n) *dropout* = **moalu**
mobbot ['mòb-bòt] (n) *love; affection* [A. maḣabba]
moca ['mòsā] (n) *small packet*
mocjid ['mòs-jīd] (n) *mosque* [A. masjiɖ]
mocola ['mòsòlā] (n) *topic; issue* [A. mas'ala – *question*]
mocra- ['mòsrā] (vi) *get wrenched; get sprained* | **mocrai ja-** – *get wrenched; get sprained* : tar fau mocrai gece – *he's sprained his ankle* [B. måcka-]
moɖ ['mòɖ] (n) *spirits; alcohol* [B. måɖ < O. maɖa]
moɖina ['mòɖīnā] (n) *Medina* [A. maɖīna]
moɖkur ['mòɖkūr] (n) *drinker of alcohol* = **moɖ + kur**
moɖu ['mòɖū] (n) *honey* [B. måɖhu < S. maɖhu]
moeɖa ['mòyɖā] (n) *refined wheat flour* [B. måyɖa < P. maida]
moeɖan ['mòyɖān] (n) *open field; village green* [P. maidān]
moela ['mòylā] (n) *dirt; rubbish* | moela caf kori lei – *let's clean up the mess* : moela kunano falaitam? – *where shall I put the rubbish?* : ator moela – *dirt on one's hands* : kanor moela – *ear wax* ¶ **moela** (adj) *dirty; darkened* | moela kafor – *dirty clothes* : tumar at moela – *your hands are dirty* : tar ceara moela oi gece – *his complexion has got darker* : **moela kor-/moela kori le-** – *make dirty; sully* : ɖeko, jama moela kori libae – *watch out or you'll get your clothes all dirty* [B. måyla]
moe-murobbi ['mòymūròb-bī] (n) *elders* = **murobbi**
moena ['mòynā] (n) *mynah (bird)* | monor moena – *pet; sweetheart* [B. måyna]
mof [mòf] (n) *mop* | **mof mar-** – *wield a mop; do the mopping* : kicino jaio na, mof marci – *don't go in the kitchen, I've just mopped it* [E.]
mogoj ['mògòz] (n) *brain* [P. maġz – *pith; kernel; brain*]
moi [mòɪ] (n) *mother's sister; mother's boin; step-mother* | amar mar hotin amar moi – *my mother's co-wife is my stepmother* : moir goror bai-bun – *cousins on one's mother's sister's side* [B. masi]
moiɖɖe ['mòɪɖ-ɖɛ] (n adv) *inside; within* | goror moiɖɖe tolet – *the toilet is inside the house* : ek aftar moiɖɖe – *within a week* : **moiɖɖe moiɖɖe / maje moiɖɖe** – *from time to time; sometimes* : tara moiɖɖe moiɖɖe ae – *they sometimes come* < **moiɖɖo**
moiɖɖo ['mòɪɖ-ɖò] (adj) *median; middle* [B. måɖɖha < S. maɖhya]
moiɖɖokan ['mòɪɖ-ɖòɣān] (n) *middle* = **moiɖɖo + kan** [3]
moiɖɖokano ['mòɪɖ-ɖòɣānò] (n adv) *inside* < **moiɖɖokan**
moiɖɖorait ['mòɪɖ-ɖò-rāɪt] (n) *middle of the night; late night* = **moiɖɖo + rait**
moiɖɖosto ['mòɪɖ-ɖòs-tò] (adj) *situated in between* ¶ **moiɖɖosto** (n) *intermediary; middleman* | ou befare tain moiɖɖosto acla – *he was the middleman in this affair; he acted as broker in this matter* [B. måɖɖhasthå < S. maɖhyastha]
moila ['mòɪlā] (n) *woman* [B. måhila]
moja ['mòzā, 'mòjā] (n) *enjoyment; delicious taste* | je moja! – *what a delight! how delicious!* : kaitam cai na, moja nae! – *I don't want to eat it, it isn't nice!* : cigret kanit moja kita? – *what pleasure is there in smoking?* : **mojar** – *of fun; of pleasant taste; nice* : mojar kela – *games which are good fun* : mojar kota – *amusing talk; a funny thing* : mojar kaini –

an enjoyable story : mojar kani – *delicious food* : mojar manus – *an entertaining person* : **moja fa-** – *get enjoyment* : kauka, moja faiba – *have some, you'll enjoy it* : tara torkatorkit moja fae – *they take pleasure in arguing* : **moja kor-** – *enjoy oneself; have fun* : hurutae bato moja korer – *the children are having fun in the bath* : **moja ɖek-** – *observe the fun; realise it isn't funny after all* : tara moja·ta ɖekto – *they want to see the fun* : moja ɖekouka ibla! – *now just see what it's like!* [P. maza]

mojbur ['mòzbūr] (adj) *forced; compelled* [A. majbūr]
mojburi ['mòzbūrī] (n) *compulsion; force majeure* [P. majbūrī]
mojbut ['mòzbūt] (adj) *firm; sturdy* [A. maƉbūṭ – *regulated; accurate*]
mojud ['mòzūɖ, 'mòjūɖ] (adj) *available* [A. maujūd – *found present*]
mojur ['mòzūr, 'mòjūr] (n) *labourer* [P. mozdūr – *paid worker*]
mokka ['mòk-kā] (n) *Mecca* [A. makka]
mokkel ['mòk-kɛl] (n) *(lawyer's) client* [A. muwakkil]
mokoɖma ['mòχòɖmā] (n) *lawsuit* | **mokoɖma kor-** – *start a lawsuit* : cacar ufre tara mokoɖma korce – *they've filed a suit against uncle* [A. muqaddama – *submission*]
mokru ['mòχ-rū] (adj) *not halal, but also not haram* [A. makrūh – *reprehensible*]
moktob ['mòχ-tòb] (n) *Islamic primary school* [A. maktab – *place of study*]
mol [mòl] (n) *dirt; excrement* [B. mål < O. mala]
mola ['mòlā] (n) *neighbourhood* [A. maḥalla]
molaim ['mòlāɪm] (adj) *soft, smooth* [A. mulayyin – *softening, aperient*]
mol-mutro ['mòlmūtrò] (n) *excreta* [B. mål-mutrå]
molom ['mòlòm] (n) *ointment* [A. marham]
mombatti ['mòm-bāt-tī] (n) *candle* = **mumbatti**
momota ['mòmòtā] (n) *affection* | tair lagi afnar momota nae ni? – *don't you feel any affection for her?* [B. måmåta < S. mamatā – *self-interest*]
mommoɖ ['mòm-mòɖ] (n) *Muhammad* | hojrot mommoɖ – *His Excellency Muhammad; the Lord Muhammad* [A. muḥammad]
mon [mòn] *heart; spirits; mind* | kusir mon – *a cheerful heart* : amar mon karaf – *I feel down-hearted* : amar mon bala nae – *I feel out of sorts* : tar mon·ta bala nae – *he is depressed / he is malicious* : tair monor goti bala – *her state of mind is good; she's in a cheerful mood* : **mone mone** – *in one's heart; in one's mind* : tara mone mone iŋsa kore – *deep down inside they are jealous* : afnare mone mone tukaiclam – *I was thinking of trying to contact you* : **mon ɖia** – *with all one's heart* : ami mon ɖia bissas kori – *I believe with all my heart* : **mon moto** – *according to one's heart; as one wishes* : he tar mon moto cole – *he does just as he pleases* : kam·ta afnar mon moto oice ni? – *was the job done to your satisfaction?* : **monor maje** – *in one's mind* : tar monor maje kita buji na – *I can't understand what he's thinking of* : amar monor maje acil jaitam – *I had a mind to go* : **mon oe** – *it seems; it comes to mind* : tara gece gi ni? mon oe – *have they gone? I think so* : akta mon oilo tan kota – *I suddenly remembered about him* : **(kar) mono ace** – *(someone) remembers* : tik ace, amar mono ace – *it's all right, I'm remembering* : tain kita koicla amar mono nae – *I can't recall what she said* : ami koitam mono nae .. – *I forgot to mention ..* : tumar mono takbo ni? – *will you remember?* : **mone loe** – *it seems; one thinks* : tara aice mone loe – *I think they've arrived* : baro·ta bajce ni? mone loe na – *is it twelve o'clock yet? I don't think so* : **mone koe** – *it seems; one thinks* : mone koe tara aito nae – *I guess they're not going to come* : kita mone koe afnar? – *what do you think?* : **mon cae/mone cae** – *one wishes* : amar mon cae bat kaitam – *I feel like eating some rice* : **mon gole** – *one's heart softens; one takes pity* : baicca·tare ɖeki tan mon golce – *when she saw the child she was moved* : karon hunia tan mon golcil – *on hearing the reason he relented* : **mone kor-** – *think; consider; take to heart* : afne kita mone koroin? – *what do you think?* : tain ar kunta mone korta faroin – *he may think something else; he may feel otherwise* : kunta mone koroin na jen – *please don't mind* : **mone an-** – *take to heart* : mone kunta anoin na jen – *please don't mind* [B. mån < O. manas]
monɖir ['mònɖīr] (n) *Hindu temple* [B. månɖir]

mondo ['mònɖò] (adj) *bad* | afnar soril kita? monɖo nae – *what's your health like? not bad* : **monɖe bala** – *good with bad; not so bad, considering* : kila acoin? monɖe bala – *how are you? not so bad* : **mondo kita?** – *what the heck; yes, why not?* : afnar gari boɖlaita ni? monɖo kita – *you're going to change your car? well, no harm in that* : **bala mondo** – *good and bad; an average state of affairs* : bala monɖo milaia coler – *things are going along, mixing good and bad; things are so-so* : tarare bala monɖo jikaici – *I asked them how things were* : bala monɖo buje na he – *he can't distinguish good from bad; he has no sense* : **mondo ko-** – *speak ill* : keur monɖo koio na, baba – *never speak ill of anybody, son* : ola korle mainse monɖo koibo – *if you act like that, people will make negative comments* [B. månɖå < S. manɖa – *slow*]
moni [¹] ['mònī] (n) *jewel* [B. måni < S. maṇi]
moni [²] (n) *sperm* [U. manī < A. minā]
monisi ['mònīšī] (adj) *offended* | **monisi o-** – *be offended; take offence* : afne monisi oiba na – *you mustn't take offence* [O. manīšī – *thoughtful*]
monjil ['mònzīl, 'mònjīl] (n) *mansion; section of the Quran* | hokk monjil – *Haque Mansion* : sat monjil – *the seven large reciting sections of the Holy Quran* [A. manzīl – *halting place*]
monjur ['mònzūr, 'mònjūr] (adj) *authorized; granted* | amar cutti monjur oi gece – *my period of leave has been approved* [A. manźūr – *seen*]
mon-mejaj ['mòn-mɛzāz, 'mòn-mɛjāz, 'mòn-mɛjāj] (n) *mood* = **mon** + **mejaj**
mon-mijaj ['mòn-mīzāz, 'mòn-mīzāj, 'mòn-mījāj] (n) *mood* = **mon** + **mijaj**
monosa ['mònòšā] (n) *intention* [U. manšā < A. manšā' – *origin*]
monosto ['mònòstò] (adj) *kept in mind* | **monosto kor-** – *intend* : ami jaitam monosto korclam – *I had been intending to go* [B. månåsthå < O. manastha]
montri ['mòntrī] (n) *(government) minister* [B. måntri < S. mantri – *advisor*]
montro ['mòntrò] (n) *incantation; magic spell* [B. måntrå < S. mantra – *sacred text*]
monukti ['mònūktī] (adv) *on an impulse*
moŋgol ['mòŋgòl] (n) *Mars; prosperity* | afnar moŋgol kamona kori – *I wish you prosperity; I wish you well* [B. måŋgål < S. maŋgala]
moŋgolbar ['mòŋgòl-bār] (n) *Tuesday* [B. måŋgålbar]
moolla ['mò-òl-lā] (n) *locality; quarter (of a city)* [A. mahalla]
moor ['mò-òr] (n) *dowry* [P. mahr]
mor [mòr] (pron adj) *my* = **amar**
mor- (vi) *die; be doomed; be rendered useless* | tain kun ɖin morcoin? – *when did he die?* : huruta jaibar lagi morer – *the children are dying to go* : ɖeko, morbae! – *watch out or you'll come to a sticky end!* : morci! – *I'm done for!* : tain kota ɖia morcoin – *by making that promise he sealed his own fate* : cinta koroin na jen, afnar foesa morto nae – *don't worry, your money won't lose its value* : amar rin morce – *my debts have been wiped out* : karen morce – *the electricity supply has gone down* : **mori ja-** – *die* : he birir lagi mori jar – *he's desperate for a smoke* [B. mår-]
mora ['mòrā] (v adj) *dead* < **mor-**
morda [¹] ['mòrɖā] (n) *male* [P. mard – *man*]
morda [²] (n) *corpse* [P. marda]
more ['mòrɛ] (pron) *me; to me* = **amare**
moric ['mòrīs] (n) *chilli* [B. måric]
morji ['mòrjī] (n) *whim; desire; grace* | afnar morji – *as you wish* : koɖar morji – *by the grace of God* [A. marÐāh – *pleasure* × murÐi – *pleasant*]
morjada ['mòrjāɖā] (n) *respect; honour* [B. mårjaɖa < S. maryādā – *bounds of custom*]
morjid ['mòrjīɖ] (n) *mosque* = **mocjiɖ**
mormi ['mòrmī] (adj) *spiritual; mystic* [B. mårmi]
mormo ['mòrmò] (n) *soft core* [B. mårmå < S. marma]
moron ['mòròn] (v n) *death* | moron kalo – *at the time of death* : moronor somoe – *at the time of death* < **mor-**

morum ['mòrūm] (adj) *deceased; late* [A. marḥūm – *who has been shown mercy*]
mosa ['mòšā] (n) *mosquito* [B. måsa]
mosa-maci ['mòšāmāsī] (n) *troublesome insects* = **mosa + maci**
mosari ['mòšārī] (n) *mosquito net* [B. måsari]
mosla ['mòš-lā] (n) *spices* | gorom mosla – *aromatic spice mixture* : fanor mosla – *condiments to accompany paan and betelnut* : **mosla de-** – *add spices* : maco mosla kita diclae? – *what spices did you put in the fish curry?* = **mosola**
mosola ['mòšòlā] (n) *spices* [U. masāla < A. maṣāliḥ – *necessary things*]
most [mòst] (adj) *intoxicated* [P. mast]
mosti ['mòstī] (n) *intoxication* [P. mastī]
mosto ['mòs-tò] (adj) *great* | mosto ek kumir – *a huge great crocodile* ¶ **mosto** (adv) *exceedingly* | mosto boro – *very big* [B. måstå < S. mastaka]
motk- ['mòtk] (vi) *get wrenched* | **motki ja-** – *get wrenched* : tar fau motki gece – *he's sprained his ankle* [B. måtka- – *snap*]
motor ['mòtòr] (n) *pea* [B. måtår]
mot [mòt] (n) *opinion* | afnar mot kita? – *what's your opinion?* : «joto mot toto fot» – *there are as many ways as there are points of view* : **(kar) mote** – *in (someone's) opinion* : amar mote bala oice – *in my opinion it was all to the good* [B. måt]
motamot ['mòtāmòt] (n) *opinion* = **mot**
motlob ['mòtlòb] (n) *motive; aim; meaning* | tan motlob kita? – *what's his motive? what's he after?* : er motlob kita? – *what does it mean?* : **motlob kor-** – *form a plan; plot* : tara motlob korer, amrar jaga loi lito – *they are scheming to take over our landholding* [A. maṭlab – *pursuit; demand*]
motlobi ['mòtlòbī] (adj) *conniving; self-interested* = **motlob + -i** ²
moto ['mòtò] (n adv) *in the sense; alike; as; in accordance* | tain afnar moto – *he's like you* : tain cacar moto gorib – *he's poor like uncle; he's as poor as uncle* : ita kaibar moto nae – *this is not fit for eating* : tain niom moto kam korcoin – *he has acted in accordance with the rules* : afnar subiḍa moto korouka – *do it at your convenience* : tain nijor moto coloin – *he goes his own way* : amra santi moto jaimu – *we'll go in a relaxed way* [B. måtå]
moton (n adv) *alike* = **moto**
mou ¹ [môu] (n) *honey* [B. mou]
mou ² (n) *breath* | **mou fala-** – *expel breath; breathe* : mou falaibar jaega nae – *there's no room to breathe* cf **mua**
moucom ['môusòm] (n) *season* [A. mausim]
mouja ['môuzā, 'môujā] (n) *village area; parish* [A. mauÐi¿ – *place, locality*]
moujud ['môujūḍ] (adj) *existing; available* [A. maujūd – *found*]
mouka ['môukā] (n) *opportunity* [A. mauqi¿ – *occasion*]
moula ['môulā] (n) *Lord; God* [A. maulā – *protector; lord*]
moulana ['môulānā] (n) *respected leader in faith* (common respectful title for Muslim clerics) [A. maulānā – *our lord*]
moulobi ['môulòbī] (n) *Muslim cleric* [A. maulawī – *follower of a Maula*]
moulud ['môulūḍ] (n) *Muslim social celebration* | moulud sorif – *formal party in celebration of the Prophet's life* [A. maulūd – *born*]
moumaci ['môumāsī] (n) *honeybee* [B. moumaci]
mour [môur] (n) *peacock* [H. mor]
mout [môut] (n) *death* [A. maut]
mouua ['môuŵā] (n) *mother's sister's husband; husband of moi*
mua ['mūā] (n) *breath* | **mua fala-** – *expel breath; breathe* cf **mou** ²
muajjen ['mūāj-jɛn] (n) *muezzin* [A. mu'aððin – *caller (to prayer)*]
mubail ['mūbāıl] (n) *mobile phone* [E.]
mubarok ['mūbāròχ] (adj) *blessed* [A. mubārak]
muc [mūs] (n) *moustache* [B. moc]
muca ['mūsā] (n) Moses [A. mūsā]

mucafir ['mūsāfīr] (n) *traveller* [A. musāfir]
mucala ['mūsālā] (n) *man with a moustache* = **muc + -ala**
mucibot ['mūsībòt] (n) *perilous situation* [A. muṣība – *calamity*]
mucolli ['mūsòl-lī] (n) *practising Muslim* [A. muṣallī – *one who prays*]
mucolman ['mūsòl-mān] (n) *Muslim* [P. musalmān]
mucolmani ['mūsòl-mānī] (n) *circumcision* | **(kar) mucolmani oe** – *(someone) gets circumcised* : aij tan fuar mucolmani oice – *today his son was circumcised* : **mucolmani kor-** – *perform the circumcision ceremony* [P. musalmānī – *Muslim practice; induction to Muslim faith community*]
muɗi ['mūɗī] (n) *grocer* | muɗir ɗukan – *grocery shop* [H. moɗī]
mufot ['mūfòt] (adj) *free of charge* [P. muft]
mugrib ['mūg-rīb] (n) *sunset; dusk* | mugribor okt – *the time for the sunset prayer* : mugribor nomaj – *the maghrib or sunset prayer* [A. maġrib – *time or place of sunset*]
muillo ['mūɪl-lɪò] (n) *value* = **mullo**
muja ['mūzā, 'mūjā] (n) *sock; socks* [P. mūza]
mujaid ['mūjāɪd, 'mūzāɪd] (n) *one who strives in the service of Islam* [A. mujāhiɗ]
muk [mūk] (n) *mouth; face; stopper* | muk kulo – *open your mouth* : tumar muk saf koro – *clean your face* : tar muk fatla – *his mouth is lightweight; he talks carelessly* : butolor muk kuae? – *where's the cap of the bottle?* : **muko** – *in one's mouth; on one's face* : tumar muko kita? – *what have you got in your mouth?* : bour muko oloiɗ – *the bride has turmeric on her face* : **muke ɗi** – *through one's mouth* : kilan kota tar muke ɗi ae – *such odd remarks come out of his mouth* : **(kar) mukor ufre** – *in (someone's) face* : amar mukor ufre na korcoin – *he contradicted me to my face* : **muk kor-** – *direct one's face* : tara janla bae muk korce – *they turned to face the window* : **muko an-** – *mention* : i kota muko anoin na jen – *please don't mention that* : **muko ɗe-** – *put in one's mouth* : kolom muko ɗio na – *don't put your pen in your mouth* : **muk ɗeka-** – *show one's face* : tan muk ɗekaita farra na – *he daren't show his face* [B. mukh < O. mukha]
muka¹ ['mūkā] (n) *stopper; cap (of bottle or jar)* < **muk**
muka² (adj) *facing; oriented* | ɗokkin muka gor – *south-facing house* ¶ **muka** (adv) *in a direction* | tain amar muka caicoin – *he looked in my direction* < **muk**
mukabela ['mūkābɛlā] (n) *confrontation* | **mukabela kor-** – *face; confront* : tara ɗusmonre mukabela korce – *they faced the enemy* ¶ **mukabela** (n adv) *in front; opposite* | tain amar mukabela boicla – *he was seated opposite me* [A. muqābala]
mukam ['mūkām] (n) *shrine of a Muslim saint* [A. maqām – *site, place*]
muki ['mūkī] (n) *a type of edible arum tuber (Colocasia esculenta)*
mukoir ['mūkòɪr] (n) *showing of the face; look-in* | **mukoir ɗe-/mukoir ɗi la-** – *look in; drop by* : tain biane ek mukoir ɗi laicla – *he dropped in this morning*
mukosto ['mūkòstò] (adj) *known by heart* | **mukosto oe / mukosto oi jae** – *gets known by heart* : cura·ta tar mukosto oi gece – *he's got that verse by heart* : gan·ta amar mukosto – *I know the song by heart* : **mukosto kor-** – *learn by heart* : iacin cura mukosto korce – *she's memorized sura Ya Sin* [B. mukhåsthå < S. mukhastha – *placed in the mouth*]
mukri ['mūkrī] (adj) *oral* | tan loge amar mukri kota roice – *I've got an oral agreement with him* : **mukri oe / mukri oi jae** – *gets learned by heart* : gan·ta amar mukri oi gece – *I've learned the song by heart* [B. mukhårit < S. mukharita]
mukta ['mūktā] (n) *pearl* [B. mukta < S. muktā]
mukti ['mūktī] (n) *liberation; freedom* | **mukti fa-** – *achieve liberation; get one's freedom* [B. mukti < S. mukti]
mukto ['mūktò] (adj) *liberated; free* [B. muktå < S. mukta]
mul [mūl] (n) *root; origin; capital* | gacor mul – *root of a plant* : binasor mul – *root cause of a disaster* : sottoir ajar fon mul - £70,000 *capital* : **mul taki** – *from the very beginning* : ami mul taki koici, oito nae – *I told you from the very outset that it wouldn't work* ¶ **mul** (adj) *of the root; basic* | mul kota – *fundamental point; the main thing* : mul biafar – *the root of the matter* : mul karon – *the basic reason* : mul foesa – *initial capital* [B. mul]

mula ['mūlā] (n) *radish* [B. mula < O. mūlā]
mulakat ['mūlāχāt] (n) *encounter* | **mulakat kor-** – *meet* : tan loge mulakat korta oimu – *I must meet up with him* [A. mulāqa]
mule ['mūlɛ] (n adv) *at the root; basically; originally* | mule tara karbari – *basically they're business people* : amra mule jantam na – *at the outset we didn't know* : **mule-u** – *at the very beginning; from the beginning* : ami mule-u koiclam – *I said so right at the beginning* : tar kam·ta korbar irađa mule-u acil na – *he never had any intention of doing the job from the word go* < **mul**
mulla ['mūl-lā] (n) *cleric; mullah* [P. mullā]
mullagiri ['mūl-lā-gīrī] (n) *acting as a mullah* | **mullagiri kor-** – *work as a mullah* : tain age mullagiri korta – *he used to be a mullah* [P. mullāgārī]
mullo ['mūl-lò] (n) *value* | ou gorir mullo koto oibo? – *what would be the value of this clock? how much would this clock be worth?* : hou samanar bout mullo – *those pieces of furniture are very valuable* [B. mullå < S. mūlya – *price*]
mulloban ['mūl-lòbān] (adj) *valuable; precious* [B. mullåban < S. mūlyavāna]
mulluk ['mūl-lūk] (n) *kingdom; country* | «jur jar, mulluk tar – *whoever holds the power holds the country* [A. mulk]
mum [mūm] (n) *wax* [P. mūm]
mumin ['mūmīn] (n) *faithful Muslim* [A. mu'mīn – *believer*]
munafa ['mūnāfā] (n) *profit; gain* | **munafa kor-** – *make profit* [A. manāfiⱬ - *advantages, gains*]
munafik ['mūnāfīk] (n) *dissembler; hypocrite* [A. munāfiq]
munajat ['mūnāzāt, 'mūnājāt] (n) *personal prayer* [A. munājāh – *tête-à-tête*]
muorrom [mū 'òr-ròm] (n) *Muharram (first month in the Muslim calendar); Muharram (Muslim festival commemorating the Battle of Karbala)* [A. muḥarram – *declared sacrosanct*]
mur [mūr] (n) *bend; fold; road junction* | kaforo mur đeka jae – *a fold in the cloth is visible* : đui rastar mur – *junction of two roads; crossroads* : **mure** – *at a junction* : mure tamaiba – *stop (your vehicle) at the junction* : **mur de-/mur đi la-** – *bend; fold* : kagjo mur đein na jen – *please don't fold the paper* [B. moɽ]
mura¹ ['mūrā] (n) *stump; head; heel* | gacor mura – *tree stump* : macor mura – *fish head* : faur mura – *heel of the foot* [B. muɽa]
mura² (n) *bend* = **mur**
mura- (vt) *bend* | **murai le-** – *bend; twist* : fuae tar fau murai lice – *the boy has sprained his ankle* [B. muɽa-]
murđa ['mūrđā] (n) *male* | afnar bilai ota magi na murđa? – *is that cat of yours a female or a male?* [P. mard – *man*]
murga ['mūr-gā] (n) *male fowl; cock* [U. murgā < P. murġ – *bird*]
murgi ['mūr-gī] (n) *fowl; hen* | joŋli murgi – *wild jungle fowl* : enda-ala murgi – *laying hen* : murgir guc – *chicken meat* : murgir enda – *hen's eggs* [U. murgī < P. murġ]
muri ['mūrī] (n) *popped rice* [B. muɽi]
murid ['mūrīd] (n) *(Sufi) disciple* [A. murīd – *aspirant*]
murmura ['mūr-mūrā] (n) *cartilage (in meat)*
murobbi ['mūròb-bī] (n) *person of a senior generation; elder* | murobbire calam đitae – *you should greet your elders with a salaam* : murobbi manus, boibar đeuka – *here's an elderly person, so please make space for them to sit* [A. murabbi – *one who rears (children)*]
murobbiana ['mūròb-bī-ānā] (n) *acting like an elder; condescending manners*
murug ['mūrūg] (n) *male fowl; cock* [P. murġ – *bird*]
muskil ['mūš-kīl] (n) *awkwardness; difficulty* | muskil oi gece – *a tricky situation has arisen* : ino anat muskil oibo – *there will be difficulties in bringing it here* : muskilor maje forci – *I've run into a load of problems* : muskilor biafar – *an awkward business* : koto boro muskil! – *oh, what a nuisance!* [A. muškil – *difficult* × muškila – *difficulty*]
mussid ['mūš-šīd] (n) *(Sufi) master* [A. muršid – *spiritual guide*]
musti ['mūš-tī] (n) *fist* [B. musti < S. muśti]

mustime ['mūš-tīmɛ] (adv) *in small quantity* | sufari roice ni? mustime kok·ta – *are there any betelnuts left? only a very few*   [H. mušti maiⁿ - *in the fist*]
mut [mūt] (n) *total* | mut koto oice? – *how much is the total?* : mut egaro fon – *the total is eleven pounds* : **mutor ufre** – *on the whole; in sum*: mutor ufre bala coler – *all said and done, things are going quite well* : **mut kor-** – *make a total; add up* : one mut korouka, koto oice – *now add up and see how much it comes to* ¶ **mut** (adj) *total; overall* | mut foriman – *the total amount* : mut koroc – *total expenditure; overall cost* : mut karbar – *the whole business* : **mut kota** – *the overall point* : mut kota, bul oi gece – *the bottom line is that there has been a mistake* : mut kota oilo, tara aito nae – *it boils down to this: they're not going to come* : somoe gece gi, mut kota – *in other words it's too late* ¶ **mut** (adv) *in total* | mut koe·ta? – *how many are there in total?* : mut baro·ta – *twelve in all*   [B. mot]
muta¹ ['mūtā] (adj) *fat; coarse; bulky; great* | tar fet muta – *he has a fat belly* : muta kafor – *coarse cloth* : muta cear – *a bulky chair* : muta basko – *a great big box* : muta kam – *a sizeable task* : muta karbar – *a significant business* : muta aoaj – *a loud noise* : muta beton – *a hefty salary*   [B. mota]
muta² (n) *(closed) fist* | **muta kor-** – *clench one's fist* : amar at muta kortam fari na – *I can't close my fist*   [B. mutha < O. muśti]
mutamuti ['mūtāmūtī] (adv) *more or less* | mutamuti tik – *more or less correct; pretty much all right* : mutamuti boro – *fairly large* : tan soril mutamuti bala – *her health is fairly good* = **mut**
mutasuta ['mūtāšūtā] (adj) *fat; corpulent*   = **muta**¹
mute ['mūtɛ] (n adv) *in total; all in all; only* | mute sob tik – *overall, all's well* : fac·jon aicoin mute – *five people came in all* : mute fac·jon? – *five in all? only five?* : **mute-u na / mute-u nae** – *not at all* : tara mute-u kam kore na – *they do no work at all* : ɖin·ta mute-u bala nae – *the weather is not at all good*   < **mut**
muti ['mūtī] (n) *fist; fistful* | ek muti cail – *a handful of rice*   [B. muthi < O. muśti]
mutmat ['mūt-māt] (adv) *in total; all in all* | mutmat focis·jon amra – *there are twenty-five of us in total* : mutmat tik ace hokolta – *everything is all right on the whole*   = **mut**
muto¹ ['mūtò] (adj) *fat*   = **muta**¹
muto² (n) *handful*   = **muti**
mut [mūt] (n) *urine*   = **mutro**
mut- (vi) *urinate* | he beto mutce – *he has wet his bed* : amma, muttam! – *Mum, I want to go to the toilet!* : **muti le-** – *urinate*
mutfecra ['mūt-fɛs-rā] (n) *measles*
mutro ['mūtrò] (n) *urine*   [B. mutrå < S. mūtra]

n

na [nā] (int) *no* | afne kamo ni? na – *are you employed? no* : afne ca kaita ni? ji na – *would you like to have some tea? no, thanks* : sađ đitam? na na na! – *may I help? oh, no, don't even think of it!* : runa ance; na, minae ance – *Runa got it; no, it was Mina who got it* : kita oice? na, kelanit aclam – *what's the matter? oh nothing, I was just playing* ¶ **na** (n) *negation; a spoken "no"* | ha na ek·ta kouka – *please say either yes or no* : na kor- – *say no; give a refusal; make a prohibition* : tain na koroin – *he says no; he refuses* : abba na korcoin – *Dad has vetoed it* : ei! na korci! – *hey, I told you not to do that!* : **na kori đe-** – *give a refusal* : tare na kori đici – *I've said no to him* : cafcofa na kori đeuka – *give them a clear refusal* [B. na [1]]

na [2] (adv) *not;* (with present imperative) *why not* | ami jani na – *I do not know* : tain kunta korcoin na – *he has not done anything* : ota na – *not that one* : buđbare na – *not on Monday* : kita koila? afnare na – *what was that you said? oh, I wasn't addressing you* : jaio na – *do not go* : jao na – *why don't you go* : đekuk na – *why no let them see* : na đeke! – *what does it matter if they do see!* : na take! – *it doesn't matter, let it be!* : **na .. na ..** – *neither .. nor ..* : na gorom na tanda – *neither hot nor cold* : na ace cail na ace dail – *there is neither rice nor dhal* : na jane baŋla na jane iŋlis – *he knows neither Bengali nor English*: **na ni?** – *is it not so?* : aij buđbar na ni? – *it's Wednesday today, isn't it?* : afne kail aiba na ni? – *you will come tomorrow, won't you?* : **.. ni na / .. ni na na** – *whether .. or not* : jani na, aij meg đibo ni na – *I don't know whether it will rain or not* : tara jikaice, afne jaita ni na – *they asked whether or not you'd be going* : ke koito fare, dorojat haca tala mara acil ni na na – *who can say whether the door was really locked or not* [B. na [2]] **Note**: Negative particle. See also **nae**.

na [3] (conj) *or else* | ekđin na ekđin – *one day or another; someday* : ek·ta loita na đui·ta? – *will you take one or two?* : kun somoe gucol korta, kanir age na bađe? – *when do you want to have a bath, before or after the meal?* : jani na, tara roito na jaito – *I don't know whether they'll stay or go* : jikauka, tai korce na ar keu korce – *ask whether it was she who did it or someone else* : **na kita?** – *or what? don't you agree?* : citi·kan arai licoin na kita? – *have you lost the letter, or what?* : one jai gi, na kita? – *let's make a move now. what do you say?* [B. na [3]]

na- (vi) *bathe (in open water)* | afne naicoin ni? – *have you had your dip (in the pond or river)?* [B. na-]

nabalig ['nābālīġ] (adj) *juvenile; under-age* [P. nā + A. bāliġ – *reaching legal age*]

nabi ['nābī] (n) *navel* [B. nabhi < S. nābhi]

nac [1] [nās] (n) *dance; stage performance* | futulor nac – *puppet show* : **nac đeka-** – *dance; put on a dance performance* : hurutae nac đekaice – *the children performed some dancing* [B. nac]

nac [2] (n) *nurse* | nac amrar goro ain – *the nurse comes to our house* [E.]

nac- (vi) *dance* [B. nac-]

naca- ['nāsā] (vt) *cause to dance; lead on a song and dance* | gaur mainse tane koto nacaice – *the village people gave him a lot of bother* [B. naca-]

nacanaci ['nāsānāsī] (n) *dancing about* < **nac-**

nacar ['nāsār] (adj) *destitute* [P. nācār – *helpless*]

nacari [1] ['nāsārī] (n) *distressed circumstances* [P. nācārī]

nacari [2] (n) *nursery* | tai nacarit jae – *she goes to nursery school* [E.]

nacij ['nāsīz] (adj) *worthless* [P. nācīz]

nađan ['nāđān] (n) *good-for-nothing* [P. nādān – *ignoramus*]

nae [1] [nāɛ] (adv) *not in existence; not* | đeu nae – *goblins do not exist* : amar baf nae – *my father is not alive* : tan gari nae – *he does not have a car* : đuđ nae – *there's no milk* : ekebare nae na – *it's not that there's none at all; there is a little bit* : ou kafor sunđor nae – *this cloth is not pretty* : tara mucolman nae – *they are not Muslims* : tara jaito nae – *they*

will not go : aij meg ḋito nae – *it will not rain today* : **nae ni?** – *is it not so?* : tolet ace, nae ni? – *there is a toilet, isn't there?* : aij buḋbar nae ni? – *it's Wednesday today, isn't it?* : afne ḋekta nae ni? – *don't you want to have a look?* : tumra jaitae nae ni? – *aren't you going to go?* : **nae o-/nae oi ja-** – *become non-existent; vanish* : amar kolom nae oi gece – *my pen has gone missing* : tain maje maje nae oi jain – *he sometimes disappears*   [B. nai]
Note: Negative particle: (1) serving on its own as the present tense of **ac-** for "is not", "are not", "am not", and (2) used with all other verbs to negate the habitual tense only (e.g. **korta nae**).

nae ² (conj) *or else* | tain aita acla nae fon korta acla – *he ought to have come, or else telephoned*   = **na** ³ + **oe**
nafit ['nāfĭt] (n) *barber*   [B. napit < S. nāpita]
naformani ['nāfòr-mānī] (n) *waywardness; immorality*   [P. nā farmānī – *disobedience*]
nafta ['nāf-tā] (n) *barber* (used as a term of abuse)   = **nafit**
naga ['nāgā] (n) *Naga* | naga moric – *Naga chilli (very hot type of chilli)*
nagat ['nāgāt] (post) *up to; by* | buḋbar nagat bar caimu – *I'll wait until Wednesday* : fac·ta nagat ses oibo – *it will end towards five o'clock*   = **lagat** ²
nagorik ['nāgòrīk] (n) *citizen*   [B. nagårik < S. nāgarika]
nagra ['nāg-rā] (n) *soft leather shoe*   [B. nagra]
nagri ['nāg-rī] (n/adj) *(pertaining to) a simplified form of the Devnagari script (used uniquely in the Sylhet area for recording ballads)*   [S. ḋevanagarī]
nai [nāı] (adv) *not* | ami kusi nai – *I am not pleased* : amra hurumanus nai – *we are not children*   Note: Arguably **nai** and **nae** are parts of a defective verb **na-** "not to be".
naile ['nāılɛ] (adv) *otherwise; alternatively* | takle ace naile nae – *if it is it is, if it ain't it ain't* : one ses koro, naile osubiḋa oibo – *finish it now, otherwise there'll be problems* : kail naile forhu – *tomorrow, or else the day after* : naile ino takta faroin – *alternatively you could stay here* : aij roibbar naile gelam ne – *if today wasn't Sunday I'd have gone* : tain naile ami morlam ne – *if it wasn't for him I'd have died* : bouka naile – *well then, why don't you sit down*   = **na** ² + **oile**
naior ['nāıòr] (n) *home of a married woman's kin* | **naior ja-** – (of a woman) *go to the home of one's parents or relatives* : bou naior gece – *daughter-in-law has gone to visit her kin* : **naior ḋe-** – *send (a woman) to the home of her parents or relatives* : tain naior ḋein na – *he won't let her go and visit her parents*   [B. naighår < O. jñāti gr̥ha]
naiori ['nāıòrī] (n) *married woman on a visit to her kin*   < **naior**
najaej ['nājāɛz] (adj) *not permitted; unpermissible*   [P. nā + A. jā'iz – *permissible*]
najeal ['nāzéāl] (adj) *sorely tried; harassed* | **najeal kor-** – *torment; harass* : mukti baini fak armire najeal korcil – *the liberation fighters harassed the Pakistan army*   [P. hāl-e-naz – *dire straits* < A. ḥāl – *condition* + A. nazʿ – *death struggle*]
najic ['nāzīs, 'nājīs] (adj) *unclean*   [A. najis]
najil ['nāzīl, 'nājīl] (adj) *revealed (scriptures)* | **najil o-** - *(scripture) be revealed*   [U. nāzil – *revealed* < A. nuzūl – *descent; revelation*]
nak [nāχ] (n) *nose* | tumar nak fuco! – *wipe your nose!* : amar nak bonḋ oi gece – *my nose is blocked* : nakor ful – *nose ornament* : aŋgul nako harain na – *one shouldn't stick one's finger in one's nose* : **nake ḋi** – *through the nose* : tar nake ḋi lou forer – *blood is running through his nose; his nose is bleeding* : tar nake ḋi goler – *his nose is dribbling* : **nake lage** – *it offends the nose* : hutkir boe nake lager – *a smell of dried fish is assailing the nose; that dried fish smells awful* : **nak dake** – *the nose makes a noise* : raitku tan nak dake – *he snores at night* : **nak daka-** – *snore* : **nak jar-** – *blow one's nose* : **nak ḋeka-** – *be haughty; be snobbish*   [B. nak]
nakari ['nāχārī] (n) *tip of the nose*
nake-muke ['nāχɛmūkɛ] (adv) *all over the face* | tar nake-muke rokto – *he's got blood all over his face* : he nake-muke kar – *he's stuffing his face; he's eating greedily and messily*   < **nak, muk**
nakra- ['nāχ-rā] (vi) *snore*   cf **nak**
nakua- ['nāχŵā] (vi) *speak nasally; whine*   cf **nak**

nala ['nālā] (n) *water channel; stream* [B. nala]
nalis ['nālīš] (n) *complaint* | **nalis kor-** – *make a complaint; complain* : tara amar gece nalis korce – *they have complained to me* [P. nāliš]
nam [nām] (n) *name; reputation* | afnar nam kouka – *please tell me your name* : tair nam jani na – *I don't know her name* : hou restonor nam ace – *that restaurant has a good reputation* : .. **namor** – *having the name* .. : i namor keure cini na – *I don't know anyone of this name* : coiod namor keu acoin ni ino? – *is there anyone here with the name Syed?* : ek namor dui·jon manus – *two people with the same name* : **(keur) name** – *in the name (of someone)* : fuar name gor rakcoin – *they bought a house in their son's name* : allar name suru kori – *let's make a start in God's name* : afnar name citi aice – *a letter addressed to you has come* : **(keur) name nam** – *of the same name (as someone)* : afnar name nam tan – *he has the same name as you* : **nam oe / nam oi jae** – *one's reputation builds up* : tan bakka nam oi gece – *he's acquired quite a reputation* : **nam kor-/nam kori le-** – *make a name (for oneself)* : tain nam kori licoin – *he's established his name* : **(kar) nam kor-** – *honour (someone's) name; praise; mention* : tara afnar nam kore – *they speak well of you* : he jaibar nam-u kore na – *he doesn't even mention the idea of going* : **(kar) nam dor-** – *mention (someone's) name; address (someone) by name* : tar batijar nam-u dorcoin na – *he didn't even mention his nephew* : baisabre nam dori dakoin na – *you aren't supposed to address an elder brother by name*: **allar nam lo-** – *take God's name; say "bismillah"* : tara allar nam loia ruana dice – *they said "bismillah" and set off* : **nam rak-/nam raki le-** – *bestow a name; name* : gedir nam rakcoin ni? – *have you given the baby a name yet?* : noea goror lagi sundor ek·ta nam raki louka – *please choose a nice name for the new house* [B. nam]
-nama ['nāmā] (n) *deed; document* [P. nāma – *record*]
nami ['nāmī] (adj) *well-known* [P. nāmī]
namjada ['nām-zādā, 'nām-jādā] (adj) *famous* [P. nāmzad – *nominated*]
namjari ['nām-zārī, 'nām-jārī] (n) *(land) registration* = **nam + jari**
namkora ['nām-xòrā] (adj) *famous* = **nam + kora** ¹
nam-nima ['nām-nīmā] (n) *name* = **nam**
nam-tikana ['nām-tīkāna] (n) *name and address* = **nam + tikana**
nan [nān] (n) *leavened white flatbread* [P. nān – *bread*]
nana ¹ ['nānā] (adj) *various* [B. nana < O. nānā]
nana ² (n) *maternal grandfather; great-uncle* (Muslim kinship term for one's mother's father, or any brother or same-generation male cousin of either parent of one's mother)
nanan ['nānān] (adj) *various* | nanan kicimor fol – *various types of fruit* : nanan jator manus – *people of various kinds or nations* : nanan babe – *in various ways* = **nana** ¹
nananta ['nānāntā] (pron) *various things* | nananta lagbo – *various different things will be needed* : tara nananta matce – *they said all sorts of things* = **nanan + -ta** ²
nani ['nānī] (n) *maternal grandmother; great-aunt* (Muslim kinship term for one's mother's mother, or any brother or same-generation female cousin of either parent of one's mother, or the wife of any *nana*.)
nao ['nāò] (v) *take* (present imperative) < **ne-**
naracara ['nārāsārā] (n) *moving about; movement* = **laracara**
naraj ['nārāz, 'nārāj] (adj) *displeased* | **naraj o-/naraj oi ja-** – *be displeased; get disgruntled* : naraj oin na jen – *please don't be offended* [P. nārāzī]
nari ¹ ['nārī] (n) *woman* [B. nari < S. nārī]
nari ² (n) *entrails* [B. nari]
nari-buri ['nārībūrī] (n) *entrails* = **nari** ² + **buri** ²
nariul ['nārīūl] (n) *coconut* [H. nāriyal]
nas [nāš] (n) *ruination* | **nas o-/nas oi ja-** – *be ruined; get spoilt* : amar hokolti nas oi gece – *everything has been ruined for me; my life is in ruins* : **nas kor-/nas kori le-** – *ruin* : rajai nas kori lico tumra – *you lot have ruined the bed cover* [B. nas < S. nāša]
nasa- ['nāšā] (vt) *ruin* | tara nasaice amare – *they've ruined me* cf **nas**
nasfoti ['nāšfòtī] (n) *pear* [P. nāšpātī]

nasiḋ ['nāšīḋ] (n) *Muslim religious song*   [A. našīd]
nasta ['nāstā] (n) *light refreshment; snack; breakfast* | ca nasta kaia jaiba – *do have tea and snacks before you go* : **nasta kor-** – *have breakfast; have a snack* : nasta korcoin ni? – *have you had your breakfast?*   [P. nāšitāī – *breakfast*]
nat [nāt] (n) *(engineering) nut*   [E.]
nata ['nātā] (adj) *spoilt* | **nata o-/nata oi ja-** – *be spoilt* : kainci nata oi gece – *the scissors are no good any more* : **nata kor-/nata kori le-** – *spoil* : ḋeko, cear nata kori libae – *watch out or you'll wreck the chair* = **nosto**
nat-boltu ['nāt-bòl-tu] (n) *nuts and bolts*
natok ['nātòχ] (n) *stage drama*   [B. natåk < S. nātaka]
natbou ['nāt-bôu] (n) *grandson's wife* = **nati + bou**
nati ['nātī] (n) *grandson; great-nephew*   [B. nati]
natin ['nātīn] (n) *granddaughter; great-niece*   [B. natni]
natinaton ['nātīnātòn] (n) *grandchildren*
natinosa ['nātīnòšā] (n) *grandchildren*
natjamai ['nāt-jāmāɪ] (n) *granddaughter's husband*   = **natin + jamai**
nau [nāu] (n) *boat*   [B. nao < S. nau]
naujubilla ['nāuzūbīl-lā] (int) *God help us!*   [A. na¿ūÐu bi l-lāh – *we seek refuge in God*]
ne [nɛ] (adv) *indeed* | farle gelam ne – *had I been able I would indeed have gone* : age aile ḋekla ne – *if you'd come sooner you would have seen* : tik ace, ḋimu ne – *it's all right, I will give it to you*   Note: A particle used to back up the verb, in a sentence where a hypothetical or future event is referred to. Used only with the future tense or hypothetical-historic tense.
ne- (vt) *take; get* | e huruṭṭa! neo aia! – *hey, children, come and get it!* : ei nao – *here you are, take it* : o neo cai! – *well I say, fancy that!* : tan noea leḋar loge kori nicoin – *he took his new suitcase with him* : **ne- gi** – *take; go off with* : nei gi? – *may I take it?* : neuka gi – *go on, take it; please do take it* : amar kolom nice gi – *he's gone off with my pen*   [B. ne-]
neijjo ['nɛɪj-jò] (adj) *fair* | neijjo bicar – *fair trial* : neijjo ḋam – *a fair price* : tain neijjo kota koicoin – *he has said fair words; he has spoken truly*   [B. nejjo < S. nyāyya – *just*]
nek [nɛk] (adj) *virtuous*   [P. nek]
neki ['nɛkī] (n) *virtue; merit; moral credit* | afnar neki oibo – *you will acquire merit (for doing so)* : tain neki lutra – *he's reaping moral credit*   [P. nekī]
neo ['nɛò] (v) *take* (future imperative)   < **ne-**
nera ['nɛrā] (adj) *bald*   [B. neṛa]
nesa ['nɛšā] (n) *addiction; intoxication; inebriation* | tan gua kanir nesa – *she's addicted to chewing betelnut* : tar ganjar nesa oi gece – *he's got hooked on cannabis* : bidio ḋekar nesa cartae oibae – *you must kick the habit of watching videos* : tara ek nesar maje – *they're intoxicated; they're high*   [A. nišwa – *intoxication*]
neta ['nɛtā] (n) *leader*   [B. neta < S. netā]
neul [nɛul] (n) *mongoose*   [B. neul]
ni¹ [nī] (int) *is it so?* | aij sombar ni? – *today's Monday, is it?* : iguin afnar ni? – *these are yours, are they?* : keu aicla ni? – *did anyone come?* : afne kusi ni? – *are you pleased?* : oice ni? – *is that it? are you done?* : sunḋor ni koin! – *so you think that's pretty, do you!* : aito ni koice? – *did they say they were coming?*   Note: An interrogative particle whose only function is to signal that what is being uttered is a question.
ni² (conj) *or else* | sombar ni moŋgolbar, buli lici – *I've forgotten whether it was Monday or Tuesday* : tain roita ni jaita? – *will he stay or will he go?* : lal·ta ni kala·ta, kun·ta? – *which one, the red or the black?* : **.. ni na / .. ni na na** – *whether .. or not* : ke jane, tara taiar ni na – *who knows whether they're ready or not* : acoin ni na, koitam fari na – *I can't say whether she's here or not* : jani liba, tain raji ni na na – *find out whether or not he's willing*   cf **na³**
-ni (noun suffix) *female form; -ess* | ḋaktorni – *lady doctor* : mastorni – *female teacher*
niae ['nīāɛ] (n) *fairness*   [B. nnay < S. nyāya]
niamot ['nīāmòt] (n) *divine bounty*   [A. ni¿ma – *favour*]

nib- [nīb] (vi) *cease to burn; die out* | **nibi ja-** – *stop burning; go out* : aguin nibi jar – *the fire is dying down* : batti nibi gece – *the lights have gone out* [B. nibh-]
niba- ['nībā] (vt) *extinguish; put out* | batti nibaitam ni? – *shall I turn the lights out?* : **nibai de-** – *extinguish; put out* : aguin nibai dice – *they've put the fire out* [B. nibha-]
nic [nīs] (n) *low part; underneath; lower storey* | nic tone beg bair korouka – *get a bag from underneath* : tara nic taki ufre aice – *they've come up from downstairs* : **nicor** – *of below; of downstairs* : nicor droaro dekouka – *look in the bottom drawer* : nicor janla kula – *the downstairs window is open* : **nice** – *below; underneath; downstairs* : nice kagoj ace – *there's some paper underneath* : tara nice gece – *they've gone downstairs* [B. nic]
nica ['nīsā] (adj) *low* | nica deoal – *a low wall* : doroja ektu nica – *the doorway is rather low* : **nica kor-/nica kori le-** – *make lower; lower; keep low* : mata nica kori louka – *keep your head down* [B. nicu]
niccoe ['nīt-tšòɛ] (adv) *certainly; undoubtedly* | amra niccoe jaimu – *we shall certainly go* : afnar kota niccoe tik ace – *what you said is surely correct* [B. niscåy < S. niščaya – *ascertainment*]
nice ['nīsɛ] (n adv) *below; underneath; downstairs* | nice dekouka – *look underneath* : tain nice gecoin – *she's gone downstairs* : kicin·ta nice – *the kitchen is downstairs* : tebulor nice kita – *there's something under the table* : dos bocoror nice – *under ten years; less than ten years* : foncasor nice – *less than fifty* < **nic**
nictala ['nīs-tālā] (n) *ground floor* = **nic + tala ²**
nicu ['nīsū] *low; lowered* | mata nicu kor- – *lower one's head* [B. nicu]
nid ['nīd] (n) *sleep; sleepiness* | nid lage – *sleepiness is felt* : amar nid lager – *I'm feeling sleepy* [B. nidra < S. nidrā]
niddes ['nīd-dɛš] (n) *indication; directions* = **nirdes**
nihat ['nīhāt] (adv) *extremely* | nihat sundor – *extremely beautiful* : nihat sorol – *exceedingly simple-minded* [A. nihāya – *extremity*]
nij [nīz, nīj] (pron) *oneself* | **nijor** – *of oneself; one's own* : tumar nijor juta ano – *fetch your own shoes* : gor afnar nijor ni? – *is it your own house?* : tar nijor dus – *it's his own fault* : **nije** – *oneself* (instrumental) : tain nije korcla – *he did it himself* : ami nije jaimu – *I shall go myself* : tai nije koicil – *she herself said so* : **nije nije** – *by oneself; on one's own* : tai nije nije hiki lice – *she has learned it all on her own* : tumi nije nije kortae – *you're supposed to do it by yourself* : **nijere** – *(to) oneself* (objective) : afne nijere kosto dira – *you're giving yourself trouble* : he nijere cine na – *he doesn't know himself* : **nijera** – *oneselves* : tara nijera befsa korto – *they want to start a business themselves* : amra nijera jaitam farmu – *we'll be able to find the way ourselves* : **nijerar** – *of oneselves; ones' own* : tarar nijerar gor ace – *they have a house of their own* [B. nij]
nijnam ['nīz-nām] (n) *proper name*
nika ['nīkā] (n) *wedding* [A. nikāh]
nikal- ['nīkāl] (v) *get out; draw out* | befsa taki foesa nikalce – *they got money out of the business* [H. nikāl-]
nikot ['nīkòt] (adj) *close* | nikot aittio – *close relative* [B. nikåt < S. nikata]
nikotborti ['nīkòt-bòr-tī] (adj) *nearby; neighbouring* | nikotborti bari – *neighbouring homestead* : dukan nikotborti – *a shop is nearby* [B. nikåtbårti]
nikote ['nīkòtɛ] (adv) *nearby; close by* | tarar gor nikote – *their house is nearby* : mocjidor nikote madrasa – *the school is close to the mosque* < **nikot**
nil [nīl] (n/adj) *blue* [B. nil < O. nīla]
nim [nīm] (adv) *in part; half* | nim raji – *partially in agreement; half willing* : nim mulla – *mullah who is incompletely qualified* [P. nīm – *half*]
nimok ['nīmòχ] (n) *salt* [P. namak]
nimok-haram ['nīmòχ-hārām] (adj) *ungrateful (to a benefactor); treacherous*
nin [nīn] (adj) *deep* | fani·ta nin ace – *the water is deep* [O. nimna – *low; deep*]
ninda ['nīndā] (n) *censure; criticism* | **ninda kor-** – *criticize; disparage* : tara kanoka cacir ninda kore – *they criticize auntie gratuitously* [B. ninda < S. nindā – *blame*]

niom ['nīòm] (n) *rule; usual practice* | kelar niom manta oiba – *you have to observe the rules of the game* : he niom omainno korce – *he has broken the rules* : ou ofisor niom bala – *the system in this office is a good one* : dain at ɖi kanir niom amrar – *our custom is to eat with the right hand* : tan ɖos·tat gumanir niom – *his habit is to go to bed at ten o'clock* : **niom nae** – *there is no rule; it is against the rules* : mocjiɖo juta finɖar niom nae – *it's not the done thing to wear shoes in the mosque* : ino kelaibar niom nae – *you're not supposed to play here* : **niomor bitre** – *within the rules* : **niom kor-** – *make a rule; adopt a practice* : ruj ek gonta atibar niom korci – *I've made it a rule to have an hour's walk each day* [B. niyâm < S. niyama – *regulation*]
niom-kanun ['nīòm-χānūn] (n) *rules and regulations* = **niom + kanun**
niontron ['nīòn-tròn] (n) *control* | niontronor bitre – *under control* : niontronor baire – *out of control* : **niontron kor-** – *control* [B. niyântrân < S. niyantraṇa – *restraining*]
niot ['nīòt] (n) *intention; plan* | afnar niot kita? – *what are your intentions?* : tar niot bala nae – *his intentions are no good* : nomajor niot – *formal intention to pray (a prescribed prelude to prayer)* : rujar niot – *intention to fast* : **(kar) niot ace** – *(someone) has an intention* : tan ɖeso jaoar niot – *he intends to go to Bangladesh* : amar befsa korar niot acil na – *I had no intention of going into business* : **niot kor-** – *form an intention; make a resolution* : amra niot korci, gari loitam – *we have decided we should buy a car* : tain etimkana korar niot korcoin – *she has resolved to set up an orphanage* [A. niyya]
nira- ['nīrā] (v) *do weeding with a hoe*
niraɖara ['nīrāɖārā] (adv) *in a continuous stream* | niraɖara fani forer – *water is streaming down* : niraɖara koroc oe – *expenditure continues relentlessly* [O. nir-ɖhārā – *outflow*]
nirafot ['nīrāfòt] (adj) *free of danger* [B. nirapâɖ < S. nirāpaɖa]
nirafotta ['nīrāfòttā] (n) *freedom from danger; safety; security* : ino nirafotta nae – *there's no security here; this place is unsafe* [B. nirapâtta < S. nirāpattā]
nirai ['nīrāi] (adj) *peaceful; quiet* | nirai jaega – *a quiet spot* : fua·ta ekere nirai – *the boy is very quiet indeed* ¶ **nirai** (adv) *peacefully; quietly* | huruta nirai boi takce – *the children have stayed sitting there quietly* [B. nirihâ < S. nirīha – *inert*]
niraicirai ['nīrāisīrāi] (adj/adv) *peaceful(ly); quiet(ly)* = **nirai**
niramis ['nīrāmīš] (n) *vegetarian food* [B. niramis < S. nirāmiśa – *meatless*]
nirani ['nīrānī] (v n) *hoeing; weeding* < **nira-**
niranobboi ['nīrānòb-bòi] (nº) *ninety-nine* [B. niranâbbâi]
niras ['nīrāš] (adj) *devoid of hope* | **niras o-/niras oi ja-** – *lose hope* : oto sokal niras oin na jen – *don't give up hope so soon* [B. niras < S. nirāśa]
nirbor ['nīr-bòr] (adj) *dependent* | tara amar ufre nirbor – *they rely on me / they are my dependants* : **nirbor kor-** – *depend* : tara afnar ufre nirbor kore – *they depend on you* : abaoar ufre nirbor kore – *it depends on the weather* [B. nirbhâr]
nirɖes ['nīrɖɛš] (n) *indication; directions* [B. nirɖes < S. nirɖeśa]
niribili ['nīrībīlī] (n) *tranquillity; peace and quiet* | ino niribili nae – *there's no peace here* : niribilir maje taktam cai – *we want to live in peace and quiet* ¶ **niribili** (adj) *tranquil; peaceful* | niribili jaega – *a tranquil spot* [B. niribili < O. nirālaya – *quiet place*]
nisan [nī'š'ān] (n) *signal; flag* [P. nišān – *sign*]
nisani ['nīšānī] (n) *sign; symbol* [B. nisani < P. nišānī]
niseɖ¹ ['nīšɛɖ] (n) *prohibition; ban* | **niseɖ kor-** – *prohibit; forbid; say no* : amra jaitam tain niseɖ korcoin – *he has forbidden us to go* : tare niseɖ korouka, ino kelaito nae – *tell him he's not to play here* [B. niseɖh < S. niśeɖha]
niseɖ² (adj) *prohibited; forbidden* | ino cigret kaoa niseɖ – *smoking is prohibited here* : mocjiɖo juta finɖa niseɖ – *wearing shoes in the mosque is forbidden* [B. nisiɖɖhâ < S. niśiɖɖha]
nisokti ['nīšòχtī] (n) *weakness* | **nisokti lage** – *one feels weak* [B. nisâkti < S. nihśakti]
nistur ['nīštūr] (adj) *cruel* [B. nisthur < S. niśthura]
nitanda ['nītāndā] (adj) *free of worry* | **nitanda o-/nitanda oi ja-** – *cease to worry; be relieved* : one amra nitanda oi geci – *now we can relax*

niti ['nītī] *rule; rules; morals* [B. niti < S. nīti]
noab [nò'āb] (n) *Nawab; nabob* [A. nuwwāb – *representatives*]
nobboi ['nòb-bòɪ] (nº) *ninety* [B. nåbbåi]
nobi ['nòbī] (n) *prophet* [A. nabīy]
nocib ['nòsīb] (n) *fate* | **nocib kor-** – *(of God) determine one's fate* : alla tane beest nocib koruk – *may God fate him to go to Heaven* [A. naṣīb – *share, lot*]
nociot ['nòsīòt] (n) *homily* [A. naṣīha – *sincere advice*]
noɖi ['nòɖī] (n) *river* [B. nåɖi]
noɖi-nala ['nòɖīnālā] (n) *rivers and streams* = **noɖi + nala**
noe [nòɛ] (nº) *nine* [B. nåy]
noea ['nòɛā] (adj) *new* | noea gari – *a new car* : noea catro-catri – *new pupils* : tara ino noea – *they're new here* : karfit ekere noea – *the carpet is brand new* : oalo noea roŋ ɖitam – *we want to put fresh paint on the wall* : **noea kor-/noea kori le-** – *make new* [H. nayā]
nofol ['nòfòl] (adj) *non-essential (prayers)* [A. nafl – *supererogatory deed*]
nogoɖ ['nògòɖ] (n) *cash; ready money* | nogoɖ ɖi laice – *they've paid in cash* [A. naqd]
nogor ['nògòr] (n) *township* [B. någår < S nagara]
nojɖik ['nòz-ɖīk] (adj) *close; nearby* [P. nazdīk]
nojɖike ['nòz-ɖīkɛ] (n adv) *close by; near by* < **nojɖik**
nojor ['nòzòr, 'nòjòr] (n) *sight; vision; look; evil eye* | tan nojor tik nae – *his eyesight isn't good* : **nojor fore** – *the evil eye is cast* : tar ufre nojor force – *someone has cast the evil eye on him* : **ek nojore** – *in one glance; at a glance* : ek nojore cinci tare – *I recognized him at a glance* : **nojore fore** – *it comes to one's notice* : befar·ta tan nojore forcil – *the matter came to her notice* : ek kali gor tarar nojore force – *they have noticed a house which is empty* : **nojor rak-** – *pay attention; keep an eye* : hurutar bae nojor rakoin jen – *please do keep an eye on the children* : **nojor kor-** – *look; watch over* : alla nojor korce tare – *God has looked kindly on him* : **nojor fala-** – *cast an evil eye* : tair ufre ke nojor falaice – *someone has cast the eye on her* [A. naẓar]
nokol ['nòχòl] (n) *copying; copy; imitation* | omiga gorir nokol – *an imitation Omega watch* : bidior nokol – *pirate copy of a video recording* : ɖolilor nokol – *copy of a document* : nokol rakta ni? – *do you wish to keep a copy?* : nokol bar oice – *a pirate edition has come out* : **nokol kor-** – *copy* : fotur hubuhu nokol koroin – *she makes perfect copies of pictures* : catro tara forikkat nokol korce – *the students have cheated by copying in the exam* ¶ **nokol** (adj) *copied; faked* | nokol camra – *fake leather* : nokol foesa – *counterfeit coin* : ou suna asol na nokol? – *is this gold genuine or fake?* [A. naql]
nokri ['nòχ-rī] (n) *employment* = **noukri**
noksa ['nòχ-šā] (n) *pattern; design; diagram* | tain kafror maje noksa tuloin – *she embroiders designs on cloth* : goror noksa akaira – *he's drawing a plan of the house* : **noksa kora** – *patterned; embroidered* : noksa kora kafor – *embroidered cloth* [A. naqša – *painting*]
nol [nòl] (n) *pipe* [B. nål]
noli ['nòlī] (n) *seaman's service certificate (formerly in use in the merchant navy)*
nomaj ['nòmāz, 'nòmāj] (n) *Muslim prayers* | fac okt nomaj – *the five daily prayers* : nomajor okt oi jar – *the time for prayer is approaching* : tain nomajo gecoin – *she's gone to say her prayers* : tain nomajo – *she's praying* : **nomaj for-** – *perform the prescribed prayer ritual* : afne nomaj forcoin ni? – *have you done your prayers?* [P. namāz]
nomaji ['nòmāzī] (adj) *devout; regular in prayer* = **nomaj + -i** [2]
nomaj-ruja ['nòmāz rūzā] (n) *prayers and fasting; basic religious duties* | **nomaj-ruja kor-** – *carry out one's religious duties; be pious* = **nomaj + ruja**
nomoskar ['nòmòšχār] (n) *(non-Muslim) salutation* | **nomoskar kor-** – *give a formal greeting; say good-day* ¶ **nomoskar** (int) *greetings!* [B. nåmåskar < S. namaskāra – *saying "namas"*]
nomuna ['nòmūnā] (n) *type; sort; sample* | gacor ek nomuna – *a type of tree* : ek nomuna calaki – *a sort of trick* : ki nomunar ɖail cain? – *what kind of dhal do you want?* : koto

nomunar manus – *people of so many different kinds* : kafror nomuna đi lauka – *give us a sample of the cloth* : tar kamor nomuna đekcoin ni? – *have you seen what his work is like?* : ki nomunar buđđi tar! – *what odd kinds of ideas he has!*   [P. namūna]

nonođ ['nònòđ] (n) *husband's sister*   [B. nånåđ]

nonori ['nònòrī] (n) *husband's elder sister*   = **nonođ + hori**

nor [nòr] (n) *male individual* | nor nari – *men and women* : nor međi – *male and female (animals)* : nor cora – *cock sparrow* : nor atti – *bull elephant*   [P. nar]

nor- (vi) *move*   = **lor-**

noracora ['nòrāsòrā] (n) *movement*   = **loracora**

norom ['nòròm] (adj) *soft; tender; frail* | norom gal – *soft cheeks* : norom mati – *soft earth* : tair đil norom – *her heart is tender* : **norom o-/norom oi ja-** – *become frail* : boesor loge tain norom oi gecoin – *he's become frail with age* : **norom fa-** – *detect weakness; take advantage* : afnare norom faice – *they're taking advantage of your gentility*   [P. narm]

nostami ['nòš-tāmī] (n) *spoliage; wastage*   [B. nåstami]

nosto ['nòš-tò] (adj) *spoilt* | «mege nosto lau, jiđe nosto gau» – *a gourd is spoilt by rain, a whole village is spoilt by feuding* : **nosto o-/nosto oi ja-** – *get spoilt* : afnar toki nosto oibo – *your cap will get spoilt* : fua nosto oi gece – *the lad has gone off the rails* : **nosto kor-** – *spoil; waste* : tara karfit nosto korce – *they've ruined the carpet* : tan somoe nosto kortam cai na – *I don't want to waste his time* : **nosto kori le-** – *spoil (for oneself)* : tumar juta nosto kori libae – *you're going to ruin your shoes* : **nosto kori đe-** – *spoil (for someone else)* : tara amrar iđ nosto kori đice – *they've spoilt our Eid for us*   [B. nåstå < S. naśta – *destroyed*]

notun ['nòtūn] (adj) *new*   [B. nåtun]

nouk [nôuk] (n) *fingernail; toenail*   [B. nåkh < S. nakha]

nouk-katni ['nôuk-kātnī] (n) *nail-clipper*

noukor ['nôukòr] (n) *service holder*   [P. naukar – *domestic servant*]

noukri ['nôukrī] (n) *employment*   [P. naukarī – *domestic service*]

nousa ['nôušā] (n) *bridegroom*   [P. nauša]

nu [nū] (int) *well; but listen; you know* | farle nu korlam ne – *well, I would have done it if I could* : tumi nu koilae – *but hang on, you said so yourself* : caci nu bemar – *but auntie is sick, as you know*   Note: An interjection conveying an attitude of objection or reproach.

nun [nūn] (n) *salt* | «jar nun kae, tar gun gae» – *he eats someone's bread and sings his praises; he is beholden to someone*   [B. nun < O. lavaṇa]

nuna ['nūnā] (adj) *salty*   [B. nona]

nur [nūr] (n) *light; brilliance*   [A. nūr]

O

o[1] [ò] (int) *yes*
o[2] (int) *hi; hey* | o beti, kuae jao? – *hey, girl, where are you off to?* : o ba, hunouka – *hi, man, listen / excuse me, mate, can I have a word with you*
o+[1] (adv prefix) *un-; non-* | foriskar, oforiskar – *clean, unclean* : subiɗa, osubiɗa – *convenience, inconvenience* : somoe, osomoe – *(right) time, wrong time* [B. å- < S. a-]
o+[2] (adj prefix) *this* = **ou**
-o (adv suffix) *too; also* | ota-o sunɗor – *this is pretty, too* : amra-o ɗekci – *we saw it too* : runar-o gori ace – *Runa too has got a watch* : .. -o .. -o – *both .. and* : tara mac-o kae, maŋso-o kae – *they eat both fish and meat* : tair gari-o ace, caikel-o – *she has both a car and a bicycle* : afne-o janoin, ami-o jani – *you know and so do I* : «kola-o becta, rot-o ɗekta» – *he wants to sell his bananas and watch the parade / kill two birds with one stone / have his cake and eat it*
o- (vi) *be; become; come into existence; happen; grow* | gulmal oibo – *there will be trouble* : ek baicca oice – *a baby has been born* : i ɗeso ɗan oe na – *rice doesn't grow in this country* : kita oice? – *what's happened?* : oice kita? – *what's the matter?* : kunta oice na – *nothing's happened; it doesn't matter* : kunta oito nae – *nothing will happen; it won't matter; it doesn't matter* : rait oice – *it's become night* : tain jolɗi bala oiba – *she'll get better soon* : **oe** – *it is; it is so; it is all right; it suffices* : haca ni? oe – *is that true? indeed it is* : amra aste atile oe – *it's all right if we walk slowly* : ɗeri na oile oe – *it'll be okay so long as there's no delay* : ila oe na – *it's not right like this* : hokolta tik oibo – *everything will turn out all right* : ola-u oibo – *it will be so; that must be how it is* : ek kaf ca oibo ni? – *will a cup of tea be in order?* : ino jaega oito nae – *there won't be enough room here* : i caile oito nae – *this rice won't be enough to go round* : afnar toki·ta oice na – *your headgear is not appropriate* : bala oice – *it's turned out well; it's all to the good* : oice! – *that's enough!* : oile oice – *anyway, that's that; enough is enough* : tain aicoin tin afta oice – *it's three weeks since she arrived* : bout ɗin oice, meg nae – *there's been no rain for a long time* : **oito fare** – *it may be; perhaps* : oito fare tara goro gece – *maybe they've gone home* : oile oito fare – *that's as may be* : **oito acil** – *should have been* : aij fati oito acil – *there should have been a party today* : **(ke) (korto) oe** – *(someone) has to (do)* : tain kam korta oin – *he has to work* : tara forto oe – *they have to study* : amra taktam oi – *we have to stay* : tain jaita oiba – *he will have to go* : tumi bar caitae oibae – *you'll have to wait* : tara bujto oibo – *they'll have to come to terms with it* : **oia ja-** / **oi ja-** – *become; happen* : natin boro oi jar – *granddaughter is getting older* : hokolta tik oi jaibo – *everything will turn out all right* : bakka ɗiroŋ oi gece – *much delay has occurred* : **oi ar-** / **oi gi ar-** – *have become; have taken place* : tain sef oi arcoin – *he has become a chef* : kela oi gi arce – *the match is over* [B. hå-]
oaɗɗa ['wāɗ-ɗā] (n) *promise* | **oaɗɗa kor-** – *promise* : tain oaɗɗa korcoin, aita – *he has promised to come* [A. wa¿da]
oafos ['wāfòš] (adv) *back again* | tara ebo oafos aice na – *they haven't yet come back* : **oafos de-/oafos ɗi la-** – *give back* : kagojain tanre oafos ɗi laici – *I've returned the papers to him* [P. vāpas]
oaj [wāz, wāj] (n) *sermon* | aij mocjiɗo oaj oibo – *there will be a sermon at the mosque today* : moulana sab oaj ɗicoin – *the moulana gave a sermon* [A. wa¿ż]
oal [wāl] (n) *wall* | tara samne oal ɗer – *they're putting a wall up in front* : fotu oalo gati lice – *she's pinned the picture on the wall* [B. ɗeoal × E. wall]
oalεkum ['wālεkūm] (int) *and the same to you* see **oalεkum ac calam**
oalεkum ac calam ['wālεkūm-ās-sālām] (int) *and peace upon you too* (standard reply to the greeting "as-salaam alaikum") [A. wa ¿alaikumu s-salām – *and upon ye peace*]
oalεkum calam ['wālεkūm-sālām] (int) *and peace upon you too* (standard reply to the greeting "salaam alaikum") [A. wa ¿alaikum salām – *and upon ye peace*]

oaris ['wārīš] (n) *heir* [A. wāriθ]
oarisan ['wārīšān] (n) *heirs* < **oaris**
oasta ['wās-tā] (n) *purpose* | **oaste** – *for a purpose* : allar oaste – *in the cause of God* : allar oaste foesa deuka – *please give some money for good works* [A. wāsiṭa – *medium, means*]
obab ['òbāb] (n) *shortage; lack; want* | kanir obab – *a shortage of food* : foesar obab – *a lack of money* : tara obabor maje – *they're living in want* : **(kuntar) obabe** – *for want of (something)* : somoer obabe – *for want of time* : tara fanir obabe gucol korto fare na – *for want of water they can't have a bath* [B. åbhab < S. abhāva – *non-existence*]
obae ['òbāɛ] (adv) *this way; here* | tain obae aita nae – *he won't come this way* : obae cauka! – *look this way, look over here!* : obae keu take na – *nobody lives around here* = o ² + **bae**
obaedi ['òbāɛdī] (adv) *this way; over here* = **obae + dia**
obak ['òbāχ] (adj) *astonished* [B. åbak < S. abākin – *speechless*]
obibaito [òbi 'bāɪtò] (adj) *unmarried* [B. åbibahitå < S. avivāhita]
obiggo ['òbīg-gò] (adj) *experienced; skilled* [B. åbhiggå < S. abhijña – *knowing*]
obiggota ['òbīg-gòtā] (n) *experience* [B. åbhiggåta < S. abhijñatā – *knowledge*]
obijug ['òbīzūg] (n) *objection; complaint; accusation; judicial charge* | tar ufre curir obijug – *he's on a charge of theft* : **obijug kor-** – *object; make complaint* : tan gari hono rakcoin dekia bout mainse obijug korcoin – *many people objected when they saw he'd parked his car there* [B. åbhijog < S. abhiyoga – *assault; accusation*]
obiman [òbi 'mān] (n) *umbrage; display of mortification* | **obiman kor-** – *act offended; indulge in a fit of sulking* [B. åbhiman < S. abhimāna – *self-conceit, haughtiness*]
oboela ['òbòɛlā] (n) *disregard; neglect* | **oboela kor-** – *fail to give proper regard; treat carelessly; neglect* : biat tara cacire oboela korce – *at the wedding they ignored auntie* [B. åbåhela < S. avahelā]
obos ['òbòš] (adj) *inert* | **obos o-/obos oi ja-** – *become paralysed* : tan bau at obos oi gece – *her left arm has become paralysed* [B. åbås < S. avaša – *not controlled*]
obossi ['òbòš-šī] (adv) *certainly; surely; indeed* | afne aiba? obossi aimu – *you'll come? certainly I will* : tain aiba obossi – *he'll surely come; I'm sure he'll come* : koa jae na obossi – *one can never tell, mind you* : aij korba? obossi! – *will you do it today? yes, of course!* [B. åbåsså < S. avašya – *uncontrollable*]
obosta ['òbòstā] (n) *state; situation; condition* | duniar obosta bala nae – *the state of the world is not good* : tarar obosta bala – *their (financial) situation is good; they're well off* : garir obosta bala – *the car is in good condition* : amar sorilor obosta bala nae – *my bodily condition isn't good; I'm poorly* : dekcoin, ki obosta! – *see what a state things are in!* : i jutar kunu obosta roice na – *these shoes are a write-off* : «hostar tin obosta» – *cheap has an uncertain condition; cheap means unreliable* [B. åbåstha < S. avasthā]
ocet ['òsɛt] (adj) *weak; lacking vigour* | ocet lage amar sorilo – *there's a feeling of debility in my body; I feel drained of strength* [B. åcet < S. aceta – *not conscious*]
ociot ['òsīòt] (n) *moral advice; religious guidance* [A. waṣīya – *directive*]
ocol ['òsòl] (adj) *not in running order; not mobile; obsolete* | injil ocol oi gece – *the engine is out of order* : tain ekere ocol – *he is completely without mobility* : agor reoaj ocol oi gece – *the olden day customs have died out* [B. åcål < S. acala – *not moving*]
odbut ['òd-būt] (adj) *extraordinary* | odbut kando – *an extraordinary affair* : odbut lage – *it seems astonishing; it's amazing* [B. åḋbhut < S. adbhūta – *wonderful*]
oddo ['òd-dò] (adv) *recently* [B. åḋḋå < S. adya – *today*] see **oiddo**
odikar ['òḋīkār] (n) *entitlement; right* | afnar kota koar odikar ace – *you have the right to speak* : tar ino aoar odikar nae – *he has no right to come here* [B. åḋhikar < S. adhikāra – *sovereignty; authority*]
oe ¹ [òy] (v) *exists; becomes; happens; goes on* | kita oe, amare janaiba – *let me know what happens* : kela oe – *a match takes place* : gac oe – *a plant grows* : meg oe – *rain falls* : osubida oe – *problems are experienced* see **o-**

oe² (int) *it is so; yes* | ino boraf oe? oe – *does snow fall here? yes, it does* : afne bala ni? ji oe! – *are you well? yes!* : afne janoin ni? oe, jani – *do you know that? yes, I do* : oe oe – *yes indeed* : haca ni? oe oe – *is that true? oh, yes, certainly it is* : **oe ni?** – *is that so?* < **o-**
oeran ['òyrān] (adj) *wearied; bothered; anxious; impatient* | ami oeran oi geci – *I'm flaked out* : afne oeran oila – *you have been to a lot of trouble* : afne oto oeran kene? – *why are you so bothered; why are you so impatient?* [A. ḣairān – *confused*]
oerani ['òyrānī] (n) *harassment; bother* = **oeran + -i** ¹
of [òf] (n) *day off (from work); state of being switched off* | kailku amar of – *tomorrow is my day off* : tain ofor ḋin london jain – *he goes to London on his day off* : **of lo-** – *take a day off* : sombare of loimu – *I'll have my day off on Monday; I'll take Monday off* : **of kor-** – *switch off* : tibi of koro cai – *switch off the television, will you* [E.]
ofis ['òfīš] (n) *office* | noea ofis kulce – *a new office has opened* : ofisor taim noe·ta taki fac·ta – *office hours are from nine to five* : tain ofiso kam koroin – *she works in an office* : **ofis kor-** – *be on duty in one's office* : tain koe·tat ofis koroin? – *at what time is he in his office?* [E.]
ofocoe ['òfò-sòy] (n) *needless use; wastage* [B. åpâcây < S. apacaya – *diminution*]
oforaḋ ['òfòrāḋ] (n) *transgression; offence; crime* [B. åpåraḋh < S. aparāḋha]
oforaḋi ['òfòrāḋī] (adj/n) *criminal* = **oforaḋ + -i** ³
oforiskar ['òfòrīš-χār] (adj) *unclean; dirty* [B. åpåriskar < S. apariśkāra – *making not clean*]
ofoman ['òfòmān] (n) *insult* [B. åpåman < S. apamāna]
ofsor ['òf-sòr] (n) *leisure; spare time* | tan ofsor nae – *he has no spare time* : **ofsor o-/ofsor oi ja-** – *be at leisure; take retirement* : afne ofsor ni? – *are you free?* : tain ofsor oicoin – *she's retired* : **ofsor somoe** – *in one's spare time* : tara ofsor somoe tas kelae – *they play cards in their spare time* [B. åbåsår < S. avasara – *occasion*]
ogcin ['òksīn] (pron) *these* = **o**² **+ gacain**
ogo ['ògô] (int) *hey! hello!* Note: Interjection used for hailing a woman. Informal and familiar.
ogrim ['ògrīm] (adj) *preceding; prior; paid in advance* | ogrim foesa – *advance payment* : ogrim beton – *advance wages* [B. ågrim < S. agrima]
ogrosor ['ògròsòr] (adj) *advancing* | **ogrosor o-** – *advance; move forward* : kam·ta aste aste ogrosor or – *the job is going ahead slowly* [B. ågråsår < S. agrasara – *going ahead*]
ogu ['ògū] (pron) *this* | ogu kita? – *what is this?* : ogu tan batija – *this is his nephew* : **ogue** – *this one* (instrumental) : ogue koice amare – *it was this fellow who told me* : **oguin** – *these; these ones* : oguin noea – *these ones are new* : oguintore falai ḋimu – *I'll throw these away* = **o**² **+ gu** ¹
oguin ['òguīn] (pron) *these* < **ogu**
oguinta ['òguīntā] (pron) *these* = **oguin + -ta** ²
oguta ['ògūtā] (pron) *this* = **ogu + -ta** ²
ohi ['òhī] (n) *(prophetic) inspiration* [A. waḣy]
ohon ['òhòn] (n) *this moment; now* = **okon**
oi ¹ [òɪ] (int) *there* | oi ḋeko! – *there, see!*
oi ² (adj) *this* | oi kolom kar? – *whose is this pen?* = **ou**
oia ['òɪ-ā] (v adv) *having become; while being; via; on behalf* | tain bemar oia ḋeso gecla – *having become ill, she went to Bangladesh* : afne beta oia dorain kita? – *while being a man, how can you be scared?* : tara kusi oia saḋ ḋibo – *being happy, they will help; they will be happy to help* : tain luton oia london jaiba – *he will go to London via Luton* : amar oia i kam·ta korba – *please do this on my behalf* < **o-**
oialle ['òɪ-āl-lɛ] (v adv) *having eventually become; after ultimately becoming* (conditional or habitual) | tain daktor oialle london gia takba – *after becoming a doctor she'll go and live in London* : baro·ta oialle amra gumai – *when it's twelve o'clock we go to bed* = **oia + arle**
oiari ['òɪ-ārī] (v adv) *having become* | tain cearmen oiairi bout kam koraicoin – *after becoming the Chairman he had a lot of work carried out* = **oia + ari**

oibbas ['òɪb-bāš] (n) *habit* | tair fan kanir oibbas – *she has the paan-eating habit* : amar cigretor oibbas nae – *I'm not in the habit of smoking cigarettes* : tarar oibbas oi gece – *they've got used to it* [B. åbbhas < S. abhyāsa – *practice*]
oibbes ['òɪb-bɛš] (n) *habit* = **oibbas**
oibbosto ['òɪb-bòstò] (adj) *habituated; accustomed* | **oibbosto o-/oibbosto oi ja-** – *become accustomed* : amra hunte hunte oibbosto oi geci – *from hearing it again and again we've become used to it* [B. åbbhåstå < S. abhyasta – *practised*]
oice ['òɪsɛ́] (int) *it's done; that's it; that's enough* | oice, one buji lici – *all right, I understand now* : oice! ar ɖein na jen – *that's enough, please don't give me any more (food)* : oice, oice! – *okay! that's enough! stop it now!* : oile oice – *anyway, that's that; enough is enough* < **o-**
oiɖɖo ['òɪɖ-ɖò] (adv) *recently; in the near future* | ami oiɖɖo cacar citi faici – *I recently received a letter from uncle* : tane ɖekci na oiɖɖo – *I haven't seen her recently* : tara oiɖɖo aoar kota – *they are supposed to be coming back in the near future* = **oɖɖo**
oiie ['òɪyɛ́] (adv) *likewise; even so* | oiie foesa lagbo – *even then it'll cost something* cf **oiou**
oije ['òɪ-jɛ́, 'òɪ-zɛ́] (int) *look, see there!* | oije, afnar cokkur samne – *look, there it is, right in front of you!* = **oi + je**
oilɖia ['òɪl-ɖɪā] (adj) *yellowish; yellow* cf **oloiɖ**
oile ['òɪ-lɛ] (v adv) *on becoming; in such a case; however* | tumi boro oile bujbae – *when you get older you will understand* : ɖin bala oile amra farko jai – *if the weather is good we go to the park* : manus bala, oile bul kam korce – *he's a good person, but still he did the wrong thing* : he aicil, oile kunta koice na – *he came, yet he didn't mention anything* < **o-**
oillia ['òɪl-lɪā] (adj) *yellow* = **oilɖia**
oinniae ['òɪn-nɪāy] (n) *injustice* | koto boro oinniae – *such a great injustice; how very unfair* : **oinniae kor-** – *commit an injustice; do something wrong* : oinniae korci, ɖoea kori maf korouka – *I did wrong, but please do forgive me* ¶ **oinniae** (adj) *unjust* | oinniae beboar – *unfair behaviour* [B. ånnay < S. anyāya – *unjust action*]
oinno ['òɪn-nɪò] (adj) *other; different* | oinno somoe koimu – *I'll tell you some other time* : aij oinno ek·jon aicoin – *a different person came today* [B. ånnå < O. anya]
oiou ['òɪ-ū] (adv) *likewise; even so* | iguin oiou baɖ – *these ones are likewise no good* : kail oiou jana lagbo – *even so, we'll have to go tomorrow* = **ou + -u**
oittacar ['òɪt-tɪā-sār] (n) *oppression; abuse; tyranny* | **oittacar kor-** – *practise oppression; be tyrannical* [B. åttacar < S. atyācāra – *acting outside proper norms*]
ojana ['òzānā, 'òjānā] (adj) *unknown* [B. åjana]
ojor ['òzòr, 'òjòr] (n) *excuse* | tara ojor ɖekaice – *they made excuses* : tain ojor tukain – *he's looking for an excuse* [A. ¿uðr]
ojota ['òzòtā, 'òjòtā] (adj) *inappropriate; unnecessary* | ojota matamati – *uncalled-for talk* : ojota jamela – *unnecessary bother* : ojota cinta koroin na jen – *please don't give yourself unnecessary worries* [B. åjåtha < S. ajathā – *not correct*]
oju ['òzū, 'òjū] (n) *Muslim ritual ablution (as a preliminary to prayer)* | afnar oju oice ni? – *have you had your ablutions?* : amar oju roice – *I'm still in a state of ritual cleanliness (since the last time I did my ablutions)* : **oju kor-** – *perform ritual ablution* [A. wuÐu']
ojuat ['òzū-āt, 'òjū-āt] (n) *explanations* | **ojuat deka-** – *offer explanations; make excuses* : tara kali ojuat ɖekae – *they keep making excuses* [A. wujūhāt – *reasons*]
okan[1] ['òχān] (pron) *this* | okan afnar ni? – *is this yours?* : **oknain / oknin** – *these* : oknain cai na – *I don't want these* = **o**[2] **+ kan**[2]
okan[2] (n) *this place; here* | okan taki london koto ɖur? – *how far is London from here?* : **okano** – *in this place; here* : **okanor** – *of this place* = **o**[2] **+ kan**[3]
okano ['òχānò] (n adv) *in this place; here* < **okan**[2]
okanta ['òχān-tā] (pron) *this* = **okan + -ta**[2]

oke ['òkɛ́] (int) *okay, all right* | (ending a phone conversation) oke, toraki? – *right, well I'm going to ring off now* : (hurriedly ending a phone conversation) bala takouka, bađe matmu ne, oke, clamalekum – *goodbye, talk to you later, okay, salaam alaikum* [E.]

okete ['òkɛ́tɛ́] (int) *okay, all right* | okete, jai gi – *right, I'm going now* = **oke + te**

okkor ['òk-χòr] (n) *character in Bengali writing* | okkore okkore – *letter by letter; literally* : okkor cin- – *know the Bengali characters; be literate* [B. åkkår < S. akśara – *syllable; letter*]

oknain ['òχ-nāın] (pron) *these* < **okan** [1]

oknin ['òχ-nīn] (pron) *these* < **okan** [1]

okon ['òχòn] (n) *this moment; now* | okone – *now* : okonku – *now* : okonkur – *of this moment* = **o** [2] **+ kon**

okta ['òχ-tā] (pron) *this (one)*

oktata ['òχ-tātā] (pron) *this (one)* = **okta + -ta** [2]

okt ['òχt] (n) *time (for prescribed Muslim prayer)* | fac okt – *the five times of prayer* : fac okt nomaj – *the set of five daily prayers* : mugribor okt oice – *it's time for the sunset prayer* : okt oice na ebu – *it's not yet time for the prayer* [A. waqt]

ola ['òlā] (adv) *like this; like that; such; so* | ola korouka – *do it like this* : ola đin bala – *a day like this is best* : amar bai ola – *my brother's like that* : ola faji beta – *such a tiresome man* : ola sunđor lage – *it's so beautiful* = **olakan**

olakan ['òlāχān] (adv) *like this* = **o** [2] **+ lakan**

olan ['òlān] (adv) *like this* = **olakan**

olau ['òlā-ū] (adv) *just like this* = **ola + -u**

oli ['òlī] (n) *guardian; saint* | i fuar oli nae – *this boy has no guardian* : oli ulla – *companion of God; saint* [A. wālīy – *friend; patron*]

oloiđ ['òlòıđ] (n) *turmeric* [B. håluđ < O. hariđra]

omainno ['òmāın-nıò] (adj) *disregarded* | omainno kor- – *disregard; disobey* : tara niom omainno korce – *they have broken the rules* [B. åmannå < S. amanya – *not worthy to be respected*]

omne ['òm-nɛ] (adv) *like this* | omne tik ace – *it's all right as it is* : tain omne korcoin – *he went like this* < **omon**

omola ['òmòlā] (adv) *like this* = **omon + lakan**

omon ['òmòn] (adj) *such; so* | omon manus – *such a person* : omon fagol – *such a madman* : omon sunđor – *so beautiful* [B. emån]

on [1] [òn] (n) *this place; here* | on taki siđa jauka gi – *from here go straight on* : on tone đur nae – *it's not far from here* : **ono** – *at this place; here* : ono ke takoin? – *who lives here?* : **onor** – *of this place; of here* : onor mati bala – *the soil of this place is good* : onor maje kita? – *what's inside of here?* = **okan** [2]

on [2] (n) *state of being switched on* | on kor- – *switch on* : centel hitiŋ on korcoin ni? – *have you turned the central heating on?* [E.]

one ['ònɛ] (n adv) *at this moment; now* | one kita korta? – *what will you do now?* : one jairam gi – *now I'm going; I'm off now* : one nae, bađe – *not now, later* = **okone** < **okon**

onek ['ònɛχ] (adj) *much; many* | onek foesa – *a lot of money* : onek manus – *many people* ¶ **onek** (adv) *much; very* | ou cuetar onek boro – *this sweater is much too big* : calir đor onek komce – *the price of rice has gone down a lot* : afne onek besi đicoin amare – *you've given me much too much* [B. ånek < S. aneka – *not one; many*]

onekta ['ònɛχ-tā] (pron) *much; a lot* = **onek + -ta** [2]

oniom ['ònıòm] (n) *irregular practice* | ofiso oniom cole – *irregular practices go on in the office* : **oniom kor-** – *fail to maintain regularity* : tain kanir maje besi oniom koroin – *he is too irregular in his eating habits* [B. åniåm < S. aniyama – *non-rule*]

onjan ['ònjān] (adj) *unknown* [H. anjān]

onku ['ònkū] (n adv) *now* | onku ami besto – *I'm busy now* : nomajor okt onku – *now is prayer time* : **onkur** – *of this moment; present* : onkur imam bala – *the present imam is good* : onkur lagi tik ace – *it's all right for now* = **okonku**

ono ['ònò] (n adv) *here* | ono bat ace – *there's some rice here* : beg·ta ono touka – *put the bag here* : amar ono jaega ace – *there's room at my place here* = **okano**
onuman ['ònūmān] (n) *supposition; guess* | onuman đui so – *at a guess, two hundred* : **onuman kor-** – *make a supposition; have a guess* : kirom lagce onuman korouka – *just imagine what it felt like* : onuman kora jae na, koe·jon acla – *it's impossible to guess how many people were there* : onuman kori koiclam – *I said it by guessing; I was just guessing* [B. ånuman < S. anumāna – *inference*]
onumoti ['ònūmòtī] (n) *permission* | onumoti cara – *without permission* : ticaror onumoti loia – *with the teacher's permission* : **(kar) onumoti ca-** – *ask for permission* : mabafor onumoti caico ni? – *have you asked for your parents' permission?* : **onumoti đe-/onumoti đi la-** – *give permission* [B. ånumåti < S. anumati]
onuruđ ['ònūrūđ] (n) *insistent request* | ita oilo amar onuruđ – *this is my (most urgent) request* : **onuruđ kor-** – *request insistently* : onuruđ korci, te-u đicoin na – *I made a special request but still he wouldn't give it me* [B. ånurođh < S. anurođha – *act of obliging*]
onusare ['ònūšārɛ́] (adv) *in accordance* | afnar kota onusare – *according to what you said* : hokolta ain onusare kora gece – *everything has been done in accordance with the law* [B. ånusare < S. anusāra – *accordance, conformity*]
oŋgo ['òŋ-gò] (n) *limb* [B. åŋgå < S. aŋga]
oŋko ['òŋ-kò] (n) *numerical figure; number; arithmetic; mathematics* | hesor oŋko ota sat na noe? – *is that last figure 7 or 9?* : oŋko forto fare – *he can read numerals* : oŋkot leki đeuka – *write it in figures* : muta oŋkor foesa – *a fat-figure sum of money; a large sum of money* : tain bala oŋko janoin – *he is good at arithmetic* : oŋkot tai kelasor maje ek lombor – *she's top of the class in maths* [B. åŋkå < S. aŋka – *curve; numerical figure; number*]
oŋso ['òŋ-šò] (n) *part; portion* | ou oŋso afnar – *this portion is for you* : ek oŋso taire đeuka – *give her a portion* : **besi oŋse** – *for the most part* : amra besi oŋse bat kai – *we eat rice most of the time* [B. åŋså < S. aŋša]
oŋsiđar ['òŋ-šīđār] (n) *part-owner; shareholder* [B. åŋsiđar]
orđđek ['òrđ-dɛχ] (n°) *one half* | orđđek ruti – *half a chapati* : barir orđđek – *one half of the homestead* : **orđđek kor-/orđđek kori le-** – *reduce to halves; halve* : kafor orđđek kori lici – *I've cut the cloth in half* [B. årđhek < O. arđhika]
ore ['òrɛ́] (int) *oh* | ore baf to baf! – *oh, goodness!*
orin ['òrīn] (n) *deer* [B. hårin < S. hariṇa]
oriŋ ['òrīŋ] (n) *deer* = **orin**
orto ['òr-tò] (n) *signification; meaning* | tefiŋ orto kita? – *what does "tapping" mean?* : itar kunu orto nae – *this has no meaning* : ami kunu orto buji na – *I can't make head or tail of it* : **orto kor-** – *extract meaning; explain the meaning* : ou aiator orto koro – *give the meaning of this Quranic verse* [B. årthå < S. artha – *aim; meaning; wealth*]
osađaron ['òšāđāròn] (adj) *uncommon; unusual* [B. åsađharån < S. asādhāraṇa]
osanti ['òšāntī] (n) *discomfiture; unease* | tara boro osantir maje – *they're in a stressful situation* : **osanti kore** – *unease is felt* : raitku amar osanti kore – *at night I feel ill at ease / restless / uncomfortable* [B. åsanti < S. ašānti – *non-peace*]
oses ['òšɛš] (adj) *endless* [B. åses < S. ašeśa]
osikar ['òšīkār] (n) *denial; refusal* | **osikar kor-** – *deny; refuse* : he nicil kori osikar kore – *he denies that he took it* : tara jaito osikar kore – *they say they won't go; they refuse to go* ¶ **osikar** (adj) *not in agreement* | tain osikar oita faroin – *he may disagree* : tara hokoloe osikar – *they all refuse to agree to it* [B. åsikar < S. asvīkāra – *non-owning*]
osombob ['òšòmbòb] (adj) *inconceivable; impossible* | osombob kota – *an unthinkable notion; an impossibility* : amar lagi ita osombob – *as far as I'm concerned it's out of the question* : ki osombob! – *how ridiculous; how outrageous!* ¶ **osombob** (adv) *unbelievably; impossibly* | aij osombob gorom coler – *it's incredibly hot today* : tain osombob jal kain – *she eats unbelievably peppery food* [B. åsåmbhåb < S. asambhava – *non-existence* × asambhāvya – *non-existent*]
osot ['òšòt] (adj) *dishonest* | [B. åsåt < S. asat]

ostasi ['òstāšī] (n°) *eighty-eight*   [B. åstasi]
ostaii ['òstā-ī] (adj) *impermanent; temporary; transient* | ostaii bebosta – *a temporary arrangement* : amra ino ostaii – *we're impermanent here; we're not permanently settled here*   [B. åsthayi < S. asthayī]
oste ['òstɛ] (adv) *softly; slowly*   = **aste**
ostir ['òstīr] (adj) *restless; impatient*   [B. åsthir < S. asthira – *not fixed*]
ostro ['òstrò] (n) *weapon*   [B. åstrå < S. astra]
osubiɖa ['òšūbīɖā] (n) *inconvenience; problem* | osubiɖa kita? – *what's the problem?* : subiɖa osubiɖa bujta oiba – *you must weigh up the pros and cons* : tara osubiɖar maje – *they're in difficulties; they're having problems* : **osubiɖa oe** – *inconvenience is felt; problems arise* : afnar hono boite osubiɖa oibo – *you won't be comfortable sitting there* : osubiɖa oile koiba – *if there's any problem please say so* : **osubiɖa ace** – *there are problems; there are objections* : tan jaite osubiɖa (ace) – *it's awkward for her to go* : amar kunu osubiɖa nae – *there's no problem for me* : afnare koite osubiɖa nae – *there's no harm in my telling you* : na, amar osubiɖa ace – *no, I object* : **osubiɖa kor-** – *make problems* : laga goror manus osubiɖa korto fare – *the next door neighbours may create problems*   [B. åsubiɖa < S. asuviḍhā – *non-convenience*]
osuk ['òšūk] (n) *illness* | fetor osuk – *stomach trouble* : hator osuk – *heart disease* : tair osuk kita oice? – *what illness has she got?* : **osuk kore** – *illness occurs* : cacir osuk korce – *aunt has fallen ill*   [B. åsukh < S. asukha – *non-ease; affliction*]
osuk-bisuk ['òšūk-bīšūk] (n) *illnesses*   = **osuk**
osusto ['òšūs-tò] (adj) *ill*   [B. åsusthå < S. asustha – *unwell*]
ota ['òtā] (pron) *this (one)*
ota ['òtā] (pron) *this (one)* | ota kita? – *what's this?* : ota gori – *it's a watch* : beg ota amar tain ɖi lauka – *please hand me the bag; let me carry that bag* : cafi ota kar? – *whose is this key?* : **otain** – *these (ones)*   = **o ² + -ta ²**
oti ['òtī] (adv) *highly; extremely* | oti sunɖor gor – *a really beautiful house* : oti bala manus – *a very good person* : oti suja – *extremely simple*   [B. åti < S. ati]
otil ['òtīl] (adv) *now* | otil kortam kita? – *now what am I to do?* : **otilku** – *now* : otilku meg ɖer – *now it's raining*   = **o ² + til**
otiri ['òtīrī] (adv) *now; yet* | tain otiri aicoin na – *he hasn't come yet*   = **o ² + titi**
otirikto ['òtīrīk-tò] (adv) *too much*   [B. åtiriktå < S. ati-rikta – *left with excess*]
otiriti ['òtīrītī] (adv) *now*   = **otiri**
otit ['òtīt] (a) *past* | otit ɖin – *past days* : fara·ta otit oice – *the crisis is past* ¶ **otit** (n) *the past* | otitor kobor jane na tara – *they know nothing about the past*   [B. åtit < S. atīta]
oto ['òtò] (adj) *so many; so much* | oto ful! – *so many flowers!* : oto ɖuɖ ɖio na – *don't put so much milk in* : oto ɖeri? – *so much delay? why so late?* : **oto·ta** – *so much* : oto·ta cai na – *I don't want so much* : **oto·guin / oto·gula** – *so many* : oto·gula kita korta? – *where will you do with so many?* : **oto·tuk / oto·tuku** – *just so much* : afne oto·tuku kaicoin – *you only ate that much* : **oto·jon** – *so many (people)* : oto·jon kuae boiba? – *where can so many people sit?* ¶ **oto** (adv) *so much; so* | oto besi kani bala nae – *it's not good to eat so much* : oto bala furi tai! – *such a good girl she is!* : oto gumain! – *he sleeps so much!*   [B. etå]
otokan ['òtòχān] (pron/adv) *such amount; so much* | otokan cai na – *I don't want this much* : tain otokan koita faroin na – *he can't tell so much; he doesn't really know*   = **oto + kan ²**
otokuni ['òtòkūnī] (adj) *so diminutive; tiny* | otokuni furi – *a very small girl* : otokuni bat kaicoin – *you've only eaten a tiny bit of rice*
otori ['òtòrī] (adv) *now; yet*   = **otiri**
otoriti ['òtòrītī] (adv) *now; yet*   = **otiriti**
ototuku ['òtòtūkū] (pron/adv) *such small amount; so little*   = **oto + tuku**
otota ['òtòtā] (pron/adv) *so much* | otota kaio na – *don't eat so much* : oilɖia otota cole na – *yellow doesn't do so well; yellow isn't that popular*   = **oto + -ta ²**

ou [ôū] (adj) *this* | ou am bala – *this mango is a good one* : tara ou goro take – *they live in this house* ¶ **ou** (pron) *this; just this* | ou dilo tumare? – *is this all they gave you?* : ou ni kota? – *is this it? is that all?* ¶ **ou** (adv) *thus; just so; just now; more or less* | ou bala – *it's best like this* : ou ses – *and so is the end; that's the lot* : ou aicoin – *she's just come in* : ou gela tain – *he just went out* : ou raki lilam – *so I just bought it* : tik ace? ou tik – *you all right? more or less so* : **ou .. ou ..** – *on one hand .. on the other hand ..* : ou asoin, ou kandoin – *one minute she laughs, next minute she cries*
ougu ['ôūgū] (pron) *this (one)* = **ou + gu** [1]
ouguin ['ôūgūın] (pron) *these (ones)* < **ougu**
oukan ['ôūχān] (pron) *this (one)* = **ou + kan** [2]
oula ['ôūlā] (adv) *like this* = **ola**
ousud ['ôūšūd] (n) *medicine* | gumor ousud – *sleeping tablets* : ousudor butol – *medicine bottle* : afnar ousud kauka – *take your medicine* [B. ousådh < S. auśadha]
outa ['ôūtā] (pron) *this (one)* = **ou + ta**
outa ['ôūtā] (pron) *this (one)* = **ou + -ta** [2]
outaouta ['ôūtā-ôūtā] (pron) *this and that*

r

rae [rāy] (n) *verdict; judgment* | ou kecit rae oice na ebo – *a verdict hasn't yet been reached in this case* : **rae de-** – *pass judgment* : joje rae dicoin – *the judge has handed down a decision; the judge has given his ruling* [A. ra'y – *view; opinion*]

rag [rāg, rāk] (n) *anger; irascibility* | cacar rag besi – *uncle has a hot temper* : tain ragor ufre nananta maticoin – *he said things in anger* : **rag oe / rag oi jae** – *one gets angry* : tumar ufre abbar rag oi gece / tumar ufre abbar rag – *Dad is cross with you* : **rag ute** – *one's anger is aroused* : cacar rag utce – *uncle's got annoyed* : ola kota hunle amar rag ute – *when I hear things like that my hackles rise* : **rag tul-** – *provoke anger* : tumra kanoka tan rag tulo kene – *why do you annoy him unnecessarily?* : kobordar, kuttar rag tulio na – *beware, don't incite a dog to anger* : **rag kor- / rag kori le-** – *get angry; lose one's temper* : miasab tar ufre rag kori licoin – *the mullah got angry with him* : rag koroin na jen – *please don't be cross* [B. rag < S. rāga – *colour; mood*]

rag- (vi) *get angry* | **ragi ja-** – *get angry* : caca maje maje ragi jain – *uncle sometimes loses his temper* [B. rag-]

raga- ['rāgā] (vt) *make angry; annoy; vex* | kuttare ragaio na – *don't annoy the dog* : **ragai de-** – *make angry; annoy; vex* : onku abbare ragai dico – *now you've made Dad angry* [B. raga-]

ragaragi ['rāgārāgī] (n) *state of being angry; display of anger* | **ragaragi kor-** – *be angry; rant and rave* < **rag-**

ragi ['rāgī] (adj) *irascible* [B. ragi]

ragua ['rāgwā] (adj) *irascible* ¶ **ragua** (n) *irascible person; crosspatch* < **rag-**

rai[1] [rāi] (n) *mustard (plant); rape (plant)* [B. rai]

rai[2] (n) *widow* = **rari**

raijjir ['rāıj-jīr] (adj) *of great extent; abundant; copious* | tara raijjir kani taiar korcil – *they had prepared masses of food* : dadar raijjir foesa ace – *great uncle has loads of money* ¶ **raijjir** (adv) *exceedingly* | aij raijjir gorom lager – *it's awfully hot today* : tarar gor raijjir boro – *their house is extremely big* < **raijjo**

raijjirta ['rāıj-jīr-tā] (pron) *a huge amount; a lot* = **raijjir + -ta**[2]

raijjo ['rāıj-jò] (n) *kingdom* [B. rajjå < S. rājya]

raikkos ['rāık-kòš] (n) *ogre; greedy eater* [B. rakkås < S. rākśasa – *demon*]

raiot ['rāıòt] (n) *ensemble of tenants on a landowner's estate* [A. ra؟īya – *herd; flock*]

rait ['rāıt] (n) *night* | tara rait takte gece gi – *they departed while it was still night* : tain dui rait takba – *he will stay for two nights* : amra sara rait jagci – *we were awake all night* : **rait oe / rait oi jae** – *night falls; night deepens* : rait oi jar – *night is falling* : bakka rait oi gece – *the night is far advanced* : besi rait oi gecil – *it was too late in the night* : **raitku** – *in the night; at night* : tara raitku kelae – *they play at night time* : **raitkur** – *of the night* : raitkur gari – *the night train* : raitkur kam – *night work* [B. rat < O. ratri]

rait-din ['rāıt-dīn] (n) *day and night* ¶ **rait-din** (adv) *by day and by night; all day and all night* | tain rait-din kam koroin – *she works night and day* : rait-din cobbis gonta – *twenty-four hours a day* ¶ **rait-din** (adj) *like day and night; totally contrasting* | rait-din bebodan – *a difference as of night and day; total difference* : rait-din beskom – *absolute disparity* = **rait + din**[1]

raj [rāz] (n) *rule; government* | ram raj – *when Rama ruled; the days of antiquity* : bitisor raj – *the period of British rule in India* [B. raj < S. rājan]

raj+ (adj prefix) *imperial; leading; top class* [S. rāja-]

raja ['rāzā, 'rājā] (n) *king* | raja ar forja – *a king and his subjects* [B. raja < S. rājan]

rajai ['rāzāı, 'rājāı] (n) *bedspread* [P. razāī]

rajas ['rāzāš, 'rājāš] (n) *goose; swan* = **raj-+ as**[2]

rajdani ['rāzdānī] (n) *capital (city)* [B. rajdhani < S. rājadhānika – *king's abode*]

raji ['rāzī, 'rājī] (adj) *consenting; agreeable* | **raji o-** – *agree; be willing* : caca raji oicoin afnar kotae – *uncle has agreed to your proposal* : tara jaito raji nae – *they are not willing to go* : he bujto raji nae – *he refuses to listen to reason* : **raji kora-** – *get to agree* : amra cacire raji koraitam oimu – *we shall have to get auntie to agree* : tain takta kori raji koraici – *we have persuaded him to stay* [A. rāĐī – *satisfied*]
rajjir ['rāj-jīr] (adj) *of great extent; abundant* = **raijjir**
rajmistri ['rāz-mīstrī] (n) *mason; bricklayer* = **raj-** + **mistri**
rajniti ['rāznītī] (n) *politics* [B. rajniti < S. rajanīti]
rak [rāk] (n) *anger* = **rag**
rak- (v) *keep; put away; accept; buy up; halt* | ou citi rakta ni? – *do you want to keep this letter?* : afnar tikit fogeto rakoin jen – *keep your ticket in your pocket* : tan lagi calon rakci – *I've saved some curry for him* : citi·kan cain dia rakce – *she accepted the letter against her signature* : tar foesa ek feni raktam nai – *I won't accept a penny of his money* : tara bout jaga rakce – *they have bought up a lot of land* : gari sofor samne rakcil – *he stopped the car in front of the shop* : rakouka! – *stop; hang on; wait a minute!* : (on telephone) one raki – *I'm going to hang up now* : beta jalaia rake na – *that fellow won't stop bothering me* : **kori rak-** – *do in readiness* : tara karfit saf kori rakce - *they've cleaned the carpet (in preparation)* : ca malaia raktam ni? – *shall I get the tea ready?* : amar tikana liki rakouka – *make a note of my address* : tarare janaia rakci – *I have informed them in advance* : **raki le-** – *keep; accept; buy up; halt* : tara amar fasfut raki lice – *they have kept hold of my passport* : amar lombor·ta raki louka – *take down my number* : foesa raki louka! – *go on, take your money!* : tara reston raki lito – *they want to buy the restaurant* : **raki de-** – *put down; hang up; stop* : afnar beg raki deuka – *why not put your bag down* : gari mure raki deuka – *please stop the car at the crossroads* : tai akta raki dice – *she suddenly hung up* [B. rakh-]
raka- ['rāχā] (vt) *cause to keep; force to accept* [B. rakha-]
rakat ['rāχāt] (n) *section of Muslim prayer ritual* [A. rak¿a – *bowing of body*]
ran [rān] (n) *thigh (of meat)* [P. rān – *thigh*]
rand- ['rānd] (v) *cook* | kurma kila randoin? – *how do you cook korma?* : tain murgi randicoin – *she has cooked some chicken* : **randat** – *engaged in cooking* : tain randat – *she's cooking* : **randi le-** – *do the cooking* : amra biankur balae randi lici – *we got all the cooking done in the morning* [B. raⁿdh-]
randa ['rāndā] (v n) *cooking* < **rand-**
rani ['rānī] (n) *queen* [B. rani]
ranna ['rān-nā] (n) *cooking* | **ranna kor-/ranna kori le-** – *cook; do the cooking* : tain ranna kori lira – *he is getting on with the cooking* = **randa**
ranna-bara ['rān-nā-bārā] (n) *cooking* = **randa**
rari ['rārī] (n) *widow* [B. raⁿṛ < O. randā]
rasta ['rāstā] (n) *road; street; way* | kula rasta – *a clear road* : rasta kali – *the street is empty* : rasta bala nae – *the road is in poor condition* : rasta janoin ni? – *do you know the way?* : tara rasta buli licil – *they lost their way* : (korbar) kunu rasta deki na – *I see no way (of doing something)* : tin dinor rasta – *three days' journey* : **rastar maje** – *on the road; on the way* : amra rastar maje kai limu – *we'll eat on the way* : **rastat** – *in the roadway* : tain rastat ubaicoin – *he is standing in the road* : **rasta de-/rasta di la-** – *make way (for someone); allow free passage* : tura rasta deuka – *please let me squeeze past* [P. rāsta – *row*]
rasta-gat ['rāstāgāt] (n) *roads; streets* = **rasta + gat**
re [ré] (int) *o! hey!* | abdul malik re! – *o, Abdul Malik!* : baba re! – *oh heavens!* : kita re, bala ni? – *hey there, how are you?* : na re beta! – *oh no, dear fellow!* : a re fut! – *come along, sonny!*
reai ['reāi] (n) *respite; relief* | kosto taki reai faitam kila? – *how can I get relief from all the stress?* : **reai nae** – *there is no escape* : one reai nae, afne jaita oiba – *there's no way out now, you'll just have to go* : **reai fa-** – *get relief* [P. rahāī – *deliverance*]

reba ['rɛbā] (int) *dear father; dear son; dear fellow* | aicca reba, đeo na – *oh come on, Dad, give me some* : kita reba, bala aco ni? – *hello my child, how are you?* : ao reba – *come along, boy*   = **re + ba** [1]
rebu ['rɛbū] (int) *dear child* cf **reba**
redio ['rɛdìò] (n) *radio* | tara redio huner – *they are listening to the radio* : redior gan – *song broadcast on radio*   [E.]
reddi ['rɛd-dī] (adj) *worthless*   [A. raddī – *fit to be rejected*]
rejakar ['rɛzāχār, 'rɛjāχār] (n) *collaborator; quisling*   [P. rizākār – *volunteer*]
rejil ['rɛzīl, 'rɛjīl] (adj) *mean-minded*   [A. raðīl]
rek [rɛχ] (n) *rekh (measure of land)*   [B. rekh < O. rekhā – *line; mark*]
rel [rɛl] (n) *rail*   [E.]
relgari ['rɛl-gārī] (n) *railway engine; railway train*   = **rel + gari**
ren [rɛn] (n) *rent* | ou goror ren koto? – *how much is the rent for this house?* : haftat ek so fon ren đei – *we pay £100 rent each week* : ren barce – *the rent has gone up* : malike ren bolaice – *the landlord has put up the rent*   [E.]
rendi ['rɛndī] (n) *whore*   [H. randī]
rendibaji ['rɛndībāzī, 'rɛndībājī] (n) *fornication*   = **rendi + -baji**
renti ['rɛntī] (adj) *rented* | renti gor – *a rented house*   [E.]
reoaj [rɛŵāz] (n) *custom*   [A. rawāj – *circulation*]
resom ['rɛšòm] (n) *silk*   [P. rešam]
reston ['rɛštòn] (n) *restaurant*   [E.]
ricibar ['rīsībār] (n) *telephone receiver* | ricibar tulcoin na – *she didn't pick up the receiver*   [E.]
rifuji ['rīfūzī, 'rīfūjī] (n) *refugee; migrant worker*   [E.]
rijab ['rīzāb, 'rījāb] (adj) *reserved* | rijab gari – *chartered bus*   [E.]
rijek ['rīzɛχ, 'rījɛχ] (n) *daily bread (as provided by God)*   [A. rizq]
rimot ['rīmòt] (n) *remote control pad*   [E.]
rin [rīn] (n) *debt* | at ajar fon rin – *a debt of eight thousand pounds* : **rin an-** – *take out a loan* : tain beŋ taki rin ancoin – *he has borrowed money from the bank* : **rin mar-/rin mari le-** – *pay off a debt* : afne aste aste rin marta oiba – *you'll have to pay off your debts gradually*   [B. rin < S. rṇ]
rini ['rīnī] (adj) *indebted*   [B. rini]
risa ['rīšā] (n) *spite; envious malice*   [B. irsa < S. īrśyā]
risarisi ['rīšārīšī] (n) *mutual hostility*   < **risa**
rista ['rīstā] (n) *connection; relationship*   [P. rišta – *thread; bond*]
ritu ['rītū] (n) *season*   [B. ritu < S. ŕtu]
ro- [1] [rò] (vi) *remain; stay; still be; be* | kaforo đag roibo – *a stain will remain on the cloth* : ino besi din roitam nai – *I shan't stay here long* : he afnar gece roito – *he wants to stay with you* : afne roicoin ni? - *you're still here, are you?* : rouk! – *let it be!* : ola rouk – *leave it as it is* : **roice** – *has remained; still is; is* : bego cini roice – *there is still some sugar in the bag* : ino jaega roice – *there is some space here* : amrar somoe roice – *we still have some time* : afnar beg roice ni? – *have you still got your bag?* : **roia ja-/roi ja-** – *remain; stay; still be* : calon roia jaibo – *some curry will be left over* : tara london roi gece – *they are still in London*   [B. rå-]
ro- [2] (vt) *sow; plant* | iato uri roici – *we have sown some beans in the yard* : alu roicoin ni? – *have you planted your potatoes?*   [B. ro-]
robi [1] ['ròbī] (n) *the sun; Sunday* | sukro soni robi bonđ – *closed on Friday, Saturday and Sunday*   [B. råbi < S. ravi]
robi [2] (n) *springtime*   [A. rabī¿]
rocul [rò 'sūl] (n) *the prophet (Muhammad)*   [A. rasūl]
rod [ròđ] (n) *cancellation*   [A. radd – *return; rejection*]

rod-boḍol ['ròḍ-bòḍòl] (n) *alteration; change* | ḍolilo roḍ-boḍol cole na – *alterations on a deed are not allowed* : ofiso bout roḍ-boḍol oice – *many changes have taken place in the office* : **roḍ-boḍol kor-** – *make changes; alter* **roḍ + boḍol**
roftani ['ròftānī] (n) *export* [P. raftanī]
rog [ròg] (n) *blood vessel; sinews* | tar rog fuli gece – *his veins are swollen* : amar roge tan mare – *I feel tension in my sinews* [P. rag – *blood vessel*]
roibbar ['ròıb-bār] (n) *Sunday* [B. råbibar]
roiḍ ['ròıḍ] (n) *sunshine* | roiḍ utce – *the sun is shining* : roiḍ lager ni? – *is the sunshine too hot for you?* : tara roḍir maje kam korer – *they are working in the sun* : **roḍit** – *in the sunshine* : roḍit ubain na jen – *don't stand in the sun* [B. roḍ < O. rauḍra – *violent*]
rokka ['ròk-kā] (n) *salvation; deliverance; defence* | **rokka oe / rokka oi jae** – *deliverance is obtained* : rokka oi gece! – *we're saved! thank goodness!* : rokka nae – *there's no getting away from it* : ar rokka nae tumrar! – *now you're in for it, children!* : **rokka kor-** – *save (someone from something); defend* [B. råkka < S. rakṣā – *protection*]
rokom ['ròχòm] (n) *sort; kind; type* | ki rokom kafor cain? – *what kind of cloth do you want?* : jeca rokom – *any old kind* : koto rokom manus – *so many types of people* : ou rokom kagoj – *this kind of paper; paper like this* : **rokomor** – *of (different) types* : fac rokomor am – *mangoes of five different kinds* : koto rokomor osubiḍa – *so many sorts of problems* : **rokom rokom** – *various types* : ino rokom rokom sari ace – *there are various kinds of sari here* ¶ **rokom** (adv) *in a manner* | bala rokom – *in a good manner; properly* : bala rokom fori louka – *read it carefully* : kunu rokom – *in some manner* : kam·ta kunu rokom ses korce – *they finished the work any old how* : amra kunu rokom colram – *we are carrying on somehow* : ek rokom – *in a way; more or less* : fotu ek rokom oice – *the photo came out so-so* : ou rokom korouka – *do it like that* [A. raqm – *number*]
rokto ['ròχtò] (n) *blood* | tair sorilo rokto nae – *she is anaemic; she looks pasty* : tan roktor colacol bonḍ – *his blood circulation is not working properly* : tar fau taki rokto bar oice – *blood has come out of his foot; his foot is bleeding* [B. råktå < S. rakta – *red coloured*]
romjan ['ròmzān, 'ròmjān] (n) *Ramadan (Muslim month of fasting)* [A. ramaḎān]
roŋ [ròŋ] (n) *colour; paint* | ou roŋ bala fai – *I like this colour* : roŋ uti gece – *the paint has come off* : **roŋgor** – *of a colour* : nil roŋgor kafor – *blue coloured cloth* : nanan roŋgor sari – *saris of various colours* : **roŋ de-** – *apply colour; paint* : tain ḍorojat roŋ ḍira – *he is painting the door* : **roŋ laga-** – *apply colour; paint* : amra kicino roŋ lagaici – *we have painted the kitchen* [P. rang]
roŋbaj ['ròŋ-bāz, 'ròŋ-bā] (n) *fun-loving person* [P. rangbāz]
roŋgila ['ròŋ-gīlā] (adj) *coloured* [P. rangīn]
roona ['ròônā] (n) *departure* = **ruana**
ros [ròš] (n) *juice; wit; rumour* [B. rås < S. rasa]
rosiḍ[1] ['ròšīḍ] (n) *receipt (voucher)* [P. rasīd]
rosiḍ[2] (adj) *righteous* [A. rašīd]
rosik ['ròšīk] (adj) *juicy; witty; humorous* [B. råsik < S. rasika]
rossi ['ròš-šī] (n) *twine; rope* [B. råsi]
rou [ròu] (n) *a carp-like species of fish (Labeo rohita)* [B. rui]
roun ['ròun] (n) *garlic* [B. råsun]
ru [rū] (n) *body hair* [B. ro]
ru- (vt) *sow; plant* = **ro-**
ruab ['rū-āb] (n) *vainglory* [A. ru¿b – *awe*]
ruana ['rū-ānā] (n) *departure* | **ruana o-/ruana oi ja-** – *depart; set off* : tara noe·tat ruana oice – *they set off at nine o'clock* : afne kuae ruana? – *where are you off to?* : **ruana de-/ruana ḍi la-** – *depart; set off* : amra kail ruana ḍi laimu – *we shall set off tomorrow* [P. ravāna]
ruci ['rūšī] (n) *taste; liking* | afnar ruci oice ni? – *is it to your liking?* : jaitam ni? afnar ruci – *shall we go? it's as you wish* [B. ruci < S. ruci – *lustre*]
ruf [rūf] (n) *beauty* [B rup < S. rūpa]

rufa ['rūfā] (n) *silver* [B. rupa < O. rūpya]
rug [rūg] (n) *illness; disease* | betar camrar rug oi gece – *the man has got a skin disease* : tan rug kita? – *what's wrong with him?* : daktor rug dorta farcoin na – *the doctor couldn't diagnose the illness* [B. rog < S. roga]
ruga ['rūgā] (adj) *sickly; skinny* [B. roga]
rug-bearam ['rūg-bé-ārām] (n) *illnesses* = **rug + bearam**
rugi ['rūgī] (n) *sick person; patient* [B. rogi < S. rogī]
ruh [rūh] (n) *soul* [A. rūh]
ruj [rūz, rūj] (adv) *daily; every day* | amra ruj nomaj fori – *we say our prayers daily* : ruj tin bar ousud kaiba – *take the medicine three times a day* : tain ruj dos·tat kamo jain – *he goes to work at ten every day* : **ruj ruj** – *every single day* : tumar ruj ruj noea kafor lage – *you expect new clothes every single day* [P. roz – *day*]
ruja ['rūzā, 'rūjā] (n) *ritual fasting; Ramadan* | tain ruja maso deso acla – *he was in Bangladesh for Ramadan* : **ruja tak-** – *be fasting* : taintain ruja takra – *they are fasting* : ami ruja aclam – *I was fasting* : afne ruja ni? – *are you fasting?* : **ruja rak-** – *keep a fast* : romjano ruja raka lage – *one has to fast in Ramadan* : **ruja baŋ-** – *break a fast; interrupt a fast* : fani kaia ruja baŋce – *he broke his fast by drinking water* [P. roza]
rujgar ['rūzgār] (n) *livelihood* [P. rozgār – *passing of days*]
ruji ['rūzī, 'rūjī] (n) *earnings; income* | tarar kunu ruji nae – *they have no earned income* : **ruji kor-** – *earn money* : one tain bala foesa ruji koroin – *he earns good money nowadays* [P. rozī – *daily bread*]
ruk [rūk] (n) *wood* | **rukor** – *of wood; wooden* : rukor tebul – *a wooden table* : ou cear rukor nae – *this chair is not made of wood* [B. rukh < O. vŕkśa – *tree*]
rukko ['rūk-kò] (adj) *harsh; rough* | rukko kota – *harsh words* : rukko beboar – *rough manners* [B. rukkå < S. rūkśa]
ruku ['rūkū] (n) *ritual bowing (in Muslim prayer)* [A. rukūʿ]
rul [rūl] (n) *roll; reel; rule* | kagjor rul – *a roll of paper* : dui rul suta – *two rolls of thread* : rul dia mafci – *I measured it with a ruler* : **rul kora** – *rolled; reeled; ruled* : rul kora kagoj – *rolled up paper / ruled paper* [E.]
ruma ['rūmā] (n) *body hair* [B. rom < S. roma]
rumal ['rūmāl] (n) *handkerchief* [P. rūmāl]
rus [rūš] (n) *wild mood* | **ruse** – *wildly; in a hurry* : he ruse kam kore – *he works in a slapdash way* : tara ruse di laice – *they handed it over unceremoniously* : gari besi ruse calaicoin – *he drove too fast* [B. ros < S. rośa – *anger*]
ruti ['rūtī] (n) *flatbread* [H. rotī]

S

sa [šā] (n) *king* [P. šāh]
sab [šāb] (n) *master* | (to a servant) tumar sab kuae? – *where is your master?* : sabe kunta koicoin na – *the boss didn't mention anything* ¶ **sab** (suffixed to name) *mister; his honour* | ali sab – *Mr Ali* : mia sab – *the reverend mullah* : hekim sab – *his honour the judge* : boro bai sab – *respected elder brother* [A. ṣāhib]
saban ['šābān] (n) *soap* [A. ṣābun]
sabas ['šābāš] (n) *encouragement* | **sabas de-** – *give encouragement; egg on; cheer* : tain hurutare sabas dira – *he is giving the children some encouragement* ¶ **sabas** (int) *well done! bravo! congratulations!* [P. šādbāš – *congratulation*]
sabbas ['šāb-bāš] (int) *well done! bravo! congratulations!* = **sabas**
sabdan ['šāb-dān] (adj) *careful* | **sabdan o-** – *be careful* : afne sabdan oita oiba – *you must be careful* : sabdan oia jauka – *mind how you go* : **sabdan oi ja-** – *become cautious; learn caution* : one tara sabdan oi gece – *now they have become more cautious* : **sabdan kor-/sabdan kori de-** – *advise caution; give a warning* : tarare sabdan kora lagbo – *they will have to be given a caution* ¶ **sabdan** (n) *caution* | **sabdane** – *with caution* : sabdane colouka – *proceed with caution* ¶ **sabdan** (int) *be careful! watch out!* [B. sabdhan < S. sāvadhāna – *attentive*]
sad[1] [šād] (n) *taste* | tarar kanit sad nae – *their food has no taste; their food is not palatable* : **sad lage** – *it tastes good* : afne ator rannat bakka sad lage – *your cooking tastes pretty good* [B. sad < S. svāda]
sad[2] (n) *assistance* | **sad de-/sad di la-** – *give assistance; help* : amare tura sad diba ni? – *please will you lend me a hand?* [B. sahåcårjå < S. sāhacarya]
sada[1] ['šādā] (adj) *plain; pure; transparent; uncoloured; white* | sada fani kaitam – *I wish to drink plain water* : tan dil sada – *her heart is pure* : sada kagoj – *plain paper; paper with no writing on it* : sada gelas – *a transparent glass* : sada kafor – *uncoloured cloth; white cloth* : sada roŋ – *white paint* [P. sāda – *simple*]
sada[2] (n) *chewing tobacco*
sadaron ['šādāròn] (adj) *common; ordinary* | sadaron manus – *ordinary people* : sadaron kota – *common topics; everyday things* : ita sadaron kota nae – *it's unusual; it's something out of the ordinary* [B. sadharån < S. sādhāraṇa]
sada-sida ['šādāšīdā] (adj) *plain; simple; simple minded* = **sada** + **sida**
sadi ['šādī] (n) *wedding* | **sadi kor-/sadi kori le-** – *get married* : afne sadi korcoin ni? – *are you married?* [P. šādī – *merrymaking*]
sadiela ['šādīɛlā] (n) *married man* = **sadi** + **-ala**
sadin ['šādīn] (adj) *independent* [B. sadhin < S. svādhīna – *self dependent*]
sadinota ['šādīnòtā] (n) *independence* [B. sadhinåta < S. svādīnatā]
sadot ['šādòt] (n) *testimony* [A. šahāda – *act of witnessing*]
sae [šāy] (n) *consent* | **sae de-** – *give one's consent* [B. say]
saeb ['šāɛb] (n) *gentleman; husband* | hou saeb ke? – *who is that gentleman?* : amar saeb koicoin, afne boita – *my husband said you are to sit and wait for him* = **sab**
sag [šāg] (n) *greens (as food)* [H. sāg]
sagor ['šāgòr] (n) *sea; ocean* | sagor kuna – *south west* [B. sagår < S. sāgara]
sagrid ['šāgrīd] (n) *disciple* [P. šāgird]
sag-sobji ['šāk-sòbzī, 'šāk-sòbjī] (n) *greens; vegetables* = **sag** + **sobji**
saibbosto ['šāɪb-bòstò] (adj) *determined; fixed* | tarik saibbosto oice – *the date has been fixed* : **saibbosto kor-** – *determine; fix* [B. sabbåstå < S. savyavastha]
saijjo ['šāɪj-jò] (n) *help* | tara keur saijjo cae na – *they don't want help from anyone* : afne aile saijjo oibo – *it'll be a help if you come* : **saijjo kor-** – *help* : tain amare bout saijjo korcoin – *he has given me a lot of help* [B. sahajjå < S. sāhāyya]

saikkat ['šāık-kāt] (n) *face-to-face contact* | **saikkat oe** – *contact occurs* : tan loge amar saikkat oice – *I met him* ¶ **saikkat** (adj) *related by blood* | tai amar saikkat boin – *she is my own sister* [B. sakkat < S. sākśāt – *in view*]
saisto ['šāıs-tò] (n) *physical condition; health* | tar saisto bala nae – *he's not in good shape* : afnar saisto oice – *you've put on weight* [B. sasthå < S. svāsthya]
sait [šāıt] (nº) *sixty* [B. sat]
saitan ['šāıtān] (n) *Satan* [A. šaiṭān]
saja ['šāzā, 'šājā] (n) *punishment* | betar saja oice – *the man has received his punishment* : **saja de-** – *inflict punishment; punish* [P. sazā]
sakki ['šāk-kī] (n) *witness* | afne amar sakki – *you are my witness* : **sakki man-** – *agree to bear witness* : tain amar lagi sakki mancoin – *he has agreed to testify on my behalf* : **sakki mana-** – *persuade to be a witness* : tane sakki manaici – *I've got him to agree to be my witness* : **sakki de-** – *bear witness; testify* : tain kouto sakki ḍita caira na – *he doesn't wish to give evidence in court* [B. sakki < S. sākśī]
sakkor ['šāk-kòr] (n) *signature* | **sakkor de-/sakkor ḍi la-** – *give one's signature; sign* : lanir ufre sakkor ḍi lauka – *please sign on the line* : **sakkor lo-** – *obtain a signature (from someone)* : amar sakkor loice – *they took my signature* [B. sakkår < S. svākśara – *autograph*]
sal¹ [šāl] (n) *year* [P. sāl]
sal² (n) *shawl* [P. šāl]
salis ['šālīš] (n) *arbitration panel; arbitration* | tain salis manoin na – *he doesn't agree to arbitration* : salisor maiḍḍome ses oice – *it's been settled by arbitration* : **salis oe** – *arbitration takes place* : aij salis oibo – *there'll be an arbitration meeting today* : **salis boe** – *an arbitration session takes place* [A. θāliθ – *third (party)*]
salisi ['šālīšī] (n) *arbitration* < **salis**
samainno [šā'māın-nıò] (adj) *small; slight; few* | samainno befar – *a trifling matter* : samainno kota – *a few words* ¶ **samainno** (adv) *slightly; a bit* | cuetar samainno boro oice – *the sweater is slightly too large* : ami samainno gumaici – *I only slept a bit* : tain samainno kain – *she eats very little* [B. samannå < S. sāmānya – *alike; common*]
samal- ['šāmāl] (vt) *put in order* = **samla-**
samla- ['šām-lā] (vt) *put in order; save; wind up* | kagoj samlaitam ni? – *shall I tidy the papers?* : tan befsa samlaicoin – *he has wound up his business* : muk samlauka! – *mind your language!* : **samlaia rak- / samalia rak-** – *keep in order; keep safe* : ḍorkari kagjain samalia rakta acla – *you should have kept your important papers safe* [B. samla-]
samnasamni ['šāmnāšāmnī] (adv) *face to face* cf **samne**
samne ['šāmnɛ] (n adv) *in front; ahead* | samne gari ace – *there's a car in front* : goror samne manus ubat – *there are people standing in front of the house* : samne jauka – *go straight ahead* : iḍ samne – *Eid is approaching* : **samne ḍi** – *ahead; in the future* : samne ḍi befsa bala oibo – *business will get better as time goes on* < **samon**
samon ['šāmòn] (n) *front* | samon·ta kacra oi gece – *the front has got dirty* : **samnor** – *of the front; of the future; next* : samnor ḍoroja kula – *the front door is open* : samnor gari kar? – *whose is the car in front?* : samnor ḍin – *the days ahead* : samnor aftat london jaimu – *I'm going to London next week* [B. samån]
santi ['šāntī] (n) *peace; ease* | tarar goro santi nae – *there's no peace in their house* : ino santi lage – *it feels peaceful here* : amra santir maje aclam – *we were enjoying a life of ease* : **santie** – *in peace; peacefully; comfortably* : tain santie gumaira – *she is sleeping peacefully* : **santi moto** – *in a relaxed manner* : amra santi moto kam kormu – *we'll do our work at a convenient pace* : afne santi moto korouka – *take it easy, do it without feeling pressurized* : **santir** – *of peace; peaceful* : boro santir jaega – *a very peaceful place* : **santi o-/santi oi ja-** – *be pacified; feel relieved* : tain kaia santi oi gecoin – *now that he's eaten he's calmed down* : tara goro aile baḍe santi oimu – *I shall be relieved when they get home* [B. santi < S. šānti]

santo ['šāntò] (adj) *peaceful; quiet* | santo furi – *a quiet girl; a good little girl* : **santo o-/santo oi ja-** – *become quiet* : fua·ta santo oi gece – *the boy has quietened down* : santo ouka – *please calm down* [B. santå < S. šānta – *pacified*]
saos ['šāòš] (n) *courage; boldness; brazenness* | tar saos ace – *he has a lot of courage* : tar saos besi – *he is too bold* : tar saos dekcoin ni? – *see how brazen he is* : saos koto! – *what cheek!* : **(kar) saose dee** – *(one's) courage permits* : amar saose dee na – *I don't have the courage to do it* : **(kar) saos oe/saos oi jae** – *(one's) courage rises; (one's) confidence grows* : amar saos oe na koitam – *I don't have the courage to say it; I daren't say it* : one tan saos oi gece matbar – *now he has got enough confidence to speak* : **saos kor-/saos kori le-** – *pluck up courage* : gaŋ far oita saos korta farcoin na – *he couldn't pluck up enough courage to cross the river* : **saos de-/saos di la-** – *give encouragement* : forikkar age taire saos di laita – *you should encourage her before the exam* [B. sahås < S. sāhasa]
saosi ['šāòšī] (adj) *bold; daring* < **saos**
sar- [šār] (vi) *suffice* | **sare** – *it suffices; it is enough* : ek camuc dile sare – *it's enough if you put one spoonful* : afne na gele sarbo – *it will be all right if you don't go* [B. sar-]
sara ['šārā] (adj) *entire; whole* | sara jindegi london kataicoin – *he spent his entire life in England* : sara din kuae acla? – *where were you all day?* : sara gor dem oi gece – *the whole house has got damp* : koe din roicla? ek mas sara – *how long did you stay there? one whole month* [B. sara]
sarakkon ['šārāk-kòn] (adv) *all the time* [B. sarakkån]
sarata ['šārātā] (pron) *all of it; the whole lot* | sarata kai louka – *go on, eat all of it* : sarata bad oi gece – *the whole lot has got spoilt* = **sara + -ta** [2]
sare ['šārɛ] (adv) *with one half added; plus a half* | sare cair – *four and a half* : sare fac goj – *five and a half yards* : sare sat so – *seven and a half hundred; seven hundred and fifty* : sare tin ajar – *three thousand five hundred* : sare tin·ta – *three and a half (o'clock); half past three* : sare baro·ta – *half past twelve* [B. saɾe]
sari ['šārī] (n) *sari; saree* [B. saɾi]
saririk ['šārīrīk] (adj) *corporeal; bodily; physical* | tan saririk obosta bala nae – *her state of health is not good* ¶ **saririk** (n) *physical condition; health* | afnar saririk bala ni? – *are you in good health?* [B. saririk < S. šārīrika]
sarto ['šār-tò] (n) *vested interest; motive; gain* | loat sarto ace tan – *he has a motive for buying it; it's in his interests to buy it* : amar jaoat sarto nae – *I don't stand to gain anything by going* : tara sarto tukar – *they're looking to further their own interests* [B. sartå < S. svārtha – *own aim*]
sartobadi ['šār-tòbādī] (adj) *self-interested; out for gain* [B. sartåbadi]
sas [šāš] (n) *breathing* | **sas tul-** – *take a breath; breathe in* : tain sas tulta faroin na – *she can't breathe* : **sas fala-** – *release breath; breathe out* [B. sas < S. švāsa]
sason ['šāšòn] (n) *discipline; control* | **sason kor-** – *discipline; control* : tara hurutare sason kore na – *they don't keep their kids under control* [B. sasån < S. šāsana – *punishment; government*]
sasti ['šāstī] (n) *punishment* | **sasti de-** – *inflict punishment; punish* : curre sasti dita acla – *they should have punished the thief* [B. sasti < S. šāsti – *punishment; governing*]
sat [šāt] (n) *shirt* [E.]
sat [šāt] (n°) *seven* | sat fon – *seven pounds* : sat asman – *the seven heavens* : tain sat·tat utoin – *he gets up at seven o'clock* : **sat-o** – *all seven* : sof sat-o din kula – *the shop is open seven days a week* [B. sat]
satais ['šātāɪš] (n°) *twenty-seven* [B. satas]
satanno ['šātān-nò] (n°) *fifty-seven* [B. satannå]
satannobboi ['šātān-nòb-bòɪ] (n°) *ninety-seven* [B. satannåbbåi]
satasi ['šātāšī] (n°) *eighty-seven* [B. satasi]
satattoir ['šātāt-tòɪr] (n°) *seventy-seven* [B. satattår]
satcallis ['šātsāl-līš] (n°) *forty-seven* [B. satcållis]
satsotti ['šātšòt-tī] (n°) *sixty-seven* [B. satsåtti]

sattis ['šāt-tīš] (nº) *thirty-seven* [B. saitris]
sauui ['šāŵŵī] (n) *vermicelli* = **seuai**
sean [šɛ 'ān] (adj) *capable of discretion* = **sian**
seba ['šɛbā] (n) *service* | **seba kor-** – *perform service; serve* [B. seba < S. sevā]
seba-susra ['šɛbāšūsrā] (n) *service and assistance* = **seba** + **susra**
sebit ['šɛbīt] (n adv) *at ease* < **seib**
sef [šɛf] (n) *chef* | tain sef boncoin – *he has become a chef* : tain sefor kam janoin – *he has experience as a chef* [E.]
seib [šɛɪb] (n) *convenience* | **seib oe** – *convenience is felt* : ino afnar seib oito nae – *you won't feel at ease here* : **sebit** – *at ease; in comfort* : sebit bouka – *sit at ease; please make yourself comfortable* : **seib fa-** – *be at ease; be comfortable* : ino boile afne seib faiba – *if you sit here you'll be more comfortable* = **subiḋa**
sejḋa ['šɛz-ḋā] (n) *prostration (in prayer)* [A. sajda]
sek[1] [šɛχ] (n) *warming* | agunor sek louka – *get yourself some warmth from the fire* : fanir sek – *warmth from hot water* : fanir sekor butol – *hot water bottle* [B. se^{n}k]
sek[2] (n) *sheikh* [A. šaiḵ]
selai ['šɛlāi] (n) *stitching* = **silai**
seloar ['šɛlòār] (n) *pantaloons* [P. šalvār]
semla ['šɛmlā] (adj) *mid-brown; nut brown* | tair gaer roŋ semla – *she has a coffee brown skin colour* [B. semla < O. šyāmala]
sera ['šɛrā] (adj) *best; choice* [B. sera < P. sir – *head, top*]
ses [šɛš] (adj) *finished* | **ses o-/ses oi ja-** – *be finished; come to an end* : holiḋ kailku ses oibo – *the holidays will end tomorrow* : cini ses oi gece – *the sugar has run out* : amar fasfut ses oi jar – *my passport is expiring* : afnar kani ses ni? – *have you finished your meal?* : amra ḋourte ḋourte ses – *we are exhausted from running* : **ses kor-/ses kori le-** – *finish off* : afnar kiric ses korta nae? – *don't you want to finish your crisps?* : jolḋi ses koro! – *hurry up and finish!* : tan kam ses kori licoin – *she has finished her work* [B. ses < S. šeś – *remaining*]
set [šɛt] (n) *snot* | **set fala-** – *clear one's nose*
seuai ['šɛŵāɪ] (n) *brown wheat vermicelli* [H. sivaiyā^n]
sia ['šīā] (n) *a Muslim who follows the tradition of Ali; Shiite* | sia sunni – *Shiites and Sunni, the two main categories of Muslims* [A. šī¿a – *faction*]
sian [šī 'ān] (adj) *capable of discretion; mature* | sian fua – *grown lad; teenage boy* : amar furi sian oi gece – *my daughter has reached puberty* [H. sayānā < O. saŋjñāna]
siḋa ['šīḋā] (adj) *straight; straightforward; simple* | siḋa rasta – *a straight road* : siḋa kam – *a straightforward job* : siḋa manus – *a simple-minded person* ¶ **siḋa** (adv) *straight forward; straight out* | siḋa jauka – *carry on straight ahead* : tain siḋa goro gecoin – *he went straight home* : beta siḋa koi lice – *he blurted it straight out* : **siḋa kor-/siḋa kori le-** – *straighten* : tara rasta siḋa korto – *they're going to straighten the road* : tumar tai siḋa kori lao – *straighten your tie* [H. sīḋhā < O. siḋḋha – *accomplished*]
siḋḋanto ['šīḋ-ḋāntò] (n) *decision* | **siḋḋanto lo-** – *take a decision* : **siḋḋante a-** – *reach a conclusion* [B. siḋḋhantā < S. siḋḋhānta – *accomplished end*]
siḋḋo ['šīḋ-ḋò] (adj) *boiled* | siḋḋo fani – *boiled water* : siḋḋo cail – *pre-boiled rice* [B. siḋḋhå < O. siḋḋha – *accomplished*]
siggir ['šīg-gīr] (adv) *quickly* [B. sighrå < S. šīghra – *quick, rapid*]
sik [šīk] (n) *skewer; spit* | sik kobab – *kebab grilled on a skewer* [B. sik]
sika ['šīkā] (n) *macramé sling (for suspending items in storage)* [B. sika]
sikar ['šīkār] (n) *admission; acknowledgement* | **sikar o-/sikar oi ja-** – *admit; acknowledge; reach agreement* : he sikar oe na – *he won't admit anything* : tara sikar oi gece – *they have conceded the point* : afne sikar ni? – *do you agree to that?* : **sikar a-** – *come round (to another point of view); come clean* : one he sikar aice – *now he has admitted everything; now he has agreed* : **sikar kor-/sikar kori le-** – *admit (something)* : ḋus sikar koroin na – *he doesn't admit to any fault* : he curi korcil, one sikar korce – *now he admits he stole it* [B. sikar < S. svīkāra – *making one's own*]

sikarjuaf ['šīkār-jūāf] (n) *confession* | **sikarjuaf de-/sikarjuaf di la-** *– make a confession* : hese sikarjuaf di laice *– he finally confessed* = **sikar + juaf**
siki ['šīkī] (n) *quarter* [B. siki]
sikka ['šīk-kā] (n) *education* [B. sikka < S. šikśa]
sikol ['šīkòl] (n) *chain-fetters* [B. sikål < O. šŕŋkhala]
sikom ['šīkòm] (n) *belly* [P. šikam]
sil [šīl] (n) *rubber stamp* | **sil mar-** *– impress a rubber stamp* : tara fasfuto sil marce *– they stamped the passport* : **sil ka-** *– receive a rubber stamp; get stamped* : amar fasfut sil kaice na *– my passport hasn't been stamped* [E. seal]
silai ['šīlāi] (n) *stitching; sewing; tailoring* | silai kuli gece *– the stitching has come undone* : tain silair kam janoin *– she knows the art of sewing* : silair mesin *– sewing machine* : **silai kor-** *– stitch; sew* : blauj·ta nije silai korcoin *– she made the blouse herself* [H. silāī]
sima ['šīmā] (n) *limit; boundary* | tair kusir sima nae *– her joy knows no bounds* : amar doijjor sima ace *– there's a limit to my patience* : faijlamir ek·ta sima ace *– there's a limit to (one's tolerance of) silliness* : simar bitre *– within the limit* : simar baire *– beyond the limit* : **simat** *– at the limit; to the limit* : tain simat gecoin gi *– he's gone too far* : **sima caria ja-** *– go over the limit* : tara sima caria kuae gece *– they've gone way over the limit* [B. sima < S. sīmā]
simito ['šīmītò] (adj) *limited; restricted* [B. simitå < S. sīmita]
sinni ['šīn-nī] (n) *sweetmeats or puddings (prepared for sharing out as a sacrament)* | tara goro goro sinni dia gece *– they distributed sacramental food from house to house* : **sinni kor-** *– hold a prayer feast (typically to mark a birth or death)* [P. šīrīnī *– sweetmeats*]
siŋ [šīŋ] (n) *wash-basin; sink; tap* | tain siŋgo muk doira *– he's washing his face at the basin* : siŋgor fani *– tap water* [E.]
siŋo ['šīŋò] (n) *lion* [B. siŋhå < S. siŋha]
sira ['šīrā] (n) *gravy* [P. šorbā *– soup*]
siri[1] ['šīrī] (n) *whistling* | **siri de-** *– whistle*
siri[2] (n) *step; staircase; generation* | samne dui·ta siri ace *– there are two steps at the front* : siri bae uta lagbo *– we'll have to go up the stairs* : siri lamta farba ni? *– will you be able to get down the stairs?* : tin siri furbe amar boro baf acla *– three generations back there was my great grandfather* [B. siṛi]
sirik ['šīrīk] (n) *polytheism; idolatry; the major sin of associating the Deity with any other concept or being* [A. širk]
sis [šīš] (n) *lead; lead pencil* | tain sis dia lekra *– he's writing with a pencil* : sis kolom *– ballpoint pen* : kolomor sis *– pencil lead; ballpoint refill* [B. sis < O. sīsaka *– lead (metal)*]
sit [šīt] (n) *cold; winter* | sit lage *– the cold affects one; it feels cold* : sit aice *– the winter has arrived* : sitor din *– days of cold; the winter period* : sitor somoe *– (in) winter* : sitor maje *– in the cold* [B. sit < S. šīta]
slamalekum ['slāmalékūm] (int) *greetings!* = **calamalekum**
so [šò] (n°) *hundred* | ek so ek *– one hundred and one* : tin so fassait *– three hundred and sixty-five* : sare cair so *– four hundred and fifty* : ek so·ta karon *– a hundred reasons* : fac so·jon manus *– five hundred people* : sor ufre *– over one hundred* : dui sor kandat *– around two hundred* : **ek so bar** *– a hundred times; time and again; most definitely* : tumare ek so bar koici *– I've told you ever so many times* : jaitam nai ni, ek so bar jaimu! *– as to my not going, well, most certainly I shall go!* [B. så < O. šata]
so- (v) *endure* | ar soitam fari na *– I can't stand any more* : ar kotota soita? *– how much more is one supposed to put up with?* [B. såh-]
soari ['šòārī] (n) *palanquin* [P. savārī *– riding*]
sob [šòb] (adj) *all* | tara sob gorib *– all of them are poor* : furin sob ino *– all the girls are here* : **sob somoe** *– all the time; always* : amra sob somoe bat kai *– we always eat rice* [B. såb < O. sarva]

sobbonas ['sòb-bònāš] (n) *ruination; calamity; disaster* | amar sobbonas oice – *I've had a disaster; I'm ruined* ¶ **sobbonas** (int) *oh dear! oh what a nuisance!* [B. sårbånas < S. sarvanāša – *total destruction*]
sobdo ['sòbdò] (n) *sound; spoken word* | kior sobdo? – *what's that noise?* : garir sobdo huna jar – *the sound of vehicles can be heard* : ɖui tin·ta sobɖo jane – *he knows how to say a couple of words* : **sobdo kor-** – *make a sound; make a noise* : injile sobɖo korer – *the engine is making odd noises* [B. såbɖå < S. šabɖa]
sobji ['sòbzī, 'sòbjī] (n) *vegetables* [P. sabzī – *greens; greenness*]
sobta ['sòbtā] (pron) *all of it* = **sob + -ta** ²
sobuj ['sòbūz, 'sòbūj] (n/adj) *green* [P. sabz]
sobur ['sòbūr] (n) *patience; long-suffering* | tan sobur ace – *she has a lot of patience* : **sobur kor-** – *be patient; wait patiently* : sobur kora lagbo – *we'll have to be patient* : tura sobur korouka – *please bear with me one moment* [A. ṣabr]
sodor ['sòdòr] (n) *headquarters; chief subdivision (of a district)* | tara soɖoro take – *they live in the chief subdivision; they live near the capital* ¶ **sodor** (adj) *main* | soɖor ɖoroja – *main entrance* [A. ṣadr – *breast; front*]
soetan ['sòytān] (adj) *mischievous* cf **saitan**
soetani ['sòytānī] (n) *mischief* | **soetani kor-** – *do mischief; be naughty* < **soetan**
sof [sòf] (n) *shop* | ami sof taki anci – *I got it from the shop* : gua sofo mile – *betelnut is available in the shop* : ita goror nae, ita sofor – *it isn't homemade, it's shop stuff* [E.]
sofat [sòf 'āt] (n) *mediation; intercession (by prophet, with God)* [A. šafā¿a]
sofno ['sòfnò] (n) *dream* | sofnor maje ɖekci afnare – *I saw you in a dream; I dreamed about you* : **sofno dek-** – *have a dream* : afne hamesa sofno ɖekoin ni? – *do you often have dreams?* : tain foesar sofno ɖekcoin – *he dreamed about money* [B. såpnå < S. svapna]
sofon ['sòfòn] (n) *dream* = **sofno**
sofor ['sòfòr] (n) *journey* [A. safar]
sofri ['sòfrī] (n) *guava*
soi ¹ [sòɪ] (adv) *straight* | soi jauka gi – *go straight ahead* : **soi soi** – *straight ahead; right in front* : tarar gor amrar goror soi soi – *their house is right opposite ours* [A. ṣahīh – *right*]
soi ² (n) *signature* | **soi kor-** – *put one's signature; sign* : tain ɖolilo soi korcoin – *he has signed the deed* [H. sahī < A. ṣahīh – *right*]
soi ³ (n) *female companion (of a woman)* [B. såhi < S. sakhī]
soid ['sòɪd] (n) *martyr* [A. šahīd]
soidminar ['sòɪd-mīnār] (n) *language martyrs' monument* = **soid + minar**
soijjo ['sòɪj-jɪò] (adj) *bearable* | **soijjo oe** – *is bearable* : i aoaj afnar soijjo oe kila? – *how do you put up with this noise?* ¶ **soijjo** (n) *endurance* | **soijjo kor-** – *endure; bear* : tara kotota soijjo korce – *they've endured a great deal* [B. såjjå < S. sahya – *bearable*]
soil [sòɪl] (n) *body* = **soril**
soinik ['sòɪnīk] (n) *soldier* [B. såinik < S. sainika]
soi-somfotti ['sòɪšòmfot-tī] (n) *property* = **somfotti**
soit [sòɪt] (post) *together with* | tain foribar soit bar oicla – *he went out, along with his wife* : kaf ano, firic soit – *bring the cup together with its saucer* [B. såhit < S. sahita – *accompanied*]
soite ['sòɪtɛ] (post) *together with* = **soit**
soitto ['sòɪt-tɪò] (adj) *true; honest* | tan kota·kan soitto – *his words are true; what he said is true* : soitto karbar – *honest trading* : **soitto kota** – *true words; truth* : afne soitto kota koicoin – *you have spoken the truth; you are quite right* : soitto kota kouka – *tell the truth* [B. såttå < S. satya]
sojda ['sòz-dā] (n) *prostration (in prayer)* = **sejda**
sok [sòχ] (n) *fancy; liking* | afnar kunu sok acil ni? – *was there anything you specially wanted?* : amar cinema jaibar sok acil – *I was (and am) feeling like going to the cinema* : tan bidio ɖekar sok – *he loves watching videos* : **sok kori** – *as a whim; as a hobby; for fun* :

tain sok kori bagan koroin – *she does gardening as a hobby* : ami sok kori boro guddi loiclam – *I bought a big kite just for fun* [A. šauq – *desire*]
sokal ['sòχāl] (n) *morning time* | one sokal, gumaita kila – *it's morning now, how do you expect to sleep* ¶ **sokal** (adv) *early; soon* | afne boro sokal aicoin – *you have come very early; you have returned very soon* : kam·ta sokal ses oito nae – *the job won't be finished very soon* : **sokal sokal** – *very early; very soon* : tain sokal sokal utoin – *she gets up very early in the morning* : afne sokal sokal ain jen – *make sure you come as soon as possible* [B. såkal < O. sakāla]
sokale ['sòχālé] (adv) *in the morning; early* < **sokal**
sokol¹ ['sòχòl] (adj) *all* = **hokol**
sokol² (n) *appearance* [A. šakl]
sokol-ceara ['sòχòl-sɛārā] (n) *appearance* = **sokol**² + **ceara**
sokti ['sòχtī] (n) *power; strength* | tan ator sokti ace – *his arms have strength; he has strong arms* : tan ubaibar sokti nae – *he hasn't got the strength to stand* : tan mukabela korar sokti kar? – *who has the power to oppose him?* [B. såkti < S. šakti – *power*]
sokto ['sòχtò] (adj) *hard; difficult* | sokto mati – *hard ground* : sokto manus – *a hard person; an unfeeling person* : sokto kam – *hard work; a difficult task* : aij ses kora sokto oibo – *it will be hard to finish it today* [B. såktå < S. šakta – *empowered*]
soloe ['sòlòy] (n) *glowing splinter; match* [B. såla < O. šalākā – *splinter*]
som [sòm] (n) *Monday* [B. som < S. soma – *the moon*]
somadan ['sòmādān] (n) *solution (to a problem)* | somossar somadan – *the solution of a problem* [B. såmadhan < S. samadhāna – *putting together*]
somaj ['sòmāz, 'sòmāj] (n) *society* [B. såmaj < S. samāja]
soman ['sòmān] (adj) *equal; the same* | soman dam – *an equal price; the same price* : soman kota – *an equal matter; the same thing* : tan lagi rait din soman – *night and day are the same to him* : tara dui bai soman – *those two brothers are just the same* : dui jug tin soman fac – *two plus three equals five* : «ator fac aŋgul soman nae» – *the five fingers are not all the same; it takes all types to make a world* : **soman soman** – *just the same; equal in extent* : tara dui bai soman soman – *those two brothers are identical / exactly the same height* ¶ **soman** (adv) *equally* | he soman boro – *he's equally old; he's the same age* : tara dui-o·jon soman lamfa – *the two of them are equally tall; they are both of equal height* [B. såman < S. samāna]
sombabona [sòm 'bābònā] (n) *possibility* [B. såmbhabåna < S. sambhāvanā]
sombar ['sòmbār] (n) *Monday* [B. sombar]
sombob ['sòmbòb] (n) *normal state of affairs; possible circumstances* | ita sombobor bitre – *it's within the bounds of possibility* ¶ **sombob** (adj) *possible* | aij boraf fora sombob – *today snowfall is possible* : amar jaoa sombob oito nae – *my going won't be possible; I won't be able to go* : sombob oile kormu – *I'll do it if it's possible* ¶ **sombob** (adv) *possibly; probably* | tain bara gecoin gi sombob – *maybe he's gone out* : aij meg dibo ni? sombob – *will it rain today? probably* [B. såmbhåb < S. sambhava – *union; source*]
somfotti [sòm 'fòt-tī] (n) *property; real estate* | sunamgonjo tarar bout somfotti – *they own a lot of land in Sunamganj* : tar bafor somfotti kai lice – *he has consumed his father's property; he has squandered his inheritance* [B. såmpåtti < S. sampatti]
somiti ['sòmītī] (n) *association; club* [B. såmiti < S. samiti]
somj- [sòmz, 'sòmj] (v) *understand* | tara somjice na – *they haven't got the message* : **somji ja-** – *understand* : ji oe, somji geci – *yes, I have understood* [H. samajh-]
somja- ['sòmzā, 'sòmjā] (vt) *explain* | kita kortam amare somjauka – *please explain what I'm to do* : **somjai de-** – *explain* : kail bisoe·ta somjai dimu afnare – *I shall explain the matter to you tomorrow* [H. samjhā-]
somman ['sòm-mān] (n) *respect* | **somman kor-** – *respect* : cacare hokoloe somman kore – *everyone respects uncle* : **somman deka-** – *show respect* [B. såmman < S. sammāna]
somoe ['sòmòy] (n) *time* | ebu bout somoe roice – *there's still plenty of time* : tan boibar somoe nae – *she hasn't even got time to sit down* : tumi somoe nosto koro kali – *you keep*

wasting time : borisar somoe – *the time of rain; the rainy season* : one kusi korbar somoe – *now is the time for rejoicing* : somoe jar gi – *the opportune moment is slipping away* : **somoe lage** – *it takes time* : gor tulte somoe lagbo – *it will take time to erect a building* : kanit bout somoe lagce amrar – *it's taken us a long time to eat* : **somoe laga-** – *take time* : kafor finḋat oto somoe lagao – *you take such a long time to get dressed* : **somoe kate** – *time passes* : afnar somoe kate kila? – *how does your time pass? how do you spend your time?* : **somoe kata-** – *pass time* : tara tibi ḋekat raijjir somoe katae – *they spend a huge amount of time watching TV* : **somoe kor-** – *make time* : ino aoar somoe korta farcoin na – *he couldn't make time to come here* : **somoe lo-** – *obtain time* : tara ek aftar somoe loice – *they have asked for one week's grace* : **somoe ḋori** – *for a period* : amra bout somoe ḋori ubairam – *we've been waiting for a long time* ¶ **somoe** (adv) *at a time; for a time* | hou somoe tain london takta – *at that time he used to live in London* : oto somoe kuae acla? – *where were you all this time?* : jaibar somoe tain kanḋicoin – *at the time of going she wept; she wept as she went away* : aite somoe fan anouka – *please bring some paan when you come* : amra tura somoe bara takmu – *we'll be out for a short while* : **somoe somoe** – *at times; from time to time* : amra somoe somoe hutki kai – *we sometimes eat dried fish* : **somoe moto** – *at the right time* : somoe moto ain jen – *please arrive in time* [B. såmåy < S. samaya]

somonde [šò 'mònḋɛ] (n adv) *in connection; about* | tara gari somonḋe jikaice – *they asked about the car* : amar somonḋe kita koicil? – *what did they say about me?* < **somondo**

somondo [šò 'mòndò] (n) *connection; relationship; marital link* | tarar loge amrar somonḋo nae – *we have no connection with them* : tara amrar loge somonḋo korce – *they have married into our family* : **somonḋe** – *in connection; about* : hi somonḋe kunta jani na – *I don't know anything about that* [B. såmmånḋhå < S. sambanḋha]

somorton [šò 'mòr-tòn] (n) *endorsement; approval; support* | **somorton kor-** – *endorse; support* [B. såmårthån < S. samarthana – *consideration*]

somossa [šò 'mòš-šā] (n) *problem* [B. såmåssa < S. samasyā – *placing together*]

somosto ['šòmòstò] (adj) *all* | somosto kam nani eka korcoin – *granny did all the work by herself* [B. såmåstå < S. samasta – *placed together*]

sommoti ['šòm-mòtī] (n) *agreement* [B. såmmåti < S. sammati]

somudro [šò 'mūd-rò] (n) *ocean* [B. såmuḋrå < S. samuḋra]

son [šòn] (n) *calendar year* [A. sana]

sondeo ['šònḋéò] (n) *doubt; suspicion* | **sonḋeo take / sonḋeo oe** – *doubt exists* : ou befare sonḋeo roice – *there is some doubt concerning this matter* : maje maje sonḋeo oe – *one sometimes wonders* : tain korcoin ni na sonḋeo – *whether or not he did it is doubtful* : meg ḋibo, sonḋeo nae – *it will rain, no doubt about it* : **(kar) sonḋeo kore** – *(one's) doubts or suspicions arise* : tain korcoin ni na amar sonḋeo kore – *I have my suspicions as to whether he did do it* : **(kare) sonḋeo kor-** – *suspect (somebody)* : fulise tare curir ḋae sonḋeo kore – *the police suspect him of theft* [B. šånḋehå < S. sanḋeha]

sonduk ['šònḋūk] (n) *strong-box; chest* [A. ṣanḋūq]

soni ['šònī] (n) *Saturn; Saturday* | soni robi ofis bonḋ – *the office is closed on Saturday and Sunday* [B. såni < S. šani]

sonibar ['šònībār] (n) *Saturday* [B. šånibar]

sontan ['šòntān] (n) *child* [B. såntan < S. santāna – *offspring*]

sontusto ['šòntūštò] (adj) *satisfied* [B. såntustå < S. santuśta]

soŋbad ['šòŋbād] (n) *piece of news* | kusir soŋbaḋ – *a bit of good news* : morar soŋbaḋ – *news of a death* : kunu soŋbaḋ faicoin ni? – *have you received any news?* : tarare soŋbaḋ ḋici – *I've sent them a message* [B. såŋbaḋ < S. saŋvāḋa – *colloquy*]

soŋge ['šòŋ-gɛ] (n adv) *in company; alongside; with* | afnar soŋge ke acla? – *who was with you?* : tain hurutar soŋge takba – *she will stay with the children* < **soŋgo**

soŋgi ['šòŋ-gī] (n) *companion* [B. såŋgi]

soŋgit ['šòŋ-gīt] (n) *anthem; music* [B. såŋgit < S. saŋgīta]

soŋgo ['šòŋ-gò] (n) *accompaniment; company* | **soŋgo de-** – *give company; accompany* : tain afnare soŋgo d ba – *he will keep you company* : **soŋge** – *in company; alongside; with* : huruta tan soŋge gecil – *the children went together with him* [B. såŋgå < S. saŋga]

soŋgram ['šòŋ-grām] (n) *struggle; fight; battle* | sađinotar soŋgram – *the struggle for independence* [B. såŋgram < S. saŋgrāma]

soŋka ['šòŋ-kā] (n) *number* | catro-catrir mut soŋka koto? – *what is the total number of students?* : furintor soŋka besi – *the number of girls is greater; the girls are in the majority* [B. såŋkha < S. saŋkhyā – *reckoning*]

soŋsar ['šòŋ-šār] (n) *establishment in the world; household; family* | amrar soŋsar boro – *we are a large household* : coe·jonor soŋsar atbo ou goro – *a family of six could fit in this house* : tain soŋsar caria gecoin gi – *he has left this world; he has passed away* : **soŋsar kor-** – *set up in family life* : onek boes oia soŋsar korcoin – *he started a family at a late age* : **soŋsar cala-** – *run a household; manage a family* : oto boro soŋsar calain kila? – *how do you manage such a large family?* : **soŋsar cole** – *a household runs; a family gets along* : tarar soŋsar bala cole – *their family is doing all right* [B. såŋsar < S. saŋsāra – *passing through*]

sooj ['šò-òj] (adj) *easy* | koa·ta sooj – *it's easy to say that* : **sooje** – *easily* : sooje hamail jae na – *you can't get in at all easily* [B. såhåj < S. sahaja – *cognate*]

soor ['šò-òr] (n) *city; town* [P. šahr]

sora ['šòrā] (n) *Islamic legal system* [A. šarɛ]

sorab ['šòrāb] (n) *alcoholic liquor* [A. šarāb – *beverage*]

sorbot ['šòr-bòt] (n) *sweet drink* [A. šarba – *drink; draught*]

sorđar ['šòr-đār] (n) *chieftain; leader* [P. sarđār]

sorđi ['šòrđī] (n) *cold; cold in the head* | **(kar) sorđi oe** – *a cold develops (in someone)* : cacir sorđi oice – *aunt has caught a cold* : **(kar) sorđi kore / sorđi kori lee** – *a cold develops (in someone)* : amar sorđi kori lice – *I've caught a cold* : **(kar) sorđi lage** – *cold is felt (by someone)* : ino boile afnar sorđi lagto fare – *if you sit here you may catch cold* [P. sardī – *coldness*]

sorif [šò 'rīf] (adj) *noble* [A. šarīf]

soril ['šòrīl] (n) *body; health* | tan soril muta – *his physique is corpulent* : tan soril karaf – *his health is bad; he is ill* : afnar soril kita, bala ni? – *how are you?* : amar soril bala nae – *I'm not well* : amar asto sorilo bis – *I feel pain throughout my body* [B. sårir < S. šarīra]

soriot ['šòrīòt] (n) *Islamic legal system; Sharia* [A. šarī̠a]

sorisa ['šòrīšā] (n) *mustard* [B. sårisa < O. sarśapa]

sorkar ['šòrχār] (n) *government* [P. sarkār]

sorkari ['šòrχārī] (adj) *of the government; official* [P. sarkārī]

sorma- ['šòr-mā] (vi) *be ashamed; be embarrassed; be bashful* | sormao kene – *why be shy; don't be so shy* : is! sormaice! – *oh dear, she's blushing!* [H. sarmā-]

sorminđa ['šòr-mīnđā] (adj) *ashamed; bashful* | **sorminđa o-/sorminđa oi ja-** – *be put to shame* [P. šarminđa]

sorol ['šòròl] (adj) *simple; naïve* | sorol buđđi – *naïve mentality* : fua·ta ekere sorol – *the boy is quite simple-minded* [B. såråł < S. sarala – *straight*]

sorom ['šòròm] (n) *shame; embarrassment (particularly that felt by juniors in the presence of elders or women in the presence of men)* | tumar sorom nae ni? – *do you have no shame?* : sorom! – *shame on you! you shouldn't do that!* : soromor bisoe – *a matter of shame; a shameful thing* : **(kar) sorom oe/sorom lage** – *shame or embarrassment is felt (by someone)* : natir sorom lager – *grandson is feeling embarrassed* : **(kar) sorom kore** – *shame or embarrassment is felt (by someone)* : sorom kore na tumar? – *don't you feel ashamed of yourself?* : **sorom fa-/sorom fai le-** – *feel ashamed; get embarrassed* : is, sorom fai lice! – *oh dear, she's got all embarrassed!* [P. šarm]

soron ['šòròn] (n) *recollection* | **(kar) soron ace** – *(someone) has a recollection* : ke aicil, afnar soron ace ni? – *do you remember who came?* : amar soron takbo – *I shall remember; I shall bear it in mind* : bađe afnar soron oito fare, tan nam kita – *maybe later on you'll* *recall what his name is* : tair soron nae – *she can't remember* : amar soron or na – *I can't recall* : **soron kor-** – *call to mind; recall* : tikana·ta soron kortam farram na – *I can't recall the address* : **(kare) soron kora-** – *cause (someone else) to remember; remind (someone)* : kail meman aiba, cacare soron koraitam oimu – *I must remind uncle that visitors are coming tomorrow*   [B. sårån < S. smaraṇa]

sorto ['šòr-tò] (n) *condition (of an agreement)* | kabinor maje sorto leka ace – *some conditions are written in the marriage contract*   [A. šarṭ]

sosa ['šòšā] (n) *cucumber*   [B. såsa]

sossa ['šòš-šā] (n) *mustard*   = **sorisa**

sosta ['šòs-tā] (adj) *cheap*   [H. sastā]

sotkat ['šòt-χāt] (n) *short cut* | **sotkat kori** – *in brief* : tane sotkat kori bujaici – *I explained it to him briefly* : sotkat kori kouka – *say it briefly; please keep it short*   [E.]

sot [šòt] (adj) *honest*   [B. såt < S. sat – *real; true*]

soto ['šòtò] (nº) *hundred* | **soto soto** – *hundreds* : soto soto manus ar – *hundreds of people are coming*   [B. såtå < S. šata]

sotok ['šòtòχ] (n) *hundredth; hundredth of an acre; "decimal" (land measure)* | ou đage tin sotok – *this plot comprises three hundredths of an acre* : sullo sotok abadi jomi – *sixteen decimals of arable land*   [B. såtåk < S. šataka]

sotoro ['šòtòrò] (nº) *seventeen*   [B. såtårå]

sotru ['šòt-rū] (n) *enemy*   [B. såtru < S. šatru]

sotruta ['šòt-rūtā] (n) *enmity* | **sotruta kor-** – *create enmity; be hostile* : tara amrar loge kali sotruta kore – *they keep giving us aggravation*   [B. såtruta < S. šatrutā]

sotti ['šòt-tī] (adv) *truly; really* | afne gecla ni sotti? – *did you really go there?* : ji oe, sotti – *yes, indeed, no kidding* : ami sotti dekci na – *I honestly didn't see it* : kafor·kan sotti sundor – *the sari is truly beautiful* : **sotti sotti** – *really and truly* : tumi sotti sotti bia korco? – *have you really truly got married?*   [B. såtti]

sotto[1] ['šòt-tò] (adj) *true*   = **soitto**

sotto[2] (n) *existence* | **sotte** – *in existence; in view (of); in spite (of)* : nanan osubida sotte tara gece gi – *because of various problems they've gone away* : foesa taka sotte đee na – *although he does have money he doesn't pay*   [B. såttå < S. sattva]

sottoir ['šòt-tòır] (nº) *seventy*   [B. såttår]

sriŋkola ['šrīŋ-χòlā] (n) *discipline; order*   [B. sriŋkhåla < S. šŕŋkhala – *chain*]

sriti ['šrītī] (n) *recollection; memory; souvenir*   [B. sriti < S. smŕti]

staii ['stāī] (adj) *permanent*   [B. sthayi < S. sthāyī]

stan [stān] (n) *place; position*   [B. sthan < S. sthāna]

stogit ['stògīt] (adj) *postponed*   [B. sthågit < S. sthagita]

sua ['šūā] (adv) *a quarter over; a quarter past* | sua camuc – *a spoon and a quarter* : sua tin – *three and a quarter* : sua fac fon – *five and a quarter pounds* : sua fac so – *five hundred and twenty-five* : sua tin·ta – *a quarter past three*   [B. soa < O. sapađa]

suag ['šūāg] (n) *wifely affection*   [B. sohag < O. saubhāgya – *good fortune*]

subida [šū 'bīđā] (n) *favourable conditions; convenience; opportunity* | tara ino subida faice na – *they haven't found conditions suitable here* : tain befsar subida tukaira – *he's seeking opportunities for business* : afnar subida đia – *(it's linked) with your convenience; whatever suits you* : **subida oe** – *convenience exists* : ufre kam korte subida oibo – *it will be convenient to work upstairs* : afnar ino boite subida or na – *it's not comfortable for you sitting here* : **subida ace** – *suitable arrangements are in place* : hono boibar bala subida ace – *there are good seating arrangements over there* : ino rannar subida nae – *there are no facilities for cooking here* : **subida kor-/subida kori le-** – *make suitable arrangements* : hokolor gumaibar subida kori lici – *we've made sleeping arrangements for everyone*   [B. subiđha < S. suvidhā]

sud [šūd] (n) *(pecuniary) interest* | korjot sud lage – *a loan attracts interest* : **sude asole** – *including both capital and interest* : sude asole fac so tis fon – *£530 including interest* :

sud ka- – *accept payments of interest* (pejorative) : kior mucoman, sud kae – *what kind of Muslim is that, who practises usury* [P. sūd – *profit*]
sudda ['šūd-dā] (post) *along with* | tain foribar sudda gecoin gi – *he has gone, taking his family with him* : malla sudda nau dubcil – *the boat sank, together with all its crew* [B. suddhå]
suddo ['šūd-dò] (adj) *pure; refined* | suddo fani – *pure water* : suddo basa – *refined language* : suddo baŋla – *chaste Bengali* [B. suddhå < S. šuddha – *purified*]
sudkur ['šūdkūr] (n) *one who consumes interest; a person who makes immoral profits from usury* = **sud + -kur**
sudu ['šūdū] (adv) *only* | ino sudu fuain – *there are only boys here* : ami sudu bat kaimu – *I shall eat only rice* : sudu noe·jon aicla – *only nine people came* : he gumae sudu – *he does nothing but sleep* : **sudu sudu** – *for no good reason; just* : tai sudu sudu torko lagae – *she starts arguments for no reason* [B. sudhu < O. šuddha]
sufari ['šūfārī] (n) *areca palm; areca nut; betelnut* [B. supari]
sugar ['šūgār] (n) *blood sugar* | tan sugar hai oi gece – *her blood sugar level has gone high* [E.]
sui ['šūī] (n) *needle* [B. sui < O. šūcī]
suinno ['šūın-nò] (n) *vacuity; zero* = **sunno**
suja ['šūzā, 'šūjā] *straight; straightforward; simple; easy* | suja rasta – *straight road* : suja befar – *straightforward affair* : suja manus – *a simple person* : suja kam – *an easy job* : ninda kora suja – *it's easy to criticize* [B. soja < O. suddha]
suji ['šūzī, 'šūjī] (n) *semolina* [H. sūjī]
sujjo ['šūj-jò] (n) *sun* [B. surjå < S. sūrya]
sujjomuki ['šūj-jò-mūkī] (n) *sunflower* [B. surjåmukhi]
sujug ['šūzūg, 'šūjūg] (n) *opportunity* | **sujug oe** – *opportunity arises* : amar jaoar sujug oito fare – *I may get a chance to go* : ino kaibar sujug oito nae – *there won't be any chance of eating here* : **sujug mile** – *an opportunity crops up* : tair aro forbar sujug milce – *she's got the chance to study further* : **sujug fa-** – *get an opportunity* : tain boibar sujug faicla na – *she never got an opportunity to sit down* : **sujug tuka-** – *look for an opportunity* : tain befsar sujug tukaira – *he's looking for business opportunities* : **sujug kor- / sujug kori le-** – *create an opportunity* : amra hono jaoar sujug kormu – *we'll sort out an opportunity to go there* [B. sujog < S. suyoga – *auspicious juncture*]
sujug-subida ['šūjūgšūbīdā] (n) *opportunities* = **sujug + subida**
suk [šūk] (n) *happiness; ease; prosperity* | suk nae tarar – *they are in a sorry state* : tara sukor maje – *they are enjoying prosperity* [B. sukh < S. sukha]
suk-dukko ['šūk-dūk-kò] (n) *weal and woe* = **suk + dukko**
suki ['šūkī] (adj) *happy; prosperous; fortunate* | amra bout suki – *we're perfectly well off* : afne suki manus – *you're a lucky fellow* [B. sukhi < S. sukhī]
sukkur ['šūk-kūr] (n) *Venus; Friday* = **sukro**
sukkurbar ['šūk-kūrbār] (n) *Friday* = **sukrobar**
sukria ['šūkrīā] (n) *expression of thankfulness; thanks* | tain sukria janaicoin – *he expressed thanks* : allare sukria – *thanks are due to God* : **sukria adae kor-** – *give thanks (which are due)* : tan gece sukria adae korta – *you should say thankyou to her* [A. šukriya]
sukro ['šūkrò] (n) *Venus; Friday* [B. sukrå < S. šukra]
sukrobar ['šūkròbār] (n) *Friday* [B. sukråbar]
suk-santi ['šūkšāntī] (n) *peace and prosperity* = **suk + santi**
sukur ['šūkūr] (n) *expression of gratitude (to God)* [A. šukr]
sul [šūl] (n) *lance; spike* [B. sul < S. šūla]
sulki ['šūlkī] (n) *spear* cf **sul**
sullo ['šūl-lò] (n°) *sixteen* | sullo ana – *sixteen sixteenths; one whole; 100%* [B. solå]
suna ['šūnā] (n) *gold; darling* | kati suna – *pure gold; genuine gold* : kita oice suna? – *what's the matter, darling?* : **sunar** – *made of gold; golden; precious* : sunar foesa – *gold*

coin : ou aŋti sunar ni? – *is this ring made of gold?* : sunar bai – *dearest brother* : sunar mai go! – *precious mother! o my goodness!* [B. sona < S. svarṇa]

sundor ['šūn-ḍòr] (adj) *beautiful; pleasant; agreeable; fair* | sunḍor furi – *a beautiful girl* : tar ceara sunḍor – *his complexion is fair* : aij ḍin·ta sunḍor – *the weather is fine today* : ou kafor sunḍor nae – *this sari is not very pretty* : **sunḍor kori** – *beautifully; nicely* : tain gor·ta sunḍor kori hajaicoin – *she has arranged the house very attractively* : sunḍor kori leko – *write nicely* [B. sunḍår < S. sunḍara]

sundori ['šūnḍòrī] (n) *beautiful woman* [B. sunḍåri < S. sunḍarī]

sunni ['šūn-nī] (n) *one who follows orthodox Muslim tradition; Sunni* [A. sunnī]

sunno ['šūn-nò] (n) *vacuity; space; zero* | tara base sunnor maje – *the stars float in space* : ek sunno fac – *one zero five* [B. sunnå < S. šūṇya]

sunnot ['šūn-nòt] (n) *orthodox Muslim tradition (based on the example of the Prophet)* | dari raka sunnot – *keeping a beard is in the Prophetic tradition* [A. sunna]

suor ['šūòr] (n) *pig* [O. šūkara – *boar*]

sur [šūr] (n) *sound; tone; melody* | golar sur – *throat tone; voice* : afnar golar sur cinci na – *I didn't recognize your voice* : ganor sur – *song melody; musical tune* : ou ganor sur bala fai – *I like this tune* [B. sur < O. svara]

sura[1] ['šūrā] (n) *gravy* [P. šorbā – *soup*]

sura[2] (n) *chapter of the Quran; sura* | sura fatia – *sura al-Fatiha* : iacin sura – *sura Ya Sin* : sura eklac – *sura al-Ikhlas* [A. sūra]

suru ['šūrū] (n) *beginning* | rastar suru – *the beginning of the road* : larair suru – *the start of the war* : **suru taki** – *from the beginning* : ami suru taki aclam – *I was there from the start* : **suru o- / suru oi ja-** – *begin* (intransitive) : meg suru or – *it's beginning to rain* : mitiŋ suru oi gece – *the meeting has begun* : **suru kor- / suru kori le-** – *begin* (transitive) : kam suru kortam ni? – *shall we begin the job?* : tain kani suru kori licoin – *he has started eating* [A. šurū¿]

suruj ['šūrūz, 'šūrūj] (n) *sun* [B. surjå < S. sūrya]

suson ['šūšòn] (n) *exploitation* [B. sosån < S. šošaṇa – *drying up*]

susra ['šūš-rā] (n) *care; attendance* [B. susrusa < S. šušrūšā]

suste ['šūs-tɛ] (adv) *well; soundly* < **susto**

susti ['šūstī] (n) *laziness* | **susti kor-** – *be lazy* [P. sustī – *weakness*]

sustiala ['šūstīālā] (n) *lazybones* = **susti + -ala**

susto ['šūstò] (adj) *healthy* [B. susthå < S. sustha – *well set up*]

suta ['šūtā] (n) *thread* [B. suta < O. sūtra]

suti ['šūtī] (n) *cotton* [B. suti < O. sūtrita]

t

ta [tā] (quantifier) *unit; one* | tin·ta kafor – *three units of clothing* : fac·ta gor – *five units of house; five houses* : lal·ta – *the red one* : afnar·ta – *your one* : i gori·ta bala – *this particular clock is good* : din·ta bala – *the weather is fine* : kota·ta oilo.. – *the thing is this*.. : noe·ta baje – *nine ones ring; it's nine o'clock* : kela egaro·tat suru oibo – *the match will start at eleven* : baro·tar age ain jen – *make sure you come before twelve* : **tain** – *units; ones* : kafor·tain hono torakci – *I've left the clothes over there*

tai [tāɪ] (n) *place; space* | tai ɖeuka – *give some space; let me have some room* : **tait** – *on the spot* : dakaitre tait mari lice – *they killed the robber on the spot* ¶ **tai** (n adv) *in possession* | cafi afnar tai ni? – *have you got the key?* [B. thaⁿi < O. sthāman]

taif [tāɪf] (n) *typing* | afne taif janoin ni? – *do you know how to type?* : taifor leka – *typed writing; neat script* : **taif kor-** – *type* : citi ke taif korbo? – *who will type the letter?* [E.]

taifmesin ['tāɪfmɛsĩn] (n) *typewriter* [E.]

taim [tāɪm] (n) *time; scheduled time* | ami taim faici na jaibar – *I didn't get time to go* : nomajor taim oi jar – *it's nearly time for prayers* : ek·ta taim tik kori louka – *please fix a specific time* : taimor age jaimu – *we'll go before the appointed time* [E.]

tain [tāɪn] (adv) *in possession* | afnar tain raki louka – *keep it in your possession* : kolom·ta runar tain – *Runa's got the pen* = **tai**

taitel ['tāɪtɛl] (n) *Islamic clerical diploma* [E.]

tai-tik ['tāɪtīk] (adv) *in order* | hokolti tai-tik – *everything is in order* : **tai-tik kor-** – *put in order* : gor·ta tai-tik kortam oimu – *I must put the house in order* = **tik**

tai-tikana ['tāɪtīkānā] (n) *details of circumstances; certain knowledge* | tar tai-tikana kunta janoin ni? – *do you have any idea where he is or what he's doing?* : itar kunu tai-tikana nae – *there's nothing certain about it* = **tai + tikana**

taltifalti ['tāltīfāltī] (n) *dithering; evasiveness; indecisive behaviour* | **taltifalti kor-** – *act in a slippery way; mess about* : he amar loge taltifalti korer – *he's messing me about*

tan [tān] (n) *pull; attraction; shortage; regional accent* | tan ɖesor lagi tan – *he feels the pull of the motherland* : ɖui boine koto tan – *there's so much attachment between the two sisters* : amar foesar tan – *I'm short of money* : tarar mator maje kumillar tan – *their speech has a Comilla accent to it* : **tan ɖe-/tan ɖi la-** – *pull; tug* : jure tan ɖeuka! – *pull hard!* : **tan mar-** – *pull; ply the oars; take a trip* : rossit tan marouka – *pull the rope* : garit tan mari aimu – *I'll have a drive around in the car* : **tan fore / tan fori jae** – *shortage occurs* : fanir tan forto fare – *there may be a water shortage* : calir tan fori gece – *rice is in short supply* [B. tan]

tan- (v) *pull; haul; attract; draw out* | gorue gari tane – *oxen pull carts* : betae buja taner – *the man is carrying a burden* : kagojo lain tanci – *I've drawn a line on the paper* : kagoje kali tane – *the paper absorbs ink* : gorome fani tane – *the heat makes you need water* : one bicnae taner – *now bed is beckoning* : tara ilektikor lain taner – *they are running a power cable through* : **(kuntar lagi) tane** – *attraction or yearning is felt (for something)* : tair ɖesor lagi tane – *she yearns for the homeland* : tar mabafor lagi taner – *he's missing his parents* : **tani an-** – *pull along* : tara gari tani aner – *they are towing the car along* : **tani le-** – *pull* : rossi tani louka – *pull the cord* [B. tan-]

tana ['tānā] (v a) *drawn out; stretched* | tana leka – *joined-up writing* < **tan-**

tanatani ['tānātānī] (n) *pulling; shortage* | **tanatani kor-** – *pull repeatedly; have a tug of war* : tara keced loia tanatani korer – *they are fighting over a cassette* : huruta loia koto tanatani korce – *they had a tug of war over the children* : **tanatani oe / tanatani cole** – *shortage occurs* : aijkail karenor tanatani coler – *nowadays there is a shortage of electricity* < **tan-**

tanda ['tāndā] (adj) *cold; cool; calm* | tanda fani – *cold water* : tanda batas – *cool wind* : tan mata tanda – *he has a cool head* ¶ **tanda** (n) *coldness; cold season* | tandar ɖae bar oi na – *on account of the cold I don't go out* : tandar somoe tain ɖeso jain gi – *in the cold season* he goes to Bangladesh : **tanda fore** – *cold weather sets in* : ou bocor bes tanda force – *it has got really cold this year* : **tanda lage** – *cold is felt* : tanda lager ni afnar? – *are you feeling the cold?* [B. thanda]

tar[1] [tār] (n) *awareness* | **(kar) tar ace** – *one is aware* : ou somonde fura tar ace tan – *he is fully aware about this* : hou somoe amar tar acil na – *at that time I had no awareness of things* : **tar fa-/tar fai le-** – *become aware; notice; feel* : cur hamaite tain tar faicla – *he became aware when the thief broke in* : rait oice amra tar faiclam na – *we didn't realise night had fallen* : amra jekta-u kori he tar faibo – *whatever we do, he'll get wind of it* : tar fai jela fau jole – *it feels to me as if my foot was burning* : afne kila tar fain? – *what's your impression?* [B. ter]

tar[2] (n) *gesture* | **tare** – *by means of gesture* : tain tare koicoin jaitam – *he gestured to me to go* : **tare tare** – *by gestures* : he tare tare bujaice tarare – *he explained to them by means of gestures* [B. thar]

tas- [tāš] (v) *stuff; cram* | begor maje dos-baro ta am tasice – *she stuffed ten or twelve mangoes into a bag* : **tasia / taissia** – *having stuffed; in full measure* : tain tasia bat kaicoin – *he stuffed himself with rice* : he tasia kam korer – *he is working like crazy* : **tasa** – *stuffed* : bosta ekere tasa – *the sack is stuffed full* [B. thas-]

tatta ['tāt-tā] (n) *joking; jesting; teasing* | **tatta kor-** – *joke; jest* : tain amrar loge tatta koroin – *he enjoys a few jokes with us* : tatta korclam – *I was only joking* [B. thatta]

tatti ['tāt-tī] (n) *latrine; excreta* | tattir gor – *latrine hut* : **tatti kor-** – *defecate* : bilaie tatti korce – *the cat has made a mess* [H. tattī – *woven screen*]

tebu ['tɛbū] (adj) *chubby* [B. tebo]

tebul ['tɛbūl] (n) *table* | gul tebul – *round table* : tain tebulo kani dicoin – *she has placed the food on the table* : tebulor kandat bouka – *please sit at the table* : **tebul laga-** – *set a table* : tebul lagaitam ni? – *shall I set the table?* [E.]

teha ['tɛhā] (n) *taka; rupee; money* = **teka**[2]

teif ['tɛif] (n) *tape; audiotape* | teif hunta ni? – *do you want to listen to some tapes?* : **teif kor-** – *record on tape* : tarar mat teif korci – *I've recorded a tape of them talking* : **teif tul-** – *make a tape recording* : tain ganor teif tulra – *he's recording some songs* [E.]

tek- [tɛχ] (vi) *run aground; get into difficulties; get stuck* | nau tekce – *the boat has run aground* : ila korle tekba – *if you act thus you'll run into problems* : hono gia tekci – *that's where I got into difficulties* : tare loia tekcoin – *they're dreadfully lumbered with him* : bifodo tekci! – *I'm in a real fix!* [B. thek-]

teka[1] ['tɛχā] (v n) *being stuck; difficulties* | koto boro teka! – *what a fix!* : **tekat** – *in difficulties* : one nae, ami tekat – *not now, I've got enough problems* : **tekar maje** – *in difficulties* : amra boro tekar maje – *we're going through a very difficult time* < **tek-**

teka[2] (n) *taka (currency unit of Bangladesh); rupee (currency unit of India and Pakistan); money* | ek katolor dam foncas teka – *the price of one jackfruit is fifty taka* : tarar bout teka – *they have pots of money* [B. taka]

teka- (vt) *cause to run aground; put into difficulties* | afnare tekaitam cai na – *I don't want to put you into difficulties* : **tekai le-** – *put into difficulties* : tain tekai licoin amare – *he's got me into a fix* [B. theka-]

teka-foesa ['tɛχāfòyšā] (n) *money* = **teka**[2] + **foesa**

tekue ['tɛk-wɛ́] (n) *take-away food* | tekue besi cole – *take-away sells the best* ¶ **tekue** (adj) *take-away* | tekue kani – *take-away meals* [E.]

tel- [tɛl] (vt) *push; shove* | tain fuscear telra – *she is pushing a pushchair* : buddare rastat telce – *they shoved the old man onto the road* [B. thel-]

tela ['tɛlā] (v n) *pushing; shoving* | **tela mar-** – *push; shove* : dorojat tela marouka – *give the door a push* : **tela de-** – *push; shove* : kor taki tela dice – *he shoved me from behind* < **tel-**

telagari ['tɛlāgārī] (n) *push-cart* = **tela** + **gari**

telateli ['tɛlātɛlī] (n) *pushing; shoving* | **telateli kor-** – *push and shove* : telateli korrae kitar lagi? – *what are you pushing us for?* < **tel-**

telibison ['tɛlībīšòn] (n) *television* | tara telibison d̃eker – *they're watching television* : telibison on korouka cain – *please switch the TV on* [E.]
telifon ['tɛlīfòn] (n) *telephone; phone call* | telifon aice – *a phone call has come; the phone is ringing* : afnar telifon! – *a call for you!* : **telifon dor-** – *answer the phone* : tara telifon d̃ore na – *they're not answering the phone* : **telifon car-** – *hang up* : telifon carouka! – *get off the line!* : **telifon kor-** – *make a phone call* : tarar goro telifon kormu – *I'll phone their house; I'll phone them* : cacar gece telifon korcla ni? – *did you phone uncle?* : amar lagi ek·ta telifon korba – *please will you make a phone call for me* [E.]
tena ['tɛnā] (n) *rag*
tendol ['tɛndòl] (n) *lascar foreman; able bodied seaman* [E. ?]
teŋ [tɛŋ] (n) *leg; shank* [B. theŋ]
teŋga ['tɛŋ-gā] (adj) *sour*
teŋra¹ ['tɛŋ-rā] (adj) *caustic*
teŋra² (n) *a species of fish (Mystus tengara)* [B. teɽa]
tera ['tɛrā] (adj) *crooked; peevish* | fotu tera oi gece – *the picture is crooked* : amar loge tera oico kene? – *why are you being so peevish with me?* [B. teɽa]
teski ['tɛskī] (n) *taxi; car* | teski dakouka – *please call a taxi* : tarar goro teski ace – *they've got a car* [E.]
testa ['tɛstā] (n) *endeavour; attempt* | testar fol – *the fruits of endeavour* : **testat** – *in the process of endeavouring* : tain bisa loar testat – *she's trying to get a visa* : **testa kor-** – *make efforts; try* : tain kamor lagi testa korra – *he's trying for a job* : ami aibar testa kormu – *I'll try to come* : tara bout testa korcil ses korto – *they tried very hard to finish* = **cesta**
tibi ['tībī] (n) *television* | amra besi tibi d̃eki na – *we don't watch much TV* [E.]
tif [tīf] (n) *fingertip; thumb print* | **tif d̃e-/tif d̃i la-** – *make a thumb impression* : tain d̃olilo tif d̃i laicla – *he had signed the deed with a thumb mark* [E. tip]
tif- (vt) *press with a fingertip* < **tif**
tifa ['tīfā] (v n) *pressing with a fingertip* | **tifa mar-** – *press with a fingertip* : gutit tifa marouka – *press the button (with your finger)* < **tif-**
tifkol ['tīfχòl] (n) *tubewell* = **tif + kol**
tifsoi ['tīfsòɪ] (n) *thumb impression as signature* | **tifsoi d̃e-/tifsoi d̃i la-** – *sign by means of a thumb impression* : leka na janle tifsoi d̃ena lage – *if someone can't write they have to sign with their thumb print* = **tif + soi**
tig¹ [tīg] (adj) *correct* = **tik**
tig² (n) *tick (mark)* | **tig d̃e-** – *give a tick; tick* : ticar katat tig d̃icoin – *the teacher ticked the workbook* : **tig mar-** – *apply a tick; tick* : kali goro tig marouka – *tick the box* [E.]
tik [tīk] (adj) *correct; all right* | tan kota tik – *what he said is correct* : afne tik somoe aicoin – *you've come at the right time* : i gorir taim tik nae – *the time by this clock is not right* : tik acoin? bilkul tik – *are you all right? perfectly all right* : **tik ace** – *it's all right* : hokolti tik ace ni? – *is everything all right?* : tik ace, bad̃e kormu ne – *it's okay, I'll do it later* : **tik nae** – *there's no certainty* : tan aoar kunu tik nae – *there's nothing certain about his coming* : aij meg d̃ibo ni na tik nae – *whether or not it will rain today is open to doubt*
¶ **tik** (adv) *correctly; exactly; really* | mesin tik cole na – *the machine doesn't function properly* : ami jani na tik – *I don't really know* : ota tik beguni nae – *this isn't exactly purple in colour* : tik baro·tat ain jen – *please come at twelve o'clock precisely* : **tik-ou** – *indeed; really and truly* : tik-ou gece gi tara – *they really have gone* : amar d̃us, tik-ou – *it was my fault, indeed it was* : **tik o-/tik oi ja-** – *become all right; get remedied; be made certain* : afne jold̃i tik oi jaiba – *you will soon get better* : gari tik oice ni? – *has the car been repaired?* : amrar jaoar tarik tik oi gece – *our departure date has been fixed* : **tik kor-/tik kori le-** – *put right; remedy; make certain* : tumar cul tik koro – *tidy up your hair* : tara gari tik korer – *they're fixing the car* : amar fasfut tik kortam oimu – *I'll have to get my passport in order* : biar tarik tik kori licoin ni? – *have you fixed the date for the wedding?* : **tik kori** – *correctly; precisely; properly* : tik kori koo – *say it correctly / tell the full truth / be specific* : he tik kori boito cae na – *he refuses to sit properly* : kagojain tik kori rakta

217

oiba – *you'll have to keep the papers in proper order* : **tik kori de-** – *put right; repair* : tain gori·ta tik kori diba – *he will repair the clock* : **tik kora-** – *have corrected; get fixed* : amar cosma tik koraitam aclam – *I should have got my glasses repaired* [B. thik]

tik- (vi) *hold out; endure; turn out right* | ou roŋ bout din tikbo – *this paint will last a long time* : tarar bia tikto nae – *their marriage isn't going to last* : afnar kota tikce – *what you said has turned out to be correct* [B. thik-]

tika ['tīkā] (n) *injection* [B. tika]

tikana ['tīkānā] (n) *certain knowledge; information on whereabouts; address* | tain aiba ni na, kunu tikana nae – *there's no knowing whether or not he'll come* : tar kunu tikana jani na – *I know nothing of his whereabouts* : afnar noea tikana kouka – *please tell me your new address* [B. thikana]

tikit ['tīkīt] (n) *ticket; postage stamp* | jaoa-aoar tikit – *return ticket* : jaoar tikit – *one-way ticket* : kamor ufre tikit lagauka – *stick a stamp on the envelope* : **tikit kat-** – *book a ticket* : bimano tikit katcoin – *she's booked her ticket on Bangladesh Biman* : **tikit kor-** – *book a ticket* : dakar tikit kortam – *I want to book a ticket to Dhaka* [E.]

tiktak ['tīktāk] (adj) *correct* | **tiktak o-/tiktak oi ja-** – *become all right; be fixed* : hokolti tiktak oi gece – *everything has been sorted out* : **tiktak kor-/tiktak kori le-** – *put right; fix* : amrar jaoar tarik tiktak korci – *we've fixed the date for our departure* = **tik**

tiktiki ['tīk-tīkī] (n) *wall gecko; eavesdropper* [B. tiktiki]

tila ['tīlā] (n) *hillock* [B. tila]

tin [tīn] (n) *tin; corrugated iron sheet* | biskutor tin – *biscuit tin* : tinor gor – *house clad with corrugated iron sheeting* [E.]

tog [tòg] (n) *cheating; fraud; scam* | tog, ita – *this is a scam* [B. thåk]

tog- (vt) *dupe; cheat* | **togi le-** – *dupe; cheat* : tara amrare balatike togi lice – *they have well and truly cheated us* [B. thåka-]

toga ['tògā] (v n) *duping; cheating* | **toga de-** – *dupe; cheat* : **toga ka-** – *be duped; be cheated* : tarar gece toga kain na jen – *be careful not to be cheated by them* < **tog-**

toga- (vt) *dupe; cheat* = **tog-**

togabaji ['tògābāzī] (n) *cheating; fraud* = **toga + -baji**

togbaj ['tòg-bāz] (n) *cheat; fraudster* = **tog + -baj**

tok [tòχ] (n) *sourness* | tok lage – *it tastes sour* [B. tåk]

tokabaji ['tòχābāzī] (n) *cheating; fraud* = **togabaji**

tokkor ['tòk-kòr] (n) *clashing; clash* [B. tåkkår]

tometu ['tòmεtū] (n) *tomato* [E.]

tuk [tūk] (quantifier) *small amount* = **tuku**

tuka[1] ['tūkā] (n) *chit; note* [B. toka]

tuka[2] (n) *knocking* | **tuka mar-** – *knock* : ke dorojat tuka marer – *someone is knocking at the door* [B. thoka]

tukitaki ['tūkītākī] (adj) *small and various* | tain tukitaki kam koroin – *he does odd jobs* : ledaro tukitaki jinis roice – *there are some odds and ends in the suitcase*

tukra ['tūkrā] (n) *piece; bit* | arok tukra mac kauka – *do have another piece of fish* : kaforor tukra kuae? – *where's that bit of cloth?* : **tukra tukra oi ja-** – *come to pieces* : kof baŋgia tukra tukra oi gece – *the cup has broken into pieces* : **tukra tukra kor-** – *reduce to pieces* : guc katia tukra tukra korcoin – *he cut the meat into pieces* [B. tukra]

tukra- (vt) *cut into pieces*

tuku ['tūkū] (quantifier) *small amount* | ek·tuku santi – *a little bit of peace* : kam·tuku kori lici – *I have done that little job* : tumar·tuku nao gi – *here, take your bit* [B. tuku]

tukuta ['tūkūtā] (quantifier) *small amount* | amar lagi o·tukuta koroin jen – *please do that one little thing for me* = **tuku + -ta**[2]

tul[1] [tūl] (n) *bag; pouch; capsule* | foesar tul – *moneybag* : tabijor tul – *amulet cartridge* [B. thuli]

tul[2] (n) *stool* [E.]

tultuli ['tūltūlī] (n) *paper bag*

tuma[1] ['tūmā] (n) *piece*
tuma[2] (n) *blister*
tuŋga ['tūŋ-gā] (n) *paper bag*
tuŋi ['tūŋī] (n) *paper bag*
tusa ['tūšā] (n) *blister*   [B. thusi]
tusi ['tūšī] (n) *blow; punch* | **tusi mar-** – *punch* : betare kok bar tusi marce – *he punched the man several times*
tut [tūt] (n) *lip*   [B. thoⁿt]
tutfalis ['tūtfālīš] (n) *lipstick*   = **tut** + **falis**

t

ta (pron) *it; that* | ta jani – *I know that* : ta tik – *that's true* : ta oile – *if that is so; in that case* : ja faro ta koro – *do what you can* : tar baḍe – *after that* : **ta-o** – *that too* : ta-o tik – *that's also true* : **ta-u** – *even that* : amra ta-u mantam raji – *we are willing to accept even that* [B. ta]

-ta [1] (noun suffix) *-ity; innate quality* | sorol, sorolota – *simple, simplicity* : sotru, sotruta – *enemy, enmity* [B. –ta < S. -tā]

-ta [2] (pron suffix) *entity* | bout, boutta – *much, a lot* : hokol, hokolta – *all, everything* : ou, outa – *this, this one*

taba ['tābā] (n) *thump* | **taba mar-** – *thump* : ḑorojat ke taba mare? – *who's that thumping on the door?* [B. thaba]

taba- (vt) *pack up; tidy away* | **tabai le-** – *pack up; tidy away* : tumar mal tabai lico ni? – *have you tidied your stuff away?*

tabij ['tābīz, 'tābīj] (n) *capsule containing a prayer or Quranic quotation, worn on the person as a protection against evil* [A. ta¿wīð – *divine protection*]

taf [tāf] (n) *heat* | **taf fore** – *hot weather descends* : aij bakka taf force – *it's very hot today* : **taf ute** – *fever arises* : cacir taf utce – *auntie has got a fever* [B. tap < S. tāpa]

taffur ['tāp-pūr] (n) *slap* | **taffur ḍe-** – *slap; smack* : **taffur mar-** – *slap; smack* : **taffur laga-** – *administer a slap* [B. thappāṛ]

tagḍa ['tāg-ḍā] (n) *insistent urging* | **tagḍa kor-** – *hustle; press for action* : **tagḍa ḍe-** – *hustle; press for action* : tan mokkel hokol tagḍa ḍer – *his clients are stepping up the pressure* ¶ **tagḍa** (adv) *urgently; quickly; soon* | tagḍa ses kori louka – *finish it quickly* : amra tagḍa aimu – *we'll come back very soon* [? A. taqāÐī – *prosecution; execution*]

tai [1] [tāi] (pron) *she* (familiar) | tai amar huru boin : *she is my younger sister* : tai iskulo fore – *she goes to school* : tair nam seli – *her name is Shelly* : taire cinoin ni? – *do you know her?* : **tara** – *they* (familiar); *she* (respectful) : tara amar huru – *they are younger than me* : tara afnar kita lage? – *what relation of yours is the lady?* : **tai beti** – *she* : tai beti kita koe? – *what does she say?* : **tar beti** – *she* : tar beti nije jane – *she herself knows it*

tai [2] (adv) *thus; so* | tai cole – *that's how it goes* : afne dakcoin, tai aici – *you called me, so I came* [B. tai]

taiar ['tāyār] (adj) *prepared; ready; made* | afne taiar ni? – *are you ready?* : hokolti taiar – *everything's prepared* : ikan lakrir taiar – *this is made of wood* : **taiar o-/taiar oi ja-** – *get prepared; be made* : amra egaro·tat taiar oimu – *we'll get ready at eleven* : kani taiar oi gece – *the meal is all ready* : gor bout age taiar oicil – *the house had been constructed long ago* : **taiar kor-/taiar kori le-** – *prepare; make* : afnar bicna taiar korci – *I've prepared your bed* : tain suji taiar korcoin – *she's made some semolina* : ca taiar kora – *the tea's already made* [P. tayyār]

taiari ['tāyārī] (n) *preparation; construction* | tain fulob taiari janoin – *she knows how to make pulao* : ou gor rukor taiari – *this house is of wooden construction* [P. tayyārī]

taii ['tāyī] (adj) *permanent* = **staii**

taikkia ['tāik-kiā] (v adv) *having remained; while remaining* | hono taikkia kam kormu – *I shall do the work while staying there* : he goro taikkia fore – *he studies at home* < **tak-**

tain [tāɪn] (pron) *he / she* (honorific) | tain amar boro caca – *he is my senior uncle* : tain london takoin – *she lives in London* : **tanir / tainor / tanor / tan** – *of him; of her; his; her* : tanor boes sottoir – *her age is seventy* : tan huruta nae – *he has no children* : tan samne bouka – *sit in front of him* : **tanre / tane** – *to him; to her; him; her* : tane kunta koici na – *I didn't say anything to her* : **taintain** – *they* (honorific) : taintain amrar murobbi – *they are our elders* : **tantanor** – *of them; their* : tantanor nam janoin ni? – *do you know their names?* : **tantanre** – *to them; them* : tantanre boibar ḍeuka – *let them sit down* [B. tini]

tais [tāɪš] (n) *uncomfortable sensation* | **tais kore** – *it hurts; it burns; it irritates* [O. tŕśā – *thirst*]

taja ['tāzā, 'tājā] (adj) *fresh; blooming* | taja am – *fresh mangoes* : taja baicca – *a healthy child* : taja soril – *a strong physique*   [P. tāza]

tajjob ['tāj-jòb] (n) *amazement* | **tajjob lage** – *it's amazing*   [A. ta¿ajjub]

tajuđ ['tāzūđ, 'tājūđ] (n) *nocturnal prayers*   [A. tahajjud – *prayer vigil*]

tak [tāχ] (n) *astonishment*   [B. tak < O. tarka – *deliberation*]

tak- (vi) *remain; dwell; be* | kanir bađe calon takbo – *after the meal some curry will remain* : tara tin đin london takcil – *they stayed in London for three days* : amra folato taki – *we live in a flat* : dicemboro tanda takbo – *it will be cold in December* : tara hariđin besto take – *they are busy all day* : bego foesa takto fare – *there may be some money in the bag* : ola takuk / ola tauk – *let it be; let's leave it at that* : **(kar) take** – *(someone) habitually has* : tan somoe take na – *he never has any time* : age tarar baratia takto : *they used to have lodgers* : ek đin amrar nijerar gor takbo – *one day we shall have a house of our own* : menot korle tumar foesa taklo ne – *if you had worked hard you would have some money* : **taki ja-** – *remain; stay put* : caca ino taki jaiba – *uncle will remain here* : ita đoile-o kacra taki jae – *even if you wash it, some dirt remains* : ola taki jauk – *let it stay the way it is*   [B. tak-]
Note: Replaces **ac-** in the future and habitual tenses. It is often replaced by **ro-** in the perfect, pluperfect and historic tenses.

taka- ['tāχā] (vi) *stare; look* | amar bae takao kene? – *why are you staring at me?* : takaio na! – *don't look!* : **takai ro-** – *keep staring; gawp* : hunia bicara takai roicil – *on hearing that the poor fellow was left goggle-eyed*   [B. taka-]

taki ['tākī] (v adv) *having remained; having been; being; from; than* | tain fac minit taki gecoin – *after stopping for five minutes he went away* : tain kusi taki bejar oicoin – *having been pleased, he then became cross* : tara on taki bagce – *they have fled from (having been) here* : sof taki fol anci – *I've brought some fruit from the shop* : ofis noe·ta taki fac·ta fojonto kula – *the office is open from nine to five* : caca bian taki ubat – *uncle has been waiting since the morning* : tai amar taki lamfa – *she is taller than me* : tain bejar taki đukkit besi – *he is offended rather than angry* < **tak-**

takle ['tākl ɛ] (v adv) *in case of (something) remaining or being; if it is so; even so* | somoe takle jaimu – *if there is any time left, I will go* : osubiđa takle koiba – *if there is any problem, do say so* : tain manus bala, takle akol-buđđi kom – *he's a good person, but even so he lacks common sense* : tar foesa ace, takle kam ae na – *he has money, yet it serves no purpose* : takle kita oibo? – *well, so what?*   < **tak-**

takot ['tāχòt] (n) *ability; power* | đeki tumar takot koto! – *let's see how much you really are capable of!* : tar bujbar takot nae – *he is powerless to understand*   [A. ţāqa]

takte ['tāχtɛ] (v adv) *while remaining; while being* | tarar goro takte kai liclam – *while we were at their house we had lunch* : he furu takte tar baf morcla – *his father died while he was small* : foesa takte ufas take – *despite having money he starves himself* : đin takte ses kori lei – *let's finish while it's still daytime*   < **tak-**

tal[1] [tāl] (n) *palmyra (tree)*   [B. tal]

tal[2] (n) *rhythm; sense* | tar kamor maje tal nae – *there is no regularity in his way of working* : **tale** – *in a rhythm; purposefully engaged* : tain foesar malanir tale – *he's on a mission to make pots of money* : tara soetanir tale – *they're up to no good* : **tal mile** – *the rhythm matches; there is harmony* : tarar maje tal mile na – *they aren't on the same wavelength* : **tal đe-** – *beat time; clap in rhythm* : **tal rak-** – *keep in time; keep in step* : tara keur loge tal rake na – *they don't coordinate with anyone* : **tal mila-** – *adjust to a rhythm; fall in step* : beta tarar loge tal milaice – *he's started colluding with them* : **(kar) tale col-** – *move in time (with someone)* : bocor tale coltam oimu – *I'll have to go along with what the boss wants* : hurutar tale colta kila? – *how could you possibly keep up with the younger generation?*   [B. tal < S. tāla]

tal[3] (n) *platter; plate; flat dish containing a display of food*   [B. thal]

tala[1] ['tālā] (n) *lock; padlock* | tala bançe – *the lock has broken* : **tala đe-** – *lock; padlock* : đorojat tala đeoa – *the door is padlocked* : **tala mar-** – *lock; padlock* : đorojat tala marcoin ni? – *have you locked the door?* : **tala laga-** – *fit a padlock; lock* : tain leđaro tala lagaia toicoin – *he's put a padlock on his suitcase and left it; he's left his case padlocked* : **tala kul-** – *take off a padlock; unlock* : ana cafie amra tala kultam kila? – *how can we undo the lock without a key?* [B. tala]

tala ² (adjectival phrase) (of God) *who is Most Exalted* | alla tala – *God who is Most Exalted; God on High* [A. ta¿ālā – *he is exalted*]

tala ³ (n) *platter; plate* [B. thala]

-tala (noun suffix) *storey* | tintala – *third storey (second floor)* : tara factalat take – *they live on the fifth level (fourth floor)* ¶ **-tala** (adj suffix) *storeyed* | tintala gor – *a three-storeyed house* : noea bildiŋ terotala – *the new building is thirteen-storeyed* [B. tåla]

talab ['tālāb] (n) *reservoir* [P. talāb]

talabi ['tālābī] (n) *magical treatment (of ailments)* | **talabi kora-** – *obtain the services of magicians to counteract black magic* [A. talāfī – *remedy, redress*]

tala-borton ['tālābòrtòn] (n) *crockery* = **tala** ³ + **borton**

talak ['tālāχ] (n) *divorce* | tin talak – *divorce by stating three times "I divorce you"* : **talak de-/talak di la-** – *divorce (one's spouse)* : kobic betae tar boure talak di laice – *the evil fellow has divorced his wife* [A. talāq]

tali ['tālī] (n) *percussion of the hands; clapping* | **tali mar-** – *clap* [B. tali]

talim ['tālīm] (n) *teaching; coaching* [A. ta¿līm]

talinali ['tālīnālī] (n) *pestering* | **talinali kor-** – *pester*

tallas ['tāl-lāš] (n) *searching* | **tallas kor-** – *search* : bout tallas korci, faici na citi·kan – *I've searched all over but couldn't find the letter* : tain afnar tallas korra – *he's looking for you* [P. talāš]

talluk ['tāl-lūk] (n) *land estate; domain; territory* [P. taalluqa – *estate; administrative area* < A. ta¿alluqa – *something connected; appurtenance*]

taloi ['tālòı] (n) *sibling's spouse's father* [B. talui < O. tatgu – *fatherly*]

talukdar ['tālūkdār] (n) *estate owner; landowner* [P. taaluqadār]

tam [tām] (n) *food* [A. ta¿m]

tam- [tām] (vi) *stop; come to a halt* | bac ino tame – *the bus stops here* : foto tamcil – *they stopped on the way* : meg tamce – *the rain has stopped* : tamouka ek minit – *please hold on a moment* : **tami ja-** – *stop; come to a halt* : gari istesono tami gece – *the train has stopped at the station* [B. tham-]

tama ['tāmā] (n) *copper* [B. tama < O. tāmra]

tama- (vt) *stop; bring to a halt* | gari tamauka! – *stop the car!* : fulise tamaice tare – *the police made him stop* : **tamai le-** – *stop; bring to a halt* : sofor samne gari tamai louka – *please stop the car in front of the shop* [B. thama-]

tamam ['tāmām] (adj) *whole; entire* | tamam dunia – *the whole world* [A. tamām]

tamsa ['tāmšā] (n) *fun; tomfoolery* | tamsa deko! – *observe the tomfoolery; just see how they're fooling around!* : **tamsa kor-** – *fool about* : tara amrar loge tamsa korer – *they're just mucking us about* [P. tamāšā – *show* < ? A. tamāšī – *conformity*]

tamuk ['tāmūk] (n) *tobacco* | **tamuk ka-** – *smoke tobacco (in a hookah)* [Pg. tabaco]

tan [tān] (pron) *his; her* (honorific) < **tain**

tana ['tānā] (n) *police station; police district* | nobigonj tana – *Nabiganj Thana; Nabiganj Police Station; Nabiganj P.S.* : tara catok tanar basinda – *they are residents of Chatak Thana* : tanar oci – *officer in charge of a police station* [B. thana < O. sthāna]

tankila ['tānkīlā] (n) *established resident* [? A. tamkīn – *establishment*]

tantan ['tāntān] (pron adj) *their* (honorific) < **tain**

tantanor ['tāntānòr] (pron adj) *their* (honorific) < **tain**

tar ¹ [tār] (pron adj) *of him; his; of it; its* | tar nam abul – *his name is Abul* : tar samne cear – *there's a chair in front of him* : tar lagi cinta koroin na jen – *don't worry on account of it* : **tar beta** – *he (himself)* : tar beta jane – *he knows* < **ta** cf **he**

tar ² (n) *wire* [P. tār]

tara ¹ ['tārā] (pron) *they;* (polite) *she* | tara kandat take – *they live nearby* : (as an indication of plurality) kamla tara bondo – *the workers are in the field* : mina tara kuae? – *where are Mina* *and all them?* : raju tara ebo jane na – *Raju and his lot don't know yet* : (polite form for "she") tara ufre gece – *she's gone upstairs* : **tarar** – *their* : tarar gor hono – *their house is over there* : **tarare** – *them; to them* : tarare koimu – *I'll tell them* : **tara tara** – *they (as distinct from anyone else)* : tara tara jaibo – *they'll go on their own* : tara tara dorbar kore – *they quarrel among themselves* < **ta** cf **he**

tara² (n) *star* [B. tara < S. tārakā]

tara³ (n) *haste; hurry* [B. taɽa]

taratari ['tārātārī] (n) *haste; hurry* | **taratari kor-** – *make haste; hurry* : taratari koro! – *hurry up!* < **tara²**

taraura ['tārā-ūrā] (n) *haste; hurry* | taraura kita? – *what's the hurry?* : taraura nae – *there's no rush*: **taraura kor-** – *make haste; hustle and bustle* < **tara²** + **ura**

tarfin ['tārfīn] (n) *turpentine* [E.]

tarif ['tārīf] (n) *favourable mention; good name* | afnar tarif hunci – *I've heard good things about you* : tan tarif ace – *he has a good reputation* : afnar tarif? – (very polite) *what is your name?* : **(kar) tarif kor-** – *speak kindly (of someone); praise (someone)* : tain afnar tarif koroin – *he speaks highly of you* [A. ta¿rīf – *introduction*]

tarik ['tārīk] (n) *date; appointment* | aij koto tarik? – *what date is it today?* : kail dos tarik acil – *yesterday was the 10ᵗʰ* : kail foela tarik oibo – *it will be the 1ˢᵗ of the month tomorrow* : jun masor funro tarik – *15ᵗʰ June* : daktoror tarik mic korci – *I missed my appointment at the doctor's* : **tarik fore** – *the appointed day arrives* : kail denticor tarik forbo – *tomorrow will be the day for the dentist* : aij tarik force – *today's the day (of the appointment)* : **(kar loge) tarik kor-** – *make a date; fix an appointment (with someone)* : tan loge tarik kormu – *I'll make a date with him* [A. tārīk̠]

tarkari ['tārχārī] (n) *vegetables; vegetable dish* [U. tarkārī < P. tarra]

tas [tāš] (n) *playing-cards* | **tas kela-** – *play cards* [A. t̤ās – *dicing bowl*]

taua ['tāw̃ā] (n) *grilling pan* [P. tāva]

tauk [tāuk] (v) *let it be* = **takuk** = **tak-**

te [té] (conj) *then; in that case* | tara mane te bala – *if they agree then that's fine* : cain te koin jen – *if you want some, then do say so* : tumar bala lage na te jao gi – *if you don't like it, then go away* : te tik ace – *it's all right, then* : te jao! – *in that case, no problem!* : auka te! – *come along, then!* : tain gela kuae te? – *so now where's he got to?* [B. tåbe]

tear ['téār] (adj) *prepared; ready* = **taiar**

tebu ['tɛbū] (conj) *even then; but still* | koto bujaici, tebu bujoin na – *I've explained at great length, but still he doesn't understand* : tebu besi bala fai na tare – *even so, I don't really like him* [B. tåbu]

tefanno ['tɛfan-nò] (n°) *fifty-three* [B. tipannå]

teij [tɛɪz] (n) *vigour* [B. tej < O. tejas]

taijfatta ['tɛɪz-fāt-tā] (n) *bay leaf* [B. tejpata]

teis [tɛɪš] (n°) *twenty-three* [B. teis]

tekta- ['tɛχtā] (vt) *importune; bother* | afnare tektaici – *sorry I've been a bother to you* : (to a child) tumar cacare ar tektaio na – *stop pestering your uncle* : **tektai le-** – *importune; bother* : bicara amare tektai ler – *that fellow is plaguing me* cf **tekto**

tekto ['tɛχtò] (adj) *inconvenienced* | **tekto kor-/tekto kori le-** – *importune; bother; embarrass* : tane korjor lagi tekto korer – *they're pestering him for a loan* : amare tekto kori licoin – *you've put me on the spot* [B. tektå < S. tyakta – *abandoned*]

tel [tɛl] (n) *oil; petrol* | joitunor tel – *olive oil* : sujjomukir tel – *sunflower oil* : garir tel lagbo – *the car needs petrol* : **tel de-** – *apply oil; add petrol* : matat tel dao na kene? – *why don't you oil your hair?* : injilo tel dita oiba – *you'll have to oil the engine* : tel dicoin ni? – *have you put petrol in?* [B. tel < O. taila]

telala ['tɛlālā] (n) *oilman* = **tel** + **-ala**

telcura ['tɛlsūrā] (n) *cockroach* = **tel** + **cura**

telibison ['tɛlībīšòn] (n) *television* | telibison dekta ni? – *do you want to watch television?* : telibison of koro – *turn the TV off* = **telibison**

telifun ['tɛlīfūn] (n) *telephone; phone call* | telifun aice – *a phone call has come; the phone is ringing* : afnar telifun! – *a call for you!* : **telifun dor-** – *answer the phone* : tara telifun dore na – *they're not answering the phone* : **telifun car-** – *hang up the phone* : telifun carcoin – *he's hung up* : **telifun kor-** – *make a phone call* : tarar goro telifun kormu – *I'll phone their house; I'll phone them* : cacir gece telifun korcla ni? – *did you phone auntie?* = **telifon**
tena ['tɛnā] (n) *rag* [B. tena]
tera ['tɛrā] (n) *star* [B. tara < O. taraka]
terabi ['tɛrābī] (n) *night prayers during Ramadan* [A. tarāwīh]
tero ['tɛrò] (nº) *thirteen* [B. terå]
tesosti ['tɛšòstī] (nº) *sixty-three* = **tesotti**
tesotti ['tɛšòt-tī] (nº) *sixty-three* [B. tesåtti]
tetallis ['tɛtāl-līš] (nº) *forty-three* [B. tetallis]
tetoi ['tɛtòɪ] (n) *tamarind* [B. teⁿtul < O. tintidī]
tetris ['tɛtrīš] (nº) *thirty-three* [B. tetris]
tettis ['tɛt-tīš] (nº) *thirty-three* = **tetris**
teu [tɛu] (conj) *even then; but still* | tara bemar, teu kamo jae – *she's ill, but even so she goes to work* : koto tukaici, teu faici na – *I looked hard but still I couldn't find it* : dimu dimu kore, teu dee na – *he keeps saying he'll give it to me, yet he never does* : teu tik nae – *even so, it's not right* = **tebu**
-ti (pron suffix) *entity* | bout, boutti – *much, a lot* : hokol, hokolti – *all, everything*
tiar ['tīār] (adj) *prepared; ready* = **taiar**
tiattoir ['tīāt-tòɪr] (nº) *seventy-three* [B. tiattâr]
tibbot ['tīb-bòt] (n) *Tibet* [B. tibbåt]
tikisa ['tīkīšā] (n) *medical treatment* | **tikisa cole** – *treatment is in progress* : cacir hator bemaror lagi tikisa coler – *aunt is receiving treatment for her heart disease* : **tikisa kor-** – *give treatment* : daktor era bicarar tikisa korer – *the doctors are giving the man treatment* : **tikisa kora-** – *get treatment carried out* : afnar sasor osubidar lagi tikisa koraita acla – *you should have sought treatment for your breathing problems* [B. cikitša < S. cikitšā]
til [tīl] (n) *sesame plant; sesame seed; skin mark* | ek cimti til – *a pinch of sesame seeds* : tilor tel – *sesame oil* : tair muko til – *she has freckles on her face* : **ek til** – *one sesame seed; a tiny amount; a moment* : ek til lobon roice – *a wee bit of salt is left* : ek til ubauka – *please wait a moment* : **tile tile** – *in tiny amounts; bit by bit; moment by moment* : tile tile bout foesa jomce – *bit by bit, much money has accumulated* : tain tile tile morra – *he is slowly dying* [B. til < O. tila]
tilaot ['tīlāòt] (n) *recitation (of verses from the Quran)* | **tilaot kor-** – *recite from the Quran* : tain ruj tura tilaot koroin – *she recites a bit of the Quran every day* [A. tilāwa]
tilismati ['tīlīs-mātī] (n) *magic* [P. tilismātī < A. ṭilasmāt – *talismans*]
tin [tīn] (nº) *three* | tin bocor – *three years* : tin·jon manus – *three people* : bial tin·ta – *3 p.m.* : tin bera lagbo – *lots of complications will arise* : ou jutar tin obosta – *these shoes are in an awful state* : **tin cair** – *three or four; a few* : tin cair din bade – *after three or four days* : tin cair·ta aefol – *a few apples* : bur tin·ta cair·ta – *at three or four in the morning* [B. tin]
tintala ['tīntālā] (adj) *three-storeyed* = **tin + -tala**
tirannobboi ['tīrān-nòb-bòɪ] (nº) *ninety-three* [B. tirannåbbåi]
tiras ['tīrāš] (n) *thirst* | fanir tiras – *thirst for water* : **tiras lage** – *thirst is felt* : afnar tiras lagce ni? – *have you started feeling thirsty?* : **tiras mite / tiras miti jae** – *thirst is quenched* : ca kauka, afnar tiras miti jaibo – *have some tea and your thirst will go* [O. tŕśā]
tirasi ['tīrāšī] (nº) *eighty-three* [B. tirasi]
tiri¹ ['tīrī] (n) *woman; wife* [B. stri < S. strī]
tiri² (n) *time* = **titi**
tiris ['tīrīš] (nº) *thirty* [B. tris]
tis [tīš] (nº) *thirty* = **tiris**

tisa ['tīšā] (adj) *(month) having thirty days* | ou mas tisa na ektisa? – *does this month have 30 days or 31?* < **tis**
titi ['tītī] (n) *time* [B. tithi < S. tithi – *one thirtieth of a lunar month*]
titkini ['tīt-kīnī] (n) *tiddler (fish)*
titta ['tīt-tā] (adj) *bitter* | **titta lage** – *it tastes bitter* [B. tita < O. tikta]
to [tò] (conj) *then; but then* | age kauka, to hutiba – *have your meal first, then you can go to bed* : tane forae ɗekci, to tan nam jani na – *I've often seen him, but I don't know his name* : tair ma ace to baf nae – *her mother is alive but not her father* : to kita korba? – *so what will you do then?* : to? – *so then?* [B. tåbe]
to- (vt) *put; put down; put aside; leave* | citi kunano toici, iaiɗ nae – *I can't remember where I put the letter* : kolom muko toio na – *don't put your pen in your mouth* : beg hono touka – *leave your bag there* : afnar kut toita ni? – *do you want to take off your coat?* : hou kota touka! – *please let that subject drop!* : tan kota muk taki toe na – *she never stops talking about him* : **toia** – *having left; leaving aside* : kam toia gece gi – *leaving work undone, he went away* : tara cacire toia kaicil – *leaving auntie out, they ate on their own* : asol toia nokol loice – *he passed over the real thing and bought a cheap imitation* [B. thu-]
toaj ['tòāz, 'tòāj] (n) *ingratiating deference* | **(kar) toaj kor-** – *fawn (on someone)* : cearmenor toaj kore kali – *he keeps fawning on the chairman* [A. tawāḌuᵢ - *humbleness*]
toal ['tòāl] (n) *towel* [Pg. toalha]
tobɗul ['tòb-ɗūl] (adj) *confused; non-plussed* [O. stabdha – *rigid; paralysed*]
tobil ['tòbīl] (n) *ready money; funds; fund* = **tohbil**
tobiot ['tòbīòt] (n) *nature; disposition* [A. ṭabīᵢa]
tobla ['tòblā] (n) *floor drum; tabla* [A. ṭabla]
toblig ['tòblīg, 'tòblīk] (n) *proselytizing; Islamic missionary work* [A. tablīġ – *transmission*]
tobu ['tòbū] (conj) *even then; but still* [B. tåbu] cf **tebu, teu, tou**
tocbi ['tòs-bī] (n) *chaplet of prayer beads; rosary* | **tocbi for-** – *recite "subhanallah" repeatedly, counting the times on one's prayer beads* [A. tasbīḥ – *doing "subhana"*]
toclim ['tòs-līm] (n) *saying "salaam alaikum"; salutation* [A. taslīm – *doing "salaam"*]
tofat ['tòfāt] (n) *difference* | ou ɗu·gur maje tofat nae – *there's no difference between these two* : aij ni kail, tofat kita? – *today or tomorrow, what difference does it make?* : rait ɗin tofat – *the difference between night and day* : ɗui bair maje rait ɗin tofat – *the two brothers are complete opposites* [A. tafāwut]
tofon ['tòfòn] (n) *lungi, sarong* [P. tah-band]
tohbil ['tòhbīl] (n) *ready money; funds; fund* [A. taḥwīl – *bill of exchange*]
toiar ['tòɪ-ār] (adj) *prepared; ready; made* | afne toiar ni? – *are you ready?* : hokolti toiar – *everything's prepared* : ikan lakrir toiar – *this is made of wood* : **toiar o-/toiar oi ja-** – *get prepared; be made* : amra egaro·tat toiar oimu – *we'll get ready at eleven* : kani toiar oi gece – *the meal is all ready* : gor bout age toiar oicil – *the house had been constructed long ago* : **toiar kor-** – *prepare; make* : afnar bicna toiar korci – *I've prepared your bed* : tain suji toiar korcoin – *she's made some semolina* : ca toiar kora – *the tea's already made* = **taiar**
toiari ['tòɪ-ārī] (n) *preparation* = **taiari**
toitor ['tòɪtòr] (n) *partridge; guinea-fowl* [B. titir < O. tittira]
tok (post) *until; up to* | kail tok – *until tomorrow* : tain aoa tok – *until he arrives* : london tok – *as far as London* [H. tak]
tokɗir ['tòχdīr] (n) *pre-ordained fate* [A. taqdīr]
toki ['tòkī] (n) *cap* [P. tāqī]
toklif ['tòχlīf] (n) *trouble; inconvenience* | **(kar) toklif oe** – *inconvenience is suffered (by someone)* : afnar toklif oice – *you've been put to a lot of trouble* : **toklif kor-** – *give trouble; bother* : tan toklif kortam cai na – *I don't want to bother him* [A. taklīf]
tokon ['tòχòn] (adv) *at that time; then* [B. tåkhån]
tokt ['tòχt] (n) *throne* [P. taḳt]
tokta ['tòχtā] (n) *plank* [P. taḳta]

tol [tòl] (n) *bottom* | baltir tol – *bottom of the bucket* : doriar tol – *bottom of the sea; sea bed* : **tol fa-** – *reach the bottom; touch the bottom* : dub dia gaŋgor tol faicla – *he dived down and touched the river bed* : **tole** – *at the bottom; below; underneath* : tole fattoir ace – *there are stones at the bottom* [B. tål < O. tala]
tol- (vi) *go under; sink* | **toli ja-** – *go under; sink* : nau toli gece – *the boat has sunk*
tola ['tòlā] (n) *bottom; underside; low place* | bortonor tola – *bottom of a plate* : faur tola – *underside of the foot; sole* [B. tåla]
tola- (vt) *cause to go under; cause to sink* | lafalafi korle nau tolaibae – *if you jump about you're going to make the boat sink*
tole ['tòlɛ] (n adv) *at the bottom; below; underneath; downstairs; in support* | kagoj tole fori gece – *the paper has fallen down below* : tole ke takoin? – *who lives on the floor below?* : gacor tole manus boice – *people have sat down under the tree* : tan garir tole bout korcira – *he is spending a lot on his car* : **tole tole** – *under cover; in secret* : tara tole tole iŋsa kore – *they are secretly jealous* < **tol**
tolob ['tòlòb] (n) *demand; wage* | **tolob kor-** – *demand* : tara foesa tolob korce – *they have demanded money* : **tolob fa-** – *receive wages* : afne tolob koto fain? – *how much do you receive in wages?* [A. ṭalab – *quest; demand*]
tolof ['tòlòf] (n) *demand; wage* = **tolob**
tomot ['tòmòt] (n) *slander* [A. tuhma]
tona ['tònā] (v n) *putting; leaving* < **to-**
tonai ['tònāɪ] (n) *body; physique; health* | betar tonai muta – *his body is stout; he is heavily built* : cacir tonai durbol oi gece – *aunt has become physically weak* [O. tanu]
tone ['tònɛ] (v adv) *from* | ami sof tone fiaij anmu – *I'll get onions from the shop* : tara kuae tone aice? – *where have they come from?* : ruja kail tone suru – *fasting will start from tomorrow* : on tone london bakka dur – *London is very far from here* < **tona**
tor ['tòr] (pron adj) *thy; your* (intimate) < **tui**
tora ['tòrā] (pron) *you lot* (intimate) < **tui**
torak- ['tòràχ] (vt) *leave; put; put down* | beg ono torakouka – *leave the bag here* : catti goro falai torakcoin – *he's left his umbrella at home* : kagjain almarit toraktam ni? – *shall I put the papers in the cupboard?* : ricibar lamai torakce – *she's put the receiver down* : (very polite) afnar tosrif torakouka – *please sit yourself down* [A. ṭark – *abandonment*]
torbuj ['tòr-būz, 'tòr-būj] (n) *watermelon* [P. tarbūz]
torikot ['tòrīkòt] (n) *mystic path; mysticism* [A. ṭarīqa – *path, way*]
tori-torkari ['tòrītòrχārī] (n) *vegetables* = **tarkari**
torjoma ['tòr-jòmā] (n) *translation* [A. tarjama]
torkari ['tòrχāī] (n) *vegetables* = **tarkari**
torko ['tòrχò] (n) *argument* | **torko kor-** – *argue* : he kali kali torko kore – *he argues for the sake of it* : **torko laga-** – *start an argument* : kani loia torko lagaice – *he provoked an argument about the food* [B. tårkå < S. tarka – *reasoning*]
torof ['tòròf] (n) *side; behalf* | tain amar torof dorcoin – *he has taken my side* : **(kar) torof taki** – *from (someone's) side; on (someone's) behalf* : amar torof taki colam koiba – *please give them a salutation on my behalf* [A. ṭaraf – *extremity; side*]
tosrif [tòs 'rīf] (n) *honourable self* (very polite) | afnar tosrif tura ficaita jodin – *if you could very kindly move yourself back a wee bit* [A. tašrif – *honouring*]
tosturi ['tòstūrī] (n) *saucer* [P. tastarī]
toto ['tòtò] (adj/adv) *that much* cf **joto**
tou ['tòū] (conj) *and then; even then; but still* | arbar tukaici, tou faici – *I searched again, and then I found it* : tar fet karaf, tou kaito car – *his stomach is upset, but still he wants to eat* : tou bala – *even so, it's a good thing* : **tou gia** – *and then; and only then* : tare dekci, tou gia iaid oice – *I saw him, and only then did I remember* = **tobu**
touba ['tòūbā] (n) *repentance* | **touba kor-** – *express contrition* : he barbar touba korce – *he said again and again how sorry he was* ¶ **touba** (int) *God forgive me* | touba touba! – *perish the thought!* [A. touba]

toufik ['tòūfīk] (n) *good fortune; God-given ability* | tarar hojo jaibar toufik nae – *they aren't lucky enough to be able to go on Hajj* : alla tane bujbar toufik deuk – *may God give him the power to understand* [A. taufīq – *endowment with capacity; success*]

tourit ['tòūrīt] (n) *the Torah* [A. taurāh]

tu [tū] (n) *spittle* | **tu fala-** – *expectorate; spit* ¶ **tu** (int) *ugh; yuck* [B. thu < O. thut]

tufan ['tūfān] (n) *storm* [A. țūfān – *flood*]

tui [tūī] (pron) *thou; you* (intimate) | tui kita koroc? – *what are you doing?* : kaiti ni tui? – *do you want to eat?* : **tor** – *thy; your; of you* : tor baire koc aito – *tell your brother to come here* : tor lagi gumaiam fari na – *I can't sleep because of you* : **tore** – *(to) thee; (to) you* : tore kunta ditam nae – *I'm not going to give you anything* : **tuin** – *you* (plural or singular) : tuin bara kelaiti – *you should play outside* : **tora** – *you* (plural) : tora kita cac? – *what do you lot want?* : **torar** – *your; of you* (plural) : torar juta kuae? – *where are your shoes, all of you?* : **torare** – *(to) you* (plural) : torare kicca hunaimu – *I'll tell you all a story* [B. tui] Note: Used only to address one's own children, servants or very intimate friends.

tuin [tūīn] (pron) *thou, ye; you* (intimate) < **tui**

tuk [tūk] (n) *anger* | **tuk mar-** – *lose one's temper* : tain akta tuk marcla – *he suddenly got angry* [O. tīkśṇatā – *pungency; hotness*]

tuk- [tūk] (vi) *come to light* | furan dolil tukce – *some old deeds have turned up*

tuka- ['tūkā] (vt) *seek; search for* | afne kita tukaira? – *what are you looking for?* : **tukaia fa-** – *find (after searching)* : dolil·kan tukaia faici – *I found the document*

tukatuki ['tūkātūkī] (n) *searching* < **tuka-**

tul- [tūl] (vt) *raise; lift; erect; pick up; pull up; rouse; remove* | tumar at tulo – *raise your arm* : tain tosturi muko tulcoin – *she raised the saucer to her lips* : beg ota tultam fari na – *I can't lift this bag* : mati taki kagoj tulra – *he's picking papers up from the floor* : tara amrare garit tulto koice – *they said they'd pick us up in their car* : tara gor tuler – *they're putting up a house* : meg der, catti tulouka – *it's raining, put your umbrella* : aij alu tulmu – *today we're going to dig up the potatoes* : hou kota tuloin na jen – *please don't bring up that subject* : tare gum taki tultam ni? – *shall I wake him up?* : baiccaintore sat·tat tuloin – *she gets the children up at 7 o'clock* : tara lamfa bil tulce – *they've run up a big bill* : soetane cacar rag tuler – *the wicked fellow is winding uncle up* : tain mocjidor lagi foesa tulra – *he's collecting money for the mosque* : ami beŋ taki foesa tultam – *I want to draw some money from the bank* : ke kagoj taki leka tulce – *someone has erased some words from the paper* : ek·ta fotu tulouka – *please take a photo* : tantanor mat tulci – *I've recorded their conversation* : bicara bidio tuler – *the man's making a video recording* : **tuli le-** – *raise; lift; erect; pick up; pull up; rouse; remove* : afnar fau tuli louka – *please will you lift up your foot* : tara gor tuli ler – *they're erecting a shed* : aste, bebire tuli libae! – *quiet, you'll wake the baby!* : fotu tuli lici – *we've taken some photographs* : ou roŋ tuli litam – *I want to remove this paint* : tara befsa tuli lice – *they've wound up the business* : **tuli de-** – *lift up* : cacire baco tuli dicoin – *he got aunt onto her bus* [B. tul-] cf **uta-**

tula [¹'tūlā] (v n) *raising* | **tula de-** – *give a lift up* : tula deo amare! – *lift me up!* < **tul-**

tula ² (n) *cotton wool* [B. tula < O. tūla]

tula- (vt) *cause to be raised* (causative form of **tul-** in all meanings) | gor tulaicoin – *he's had a shed put up* : amra fotu tulaimu – *we'll have a photo taken*

tulona ['tūlònā] (n) *comparison; criticism* | **tulona kor-** – *make comparisons; criticise* : tain kali tulona koroin – *he keeps criticising* [B. tulåna < S. tulanā – *raising; weighing up*]

tumi ['tūmī] (pron) *you* (familiar) | tumi hokolor huru – *you're the youngest (of all)* : **tumar** – *your; of you* :tumar boes koto? – *how old are you?* : bobisot tumar samne – *the future is in front of you* : **tumare** – *(to) you* : ekta koitam tumare – *there's something I want to tell you* : **tumra / tumitain** – *you* (plural) : tumra kaico ni? – *have you all eaten?* : tumitain huru roice – *you're still young, all of you* : **tumrar** – *your; of you* (plural) : tumrar mabaf hokol aira – *your parents are all coming* : **tumrare** – *(to) you* (plural) : tumrare fotu dekaimu – *I'll show you all some pictures* [B. tumi] Note: Used to address juniors, close relatives and friends. Not to be used when addressing adult strangers.

tura ['tūrā] (adj) *some; a little* | tain tura bat kaicoin – *she has eaten a little rice* : tura somoe roice – *a little time is left* ¶ **tura** (adv) *somewhat; a little* | tura boro lage – *it seems a little too big* : tar bearam tura komce – *his illness has subsided a bit* : tura bar caitam ni? – *shall we wait a little?* ¶ **tura** (pron) *a little bit* | tura roice – *there's a little bit left* : aro tura lagbo – *we'll need a bit more* : **tura tura** – *just a little bit* : ami tura tura buji – *I can understand a wee bit*   [H. thoṛā]
turaturi ['tūrātūrī] (adv) *a little*   = **tura**
turost ['tūròst] (adj) *agitated*   [B. tråstå < S. trasta – *alarmed*]
tusok ['tūšòχ] (n) *mattress*   [P. tošak]
tusto ['tūš-tò] (adj) *satisfied*   [B. tustå < S. tuśta]
tuta ['tūtā] (n) *parrot*   [B. tota < P. tūtī]
tutla ['tūt-lā] (adj) *afflicted by stuttering*   [B. toṭla]
tutla- (vi) *stutter; stammer*
tutu ['tūtū] (n) *spittle* | **tutu fala-** – *expectorate; spit*   [B. thuthu]

u

-u (adv suffix) *particularly; indeed* (giving emphasis to the attached word) | one bat kaita-u – *he does want to eat rice now* : one bat-u kaita – *he wants to eat rice now* : one-u bat kaita – *he wants to eat rice now* : afne-u koicla – *it was you who said it* : amra jaitam-u – *we definitely want to go* : hokole-u janoin – *absolutely everyone knows* : haca-u – *that's true indeed* : ola-u oibo – *yes, it must indeed be so*

uba ['ūbā] (v n) *standing* | **ubat** – *standing; hanging about* : afne ubat acla na boat acla? – *were you standing or sitting?* : tain egaro·ta taki ubat – *he's been waiting since eleven o'clock* : tik ace, amra ubat takmu – *it's all right, we'll remain standing* < **uba-**

uba- (vi) *stand up; be standing; hang about; wait* | tain ubaicoin – *he has stood up; he is standing* : tain ubaira – *he is standing; he is waiting* : ek minit ubauka – *please hang on a minute* : tarar lagi ubaitam nai – *we won't wait for them* : ubauka, ami bujci na – *hang on, I haven't got what you meant* : **ubai tak-** / **ubai ro-** – *remain standing; be left standing* : tain rastat ubai roicoin – *he's standing there in the road* : ubai takta oiba – *you'll have to stay standing* : **ubaia rak-** – *keep (someone) standing / waiting* : cacire ubaia rakcoin kene? – *why have you kept auntie waiting?*

ubauba ['ūbā-ūbā] (adv) *after a short wait; without delay* | ubauba kam ses oibo – *the job will be finished while you wait* : afne ubauba jaiba gi – *just a second, then you can go* < **uba-**

uca ['ū-sā] (adj) *high; lofty* [B. uⁿca < O. ucca]

ucal ['ū-sāl] (n) *regurgitation; wave of nausea* | dekia amar ucal utcil – *when I saw it I felt like throwing up* [H. uchāl – *upwelling*]

ucilla [ū 'sīl-lā] (n) *expedients; means; initiative* | kunta faite oile ucilla lage – *if you want to achieve anything you need to find ways and means* : afnar ucillae kam boni gece – *thanks to your initiative the job has been done* : **ucilla kor-** – *seek ways and means; use initiative* : loita oile ucilla korta oiba – *if you want to get it you must put your mind to it* [A. wasīla – *expedient*]

ucit [ū 'sīt] (adj) *right and proper* | ucit kota – *apt words; a cogent remark* : afnar jaoa·ta ucit – *you really ought to go* : kunta koa ucit acil tar – *he should have said something* : torko lagani ucit nae – *it's not right to start an argument* [B. ucit < S. ucita – *pleasant; proper*]

uda ['ūdā] (adj) *damp* [O. uda – *wet*]

uddar ['ūd-dār] (n) *deliverance; salvation* | amrar lagi uddar nae – *there's no way out for us* : **uddar o-/uddar oi ja-** – *be saved* : afne uddar oi gecoin – *you've been saved; you're lucky to be out of it* : **uddar kor-** – *save; rescue* : becarire bifot taki uddar korce – *they rescued the poor woman from her perilous situation* [B. uddar < S. uddhāra – *raising*]

udla ['ūdlā] (adj) *naked* [B. udla]

udla- (vi) *bare oneself; go around naked* | udlaicoc kene, be? – *oh, why have you taken all your clothes off, child?*

uf [ūf] (int) *oh! ow! ouch!*

ufae ['ūfāy] (n) *way; recourse* | ufae ace – *there are ways and means* : ufae nae – *there's nothing one can do* : ufae tukaitam oimu – *I'll have to find a way* : tan jaoar ufae nae – *there's no way he can go* : ar ufae nae – *there's no other way out* : one ufae kita? – *now what's to be done?* [B. upay < S. upāya – *expedient*]

ufas ['ūfāš] (n) *not eating; fasting* | tain dui din dori ufas – *he hasn't eaten for two days* : **ufas tak-** / **ufas ro-** – *remain without eating* : tain forae ufas takoin – *she often goes without food* : afne ufas ni? – *have you not eaten?* [B. upos < S. upavāsa]

ufat ['ūfāt] (n) *death* [A. wafāh]

ufoar ['ūfòār] (n) *gift; present* [B. upåhar < S. upahāra]

ufor ['ūfòr] (n) *topside; upper floor* | tebulor ufor·ta nata oi gece – *the table top has got spoilt* : he ufor taki forcil – *he fell from the first floor* : **ufror** – *of the top; of the upper* *floor; upper* : ufror rum kali – *the upstairs room is empty* : ufror cuic marouka – *turn off the upper switch* : **ufre** – *on top; upstairs; above* : ufre dakni takto – *there should be a lid on top* : ufre jaita faroin – *you may go upstairs*   [B. upår]

ufortala ['ūfòr-tālā] (n) *upper storey; upper floor* = **ufor** + **-tala**

ufostit ['ūfòs-tīt] (adj) *present* | mitiŋo ke ke ufostit acla? – *which people were present at the meeting?* : **ufostit somoe** – *the present; at present* : ufostit somoe kunta koitam nai – *I won't say anything at present*   [B. upåsthit < S. upasthita]

ufre ['ūf-rɛ́] (n adv) *on top; on; over; above; up; upstairs* | tebulor ufre – *on the table* : afnar matar ufre – *above your head* : ek sor ufre – *over one hundred* : noe·tar ufre oi gece – *it's past nine o'clock* : ufre cauka – *look up* : ufre jauka – *go upstairs* : gacor ufre boi lekcoin – *she's written a book about plants* : emrikar ufre bijnic korcoin – *he's set up a business on American soil* : tain amar ufre bejar – *he's cross with me* : ita afnar ufre – *it's up to you* : tar ufre cari ɗeuka – *leave it to him* : kun kotar ufre tarare cafi ɗi laicla? – *on what grounds did you let them have a key?* : ragor ufre nananta koita faroin – *he may say all sorts of things in anger* : bicara kealor ufre cole – *that fellow always acts on impulse*   < **ufor**

ufri ['ūfrī] (adj) *additional; paranormal* | tara ufri foesa kamae – *they make money on the side* : ufri cul – *added-on hair; false hair* : ufri bemar – *illness of psychic origin* = **ufor** + **-i** ²

ufta ['ūftā] (adj) *contrary* | ufta kota – *words of disagreement* : ufta batas – *contrary wind; head wind* : ufta bab – *hostile mood* ¶ **ufta** (adv) *in a contrary manner; against the flow* | nau ufta coler – *the boat is sailing upstream* : beta kali ufta mate – *he talks contrarily; he keeps disagreeing or contradicting*   cf **ufut**

ufte ['ūftɛ] (adv) *on the contrary* | foesa ɗee na, ufte ɗabi kore – *he doesn't pay up, but on the contrary he demands money*   < **ufta**

ufut ['ūfūt] (adj) *face down* | bicara ufut acil na cit? – *was he lying face down or face up?* : tara rugire ufut kori rakcil – *they kept the patient face down*   [B. upuɽ < O. avamūrḍha]

ujagiri ['ūzāgīrī, 'ūjāgīrī] (n) *act of staying awake; vigil* | **ujagiri kor-** – *stay awake (at night); keep a vigil*   cf **jag-**

ugro ['ūg-rò] (adj) *uncivil; rough in behaviour*   [B. ugrå < S. ugra – *potent, fierce*]

ujir ['ūzīr, 'ūjīr] (n) *vizier; minister*   [A. wazīr]

ujon ['ūzòn, 'ūjòn] (n) *weight* | afnar ujon koto? – *what is your weight?* : ou foketor ujon besi – *this packet weighs too much* : **ujon kor-** – *weigh* : begor ujon korci na – *I haven't weighed the bag* : **ujon maf-** – *weigh* : aij afnar ujon mafta ni? – *do you want to check your weight today?*   [A. wazn]

uju ['ūzū] (n) *ritual ablution as a preliminary to Muslim prayers*   [A. wuḌū¿]

ukil ['ūkīl] (n) *lawyer*   [A. wakīl – *agent; representative*]

ukuin ['ūkūin] (n) *louse* | ou fuar culo ukuin oi gece – *this boy has got lice in his hair* : **ukuin bac-** – *pick out lice or nits* : ukuin baca lagbo – *the nits will have to be picked out*   [B. ukun]

ukum ['ūkūm] (n) *command* | koɗar ukum oile.. – *if God so commands..*   = **hukum**

ul [ūl] (n) *wool* | **ulor** – *of wool; woollen* : ulor atmuja – *woollen gloves*   [E.]

ullu ['ūl-lū] (n) *great owl; idiot*   [H. ullū]

ulos ['ūlòš] (n) *bed-bug*

ulot-falot ['ūlòt-fālòt] (adj) *upside down and back to front; in disorder* | amar kagoj-fotro ulot-falot oi gece – *my papers have got all mixed up*   cf **ulta-falta**

ult- (vi) *turn upside down; become reversed* | nau ultice – *the boat has turned turtle* : **ulti ja-** – *turn upside down; become reversed* : gelas ulti jaibo – *the glass is going to tip over* : jama ulti gece – *the shirt has got inside out*

ulta ['ūltā] (v adj) *reversed; upside down; inside out; back to front*   < **ult-** cf **ulto**

ulta- (vt) *reverse; turn over; turn upside down; turn inside out; turn back to front* | fata ultauka – *turn over the page* : tara tin·ta gari ultaice – *they turned three cars upside down* : joje rae ultaita faroin – *the judge may overturn the judgment* : tumar atmuja ultairae kitar lagi? – *why are you turning your gloves inside out?*   [B. ulta-]

ulta-falta ['ūltāfālta] (adj) *reversed; upside down; inside out; back to front; in disorder* | cear tebul ulta-falta oi gece – *the chairs and tables are in disarray* = **ulta + falta**
ulto ['ūltò] (adj) *reversed; upside down; inside out; back to front; one after next in a series* | ulto gari – *an upside down cart* : tumar kut ulto – *your coat is inside out* : tar toki ulto – *his cap is back to front* : amra ulto afta aimu – *we'll come the week after next* ¶ **ulto** (adv) *the wrong way; in reverse order* | afne kagoj·kan ulto dorcoin – *you're holding the paper upside down* : tar toki ulto finde – *he wears his cap back to front* : tumar juta ulto lagaio na – *don't put your shoes on the wrong foot* : gari ulto coler – *the car is going backwards* = **ulta**
ulu ['ūlū] (n) *ululation* | **ulu kor-** – *ululate; go "lu-lu-lu-lu"* (*an ancient traditional Hindu way of propitiating the spirits at dusk*) [B. ulu]
um [ūm] (n) *heat; warmth* [O. uśma]
ummot ['ūm-mòt] (n) *the Muslim faith community* [A.'umma]
umrau ['ūm-rāu] (n) *the short pilgrimage to Mecca (performed outside the month of Dhul Hijja)* | umrau hoj – *the umra pilgrimage* [A. ¿umra]
umta ['ūmtā] (n) *heat; warmth* | rodit umta lage – *it feels hot in the sun* [O. uśmatā]
unaraia ['ūnārāıā] (n) *unlucky person*
uncallis ['ūn-sāl-līš] (n°) *thirty-nine* [B. uncållis]
unda ['ūndā] (adj) *bent down* | tar mata unda – *his head is bowed* : **unda o-** – *bend down* : hamaite unda oa lage – *you have to bend down to enter* [H. auⁿdhā < O. avamūrdha]
undur ['ūndūr] (n) *mouse; rat* | goror maje undur oi gece – *the house has got infested with mice* [O. undura]
unnois ['ūn-nòıš] (n°) *nineteen* [B. unis]
unnois-bis ['ūn-nòıš-bīš] (n) *discrepancy; lack of accuracy* | isabor maje unnois-bis oi gece – *there's some irregularity in the accounts* = **unnois + bis**
unnoti ['ūn-nòtī] (n) *improvement* | tar kamor maje unnoti oice – *there's been some improvement in his work* : **unnoti kor-** – *improve; get better* : fuae oŋkot unnoti korer – *the boy is getting better at maths* [B. unnåti < S. unnati]
unoasi ['ūnòāšī] (n°) *seventy-nine* [B. unåasi]
unofoncas ['ūnòfòn-sāš] (n°) *forty-nine* [B. unåpåncas]
unonobboi ['ūnònòb-bòı] (n°) *eighty-nine* [B. unånåbbåi]
unosait ['ūnòšāıt] (n°) *fifty-nine* [B. unåsat]
unosottoir ['ūnòšòt-tòır] (n°) *sixty-nine* [B. unåsåttår]
untis ['ūntīš] (n°) *twenty-nine* [B. untris]
ur-[1] (vi) *fly* | asmanor maje felen ure – *planes fly in the sky* : **uri ja-** – *fly; fly away; be blown away; be blown up*: cator tin uri gecil – *the tin roofing was blown away* : larait koto ful uri gece – *many bridges were blown up in the war* [B. uṛ-]
ur-[2] (vi) *hasten; hurry*
ura ['ūrā] (v n) *haste; hurry* < **ur-**[2]
ura- ['ūrā] (vt) *cause to fly; blow away; blow up; squander* | fuainte guddi urar – *the boys are flying kites* : gec futia gor uraice – *gas exploded and blew up the house* : tara kali foesa urae – *they keep squandering money* : **urai de-** – *put to flight; blow up; squander* : bol urai dice – *he sent the ball flying* : bumae gari urai dibo – *the bomb will blow the car sky high* : bicara foesa urai der – *the fellow is chucking money away* [B. uṛa-]
ural ['ūrāl] (n) *flying; flight* | **ural de-** – *take off; fly away* : koutor ural dice – *the pigeon has flown away* < **ur-**[1]
urat ['ūrāt] (n) *thigh* [B. uråt < O. ūru]
uratara ['ūrātārā] (n) *haste; hurry* = **taraura**
urauri ['ūrā-ūrī] (n) *haste; hurry* | urauri nae – *there's no hurry* : oto urauri kita? – *what's all the hurry?* : uraurir maje tikitor kota fauri liclam – *in the rush I forgot the tickets* < **ur-**[2]
urdoŋgi ['ūrdòŋ-gī] (adj) *hemiplegic* | urdoŋgi bemar – *hemiplegia* : urdoŋgi batas – *stroke* : tan urdoŋgi batas lagce – *she's suffered a stroke* [B. årdhåŋgi < S. ardhaŋgī]

ure ['ūrɛ] (int) *oh* | ure baf to baf! – *oh heavens!* : ure alla! – *oh God!*
uri ['ūrī] (n) *(green) bean; beans* | urir bici – *bean seeds; beans* [Pk. udiḍa]
uruc ['ūrūs] (n) *festival held at the shrine of a Muslim saint* [A. ¿urs – *wedding feast*]
ururi ['ūrūrī] (adj) *ready to fly*   < **ur-** ¹
ustaḍ [ūs 'tāḍ] (n) *guru; Islamic teacher* [P. ustād]
ustar ['ūstār] (n) *stumbling* | **ustar ka-** – *trip up; stumble* : ustar kaia forcla – *he tripped and fell*
ut (n) *camel* [B. ut < O. uśtra]
ut- (vi) *go up; get up; wake up; rise up; show up; put up; crop up* | ufre utouka – *go upstairs* : cear taki uta lagbo – *you'll have to get up off your chair* : tain utcoin na ebu – *he hasn't woken up yet* : amar rag uter – *my temper is rising* : bil uter – *the bill is mounting up* : tain embacit gia utcla – *he showed up at the embassy* : bajaro mac ute na besi – *not much fish turns up on the market* : ami tan goro utci – *I've put up at his house* : bakor utce – *the coriander has come up* : aij ileksonor kota utcil – *today the subject of elections cropped up* : afnar fotu bala utce – *your photo has come out well* : **uti ja-** – *get up; get up and go; be removed* : tain uti gecoin – *he has woken up / he has got up* : bakka somoe boici, one uti jaitam – *we've sat for quite a while, now I'm going to get up and go* : ofis on taki uti gece – *the office has moved from here* : he amar mon taki uti gece – *he has gone from my heart; I no longer care about him* [B. uth-]
uta ['ūtā] (v n) *going up; rising*   < **ut-**
uta- (vt) *cause to go up; lift up; put up; wake up; remove* | tumar at utao – *put up your hand* : tarare utaitam cai na – *I don't want to wake them* : mal·ta garit utaimu – *we'll load the goods onto the van* : tar camana on taki utaice – *he's removed his belongings from here* : amra fotu utaimu – *we'll take a photograph* : **utai le-** – *awaken; remove* : tarare utai litam oimu – *I'll have to wake them* : tan befsa utai licoin – *he's packed up his business* : **utai de-** – *put up; help on board; get rid of* : minare garit utai ḍici – *we put Mina onto her train* : agor ain·ta utai ḍice – *they've scrapped the previous law* [B. utha-] cf **tul-**
uta-lama ['ūtālāmā] (n) *going up and coming down; rising and falling; fluctuation*   = **uta + lama** ¹
utan ['ūtān] (n) *courtyard of a village homestead* [B. uthan]
utla ['ūtlā] (n) *migrant; new settler* [H. uthallū]
utra ['ūtrā] (n) *migrant; new settler*   = **utla**
utka ['ūtkā] (n) *retching; inclination to vomit* | amar utka utce – *I feel like throwing up* : amar utka utka lage – *I feel queasy*
uttoir ¹ ['ūt-tòir] (adj) *northern* | uttoir ḍig – *northerly direction*: uttoir ḍige – *in a northerly direction; northwards* ¶ **uttoir** (n) *the north* | uttoir ḍokkin fub foccim – *North, South, East and West* : **uttoror** – *of the north; northern* : uttoror gor – *the building on the northern side of the compound* [B. uttår < S. uttara – *upper; northern; subsequent*]
uttoir ² (n) *reply; answer* | one-u uttoir cai – *I want an answer now* : uttoir faici na ebu – *I haven't had a reply yet* : **uttoir de-/uttoir di la-** – *give a reply* : tain kunu uttoir ḍicoin na – *he hasn't answered* [B. uttår < S. uttara – *subsequent item; reply*]
utukuni ['ūtūkūnī] (adj) *so small; as small as this; tiny*   = **otokani**
ututi ['ūtūtī] (pron/adv) *so little; a wee bit*   = **otota**

CPSIA information can be obtained
at www.ICGtesting.com
Printed in the USA
LVOW10s1445130617
537959LV00023B/521/P